7170
P9-EDR-295

Dictionary of Literary Biography • Volume Sixty-six

German Fiction Writers, 1885-1913

Part 2: M-Z

Dictionary of Literary Biography

1: *The American Renaissance in New England,* edited by Joel Myerson (1978)

2: *American Novelists Since World War II,* edited by Jeffrey Helterman and Richard Layman (1978)

3: *Antebellum Writers in New York and the South,* edited by Joel Myerson (1979)

4: *American Writers in Paris, 1920-1939,* edited by Karen Lane Rood (1980)

5: *American Poets Since World War II,* 2 parts, edited by Donald J. Greiner (1980)

6: *American Novelists Since World War II,* Second Series, edited by James E. Kibler, Jr. (1980)

7: *Twentieth-Century American Dramatists,* 2 parts, edited by John MacNicholas (1981)

8: *Twentieth-Century American Science-Fiction Writers,* 2 parts, edited by David Cowart and Thomas L. Wymer (1981)

9: *American Novelists, 1910-1945,* 3 parts, edited by James J. Martine (1981)

10: *Modern British Dramatists, 1900-1945,* 2 parts, edited by Stanley Weintraub (1982)

11: *American Humorists, 1800-1950,* 2 parts, edited by Stanley Trachtenberg (1982)

12: *American Realists and Naturalists,* edited by Donald Pizer and Earl N. Harbert (1982)

13: *British Dramatists Since World War II,* 2 parts, edited by Stanley Weintraub (1982)

14: *British Novelists Since 1960,* 2 parts, edited by Jay L. Halio (1983)

15: *British Novelists, 1930-1959,* 2 parts, edited by Bernard Oldsey (1983)

16: *The Beats: Literary Bohemians in Postwar America,* 2 parts, edited by Ann Charters (1983)

17: *Twentieth-Century American Historians,* edited by Clyde N. Wilson (1983)

18: *Victorian Novelists After 1885,* edited by Ira B. Nadel and William E. Fredeman (1983)

19: *British Poets, 1880-1914,* edited by Donald E. Stanford (1983)

20: *British Poets, 1914-1945,* edited by Donald E. Stanford (1983)

21: *Victorian Novelists Before 1885,* edited by Ira B. Nadel and William E. Fredeman (1983)

22: *American Writers for Children, 1900-1960,* edited by John Cech (1983)

23: *American Newspaper Journalists, 1873-1900,* edited by Perry J. Ashley (1983)

24: *American Colonial Writers, 1606-1734,* edited by Emory Elliott (1984)

25: *American Newspaper Journalists, 1901-1925,* edited by Perry J. Ashley (1984)

26: *American Screenwriters,* edited by Robert E. Morsberger, Stephen O. Lesser, and Randall Clark (1984)

27: *Poets of Great Britain and Ireland, 1945-1960,* edited by Vincent B. Sherry, Jr. (1984)

28: *Twentieth-Century American-Jewish Fiction Writers,* edited by Daniel Walden (1984)

29: *American Newspaper Journalists, 1926-1950,* edited by Perry J. Ashley (1984)

30: *American Historians, 1607-1865,* edited by Clyde N. Wilson (1984)

31: *American Colonial Writers, 1735-1781,* edited by Emory Elliott (1984)

32: *Victorian Poets Before 1850,* edited by William E. Fredeman and Ira B. Nadel (1984)

33: *Afro-American Fiction Writers After 1955,* edited by Thadious M. Davis and Trudier Harris (1984)

34: *British Novelists, 1890-1929: Traditionalists,* edited by Thomas F. Staley (1985)

35: *Victorian Poets After 1850,* edited by William E. Fredeman and Ira B. Nadel (1985)

36: *British Novelists, 1890-1929: Modernists,* edited by Thomas F. Staley (1985)

37: *American Writers of the Early Republic,* edited by Emory Elliott (1985)

38: *Afro-American Writers After 1955: Dramatists and Prose Writers,* edited by Thadious M. Davis and Trudier Harris (1985)

39: *British Novelists, 1660-1800,* 2 parts, edited by Martin C. Battestin (1985)

40: *Poets of Great Britain and Ireland Since 1960,* 2 parts, edited by Vincent B. Sherry, Jr. (1985)

41: *Afro-American Poets Since 1955,* edited by Trudier Harris and Thadious M. Davis (1985)

42: *American Writers for Children Before 1900,* edited by Glenn E. Estes (1985)

43: *American Newspaper Journalists, 1690-1872,* edited by Perry J. Ashley (1986)

44: *American Screenwriters,* Second Series, edited by Randall Clark, Robert E. Morsberger, and Stephen O. Lesser (1986)

45: *American Poets, 1880-1945,* First Series, edited by Peter Quartermain (1986)

46: *American Literary Publishing Houses, 1900-1980: Trade and Paperback,* edited by Peter Dzwonkoski (1986)

47: *American Historians, 1866-1912,* edited by Clyde N. Wilson (1986)

48: *American Poets, 1880-1945,* Second Series, edited by Peter Quartermain (1986)

49: *American Literary Publishing Houses, 1638-1899,* 2 parts, edited by Peter Dzwonkoski (1986)

50: *Afro-American Writers Before the Harlem Renaissance,* edited by Trudier Harris (1986)

51: *Afro-American Writers from the Harlem Renaissance to 1940,* edited by Trudier Harris (1987)

52: *American Writers for Children Since 1960: Fiction,* edited by Glenn E. Estes (1986)

53: *Canadian Writers Since 1960,* First Series, edited by W. H. New (1986)

54: *American Poets, 1880-1945,* Third Series, 2 parts, edited by Peter Quartermain (1987)

55: *Victorian Prose Writers Before 1867,* edited by William B. Thesing (1987)

56: *German Fiction Writers, 1914-1945,* edited by James Hardin (1987)

57: *Victorian Prose Writers After 1867,* edited by William B. Thesing (1987)

58: *Jacobean and Caroline Dramatists,* edited by Fredson Bowers (1987)

59: *American Literary Critics and Scholars, 1800-1850,* edited by John W. Rathbun and Monica M. Grecu (1987)

60: *Canadian Writers Since 1960,* Second Series, edited by W. H. New (1987)

61: *American Writers for Children Since 1960: Poets, Illustrators, and Nonfiction Authors,* edited by Glenn E. Estes (1987)

62: *Elizabethan Dramatists,* edited by Fredson Bowers (1987)

63: *Modern American Critics, 1920-1955,* edited by Gregory S. Jay (1988)

64: *American Literary Critics and Scholars, 1850-1880,* edited by John W. Rathbun and Monica M. Grecu (1988)

65: *French Novelists, 1900-1930,* edited by Catharine Savage Brosman (1988)

66: *German Fiction Writers, 1885-1913,* 2 parts, edited by James Hardin (1988)

Documentary Series

1: *Sherwood Anderson, Willa Cather, John Dos Passos, Theodore Dreiser, F. Scott Fitzgerald, Ernest Hemingway, Sinclair Lewis,* edited by Margaret A. Van Antwerp (1982)

2: *James Gould Cozzens, James T. Farrell, William Faulkner, John O'Hara, John Steinbeck, Thomas Wolfe, Richard Wright,* edited by Margaret A. Van Antwerp (1982)

3: *Saul Bellow, Jack Kerouac, Norman Mailer, Vladimir Nabokov, John Updike, Kurt Vonnegut,* edited by Mary Bruccoli (1983)

4: *Tennessee Williams,* edited by Margaret A. Van Antwerp and Sally Johns (1984)

Yearbooks

1980, edited by Karen L. Rood, Jean W. Ross, and Richard Ziegfeld (1981)

1981, edited by Karen L. Rood, Jean W. Ross, and Richard Ziegfeld (1982)

1982, edited by Richard Ziegfeld; associate editors: Jean W. Ross and Lynne C. Zeigler (1983)

1983, edited by Mary Bruccoli and Jean W. Ross; associate editor: Richard Ziegfeld (1984)

1984, edited by Jean W. Ross (1985)

1985, edited by Jean W. Ross (1986)

1986, edited by J. M. Brook (1987)

Concise Series

The New Consciousness, 1941-1968 (1987)

Dictionary of Literary Biography • Volume Sixty-six

German Fiction Writers, 1885-1913

Part 2: M-Z

Edited by
James Hardin
University of South Carolina

A Bruccoli Clark Layman Book
Gale Research Company • Book Tower • Detroit, Michigan 48226

Matthew J. Bruccoli and Richard Layman, *Editorial Directors*
C. E. Frazer Clark, Jr., *Managing Editor*

Manufactured by Edwards Brothers, Inc.
Ann Arbor, Michigan
Printed in the United States of America

Library of Congress Cataloging-in-Publication Data

German fiction writers, 1885-1913.

(Dictionary of literary biography; v. 66)

"A Bruccoli Clark Layman book."
Includes index.
1. German fiction—19th century—History and criticism. 2. German fiction—20th century—History and criticism. 3. German fiction—19th century—Bio-bibliography. 5. Novelists, German—19th century—Biography-Dictionaries. 6. Novelists, German—20th century—Biography—Dictionaries. I. Hardin, James N. II. Series.

PT771.G47 1988 883'.8'09 [B] 87-29300
ISBN 0-8103-1744-3

Contents

Contents

Dictionary of Literary Biography • Volume Sixty-six

German Fiction Writers, 1885-1913

Part 2: M-Z

Dictionary of Literary Biography

Heinrich Mann
(27 March 1871-12 March 1950)

Michael M. Metzger
State University of New York at Buffalo

BOOKS: *In einer Familie: Roman* (Munich: Albert, 1894; revised, Berlin: Ullstein, 1924);

Das Wunderbare und andere Novellen (Paris, Leipzig & Munich: Langen, 1897);

Ein Verbrechen und andere Geschichten (Leipzig-Reudnitz: Baum, 1898);

Im Schlaraffenland: Ein Roman unter feinen Leuten (Munich: Langen, 1900); translated by Axton D. B. Clark as *In the Land of Cockaigne* (New York: Macauley, 1929); translation republished as *Berlin: The Land of Cockaigne* (London: Gollancz, 1929);

Die Göttinnen oder Die drei Romane der Herzogin von Assy, 3 volumes: *Diana; Minerva; Venus* (Munich: Langen, 1903); volume 1 translated by Erich Posselt and Emmet Glore as *Diana* (New York: Coward-McCann, 1929);

Die Jagd nach Liebe: Roman (Munich: Langen, 1903);

Professor Unrat oder das Ende eines Tyrannen: Roman (Munich: Langen, 1905); republished as *Der blaue Engel* (Berlin: Weichert, 1951); translated anonymously as *The Blue Angel* (London: Reader's Library, 1931); translation republished as *Small Town Tyrant* (New York: Creative Age Press, 1944); retranslated by Wirt Williams as *The Blue Angel* (New York: New American Library, 1959);

Flöten und Dolche: Novellen (Munich: Langen, 1905); "Pippo Spano" translated by Basil

Heinrich Mann (Ullstein)

Creighton in *Tellers of Tales*, edited by W. Somerset Maugham (New York: Doubleday, Doran, 1939), pp. 780-808; "Drei-Minuten-

Roman" translated by Victor Lange as "Three Minute Novel," in *Great German Short Novels and Stories* (New York: Random House, 1952), pp. 396-400;

Eine Freundschaft: Gustav Flaubert und George Sand (Munich: Bonsels, 1905);

Mnais und Ginevra (Munich & Leipzig: Piper, 1906);

Schauspielerin: Novelle (Vienna & Leipzig: Wiener Verlag, 1906);

Stürmische Morgen: Novellen (Munich: Langen, 1906); "Abdankung" translated by Rolf N. Linn as "Abdication," *Spectrum,* 4 (Spring-Summer 1960);

Zwischen den Rassen: Ein Roman (Munich: Langen, 1907);

Die Bösen (Leipzig: Insel, 1908);

Die kleine Stadt: Roman (Leipzig: Insel, 1909); translated by Winifred Ray as *The Little Town* (London: Secker, 1930; Boston: Houghton Mifflin, 1931);

Gesammelte Werke, 4 volumes (Berlin: Cassirer, 1909);

Varieté: Ein Akt (Berlin: Cassirer, 1910);

Das Herz: Novellen (Leipzig: Insel, 1910);

Die Rückkehr vom Hades: Novellen (Leipzig: Insel, 1911);

Schauspielerin: Drama in 3 Akten (Berlin: Cassirer, 1911);

Die große Liebe: Drama in 4 Akten (Berlin: Cassirer, 1912);

Auferstehung: Novelle (Leipzig: Insel, 1913);

Madame Legros: Drama in 3 Akten (Berlin: Cassirer, 1913);

Brabach: Drama in 3 Akten (Leipzig: Wolff, 1917);

Gesammelte Romane und Novellen, 10 volumes (Leipzig: Wolff, 1917);

Die Novellen, 2 volumes (Munich: Wolff, 1917);

Die Armen: Roman (Leipzig: Wolff, 1917);

Bunte Gesellschaft: Novellen (Munich: Langen, 1917);

Der Untertan: Roman (Leipzig: Wolff, 1918); translated by Ernest Boyd as *The Patrioteer* (New York: Harcourt, 1929); translation republished as *Little Superman* (New York: Creative Age Press, 1945); translation republished as *Man of Straw* (London: Hutchinson, 1947);

Drei Akte: Der Tyrann; Die Unschuldige; Varieté (Leipzig: Wolff, 1918);

Der Weg zur Macht: Drama in 3 Akten (Leipzig: Wolff, 1919);

Der Sohn: Novelle (Hannover: Steegemann, 1919);

Macht und Mensch (Munich: Wolff, 1919);

Die Ehrgeizige: Novelle (Munich: Roland, 1920);

Die Tote und andere Novellen (Munich: Recht, 1920);

Diktatur der Vernunft (Berlin: Die Schmiede, 1923);

Abrechnungen: Sieben Novellen (Berlin: Propyläen, 1924);

Der Jüngling: Novellen (Munich: Langes, 1924);

Das gastliche Haus: Komödie in 3 Akten (Munich: Langes, 1924);

Der Kopf: Roman (Berlin, Vienna & Leipzig: Zsolnay, 1925);

Kobes: Mit 10 Lithographien von Georg Grosz (Berlin: Propyläen, 1925);

Gesammelte Werke, 13 volumes (Berlin, Vienna & Leipzig: Zsolnay, 1925-1932);

Liliane und Paul: Novelle (Berlin, Vienna & Leipzig: Zsolnay, 1926);

Suturp (Berlin: Wegweiser-Verlag, 1928);

Mutter Marie: Roman (Berlin, Vienna & Leipzig: Zsolnay, 1927); translated by Whittaker Chambers as *Mother Mary* (New York: Simon & Schuster, 1928);

Eugénie oder die Bürgerzeit: Roman (Berlin, Vienna & Leipzig: Zsolnay, 1928); translated by Arthur J. Ashton as *The Royal Woman* (New York: Macauley, 1930);

Sieben Jahre: Chronik der Gedanken und Vorgänge (Berlin, Vienna & Leipzig: Zsolnay, 1929);

Sie sind jung (Berlin, Vienna & Leipzig: Zsolnay, 1929);

Der Tyrann; Die Branzilla: Novellen (Leipzig: Reclam, 1929);

Die große Sache: Roman (Berlin: Kiepenheuer, 1930);

Geist und Tat: Franzosen 1780-1930 (Berlin: Kiepenheuer, 1931);

Ein ernstes Leben: Roman (Berlin, Vienna & Leipzig: Zsolnay, 1932); translated by Edwin and Willa Muir as *The Hill of Lies* (London: Jarrolds, 1934; New York: Dutton, 1935);

Das öffentliche Leben (Berlin, Vienna & Leipzig: Zsolnay, 1932);

Die Welt der Herzen: Novellen (Berlin: Kiepenheuer, 1932);

Das Bekenntnis zum Übernationalen (Berlin, Vienna & Leipzig: Zsolnay, 1933);

Der Haß: Deutsche Zeitgeschichte (Amsterdam: Querido, 1933);

Heinrich Mann und ein junger Deutscher: Der Sinn dieser Emigration (Paris: Europäischer Merkur, 1934);

Die Jugend des Königs Henri Quatre: Roman (Amsterdam: Querido, 1935); translated by Eric Sutton as *Young Henry of Navarre* (New York:

Drawing by Mann of the death of his father in 1891 (Heinrich-Mann-Archiv, Akademie der Künste der DDR, Berlin)

"Waldidylle" (Forest Idyll), a youthful drawing by Mann (Vicktor Mann, Wir waren Fünf, *1964)*

Knopf, 1937); translation republished as *King Wren: The Youth of Henri IV* (London: Secker & Warburg, 1937);

Es kommt der Tag: Deutsches Lesebuch (Zurich: Europa-Verlag, 1936);

Hilfe für die Opfer des Faschismus: Rede 1937 (Paris: Überparteilicher deutscher Hilfsausschuß, 1937);

Die Vollendung des Königs Henri Quatre (Kiev: State Press for National Minorities of the USSR, 1938); translated by Sutton as *Henri Quatre, King of France,* 2 volumes (London: Secker & Warburg, 1938-1939); translation republished as *Henry, King of France* (New York: Knopf, 1939);

Mut: Essays (Paris: Éditions du 10 mai, 1939);

Lidice: Roman (Mexico City: Editorial "El Libro Libre," 1943);

Ein Zeitalter wird besichtigt (Stockholm: Neuer Verlag, 1945);

Voltaire–Goethe (Weimar: Verlag Werden und Wirken, 1947);

Der Atem: Roman (Amsterdam: Querido, 1949);

Ausgewählte Werke in Einzelausgaben, edited by Alfred Kantorowicz, 13 volumes (Berlin: Aufbau, 1951-1962);

Geist und Tat: Ein Brevier, edited by Kantorowicz (Berlin: Aufbau, 1953);

Eine Liebesgeschichte: Novelle (Munich: Weismann, 1953);

Empfang bei der Welt: Roman (Berlin: Aufbau, 1956);

Das gestohlene Dokument und andere Novellen (Berlin: Aufbau, 1957);

Gesammelte Werke in Einzelausgaben, 14 volumes (Hamburg: Claassen, 1958-1966);

Die traurige Geschichte von Friedrich dem Großen: Fragment (Berlin: Aufbau, 1960);

Das Stelldichein; Die roten Schuhen (Munich: Dobbeck, 1960);

Gesammelte Werke, edited by the Akademie der Künste der DDR, 24 volumes published (Berlin: Aufbau, 1965-);

Werkauswahl in zehn Bänden, 10 volumes (Düsseldorf: Claassen, 1976).

OTHER: Alfred Capus, *Wer zuletzt lacht. . . : Roman. Aus dem Französischen,* translated by Mann (Munich: Langen, 1901);

Anatole France, *Komödiantengeschichte: Roman. Aus dem Französischen,* translated by Mann (Munich: Langen, 1904);

Pierre Ambroise François Choderlos de Laclos, *Gefährliche Freundschaften,* translated by Mann, 2 volumes (Berlin & Leipzig: Verlag der Funken, 1905); republished as *Schlimme Liebschaften* (Leipzig: Insel, 1920); republished as *Gefährliche Liebschaften* (Leipzig: Insel, 1926);

Albert Jamet, *Der Unbekannte Soldat spricht,* translated by Hermynia zur Mühlen, foreword by Mann (Vienna: Prager, 1932);

Gerhart Seger, *Oranienburg: Erster authentischer Bericht eines aus dem Konzentrationslager Geflüchteten,* foreword by Mann (Karlsbad: Graphia, 1934);

Hans A. Joachim, *Die Stimme Victor Hugos: Hörspiel,* afterword by Mann (Paris: Editions du Phénix, 1935);

Felix Fechenbach, *Mein Herz schlägt weiter: Briefe aus der Schutzhaft,* foreword by Mann (St. Gallen: Kulturverlag, 1936);

Manuel Humbert, *Adolf Hitlers "Mein Kampf": Dichtung und Wahrheit,* foreword by Mann (Paris: Pariser Tageblatt, 1936);

The Living Thought of Nietzsche, edited by Mann (London: Cassell, 1939);

Der Pogrom, foreword by Mann (Zurich & Paris: Verlag für soziale Literatur, 1939);

Deutsche Stimmen zu 1789, foreword by Mann (Paris: Deutsches Kulturkartell, 1939);

Ernst Busch, *Lied der Zeit: Lieder, Balladen und Kantaten aus Deutschland von 1914 bis 1945,* foreword by Mann (Berlin-Niederschönhausen: Verlag Lied der Zeit, 1946);

Morgenröte: Ein Lesebuch, introduction by Mann (New York: Aurora, 1947);

Victor Hugo, *Dreiundneunzig,* afterword by Mann (Leipzig & Munich: List, 1949).

More persistently than any other major writer of his generation, Heinrich Mann opposed social injustice and the spiritual decline of Germany's culture during the Wilhelmine era before World War I and during the Weimar Republic. He was also a vehement, prophetic enemy of National Socialism. With a satiric realism that heightens the reader's tragic awareness, his best works lay bare the ideological and societal roots of the delusions that gave to German history in his lifetime its catastrophic bent.

Luiz Heinrich Mann was born in the north German port of Lübeck in 1871, the year Bismarck unified Germany under the contradictory auspices of militaristic Prussian autocracy and laissez-faire industrial capitalism. His father, Thomas Johann Heinrich Mann, scion of a respected mercantile dynasty, was a senator, a member of the Hanseatic city's ruling body. His

Heinrich and Thomas Mann in 1900 (Thomas-Mann-Archiv, Zurich)

Mann in 1903, holding a volume from his trilogy Die Göttinnen *(Deutsche Akademie der Künste, Abteilung Literaturarchiv, Berlin)*

Mann's self-portrait in pencil, circa 1905 (Deutsche Akademie der Künste, Abteilung Literaturarchiv, Berlin)

mother, Julia da Silva-Bruhns Mann, had been born in Brazil to a colonial entrepreneur from Lübeck and his Brazilian wife. Mann received from this side of his heritage not only his first name but also, like his younger brother Thomas, the sense of living "between two races," of carrying within himself opposing forces of disciplined rationality and a passion for the exotic, a craving at once for independence and communion. With Thomas a close, sometimes combative, relationship endured throughout his life. He was devoted to his sister Carla, an actress who committed suicide in 1910.

Although as the eldest son Mann seemed destined to become a merchant, he early inclined toward an artistic career, first as a painter, then as a writer. After he left the gymnasium in 1889 his father apprenticed him to a bookseller in Dresden and the following year to the publishing house of S. Fischer in Berlin, where he also attended the university. Upon his father's death in 1891 the family business was sold, there being no heir able to carry it on; his share of the proceeds left Mann financially independent to pursue a career as a writer. In 1893 the family moved to Munich, the chief artistic center in Germany. Partly because of problems with his health Mann led a peripatetic life, staying for long periods in France and Italy, particularly in Rome, until he settled in Munich in 1914.

Book reviews by Mann had appeared in German literary journals as early as 1891; in 1894 his first novel, *In einer Familie* (In a Family) was published, followed in 1897 and 1898 by collections of novellas and short stories. Like his brother he combined a fertile creative imagination with self-discipline to maintain a copious and many-sided productivity that was to continue almost unabated until his death. The period from 1900 until World War I, however, was the most significant for his artistic and intellectual development.

Of the three great European novelistic traditions of the nineteenth century that influenced German writers–the English of Scott and Dickens, the Russian of Tolstoy and Dostoyevski, and the French of Stendhal, Balzac, Flaubert, and Zola–Mann chose the last as his model. Accordingly, his novels are characterized by the narrator's seemingly unrelenting objectivity; his characters and their actions are regarded from a distance that is fastidiously maintained. Satiric irony and a tendency to polemical caricature are hallmarks of his works, especially the earlier ones. Minute and stylistically brilliant description and direct rendering of dialogue take precedence over analyses of states of mind. Mann admired the French authors for their clarity and intellectual conviction, their grasp of an individual's fate as arising not only from his own ideas and volition but also from the historical era and society in which he lives. He prized Zola's devotion to the cause of justice.

Mann rejected both naturalism and symbolism, the predominant artistic tendencies in Germany in the late nineteenth century; he was repelled by the materialist determinism of the former and the decadent resignation of the latter. Typically for his generation, he was strongly influenced by Nietzsche, but also by the French author Paul Bourget. His early thinking followed conservative lines, defending traditional social values against the upheavals brought about by Germany's rapid economic development. Nietzschean longing for a lost primal vitality and wholeness of humanity underlies Mann's wittily scornful depictions of bourgeois society at the turn of the century. Men and women lustfully pursue wealth, power, and sensual pleasure, seem-

Die kleine Stadt

I

Der Advokat Belotti trat schwänzelnd an den Tisch vor de[illegible]
[illegible] mit dem Taschentuch von seinem kurzen Hals und sagte
[illegible] Fortschritt [illegible]

„Die Post hat wieder Verspätung." [illegible]

„Jawohl," machten Apotheker und Gemeindesekretär, und da [illegible]
[illegible] mehr zu sagen blieb, schwiegen sie. [illegible] der Reisenden [illegible]

„Es wird doch nichts geschehen sein?"

Die Anderen stießen unwillig den Atem aus. Der [illegible]
Carabinieri [illegible] legte mit Nachsicht, weil er sich von einem Fremden [illegible]
große Sicherheit der Straßen dar. Zwei seiner Leute begleiteten [illegible]
[illegible] Pferde die Post, und nur einmal hatten sie einzugreifen [illegible]
[illegible] wollte ein Bauer seinen Platz nicht bezahlen und zog gegen [illegible]
Kutscher das Messer.

„Solche Leute haben wenig Erziehung," erklärte der [illegible]

„Ein langweiliges Handwerk, das Ihre," rief der Apotheker [illegible]
[illegible] mit seiner braven Stimme. „[illegible] aus dem Grabe[illegible]
[illegible] mit seiner [illegible] zurück[illegible]. Als wir dabei waren [illegible]
[illegible] und eine [illegible] Wie, Achille?"
[illegible] anders zu. [illegible]

Der Wirt rief von drinnen:

„[illegible]" [illegible] stützte die Last seines Bauches auf [illegible]
Er [illegible] heraus, [illegible] Munde, worin die Zunge [illegible]
[illegible] und wartete mit offenem [illegible]

„Wie, mein Alter?" und der Apotheker klopfte ihm auf [illegible]

„Vor diesen Füßen ist manche Granate geplatzt. In Bezzecc[illegible]
[illegible] beiden der General Garibaldi selber stand. Die [illegible]
[illegible] als gleich bei [illegible] wir springen zurück, versteht sich; der General aber rührte sich [illegible]
[illegible] ‚Freunde,' sagt er zu uns, und, Achille, wir [illegible]
[illegible]

„Das ist die reine Wahrheit," sagte der Wirt, und voll Würde [illegible]

First page from the manuscript for Die kleine Stadt *(1909), widely regarded as Mann's most artistically successful work (Deutsche Akademie der Künste, Abteilung Literaturarchiv, Berlin)*

Der Untertan
Geschichte der öffentlichen Seele unter Wilhelm II.

[illegible]

Die Macht

I

[illegible]

Diederich Heßling war ein weiches Kind, das am liebsten träumte, sich vor allem fürchtete und viel an den Ohren litt. Ungern verließ er im Winter die warme Stube, im Sommer den engen Garten, der nach den Lumpen der Papierfabrik roch und über dessen Goldregen- und Fliederbäumen das höhere Fachwerk der alten Häuser stand. Wenn Diederich vom Märchenbuch, dem geliebten Märchenbuch aufsah, erschrak er [illegible] sehr. Neben ihm auf der Bank hatte ganz deutlich eine Kröte gesessen, halb so groß wie er selbst! Oder an der Mauer drüben [illegible] zum Bauch in der Erde ein Gnom und schielte her!

Fürchterlicher als Gnom und Kröte war der Vater, und obendrein sollte man ihn lieben. Diederich liebte ihn. Wenn er genascht oder gelogen hatte, [illegible] er sich solange schmatzend und scheu wedelnd am Schreibpult [illegible], bis Herr Heßling etwas merkte und den Stock von der Wand nahm. [illegible] nicht herausgekommene Unfall mischte in Diederichs Ergebenheit und Vertrauen einen Zweifel. Als der Vater einmal mit seinem [illegible] Bein die Treppe herunterfiel, klatschte der Sohn wie toll in die Hände, — worauf er weglief.

Kam er nach einer Abstrafung mit gedunsenem Gesicht und unter Geheul an der Werkstätte vorbei, dann lachten die Arbeiter. Sofort aber streckte Diederich nach ihnen die Zunge aus und stampfte. „Er war sich bewußt: [illegible] ist mein Papa! Ihr wärt froh, wenn ihr auch Prügel von ihm bekommen [illegible]. Aber dafür seid ihr viel zu [illegible] wenig."

Er bewegte sich zwischen ihnen, wie ein launenhafter Pascha; drohte ihnen, es dem Vater zu melden, daß sie sich Bier holten, und bald ließ er sich [illegible] die Stunde [illegible], zu der Herr Heßling zurückkehrte.

First page from the manuscript for Der Untertan *(1918), Mann's satire of Wilhelmine Germany (Deutsche Akademie der Künste, Abteilung Literaturarchiv, Berlin)*

ingly the only real goals of existence; but they give up these quests in fits of nihilistic boredom, only to resume them when opportunity beckons. No purpose in living beyond self-gratification seems possible.

His youthful good looks and innocently pliable opportunism ideally equip Andreas Zumsee, the protagonist of *Im Schlaraffenland* (1900; translated as *In the Land of Cockaigne,* 1929), to succeed in just such a world. "Cockaigne" is Berlin, the political and financial capital of the empire, populated by unscrupulous nouveau-riche financiers, corrupt journalists serving their speculative interests, and officers, artists, and actors who entertain and console the financiers' and journalists' chronically bored wives. Andreas becomes the lover of Adelheid Türkheimer, the wife of a wealthy banker. She launches his career as a dramatist, and he becomes accepted in the best social circles. When her affections pall, Andreas brings about his own downfall by having an affair with a working-class girl, the mistress of Adelheid's husband. The Türkheimers close ranks and force their former young paramours to marry, giving Andreas a job as a journalist. For his presumptuousness he is condemned to life in the lower middle classes. Mann vividly depicts a situation in which persons and objects are made to reveal their frequently grotesque natures. Although the novel clearly derives from Maupassant's *Bel-Ami* (1885; translated, 1891), its satiric temper rather calls to mind Voltaire or even Swift.

Commentators usually regard *Die Jagd nach Liebe* (The Pursuit of Love, 1903) as a counterpart to *Im Schlaraffenland,* set in Munich rather than Berlin. Although both novels analyze life among the upper classes with pessimistic irony, *Die Jagd nach Liebe* centers on love in a culture that equates it solely with sexual gratification, which in its turn has become a commodity interchangeable with money and power. Mann returns to this concern with love throughout his oeuvre, making it his central theme and treating it, depending on the context and period of his life, elegiacally or cynically as a simple matter of fact about which only fools have illusions. In *Die Jagd nach Liebe,* incapacity to love manifests itself in various characters as perversion, sentimentality, or tragedy. Claude Marehn, a rich, feckless young man, hopes to find salvation from an empty life in the consummation of his love for the aspiring actress Ute Ende. Her ambitions absorb Ute completely, however, and she treats Claude only as a brotherly confidant who pays her bills. Although she claims that she wishes to succeed through her talent alone and not by resorting to the wiles used by others, she does not conceal from Claude that his guardian Panier has seduced her as the price for advancing her career. The elderly satyr Panier possesses the brutish vitality in sexual and financial matters that Claude and his generation, crippled by too much reflection, lack. Claude seeks oblivion in travel, gambling, and love affairs. Vitiated by his obsession for Ute, his soul remains barren even as he responds to but inwardly betrays the sincere passion of other women. Finally, Claude becomes mortally ill. Now that he is disfigured and foul-smelling, Ute attempts the supreme role of her otherwise mediocre career: professing regret for what she has done to Claude, she declares her love and gives herself to him on his deathbed in hopes that she will inherit his fortune.

In his trilogy *Die Göttinnen* (The Goddesses, 1903), Mann explores the futility of attempting to live as though such creatures as Ute are harmless aesthetic phenomena to whose corrosive moral effects the superior individual is immune. The Duchess Violante von Assy possesses wealth, intelligence, and, most fatefully, demonic beauty that enslaves all who behold it. In the cause of her desire to transfigure the world in aesthetic grandeur, many sacrifice their lives–some with noble purpose, others in gruesome vanity–while Violante remains the essentially frigid and passive center of the hopes kindled by her beauty. This noblewoman-adventuress partakes of mythic identities in three novels. In *Diana*–named for the protectress of slaves and women–Violante joins in a plot to overthrow the monarch of her native Dalmatia and make her queen instead. Her wish to bring "liberty, justice, prosperity, and enlightenment" to her land arises less from political than from aesthetic motives: she believes that the beauty of her people deserves their being endowed with these rights; "godly" whim precludes concern with their real needs. The comic-opera conspiracy fails, and Violante flees to Italy, where she becomes the object of intrigues by the nobility and clergy. *Minerva*–named for the protectress of artists and artisans–shows Violante at the center of an extravagant cult of artistry. Painters, sculptors, and poets, modeled on contemporary advocates of symbolism and the associated art nouveau, proclaim allegiance to an ideal *paradis artificiel* of the soul, exalted beyond the meanness of the empirical world. Their lives, how-

The Czech actress Maria Kanová, whom Mann married on 12 August 1914 (Deutsche Akademie der Künste, Abteilung Literaturarchiv, Berlin)

Mann with his daughter Leonie (Marta Feuchtwanger, Pacific Palisades)

ever, reveal them to be pathetically vulnerable to the world's enticements and sufferings, with money, desire, and power their guiding obsessions. In *Venus,* finally, Violante goads her myriad suitors to ever greater extravagance and bestiality. Here Mann sardonically exposes the absurdity and horror of the neoromantic idea that love and death may be united in a moment of supreme beauty by showing, in an orgy of bloody degradation, the consequences of translating it into reality. Deserted, her beauty about to fade, Violante dies in isolation and agonizing barrenness, the price of having lived a life that was her great work of art, a life whose ambivalence between aesthetic grandeur and moral revulsion not even she could reconcile.

Mann's most famous novella, "Pippo Spano," written in 1903 and published in the collection *Flöten und Dolche* (Flutes and Daggers, 1905), reveals his skepticism about the relationship of the artist, the aesthetic personality par excellence, to the realities of life. Mario Malvolto, a popular young dramatist, is amazed to find that his art gives him real power over others, especially Gemma, a young noblewoman who falls in love with him. To his mind he has adopted to best effect the bold opportunism of the Italian Renaissance typified by the mercenary captain Pippo Spano, whose portrait watches over the action in enigmatic silence. Mario soon finds that Gemma, unwilling to distinguish between the artist and the man, lives more ardently for his art than for his love. When their affair becomes a public scandal, Mario and Gemma plan joint suicide by his hand. He kills Gemma but cannot shoot himself. Unable to act as love and honor demand, Mario is merely "a comedian who has forgotten his lines." Failure as a man cannot be morally compensated for by artistic success. "Pippo Spano" signalizes a turning point in Mann's thinking toward the conviction that the artist must answer for the consequences of his works as moral acts, that he must not only analyze and judge the world but help in changing it for the better.

If exposure of repressive institutions can help to make society more humane, then *Professor Unrat oder das Ende eines Tyrannen* (Professor Unrat or the End of a Tyrant, 1905; translated as *The Blue Angel,* 1931) was the first major work to incorporate this change in Mann's artistic purposes. The Professor, a teacher in a gymnasium in the Lübeck of Mann's childhood, has been the malevolent scourge of the city's youth for twenty-five years, destroying with pedantry any inspiration they derive from their schooling and ruining their future careers as punishment for the slightest offense against his whims. His name is Raat, but his students call him "Unrat" (refuse, filth). As his tyranny holds sway in the school, he tries to control the world outside by speaking of all matters in set bureaucratic phrases or the adolescent vocabulary of the classroom. His crabbed life takes a new turn when he falls in love with the "artiste" Rosa Fröhlich, a singer in the dubious café The Blue Angel. In her honesty and directness of feeling she is the opposite of Unrat: he does touch her, however, with the wooden honorableness of his intentions. They marry; and until he is dismissed for conduct unbecoming an educator Unrat leads a double life, acting as Rosa's factotum and guardian of her honor at night and oppressing his pupils by day. Neither love nor the loss of his position changes Unrat's nature. The home of this odd couple becomes a club where the most distinguished gentlemen of the town, most of them Unrat's former pupils, may spend their evenings drinking and gambling in the company of women of easy virtue. Revealing the anarchy that is the obverse of his tyranny, Unrat delights in corrupting leading citizens, profiting from the financial ruin of some of them. Society tolerates transgression of its moral code, but not of its deep concern for property; bourgeois "respectability" is restored when Unrat is arrested for stealing the wallet of his wife's lover. A trenchant study of a man driven even in love by frustrated aggression, as both agent and victim of a hypocritical, repressive society, *Professor Unrat* remains one of Mann's most accessible works.

Zwischen den Rassen (Between the Races, 1907) reflects Mann's ideological position and his sense of being an outsider. In depicting its heroine, Lola Gabriel, who is of German-Brazilian parentage, Mann drew heavily on the circumstances of his mother's youth and on the life of the German-Argentinian Ines Schmied, to whom he was then engaged. Lola is drawn alternately to the Italian noble Pardi, a ruthless man of action, and the sensitive German humanist Arnold Acton, who is critical of Pardi and his political principles. She marries Pardi, accepting his inevitable abuses and betrayals as retribution for following her vital drives rather than her humane reason. Acton wins her love by challenging Pardi to a duel whose outcome is unresolved at novel's end. He represents a hope for Mann: the intellectual finally aroused to challenge both brutal amorality

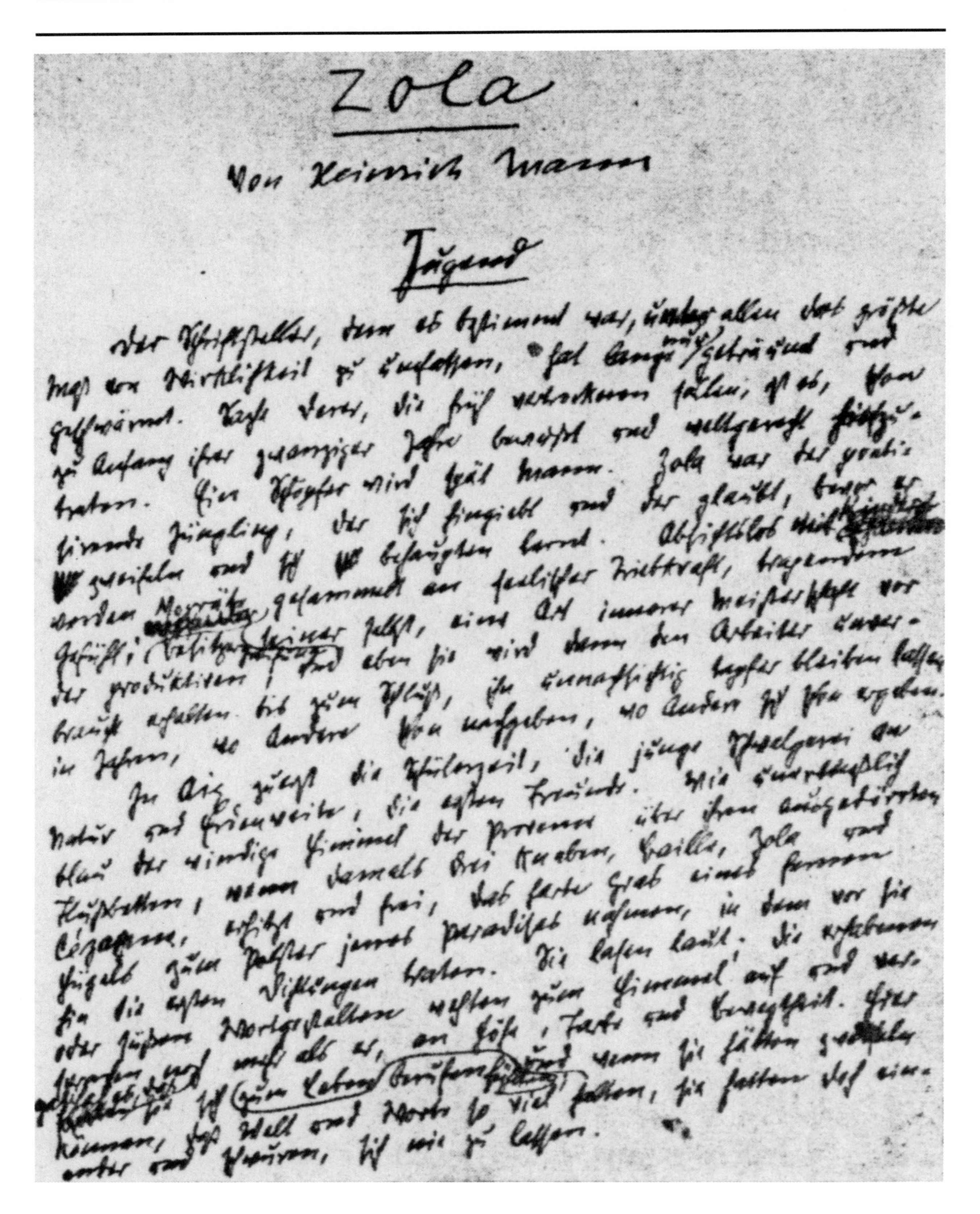

Zola

Von Heinrich Mann

Jugend

First page from the manuscript for Mann's essay "Zola," published in 1915 in the journal Die weißen Blätter *(Deutsche Akademie der Künste, Abteilung Literaturarchiv, Berlin)*

Mann in 1920

Heinrich and Thomas Mann in Berlin, 1920s (Ullstein)

and Germany's infatuation with materialism, an infatuation that had paralyzed the political will of its people and put their strength at the disposal of an unscrupulous, power-intoxicated elite that could lead them to disaster.

His years outside Germany, especially living "like the common people" in Rome, gave Mann unique opportunities to observe other societies. To him, Italy after its unification in 1860 was a hopeful example of what the democratic instincts of a people could bring about: a republic based on communities of autonomous individuals who, in an atmosphere of mutual respect, make decisions affecting their lives by general consent and resolve differences in the common interest. Although such cities existed in Germany, and included Lübeck, their democratic institutions were being displaced by the centralized autocracy of the Second Reich, a trend fostered also by industrialization. Mann's "hymn to democracy" in this sense was his novel *Die kleine Stadt* (1909; translated as *The Little Town,* 1930); widely regarded as his artistically best work, it is distinguished by genial, tolerant humor. That his homeland was the political antipode of Mann's ideal is revealed by the fact that the novel's publisher refused to let the word *democracy* appear in its advertisements so as not to offend the public's faith in the authoritarian national state. The book was a commercial failure at the time of its publication but was better received in later years. In the novel, the arrival of an itinerant opera troupe in a small city in the hills outside Rome sharpens traditional differences between the town's ideological factions: the "progressives," who favor innovation and a secular society and who invited the players; and the "conservatives," who espouse tradition and piety and who try first to prevent, then to sabotage the performance. About a hundred skillfully individualized characters figure in complex relationships of love and hate, alliance and rivalry. The central chapter depicts the operatic performance, which the townspeople comment upon not as "art" but as something arising from and affecting their own lives. In this society culture is truly popular, not the domain of a particular class. No barrier of consciousness separates the artist from society. Although tensions mount to a point approaching civil conflict, compromise and reconciliation are finally achieved–not by an external authority but through the common sense and respect for human dignity of the people themselves.

While living abroad Mann became ever more convinced of the innate dishonesty and cruelty of the German socioeconomic system. He concluded that only a democratic republic could better the lot of the people, releasing them from psychological bondage to the power structure that made them, in effect, conspire in their own subjection. But Mann understood that the democracy of *Die kleine Stadt* arose from the special character of the Italian people; he was scathingly pessimistic about the capability of his countrymen to develop similar political institutions, as they had been "deformed" by their history and their veneration of "great men" into a nation of submissive underlings. Most pernicious to Mann was an intellectual tradition in which freedom and justice were abstractions to be striven for by certain individuals through self-improvement; these ideals were held to be achievable by the whole society, if at all, only through a lengthy evolutionary process. Around 1910 France became for Mann the model possibility of Humanity emancipating itself by acting according to its collective practical reason. Mann's criticism of Germany's situation, aesthetically motivated in earlier novels, began to concentrate increasingly on political and social questions; jaundiced conservatism was replaced by an ever more radical view of the duty of the writer in his own time. In both phases of Mann's thinking the adversary was the autocratic, materialist Wilhelmine Reich; the goal was the achievement by mankind of its highest potential.

"Geist und Tat" (Intellect and Action) and *Voltaire–Goethe,* provocatively uncompromising essays written in 1910, contain the nucleus of Mann's sense of the supreme task of the intellectual: to bring a nation to follow the demands of critical reason for truth and justice, as France had done in 1789. In "Geist und Tat" (published in the collection *Macht und Mensch* [Power and Man, 1919]) he says: "Dies Volk machte die Revolution nicht, solange es nur hungerte: es machte sie, als es erfuhr, daß es eine Gerechtigkeit und Wahrheit gäbe, die in ihm beleidigt seien. . . . Die Geschichte hat keinen anderen Sinn mehr, als jener großen Stunde Dauer zu geben und dem Geist, der das Geschlecht jenes Jahres beseelte, die Welt zum Körper. . . . Denn der Geist ist nichts Erhaltendes und gibt keine Vorrechte. Er zersetzt, er ist gleichmacherisch; und über die Trümmer von hundert Zwingburgen drängt er den letzten Erfüllungen der Wahrheit und Gerechtigkeit entgegen, ihrer Vollendung, und sei es die des Todes" (This people did not make a revolution as long as it was only hungry, but rather when it learned that Justice and Truth ex-

Félix Bertaux, Pierre Viénot, and Mann at the 1923 Les Décades de Pontigny, a yearly gathering of intellectuals started in 1905 by Paul Desjardins (Archive des Centre Culturel International de Cerisy-la-Salle)

Mann in 1923 (Archiv des Centre Culturel International de Cerisy-la-Salle)

isted, to which its own situation was an affront. . . . History has no other significance than to give permanence to that great moment and to give to the intellect, which inspired that generation, the world as its incarnation. . . . For the intellect does not conserve and grants no privileges. It subverts, it is egalitarian; and over the ruins of a hundred fortresses it presses on toward the final realization of Truth and Justice, their fulfillment, even though it may be that of death).

In *Voltaire–Goethe* (published separately in 1947) he praises the French philosopher's radical intellectuality and his rebellion against the inertia of nature and human institutions as being more fruitful for the dignity and liberation of mankind than Goethe's scientific objectivity and cautious rejection of abrupt change. Such iconoclasm allied Mann with members of the expressionist movement, and his essays were published in its journals *Die Aktion* and *Pan*.

For a time Mann gained wider renown as a playwright than as a novelist. He wrote the psychological dramas *Schauspielerin* (Actress, 1911) and *Die große Liebe* (The Great Love Affair, 1912); two plays dealing with the French Revolution and its aftermath, *Madame Legros* (1913) and *Der Weg zur Macht* (The Path to Power, 1919); and a tragedy of unscrupulous materialism, *Brabach* (1917). During this especially happy phase of his life Mann met the Czech actress Maria Kanová, whom he married in August 1914. Their daughter Leonie was born in 1916.

On the day following his marriage, thanks to the inflamed patriotism of the early days of World War I, serialization was discontinued of the masterpiece that was to bring Mann his most widespread acclaim when it was published as a book in 1918: *Der Untertan* (The Subject; translated as *The Patrioteer,* 1929). Kurt Tucholsky praised the novel as "the herbarium of German manhood" because of the precision with which Mann analyzed the forces that gave to Wilhelmine society its repressive, servile character. The development of Diederich Heßling is the central concern of this richly detailed parody of the bildungsroman, the novel of a young man's spiritual cultivation that had found its greatest exponents in Goethe, Eichendorff, and Keller. Diederich, a sickly and sentimental child, is formed successively by his family, his schooling, his university fraternity, and the worlds of business and politics into a model loyal subject of the Kaiser. He comes to respect, even to love, only those who treat him with arbitrary harshness and deceit. Heßling's cowed adoration of Wilhelm II is a paradigm for the results of this education, which has taught him that the reward for subjection of the individual to the will of the more powerful, for his conformity to collective norms, is the license to exploit those weaker than he. Hypocrisy, duplicity, and ruthless opportunism characterize Heßling's relations with his family and with women; toward the employees of his paper mill he is a rapacious tyrant. Eventually he becomes secure in the knowledge that despite the apparently adversarial roles played by some, all elements of the power structure–including the Social Democratic leaders of his workers–are corruptible and interested chiefly in maintaining the privileges of the few, regardless of the cost to the many.

Der Untertan was an immediate best-seller when the war was over; 100,000 copies had been printed by the end of 1918. Many readers found in it at least a partial explanation of the tragedy that had befallen the nation. Mann later conceived of *Der Untertan* as the "Novel of the Bourgeoisie," the first in a trilogy he called "Das Kaiserreich: Die Romane der deutschen Gesellschaft im Zeitalter Wilhelms II" (The Empire: Novels of German Society in the Age of Wilhelm II). The second, *Die Armen* (The Poor, 1917), the "Novel of the Proletarian," deals with working-class conditions, although both the plot and the depictions of proletarian life are overidealistic. In possession of a document proving that Heßling does not have full legal title, Karl Balrich hopes to gain ownership of the paper mill for his fellow workers in a lawsuit. Wishing to become the workers' attorney in the case, he begins learning Latin as the first step toward the law degree that will enable him to secure justice. Circumstances, Heßling's chicanery, and–especially–the workers' lack of solidarity defeat him. Karl joins the army when the war begins. He has learned that he was mistaken in trying to transcend his class to gain redress for individual grievances through the society's institutions. He hopes to join the collective struggle for the rights of the proletariat when peace comes. Because of this patriotic but ambiguous conclusion the novel could be published during the war.

The third novel in the trilogy, *Der Kopf* (The Head, 1925), the "Novel of the Leaders," concerns the lives of two friends between 1891 and 1914: the idealistic, sensual Terra and the accommodating pragmatist Mangolf. Many readers see in this novel a fictional treatment of the differ-

Mann and Nelly Kroeger on the beach at Nice in 1930, the year of Mann's divorce from his first wife (Marta Feuchtwanger, Pacific Palisades, California)

Emil Jannings as the professor in the 1930 film Der blaue Engel, *based on Mann's 1905 novel* Professor Unrat

ences between Mann and his brother Thomas. Mangolf pursues power by all means and eventually becomes Imperial Chancellor; Terra is his perpetual adversary as a publicist, a coal magnate, and a member of the Reichstag. The start of the war makes clear to both the tragic absurdity of their lives, and they commit suicide together. Around this plot Mann constructed a complex and often improbable roman à clef that purports to expose the cupidity and psychological corruption of Germany's former rulers. Although he lavished much care on *Der Kopf,* the novel is generally regarded as a failure.

The war further disrupted the relationship between Heinrich and Thomas Mann, which had been difficult for at least a decade. Both had been aware since youth of essential disparities in their temperaments, which became evident in their art and social and political attitudes. Heinrich was the more evidently passionate and critical of the two, satirizing institutions hallowed by the bourgeoisie and espousing the values of social justice and popular democracy. Thomas, while critical in his own way, appeared to be less dissatisfied with things as they were; he seemed to be more understanding, if with affectionate irony, of the souls of his fellow Germans as revealed in their culture and more ready to perpetuate tradition than to break with it forcibly. Like many German writers of the time, Thomas Mann defended his nation's role in the war almost until its end; Heinrich, on the other hand, saw in the war only universal catastrophe. The brothers began seeing veiled personal attacks in each other's writings, and soon they were not on speaking terms. Only in 1922, when Heinrich fell seriously ill, did a reconciliation come about. From then on, although a certain distance remained, Heinrich and Thomas Mann made common cause, particularly in defending the Weimar Republic.

In the tumultuous political aftermath of World War I Heinrich Mann emerged as a leading advocate of reason and moderation in Germany. His criticisms of arrogant, saber-rattling nationalism and of imperialistic capitalism had proven to be tragically correct. During the 1920s he dedicated his writing almost exclusively to helping Germany to find her place within a new community of Europe and to become a more humane and socially just nation. In articles, lectures, and essays he worked incessantly for reconciliation and cooperation between France and Germany and toward a tolerant and decent democratic society, a constitutional republic free from the totalitarianism of either fascism or communism. Always a critic of capitalism, he believed that the best hope for Germany and Europe lay in a program of democratic socialism, finding both "American" free enterprise and "Russian" communism to be alien to the traditions and interests of an autonomous, vital Europe. During these years Mann wrote in "Unser Einfluß und diese Zeit" (Our Influence and This Time), collected in the volume *Sieben Jahre* (Seven Years, 1929): "Literatur ist niemals nur Kunst, eine bei ihrer Entstehung schon überzeitliche Dichtung gibt es nicht. Sie kann so kindlich nicht geliebt werden wie Musik. Denn sie ist Gewissen–das aus der Welt hervorgehobene und vor sie hingestellte Gewissen. Es wirkt und handelt immer" (Literature is never solely a form of art; there is no such thing as a work that stands outside of its age at the time it is written. It cannot be loved in as childlike a way as music. For it is conscience–conscience that has been lifted out of the world and that now confronts it. It is perpetually at work and in action).

Like *Der Kopf,* Mann's novels of the Weimar period have not met with critical esteem; most of them are considered seriously flawed attempts to project the possibility of humane, ethical action into the turmoil of contemporary Germany, an artistic undertaking about which Mann himself was skeptical. *Eugénie oder die Bürgerzeit* (Eugénie or the Bourgeois Era, 1928; translated as *The Royal Woman,* 1930), set in Lübeck in 1873 and evocative of the world and style of Theodor Fontane, is better regarded than Mann's other novels of this period. The action centers on a "play within the play" about the recently deposed Emperor Napoleon III of France and the Empress Eugénie that is instrumental in the downfall of an unscrupulous speculator and in making his victims, a wealthy patrician family, reflect about their own social morality. Two novels with a contemporary setting deal with the problematic relations of parents and children in a new age. *Mutter Marie* (1927; translated as *Mother Mary,* 1928) tells of the spiritual conversion of a woman who, repenting her almost incestuous love for her long-lost son, sacrifices her interests and even risks her life to secure his happiness. In *Die große Sache* (The Big Deal, 1930) an engineer teaches his materialistic children by means of a deception that the true goal of life is joy, satisfaction brought about by genuine accomplishment–by truly working for a living and not merely profiting from the deeds of

Nelly Kroeger and Mann, 1930 (Marta Feuchtwanger, Pacific Palisades, California)

Mann listening to a tribute from Lion Feuchtwanger at a celebration of Mann's sixtieth birthday in 1931 (Marta Feuchtwanger, Pacific Palisades, California)

Mann, André Gide, and Michael Gold at the International Writers' Congress for the Defense of Culture, Paris, 1935 (Marta Feuchtwanger, Pacific Palisades, California)

others. *Ein ernstes Leben* (A Serious Life, 1932; translated as *The Hill of Lies,* 1934) is about a young woman who falls victim to thieves who make her appear guilty of their crimes and is vindicated by a kindly police inspector. These novels plead for social reconciliation, especially between the older generation, who had known the world before the war, and the young, who had not. This good intention is marred by contrived plots and turgid writing.

Even during the brief period of economic well-being enjoyed by the Weimar Republic Mann's advocacy of democracy, socialism, and European cosmopolitanism represented a minority position in Germany, where resentment still ran high against the Treaty of Versailles and the belief was widely held that the war could have been won had it not been for a political "stab in the back" by Social Democrats on the home front. As politics became radicalized during the Depression Mann was attacked ever more virulently, especially by the National Socialists and their allies of the ultranationalist right. Nonetheless, his reputation as a writer and political thinker was at its zenith during these years, and he was widely regarded throughout Europe as representing the best of the German intellectual tradition. Although he never seriously entertained the idea, the suggestion was made that Mann run for president of the republic in the 1932 election. With his deep appreciation of French culture and his excellent command of the language, he served as an unofficial "cultural ambassador" to France and contributed to improved relations between the two nations.

Mann moved from Munich to Berlin in 1928; shortly thereafter his marriage ended in divorce. In 1930 the film *Der blaue Engel* (English version: *The Blue Angel*) based on *Professor Unrat* and starring Marlene Dietrich and Emil Jannings, was produced. The recasting of Unrat as a tragic figure and the suppression of socially critical content, together with the brilliance of the actors and director, brought worldwide popularity to the film, which still ranks as a classic. (In his memoirs Mann reported, as a sign of Germans' hos-

Mann in 1936, during his exile in France (Deutsche Akademie der Künste, Abteilung Literaturarchiv, Berlin)

Mann and Nelly Kroeger in California, 1938. They were married the following year (Thomas-Mann-Archiv).

Mann in Los Angeles during the 1940s (S.V.-Bilderdienst, Munich)

tility toward him in 1933, brisk sales of a jumping-jack doll with his head and Marlene Dietrich's legs. He wryly commented that the Nazis' hatred had made him better known than anything he had ever done.)

Mann was elected president of the Literary Section of the Prussian Academy of the Arts in 1931; that year he received widespread tributes on the occasion of his sixtieth birthday. Shortly before Adolf Hitler was appointed chancellor of Germany on 31 January 1933 Mann joined Albert Einstein and Käthe Kollwitz in an appeal to the Social Democratic and Communist parties to unite in efforts to prevent the Nazis from taking power. On 15 February, under official pressure, the Prussian Academy demanded Mann's resignation. On the pretext of taking a trip to Frankfurt, he left Germany on 21 February. He settled on the French Riviera where he was soon joined by Nelly Kroeger, on whom he had based the heroine of *Ein ernstes Leben*. Mann was one of the first to have his German citizenship canceled. He was soon made a citizen of Czechoslovakia.

During his seven years in France Mann ceaselessly attempted to rally democratic forces against fascism. He wrote regularly for French journals, lectured, and participated in rallies; although he was not a communist, he supported the Popular Front movement. Disappointed by the failure of German socialists and communists to unite to prevent the Nazis from coming to power in Germany, he still believed that only such coalitions could prevent fascists from taking over still more countries. His major literary accomplishment in France was the completion of *Die Jugend des Königs Henri Quatre* (1935; translated as *Young Henry of Navarre*, 1937) and *Die Vollendung des Königs Henri Quatre* (The Fulfillment of King

Mann, circa 1945 (S.V.-Bilderdienst, Munich)

Henry IV, 1938; translated as *Henri Quatre, King of France,* 1938-1939). Mann was moved to write historical novels about the sixteenth-century French king Henry IV because, in contrast to the men in power in Mann's own age, his greatness had lain in his humane concern for the welfare of his people, his capacity to love, and his burning desire to bring about peace and reconciliation between warring religious and social factions.

After the fall of Paris in June 1940 Mann knew that he had to leave Europe. In September he and Nelly, whom he had married the previous year, together with his nephew Golo, Franz Werfel, and Alma Mahler-Werfel, made their way on foot through the Pyrenees to the Spanish border. From Spain they went to Portugal, where they boarded a ship that arrived in New York on 13 October. Thomas Mann had come to the United States in 1938. Soon both brothers settled on the outskirts of Los Angeles.

Whereas Thomas was much in demand as a lecturer and guest professor, Heinrich was barely known in the United States. After a year as a writer at the Warner Brothers studio he became financially dependent on his brother and on his wife's work as a nurse. Despite his advanced age and almost total isolation he continued to write, producing a remarkable personal history, *Ein Zeitalter wird besichtigt* (Portrait of an Epoch, 1945), and three novels.

Lidice (1943) is named for the town in Czechoslovakia that was razed, and whose inhabitants were shot or deported, at Hitler's orders in 1942 as retribution for the assassination of Reinhard Heydrich, the Nazi Protector of Bohemia-Moravia. In a seriocomic vein that many find inappropriate, Mann fictionalizes these events as the outcome of the impersonation of Heydrich by a Czech student who usurps power in Prague for a time. He eases the lot of his countrymen, deceiving the Gestapo into murdering the real Heydrich. In the novel, which consists mainly of dialogues, Heydrich emerges as a monstrous descendant of Unrat and Heßling. The destruction of Lidice is commemorated as a sacrifice for freedom.

In California Mann completed *Der Atem,* (Breath, 1949) and *Empfang bei der Welt* (Reception in the World, 1956). Both novels recapitulate themes and techniques from earlier works, sometimes carrying them to heights of satiric surrealism that Thomas Mann was to call "the avantgardism of old age." *Der Atem* is set in Nice at the start of World War II; the central figure is an impoverished, eccentric countess who is dying of consumption. Much of the novel is concerned with her memories; the crises of contemporary Europe are shown through various financial and political intrigues. The countess symbolizes the poignant transfiguration of a European society that is about to disappear forever. *Empfang bei der Welt* comments with bitter humor on the function of art in a world obsessed with power and money. Despite its setting in an indefinite, modernistically conceived "here and now," the tone and targets of the novel's satire are reminiscent of Mann's earlier works. An extensive fragment of a third novel, *Die traurige Geschichte von Friedrich dem Großen* (The Sad Story of Frederick the Great, 1960) was published posthumously. Composed, like *Lidice,* of dialogues, it was conceived by Mann as a negative counterpart from German history to his celebration of Henry IV.

In 1944 his wife committed suicide, a blow from which Mann never recovered. Following the end of the war in 1945 he felt that the political climate in America was becoming less tolerant because of a pervasive fear of communism. The newly founded German Democratic Republic awarded Mann its National Prize for Literature and Art in 1949 and invited him to become the first president of the German Academy of the Arts in East Berlin. Mann accepted, but as he pre-

Die rothen Schuhe

von Heinrich Mann

I

Beide Geschwister waren nur mit Mühe zu Hause zu halten. Was ist mit grossen, ausgewachsenen Menschen zu thun, die weder die Schule beenden, noch einen bürgerlichen Beruf wählen, noch etwa heirathen wollen. Drohungen der Eltern bewirken höchstens, dass sie durchgehen. Grade wird der Sohn noch aufgefangen.
»Wir haben euch nicht nöthig. Ich bringe mich allein durch. In vier Wochen bin ich gemacht — wie heute jeder Jugendliche, der es richtig anfasst, womöglich anständig, sonst anders. Vorurtheile ausgeschlossen. Wir haben neue Erlebnisse, ein neues Weltbild. Was wisst ihr von unseren geistigen Voraussetzungen!«

Ob er denn sogar für seine Schwester die Verantwortung tragen wolle, fragten die schwergeprüften Eltern.

»Dann hole ich auch sie ab, — grade weil ich für ihre seelischen Rechte hafte. Übrigens sie mit ihrem Talent braucht euch erst recht nicht.«

Denn Berthold war mit dem dramatischen Talent Luisens vollauf vertraut. Was er nicht kannte, waren nur ihre Beziehungen zu seinem Schulfreund Max. Eines Abends, er war wieder einmal zum Durchgehen fertig und wollte von ihr Abschied nehmen: — in der Thür fuhr er zurück. Wuth verzerrte sein Gesicht so ungeheuerlich, dass die Schwester, schon bereit, gegen ihn vorzugehen, ergriffen stillhielt. Der Bruder stellte an den Freund eine unvorhergesehene Frage: »Denkst du Luise zu heirathen?«

Das Liebespaar sah sich erstaunt an. Worauf Max: »Ich befinde mich in vollster Übereinstimmung mit Luise, wenn ich nein sage.« Da ward Berthold stürmisch. Sie erkannten den Verächter bürgerlicher Sitte nicht wieder. »Und du willst durchgehn? Wir haben doch einfach dasselbe vor.« Es sei nicht dasselbe, sagte Berthold. Zuletzt entschied Max: »Es ist vorzuziehen, dass ich gehe. Mit deiner Schwester verständigt

First page from the manuscript for Mann's short story "Die roten Schuhe," published in 1960 (Karl Lemke, Heinrich Mann, *1970)*

pared to return to Germany he died of a stroke on 12 March 1950. In 1961, in honor of the ninetieth anniversary of his birth, his ashes were transferred to the Dorotheenstadt Cemetery in East Berlin, where they are interred near the grave of Bertolt Brecht.

Letters:

Thomas Mann/Heinrich Mann, Briefwechsel 1900-1949, edited by Hans Wysling (Frankfurt am Main: Fischer, 1984).

Bibliography:

Edith Zenker, *Heinrich-Mann-Bibliographie: Werke* (Berlin & Weimar: Aufbau-Verlag, 1967).

Biographies:

Klaus Schröter, *Heinrich Mann* (Hamburg: Rowohlt, 1967);

Nigel Hamilton, *The Brothers Mann: The Lives of Heinrich and Thomas Mann 1871-1950 and 1875-1955* (London: Secker & Warburg, 1978).

References:

Sigrid Anger, ed., *Heinrich Mann 1871-1950: Leben und Werk in Dokumenten und Bildern* (Berlin & Weimar: Aufbau, 1971);

Heinz Ludwig Arnold, ed., *Heinrich Mann: Sonderband aus der Reihe TEXT + KRITIK* (Munich: Boorberg, 1971);

André Banuls, *Heinrich Mann* (Stuttgart: Kohlhammer, 1970);

Hugo Dittberner, *Heinrich Mann: Eine kritische Einführung in die Forschung* (Frankfurt am Main: Athenäum Fischer Taschenbuch, 1974);

Volker Ebersbach, *Heinrich Mann: Leben, Werk, Wirken* (Frankfurt am Main: Röderberg, 1978);

Jürgen Haupt, *Heinrich Mann* (Stuttgart: Metzler, 1980);

Brigitte Hocke, *Heinrich Mann* (Leipzig: VEB Bibliographisches Institut, 1983);

Herbert Ihering, *Heinrich Mann: Sein Werk und sein Leben* (Berlin: Aufbau, 1952);

Rolf N. Linn, *Heinrich Mann* (New York: Twayne, 1967);

Siegfried Sudhof, "Heinrich Mann," in *Deutsche Dichter der Moderne: Ihr Leben und Werk,* edited by Benno von Wiese (Berlin: Schmidt, 1969);

Ulrich Weisstein, *Heinrich Mann: Eine historisch-kritische Einführung in sein dichterisches Werk* (Tübingen: Niemeyer, 1962);

Renate Werner, *Skeptizismus, Asthetizismus, Aktivismus: Der frühe Heinrich Mann* (Düsseldorf: Bertelsmann, 1972);

Renate Werner, ed., *Heinrich Mann: Texte zu seiner Wirkungsgeschichte in Deutschland* (Tübingen: Niemeyer, 1977).

Papers:

The greatest part of the literary archive of Heinrich Mann is housed in the Literaturarchiv of the Deutsche Akademie der Künste, Berlin, German Democratic Republic. Letters and other materials are also held at the Deutsches Literaturarchiv at the Schiller-Nationalmuseum, Marbach am Neckar; the Akademie der Künste, West Berlin; and the Deutsche Bibliothek, Frankfurt am Main, all in the Federal Republic of Germany.

Thomas Mann

(6 June 1875-12 August 1955)

Dieter W. Adolphs
Michigan Technological University

and

Egon Schwarz
Washington University

SELECTED BOOKS: *Der kleine Herr Friedemann: Novellen* (Berlin: Fischer, 1898); title story translated by Herman George Scheffauer as "Little Herr Friedemann" in *Children and Fools* (New York: Knopf, 1928);

Buddenbrooks: Verfall einer Familie. Roman, 2 volumes (Berlin: Fischer, 1901); translated by H. T. Lowe-Porter as *Buddenbrooks,* 2 volumes (New York: Knopf, 1924);

Tristan: Sechs Novellen (Berlin: Fischer, 1903); title story translated by Kenneth Burke in *Death in Venice* (New York: Knopf, 1925); "Tonio Kröger" translated by B. Q. Morgan in *The German Classics of the 19th and 20th Centuries,* edited by Kuno Francke and William Guild Howard, volume 19 (New York: German Publications Society, 1914);

Fiorenza (Berlin: Fischer, 1906);

Bilse und ich (Munich: Bonsels, 1906);

Königliche Hoheit (Berlin: Fischer, 1909); translated by A. Cecil Curtis as *Royal Highness: A Novel of German Court Life* (New York: Knopf, 1916);

Der kleine Herr Friedemann und andere Novellen (Berlin: Fischer, 1909);

Der Tod in Venedig: Novelle (Munich: Hyperion, 1912); translated by Burke as *Death in Venice* (New York: Knopf, 1925);

Das Wunderkind: Novellen (Berlin: Fischer, 1914); title story translated by Scheffauer as "The Infant Prodigy" in *Children and Fools* (New York: Knopf, 1928);

Friedrich und die große Koalition (Berlin: Fischer, 1915);

Betrachtungen eines Unpolitischen (Berlin: Fischer, 1918); translated by Walter D. Morris as *Reflections of a Nonpolitical Man* (New York: Ungar, 1983);

Herr und Hund; Gesang vom Kindchen: Zwei Idyllen (Berlin: Fischer, 1919); translated by Scheffauer as *Bashan and I* (London: Collins, 1923); translation republished as *A Man and His Dog* (New York: Knopf, 1930);

Thomas Mann (Ullstein)

Wälsungenblut (Munich: Phantasus, 1921);

Bekenntnisse des Hochstaplers Felix Krull: Buch der Kindheit (Vienna: Rikola, 1922; enlarged, Amsterdam: Querido, 1937); enlarged as *Bekenntnisse des Hochstaplers Felix Krull: Der Memoiren erster Teil* (Frankfurt am Main:

Fischer, 1954); translated by Denver Lindley as *Confessions of Felix Krull, Confidence Man: The Early Years* (New York: Knopf, 1955);

Novellen, 2 volumes (Berlin: Fischer, 1922);

Rede und Antwort: Gesammelte Abhandlungen und kleine Aufsätze (Berlin: Fischer, 1922);

Goethe und Tolstoj: Vortrag (Aachen: Verlag "Die Kuppel," 1923); revised as *Goethe und Tolstoj: Zum Problem der Humanität* (Vienna: Bermann-Fischer, 1932);

Von deutscher Republik (Berlin: Fischer, 1923);

Okkulte Erlebnisse (Berlin: Häger, 1924);

Der Zauberberg: Roman, 2 volumes (Berlin: Fischer, 1924); translated by Lowe-Porter as *The Magic Mountain,* 2 volumes (New York: Knopf, 1927);

Bemühungen: Neue Folge der gesammelten Abhandlungen und kleinen Aufsätze (Berlin: Fischer, 1925);

Gesammelte Werke in zehn Bänden, 10 volumes (Berlin: Fischer, 1925);

Lübeck als geistige Lebensform (Lübeck: Quitzow, 1926);

Kino: Romanfragment (Gera: Blau, 1926);

Pariser Rechenschaft (Berlin: Fischer, 1926);

Unordnung und frühes Leid (Berlin: Fischer, 1926); translated by Scheffauer as *Early Sorrow* (London: Secker, 1929);

Ausgewählte Prosa, edited by J. van Dam (Groningen & The Hague: Wolters, 1927);

Die erzählenden Schriften, 3 volumes (Berlin: Fischer, 1928);

Zwei Festreden (Leipzig: Reclam, 1928);

Children and Fools, translated by Scheffauer (New York: Knopf, 1928);

Hundert Jahre Reclam: Festrede (Leipzig: Reclam, 1928);

Sieben Aufsätze (Berlin: Fischer, 1929);

Mario und der Zauberer: Ein tragisches Reiseerlebnis (Berlin: Fischer, 1930); translated by Lowe-Porter as *Mario and the Magician* (London: Secker, 1930; New York: Knopf, 1931);

Lebensabriß (Paris: Harrison, 1930); translated by Lowe-Porter as *A Sketch of My Life* (New York: Knopf, 1960);

Die Forderung des Tages: Reden und Aufsätze aus den Jahren 1925-1929 (Berlin: Fischer, 1930);

Deutsche Ansprache: Ein Appell an die Vernunft (Berlin: Fischer, 1930);

Goethe als Repräsentant des bürgerlichen Zeitalters: Rede (Vienna: Bermann-Fischer, 1932);

Goethes Laufbahn als Schriftsteller: Vortrag (Munich: Oldenbourg, 1933);

Die Geschichten Jaakobs (Berlin: Fischer, 1933); translated by Lowe-Porter as *Joseph and His Brothers* (New York: Knopf, 1934);

Past Masters and Other Papers, translated by Lowe-Porter (New York: Knopf, 1933);

Der junge Joseph (Berlin: Fischer, 1934); translated by Lowe-Porter as *Young Joseph* (New York: Knopf, 1935; London: Secker, 1935);

Leiden und Größe der Meister (Berlin: Fischer, 1935);

Freud und die Zukunft: Vortrag (Vienna: Bermann-Fischer, 1936);

Joseph in Ägypten (Vienna: Bermann-Fischer, 1936); translated by Lowe-Porter as *Joseph in Egypt* (New York: Knopf, 1938; London: Secker, 1938);

Stories of Three Decades, translated by Lowe-Porter (New York: Knopf, 1936);

Ein Briefwechsel (Zurich: Oprecht, 1937); translated by Lowe-Porter as *An Exchange of Letters* (New York: Knopf, 1937);

Freud, Goethe, Wagner: Three Essays, translated by Lowe-Porter (New York: Knopf, 1937);

Stockholmer Gesamtausgabe der Werke, 12 volumes (Stockholm: Bermann-Fischer, 1938-1956);

Dieser Friede (Stockholm: Bermann-Fischer, 1938); translated by Lowe-Porter as *This Peace* (New York: Knopf, 1938);

Schopenhauer (Stockholm: Bermann-Fischer, 1938);

Vom künftigen Sieg der Demokratie (Zurich: Oprecht, 1938); translated by Agnes E. Meyer as *The Coming Victory of Democracy* (London: Secker & Warburg, 1938);

Achtung, Europa! Aufsätze zur Zeit (Stockholm: Bermann-Fischer, 1938);

Einführung in den Zauberberg für Studenten der Universität Princeton (Stockholm: Bermann-Fischer, 1939);

Lotte in Weimar (Stockholm: Bermann-Fischer, 1939); translated by Lowe-Porter as *The Beloved Returns* (New York: Knopf, 1940); translation republished as *Lotte in Weimar* (London: Secker & Warburg, 1940);

The Problem of Freedom (New Brunswick, N.J.: Rutgers University Press, 1939); translated into German as *Das Problem der Freiheit* (Stockholm: Bermann-Fischer, 1939);

Die vertauschten Köpfe: Eine indische Legende (Stockholm: Bermann-Fischer, 1940); translated by Lowe-Porter as *The Transposed Heads: A Legend of India* (New York: Knopf, 1941);

Dieser Krieg: Aufsatz (Stockholm: Bermann-Fischer, 1940); translated by Eric Sutton as

Mann's parents, Julia and Thomas Johann Heinrich Mann (Thomas-Mann-Archiv, Zurich)

This War (New York: Knopf, 1940; London: Secker & Warburg, 1940);

War and Democracy (Los Angeles: The Friends of the Colleges at Claremont, 1940);

Order of the Day: Political Essays and Speeches of Two Decades, translated by Lowe-Porter, Meyer, and Eric Sutton (New York: Knopf, 1942);

Deutsche Hörer! 25 Radiosendungen nach Deutschland (Stockholm: Bermann-Fischer, 1942); translated by Lowe-Porter as *Listen, Germany! Twenty-five Radio Messages to the German People over B.B.C.* (New York: Knopf, 1943); German version enlarged as *Deutsche Hörer! 55 Radiosendungen nach Deutschland* (Stockholm: Bermann-Fischer, 1945);

Joseph, der Ernährer (Stockholm: Bermann-Fischer, 1943); translated by Lowe-Porter as *Joseph the Provider* (New York: Knopf, 1944);

Das Gesetz: Erzählung (Stockholm: Bermann-Fischer, 1944); translated by Lowe-Porter as *The Tables of the Law* (New York: Knopf, 1945);

The War and the Future (Washington, D.C.: Library of Congress, 1944);

Adel des Geistes: Sechzehn Versuche zum Problem der Humanität (Stockholm: Bermann-Fischer, 1945); translated by Lowe-Porter as *Essays of Three Decades* (New York: Knopf, 1947); German version enlarged as *Adel des Geistes: Zwanzig Versuche zum Problem der Humanität* (Berlin: Aufbau, 1955);

Leiden an Deutschland: Tagebuchblätter aus den Jahren 1933 und 1934 (Los Angeles: Pazifische Presse/New York: Rosenberg, 1946);

Ein Streitgespräch über die äußere und innere Emigration, by Mann, Frank Thieß, and Walter von Molo (Dortmund: Druckschriften-Vertriebsdienst, 1946);

Deutschland und die Deutschen: Vortrag (Stockholm: Bermann-Fischer, 1947);

Doktor Faustus: Das Leben des deutschen Tonsetzers Adrian Leverkühn, erzählt von einem Freunde (Stockholm: Bermann-Fischer, 1947); translated by Lowe-Porter as *Doctor Faustus: The*

View of Lübeck, Mann's birthplace and the setting for his novel Buddenbrooks *(Thomas-Mann-Archiv, Zurich)*

Mann (second from left) with his younger sisters Julia and Carla and his older brother Heinrich, circa 1885 (Thomas-Mann-Archiv, Zurich)

Mann as a student at the Katharineum in Lübeck, 1893

Life of the German Composer, Adrian Leverkühn, as Told by a Friend (New York: Knopf, 1948);

Nietzsches Philosophie im Lichte unserer Erfahrung: Vortrag (Berlin: Suhrkamp, 1948);

Neue Studien (Stockholm: Bermann-Fischer, 1948);

Die Entstehung des Doktor Faustus: Roman eines Romans (Amsterdam: Bermann-Fischer, 1949); translated by Richard and Clara Winston as *The Story of a Novel: The Genesis of Doctor Faustus* (New York: Knopf, 1961);

Goethe und die Demokratie (Zurich: Oprecht, 1949);

Ansprache im Goethe-Jahr 1949 (Frankfurt am Main: Suhrkamp, 1949; Weimar: Thüringer Volksverlag, 1949);

Goethe / Wetzlar / Werther (Copenhagen: Rosenkilde og Bagger, 1950);

Michelangelo in seinen Dichtungen (Cellerina: Quos Ego Verlag, 1950);

Meine Zeit: 1875-1950. Vortrag (Frankfurt am Main: Fischer, 1950);

Der Erwählte: Roman (Frankfurt am Main: Fischer, 1951); translated by Lowe-Porter as *The Holy Sinner* (New York: Knopf, 1951);

Lob der Vergänglichkeit (Frankfurt am Main: Fischer, 1952);

Die Begegnung: Erzählung (Olten: Vereinigung Oltner Bücherfreunde, 1953);

Die Betrogene: Erzählung (Frankfurt am Main: Fischer, 1953); translated by Willard R. Trask as *The Black Swan* (New York: Knopf, 1954);

Gerhart Hauptmann: Rede, gehalten am 9. November 1952 im Rahmen der Frankfurter Gerhart-Hauptmann-Woche (Gütersloh: Bertelsmann, 1953);

Der Künstler und die Gesellschaft: Vortrag (Vienna: Frick, 1953);

Altes und Neues: Kleine Prosa aus fünf Jahrzehnten (Frankfurt am Main: Fischer, 1953);

Ansprache im Schillerjahr 1955 (Berlin: Aufbau, 1955);

Das Eisenbahnunglück: Novellen (Munich: Piper, 1955);

Gesammelte Werke in zwölf Bänden, 12 volumes (Berlin: Aufbau, 1955);

Versuch über Schiller: Seinem Andenken zum 150. Todestag in Liebe gewidmet (Frankfurt am Main: Fischer, 1955);

Nachlese: Prosa 1951-1955 (Frankfurt am Main: Fischer, 1956);

Meerfahrt mit Don Quijote (Wiesbaden: Insel, 1956);

Das erzählerische Werk: Taschenbuchausgabe in zwölf Bänden, 12 volumes (Frankfurt am Main: Fischer, 1957);

Sorge um Deutschland: Sechs Essays (Frankfurt am Main: Fischer, 1957);

Erzählungen (Frankfurt am Main: Fischer, 1958);

Last Essays, translated by Richard and Clara Winston, Tania and James Stern, and Lowe-Porter (New York: Knopf, 1959);

Gesammelte Werke in dreizehn Bänden, 13 volumes (Frankfurt am Main: Fischer, 1960-1974);

Stories of a Lifetime, translated by Lowe-Porter, 2 volumes (London: Secker & Warburg, 1961);

Drawings by Mann for "Bilderbuch für artige Kinder," a gift book by Thomas and Heinrich Mann for their sister Carla's confirmation in 1897 (Viktor Mann, Wir waren fünf, *1964)*

Das essayistische Werk, edited by Hans Bürgin, 8 volumes (Frankfurt am Main: Fischer, 1968);

Notizen: Zu Felix Krull, Königliche Hoheit, Versuch über das Theater, Maja, Geist und Kultur, Ein Elender, Betrachtungen eines Unpolitischen, Doktor Faustus und anderen Werken, edited by Hans Wysling (Heidelberg: Winter, 1973);

Romane und Erzählungen, 10 volumes (Berlin: Aufbau, 1974-1975);

Thomas Mann: Tagebücher 1918-1921; 1933-1934; 1935-1936; 1937-1939; 1940-1943; 1944-1946, edited by Peter de Mendelssohn, 6 volumes published (Frankfurt am Main: Fischer, 1977-); partially translated by Richard, Clara, and Krishna Winston, edited by Hermann Kesten as *Thomas Mann Diaries: 1918-1939,* 1 volume (New York: Abrams, 1982);

Gesammelte Werke in Einzelbänden, edited by de Mendelssohn, 14 volumes published (Frankfurt am Main: Fischer, 1980-).

OTHER: E. von Mendelssohn, *Nacht und Tag: Roman,* edited by Mann (Leipzig: Verlag der weißen Bücher, 1914);

Johann Wolfgang von Goethe, *Die Wahlverwantschaften,* afterword by Mann (Leipzig: List, 1925);

Theodor Fontane, *Ausgewählte Werke,* introduction by Mann, 6 volumes (Leipzig: Reclam, 1929);

M. Karlweis, *Jakob Wassermann: Bild, Kampf und Werke,* introduction by Mann (Amsterdam: Querido, 1935);

Erika Mann, *Zehn Millionen Kinder: Die Erziehung der Jugend im Dritten Reich,* foreword by Mann (Amsterdam: Querido, 1938);

Martin Niemöller, *"God is My Fuehrer": Being the Last 28 Sermons,* preface by Mann (New York: Philosophical Library and Alliance Book Corp., 1941);

The Short Novels of Dostoevsky, translated by Constance Garnett, introduction by Mann (New York: Dial Press, 1945);

Dust jacket for Mann's first published book, a collection of short stories

Self-portrait of Mann sketched by Mann on a title page of Der kleine Herr Friedemann *(Deutsche Akademie der Künste, Abteilung Literaturarchiv, Berlin)*

Mann, circa 1900

Dust jacket for the first edition of the 1901 novel that gained Mann his fame

Mann in 1900 (Thomas-Mann-Archiv, Zurich)

Dust jacket for the 1903 collection in which Mann's story "Tonio Kröger" first appeared

So ward ich [illegible] und kalt gestählt,
und [illegible] ich jetzt
die Welt [illegible], von [illegible]:
[illegible] hat das [illegible] Herz
[illegible] und [illegible] und Traum,
[illegible] hat [illegible] Teil von Schmerz
Und in das Leben [illegible];
Ihm ward die gewaltige [illegible]
zum Mittel nur,
Aus eigner Kraft sich eine Welt zu bauen.

I

Rom
Mitte Oktober 1897

1. ([illegible])

"Was ist das. – Was – ist das ..."

"Je, den Düwel ook, c'est la question, ma très chère demoiselle!"

Die Consulin Buddenbrook, neben ihrer Schwiegermutter auf dem geradlinigen, weiß lackierten und mit einem goldenen Löwenkopf verzierten Sofa, dessen Polster hellgelb überzogen waren, warf einen Blick auf ihren Gatten, der in einem Armsessel bei ihr saß, und kam ihrer kleinen Tochter zu Hilfe, die der Großvater am Fenster auf den Knieen hielt.

"Tony!" sagte sie, "ich glaube, daß mich Gott –"

Und die kleine Antonie, achtjährig und zartgebaut, in einem [illegible] gearbeiteten Kleidchen aus einer Art ganz leichter, changierender Seide, den hübschen Blondkopf ein wenig vom Gesichte des Großvaters abgewandt, blickte aus ihren hellblauen Augen angestrengt nachdenkend und ohne etwas zu sehen ins Zimmer hinein, wiederholte noch einmal: "Was ist das", sprach darauf langsam: "Ich glaube, daß mich Gott", fügte, während ihr Gesichtchen sich aufklärte, rasch hinzu: "– geschaffen hat samt allen Creaturen", war plötzlich auf glatte Bahn geraten und schnurrte nun, glückstrahlend und unaufhaltsam, den ganzen Artikel daher, getreu nach dem Katechismus, wie er soeben, Anno 1835, unter Genehmigung eines hohen und wohlweisen Senates, neu revidiert herausgegeben war – schnell und dennoch mit deutlicher Aussprache eines jeden Buchstaben, wie sie es bei [illegible] in der Schule gelernt hatte. Wenn man im Gange war, dachte sie, war es ein Gefühl, wie wenn man im Winter auf dem kleinen Handschlitten mit den Brüdern den Jerusalemsberg hinunterfuhr: es vergingen einem gerade so die Gedanken dabei und man konnte nicht einhalten, wenn man es auch wollte.

First page from the manuscript for Buddenbrooks *(Thomas-Mann-Archiv, Zurich)*

Adelbert von Chamisso, *Gedichte; Peter Schlemihls wundersame Geschichte,* introduction by Mann (Oldenburg & Mainz: Lehrmittel-Verlag, 1947);

Frans Masereel, *Jeunesse,* introduction by Mann (Zurich: Oprecht, 1948);

Arthur Schopenhauer, *Die Welt als Wille und Vorstellung,* edited by Mann (Zurich: Claassen, 1948);

Alfred Kantorowicz, *Suchende Jugend: Briefwechsel mit jungen Leuten,* introduction by Mann (Berlin: Kantorowicz, 1949);

Klaus Mann zum Gedächtnis, foreword by Mann (Amsterdam: Querido, 1950);

Sigmund Freud, *Abriß der Psychoanalyse; Das Unbehagen in der Kultur,* afterword by Mann (Frankfurt am Main & Hamburg: Fischer, 1953);

José María Corredor, *Gespräche mit Casals,* foreword by Mann (Bern: Scherz, 1954);

Die schönsten Erzählungen der Welt: Hausbuch unvergänglicher Prosa, introduction by Mann, 2 volumes (Munich, Vienna & Basel: Desch, 1955-1956);

Alexander Moriz Frey, *Kleine Menagerie,* foreword by Mann (Wiesbaden: Limes, 1955);

Und die Flamme soll euch nicht versengen: Letzte Briefe zum Tode Verurteilter aus dem europäischen Widerstand, edited by Piero Malvezzi and Giovanni Pirelli, translated by U. Muth and P. Michael, foreword by Mann (Zurich: Steinberg, 1955);

Heinrich von Kleist, *Die Erzählungen,* foreword by Mann (Frankfurt am Main: Fischer, 1956);

Masereel, *Mein Stundenbuch,* foreword by Mann (Munich: List, 1957).

Thomas Mann is one of the most celebrated German writers in history, and he experienced this phenomenal acclaim within his own lifetime. In 1938, the year he left Europe for exile in the United States, Mann was sixty-three years old, with seventeen years of great productivity ahead of him; he could be regarded as having reached the middle of his literary career.

Mann was one of the few German-speaking intellectuals who received a warm welcome in the United States; within a short time he was fully integrated into American society. Even before his exile Mann was well known to Americans as the winner of the 1929 Nobel Prize for literature. His name had again been brought to the American public's attention when he made his second trip to the United States in 1935, during which Harvard University awarded him an honorary doctorate and President Roosevelt received him in the White House. His decision to settle in the United States was influenced by an invitation to become an honorary faculty member at Princeton University. He traveled all over the continent, delivering widely publicized speeches. One of the most prestigious American publishers, Alfred A. Knopf, had already hired Helen T. Lowe-Porter to translate Mann's works into English, enabling him to address himself to a large circle of people who were interested both in his literary works and in his political views. As an articulate and passionate opponent of fascism and as an outspoken partisan of Roosevelt's policies at home and abroad, he exercised a considerable influence on the country he had chosen as his residence.

The reasons he gave the students at Princeton for the success of his novels in Germany also explain the enormous interest he elicited in the United States. Characterizing his novel *Der Zauberberg* (1924; translated as *The Magic Mountain,* 1927), which had been placed next to the works of Cervantes and Voltaire in a course on world literature, Mann explained that "the subject matter of *The Magic Mountain* was not by its nature suitable for the masses. But with the bulk of the educated classes these were burning questions, and the national crisis had produced in the general public precisely that alchemical keying up in which had consisted the actual adventure of young Hans Castorp. Yes, certainly the German reader recognized himself in the simple-minded but shrewd young hero of the novel. He could and would be guided by him."

Mann's works represent a successful synthesis of the artist's egotistical need to produce and the world citizen's desire to express his ideas in a universally intelligible way. He saw *Der Zauberberg* as a document of the "europäischen Seelenverfassung und geistigen Problematik im ersten Drittel des zwanzigsten Jahrhunderts" (European mentality and intellectual dilemma of the first third of the twentieth century). He realized that for a work to be successful, the artistic wishes of the author and the concerns of the times must be fused into one whole. To achieve this aim, Mann consciously assumed the task of representing Germany's venerable cultural tradition in the intellectual world.

After receiving the Nobel Prize Mann regarded it as his responsibility to play the role of diplomat for the "good" Germany, particularly in the face of the historical catastrophe he saw com-

Katja Pringsheim in 1905, the year of her marriage to Mann (Thomas-Mann-Archiv, Zurich)

Mann with his daughter Erika, circa 1907

The Mann family at their country house in Bad Tölz, 1909. Left to right: Katja holding Golo, Erika, Thomas, and Klaus

Mann (center, rear) in 1915 at the home of his publisher Samuel Fischer in Garmisch. Fischer is standing at left; the writer and translator Hans Reisiger, one of Mann's closest friends, is in front of Mann; the writer Annette Kolb stands at right with her arm around Fischer's daughter Brigitte.

Mann in the workroom of his house in California, 1947 (Thomas-Mann-Archiv, Zurich)

First two pages from the diary Mann began on 11 September 1918. Mann kept diaries from the time he was a student in Lübeck until shortly before his death in 1955, but destroyed those written before 1918 and from 1922 through 1932

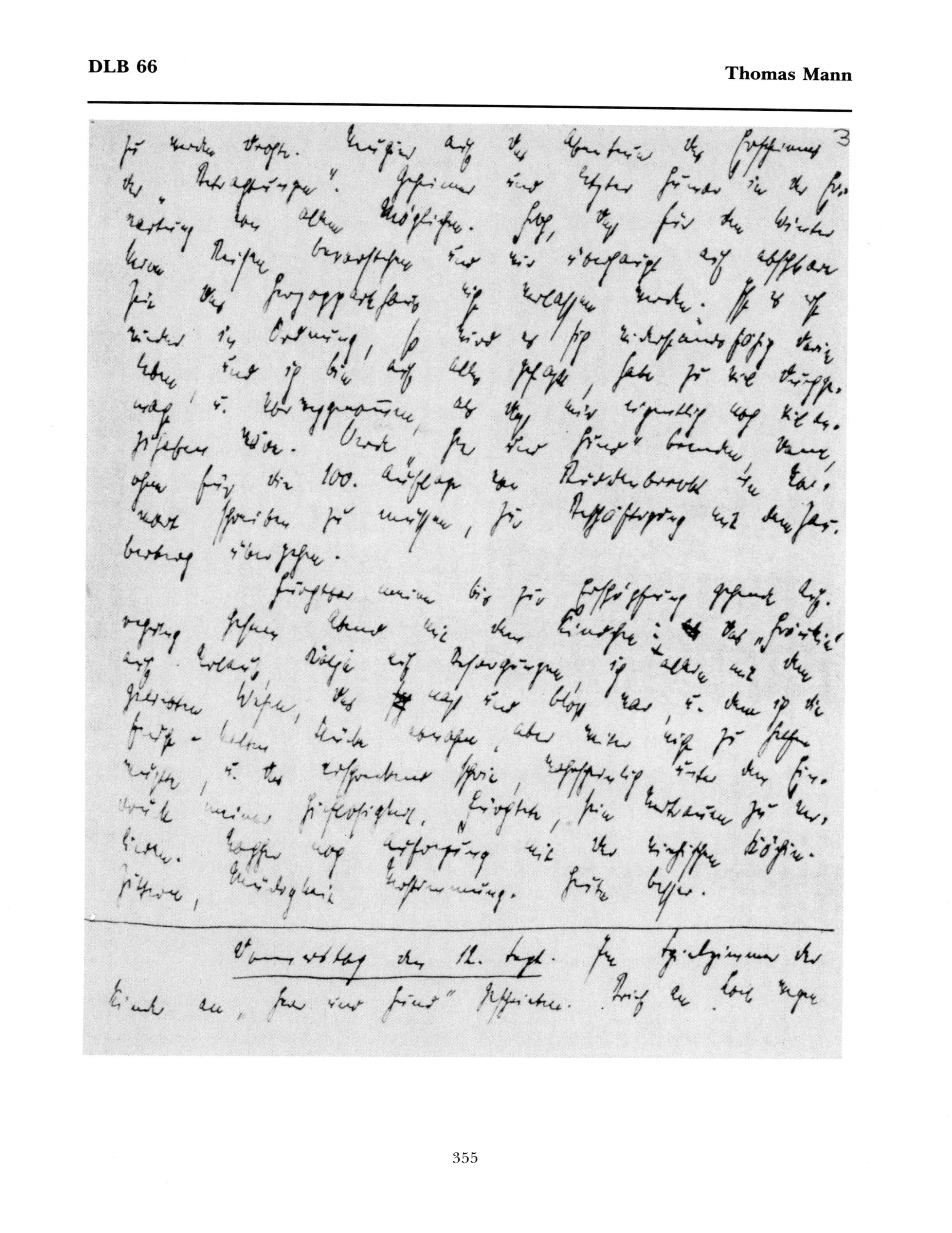

Dust jacket by G. W. Roeßner for Mann's collection of two "idylls," published in 1919

ing. Americans harbored no suspicion that Mann might be a National Socialist, and, unlike many contemporary intellectuals, he did not look to Moscow for a utopian solution, either. His hopes were dependent on the "American model" that he was more willing to embrace than many of his fellow immigrants. No other German-speaking author, with the exception perhaps of Goethe, knew how to exploit the position of representative of German culture as well as Mann.

During the Middle Ages Mann's hometown of Lübeck, a port in the extreme southwest corner of the Baltic Sea, had been one of the most important cities of the Hanse, a commercial association whose power extended from England to Scandinavia to Russia. Even after the collapse of the Hanse in the seventeenth century, Lübeck maintained its political independence and commercial significance. Since trade was at the core of the city's life, it was the wealthy merchant families who determined its political and financial fate, and it was from them that the members of the city parliament were selected. The wealthy Bürger (upper-class citizens) often functioned as the consuls of other European states and their colonies. Business and residential quarters were united under one roof in the larger homes, whose imposing, gabled facades dominated the city.

Johann Siegmund Mann moved from Mecklenburg to Lübeck in 1775; fifteen years later he established a small business. Through his marriage to the daughter of a Hamburg grain merchant he furthered his professional relationships and established the basis for the success of his firm, which was primarily achieved by delivering grain to the Prussian troops during the Napoleonic War from 1804 to 1814. In 1825 his son, Johann Siegmund II, married the daughter of the future mayor. It was not long before the Mann family was well established in Lübeck. After the death of his first wife, Johann Siegmund II married Elisabeth Marty; his first son from this marriage was Thomas Mann's father, Thomas Johann Heinrich Mann, who was born in 1840. One year later the house on Mengstraße, which Thomas Mann was to make famous in his novel *Buddenbrooks* (1901; translated, 1924), was built.

In 1863 Thomas Johann Heinrich Mann took over the family business and also assumed the position of consul of the Netherlands. In 1869 he became a member of the city's parliament. The same year he married Julia da Silva-Bruhns, who had been born in Brazil to a wealthy former citizen of Lübeck and his Portuguese wife; after her mother's death she had been raised in Lübeck by her father's relatives. Their first son, Luiz Heinrich, was born in 1871; their second son, officially named Paul Thomas, was born on 6 June 1875. In 1877 Thomas Johann Heinrich Mann was elected to a lifetime position as senator of the city. The same year his daughter Julia Elisabeth was born.

In the early 1870s a great economic upsurge, known as the Gründerjahre, took place in Germany. Reparations from France, which had lost the Franco-Prussian War, fueled a period of wild financial speculation. Lübeck began to industrialize; the old firms had already lost their privileges by 1866, and their anachronistic system of business was replaced by new institutions such as stock corporations. In spite of the insecure future of his firm, Mann's father was able until his death to provide his children with a glamorous lifestyle, including summers at Travemünde on the

Katja (far left) and Thomas Mann visiting Joseph von Lukács (third from left), the father of the Marxist critic Georg Lukács, in Budapest, 1922

Baltic Sea; the state of mind created by the sea is found again and again in Mann's works. In 1881, the year his daughter Carla Augusta Olga Maria was born, he built a house at Beckergrube 52. A final child, Viktor, was born in 1890.

Mann believed that his own ability to create long novels was strengthened by the lasting impression his reliable and ambitious father had made on him. Mann also observed the pleasure his father took in outer appearances and later assumed this characteristic himself. His mother exercised the primary artistic influence on both Thomas and Heinrich: she had a large repertoire of songs that she enjoyed performing for the children; she also liked to read aloud to them and told them stories from her childhood in Brazil. Thus, Julia Mann not only awakened artistic interests in her sons but also introduced them to a world foreign to their existence in Lübeck, providing them experiences and feelings beyond the horizon of other boys their own age.

The family firm was dissolved upon the death of Mann's father in 1891. At about the same time his grandmother died. Her house on Mengstraße, which had provided for Mann not only refuge from the social turmoil of his parents' home but also a retreat from the pressures of school, was sold. A year after her husband's death, Julia Mann moved to the culturally and artistically active city of Munich with her younger children. Heinrich had left home in 1888 to pursue a career as a writer. Thomas, who was not quite seventeen, remained in Lübeck to complete the sixth form at the Katharineum, which entitled him to a shortened term of military service.

In spite of these profound changes and the experience of death, which left a deep imprint on Mann, he felt a sense of liberation. He no longer had to spend long hours studying to please his father, who had hoped that he would eventually take over the family business, and could devote himself to his real interests. His closest friend was Otto Grautoff, who was a social outcast because of the bankruptcy of his father; Mann's letters to Grautoff between 1894 and 1900 are the only autobiographical source of im-

Mann in Stockholm to receive the Nobel Prize for literature in 1929 (photo: Svenska Dagbladet, Stockholm)

portance for the significant period in the author's life before the appearance of *Buddenbrooks.* It was together with Grautoff that Mann published his first works in the school paper, *Frühlingssturm,* of which the two were coeditors. Two issues of this short-lived effort appeared in 1893. After he had made several attempts at poetry, Mann's superior narrative talent became evident. His first literary endeavors portray an inexperienced person who feels frustrated by the inability of others to respond to his feelings of love.

In Lübeck Mann had his first and immediately intense encounter with the operatic music of Richard Wagner. At the same time he was reading everything available, particularly Schiller and Heine.

Immediately upon receiving his diploma in 1894 Mann left Lübeck to join his family in Munich. The move marked his dissociation from the upper-class mores and values of the nineteenth century and his entry into the modern era. In contrast to Lübeck, Munich was one of the great centers of a developing Germany. The suburb of Schwabing, where farmers and tradesmen lived in close proximity to the well-to-do middle class, was being invaded by artists, who brought with them an atmosphere of liberalism. Elite circles such as that around the poet Stefan George believed themselves exempt from conventional social mores on account of their aesthetic superiority and developed an ideology of "art for the sake of art." This atmosphere provided the basis for what is known as "decadent" art and literature.

Within a short time Mann was well acclimated to life in Munich; through his mother's circle of friends he came to know many artists and intellectuals. He took a position with a fire insurance company, the Süddeutsche Feuerversicherungsbank. During office hours he secretly wrote a short story, "Gefallen" (Fallen).

Although Mann later rejected this piece, it marks a significant step in his career since it was published in October 1894 in the respected periodical *Die Gesellschaft,* where it attracted the attention of the influential writer and editor Richard Dehmel. Dehmel wrote to Mann, praising his work, and later visited him. Such recognition strengthened Mann's standing in the artistic circles of Munich and encouraged him to embark on a literary career unencumbered by gainful but time-consuming employment. He gave notice at the insurance company and registered for several courses at the Technische Universität in Munich. The lectures and seminars he attended more or less regularly from November 1894 to June 1895 provided important material for many of his future writings; Professor Wilhelm Hertz's lectures on German mythology and literature of the Middle Ages inspired as late a novel as *Der Erwählte* (The Chosen One, 1951; translated as *The Holy Sinner,* 1951).

Mann's short story "Der Wille zum Glück" (The Will to Be Happy) appeared in the August/September 1896 issue of the recently founded magazine *Simplicissimus.* Two other stories, which were later lost, were sent to Dehmel, who offered encouragement but failed to publish them. Mann, however, was little concerned with immediate success, and concentrated on sharpening his writing skills and expanding his literary knowledge; his notebooks from this period document a strong interest in Nietzsche and Schopenhauer.

The success of "Gefallen" improved Mann's relationship with his older brother. During his last school years Mann had not felt that he was taken seriously by Heinrich, who had already established himself as a writer; but in 1895 the brothers traveled to Italy, returning there in October 1896 for what would become an eighteen-month stay. In Rome Thomas finished a short story,

Mann's Nobel Prize citation (Thomas-Mann-Archiv, Zurich)

"Der kleine Herr Friedemann" (translated as "Little Herr Friedemann," 1928), which he sent to the periodical *Neue deutsche Rundschau* of the influential S. Fischer publishing house. The editor, Oskar Bie, accepted the piece and requested that Mann send him all his previously written works so that they could be published as a collection. Before his return to Munich in the spring of 1898 the collection appeared under the title *Der kleine Herr Friedemann.*

In these stories two spheres are presented in opposition to one another. On the one hand, there is the world of the successful hero who follows traditional, socially acceptable paths. The action serves primarily to show how he improves his position in society, catering to well-tested societal norms. This type strives for what is acknowledged by all as good and right. Within his limited realm of family and professional life, he searches for happiness. This is the "banale Bürger" (commonplace citizen). The second world is that of the outsider who expects something more from life. He looks down on the commonplace citizen, but at the same time admires his strength and the naive self-confidence. The perspective of the outsider reveals that the concepts of happiness and love are empty ideals in view of the "normal" social reality. The story "Enttäuschung" (Disillusionment) is paradigmatic for the entire collection: disillusionment stems from the realization that life does not correspond to commonly held ideals. The aesthetics of decadence requires the rejection of banal social reality and concentration on the feelings of the sensitive individual. To the extent that they do not correspond to the "average," Mann's main characters can be seen as decadent; but they do not fill the bill completely because they do not make a cult of their heightened awareness or create an artistic principle out of their choice of life-style. They suffer because they are aware of an unbridgeable gap between their own lives and normal existence. They can enjoy neither the pleasures of narcissistic reflection nor the pathos of art for the sake of art; they are always in a state of gnawing self-doubt. Hardly have they been confronted with the outside world when they feel that their weaknesses have been exposed: they have re-

Dust jacket for Mann's 1930 novella about an evil hypnotist, generally considered to be an allegorical warning of the danger of fascism

moved themselves so completely from society that they can no longer participate in its life; at the same time, their search for inner fulfillment has been equally unsuccessful.

The stories of *Der kleine Herr Friedemann* present varied perspectives on the outsider's existence. Johannes Friedemann in "Der kleine Herr Friedemann" is physically an outsider from the very outset; a cripple, he attempts to find happiness outside of family and work. For a time he finds pleasure in nature and music. The narrator of "Der Bajazzo" (The Dilettante) intentionally distances himself from others because he feels superior to them. His artistic tendencies, however, are unproductive. Socially prominent women always see through the Bajazzo and Friedemann. These childless females enjoy success without having fulfilled the traditional female role; they are cruel and without compassion for weakness. They relentlessly show their superiority, giving men a feeling that their happiness is based on lies and deceit. The love, hate, and rage of the male characters in Mann's early works are initially directed at life, then toward the female characters, and finally internalized as doubt, disgust, and self-hate.

This first collection reveals a thematic and structural unity through which Mann presents a common world. This unity is characteristic of all of his works. It is accomplished by various means, among them the stylistic element that has become famous through Mann's oeuvre: the leitmotiv. The linking of individual pieces of Mann's first collection by common settings, such as Lübeck, Munich, and Italy, and the repetition of names, such as Gerda for Johannes Friedemann's mother as well as for the mother of Hanno in *Buddenbrooks,* can be seen as the beginning of the leitmotiv.

A parallel between Mann's literary leitmotiv and Wagner's musical one has often been pointed out by critics. Both devices serve a similar function: to create thematic and structural unity by guiding the reader or listener's attention to an artificial connection between details. While the musical leitmotiv can link a new and old theme by combining the two, the literary leitmotiv lacks this possibility because only one theme can be developed within the narration at a time. Mann's peculiar use of the leitmotiv turns this apparent disadvantage into a powerful means of narration. By using motifs which contradict each other, Mann undermines and exposes as an illusion the supposed omniscience of the narrator. The reader always has to be aware of the dialectical function of the stereotypes Mann uses: to first create powerful images, and then, in a second step, to mercilessly unmask these images as illusions.

Mann had begun writing *Buddenbrooks* in 1897, completing it in August 1900. In October he began a one-year enlistment in the Royal Bavarian Infantry but was discharged as unfit in December. The publisher Samuel Fischer was appalled at the length of the manuscript of *Buddenbrooks* and demanded radical cuts, but the young author insisted on an unabridged printing. The publisher's agreement to do so was one of the most important decisions in the company's history. While the first two-volume edition of 1,000 copies sold slowly, the second printing, in an inexpensive one-volume edition, exploded like a bombshell.

In *Buddenbrooks* the characters represent different generations as they develop within a historical framework. The novel, which tells the story

Mann with his daughter Erika in Munich in 1933, shortly before the Mann family was forced into exile by the rise to power of the Nazis

of a merchant's family, begins with the founding of the Johann Buddenbrook firm and ends with the death of Hanno, the only heir of the fourth generation. The details are generally those of Mann's family's history and the social life of Lübeck. The story opens in 1835, just after the Buddenbrook family has moved into a house on Mengstraße. Three generations are living together: the founder of the family firm is seventy years old and heads the business together with his twenty-five-year-old son, Johann II. Nine-year-old Thomas, his brother Christian, and his sister Tony participate in the celebration of the new home in the company of friends and members of the two older Buddenbrook generations. These festivities are described in great detail; through this gathering the basic themes of the novel are revealed and the differences of the three generations are emphasized. The founder of the firm still thinks in a way that reflects the ideals of the Napoleonic era. His son, Consul Johann Buddenbrook, is completely adapted to modern times and follows the practical ideals of his position. But his father senses the potential for evil in this practice. He regrets the fading away of the classical education based on the humanities and its replacement by a technical, goal-oriented system. His grandson Thomas is brought up under the new system: his father sends him to the Realgymnasium (a school combining a classical with a practical modern education), which prepares him to be a businessman.

The subtitle of the novel is *Verfall einer Familie* (Decline of a Family): the Buddenbrooks are subject to an inner dynamic which brings about the demise of the family and makes its final collapse inevitable. Johann Buddenbrook establishes a tradition by founding a family firm that requires different generations to work together. The principles of this tradition secure the success of the business; the symbol of the tradition is the house on Mengstraße, where the most important achievements in the family history are recorded chronologically in the Gutenberg Bible. But the succeeding generations have increasing difficulty abiding by the traditional laws of the

(1933)

(1934)

(1936)

Dust jackets by Kurt Walser for the first three volumes in Mann's tetralogy based on the biblical story of Joseph

Bruno Walter, Mann, and Arturo Toscanini at Stefan Zweig's home in Salzburg, 1935 (by permission of Dr. Hans-Otto Mayer)

firm. The leitmotiv of bad teeth makes it easier to comprehend this change: when bad teeth are mentioned, other difficulties are sure to follow. This leitmotiv is well illustrated by the fate of Thomas Buddenbrook. He is prosperous–he breaks all records in the firm's history, in the face of many obstacles, and also becomes a senator. Thus it is apparent that the Buddenbrooks do not decline because of financial trouble but because of their physical and mental weakness. In the first part of the novel the reader learns that Thomas has bad teeth; later, before his fiftieth birthday, he goes to the dentist and dies on the way home of a complete physical breakdown, symbolized by a decayed, hollow tooth.

The house on the Mengstraße also serves as a leitmotiv. It first belongs to the wealthy Ratenkamp family, who experience their decline within its shelter. This fate is inherited by the Buddenbrooks when they move in, and the reader can only assume that the ever-growing Hagenström family will die out just like the Ratenkamps and Buddenbrooks after they buy the house in 1871.

Another leitmotiv in *Buddenbrooks* is happiness. To an ever-increasing degree the interests of the firm force the family members to renounce their personal happiness. The main victim of this denial of happiness and love is Thomas's sister Tony, who was modeled after Mann's aunt, Elisabeth Amalia Hyppolitha. The greatest happiness in Tony's life is her love for Morten Schwarzkopf, who comes from a modest background. Together with him Tony experiences the beauty of the sea, and from him she learns about the political liberation movements stirring in the country. Cruelly torn away from this relationship by her family, she is forced into two unfortunate marriages that cause financial loss as well as loss of prestige. Yet it is Tony her-

Katja and Thomas Mann in St. Moritz, February 1935 (Stadtbibliothek, Munich)

self who feels the need to protect the family tradition. She upholds the principles of the firm even though they have become empty of meaning; just how blind Tony is to reality is revealed by the fact that she continues to repeat the leftist slogans of her young love, Schwarzkopf, which are quite incongruous with her otherwise patrician worldview.

In Hanno's education the prophecy of his grandfather is fulfilled: the new school system, representing modern times, is incompatible with the cultivated spirit and intellect of the Buddenbrooks. The classical education that had fused a refined life-style with class consciousness has disintegrated–all that is left is an empty striving for success. The somewhat morbid Hanno suffers under the narrow-minded perspective of his teachers and seeks escape in nature during vacations at the Baltic Sea and through the music of Wagner. He perceives school as never-ending harassment. Hanno's education marks the end of the days of the patricians and the point of departure for art in the coming twentieth century. The second chapter of the last section of the novel, which ends with the words "Dies war ein Tag aus dem Leben des kleinen Johann" (This was one day in the life of little Johann), is a literary document of intellectual oppression through education. Hanno dies at the age of fifteen.

Only women remain alive at the conclusion of the novel; they represent a static element in contrast to the male characters. Gerda, Thomas's widow, with her passion for music and her symbolic origins on the edge of the North Sea, is subtly stylized into a harbinger of dissolution and death. After her husband and her son have died she leaves the culturally inactive city of Lübeck. Tony remains the only proof of the Buddenbrooks' former existence.

The major character of Mann's novella "Tonio Kröger" (published in *Tristan: Sechs Novellen*, 1903; translated, 1914) shares his last name with the in-laws of Thomas Buddenbrook; his first name represents the Latin heritage of Mann's mother. For Mann the South symbolized a purely aesthetic world. Tonio's mother is musical and inspires her son to write at a very early age. Because of his Latin appearance and his literary interests he becomes an outsider at school. Later in life he must fight inner conflicts: he could follow the path of the artist and completely remove himself from society; this choice, however, would deny the Nordic and social side of his heritage. In accepting the fact that he is an outsider and yet remaining within society, Tonio has a chance to find love and happiness. The love which the average person experiences presupposes a certain naiveté which Tonio has lost. Instead, he strives for a sublimated form of love, a special kind of art that expresses social sympathy.

Mann identified with the bourgeois tradition of humanism as defined in this story. In *Buddenbrooks* he showed that the traditional ideals of the upper classes were either an illusion or a reflection of self-interest; at the same time, he was unable to renounce the need to portray ideals that were so much a part of his heritage. He wanted to speak for everyone, without a fixed point of view. He belonged neither to the capitalists, as represented by the Hagenströms, nor to the left-leaning liberals such as Morten Schwarzkopf. After his father's death and the demise of his social group Mann lost any firm political orientation; art remained his only means of speaking out. "Tonio Kröger" documents Mann's path away from the disillusioned romanticism of his first collection of stories toward a new artistic intellectualism.

In the spring of 1903 Mann was introduced to the wealthy Pringsheim family. Alfred Pringsheim, of Jewish descent, was a mathematician at the University of Munich and a member of a group of Wagner worshippers. His mansion was one of the most significant sites for intellectual and artistic meetings in Munich. Pringsheim's daughter Katharina (Katja) was nineteen years old when Mann met her. They were married on 11 February 1905 and had six children: Erika was born in 1905, Klaus in 1906, Golo in 1909, Monika in 1910, Elisabeth in 1918, and Michael in 1919.

Mann's marriage enabled him to resume the way of life he had loved so much during his childhood. In *Lebensabriß* (1930; translated as *A Sketch of My Life,* 1960) he says: "Die Atmosphäre des großen Familienhauses, die mir die Umstände meiner Kindheit vergegenwärtigte, bezauberte mich. Das im Geist kaufmännischer Kultureleganz Vertraute fand ich hier ins Prunkhaft-Künstlerische und Literarische modänisiert und vergeistigt" (The atmosphere of the large home, which brought back my childhood memories as if they were real again, totally enchanted me. The familiar spirit of the elegance of the cultured businessman's world was enhanced and transmuted into the luxurious glamor of artistic and literary life). Through the Pringsheim family Mann was introduced to the most affluent circles of Munich and Berlin society. In addition, Katja's father presented the young couple with a royally furnished apartment in Schwabing and supported them financially for years.

Katja Mann became Mann's partner in his intellectual enterprise. Her self-assured personality complemented his ambitious but sensitive nature. She assumed the social responsibilities for her famous husband, kept his mornings free from intrusions so that he could work on his literary projects, managed his financial affairs, and even intervened when she felt that he was being manipulated or was simply saying too much in interviews. Life without Katja seemed utterly unimaginable to him.

Neither Mann nor his wife had much contact with people from the lower classes, which might have provided them with insight into another way of life. Katja had attended private schools reserved for the upper classes; her ideas on public education show the distance that separated her from the less privileged. In her memoirs (1974) she says, "Wenn man alleine lernt, lernt man schneller. In der Schule muß man sich immer nach dem Durchschnitt oder dem Unterdurchschnitt richten, und ich gehörte zum oberen Durchschnitt" (If you study privately you will learn much faster. In school you always have to be oriented toward the average achiever or the less-than-average achiever, and I belonged to the above-average group).

Mann's next major work, the drama *Fiorenza* (1906), deals with the intellectual and political conflict between Lorenzo the Magnificent, the glorious figure of the Florentine High Renaissance, and Girolamo Savonarola, the prior of San Marco, who condemns the humanists' excessive enjoyment of life and "decadent" art. While Savonarola is seen as an ascetic and a rigid moralist who is about to draw the masses away from Lorenzo, the latter seems to be an aesthete who supports art for art's sake and lacks any responsibility to lead his people to a moderate and moral life. Only at the end do the opponents meet, when Savonarola visits Lorenzo on his deathbed. Now it becomes apparent that the two men have much in common. In Lorenzo's view, Savonarola and he are brothers through an elective affinity: their fragile natures, which are only to be overcome by means of artistic fame or political power.

Lorenzo says, "Wär' ich schön geboren, nie hätte ich zum Herrn der Schönheit mich gemacht. Die Hemmung ist des Willens bester Freund" (Had I been born beautiful, I would never have made myself the lord of beauty. Hindrance is the will's best friend). He has no sense of smell and calls himself a cripple who does not know the scent of the rose or of a woman. His will to rule over the people's aesthetic taste stems from this personal shortcoming, just as Savonarola's desire for ethical and political leadership is a reaction to his personal weakness; the artist's work is seen as a form of sublimation. Shortly before his death Lorenzo identifies with the prior's confession: "Das Leiden darf nicht umsonst gewesen sein. Ruhm muß es bringen!" (My sufferings must not have been in vain. They must bring me fame!).

For the first time, Mann is openly confessing his own need for recognition. He accepts his new role as the famous man admired by the masses, but at the same time wants to make clear

Katja and Thomas Mann with their children (from left) Klaus, Elisabeth, Michael, and Erika in Munich in the early 1930s (Stadtbibliothek, Munich)

Mann with producer Carl Laemmle and directors Max Reinhardt and Ernst Lubitsch in Hollywood, 1938 (Thomas-Mann-Archiv, Zurich)

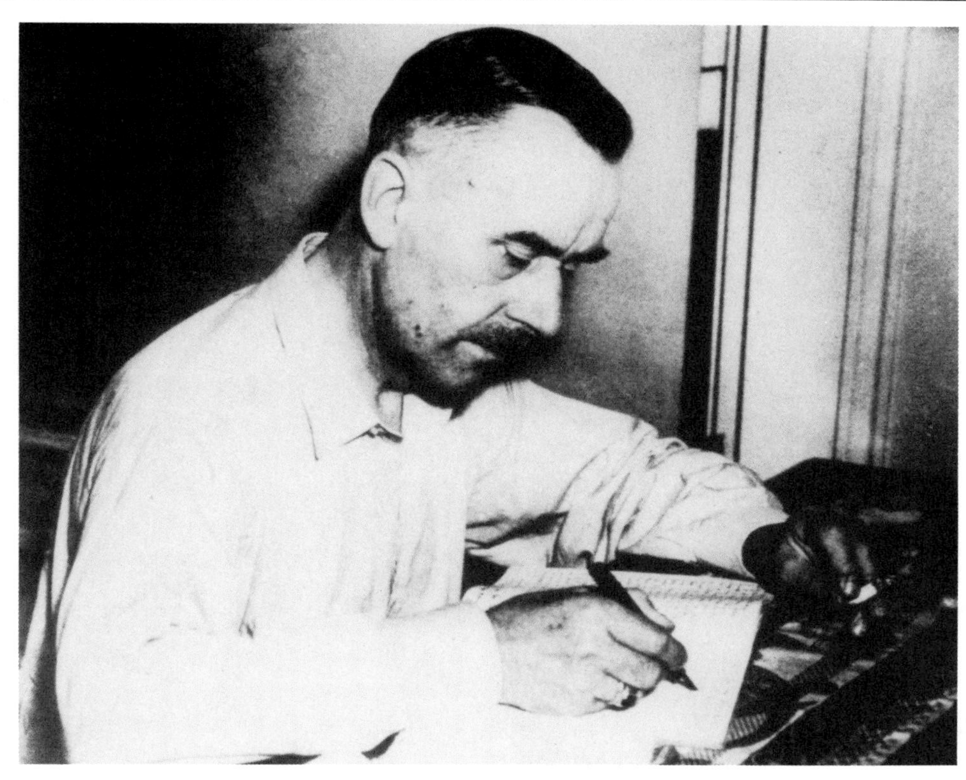

Mann writing in his diary, Princeton, 1939 (Princeton University Library)

Albert Einstein and Mann in Princeton, 1939 (Thomas Mann-Sammlung, Dr. Hans-Otto Mayer, Düsseldorf)

Dust jacket by Yngve Berg for Mann's 1939 novel based on the 1816 meeting of Goethe and Lotte Kestner, a woman he had loved forty-four years earlier

Mann in Saltsjöbaden, Sweden, 1939, where he was to be the German delegate at a meeting of the P.E.N. Club Congress; the meeting did not take place (Thomas-Mann-Archiv, Zurich).

Joseph der Ernährer

Inhalt:

Vorspiel in oberen Rängen (S. 1–11)

Erstes Hauptstück: Die andere Grube
(S. 12–73) Joseph kennt seine Tränen
Der Amtmann über das Gefängnis
Von Güte und Klugheit
Die Herren
Vom stechenden Wurm
Joseph hilft aus als Deuter

Zweites Hauptstück: Die Berufung
(S. 74–112) Neb-nef-nezem
Der Eilbote
Von Licht und Schwärze
Die Träume des Pharao

Drittes Hauptstück: Die kretische Laube
(S. 112–190) Die Einführung
Das Kind der Höhle

Manuscript for Mann's table of contents for Joseph der Ernährer *(1943), the final volume in his Joseph tetralogy (Thomas-Mann-Archiv, Zurich)*

Mann's favorite photograph of himself, taken in California in 1944 (by permission of Dr. Hans-Otto Mayer)

Katja and Thomas Mann with their grandchildren Frido and Toni in California, 1945

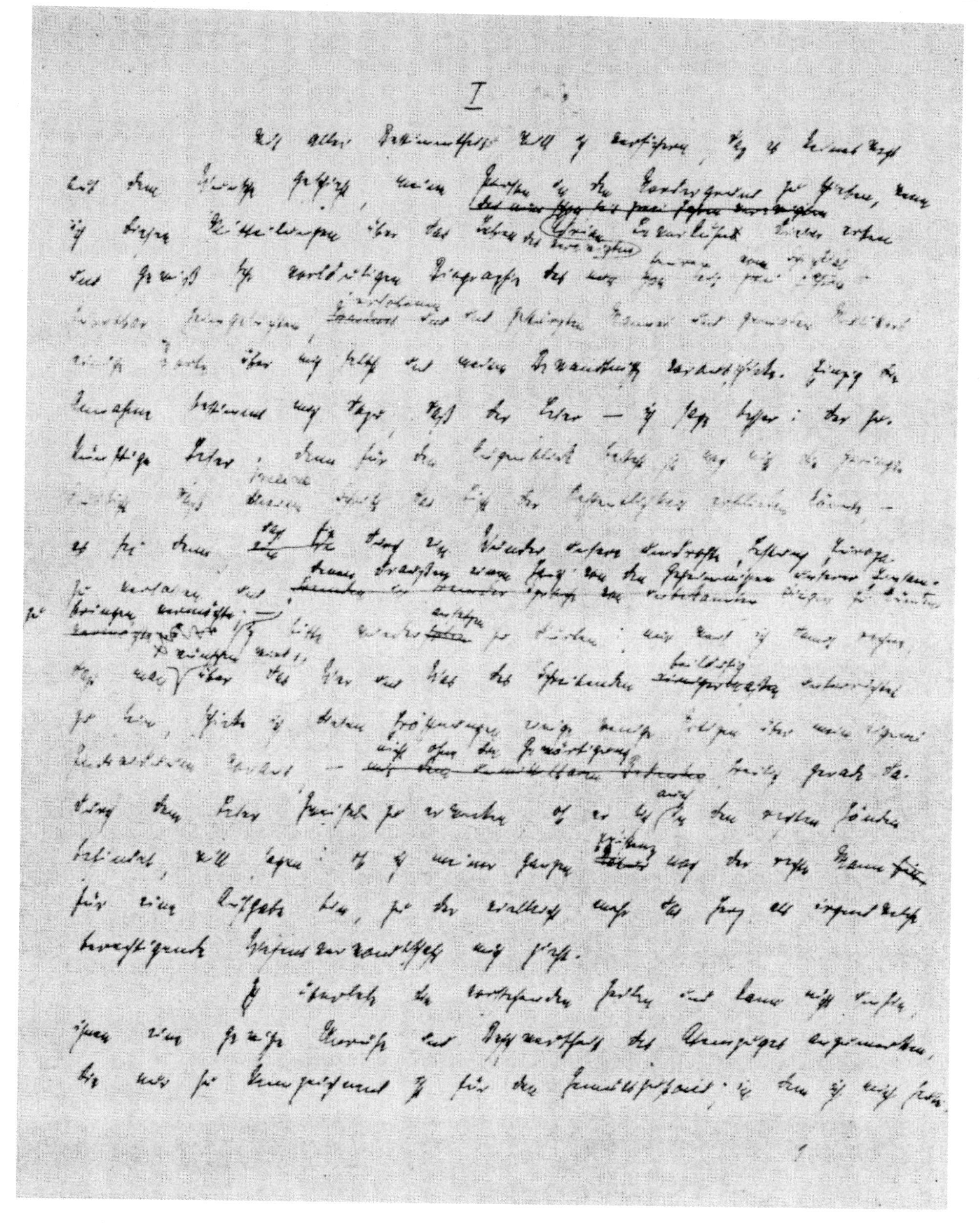

First page from the manuscript for Mann's novel Doktor Faustus *(1947) (Thomas-Mann-Archiv, Zurich)*

that glory and power are dangerous illusions. Thus, he links these themes with the leitmotiv of the great figure who is physically handicapped from birth and suffers from illness.

Fiorenza was Mann's only experiment with the dramatic form. It was performed in Frankfurt and Munich and was a moderate success; but Mann referred to it as a "dramatic novella," realizing that it was not well suited for the traditional stage. In its depiction of the confrontation between opposing artistic and ideological tenets, portrayed as a debate between individuals who represent these contradictory attitudes, *Fiorenza* prefigures *Der Zauberberg*.

In 1906 Mann wrote *Wälsungenblut* (The Blood of the Walsungs), which deals with incestuous love. He was forced to retract the work before the copies of *Die neue Rundschau* which contained it had arrived in the bookstores. He had used the stereotype of the rich Jew and his tastelessly "bedecked" wife, and even before publication the news spread around Munich that Mann had written the story as a satire of his wife's family. The public could not believe that Katja Mann's father was not identical with the Jewish Wagner-worshiper in *Wälsungenblut;* and even though his mother-in-law had approved the publication, her husband, who was not fond of his son-in-law's "loose" literary career, became so outraged that Mann had no choice but to withdraw the work. The story did not appear until 1921, and then only in a private edition.

In the novel *Königliche Hoheit* (1909; translated as *Royal Highness,* 1916) Mann once again varies two of his favorite themes, the outsider and happiness. Like Tonio Kröger, Prince Klaus Heinrich experiences exclusion from his peer group; once again, the protagonist is suffering from a physical handicap, this time atrophy of his left hand. He is able to turn his feelings as an outsider into a positive attitude: when he assumes the throne he does not become a cynical tyrant but a kindhearted ruler. He finds happiness in marriage to Imma Spoelmann, who is also an outsider because of her American Indian ancestry. His wife's wealth enables Klaus Heinrich to reform his destitute land. *Königliche Hoheit* marks the turning point in Mann's development from an apolitical aesthete and pessimistic critic of culture to a nationalistic monarchist–an orientation to which he held for ten years out of loyalty to traditional values.

The novella *Der Tod in Venedig* (1912; translated as *Death in Venice,* 1925) describes the decline of a celebrated writer, Gustav Aschenbach. The erotic excitement of decaying Venice and the allure of the handsome boy Tadzio render Aschenbach incapable of leaving. As a result of his decision to stay in the plague-infested city he becomes a victim of the disease. The work reveals the homoerotic fantasies of an author who could never openly admit his sexual propensity. The moral standards of his time did not allow him actual fulfillment of his desires; instead, the boys and young men who aroused his fantasies repeatedly found entrance into his literary works. Tadzio is the name of a Polish boy Mann had glimpsed at the Lido, the beach on the Adriatic Sea near Venice.

At the end of the novella Aschenbach dies in his canopied beach chair, watching his beloved Tadzio, who seems to be summoning him into the sea. The public will remember the great man as a model of artistic and personal self-discipline, while his actual end is rather undignified. Artistic beauty has revealed itself to be an illusion; it is the basis for the artist's fame, but not a true picture of his inner self.

Aschenbach succumbs to the erotic impulses which he had repressed in the interest of a disciplined classical art. The taming of the artist's drives by means of a rigorous self-discipline may result in a purified classicism–for a while; but beauty, no matter how spiritualized, is inextricably bound up with the artist's erotic subconscious. Mann's modern-day Venice is imperceptibly transformed into a classical landscape where the ancient gods Apollo and Dionysus wage a battle for Aschenbach's soul.

The outbreak of World War I forced Mann to deal explicitly with politics. He became an ally of the patriotic monarchists with his essay *Friedrich und die große Koalition* (Frederick and the Great Coalition, 1915), in which he demonstrated the qualities of the German spirit as exemplified by Frederick the Great. He was suddenly identified with a group of loyalist writers who saw Germany as a country with high moral qualities that was being unfairly attacked.

While Mann was making plans for a book which would reawaken the ideals of the nineteenth century and celebrate the moral and apolitical characteristics of the German spirit, he encountered an unexpected opponent in his own brother, Heinrich, whose 1915 essay "Zola" cast France as an ally in the struggle for democracy.

Mann in 1946 (Camera Press, London)

Heinrich Mann felt that it was the responsibility of all intellectuals to lend support for democratization and thereby accelerate a process hampered by autocratic Germany. Artists such as his brother Thomas were depicted as parasites who could not break away from their old financial supporters. This criticism hurt Thomas Mann deeply. He wanted to be right at any cost, even without being fully convinced of his own position. But as it became increasingly clear that Germany would lose the war, Mann realized that the time for support for conservatism was over. The only thing yet to be done was to secure his personal integrity; there were no longer any political interests worth defending. Thus, his book was finally completed as the intellectual retreat of an artist who could no longer defend traditional values politically but rather as a reflection of his own apolitical conscience.

When the voluminous work appeared in 1918 under the title *Betrachtungen eines Unpolitischen* (translated as *Reflections of a Nonpolitical Man,* 1983), its great success was an irony of fate. The book was enthusiastically adopted by the antidemocratic forces in Germany at a moment when its author was trying to adjust to the coming of democracy. In 1922 he publicly declared his allegiance to the new system in the speech *Von deutscher Republik* (Of the German Republic, 1923). From that day forward he was placed in a difficult position between the disappointed conservatives, on the one hand, and the German Democrats, who would hold him suspect for a long time to come, on the other.

After a relatively unproductive period, Mann completed *Der Zauberberg* in 1924. When he had first planned it in 1912, he had thought of it as a brief humorous pendant–he called it a "satyr play"–to the tragic novella *Der Tod in Venedig.* But the doom signaled by Gustav Aschenbach's downfall had become reality at the end of the war. Thus, what was originally conceived as a short story became Mann's third swan song; this time not to the upper class of Lübeck nor to the nineteenth-century artist, but to the entire prewar culture.

The beginning of the novel is indicative of the complex interplay it presents between the past, the present, and the future. The narrator points out a special feature of the German language: while the simple past tense can be used in English to refer to recent events, its German equivalent is mainly reserved for storytelling purposes. The narrator emphasizes the irrecoverability of the world depicted in his story by calling himself "den raunenden Beschwörer des Imperfekts" (the murmuring conjurator of the simple past tense). He points out that the era portrayed in the story is not separated from the present by a long period of time–in fact, it is rather recent–but by the cataclysm of World War I, which has ushered in a new and completely different era.

The novel is more than a mourning of the past; it also attempts to remind the new culture of its historical dimensions. It begins in 1907 at the tuberculosis sanatorium Berghof in Davos, a luxurious resort for the upper classes in a remote area of the Swiss Alps. Its inhabitants represent the various national mentalities and intellectual currents of the prewar period. The protagonist, the inexperienced young German engineer Hans Castorp, is so absorbed by the uncanny atmosphere of the Berghof that he feels as if he is caught in a magical circle. Initially, he intends to stay only three weeks to visit his cousin Joachim Ziemßen, whose military career has been interrupted by tuberculosis. Ziemßen returns to the army, but he has to come back to the sanatorium, where he dies. Castorp, entranced by the Magic Mountain, remains in Davos; seven years later, long after the death of his cousin, it is only World War I that can remove him from this world. He is called back to everyday life to fight in the Great War.

In many respects the novel can be compared to the classical German bildungsroman or educational novel. Like Goethe's Wilhelm Meister, Castorp becomes a more educated and responsible individual after the years of exposure to all the trends of his time and culture. First of all, he experiences the difference between objective and subjective time: the former can be measured mechanically and subjects the human being to the law of cause and effect; the latter depends on the intensity of feelings and alternately stagnates and rushes. Subjective time is the basis for human perception, enabling Castorp to broaden his horizon and understand the intellectual heritage of his culture. The Magic Mountain with its international atmosphere enables him to realize that Germany's fate is bound to a common European tradition. Castorp gains a perspective from which he can appreciate what initially was completely strange and forbidding to his pragmatic and technically oriented mind.

During the first year of his stay Castorp becomes completely part of the Berghof routine. Wrapped in blankets, he rests for hours on his private balcony, just like the patients, who are acclimated to such a degree that their former lives in the lower altitudes have become unimaginable. While the original purpose of their stay was to escape death from tuberculosis, they are caught in a vicious circle: the Berghof can prolong their lives to a degree, but they are still hopelessly in the clutches of death. The luxurious life-style deceives them and serves the interest of the Berghof management, which quietly removes the corpses of the deceased on sleds at night, unnoticed by survivors.

There are frequent festivities, some of them carried to bacchanalian excess. But the main social events are the regular meals, which are too opulent to qualify as a healthy diet. As in the outside world, the patients are divided into social and ethnic groups, represented by seven dinner tables. When he leaves the sanatorium, Castrop

Mann in 1954 at his home in Kilchberg, near Zurich, where he moved in 1952 (photo Atlantis)

will have eaten at every table, even the "schlechten Russentisch" (the bad Russian table).

Castorp's most significant insights stem from his increasingly active inclusion in the intellectual battles between the Italian humanist Settembrini and the rigid dogmatist and ascetic Naphta. Mann's descriptions of Settembrini and Naphta are suffused with irony and humor: the hedonistic humanist's life-style is extremely modest, while the radical ascetic lives in a stylish and comfortable apartment. Their ideological confrontation cannot be settled by arguments: in a pistol duel, Naphta shoots himself after Settembrini refuses to aim at him. It is not the rigid moralist who survives, as in *Fiorenza,* but the physically weakened humanist with self-doubts that derive from his commitment to a cosmopolitan intellectualism.

In addition to the seven dinner tables and the intellectual dispute, Castorp is exposed to three other powerful influences. First, he develops a critical attitude toward science as a result of his observations of Dr. Behrens, the head physician, a traditional medical doctor who apparently acts more in the interest of the institution's management than in that of his patients, and his assistant, Dr. Krokowski, a follower of a popularized form of psychoanalysis that Ziemßen calls "Seelenzergliederung" (dismemberment of the soul), an approach that only reinforces his patients' illusions.

The appearance of Clawdia Chauchat is another key experience for Castorp. Her Eastern heritage and fluent knowledge of French upset the balance Mann's previous works had established between "Northern" and "Southern" values, the German tradition of self-command and the Latin dedication to art. Clawdia's unpunctuality and sensuality irritate Castorp, who tries to hide his insecurity behind a feeling

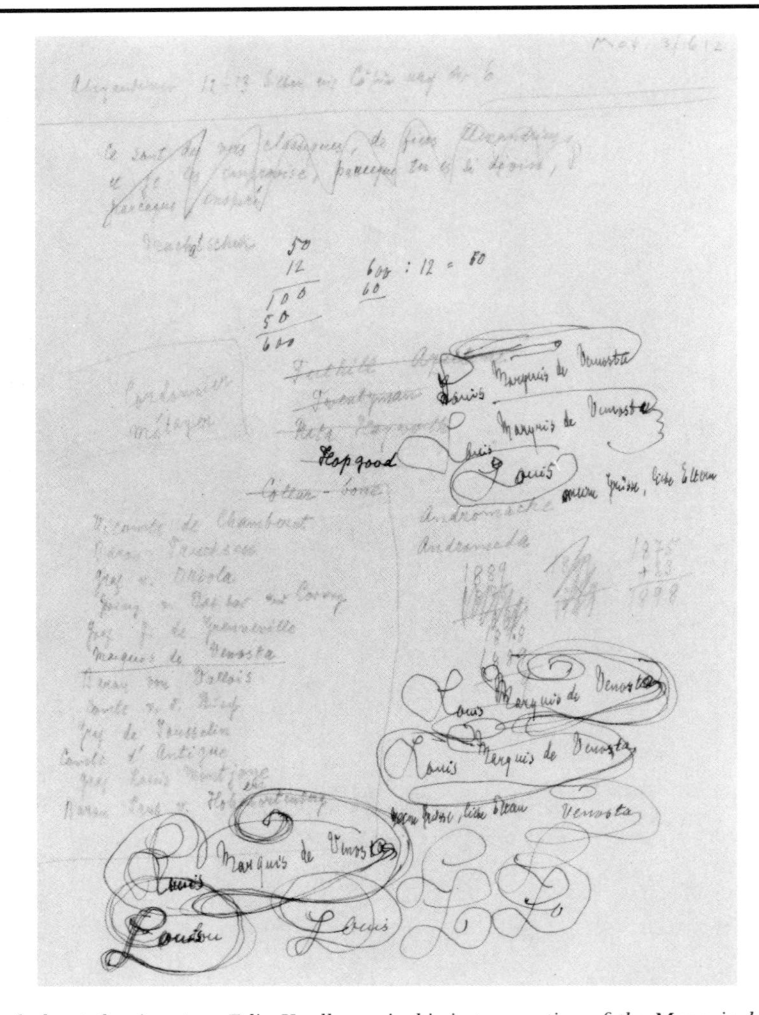

Page on which Mann worked out the signature Felix Krull uses in his impersonation of the Marquis de Venosta in Bekenntnisse des Hochstaplers Felix Krull *(1954), Mann's last novel (Thomas-Mann-Archiv, Zurich)*

of cultural superiority. He harbors a chauvinistic prejudice against Clawdia's native Russia, and finds her behavior uncivilized and uncouth. Clawdia tries to avenge herself by forcing Castorp to speak in French, but she cannot destroy his self-respect; she only strengthens him by refuting his initial prejudice. Castorp's love affair with Clawdia is indicative of Mann's enormous intellectual development in the years between the *Betrachtungen eines Unpolitischen* and the completion of *Der Zauberberg*.

Finally, Castorp is extremely impressed with his successor as Clawdia's lover, the giant Mynheer Peeperkorn. Peeperkorn is the epitome of the strong personality. His lack of intellectuality, symbolized by his incapacity for articulate speech, is compensated for by his cult of vitalism. Peeperkorn commits suicide when he feels his sexual powers falter; Castorp is repulsed by this demeaning death and realizes that the ideal of a great personality stems from the exaggeration of the individual.

Before Castorp leaves the Magic Mountain to become a foot soldier in the chaos of World War I he has a vision during a snowstorm of a peaceable mankind, civilized and humane, albeit with a sinister, indeed murderous secret under the pleasant surface. The vision gives way to daydreaming and finally the verbalization of problems central to the novel. In the course of these musings the reader finds the only italicized sentence in the book; it says that for the sake of love, man is not to grant death power over his thoughts. Stripped of its symbolism this passage contains Mann's confession that in *Der Zauberberg* he has subjected his romantic German heritage to a final scrutiny, deciding to relegate it to second place behind the democratic and life-

Mann and his wife visiting his old school, the Katharineum in Lübeck, May 1955

The Manns in Lübeck, May 1955 (Presse-Bild Hans Kripgans, Lübeck)

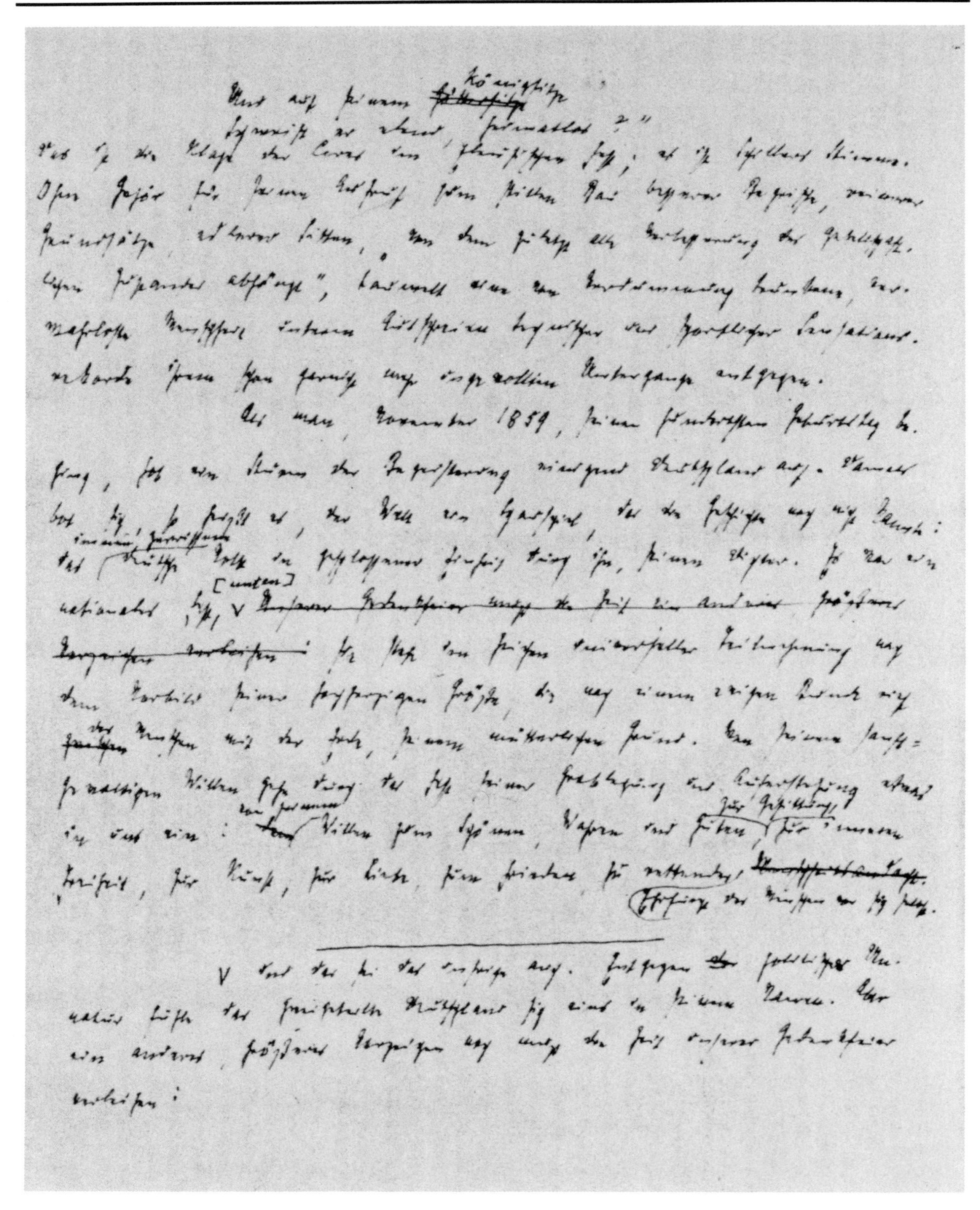

Page from the manuscript for Versuch über Schiller *(1955), one of Mann's last works (Thomas-Mann-Archiv, Zurich)*

Mann at his desk in Kilchberg, 1955 (photo: Fritz Eschen, Berlin)

enhancing virtues of western European culture. It can be argued that the impact of this message is weakened by the narrator's explicit assertion that shortly after escaping from the storm Castorp forgets the vision, and by the fact that the book continues for several more chapters. But in the course of these chapters the message turns up again in only slightly modified form, so that the conclusion is permissible that it retains its validity even if Castorp himself cannot live up to it. At the end of the novel he is left to an uncertain fate in the midst of a merciless battle.

Der Zauberberg shows the self-destructive powers hidden in culture; at the same time, it appeals to the moral values of culture, without which the world would be totally lost. In this work Mann's narrative techniques sparkle at their most brilliant. The narrator, the characters, and the world created are constantly relativized through irony so that it is impossible for the reader to maintain any fixed point of reference. The characters exist behind masks: their individual fates seem to adhere to historically predetermined roles. But even these roles receive a new individuation through the narration. The story is an exercise in dialectical hermeneutics: without tradition the people would have no identity, but the tradition must incessantly be reinterpreted and related to the present lest it become a simple stereotype.

All of this does not make it easy for the reader, particularly if he must rely on a translation. The constant switching between historical patterns and individual fates is achieved through Mann's use of language, which is significant to the smallest detail. Certain references, such as the one to the function of the German simple past tense, have to be left out unless the text is to be encumbered by lengthy footnotes (in *The Magic Mountain* "den raunenden Beschwörer des Imperfekts" is translated as "the rounding wizard of times gone by").

Another difficulty is caused by the use of the leitmotiv. Repeated phrases such as "blond

Mann in May 1955 (Conti-Press, Hamburg)

und blauäugig" (blond and blue-eyed) connect parts of the text; they often have not been recognized by the translator, or their different contexts did not allow for the exact repetition of the former phrase. The names of characters, such as Clawdia Chauchat (hotcat) or Hermine Kleefeld (cloverfield), are related to their personalities in ways that are only apparent in the original German. Some passages imitate the language of special social groups or particular styles of art to such an extent that it is impossible to determine the line between parody and seriousness. Every translation of Mann's works is necessarily an interpretation that limits and reduces the vast and rich tapestry of his language. The English translations concentrate almost exclusively on the story line and, consequently, do not let the reader see how resolutely the German text relativizes the plot through irony.

Today, even German-speaking readers are separated from Mann's text by a great historical and cultural distance. The original readers of the work were privileged bourgeois citizens educated in the humanities in a style that no longer exists. They were well acquainted with mythology and texts of world literature as well as the biographies of people such as Goethe and Nietzsche. The modern reader is often unaware of the allusions to this tradition, nor will he suspect, for example, that Peeperkorn is modeled on the dramatist Gerhart Hauptmann. This cultural distance does not make the story less interesting than it was for the reader of 1924, but it reduces the significance of the intended irony. Even if the modern reader is aware of the cultural background, he will experience the humor in a different way than Mann intended–in analogy to a joke which requires extensive explanation to be appreciated. In spite of these obstacles to full understanding, Mann's texts retain much of their original luster and, on the whole, their many levels of significance.

In 1926 Mann was elected a member of the Literary Section of the Prussian Academy of Art. After *Der Zauberberg* he returned to the present, the era of the Weimar Republic, which is reflected in two of his works. The economic depression and the rise of National Socialism provided the background for these short stories. In *Unordnung und frühes Leid* (Disorder and Early Sorrow, 1926; translated as *Early Sorrow,* 1929), the economic crisis forms the background. The story centers on a family whose life-style has been severely reduced and which is undergoing a generational conflict. The children see in their magnificent villa only the relic of a bygone time; the values their parents associate with the house are foreign to them. The inner tensions of the father, Abel Cornelius, a history professor who has to reconcile his rigorous self-expectations as a scholar with his mystical inclinations, constitute a subtheme. The main theme is the painful process of his separation from the youngest daughter, Lorchen; he is forced to witness her loss of childish naiveté without being able to keep the distance between them from growing. Lorchen is Mann's typical child figure: she lacks the "normal" childlike characteristics. In the eyes of her brothers and sisters she is too young to be taken seriously; in reality, she already possesses the self-awareness and eros that tragically separate her from her siblings and her father, whom she loves dearly.

The story *Mario und der Zauberer* (1930; translated as *Mario and the Magician,* 1931) is based on experiences Mann and his family had as vacationers in Mussolini's Italy. In the story a family wit-

Mann accepting honorary citizenship of Lübeck, 21 May 1955 (by permission of Dr. Hans-Otto Mayer)

Mann and his wife meeting the Italian novelist Alberto Moravia in Rome, April 1953 (Thomas-Mann-Archiv, Zurich)

nesses a murder: a magician / hypnotist humiliates his audience of vacationers and townspeople until the uneducated young waiter Mario draws a revolver and puts an end to the terror. The narrator, who confesses that he, too, had come under the hypnotic spell of the demogogic entertainer, hopes that his children have misunderstood the episode as a simple stunt. The story does not answer the question whether the parents have done the right thing by protecting the children from the truth of the situation. *Mario und der Zauberer* was later acknowledged as Mann's warning against fascism, already in power in Italy and threatening to take over Germany.

Mario und der Zauberer reflects an incident of injured vanity Mann suffered in Italy, when his family was refused permission to dine on the same hotel terrace as the Italian aristocracy. Something similar happened on 10 December 1929, when Mann was awarded the Nobel Prize in Stockholm: King Gustav V gave preferential treatment to the one aristocrat among the winners. Fifty years later Katja Mann still remembered this event as a grievous insult. Mann had defended democracy undauntedly throughout the Weimar period, but he had to experience what it meant to be discriminated against before he could really stand up for it emotionally.

In 1921 and 1925 Mann had written essays on Goethe and Tolstoy in which he attempted to bind the realism of the nineteenth century to the older tradition of German classicism. In the course of this work he became receptive to the suggestion in Goethe's autobiography *Aus meinem Leben: Dichtung und Wahrheit* (From My Life: Prose and Truth, 1811-1814, 1833; translated as *Autobiography of Goethe,* 1846) that the Biblical story of Joseph be recast as a historical novel. In 1926 Mann began a project based on a section of Genesis that resulted in a mammoth tetralogy. Seventeen years would be devoted to this effort. He made an intensive study of the era in question and took a three-month tour of the historical sites referred to in the Bible. In 1933 the first of the four volumes appeared: *Die Geschichten Jaakobs* (The Tales of Jacob; translated as *Joseph and His Brothers,* 1934), in which the origin of the historical tradition from which Joseph derives is described. *Der junge Joseph* (translated as *Young Joseph,* 1935) and *Joseph in Ägypten* (translated as *Joseph in Egypt,* 1938) followed in 1934 and 1936, respectively. The final volume, *Joseph, der Ernährer* (translated as *Joseph the Provider,* 1944), was not published until 1943.

The last three works were written abroad. Mann left Germany on 11 February 1933 on a lecture tour and remained in exile. Despite his great influence during the Weimar years, which he had repeatedly used to warn his countrymen against the rising tide of National Socialism, at heart Mann had remained the "unpolitical German." His political ideas strike the modern reader as alarming in their optimistic naiveté. When one reads his interviews of the period one is amazed to see the extent to which he minimized the dangers of militarism and political extremism. In 1928 he had still believed that National Socialism, in spite of all the bloody rioting, need not be taken seriously. As late as 1932 he was still of the opinion that the Nazi threat would be short lived. Soon after Hitler became chancellor, Mann gave a lecture in Munich on Richard Wagner titled "Leiden und Größe Richard Wagners" (Sufferings and Greatness of Richard Wagner), in which he upheld the essence of German culture against ideological abuse. The speech greatly fanned the hostility of the new regime and its sympathizers. Still, Mann might have returned to Germany after his foreign lecture tour had it not been for the warnings of his oldest children, Klaus and Erika, who were fervent antinationalists. A letter of March 1933 reveals the depth of his fear that he would never be able to "breathe the air" of Germany again. In exile he regarded it as his mission to represent Germany's "good element" against the destructive powers of its current rulers.

At first he stayed in Sanary-sur-Mer on the French Riviera, where many refugee writers had taken up residence; in the early fall of 1933 he moved to Küsnacht, near Zurich, where he lived until his move to the United States in 1938. On 19 December 1936 his honorary doctorate, which he had received in 1919, was revoked by the philosophical faculty of Bonn University; Mann published the letter informing him of the revocation, along with his reply, as *Ein Briefwechsel* (1937; translated as *An Exchange of Letters,* 1937). In 1937 he was awarded Czechoslovakia's Herder Prize for exiled writers. In Küsnacht he began a novel about Goethe, *Lotte in Weimar* (translated as *The Beloved Returns,* 1940), which was completed at Princeton and published in 1939. Goethe is portrayed as an isolated intellectual giant in the small-town atmosphere of eighteenth-century Weimar who is visited by a woman he had loved and lost forty years earlier: Charlotte Kestner (neé Buff), who served as the model for Charlotte in his

Der Erwählte

Wer läutet?

Glockenschall, Glockenschwall supra urbem, über der ganzen Stadt, in ihren von Klang überfüllten Lüften! Glocken, Glocken, sie schwingen und schaukeln, wogen und wiegen ausholend an ihren Balken, in ihren Stühlen, hundertstimmig, in babylonischem Durcheinander. Schwer und geschwind, brummend und bimmelnd, – da ist nicht Zeitmaß noch Einklang, sie reden auf einmal und alle einander ins Wort, ins Wort auch sich selber: an dröhnen die Klöppel und lassen nicht Zeit dem erregten Metall, daß es ausdröhne, da dröhnen sie pendelnd an am anderen Rande, ins eigene Gedröhne, also daß, wenn's noch hallt "In te Domine speravi", so hallt es auch schon "Beati, quorum tecta sunt peccata", hinein aber klingelt es hell von kleineren Stätten, als rühre der Meßbub das Wandlungsglöcklein.

Von den hohen Türmen läutet es und aus der Tiefe, von den sieben [illegible] Orten der Wallfahrt und allen Pfarrkirchen der sieben Sprengel, vom Quartier läutet's, von dem Heiligtume des Lateran und von Sankt Johannes im Lateran; es läutet über dem Grabe dessen, der die Schlüssel führt, im Vatikanischen Hügel, von Santa Maria Maggiore, in Foro, in Domnica, in Cosmedin und in Trastevere; von Ara Celi, Sankt Paulus außer der Mauer, Sankt Peter in Banden und vom Haus zum hochheiligen Kreuz in Jerusalem. Aber auch von den Kapellen der Friedhöfe, den Dächern der Saalkirchen und Oratorien in den Gassen läutet es auf. Wer nennt die Namen und weiß die Titel? Wie es läutet,

First page from the manuscript for Der Erwählte *(1951) (Thomas-Mann-Archiv, Zurich)*

novel *Die Leiden des jungen Werthers* (1774; translated as *The Sorrows of Werther,* 1786). At an early stage of his life, impressed with the sage's productivity, Mann had taken Goethe as a model. He had especially been inspired by Goethe's ability to balance his often contradictory inner forces and achieve mental harmony even in his most trying moments.

The Joseph project corresponded well to the concerns of the time. Joseph is banned by his brothers to Egypt. Having grown up in the mythical world of Israel, he is struck by the modernity and complexity of the Egyptian civilization. Thanks to this new horizon he can free himself from the mythical entanglement. He does not give up his own culture, but his new experiences make it possible for him to show his people a way into the future. Like Prince Klaus Heinrich, he avoids becoming a despotic patriarch and finds his identity as a wise statesman. Thus, the ending of the fourth Joseph novel, *Joseph, der Ernährer,* elaborates on a theme Mann had used thirty-five years previously in *Königliche Hoheit;* by 1943 he had given up the idea of an elitist and aristocratic leadership. While *Königliche Hoheit* was the literary prelude to an ideological defense of nationalistic politics, the Joseph novels try to work against the nationalists' attempt to use a distorted view of history and culture as a support for their ideology.

From 1940 until 1952 Mann lived in a luxurious home in Pacific Palisades, California. He became an American citizen on 23 June 1944. On 25 January 1947 his honorary doctorate was restored by Bonn University. He received many other honorary doctorates and awards from American and European institutions between 1939 and his death in 1955, including membership in the Accademia Nazionale dei Lincei in Rome in 1947, the Goethe Prize of Weimar in 1949, membership in the Academy of Arts and Letters in New York City in 1951, and the Officer's Cross of the Legion of Honor of France in 1952.

With the completion of *Joseph, der Ernährer* and a short story about Moses, *Das Gesetz* (1944; translated as *The Tables of the Law,* 1945), Mann's biblical writings were finished. His next novel, *Doktor Faustus: Das Leben des deutschen Tonsetzers Adrian Leverkühn, erzählt von einem Freunde* (1947; translated as *Doctor Faustus: The Life of the German Composer, Adrian Leverkühn, as Told by a Friend,* 1948), was his last swan song–a farewell to German culture and its intellectual tradition. In this story Germany's downfall is reflected in the fate of the composer Adrian Leverkühn.

The initiated reader of Mann's works will immediately recognize Lübeck society in the fictional town of Kaisersaschern. Mann completes the circle of his personal development by describing the upbringing of a young man with artistic ambitions in a traditional German environment, surroundings just like Hanno Buddenbrook's and Tonio Kröger's in the stories completed more than forty years before. Many themes are used again in the fashion of the leitmotiv, but the intellectual framework has changed completely.

This change is particularly reflected by the narrative perspective: for the first time, Mann uses a first-person narrator for a novel. Adrian Leverkühn's friend Serenus Zeitblom, Ph.D., a professor of literature, represents the educated German who is well versed in history and aware of the coming catastrophes of National Socialism and World War II but is paralyzed when it comes to taking action against these developments. A comparison of *Doktor Faustus* with *Mario und der Zauberer* shows that Mann's criticism of German intellectuals remained the same during the entire period of European fascism.

The hope he had expressed in *Der Zauberberg* that Germany could maintain a cooperative and mediating position in the middle of Europe had been cruelly disappointed. Mann's predominantly aesthetic comprehension of history did not allow for new explanations of Germany's Nazi aberration. Instead, he returned to his older concept of tragic fate: Leverkühn's end appears to be as inevitable as Thomas Buddenbrook's or Gustav Aschenbach's.

In contrast to Zeitblom, who is a passive intellectual with a bourgeois life-style and modest scholarly ambitions, Leverkühn is driven to produce art that has never existed before; and he is not afraid of unleashing self-destructive forces to do so. Leverkühn is the prototype of the German character who has to go his own way without concern for his own destruction or that of others.

Mann always had conflicting feelings about music, especially about the love of his childhood and youth, Wagner. He could not withstand the stunning power of Wagner's music, but at the same time, he realized the danger of its overwhelming sensuality and irrationality. In 1903 he had expressed this concern in literary form in "Tristan" (translated, 1925), the title story in the collection that included "Tonio Kröger." Adrian Leverkühn strongly opposes Wagner. Arnold

Mann in the 1950s (photo Caskey)

Schönberg's rationalistic twelve-tone music, which attempts to exclude any element of arbitrariness, is attributed in the novel to Leverkühn. His striving to reach this goal stands for the desire of the German character to accomplish the impossible.

To emphasize Leverkühn's dilemma as specifically German, Mann uses the greatest theme contributed by Germany to world literature, the Faust motif stemming from the Middle Ages. Leverkühn, the new Faust, has to seal a pact with the devil if he is to create great music. Unlike Goethe in his basically optimistic *Faust,* Mann has grave doubts about the redemption of Leverkühn's soul. Like the characters in *Buddenbrooks* whose dedication to the firm entails a denial of love and happiness, Leverkühn will create great music at the price of the same renunciation. Thus, Mann reverts to the medieval view that Faust is damned. By making love to a prostitute Leverkühn contracts syphilis, which stimulates and ultimately destroys his genius: the modern version of hell is insanity.

As remarkable as the reinterpretation of the Faust legend in the light of German history is the method Mann employs, a technique he called "Montage." He had always been fond of overtly or covertly quoting from various sources in his narrative works; in this novel the propensity is carried to such lengths that practically no passage is independent of some written model. The poetry of Shakespeare and the German romantics, epistolary literature, musicians' biographies, and newspaper and magazine articles on space and deep-sea exploration, medicine, and theology are quoted verbatim or in slight adaptation to surrounding passages. It thus turns out that Adrian Leverkühn "is" not only Faust (and Zeitblom his traditional assistant, Wagner) but also Nietzsche, whose stages in life Leverkühn replicates; Luther (which makes Zeitblom an Erasmus figure); and Beethoven, Schönberg, Alban Berg, and other musicians. Leverkühn's life embodies the entire cultural development of Germany. Mann's next work of fiction, *Die Entstehung des Doktor Faustus* (1949; translated as *The Story of a Novel,* 1961), a re-

Mann's grave in Kilchberg

telling of the circumstances under which *Doktor Faustus* was written, relaxes the high standards of narration and reintroduces a certain amount of the irony to which his readers had become accustomed.

In 1949, on the occasion of Goethe's 200th birthday, Mann made speeches in both the western and the eastern parts of Germany in which he spoke out for a united nation. This message was not well received in the West. It was not understood that by preferring one side over the other Mann would have compromised his deepest convictions about Germany's indivisible tradition. Mann was deeply shocked by the cold war that followed the end of World War II in 1945 and by Senator Joseph McCarthy's persecution of liberal intellectuals. The hysteria unleashed by McCarthyism drove him from the United States, and in 1952 he moved to Kilchberg, near Zurich.

His last two novels once more brought to the fore the optimistic Thomas Mann. In *Der Erwählte* (The Chosen One, 1951; translated as *The Holy Sinner,* 1951), based on Hartmann von Aue's medieval work *Gregorius,* one of the worst sinners is chosen by God to become pope. The second novel was a work Mann had left unfinished after publishing the first chapter as a novella in 1922: *Bekenntnisse des Hochstaplers Felix Krull: Der Memoiren erster Teil* (1954; translated as *Confessions of Felix Krull, Confidence Man: The Early Years,* 1955). At the end of his life he possessed the serenity to portray the artist as a confidence man who fools both himself and society by hiding behind a succession of masks in an effort to maintain his intellectual integrity, all the while admitting the illusionary nature of his acts.

Mann's last work was the voluminous essay *Versuch über Schiller* (On Schiller, 1955). He completed the manuscript in time for it to be used for the addresses he gave in Stuttgart and Weimar in May 1955 on the occasion of the 150th anniversary of Schiller's death. In this essay Mann appeals to the optimistic side of the German character. Consequently, his last word is a manifestation of hope–in favor of Schiller's *An die Freude* (Ode to Joy, 1786) and not Leverkühn's symphony "Dr. Fausti Weheklag" (Lamentation of Dr. Faustus). When Mann returned to his hometown of Lübeck on 20 May 1955 to receive an honorary citizenship from the city, he had already returned to Tonio Kröger's enthusiasm for Schiller. Mann was conciliatory at last, in accordance with the good German character he had always tried to emulate.

The works of Mann's old age appear as youthful as "Tonio Kröger." They are further enriched by a humorous atmosphere of self-parody. It is therefore appropriate to say that Mann was taken from this world at the height of his intellectual powers. He died in Zurich on 12 August 1955 at eighty years of age, just two days after being elected to the Peace Class of the Order *Pour le mérite* by West Germany. He left many unfinished projects which will keep scholars busy for a long time to come. But the mystery of his creativity and of his life will never be completely solved.

Letters:

Briefe an Paul Amann 1915-1952, edited by Herbert Wegener (Lübeck: Schmidt-Römhild, 1959);

Thomas Mann–Karl Kerényi: Gespräch in Briefen, edited by Karl Kerényi (Zurich: Rhein, 1960);

Thomas Mann an Ernst Bertram: Briefe aus den Jahren 1910-1955, edited by Inge Jens (Pfullingen: Neske, 1960);

Briefe, 1889-1955, 3 volumes, edited by Erika Mann (Frankfurt am Main: Fischer, 1961-1965);

Thomas Mann–Heinrich Mann: Briefwechsel 1900-1949, edited by Hans Wysling (Frankfurt am Main: Fischer, 1968);

Letters of Thomas Mann, 1889-1955, edited and translated by Richard and Clara Winston (New York: Knopf, 1971);

Thomas Mann: Briefwechsel mit seinem Verleger Gottfried Bermann Fischer 1932-1955, edited by Peter de Mendelssohn (Frankfurt am Main: Fischer, 1973);

Hermann Hesse–Thomas Mann: Briefwechsel, edited by Anni Carlsson and Volker Michels (Frankfurt am Main: Suhrkamp, 1975); translated by Ralph Manheim as *The Hesse / Mann Letters, 1910-1955* (New York: Harper & Row, 1975);

An Exceptional Friendship: The Correspondence of Thomas Mann and Erich Kahler, translated by Richard and Clara Winston (Ithaca, N.Y. & London: Cornell University Press, 1975);

Thomas Mann: Briefe an Otto Grautoff, 1894-1901, und Ida Boy-Ed, 1903-1928, edited by de Mendelssohn (Frankfurt am Main: Fischer, 1975);

Die Briefe Thomas Manns, 3 volumes, edited by Hans Bürgin and Hans-Otto Mayer (Frankfurt am Main: Fischer, 1976-1982);

Thomas Mann–Alfred Neumann: Briefwechsel, edited by de Mendelssohn (Darmstadt: Schneider, 1977).

Interviews:

Frage und Antwort: Interviews mit Thomas Mann 1909-1955, edited by Volkmar Hansen and Gert Heine (Hamburg: Knaus, 1983).

Bibliography:

Hans Bürgin, *Das Werk Thomas Manns,* edited by Walter A. Reichart and Erich Neumann (Frankfurt am Main: Fischer, 1959).

Biographies:

Klaus Mann, *The Turning-Point: Thirty-Five Years in This Century* (New York: Fischer, 1943);

Viktor Mann, *Wir waren fünf: Bildnis der Familie Mann* (Konstanz: Südverlag, 1949);

Hans Mayer, *Thomas Mann: Werk und Entwicklung* (Berlin: Volk und Welt, 1950);

Erika Mann, *Das letzte Jahr: Bericht über meinen Vater* (Frankfurt am Main: Fischer, 1956); translated by Richard Graves as *The Last Year of Thomas Mann* (New York: Farrar, Straus & Cudahy, 1958);

Georg Lukács, *Thomas Mann* (Berlin: Aufbau, 1957); translated by Stanley Mitchell as *Essays on Thomas Mann* (London: Merlin Press/ New York: Grosset & Dunlap, 1964);

Julia Mann, *Aus Dodos Kindheit* (Konstanz: Rosgarten-Verlag, 1958);

Klaus Schröter, ed., *Thomas Mann in Selbstzeugnissen und Bilddokumenten* (Reinbeck: Rowohlt, 1964);

Hans Bürgin and Hans-Otto Mayer, *Thomas Mann: Eine Chronik seines Lebens* (Frankfurt am Main: Fischer, 1965); translated by Eugene Dobson as *Thomas Mann: A Chronicle of*

His Life (University: University of Alabama Press, 1969);

Eike Midell, *Thomas Mann: Versuch einer Einführung in Leben und Werk* (Leipzig: Reclam, 1966);

J. P. Stern, *Thomas Mann* (London & New York: Columbia University Press, 1967);

Schröter, ed., *Thomas Mann im Urteil seiner Zeit* (Hamburg: Wegner, 1969);

André von Gronicka, *Thomas Mann: Profile and Perspectives* (New York: Random House, 1970);

Katja Mann, *Meine ungeschriebenen Memoiren*, edited by Elisabeth Plessen and Michael Mann (Frankfurt am Main: Fischer, 1974); translated by Hunter and Hildegarde Hannum as *Unwritten Memories*(New York: Knopf, 1975);

Peter de Mendelssohn, *Der Zauberer: Das Leben des deutschen Schriftstellers Thomas Mann* (Frankfurt am Main: Fischer, 1975);

Inge Diersen, *Thomas Mann: Episches Werk, Weltanschauung, Leben* (Berlin: Aufbau, 1975);

Nigel Hamilton, *The Brothers Mann: The Lives of Heinrich and Thomas Mann, 1871-1950, 1875-1955* (New Haven: Yale University Press, 1979);

Hans Wysling, *Narzissmus und illusionäre Existenzform: Zu den Bekenntnissen des Hochstaplers Felix Krull* (Bern & Munich: Francke, 1982);

Eberhard Hilscher, *Thomas Mann: Sein Leben und sein Werk* (Berlin: Das europäische Buch, 1983).

References:

Dieter W. Adolphs, *Literarischer Erfahrungshorizont: Aufbau und Entwicklung der Erzählperspektive im Werk Thomas Manns* (Heidelberg: Winter, 1985);

T. E. Apter, *Thomas Mann: The Devil's Advocate* (New York: New York University Press, 1979);

Hendrik Balonier, *Schriftsteller in der konservativen Tradition: Thomas Mann 1914-1924* (Frankfurt am Main: Lang, 1983);

Reinhard Baumgart, *Das Ironische und die Ironie in den Werken Thomas Manns* (Munich: Hanser, 1964);

Gunilla Bergsten, *Thomas Manns Doktor Faustus: Untersuchungen zu den Quellen und zur Struktur des Romans* (Stockholm: Svenska Bokförlaget Bonniers, 1963); translated by Krishna Winston as *Thomas Mann's Doctor Faustus: The Sources and Structure of the Novel* (Chicago & London: University of Chicago Press, 1969);

Beatrix Bludau, Eckhard Heftrich, and Helmut Koopmann, eds., *Thomas Mann 1875-1975: Vorträge in München, Zürich, Lübeck* (Frankfurt am Main: Fischer, 1977);

Bernhard Blume, *Thomas Mann und Goethe* (Bern: Francke, 1949);

Francis Bulhof, *Transpersonalismus und Synchronizität: Wiederholung als Strukturelement in Thomas Manns "Zauberberg"* (Groningen: Van Dederen, 1966);

James Cleugh, *Thomas Mann: A Study* (New York: Russell, 1933);

Deutsche Blätter (Santiago de Chile), special supplement, "Huldigung an Thomas Mann zum 70. Geburtstag–Homenaje a Thomas Mann," 3 (May / June 1945);

Ulrich Dittmann, *Sprachbewußtsein und Redeform im Werk Thomas Manns: Untersuchungen zum Verhältnis des Schriftstellers zur Sprachkrise* (Stuttgart: Kohlhammer, 1969);

Ignace Feuerlicht, *Thomas Mann* (New York: Twayne, 1968);

Martin Flinker, ed., *Hommage de la France à Thomas Mann à l'occasion de son 80e anniversaire* (Paris: Flinker, 1955);

Christoph Geisler, *Naturalismus und Symbolismus im Frühwerk Thomas Manns* (Bern & Munich: Francke, 1971);

Germanic Review, special Mann issue, 25 (December 1950);

Käthe Hamburger, *Thomas Manns biblisches Werk: Der Joseph-Roman, die Moses-Erzählung "Das Gesetz"* (Munich: Nymphenburger Verlagshandlung, 1981);

Henry Hatfield, *From the Magic Mountain: Mann's Later Masterpieces* (Ithaca, N.Y. & London: Cornell University Press, 1979);

Hatfield, *Thomas Mann: An Introduction to His Fiction* (New York: New Directions, 1962);

Hatfield, ed., *Thomas Mann: A Collection of Critical Essays* (Englewood Cliffs, N.J.: Prentice-Hall, 1964);

Hellmut Haug, *Erkenntnisekel: Zum frühen Werk Thomas Manns* (Tübingen: Niemeyer, 1969);

Eckhard Heftrich, *Zauberbergmusik: Über Thomas Mann* (Frankfurt am Main: Klostermann, 1975);

Erich Heller, *The Ironic German: A Study of Thomas Mann* (Boston & Toronto: Little, Brown, 1958);

Margit Henning, *Die Ich-Form und ihre Funktion in Thomas Manns "Doktor Faustus" und in der deutschen Literatur der Gegenwart* (Tübingen: Niemeyer, 1966);

Frank Donald Hirschbach, *The Arrow and the Lyre: A Study of the Role of Love in the Works of Thomas Mann* (The Hague: Nijhoff, 1955);

R. J. Hollingdale, *Thomas Mann: A Critical Study* (Cranbury, N.J.: Associated University Press, 1971);

Klaus W. Jonas, *Fifty Years of Thomas Mann Studies: A Bibliography of Criticism* (Minneapolis: University of Minnesota Press, 1955);

Jonas, *Die Thomas-Mann-Literatur,* 2 volumes (Berlin: Schmidt, 1972, 1979);

Fritz Kaufman, *Thomas Mann: The World as Will and Representation* (Boston: Beacon, 1957);

Ernst Keller, *Der unpolitische Deutsche: Eine Studie zu den "Betrachtungen eines Unpolitischen" von Thomas Mann* (Bern & Munich: Francke, 1965);

Helmut Koopmann, *Die Entwicklung des "intellektualen" Romans bei Thomas Mann* (Bonn: Bouvier, 1962);

Koopman, *Thomas Mann: Konstanten seines literarischen Werkes* (Göttingen: Vandenhoeck, 1975);

Koopman, ed., *Thomas Mann* (Darmstadt: Wissenschaftliche Buchgesellschaft, 1975);

Hermann Kurzke, *Auf der Suche nach der verlorenen Identität: Thomas Mann und der Konservatismus* (Würzburg: Königshausen & Neumann, 1980);

Kurzke, *Thomas-Mann-Forschung 1969-1976: Ein kritischer Bericht* (Frankfurt am Main: Fischer, 1977);

Herbert Lehnert, *Thomas Mann: Fiktion, Mythos, Religion* (Stuttgart: Kohlhammer, 1965);

Lehnert, *Thomas-Mann-Forschung: Ein Bericht* (Stuttgart: Metzler, 1969);

Lehnert, "Thomas Mann in Exile 1933-1938," *Germanic Review,* 38 (1963): 277-294;

Martin H. Ludwig, *Thomas Mann: Gesellschaftliche Wirklichkeit und Weltsicht in den Buddenbrooks* (Hollfeld: Beyer, 1979);

E. L. Marson, *The Ascetic Artist: Prefigurations in Thomas Mann's "Der Tod in Venedig"* (Bern, Frankfurt am Main & Las Vegas: Lang, 1979);

Harry Matter, *Die Literatur über Thomas Mann: Eine Bibliographie 1896-1969,* 2 volumes (Berlin & Weimar: Aufbau, 1972);

James R. McWilliams, *Brother Artist: A Psychological Study of Thomas Mann's Fiction* (Lanham, Md.: University Press of America, 1983);

Gertrude Michielsen, *The Preparation of the Future: Techniques of Anticipation in the Novels of Theodor Fontane and Thomas Mann* (Bern, Frankfurt am Main & Las Vegas: Lang, 1978);

Modern Language Notes, special issue, "Thomas Mann, 1875-1975," 90, no. 3 (1975);

Charles Neider, ed., *The Stature of Thomas Mann* (New York: New Directions, 1947);

Neue Rundschau (Stockholm), special issue, "Sonderausgabe zu Thomas Manns 70. Geburtstag" (6 June 1945);

Hans W. Nicklas, *Thomas Manns Novelle "Der Tod in Venedig": Analyse des Motivzusammenhangs und der Erzählstruktur* (Marburg: Elwerz, 1968);

Ronald Peacock, *Das Leitmotiv bei Thomas Mann* (Bern: Haupt, 1934);

Heinz-Peter Pütz, *Kunst und Künstlerexistenz bei Nietzsche und Thomas Mann: Zum Problem des ästhetischen Perspektivismus in der Moderne* (Bonn: Bouvier, 1963);

Pütz, *Thomas Mann und die Tradition* (Frankfurt am Main: Athenäum, 1971);

Terence Reed, *Thomas Mann: The Uses of Tradition* (Oxford: Clarendon Press, 1974);

Klaus-Jürgen Rothenberg, *Das Problem des Realismus bei Thomas Mann: Zur Behandlung der Wirklichkeit in den "Buddenbrooks"* (Cologne & Vienna: Böhlau, 1969);

Heinz Sauereßig, *Die Entstehung des Romans Der Zauberberg: Zwei Essays und eine Dokumentation* (Biberach: Wege und Gestalten, 1965);

Sauereßig, ed., *Besichtigung des Zauberbergs* (Biberach: Wege und Gestalten, 1974);

Jürgen Scharfschwerdt, *Thomas Mann und der deutsche Bildungsroman: Eine Untersuchung zu den Problemen einer literarischen Tradition* (Stuttgart: Kohlhammer, 1967);

Oskar Seidlin, *Von Goethe zu Thomas Mann: Zwölf Versuche* (Göttingen: Vandenhoeck, 1963);

Sinn und Form, special Mann issue (1965);

Richard Thieberger, *Der Begriff der Zeit bei Thomas Mann: Vom Zauberberg zum Joseph* (Baden-Baden: Kunst und Wissenschaft, 1952);

John C. Thirwall, *In Another Language: A Record of the Thirty-Year Relationship between Thomas Mann and His English Translator, Helen Tracy Lowe-Porter* (New York: Knopf, 1966);

Thomas Mann: 1875 / 1975 (Munich: Moos, 1975);

Frédérick Tristan, ed., *Thomas Mann: Cahier dirigé par Frédérick Tristan* (Paris: Edition de l'Herne, 1973);

Hans Rudolf Vaget, *Thomas Mann: Kommentar zu sämtlichen Erzählungen* (Munich: Winkler, 1984);

Vaget and Dagmar Barnouw, *Thomas Mann: Studien zu Fragen der Rezeption* (Bern & Frankfurt am Main: Lang, 1975);

Hermann Weigand, *Thomas Mann's Novel "Der Zauberberg"* (New York & London: Appleton-Century, 1933);

Weimarer Beiträge, special Mann issue, 21, no. 9 (1975);

George Wenzel, ed., *Betrachtungen und Überblicke: Zum Werk Thomas Manns* (Berlin & Weimar: Aufbau, 1966);

Wenzel, ed., *Thomas Mann zum Gedenken* (Potsdam: Thomas-Mann-Arbeitskreis des Kulturbundes zur demokratischen Erneuerung Deutschlands, 1956);

Wenzel, ed., *Vollendung und Größe Thomas Manns: Beiträge zu Werk und Persönlichkeit* (Halle: Sprache und Literatur, 1962);

Richard Winston, *Thomas Mann: The Making of an Artist, 1875-1911* (New York: Knopf, 1981);

Wissenschaftliche Zeitschrift der Friedrich-Schiller-Universität Jena, Gesellschafts- und Sprachwissenschaftliche Reihe, special Mann issue, 25, no. 3 (1976);

Hans Wysling, *Thomas Mann heute: Sieben Vorträge* (Bern & Munich: Francke, 1976);

Michael Zeller, *Bürger oder Bourgeois? Eine literatursoziologische Studie zu Thomas Manns "Buddenbrooks" und Heinrich Manns "Im Schlaraffenland"* (Stuttgart: Klett, 1976).

Papers:

Thomas Mann's papers are in the Thomas Mann Collection, Yale University; the Thomas-Mann-Archiv, Berlin; the Thomas-Mann-Archiv, Lübeck; the Sammlung Ida Herz,Nuremberg; and the Sammlung Hans-Otto-Meyer, Düsseldorf. The main center for Thomas Mann research is the Thomas-Mann-Archiv, Eidgenössische Technische Hochschule Zürich, Schönberggasse 15, CH-8001 Zurich. The Thomas-Mann-Archiv publishes the *Blätter der Thomas Mann Gesellschaft Zürich* and the *Thomas-Mann-Studien.*

Kurt Martens

(21 January 1870-16 February 1945)

George C. Schoolfield
Yale University

BOOKS: *Sinkende Schwimmer: Novellistische Skizzen aus dem Strudel der Zeit* (Berlin: Hochsprung, 1892);

Wie ein Strahl verglimmt: Drama in einem Akt (Leipzig: Wild, 1895);

Die gehetzten Seelen: Novellen (Berlin: Fontane, 1897);

Roman aus der Décadence (Berlin: Fontane, 1898);

Aus dem Tagebuch einer Baronesse von Treuth und andere Novellen (Berlin: Fontane, 1899);

Die Vollendung: Roman (Berlin: Fleischel, 1902);

Kaspar Hauser: Drama in vier Akten (Berlin: Fleischel, 1903);

Katastrophen: Novellen (Berlin: Fleischel, 1904);

Kreislauf der Liebe: Eine Geschichte von besseren Menschen (Berlin: Fleischel, 1906);

Der Freudenmeister: Komödie in vier Akten (Berlin: Fleischel, 1907);

Drei Novellen von adeliger Lust (Berlin: Fleischel, 1909);

Literatur in Deutschland: Studien und Eindrücke (Berlin: Fleischel, 1910);

Deutschland marschiert: Ein Roman von 1813, volume 1 of *Die alten Ideale* (Berlin: Fleischel, 1913);

Pia: Der Roman ihrer zwei Welten, volume 2 of *Die alten Ideale* (Berlin: Fleischel, 1913);

Geschmack und Bildung: Kleine Essays (Berlin: Fleischel, 1914);

Verse (Munich: Bachmair, 1914);

Hier und drüben: Roman, volume 3 of *Die alten Ideale* (Leipzig: Grethlein, 1915);

Jan Friedrich: Der Roman eines Staatsmannes (Leipzig: Grethlein, 1916);

Die großen und die kleinen Leiden: Novellen (Leipzig: Grethlein, 1917);

Der Alp von Zerled: Roman (Leipzig: Grethlein, 1920);

Schura: Novelle (Berlin: Hillger, 1920);

Schonungslose Lebenschronik 1870-1900 (Vienna: Rikola, 1921);

Die Pulververschwörung 1603-1606 (Leipzig: Deutscher Verlag, 1922);

Zwischen Sumpf und Firmament: Novellen (Munich: Paetel, 1922);

Abenteuer der Seele: Novelletten (Leipzig: Reclam, 1923);

Des Geliebten doppelte Gestalt: Roman (Berlin: Scherl, 1923);

Schonungslose Lebenschronik: Zweiter Teil 1901-1923 (Vienna: Rikola, 1924);

Blausäure: Ein Schuß im Wiener Wald: Kriminal-Novellen (Berlin: Sieben Stäbe, 1929);

Gabriele Bach: Roman einer Deutschen in Paris (Berlin: Neff, 1935);

Die Tänzerin und der Blinde (Berlin: Limpert, 1935);

Feldherr in fremdem Dienst: Schicksale des Grafen Matthias von der Schulenburg: Historische Erzählung (Leipzig: Möhring, 1936);

Die junge Cosima: Roman (Leipzig: Janke, 1937);

Forsthaus Ellermoor: Roman (Dresden: Seyfert, 1937);

Verzicht und Vollendung: Roman (Berlin: Steuben, 1941).

OTHER: *Die deutsche Literatur unserer Zeit: In Charakteristiken und Proben,* edited by Martens (Munich: Rösl, 1922; enlarged, Berlin: Franke, 1933);

Sūdraka, *Vasantasena,* translated and adapted for the stage by Kurt and Herta Martens (Berlin: Drehbühne, 1943).

PERIODICAL PUBLICATION: "Im Spiegel: Autobiographische Skizze," *Das literarische Echo,* 5 (1903): 1394-1396.

Kurt Martens is mainly known to students of German literature as Thomas Mann's close friend during Mann's early Munich years. Mann's "Tonio Kröger" (1903) is dedicated to Martens in recognition of their friendship, which was encouraged by the circumstance that Martens, like Mann, was a recent arrival in the Bavarian capital and came from a patrician and conservative home. They had met when Mann, a junior editor of the journal *Simplicissimus,* accepted a story by Martens; the two young authors began to trade manuscripts and opinions. Given a "half-autobiographical" novel to read–it would become Mann's *Buddenbrooks* (1901)–Martens was filled with admiration, although as an "unverbesserlicher Desillusionist und Skeptiker" (inveterate "disillusionist" and skeptic) he at first kept his enthusiasm to himself: "Es wollte mir so vorkommen, als wäre da etwas geschrieben worden, das höher stand als die ganze erzählende Dichtung dieser Zeit" (It seemed to me as if something had been written here that exceeded all the narrative literature of the time).

For his part, Mann was quite blunt with Martens in defining the latter's strengths and limitations. Having read *Kreislauf der Liebe: Eine Geschichte von besseren Menschen* (Circulation of Love: A Story about the Better Sort of People, 1906), he wrote to Martens that the "idyll" would someday be a valuable document about the reactionary mood in Germany at the beginning of the twentieth century; yet he found that it was too dry, "mit zu wenig Ironie, Romantik, Keckheit, Höhe . . . *keine* Prosa-Dichtung, sondern ein außerordentlich anständiger Roman" (with too little irony, romanticism, boldness, elevation . . . *not* a poetic creation in prose, but an extraordinarily respectable novel). Mann's 1905 marriage to Katja Pringsheim loosened the bond of friendship. Going through Martens's *Literatur in Deutschland* (Literature in Germany, 1910), Mann was pleased at the high and unenvious praise accorded him in the essay on his and his brother Heinrich's work, but he was dismayed because Martens had brought up "Wälsungenblut" (Blood of the Volsungs)–a scandalous Wagnerian tale about a wealthy Jewish family and brother-sister incest that Mann had withdrawn from publication in a magazine in 1906 (it was finally published as a book in 1921). Furthermore, he interpreted Martens's description of the character Imma Spoelmann in Mann's novel *Königliche Hoheit* (1909; translated as *Royal Highness,* 1916)–"ein ziemlich freches, verwöhntes Persönchen minderer Rasse" (a rather impudent and spoiled little person of a lesser breed)–as a bit of sniping at his wife. "Das ist schade, denn ich konnte meiner Frau dein Buch nicht vorenthalten, und–wir hätten so nett mit einander verkehren können" (It's too bad, since I couldn't keep your book away from my wife, and–we could have visited back and forth so nicely).

Professional contacts were maintained well into the 1920s; rather condescendingly, Mann took pains to thank Martens for his words of praise in *Die deutsche Literatur unserer Zeit* (German Literature of Our Time, 1922), saying that they showed perhaps the most attractive side of Martens's character, his "Geist uneigennützigen Dienens" (spirit of unselfish serving). After Martens's move to Dresden in 1927, the link was broken; getting a telegram from Martens on his sixtieth birthday, Mann expressed surprise to the artist and writer Alfred Kubin, another friend from the Munich salad days, that "our good old Kurt Martens" was still alive. After World War II Mann learned that Martens had died during the bombing of Dresden in February 1945: "Mit 70 Jahren soll er sich damals, aus den rauchenden Trümmern seines Hauses in Blasewitz geflohen, vergiftet haben" (At the age of 70, having fled from the smoking ruins of his house in Blasewitz, he is said to have taken poison.)

Mann's brief review of the first volume of Martens's autobiography, *Schonungslose Lebenschronik* (Unsparing Chronicle of Life, 1921, 1924), was amiably neutral; he must have been flattered by Martens's tributes to his exceptional talent, yet pained by the crass revelations Martens made about himself in an often wooden and pedantic style. (A contemporary cartoon, "Schonungsloser Kurt," portrays Martens on a stage, with perfectly parted hair and trim mustache: he has stripped off all his clothes.) The burden of Martens's first volume, beginning with his birth in Leipzig in 1870 to Heinrich Oskar and Henriette Erckel Martens and ending in 1900, was the harmful effect his upbringing in boarding schools had had upon him. Some of the teachers had been excellent (he remembered those in Latin with particular thankfulness), but the headmaster was unaware of what went on outside the classroom, and Martens had early been introduced to homosexual practices. These involvements, however much Martens claims to regret them, are recounted with a great deal more ardor than are his later heterosexual adventures and the vague and hasty story of his engagement and marriage. He first attended Heyne's Institute in Tharandt in Saxony, where the majority of the pupils were the sons of officers or members of the landed nobility; he found some of them unbearably crude, but their barbarism, in contrast to that of the masses, had "Kontur, Stil, und Rasse" (contour, style, and breeding). The smaller part of the student body consisted of the children of country squires and members of Martens's own social class, official families from Leipzig and Dresden. After five years at Tharandt Martens was sent at fourteen to the royal gymnasium at Wurzen, and made the passing acquaintance of Otto Julius Bierbaum (who gave a grotesque picture of the place in his 1897 novel *Stilpe*). Then he attempted university life at Heidelberg, but the drunken brutality of his dueling fraternity repelled him, as did his first sexual experience with a woman, a prostitute.

In Berlin, however, he was impressed by the lectures of the historian Heinrich von Treitschke and formed a cult of admiration for great men, from Alexander and Buddha to Bismarck and Moltke, which he never abandoned; traces of it can be seen in his historical novels. After travel in Italy with his mother and one of his sisters–he was extraordinarily devoted to the female members of his family–and a tour of duty as a clumsy volunteer cadet with a Saxon hussar regiment (he used this experience as background for a story in *Katastrophen* [Catastrophes, 1904] about one Pöppelmann, an inadvertent hero in the "summer war" of 1866), he settled down to his legal studies in Berlin. At the same time he read extensively in contemporary French, Russian, and Scandinavian literature. Moving to Dresden in 1895, he began his career in the Saxon courts, a world he found as hollow as the others he had tried. A conversion to Roman Catholicism–its immediate cause was no doubt his reading of Joris-Karl Huysmans and of the novel *Trætte Mænd* (Tired Men, 1891) by the Norwegian Arne Garborg (a book whose hidden *anti*-Catholic argument he seems to have overlooked)–likewise failed to effect a change in his skeptical nature. Association with such literary figures as Otto Erich Hartleben and the discovery of the verse of Stefan George and Hugo von Hofmannsthal persuaded him at last that letters were his calling, and in 1896 he began work on a novel.

He says in *Schonungslose Lebenschronik* that he set out in this novel to demonstrate that it was neither empty phrasemaking nor a silly contradiction in terms to speak of a "German decadence," a strain of rot in Wilhelm II's burgeoning and blustering empire. *Roman aus der Décadence* (Novel out of the Décadence, 1898) is set in Leipzig and bears patent autobiographical features; the main figure, Just, appointed to a trainee's post in the court system, is appalled at the callousness and ignorance of the judge and attorneys. Involved in a protracted platonic relationship with Alice, the daughter of a good family, he finds sexual release with a beggar girl: he dresses her in a peplum, calls her Amaryllis, and stimulates her with a reading of Theocritus. In fact, he stimulates *himself*: like Huysmans's hero Des Esseintes in *A rebours* (1884; translated as *Against the Grain,* 1922), he needs a stage setting for maximum erotic performance. His conversion to the Roman church soon goes sour; he is put off by the vulgarity of the priest from whom he receives instruction and by his new coreligionists. Yet his devotion to the customary practices of literature's decadents is neither complete nor deep; he slowly grows estranged from his friend Erich Lüttwitz, another jurist and dilettante, as the latter begins a life of ostentatious decadence. Having inherited wealth, Erich rents an out-of-the-way mansion, decks out its interior with exquisite trappings, recruits and costumes young women (the imposing "Thusnelda," the tragic "Elvira," and Amaryllis herself) for various erotic roles, and becomes a racetrack dandy.

The novel's climax comes when Erich holds a party which, he lets it be known, will be his "death-festival." With the extravagance of his type, he hires an augmented symphony orchestra to perform Berlioz's *Symphonie fantastique;* after the last movement, the "Songe d'une nuit du Sabbath" (Dream of a Witches' Sabbath), has been played, "alle Sinne wurden, nach dem Kumulations-Prinzip von Huysmans' Herzog Des Esseintes, mit den auserlesensten Delikatessen gespeist" (all the senses were fed with the choicest delicacies, in accordance with the cumulative principle of Huysmans's Duke Des Esseintes). Then Oskar Panizza's notorious play about the court of Pope Alexander VI (Rodrigo Borgia), *Das Liebeskonzil* (The Council of Love, 1895), is performed, and the obscenities on stage drive the audience into orgiastic imitation of the performers. Erich disappears but does not kill himself; instead, he marries a lively and moneyed widow. (When Martens tried for exaggerated or colorful effects, he easily slid into the grotesque and the risible; this is the case with Erich's orgy, and the tale "Madam oder die Schattenseiten zärtlicher Gefühle" [Madam or the Dark Sides of Tender Feelings] in *Katastrophen* is another case in point. An Alpine thunderstorm sets fire to a Swiss chateau after the narrator, an artist who is the paid guest of a well-to-do middle-aged woman, has humiliated her in the course of a passionate coupling; she hangs herself as the storm rages, and he flees, "gehetzt von einem schlotternden Gespenst, dem verkohlten Leichnam einer fetten, lüsternen Frau" [pursued by a tottering phantom, the charred corpse of a fat and lustful woman].)

The passive decadent Just observes the goings-on at Erich's with his usual detachment. At the novel's end his sometime-mistress Alice, freshly wed to a dull-witted young officer, initiates a run-of-the-mill affair with him–and he, while enjoying it, concludes that Alice has become platitudinous, even in bed. Trying to give his life some content, he decides to propose to Esther, an admirable Jewess engaged in social-reform work, only to learn that she has secretly married the honest editor Tönnies, whose faulty manners and shabby clothes have long been the object of Just's friendly scorn. On the book's last page, Just toys with the notion of joining a revolutionary movement led by the Russian Dimitri Teniawsky. A childhood friend of Czar Nicholas II, Teniawsky had once planned to destroy established society by acts of terrorism, and came close (as he tells Just) to hurling a bomb into the audience at a concert. Yet the plot failed, and Teniawsky realized that the revolution must be slowly and carefully prepared and without bloodshed. After hearing Teniawsky's arguments, Just records: "Meine Antwort war das Lächeln der Auguren" (My reply was the smile of the augurs). His decision remains unknown.

For all its schematization and its dependence on recent literature for many of its effects, *Roman aus der Décadence* is an important document in its own right. Almost every decadent novel comments, however obliquely, on social and political ills–indeed, the decadent's selfish and exclusivist pose is an act of individual revolution against the time in which he lives–and Martens, in his matter-of-factness, comes closer than many of his contemporaries in making what the Belgian critic Ivan Gilkin (writing of *A rebours*) called an "effrayante analyse de la décomposition sociale" (a terrifying analysis of social decomposition). But Martens lacks that "elevation" of which Thomas Mann would speak; as Just's narrative voice is dryly unimpassioned, so Martens is incapable of making almost any of his characters or his milieu seem alive. The exception is a figure Martens himself called "etwas zu phantastisch" (perhaps too fantastic): Teniawsky's story of the unperformed terrorist deed is the most memorable passage in the book, and maybe in all of Martens's oeuvre.

Martens moved to Munich in 1899. That year he married Mary Fischer; they had a daughter, Hertha Helena. The remainder of his literary career was a long anticlimax. His criticism of German society in *Die Vollendung* (The Completion, 1902) and *Kreislauf der Liebe* and many of his novellas was never trenchant enough, perhaps because of his affection for the groups he regarded as responsible for German decay–the nobility and his own upper-bourgeois class–and because of his inability, which he admitted, to portray any aspect of German society that lay outside these realms. He regarded his stories about the nobility–*Aus dem Tagebuch einer Baronesse von Treuth* (From the Diary of a Baroness von Treuth, 1899) and *Drei Novellen von adeliger Lust* (Three Novellas about Nobility's Pleasure, 1909)–as his best works; and it may be revelatory that he did not take it at all ill when the Baltic nobleman Eduard von Keyserling told him he disliked *Roman aus der Décadence* because it had been written by an "apostate of the bourgeoisie." Even when he had descended quite patently into the ranks of entertainment writers, his concern with two social sectors, the nobility and his own, remained. *Der Alp von Zerled* (The Incubus of Zerled, 1920) circles sentimentally around the gifted lawyer Roderich, whose erotic fascination with a governess and a daughter belonging to the noble house of Zerled leads to his brutal murder at a nobleman's orders.

Martens's genuine concern with Germany's decline, in the very moment of its greatest display of grandeur, when "der Friedenskaiser reiste, ölige Reden um sich streuend, von einem erlauchten Vetter zum andern" (the emperor of peace, scattering his oily speeches far and wide, journeyed from one illustrious cousin to another), led him to produce a trilogy of historical novels, *Die alten Ideale* (The Old Ideals) from 1913 to 1915. As World War I wore on, he expressed his belief in the gifted bourgeois as a possible national savior in his best historical narration, *Jan Friedrich* (1916), about Johann Friedrich Struensee, the Altona physician who briefly became Denmark's enlightened ruler and then was subjected to a horrible death by the Danish nobility.

In 1927 Martens moved to Dresden. *Verzicht und Vollendung* (Renunciation and Completion, 1941), which the literary historian Ernst Alker saw as an act of "discreet opposition" to National Socialism, is built on the fiction that Louis XVII, "l'Orphelin du Temple," survived the French Revolution and by his moral strength triumphed over his vulgar tormenters. The dauphin Louis, the "true" blueblood who leads the restricted and responsible existence of the "true" bourgeois, may stand for a final solution of the conflict between these two social groups that appears to have concerned Martens through much of his later life. *Verzicht und Vollendung* was Martens's last published work. The novels that Karl H. Salzmann–writing an *in memoriam* in 1946–said were ready for printing never appeared. Two other manuscripts had been destroyed in the air raids on Dresden.

References:

Ernst Alker, *Die deutsche Literatur im 19. Jahrhundert: 1832-1914* (Stuttgart: Kröner, 1961), p. 762;

Jens Malte Fischer, "Kurt Martens: Roman aus der Décadence (1898)," in his *Fin de siècle: Kommentar zu einer Epoche* (Munich: Winkler, 1978), pp. 169-178;

Helmut Kreuzer, *Die Bohème: Beiträge zu ihrer Beschreibung* (Stuttgart: Metzler, 1968), pp. 96-97;

"M," "Fin-de-siècle-Konvertiten," *Hochland-Echo* (November 1903): 237-240;

Thomas Mann, *Briefe 1889-1936* (Frankfurt am Main: Fischer, 1961);

Mann, *Briefe 1948-1955 und Nachlese* (Frankfurt am Main: Fischer, 1965);

Mann, "Ein Schriftstellerleben," in volume 10 of his *Gesammelte Werke* (Frankfurt am Main: Fischer, 1960), pp. 613-616;

Peter de Mendelssohn, "Kurt Martens," in his *Der Zauberer: Das Leben des deutschen Schriftstellers Thomas Mann, I: 1875-1918* (Frankfurt am Main: Fischer, 1975), pp. 350-353;

Karl Johann Müller, "Exkurs: Thematisierung der Dekadenz: Kurt Martens 'Roman aus der Décadence' und Gerhard Ouckama-Knoops 'Die Dekadenten,' " in his *Das Dekadenzproblem in der oesterreichischen Literatur um die Jahrhundertwende* (Stuttgart: Heinz, 1977);

Karl H. Salzmann, "Kurt Martens zum Gedächtnis," *Der Zwiebelfisch,* 25, no. 2 (1946): 26-27;

Carl Hans von Weber, "Kurt Martens," *Das literarische Echo,* 5 (1903): 1387-1394.

Alfons Paquet

(26 January 1881-8 February 1944)

H. M. Waidson

BOOKS: *Schutzmann Mentrup und Anderes* (Cologne: Schmitz, 1901);

Lieder und Gesänge (Berlin: Grote, 1902);

Anatolien und seine deutschen Bahnen (Munich: Süddeutsche Verlags-Anstalt, 1906);

Auf Erden: Ein Zeit- und Reisebuch in fünf Passionen (Düsseldorf: Bagel, 1906; enlarged, Jena: Diederichs, 1908);

Das Ausstellungsproblem in der Volkswirtschaft (Jena: Fischer, 1908);

Asiatische Reibungen: Politische Studien (Munich: Verlags-Gesellschaft München, 1909);

Südsibirien und die Nordwestmongolei: Politisch-geographische Studie und Reisebericht (Jena: Fischer, 1909);

Kamerad Fleming (Frankfurt am Main: Rütten & Loening, 1911; enlarged, Berlin: Deutsche Buchgemeinschaft, 1926);

Held Namenlos (Jena: Diederichs, 1912);

Li oder im neuen Osten (Frankfurt am Main: Rütten & Loening, 1912);

Limo der große beständige Diener (Frankfurt am Main: Rütten & Loening, 1912);

Erzählungen an Bord (Frankfurt am Main: Rütten & Loening, 1913);

Der Sendling: Erzählungen und Schilderungen (Hamburg-Großborstel: Deutsche Dichter-Gedächtnis-Stiftung, 1914);

Der Kaisergedanke (Frankfurt am Main: Rütten & Loening, 1915);

Die jüdischen Kolonien in Palästina (Weimar: Kiepenheuer, 1915);

Nach Osten! (Stuttgart: Deutsche Verlags-Anstalt, 1915);

In Palästina (Jena: Diederichs, 1915);

Aus dem bolschewistischen Rußland (Frankfurt am Main: Frankfurter Societäts-Druckerei, 1919);

Im kommunistischen Rußland: Briefe aus Moskau (Jena: Diederichs, 1919);

Der Geist der russischen Revolution (Leipzig: Wolff, 1919; revised, 1920);

Das russische Gesicht (Heilbronn: Ulrich, 1920);

Alfons Paquet in 1917 (by permission of Henriette Klingmüller-Paquet)

Die Quäker (Frankfurt am Main: Frankfurter Societäts-Druckerei, 1920);

Der Rhein als Schicksal oder Das Problem der Völker (Munich: Wolff, 1920);

Die Botschaft des Rheines (Hamburg: Harms, 1922);

Delphische Wanderung (Munich: Drei Masken, 1922);

Drei Balladen (Munich: Drei Masken, 1923);

Rom oder Moskau: Sieben Aufsätze (Munich: Drei Masken, 1923);

Die Prophezeiungen (Munich: Drei Masken, 1923), translated by H. M. Waidson as *Prophecies* (Columbia, S.C.: Camden House, 1983);

Fahnen: Ein dramatischer Roman in 3 Akten (Munich: Drei Masken, 1923);

Der Rhein, eine Reise (Frankfurt am Main: Frankfurter Societäts-Druckerei, 1923);

Amerika: Hymnen, Gedichte (Leipzig-Plagwitz: Die Wölfe, 1924);

Frankfurt als Bücherstadt und das Rhein-Main-Gebiet als Heimat des Buchdrucks und des Buchgewerbes: Vortrag (Frankfurt am Main: Hanser, 1924);

Markolph oder König Salomo und der Bauer (Frankfurt am Main: Verlag des Bühnenvolksbundes, 1924);

Die neuen Ringe: Reden und Aufsätze zur deutschen Gegenwart (Frankfurt am Main: Frankfurter Societäts-Druckerei, 1924);

Ausblick auf das Meer: Zwei Erzählungen (Stuttgart: Fleischhauer & Spohn, 1925);

Lusikas Stimme: Novelle (Stuttgart, Berlin & Leipzig: Deutsche Verlags-Anstalt, 1925);

Skizze zu einem Selbstbildnis (Frankfurt am Main: Frankfurter Societäts-Druckerei, 1925);

Rhein und Menschheit (Wiesbaden: "Friede durch Recht," 1925);

Sturmflut (Berlin: Volksbühnen-Verlags- und Vertriebs G.m.b.H., 1926);

William Penn, Gründer von Pennsylvanien (Augsburg: Filser, 1927);

Städte, Landschaften und ewige Bewegung: Ein Roman ohne Helden (Hamburg-Großborstel: Deutsche Dichter-Gedächtnis-Stiftung, 1927);

Die alte Sparcasse: Ein Hundertjahrbild der Hamburger Sparcasse von 1827 (Hamburg: Trautman, 1927);

Gastechnik: Bilder eines lebenswichtigen Betriebes auf Grund einer Darstellung der Hamburger Gaswerke (Berlin: Schröder, 1928);

Der Neckar: Ein Lebensbild zu vierzig Zeichnungen (Heidelberg: Hörning, 1928);

Gesammelte Schriften: Aufsätze, volume 1: *Antwort des Rheines: Eine Ideologie* (Augsburg: Filser, 1928);

Hamburg als Ausstellungsstadt (Hamburg: Boysen & Maasch, 1929);

Frau Rat Goethe und ihre Welt (Frankfurt am Main: Englert & Schlosser, 1931);

Das Siebengestirn: Gedichte (Berlin: Rabenpresse, 1932);

Freiherr vom Stein: Chor-Dichtung (Berlin: Volkschaft-Verlag, 1933);

Politik statt Religion? Rundgespräch, by Paquet and others (Berlin: Eckart-Verlag, 1933);

Und Berlin? Abbruch und Aufbau der Reichshauptstadt (Frankfurt am Main: Societäts-Verlag, 1934);

Weltreise eines Deutschen: Landschaften, Inseln, Menschen, Städte (Berlin: Buchmeister-Verlag, 1934);

Wohin führt uns Jesus Christus? Ansprachen, by Paquet, A. Garrett, and E. Fuchs (Bad Pyrmont: Quäkerverlag, 1934);

Fluggast über Europa (Munich: Knorr & Hirth, 1935);

Ballade von George Fox (Bad Pyrmont: Quäkerverlag, 1936);

Die religiöse Gesellschaft der Freunde (Bad Pyrmont: Quäkerverlag, 1937);

Der Reiter von Damaskus (Bad Pyrmont: Quäkerverlag, 1937);

Der Frankfurter Rundhorizont: Fahrten in weiter Landschaft (Frankfurt am Main: Diesterweg, 1937);

Amerika unter dem Regenbogen (Frankfurt am Main: Frankfurter Societäts-Verlag, 1938);

Erwähnung Gottes (Bad Pyrmont: Quäkerverlag, 1939);

Gaswelt und vier andere Essays (Cologne: Staufen-Verlag, 1940);

Der Rhein: Vision und Wirklichkeit (Düsseldorf: Bagel, 1940; enlarged, 1941);

Spiel mit der Erdkugel (Česká Lípa: Kaiser, 1940);

Die Botschaft des Rheins: Erlebnis und Gedicht (Ratingen: Herm, 1941);

Melodie der Welt (Frankfurt am Main: Kramer, 1946);

Die Frankfurterin (Frankfurt am Main: Kramer, 1947);

John Woolman, ein großer Helfer (Bad Pyrmont: Friedrich, 1951);

Gedichte (Heidelberg & Darmstadt: Schneider, 1956);

Gesammelte Werke, 3 volumes, edited by Hanns Martin Elster (Stuttgart: Deutsche Verlags-Anstalt, 1970).

OTHER: Ku Hung-Ming, *Chinas Verteidigung gegen europäische Ideen: Kritische Aufsätze,* foreword by Paquet (Jena: Diederichs, 1911);

Jahrbuch des Deutschen Werkbundes 1912, edited by Paquet (Jena: Diederichs, 1912);

En détachement de travail, edited by Paquet (Frankfurt am Main: Rütten & Loening, 1917);

G. D. H. Cole and W. Mellor, *Gildensozialismus,* foreword by Paquet (Cologne: Rheinland, 1921);

John Woolman, *Die Aufzeichnungen von John Woolman: Aus der Zeit der Sklavenbefreiung,* translated by Paquet (Berlin: Quäkerverlag, 1923);

Ivan V. Kirejewski, *Rußlands Kritik an Europa,* edited by Paquet (Stuttgart: Frommann, 1923);

I. A. Gontscharow, *Oblomov,* afterword by Paquet (Leipzig: List, 1925);

Wilhelm Steinhausen, *Aus meinem Leben: Erinnerungen und Betrachtungen,* edited by Paquet (Berlin: Furche, 1926);

Land voraus!, edited by Paquet (Munich: Knorr & Hirth, 1938);

F. M. Jansen, *Rheinische Städte, rheinische Burgen,* completed by Paquet (Düsseldorf: Schwann, 1941);

Von Brest-Litovsk zur deutschen Novemberrevolution: Aus den Aufzeichnungen von Alfons Paquet, Wilhelm Groener, Albert Hopman, edited by Winfried Baumgart (Göttingen: Vandenhoeck & Ruprecht, 1971).

Alfons Paquet made considerable and varied contributions to German writing during the first four decades of the twentieth century. His novels and short stories often reflect his imaginative involvement with political and social issues. His best plays were performed in Berlin and elsewhere in Germany during the 1920s, the period which saw the culmination of his involvement in current events and of his acclaim by his literary contemporaries. His accounts of his travels to Russia, the Far East, and America are of a concrete, realistic character and of interest as documents of their time and place. He made his first contribution to the *Frankfurter Zeitung* in 1904, and continued to write for the newspaper until it ceased publication in 1943. Paquet's writings include lyrical poetry, drama, short stories, novels, essays, and accounts of a journalistic nature. His descriptive powers enabled him to treat a wide range of subjects with lively energy and a conscientious, humane sense of responsibility.

Born in Wiesbaden in 1881 to Jean and Friedericke Burger Paquet, Alfons Hermann Paquet was later to write in *Skizze zu einem Selbstbildnis* (Autobiographical Sketch, 1925): "Einige meiner Vorfahren, noch nicht ganz außerhalb des Erinnerns, waren Bäckerwirte, Kupferschmiede, Schulmeister in Landstädten, andere, die in größeren Städten lebten, waren Gerber, Advokaten, Soldaten" (Some of my forefathers, still not wholly unremembered, were bakers, coppersmiths, teachers in country towns, while others who lived in larger cities were tanners, lawyers, soldiers). His father's family came from Grenoble (his great-grandfather had taken part in the Napoleonic Wars and then settled in Luxembourg), while his mother could trace forebears in Heilbronn back to the sixteenth century. From his mother he inherited "die Lebenswärme, die die Wurzel alles Dichterischen ist" (the warmth of life which is the root of all that is poetic). His father, not wishing to encourage the boy's liking for books, took him out of school at the age of fifteen and sent him to London to be an apprentice in an uncle's clothing business. Paquet developed an enthusiasm for literature and for the exploration of strange cities, and after his return home he found difficulty in settling down as an apprentice in his father's glove business. He wrote poems, stories, and dramatic fragments whenever he had the opportunity, and his first appearance in print, a poem on Gutenberg, was published in the *Mainzer Anzeiger* in 1900.

With the publication of his first two books Paquet felt justified in leaving commerce to earn a living by writing. His volume of eleven short stories, *Schutzmann Mentrup und Anderes* (Police Officer Mentrup and Other Stories, 1901), brought him to the attention of Carl Busse and Wilhelm Schäfer, who helped him to make a start in publishing and to find work as a journalist. One of the stories in Paquet's collection, "Abendwölkchen" (Little Evening Cloud), was awarded the Golden Rose prize by the city of Cologne. A story of the tragic outcome of a love affair, it is set against the background of the London docks. The verse in *Lieder und Gesänge* (Poems and Songs, 1902) is often written in a traditional romantic style. The mood of "Wie ich abends . . ." (How in the Evening I . . .) evokes a folksong in rural setting. At other times, as in "Kummer" (Care), the poet looks into himself with feelings of despair and guilt. Although the protagonist of "Nähe" (Proximity) believes that God reveals Himself in the quiet of nature, he responds also to the stimulus of an express train that rushes past. In "Im Wandel" (Movement) the poet sees himself as a restless wanderer aware of life and the meaning of freedom, with the Divine as his goal. "Licht" (Light) is written in rhapsodic free verse. Occasionally Paquet ex-

Dust jacket for Paquet's 1923 novel about an attempt to form a utopian commune in Russia

periments with long lines of poetry, as in "Singende Seele" (Soul in Song).

Paquet began his travels while sporadically attending Heidelberg University from 1902 to 1904 and Munich University from 1904 to 1905. In 1903 he journeyed through Siberia to the Pacific Ocean. A year later he went to America to visit the world exposition in St. Louis. He was to develop an interest in the arrangement of exhibitions, as well as in the earth's underground resources and in religious sects and free churches. As his daughter Henriette Kingmüller recalls him (in a 1985 letter), he was "definitiv kein l'art pour l'art-Mensch" (definitely not an art-for-art's-sake person). He traveled through the Balkans to Turkey and Syria in 1905, returning home earlier than planned on account of illness. His broadening vision and the impressions made by his travels are reflected in his second book of verse, *Auf Erden: Ein Zeit- und Reisebuch in fünf Passionen* (On Earth: A Book of the Times and of Travel in Five Passions, 1906). Many of these poems, with their vigorous long lines, are set in America, which is described with rugged vitality. Rhapsodic, adventurous, and emphatic reactions predominate in the poems of *Held Namenlos* (Nameless Hero, 1912).

In 1906 Paquet began to study at Jena University, where he earned a Ph.D. in economics in 1908. On 18 October 1910 he married Marie-Henriette Steinhausen; they had six children: Henriette, Friederike, Sebastian, Barbara, Wilhelmine, and Bernhard.

The action of Paquet's first novel, *Kamerad Fleming* (Comrade Fleming, 1911), takes place in Paris; it is presented from the point of view of a German who becomes involved in political agitation and meets his death as a consequence. The novel's considerable number of descriptive passages are characterized by detailed realism. Paquet's concern for political principles also finds expression in *Limo, der große beständige Diener* (Limo, the Great and Constant Servant, 1912), a play set in a remote quasi-legendary state where the emperor, who orders the death of his loyal minister, subsequently admits his mistake and revises his attitudes. The play was first performed in Stuttgart in 1924. Another collection of Paquet's short stories, *Erzählungen an Bord* (Tales on Board), appeared in 1913.

Between 1916 and early 1918 Paquet lived mainly in Stockholm as a representative of the *Frankfurter Zeitung*. After visiting Finland early in 1918 he spent July-November 1918 as press attaché to the German general consulate in Moscow. His reports from Russia appeared as *Im kommunistischen Rußland: Briefe aus Moskau* (In Communist Russia: Letters from Moscow, 1919). This work is a lively and detailed account of Paquet's reactions to a period of major crisis; after ten months of Lenin's rule the Soviet promises of bread, freedom, and peace seem hollow to him. Paquet supplemented this account with *Der Geist der russischen Revolution* (The Spirit of the Russian Revolution, 1919), three lectures which he gave shortly after his return from Russia. Although he has much to say in criticism of Russian communism, he also finds positive aspects. Paquet's diaries for 4 July to 27 November 1918, edited by Winfried Baumgart in 1971, provide a more personal supplement to these two books. Further views of life and society in Russia at that time are to be found in *Rom oder Moskau: Sieben Aufsätze* (Rome or Moscow: Seven Essays, 1923). Paquet's interest in the Society of Friends is visible in one of these essays, "Die Quäker" (The Quakers) as well as in his biographical poem on George Fox in *Drei Balladen* (Three Ballads, 1923).

The Russian Revolution stimulated Paquet not only to realistic reporting and intellectual argument but also to imaginative writing. The novel *Die Prophezeiungen* (1923; translated as *Prophecies*, 1983) has qualities of mystery and fantasy and a sometimes wayward abruptness of style and narrative action. Of Paquet's writings of the 1920s, this book seems closest to expressionism. The action begins in Sweden and moves to Germany in the latter part of World War I; after two years in Africa, the novel's Swedish protagonist, Bildad, finds himself in Eastern Siberia, where he becomes a companion of Countess Rune Lewenclau, a Swedish compatriot who leads a group through Siberia to join forces in Russia with Granka Umnitsch, the leader of the "High Northern Commune" that aims at becoming a self-sufficient community. The commune plans to turn its back on industrial civilization and to have a minimum of relations with the hostile Western powers. This new, experimental society does not, however, survive the accidental death of its leader. Paquet originally intended the novel to have a sequel, "Die Erfüllungen" (The Fulfillments), but this plan was not realized.

The performance of *Fahnen: Ein dramatischer Roman in 3 Akten* (Flags: A Dramatic Novel in 3 Acts, 1923) at the Berlin Volksbühne (People's Theater) in 1924 attracted considerable attention in theatrical circles. This interest was no doubt due in part to the work of the producer, Erwin Piscator, at that time making a name for himself as an energetically radical young man of the theater. The text of the play makes an impression of narrative rather than dramatic construction, and Paquet seems to admit this flaw in his choice of subtitle: when Piscator was preparing the play for performance, he changed its subtitle to "ein episches Drama" (an epic drama), thus initiating the use of a phrase that, according to Cecil W. Davies, "Brecht made famous and upon which he constructed a whole theory of theater." *Fahnen* takes place in Chicago in 1886, a time of unrest among industrial workers there. The leading factory owner conspires with the chief of police to arrange a pretext for the arrest and execution of leading figures in the proletarian movement.

Paquet, circa 1930 (by permission of Henriette Klingmüller-Paquet)

The success of this production resulted in Piscator's being allowed to choose and produce plays at the Volksbühne for several years.

One of the works he selected was another play by Paquet, *Sturmflut* (Storm Flood, 1926), which had its first production in Berlin in 1926. *Sturmflut* takes over some names and motifs used in *Die Prophezeiungen;* the charismatic leader of a new Russia is called Granka Umnitsch, and for a time his mistress is Rune, the "aristocrat, adventuress, man-woman," as Paquet describes her in his foreword to the play. Paquet also points out that he did not conceive Granka Umnitsch as Lenin; for Lenin, he says, never had Tolstoyan traits or a vision of an unarmed society, nor did he lose contact with the masses. In *Sturmflut,* Granka Umnitsch survives and looks forward to ruling effectively in the future, an outcome that makes the ending of the play more positive than that of *Die Prophezeiungen.* Paquet considered *William Penn, Gründer von Pennsylvanien* (William Penn, Founder of Pennsylvania, 1927) the concluding play of a "trilogy of European tensions of today." Based, though not closely, on Penn's life, the play presents a viewpoint of greater sympathy with the "humane and liberal West." It was first performed in Frankfurt in 1927.

In the 1920s Paquet visited Greece, Turkey, Switzerland, Belgium, Great Britain, and Lithuania. *Städte, Landschaften und ewige Bewegung* (Cities, Landscapes and Eternal Movement, 1927) sums up some of his travel impressions. Descriptions of his early visits to czarist Russia and the Far East are followed by accounts of visits during World War I to Baltic lands and Poland (at that time under German occupation); impressions of Moscow during the revolution; descriptions of Rome, Greece, Syria, and Jerusalem; and sketches of London and finally Frankfurt. Paquet was a cautious observer with an eye for detail and an efficient prose style. He subtitled this substantial volume *Ein Roman ohne Helden* (A Novel without Heroes), explaining this phrase in his foreword: "Und es ist doch ein Roman, denn es ist kein Buch zufälliger Beschreibung. Problem und Entwicklung sind da, aber statt der Menschen treten Städte hervor als Träger der Schicksale" (And it is a novel after all, for it is not a book of chance descriptions. Problems and development are there, but instead of human beings cities step forward as bearers of fates).

In 1930 Paquet became secretary of the committee to award the Frankfurt Goethe Prize, and in this capacity he visited Sigmund Freud. His principal contribution to celebrating Goethe's fame was *Frau Rat Goethe und ihre Welt* (Frau Rat Goethe and Her World, 1931), a life of Goethe's mother in the context of eighteenth-century Frankfurt.

The last major work of fiction Paquet wrote was the still unpublished novel "Von November bis November" (From November to November), an account of the year from November 1917 to November 1918 as experienced by a journalist in Sweden, Finland, and Russia. Avoiding the fantasy of *Die Prophezeiungen,* the work has a sober realism, but the protagonist's relationship with Tamara allows the introduction of personal emotions. Many episodes in the novel have their models in incidents Paquet recorded in his diary. Only the final third of the novel takes place in Russia; the prefatory exposition in Sweden and Finland is perhaps too lengthy, but the work is challenging and authentic, significant both from a documentary point of view and as a piece of imaginative writing.

In 1933 Paquet became a member of the Society of Friends. The same year he withdrew from the Literary Section of the Prussian Academy in protest against the takeover of that body by the National Socialists. He continued to be a contributor to the *Frankfurter Zeitung,* but not of political material. In 1935 he was arrested by the Nazi authorities while traveling by train to Sweden and was held in Berlin for several days. His account of his trip to America in 1937, *Amerika unter dem Regenbogen* (America beneath the Rainbow, 1938), is a cheerful, colorful, and sometimes serene description of a visitor's impressions.

The collection of poems *Erwähnung Gottes* (Mention of God, 1939) demonstrates Paquet's concern late in his life to express himself in religious terms. These poems and those written from 1940 onward (first published in 1970 in the three-volume selection of Paquet's work) reflect a delicate, lyrical sensitivity that was wholly alienated from the officially predominating attitudes of that time. Paquet died in the early morning of 8 February 1944 in the cellar of his house in Frankfurt am Main, where he had taken shelter during an air raid. His poetry and prose form a considerable and consistent whole, revealing a mastery both of objectively descriptive approaches and of sensitive and personal lyrical forms of self-expression.

Bibliography:

Marie Henriette Paquet, Henriette Klingmüller, Sebastian Paquet, Wilhelmine Woeller-Paquet, *Bibliographie Alfons Paquet* (Frankfurt am Main: Woeller, 1958).

References:

Cecil W. Davies, *Theatre for the People: The Story of the Volksbühne* (Manchester: University Press, 1977);

B. Kossmann and M. Richter, eds., *Alfons Paquet 1881-1944* (Frankfurt am Main: Stadt- und Universitätsbibliothek, 1981).

Papers:

Alfons Paquet's papers are in the Alfons-Paquet-Archiv of the Stadt- und Universitätsbibliothek, Frankfurt am Main, Federal Republic of Germany.

Stanislaw Przybyszewski

(7 May 1868-23 November 1927)

Hanna A. Zolman

BOOKS: *Zur Psychologie des Individuums,* 2 volumes (Berlin: Fontane, 1892);

Totenmesse (Berlin: Fontane, 1893);

Das Werk des Edvard Munch: Vier Beiträge, by Przybyszewski, Franz Servaes, Willy Pastor, and Julius Meyer-Graefe, edited by Przybyszewski (Berlin: Fischer, 1894);

Vigilien (Berlin: Fischer, 1895);

De profundis (Berlin: Storm, 1895);

Homo Sapiens, 3 volumes: volume 2, *Unterwegs* (Berlin: Fontane, 1895); volume 1, *Über Bord* (Berlin: Storm, 1896); volume 3, *ImMalstrom* (Berlin: Storm, 1896); translated into Polish, 3 volumes (Lvov: Nakl Ksieg Polskiej, 1901); Polish version translated into English by Thomas Seltzer, 1 volume (New York: Knopf, 1915);

Auf den Wegen der Seele (Berlin: Kritik-Verlag, 1897);

Satans Kinder: Roman (Munich: Langen, 1897);

Die Synagoge des Satan: Ihre Entstehung, Einrichtung und jetzige Bedeutung. Ein Versuch (Berlin: Kritik-Verlag, 1897);

Epipsychidion (Berlin: Fontane, 1900);

In diesem Erdenthal der Thränen (Berlin: Rosenbaum & Hart, 1900);

Totentanz der Liebe: Vier Dramen (Berlin: Fontane, 1902)–*Das große Glück, Das goldene Vlies, Die Mutter, Die Gäste; Das große Glück* translated by Lucille Baron as *For Happiness* (Boston: Badger, 1912);

Schnee: Drama in vier Akten (Munich: Marchlewski, 1903); translated by O. F. Theis as *Snow: A Play in Four Acts* (New York: Brown, 1920);

Erdensöhne: Roman (Berlin: Fontane, 1905);

Androgyne (Berlin: Fontane, 1906);

Gelübde: Dramatische Dichtung in drei Aufzügen, bound with *Schnee* (Munich: Etzold, 1906);

Untiefen: Drama in drei Akten (Munich: Müller, 1913);

Polen und der heilige Krieg (Munich & Berlin: Müller, 1916);

Von Polens Seele: Ein Versuch (Jena: Diederichs, 1917);

Der Schrei: Roman (Munich: Müller, 1918);

Moi Wspóleczésni, 2 volumes (Warsaw: Instytut Wydawniczy, 1926, 1930); translated and abridged by Klaus Stämmler as *Erinnerungen an das literarische Berlin,* 1 volume (Munich: Winkler, 1965).

PERIODICAL PUBLICATIONS: "Psychischer Naturalismus," *Neue Deutsche Rundschau,* 5 (1894): 150-156;

"Mysterien," *Die Zukunft,* 8 (1894): 603-609;

"Franz Flaum," *Deutscher Musen-Almanach* (1897): 103-108;

"Das Geschlecht," *Die Fackel,* 239-240 (1907): 1-11.

Few German writers at the turn of the century evoked as much personal interest and critical acclaim as the Polish-born Stanislaw Przybyszewski. His fame as "der geniale Pole" (the ingenious Pole) spread from Germany to Scandinavia and most eastern European countries. The modernists in Russia acclaimed him as second only to Dostoyevski, and Young Poland and Young Czechoslovakia hailed him as the literary genius of the century. Yet he died forgotten, his books out of print.

Each succeeding generation has found in Przybyszewski's work something of contemporary value. The expressionists regarded him as a precursor; some elements in the works of Thomas Mann and Gottfried Benn are thought to be derived from him; his insight into the human psyche makes him a proto-Freudian. Currently Przybyszewski is perceived as an innovator in the field of the psychological novel and in the use of the stream of consciousness, while his theory of art and his preoccupation with human sexuality bring him close to contemporary times.

The most striking aspect of Przybyszewski's style is an extraordinary mixture of kinetic and

Stanislaw Przybyszewski in 1895, pastel and oil portrait by Edvard Munch (Oslo Kommunes Kunstsamlinger, OKK134)

static forces–a trait which applies to the writer as well as to the man. Born in 1868 to a stern peasant father and a musical, affectionate mother, raised in an ardently Catholic environment in the part of Poland under Prussian authority, a flatland rich in folklore and superstition, Przybyszewski grew to lambast religion and the code of bourgeois morality. A small-town sophisticate from the backwaters of Poland with a name few Germans could pronounce, he entered the whirlwind of metropolitan Berlin and soon charmed his artist friends with spirited conversation in a strangely attractive, accented German, an enchanter whose piano renditions of Chopin and Schumann become legendary. He was full of contradictions: passionate, unsteady, and given to bouts of hard drinking and loud skirmishes in the Berlin café Zum schwarzen Ferkel, he was also described as a melancholy man with a barely audible, melodious voice; pliable and meek in personal relations, he was intransigent in matters of art.

Przybyszewski spent his first thirteen years in the hamlet of Lojewo. He was tutored by his father, a teacher of peasant children in a one-room school; his mother taught him to play the piano and to adore Chopin's music. His avid reading and musical talent prompted his parents to send him to a gymnasium where he received a classical German education. An indifferent student, Przybyszewski preferred reading widely in European literature and writing poetry and short stories to schoolwork. He also began to write a novel. A few of the preserved juvenilia are immature rhymes about unfulfilled love, indefinite longing, and death.

While Przybyszewski was attending the gymnasium his father suffered a nervous breakdown and tried repeatedly to commit suicide. Przybyszewski helped to take care of his father, soothing him by playing the piano for hours. The interest in psychopathology stimulated by his father's illness was to lead him to study medicine and to create neurotic or near-neurotic fictional characters.

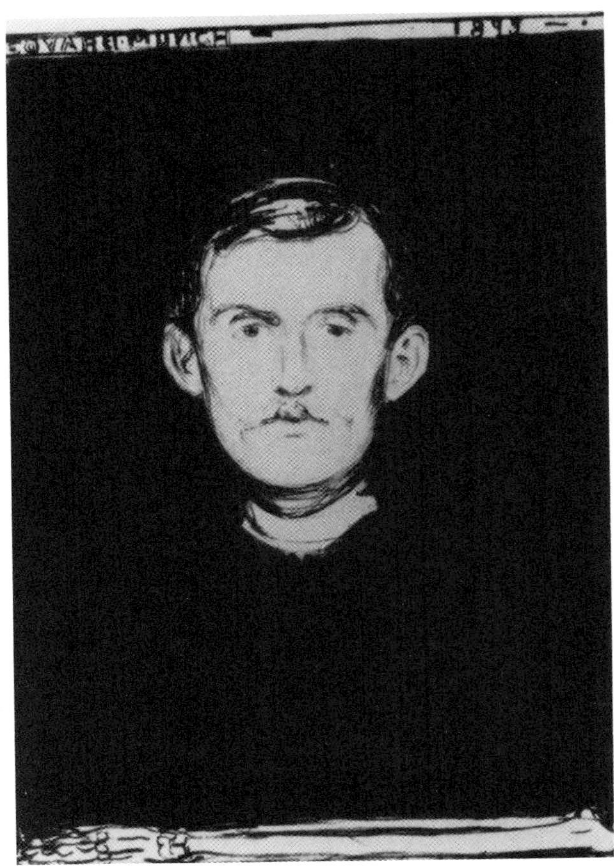

Munch's 1895 lithograph Self-portrait with Skeleton Arm. *Munch and Przybyszewski became friends in the late 1880s, while both were living in Berlin (Oslo Kommunes Kunstsamlinger, OKK192).*

The Swedish dramatist and novelist August Strindberg, another of Przybyszewski's Berlin friends, in 1890; portrait in oils by Munch (Nationalmuseum, Stockholm)

Refused a scholarship for medical study, Przybyszewski accepted a grant to study architecture at the University of Berlin; he arrived in Germany in May 1889. A year later he gave up the grant and transferred to medical school. His medical studies, combined with his immersion in Nietzsche's works, led to his first German publications: long psychological and critical essays about Chopin, Nietzsche, and the Swedish writer Ola Hansson. Collected in two volumes under the title *Zur Psychologie des Individuums* (Toward the Psychology of the Individual, 1892), the essays depict the fin-de-siècle creative individual as torn between the prevailing moral and social codes and the artist's perception of man's repressed drives, states of altered perception, and sexual and emotional ecstasy. Przybyszewski believed that this torment in the soul of the artist, whose freedom of expression is prohibited by the existing moral system, must be the subject of contemporary art.

Przybyszewski's novel approach to art at a time when naturalism reigned supreme caused a stir in the Berlin literary world and secured his standing among the influential writers and artists known as the Friedrichshagen Circle, who became his close friends. Przybyszewski soon earned the title "King of the Berlin Bohème": his endless discussions and nightlong drinking parties with his German and Scandinavian artist friends, including Edvard Munch and August Strindberg, became legendary. Under a variety of Slavic names, the figure of Przybyszewski is found in a series of romans à clef written about this period in Germany and Scandinavia, while his triangular face, unruly hair, and piercing eyes are recognizable in many of Munch's paintings.

After living for three years with Martha Foerder, who had borne him two children, in 1893 Przybyszewski married Dagny Juell, the Norwegian inamorata of Munch and Strindberg. To support two households and pay for his medical study he became the editor of and main contributor to a Polish socialist periodical in Berlin, and ghostwrote doctoral dissertations for medical students. Still, his life was far from comfortable; the writer Richard Dehmel, a lifelong friend, and others helped by inviting Przybyszewski and his wife to dinner and frequently lending them money.

Inspired by his love for Dagny, Przybyszewski created his first fictional work, *Totenmesse* (Requiem Mass, 1893), in which he acknowledged the significance of the French decadent writer Joris-Karl Huysmans, whose volume of art criticism, *Certains,* appeared in 1889, by

The Norwegian Dagny Juell, the inamorata of Munch and Strindberg, who became Przybyszewski's wife in 1893

naming the protagonist Certain. *Totenmesse* begins with the words "Am Anfang war das Geschlecht . . . " (In the beginning was sex . . .), a phrase which has been associated with Przybyszewski since the publication of this work. Certain is a cerebral type of individualist whose creativity and natural instincts, represented by sexual potency, have atrophied under the weight of his intellect. Tormented by guilt and by the dichotomy in his soul, Certain is brought to the extremes of nervous exhaustion; he commits suicide while gazing at his beloved's dead body.

Totenmesse immediately established Przybyszewski's reputation as a significant writer. The work illuminates the neuroses of the fin de siècle so penetratingly that it became a prototypical document of the epoch. Especially striking is the intermingling of scientific terminology and poetic prose which was to become the hallmark of Przybyszewski's style, a style whose beauty increased markedly in the long poems in prose

Vigilien (Vigils, 1895), *Epipsychidion* (1900), and *Androgyne* (1906).

In November 1893 the authorities suspended the socialist publication; Przybyszewski lost his job and the right to attend the university. His hopes shattered, Przybyszewski struggled for several months to find a way to support his family, but finally sent his pregnant wife home to her family in Kongsvinger, Norway. He followed a few months later, arriving in Norway in May 1894 accompanied by Munch. Preceded by his literary fame, Przybyszewski soon met many of Scandinavia's most famous artists and writers, and the evenings in the Café Grand in Christiania became as lively as those in Berlin. He formed lifelong friendships with a number of Scandinavia's most famous artists, including the Norwegian writer Knut Hamsun.

Przybyszewski's years in Norway were the most productive period in his life: he contributed regularly to a number of Berlin and Prague publications and wrote prose poems, novels, and plays. In June 1896 he was arrested in Berlin on suspicion of murdering Martha Foerder, who by then was the mother of three of his children. She had apparently committed suicide, however, and Przybyszewski was soon released. Nevertheless, the German public condemned Przybyszewski for his immoral life-style and his desertion of Martha and their children, and he never regained his former popularity in Germany. He later used the experience in the first of his "confessional" novels, *Homo Sapiens* (1895-1896; translated into Polish in 1901 and from Polish into English in 1915). Przybyszewski, Dagny, and Martha are transformed into Falk, Isa, and Maryt in the novel. Falk, a bohemian-turned-cad, believes himself to be a Nietzschean individualist; his erotic adventures cause suffering and death. The considerable critical acclaim received by the three-volume novel was based, the author complained later, on false premises. The modernists saw in Falk the self-sufficient superman ignoring the conventions of bourgeois morality and failed to perceive the irony of the novel's title.

Przybyszewski's novel *De profundis* (1895) is a poetic narration of love between a brother and sister whose feelings erupt into an irresistible sexual attraction. Unable to suppress their desires but afraid to violate the moral code, they choose death. The critical reception the work received was mixed: some admired the daring of the topic and the author's psychoanalytical acumen; others were shocked by the erotic and demonic imagery of incubi and succubi appearing in dreams and visions, and condemned Przybyszewski as an immoralist and Satanist.

A true incarnation of evil is Gordon, the protagonist of *Satans Kinder* (Satan's Children, 1897). In the guise of a social revolutionary he trains a group of misguided idealists for an act of political terrorism. Gordon is bent on destruction as proof of his power over men's minds and actions. The compact, realistic narration and the relevance of the topic to contemporary events make *Satans Kinder* as readable now as it was at the time of publication.

Impressed by the contemporary Scandinavian drama, Przybyszewski adapted the dramatic techniques of Ibsen and Strindberg to the four plays he published under the title *Totentanz der Liebe* (Love's Dance of Death, 1902). The plays depict doomed love, marital infidelity, and tragic consequences of unbridled passions.

The highlight of the Norwegian period, indeed of Przybyszewski's imaginative works in general, proved to be the poem in prose *Epipsychidion* (1900); it reveals him to be a lyric poet, a mystic, a mythmaker, and a philosopher. The writer Theodor Fontane compared the beauty of its language to that of Nietzsche's; it took a Pole, Fontane wrote, to show the Germans what could be done with their language.

Przybyszewski returned to Poland in September 1898 and began to write exclusively in his native language. His Polish publications were numerous and his contribution to Polish modernism was considerable, but as his French biographer Maxime Herman pointed out in 1939, the reputation of the man obscured the stature of the writer in his native land.

After moving to Poland Przybyszewski fathered an illegitimate child with a painter and had a liaison with Jadwiga Kasprowicz, the wife of the highly respected poet Jan Kasprowicz, who left her husband and children to live with Przybyszewski. In 1901 Przybyszewski's estranged wife, Dagny, was shot to death in Tbilisi by a young Russian, who then killed himself. The outrage of his conservative compatriots at his life-style may have prompted Przybyszewski to move to Munich in 1906 with Jadwiga Kasprowicz, whom he had married. He was unable to recapture the attention of critics or the reading public in Germany. Banished to a marginal literary existence, Przybyszewski returned to Poland after World War I and spent his last years on the lecture circuit and writing his memoirs. He died,

Dagny Juell shortly after her marriage to Przybyszewski, oil painting by Munch (Oslo Kommunes Kunstsamlinger)

sick and embittered, in the home of friends in Jaronty in 1927.

Przybyszewski's memoirs, published first in Polish (1926, 1930) and then in an abridged German translation as *Erinnerungen an das literarische Berlin* (Recollections of Literary Berlin, 1965), have led to a revival of interest in the forgotten "geniale Pole" and to a more scholarly study of his texts. His theory of art and its implementation in his best works reveal Przybyszewski as an important writer whose aesthetics reappear, with modern variations, in the works of poets and novelists of today.

Bibliography:

Stanislaw Helsztynski, *Bibliografia pism Stanislawa Przybyszewskiego* (Warsaw: Towarzystwo Przyjaciol Ksiaźki, 1968).

Biographies:

Maxime Herman, *Un Sataniste polonais, Stanislaw Przybyszewski (de 1868 à 1900)* (Paris: Belles Lettres, 1939);

Stanislaw Helsztyński, *Przybyszewski,* third edition (Warsaw: Ludowa Spoldzielnia Wydawnicza, 1973).

References:

Julius Bab, *Die Berliner Boheme* (Berlin: Seeman, 1904);

Maxime Herman, *Dostoïevski et Przybyszewski* (Lille: Santai, 1938);

K. G. Just, "Nihilismus als Stil: Zur Prosa von Stanislaw Przybyszewski," in *Wissenschaft als Dialog: Studien zur Literatur und Kunst seit der Jahrhundertwende,* edited by Renate von Hey-

Charcoal drawing by Munch, used as the vignette for Przybyszewski's 1894 poetry collection Vigilien *(Oslo Kommunes Kunstsamlinger, OKK2449)*

The Norwegian writer Knut Hamsun (pseudonym of Knut Pedersen), who became Przybyszewski's friend after the latter moved to Norway in 1894; dry-point sketch by Munch, 1896 (Oslo Kommunes Kunstsamlinger OKK40)

Jealousy *(1895), an allegorical oil painting by Munch. Przybyszewski's face appears at right (Rasmus Meyers Samlinger, Bergen).*

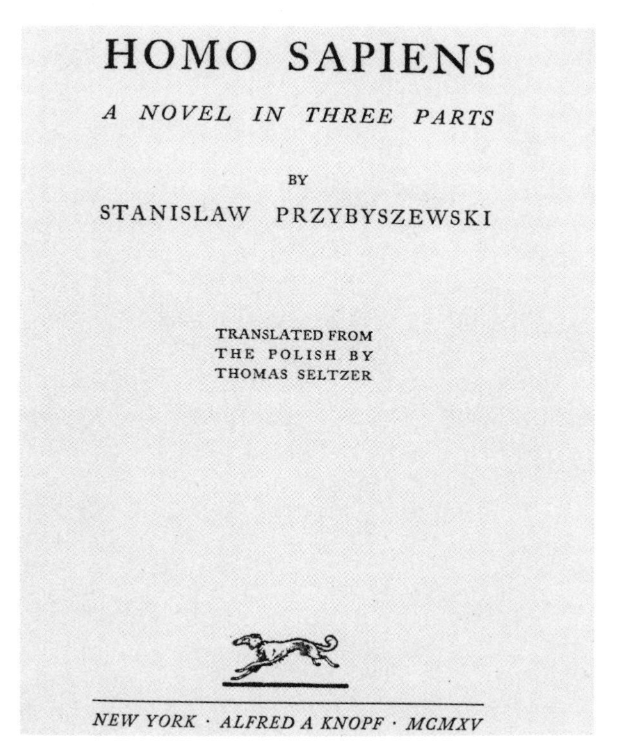

HOMO SAPIENS

A NOVEL IN THREE PARTS

BY

STANISLAW PRZYBYSZEWSKI

TRANSLATED FROM
THE POLISH BY
THOMAS SELTZER

NEW YORK · ALFRED A KNOPF · MCMXV

Title page for the English translation of Przybyszewski's autobiographical novel about a bohemian-turned-cad

debrand and Klaus Gunther Just (Stuttgart: Metzler, 1969), pp. 112-133;

A. J. Meier-Graefe, "Stanislaw Przybyszewski," *Die Gesellschaft,* 11 (1895): 1040-1045;

A. Moeller-Bruck, "De profundis," *Die Gesellschaft,* 12 (1896): 664-669;

Stanislaw Sawicki, "Stanislaw Przybyszewski und Norwegen," *Edda,* 34, no. 1 (1934): 1-19;

Manfred Schluchter, "Stanislaw Przybyszewski und seine deutschsprachigen Prosawerke 1892-1899," dissertation, University of Tübingen, 1969;

Irena Szwede, "The Works of Stanislaw Przybyszewski and Their Reception in Russia at the Beginning of the Twentieth Century," Ph.D. dissertation, Stanford University, 1970;

R. Taborski, "Stanislaw Przybyszewski und Wien," *Österreichische Osthefte,* 2 (1966): 130-137;

John Weichsel, *Stanislaw Przybyszewski: His Life and Writings* (New York: Knopf, 1915);

Hanna A. Zolman, "Stanislaw Przybyszewski and His Lyrical Universe," Ph.D. dissertation, University of California, Los Angeles, 1980.

Gabriele Reuter

(8 February 1859-16 November 1941)

Katherine R. Goodman
Brown University

BOOKS: *Glück und Geld: Roman aus dem heutigen Egypten* (Leipzig: Friedrich, 1888);

Episode Hopkins; Zu spät: Zwei Studien (Dresden: Pierson, 1889);

Kolonistenvolk: Roman aus Argentinien (Leipzig: Fock, 1891);

Aus guter Familie: Leidensgeschichte eines Mädchens (Berlin: Fischer, 1895);

Der Lebenskünstler: Novellen (Berlin: Fischer, 1897);

Frau Bürgelin und ihre Söhne: Roman (Berlin: Fischer, 1899);

Ellen von der Weiden: Ein Tagebuch (Berlin: Fischer, 1900);

Frauenseelen: Novellen (Berlin: Fischer, 1902);

Liselotte von Reckling: Roman in zwei Theilen (Berlin: Fischer, 1904);

Das böse Prinzeßchen: Ein Märchenspiel für Kinder (Berlin: Fischer, 1904);

Gunhild Kersten: Novelle (Stuttgart: Deutsche Verlags-Anstalt, 1904);

Margaretes Mission, 2 volumes (Stuttgart: Deutsche Verlags-Anstalt, 1904);

Marie von Ebner-Eschenbach (Berlin & Leipzig: Schuster & Loeffler, 1904);

Wunderliche Liebe: Novellen (Berlin: Fischer, 1905);

Annette von Droste-Hülshoff (Berlin: Bard & Marquardt, 1905);

Die Probleme der Ehe (Berlin: Schwetschke, 1907);

Der Amerikaner: Roman (Berlin: Fischer, 1907);

Eines Toten Wiederkehr und andere Novellen (Leipzig: Reclam, 1908);

Das Tränenhaus: Roman (Berlin: Fischer, 1909; revised, 1926);

Sanfte Herzen: Ein Buch für junge Mädchen (Berlin: Fischer, 1909);

Frühlingstaumel: Roman (Berlin: Fischer, 1911);

Liebe und Stimmrecht (Berlin: Fischer, 1914);

Im Sonnenland: Erzählung aus Alexandrien (Berlin: Hillger, 1914);

Ins neue Land (Berlin & Vienna: Ullstein, 1916);

Die Jugend eines Idealisten: Roman (Berlin: Fischer, 1917);

Gabriele Reuter

Was Helmut in Deutschland erlebte: Eine Jugendgeschichte (Gotha: Perthes, 1917);

Vom weiblichen Herzen: Novellen (Berlin: Hillger, 1917);

Die Herrin: Roman (Berlin: Ullstein, 1918);

Großstadtmädel: Jugendgeschichten (Berlin: Ullstein, 1920);

Vom Kinde zum Menschen: Die Geschichte meiner Jugend (Berlin: Fischer, 1922);

Benedikta: Roman (Dresden: Seyfert, 1923);

Töchter: Der Roman zweier Generationen (Berlin: Ullstein, 1927); translated by Roberts Tapley as

Daughters: The Story of Two Generations (New York: Macmillan, 1930);

Das Haus in der Antoniuskirchstraße (Berlin & Leipzig: Abel & Müller, 1928);

Irmgard und ihr Bruder: Roman (Berlin: Deutsche Buchgemeinschaft, 1930);

Vom Mädchen, das nicht lieben konnte: Roman (Berlin: Ullstein, 1933);

Grete fährt ins Glück: Erzählung (Berlin: Weisel, 1935);

Grüne Ranken um alte Bilder: Deutscher Familienroman (Berlin: Grote, 1937).

Gabriele Reuter took Wilhelminian society–the German equivalent of Victorian England–by storm in 1895 with her novel *Aus guter Familie: Leidensgeschichte eines Mädchens* (From a Good Family: The Suffering of a Young Woman). Her clear-sighted exposé of the pain and frustration of middle-class women resonated not only in the hearts of many girls and women but, to judge from Reuter's own accounts of its reception, in the hearts of many fathers. It became the catalyst for a protracted public discussion on the education and role of women in modern society. Adopted by the contemporary women's movement as one of their own, Reuter–despite her sympathy for the movement–consistently refused to view her literary works as propagandistic tools for it. Yet she repeatedly portrayed middle-class girls and women, endowing them with her own qualities of modesty and inner strength. In 1904 Thomas Mann called her "die souveränste Frau, die heute in Deutschland lebt" (the most sovereign woman living in Germany today).

Reuter was born in Alexandria, Egypt, in 1859. Her father, Karl Reuter, was a businessman who had gone there to add a trade delegation to the German embassy. It was the family of her mother, Johanne Behmer Reuter, that almost certainly inspired Reuter's interest in literature, for it included a long line of intellectuals, among them a number of women. Her great-grandmother Philippine Gatterer had been one of the famous women of the German Enlightenment in Göttingen and a daughter of the historian Johann Christoph Gatterer. Another of her ancestors, Caroline Engelhard, had written popular novels.

In 1864, for reasons of health, Johanne Reuter returned to Germany with her young children to live in Dessau. When the father's business was threatened in 1868 they were forced to rejoin him in Alexandria, and Gabriele spent

Reuter in 1907 (Ullstein)

the next four formative years in exotic, nonbourgeois surroundings. In her autobiography Reuter attributed certain broadly romantic tendencies in her works to this experience. She was so much in danger of failing to learn the "proper" behavior for a young German girl that her mother returned to Germany in 1872 to enroll Gabriele and her brother in appropriate schools in Wolfenbüttel. But Karl Reuter died suddenly, the family lost its income, and she was unable to continue at school.

The thirteen-year-old Reuter solemnly determined to take up the burden of supporting her family. Her childhood passion had been for the theater, but her father had made her promise never to go on the stage. Her mother, recalling that her ancestors had earned money by the pen, encouraged Reuter to enter a writing contest. She failed to win, but the praise and encouragement of an aunt induced her to begin writing feuilletons–mainly stories about Egypt–for the newspapers, including the conservative *Kreuzzeitung,* of which her cousin was the editor. Reuter believed the stories to be the work of a dilettante and had higher ambitions, though she did not immediately cultivate them. Instead, she let her talent lie fallow while she pursued household chores and looked after her ailing mother.

In 1879 she and her mother settled in Weimar. From the end of the eighteenth century the court there had assembled a brilliant array of intellectuals, the most famous of whom had been Goethe; other active minds had settled in this small town to live in the shadow of these influential writers, so that long after the death of Goethe Weimar still clung to its reputation as an intellectual haven. There Reuter associated regularly with an aunt and uncle and their friends. The uncle was a painter who introduced her to the world of modern art, in particular the paintings of Arnold Böcklin, who was just beginning to shock the bourgeois public with his mythic style and daring subject matter. In this circle she was also introduced to the works of Friedrich Nietzsche. Her aunt provided the young novelist with a living example of a devoted mother and wife who felt unfulfilled in these roles. Although she was a natural comedienne, her humor had been stifled in her domestic milieu, and Reuter believed that this frustration of her talent indirectly caused her early death. Almost certainly the experience with the fate of her aunt contributed heavily to her own sensitivity to the lives of bourgeois women.

Reuter had ceased writing stories of life in Egypt when her mother fell ill, but she had long planned a novel about the country. Caring for her mother had caused her own health to deteriorate, and on vacation to restore it she began writing her Egyptian novel. Her Aunt Guste helped, urging Reuter to clarify her style; she also advised her to leave out long dialogues on philosophy. Reuter named the novel "Oktavia," but the publisher gave it the more sensational title *Glück und Geld* (Happiness and Money, 1888). It was first published serially in the *Tägliche Rundschau.* Although the naturalist novelist Karl Bleibtreu praised the work, it remained relatively unknown.

Reuter considered the years 1887 to 1891 to be her artistic and personal turning point. She sought out colleagues by attending writers' conferences. At her first conference she met the critic Karl Frenzel, who told her to forget her Egyptian novellas and novels; she would always write about Egypt as an outsider, he said, when she should be writing about something she knew intimately. At another conference she met John Henry Mackay, the anarchist and disciple of the arch-individualist Max Stirner. In spite of the great philosophical differences between them, Reuter, with characteristic open-mindedness, felt that they shared the same intense longing for truth. They became good friends, and in 1891 she praised his literary works in an article for the journal *Die Gesellschaft.* Mackay urged her to lead her own life, and on his advice she moved with her mother to Munich in 1895 to escape the stifling effect of her family in Weimar.

Her reading during these years proved critical to her literary evolution. She read Charles Darwin and his German popularizer, Ernst Haeckel. She steeped herself in the philosopher of resignation, Arthur Schopenhauer. She began to read modern literature, especially the naturalists. She read Emile Zola, Edmond-Louis-Antoine and Jules-Alfred Huot de Goncourt, Gustave Flaubert, and Guy de Maupassant. De Maupassant's prose was to influence much of her later, subtly psychological fiction.

One day, in a flash of inspiration, she realized "why she was on earth": her role was to articulate what girls and women silently suffered. Although drawn to naturalism, she felt it would be hypocritical to pretend to describe the life of the proletariat, as so many German naturalists had tried to do; but the lives of middle-class women were all too familiar. She would not describe their grand passions; that had been done to excess by male authors. "Nein–die stumme Tragik des Alltags" (No–the silent tragedy of daily life) was to be her theme: "Die Tragik in dem Los des Weibes: geboren zu sein, erzogen zu werden für eine Berufung, die sie gelehrt ist, als ihr einziges Glück zu betrachten, und dieses Glück, diese Berufung wird ihr stets vor Augen gehalten und doch nie gewährt–niemals darf sie eintreten in den Tempel des Gottes, zu dessen Priesterin sie doch gebildet ist" (The tragedy of the lot of woman: to be born, to be raised for a calling which she is taught to view as her only happiness, and this happiness, this calling is always held before her eyes and yet never granted–never is she permitted to enter the temple of the God whose priestess she has been educated to be).

Having made that decision she began to write the story of a young middle-class girl. Although she drew on her own experiences, this novel would *not* portray her life; for that would be the life of a girl who became a writer. It was to be the story of a girl whose milieu prohibited her from exploring any of her interests, talents, or desires, prevented her from becoming a full human being. It would be years before she fin-

W 15 Berlin d. 4 Okt. 26
Ludwigkirchstr. 2.

Sehr geehrter Herr!

Gern gestatte ich Ihnen meine Novelle „Eines Toten Wiederkehr" für Schulzwecke in Amerika nachzudrucken. Auch mein Verleger wird, falls die Ausgabe sich auf diesen Zweck beschränkt, nichts dagegen einzuwenden haben.

Es ist mir jedesmal eine Freude wenn ich höre, dass meine Aufsätze drüben Interesse erregen und ich danke Ihnen herzlich für Ihre gütigen Worte.

Mit verbindlichem Gruss

Gabriele Reuter

Letter from Reuter to Taylor Starck, who prepared a school edition of her novella "Eines Toten Wiederkehr" for publication in the United States in 1928

ished the novel, for her own priority–as that of many of her heroines–was her concern for a loved one. Her mother's illness required her constant attention.

In the meantime, on trips to Berlin she became acquainted with the lively group of young naturalist writers in Friedrichshagen: Wilhelm Bölsche, Bruno Wille, and Julius and Heinrich Hart. Ernst von Wolzogen introduced her to the naturalist literati associated with the theater Freie Bühne and to her future publisher Samuel Fischer. She built a circle of professional friends, and, when her manuscript was finished, she gave it to them for their comments.

Despite their praise, Reuter was distraught when they discussed her novel as though it revealed only the sexual desires and frustrations of a young girl; she had tried to show the effect of bourgeois restrictions on the humanity of women. That night she stood in front of the stove for hours, trying to decide whether to destroy the manuscript. She finally decided that she had written *her* truth, that truth was different for everyone; she preserved the manuscript.

Mackay recommended the novel warmly to Fischer; Fischer liked it, but feared that it would not earn the author any money. *Aus guter Familie* turned out to be a success beyond anyone's dreams. The story of sensitive, intelligent Agathe Heidling, driven to madness and apathy by the barriers to her development erected by her family, unleashed a frenzy of debate in all parts of Germany. It exposed the fundamental inhumanity of the ideology of womanhood expressed by Agathe's well-intentioned father and current in the majority of Wilhelminian households. According to this ideology, woman was an important member of society because she was "die Wurzel, die stumme, geduldige, unbewegliche, welche kein eigenes Leben zu haben scheint und doch den Baum der Menschheit trägt" (the root, silent, patient, immobile, which appears to have no life of its own and yet bears the tree of humanity). The novel established Reuter's reputation.

Reuter's financial problems ceased; *Aus guter Familie* would go into five editions by 1897 and eighteen by 1908. Simultaneously with its first publication Reuter moved with her mother to Munich, where she met articulate feminists. She was tempted for a while to join them, but ultimately rejected that choice: she believed that her real talent lay in writing, and, convinced that writing demanded total dedication, she decided to leave the political battles to others. In 1899 she and her mother settled in Berlin, where she began to write prolifically, completing nearly a book a year for the next two decades.

Whether married, widowed, divorced, or single, Reuter's heroines repeatedly give voice to the loneliness of women and the unwillingness or inability of men to comprehend them. The heroines of the short stories in *Der Lebenskünstler* (The Artist of Life, 1897) and *Frauenseelen* (Women's Souls, 1902) either choose their isolation by rejecting unsatisfying relationships or discover it only after the hope for something more has proven illusory. Many of the men she portrays have difficultly imagining that women are human beings with minds and emotions. Occasionally, especially in *Frauenseelen,* Reuter suggests that isolation is a general human condition. But frequently, both in these stories and in her novels, even the best-intentioned men reveal a base lust which can appear merely petty or can be dangerous for the heroine.

For the most part these women learn to bear their loneliness with strength and grace, but the heroine of *Frau Bürgelin und ihre Söhne* (Mrs. Bürgelin and Her Sons, 1899), a novel much admired by Thomas Mann, is a strong-willed, divorced mother who becomes an overbearing tyrant and drives away her talented son. As in all her novels, however, Reuter's concern for evenhandedness permits sympathy even for the character least generously motivated.

Reuter is probably at her best when describing psychological nuances in women's lives, as in *Aus guter Familie* and in the novel *Ellen von der Weiden* (1900), which went through an astounding total of sixty-five editions. The mysterious, nature-loving Ellen von der Weiden marries a doctor and moves to Berlin. Her husband, worried that the life stories his patients tell will upset her, asks her not to visit the hospital. But she has dreams that are not fulfilled in her housekeeping duties, and their marriage ends in divorce, a scandal in those times. Once again Reuter's psychological acumen keeps her from placing blame on individuals; instead, she portrays them as unhappily trapped by limiting ideologies.

Nevertheless, Reuter's admiration is usually reserved for the women who escape these false ideologies, women with strength to build their own lives in the face of the most general and most intimate social pressure. The heroine of the novel *Liselotte von Reckling* (1904)–another of Thomas Mann's favorites–also experiences an unhappy marriage, though in this case she and her hus-

Reuter in 1934 (Ullstein)

band simply grow apart. In the end Liselotte chooses to live a reclusive life in communion with nature. Like Reuter, she devotes herself to the care of her mother.

Although she distanced herself from the political arena, Reuter's sympathies clearly lay with the women's movement. She wrote many essays on issues of the day, including *Die Probleme der Ehe* (The Problems of Marriage, 1907) and *Liebe und Stimmrecht* (Love and Suffrage, 1914). Reuter's nonideological commitment to the women's movement also surfaced in her two biographies of female literary figures: the contemporary Austrian dramatist and novelist Marie von Ebner-Eschenbach (1904) and the nineteenth-century poet Annette von Droste-Hülshoff (1905). In *Marie von Ebner-Eschenbach* Reuter emphasizes those qualities in the Austrian writer which she admired in her own characters: modesty, dedication, love, passion in literature, lack of self-centeredness, generosity. "Das Aufrührerische, Draufgängerische, Rücksichtslose ist ihr in jedem Sinne verdächtig" (She is suspicious of everything rebellious, reckless, unscrupulous); she is "auch im Konservatismus Idealistin" (an idealist even in conservatism).

Reuter's novel *Das Tränenhaus* (The House of Tears, 1909) takes up one of the contemporary women's movement's major goals: a home for unwed mothers. A guest in such a home, Cornelie Reimann, is haunted at night by the wailing of all the abandoned women in history, but refuses to let others use her literary talents for purposes of agitation. Yet, like the contemporary Mutterschutz (League for the Protection of Mothers), she hopes for the moral reevaluation of the social position of unwed mothers. (The 1926 revision of this novel omits the first three chapters, in which the heroine's initial resentment and anger at the irresponsibility of the father of her child is articulated.)

After World War I Reuter wrote less prolifically. Unlike many feminists of the day she had not espoused pacifism in response to the brutalities of the times. She claimed to have learned that violence arises out of our inner depths and that we are its prey until it has reached its goal, and she maintained a strong sense of German nationalism which may have been the heritage of her conservative family background.

In *Ins neue Land* (Into a New Country, 1916) a painter who had hoped to remain aloof from political events suddenly finds himself drawn into the hatred of the French culture he had studied and loved so well. After the war, having experienced and observed its personal and moral toll, he hopes to develop sensitivities in his son which are productive and not destructive.

The relationship between the individual artist and social responsibility had long been important to Reuter. She posed the question in broader cultural terms in *Die Jugend eines Idealisten* (The Youth of an Idealist, 1917). An actress retires from the stage to devote her resources to her son's goal of establishing a school for young boys; because of his experiences and those of his mother, he wishes to educate the boys to behave with more sensitivity to others. Reuter's own concern for the education of youth manifested itself in her many works of children's literature.

Reuter responded to contemporary social unrest with her novel *Benedikta* (1923). Here, as in *Die Jugend eines Idealisten*, she supports a paternalistic solution to social problems. Communism is portrayed as naive and destructive. Her conservative criticisms of social movements resemble the anarchist Mackay's concern that any state or ideology eventually restricts free human evolution.

Reuter's autobiography, *Vom Kinde zum Menschen* (From the Child to the Person, 1922), concludes with the publication of *Aus guter Familie;* little is known about Reuter's life in the period between the world wars, except that she lost her savings in the inflation of 1923 and struggled to support herself for the rest of her life. As late as 1930, in the novel *Irmgard und ihr Bruder* (Irmgard and Her Brother), she was still portraying a determined, loving woman whose individuality is ignored by the men in her life and who therefore experiences severe isolation.

During the Hitler years only two books by Reuter appeared, a book for children and a fictionalized account of her family history. Her lifelong concern for active and generous engagement on behalf of the flowering of individual human natures stood in sharp contrast to the events surrounding her in her final years. She died in Weimar in November 1941.

References:

Richard L. Johnson, "Gabriele Reuter: Romantic and Realist," in *Beyond the Eternal Feminine: Critical Essays on Women and German Literature,* edited by Susan L. Cocalis and Kay Goodman (Stuttgart: Akademischer Verlag Hans-Dieter Heinz, 1982), pp. 225-244;

Johnson, "Men's Power over Women in Gabriele Reuter's *Aus guter Familie,*" in *Gestaltet und Gestaltend: Frauen in der deutschen Literatur,* edited by Marianne Burkhard (Amsterdam: Rodopi, 1980), pp. 235-253;

Thomas Mann, "Gabriele Reuter," in his *Gesammelte Werke in 13 Bände,* volume 13 (Frankfurt am Main: Fischer, 1974), pp. 388-398.

Papers:

Gabriele Reuter's papers are at the Goethe- und Schiller-Archiv in Weimar, German Democratic Republic.

Franziska Gräfin zu Reventlow

(18 July 1871-27 July 1918)

George C. Schoolfield
Yale University

BOOKS: *Klosterjungen: Humoresken,* by Reventlow and O. Eugen Thossan (Otto Anthes) (Leipzig: Wigand, 1897);

Das Männerphantom der Frau (Zurich & Paris: Verlag der Zürcher Diskussionen, 1898);

Viragines oder Hetären? (Paris: Verlag der Zürcher Diskussionen, 1901);

Ellen Olestjerne: Eine Lebensgeschichte (Munich & Berlin: Schnabel, 1903);

Von Paul zu Pedro: Amouresken (Munich: Langen, 1912);

Herrn Dames Aufzeichnungen oder Begebenheiten aus einem merkwürdigen Stadtteil (Munich: Langen, 1913);

Der Geldkomplex: Roman (Munich: Langen, 1916);

Das Logierhaus zur schwankenden Weltkugel und andere Novellen (Munich: Langen, 1917); enlarged, and edited by Else Reventlow, as *Das Logierhaus zur schwankenden Weltkugel: Novellen und Skizzen* (Munich & Vienna: Langen-Müller, 1972);

Gesammelte Werke in einem Bande, edited by Else Reventlow (Munich: Langen, 1925);

Tagebücher 1895-1910, edited by Else Reventlow (Munich & Vienna: Langen-Müller, 1971).

PERIODICAL PUBLICATION: "Ein Bekenntnis: Skizze," *Die Gesellschaft,* 10 (1894): 317-322.

Literary reminiscences from Schwabing, the artists' quarter of Munich, are full of descriptions of "die tolle Gräfin" (the mad countess) Franziska zu Reventlow. Some of the memoirists had been her lovers, or wished they had been: Theodor Lessing called her the "Braut von ganz Schwabing" (the bride of all Schwabing). Fiction also has its share of lightly disguised–and quite disparate–portraits of her. The "Schleswig-Holstein Venus," as the erotomaniac and satirist Oskar Panizza called her, was the model for Lilly von Robicek, who lives for love alone, in Ernst von Wolzogen's best-seller *Das dritte Geschlecht* (The Third Sex, 1899). In Heinrich Mann's *Die Jagd nach Liebe* (The Hunt for Love, 1903) she is Countess Yvonne Zank, the fickle mistress of the wealthy dilettante Claude Marehn. Yvonne betrays Claude with his brutal mentor Eisenmann, yet she is soon enchanting the young man once more. Recuperating from one of her many operations, "sie behauptete, sie sei von der Richtigkeit mancher ihrer Organe nicht überzeugt; man könne ihr welche vertauscht haben, und vielleicht kamen daher ihre Abenteuer" (she claimed that she was not altogether convinced about the correctness of several of her organs; some of them could have been interchanged, and perhaps that was the source of her adventures). Claude takes her away from Munich for a lakeside vacation; the next day, she disappears with Eisenmann.

Mann's brother Thomas was less generous toward her; in "Beim Propheten" (At the Prophet's, 1914), his mocking picture of the circle around Daniel zur Höhe (who may be the poet Stefan George), he adduces "eine hinkende Dame, die sich als 'Erotikerin' vorstellen zu lassen pflegte, eine unverheiratete junge Mutter von adeliger Herkunft, die von ihrer Familie verstoßen, aber ohne alle geistigen Ansprüche war und einzig und allein auf Grund ihrer Mutterschaft in diesen Kreisen Aufnahme gefunden hatte" (a lady with a limp, who was wont to have herself presented as an "erotician," a young unmarried mother of noble descent who had been disowned by her family but who had no intellectual pretensions whatsoever, and who had been received in these circles solely and simply on the basis of her motherhood). The sentence's last jab alludes to the mystical importance some of the Munich "cosmic authors"–among them Alfred Schuler, the homosexual mythologist who believed he lived in imperial Rome–attached to the "hetaera" who had borne a son by an unknown father.

In her diary of March 1897 Reventlow claimed that the poet René (about to become Rainer Maria) Rilke put a poem into her mailbox every day, but none of these has survived; the im-

Franziska Gräfin zu Reventlow with her son Rolf in 1905 (Ullstein)

pressionistic verses on the town of Constance, dedicated to her and included in Rilke's collection *Advent* (1898), do not bespeak any passion whatsoever. Rilke's letters to her are friendly and respectful, and an 1899 epistle addressed to her infant son Rolf is an appeal to her to treasure her role as a mother. To his confidante Lou Andreas-Salomé, Rilke expressed doubts about the countess's literary ability after having read her autobiographical novel *Ellen Olestjerne* (1903): "Dieses Leben, dessen Hauptwert gerade darin liegt, gelebt worden zu sein ohne Untergang, verliert vielleicht zu sehr an Nothwendigkeit, wenn es von dem erzählt wird, der es gelenkt und gelitten hat, ohne doch daran zum Künstler geworden zu sein" (This life, whose chief value lies precisely in the fact of its having been lived without ruin, perhaps loses too much of its necessity when it is told by the person who has directed and suffered it, without having become an artist in the process). In *Von Paul zu Pedro: Amouresken* (From Paul to Pedro: Amouresques, 1912), Reventlow has her heroine write: "Ich bin, soweit ich mich erinnern kann, immer nur die irdische [Liebe] gewesen" (As far as I can recall, I have always been only earthly [love]).

Reventlow was born in 1871. Her father, Ludwig Graf zu Reventlow, had been appointed district councillor in Husum, after that town on the west coast of Schleswig had changed from Danish to Prussian rule in the war of 1864; the novella writer and poet Theodor Storm, Husum's most prominent literary citizen, was among the councillor's few friends. Her mother, Marie Gabriele Blanche Comtesse d'Allemont, was born a Rantzau and so, like the father, belonged to one of the oldest and most distinguished families of these marches between Germany and Scandinavia. Franziska's siblings lived up to the expectations their caste had of them: Agnes became the canoness of a Lutheran cloister for members of the nobility; Ludwig married a Reventlow cousin and so acquired an estate; Ernst, a naval officer turned popular historian and political writer, was elected to the Reichstag during the Weimar Republic (and was a pioneering supporter of Adolf Hitler); and Carl, Franziska's junior, inherited land and rose to the rank of major in the Prussian army. Her relationship to both her parents was strained: her father was preoccupied; her mother, a disciplinarian, rejected the unruly child's attempts at affection. At fifteen she was sent to a boarding school for "daughters of the nobility" at Altenburg, only to be expelled for insubordination; on the inside of her cupboard, in giant letters, she had printed a defiant line of verse: "Ich habe nie das Knie gebogen–den stolzen Nacken nie gebeugt" (Never have I bent my knee–and never my proud head bowed low).

In 1899 the Reventlows moved to Lübeck, where, at Franziska's request, she was enrolled in a teacher's seminary: she wanted, she argued, to bring new thoughts to youth. At about the same time her brother Carl introduced her to the Ibsen Club. Carl also served as a go-between in her platonic love affair with Emanuel Fehling, the son of a senator on the Lübeck city council and a pupil at Lübeck's Katharineum. Her letters to Fehling give an account of her reading: Henrik Ibsen (she could not understand why Ellida Wangel, in *The Lady from the Sea* [1888], was fascinated by only *one* man, the sailor); Jens Peter Jacobsen, a Danish novelist and poet (the formlessness of whose *Niels Lyhne* [1880] she loves, she says); the elegant Norwegian satirist Alexander Kielland; and another Norwegian, Arne Garborg (whose works are concerned, among other things, with the problems of male-and-female eroticism in a hypocritical society). Very much up to date, she also made her way through Zola, Tolstoy, and some of Nietzsche, Ferdinand Lassalle, and August Bebel.

These months of self-education and of dreams about freedom from parental constraint led her to run away from home on her twenty-first birthday. In Hamburg she met a young lawyer, Walter Lübke, a member of that city's chapter of the Ibsen Club, and he–perhaps inspired by the plans of Schoolmaster Arnholm for Bolette Wangel in *The Lady from the Sea*–agreed to finance a stay in Munich for her so that she could study art. After six months in Schwabing, where she became particularly popular with the Polish colony, she returned to Lübeck upon learning of her father's illness; yet her mother refused to let her see him before his death. She turned the event into a sketch for the Munich journal *Simplicissimus* in 1895, then incorporated it into *Ellen Olestjerne*. In Hamburg again, she married her Maecenas, who, unlike Ibsen's balding Arnholm, was only a little older than his protégée. Following a year of marital life with the naive Lübke (a child, conceived during the Schwabing months, was aborted by a helpful physician without her husband's being aware of her pregnancy), she persuaded him to support her in art studies in Munich. This time she threw herself with even greater zeal into free-wheeling eroticism. Her diary entry for 13 June 1895 begins: "Wieder und wieder im Venusberg. Alles, was an Sinnlichkeit und Leidenschaft in mir ist, wie im Sturm aufgewacht" (In the Mountain of Venus again and again. All the sensuality and passion I possess are awakened, as though in a tempest). At last informed of what was happening and what had happened, Lübke demanded a divorce, to Reventlow's regret. On 31 December 1896 she wrote in her diary: "Ich wollte Walter behalten und die anderen alle auch–was habe ich in der kurzen Zeit alles erlebt–einen nach dem andern. Warum fühle ich das Leben herrlich und intensiv, wenn ich viele habe? Immer das Gefühl, eigentlich gehöre ich allen" (I wanted to keep Walter and all the others, too–how much I have experienced in such a short time–one [lover] after another. Why is my sensation of living so splendid and intense when I have many? There's always a feeling of actually belonging to them all).

To her consternation she learned that she was pregnant again. The child's father, whose identity she kept secret, may have been the paleontologist Albrecht Hentschel, one of those "extremely masculine natures" of which she was fond. Her pleas to Lübke were answered with laconic refusals to see her again. An April excursion to the Lake of Constance, where she was joined by Rilke, filled her both with homesickness for Husum and the hope that her child might live, after all. Her devotion to little Rolf, born in September 1897, was admirable in the eyes of Schwabing; she was a "Madonna with the child." Nonetheless, her diaries indicate an overwhelming egomania in the possessiveness she showed to her "Mouse," her "Bubi"; before the boy's birth she wrote: "Mein Kind soll keinen Vater haben, nur mich. Und ganz" (My child shall not have a father, only me. And [me] totally).

The twelve years after "Bubi's" arrival were the most glorious of her life. She was adored by remarkable men: the philosopher Ludwig Klages, the "cosmicist," whom she first blindly admired as "der einzige Mensch, der alles versteht und der fliegen kann" (the only being who understands everything and who can fly) and then, cooling off, neatly analyzed: Klages was "am Ende doch nur ein Mensch mit Größenwahnsinn und Ichsucht und einem wundervollen Verstand" (ultimately, only a person with megalomania and egotism and a wonderful mind). Another admirer was the poet Karl Wolfskehl, who liked to dress up for masquerades as, variously, an eye-rolling Dionysus from India and a stately Homer. She gave the key to her apartment to the athletic lawyer Alfred Friess (called "Monsieur" and "Bel ami"). In 1903, after the break with Klages, who nonetheless became Rolf 's legal guardian, she entered a *mariage à trois* with the novelist Franz Hessel and the Polish glass stainer Bogdan von Suchoski; she engaged, as well, in what can only be called prostitution, for fun and profit. She appeared at a Schwabing costume party–where Stefan George reigned as Caesar–as a hermaphroditic youth, and in a 1907 letter to Franz Hessel she tells how, in Rome, guided by a charming Englishman and dressed as a catamite, she went to a bar and garnered offers from the elderly patrons.

At the same time she worked, not willingly but skillfully, as a translator, principally for the publisher Albert Langen. She translated many works by Anatole France, some by Guy de Maupassant, and the erotic novels of Marcel Prévost. In his bibliography, Johannes Székely lists almost fifty items from the French, many of them of book length, as well as a single stab at Dano-Norwegian, Bernt Lie's insignificant *Vildfugl* (Wild Bird) in 1905.

Her diaries and letters show that Reventlow had the makings of an extraordinary travel writer because of her wit, her curiosity, and the immediacy of her descriptions (for example, of Samos in 1903 and Corfu in 1906). On a bicycle trip through Italy in the summer of 1907 with "Franzl" (Hessel) and "Such" (Suchoski) and, of course, "Bubi," she had a misadventure which she depicted brilliantly but with apparent unawareness of its sordidness. At a beach pensione she gave premature birth to twin girls; one was stillborn and the other lived for a day. "Bubi [hat] . . . laut angefangen zu weinen: 'Nun stirbt es'. Aber es lebte immer noch. Als er abends im Bette lag, sang er ganz leise: 'Sybillchen, bleib' am Leben, Sybillchen, bleib' am Leben' " (Bubi began to weep, loudly: "Now it's dying." But it still kept on living. As he lay in bed in the evening, he sang, quite quietly: "Little Sybille, stay alive, stay alive, little Sybille"). In the evening, too, "all die entsetzlichen Leute" (all the terrible people) arrived to attend to the death certificate and the burial. It seemed so grotesque and uncanny that the travelers finally burst out into nervous laughter. "Die Nacht dann fest und tief geschlafen, wache gerade auf, als Such das Kind hinausträgt" (Slept deeply and well then during the night, wake up, just as Such carries the child out).

In 1910 Reventlow's financial difficulties became too much for her. With the aid of Erich Mühsam, who as a schoolboy in Lübeck had admired the adolescent countess from afar, she arranged to move to Ascona in the Swiss canton of Ticino. She was to enter into a marriage, in name only, with an alcoholic and almost totally deaf member of the Baltic-German nobility, Alexander von Rechenberg-Linten: the baron would thereby meet his aged father's demand that he have a wife, and Reventlow would get a share of the wealth that would fall into his hands. The wedding took place in June 1911, and the money was eventually received; "eine kurze Millionärsreise" (a brief millionaire's trip) to Majorca was undertaken in celebration, but upon her return Reventlow discovered that the bank where she had deposited the money had failed.

The remainder of her life was spent in struggles with creditors, and in efforts first to obtain Swiss citizenship for Rolf so that he would not have to serve in the German army, then to keep him from volunteering, and finally to extract him from service after he was drafted. Rolf later said that she went to Koblenz, where he was stationed, and persuaded him to desert to Switzerland; a more dramatic tale, allegedly told by the countess to a friend, had it that she herself rowed the young man across the Lake of Constance under fire from German patrol boats. Franziska zu Reventlow died in the summer of 1918 during an operation. Judging by her last photographs, she had kept her soft and stylish good looks.

Reventlow's literary career falls into three parts. The meager early harvest consists of a few autobiographical sketches, mostly subsumed into *Ellen Olestjerne,* and two essays on men's–and the countess's–view of women, published as pam-

Cover for the 1976 paperback edition of Reventlow's diary

phlets in Panizza's short-lived Zürcher Diskussionen series. These efforts did not provide much ammunition to feminists who argued for equal rights in the professions. The great hetaera-to-be Reventlow thought that women were most themselves, and happiest, in bed with a variety of partners of their own choosing. Professional training and zeal, she argued, quickly robbed them of their charm: "Die Energie und die Selbstverleugnung, die manche von ihnen an den Tag legen, mag ja höchst anerkennenswert sein, aber ein erfreuliches Bild ist es nicht" (The energy and self-denial many of them display may of course be admirable in the extreme, but it is not a pleasant picture).

The second phase of Reventlow's work is represented by a single book, *Ellen Olestjerne,* written at Klages's urging and for many years best known to readers of German literature because of Rilke's ambiguous review in *Die Zukunft*–a review couched in the form of a letter to "Ellen" herself, congratulating her on her exemplary bravery in telling her story. Other reviewers were shocked at the boldness, and the evident authorial approval, with which Ellen listed the men in her life, and at her somewhat disorderly passage to a liberation from family and moral strictures.

Reventlow herself was clearsighted enough to laugh at her leaden prose. In 1903, the year of the novel's appearance, she called it "ganz greulich" (quite horrible) and later confided to Mühsam that it was "ein sentimentaler Schmarren" (sentimental junk). "Das Element nordischen Heidentums in unvermischter Reinheit" (the element of Nordic heathendom in unalloyed purity) which Klages thought he saw in the book's author was expressed in the novel itself largely in Reventlow's tedious chronicling of Ellen's intrepid comings and goings, her readings, and her acquaintances (rather as in a plodding but frank work from Scandinavian naturalism, such as Amalie Skram's *Constance Ring* of 1885, or Victoria Benedictsson's *Fru Marianne* of 1887). The "Nordic-ness" Rilke perceived in it was of a different and subtler sort–Reventlow's efforts, comprising the novel's most satisfying parts, to conjure up the world of Castle Nevershuus and "die kleine nordische Küstenstadt" (the little Nordic coastal town). Here, in her occasional impressionism, Reventlow showed herself, too briefly, as an apt pupil of Rilke's great Danish model, Jens Peter Jacobsen. It has been suggested that Rilke got the idea for his own pseudo-Scandinavian novel, *Die Aufzeichnungen des Malte Laurids Brigge* (1910; translated as *The Notebooks of Malte Laurids Brigge,* 1949), from *Ellen Olestjerne.* In consideration of the disparity of quality between *Ellen Olestjerne* and Rilke's novel, it is more likely that he wrote in reaction against her book. As one of Reventlow's literary admirers, Margarete Privat, has observed, the documents and letters of the early years are far better than the equivalent passages in the novel, probably because the author, in the former, does not feel obliged to follow a sequential and unselectively detailed third-person narration. The reader breathes a sigh of relief whenever the novel has recourse to the feigned diary; yet even here, the real diaries are much livelier.

Her literary career–which Reventlow never regarded as such, for "schreibende Frauen [sind] schrecklich" (women who write [are] horrible)–was resumed in Ascona, no doubt out of financial necessity. As before, she drew upon her own life, but now with elegant lightness. In the epistolary novel *Von Paul zu Pedro: Amouresken* of 1912 a young woman of vast erotic experience and equally vast good nature develops her theory of love and her classification system of lovers in a correspondence with a male friend; their relationship has amounted, apparently, only to pleasant tearoom conversations. In the nineteen letters she sorts his more successful rivals into types: the largest class is made up of the "Pauls," almost faceless lovers, representing "immer etwas Lustiges, Belangloses, ohne Bedenken und ohne Konsequenzen" (always something amusing and unimportant, without hesitations and without consequences). Then there are the "saviors," the most difficult type to endure, men who want to save women by means of true love (Reventlow is supposed to have classified Klages under this head); the "silly boys"; the "elegant companion bulldogs"; and so forth. The "Pedro" of the title is a wealthy Sicilian who has a central and melodramatically comical part in the complex love affair of the book's latter pages. The letters end with an attempt at self-analysis: "Ich habe so viel Anlage zu passivem Glück, und dabei sind meine 'Glücke' fast immer stürmisch und bewegt" (I have such a great gift for passive happiness, and yet my "happinesses" are almost always tempestuous and stormy). The epistolary voice is not that of a femme fatale but of an amused observer, both of herself and of her myriad lovers.

Székely has surmised that Reventlow knew the *Dialogues of Hetaeras,* attributed to Lucian of Samosata, antiquity's great wit, which the eroticist Franz Blei published in a new translation in 1907. Székely might also have mentioned Pietro Aretino's lubricious *Ragionamenti* (Conversations), which came out in German in 1903. Yet, unlike Aretino's dialogues and some of Lucian's, Reventlow's letters are never pornographic–"Soll ich Ihnen 'alles' erzählen?–Nein, ich erzähle nie alles" (Should I tell you "everything"?–No, I never tell everything). She had learned much from Prévost, and *Von Paul zu Pedro* could read almost like a translation from his discreet yet impudent works were it not for the kindheartedness mixed into the German novel's plainly hedonistic spirit. Andreas-Salomé wrote a severe review of the book, taking its creator to task for failing to mention the debasement promiscuity may entail. Andreas-Salomé was quite right; the book contains no moral and blithely ignores the possible consequences of the letter writer's life. Yet anyone who has read one of Andreas-Salomé's own novels will understand why she was unable to esteem the book's lucid style and graceful wit.

The best known of Reventlow's works is *Herrn Dames Aufzeichnungen oder Begebenheiten aus einem merkwürdigen Stadtteil* (Mr. Dame's Notebooks; or, Events from a Remarkable Neighborhood, 1913), a look back at the great days–and nights–in Schwabing, a book Karl Wolfskehl praised as an authentic piece of documentation despite its fictional dress. Cursed with a name–literally, Mr. Lady–that makes him feel unsure of himself, an innocent young man leaves his journals in the keeping of an authoress; she edits them after his death in a railroad accident. Dame's observations are considerably more timid than those in Reventlow's journals. He is led through "Wahnmoching" (a name supposedly coined by "Bubi"), a place where illusion is supreme, by Dr. Sendt (based on the rational philosopher Paul Stern, with whom Reventlow corresponded after her move to Ascona). He is bowled over by the great Schwabing personalities of the countess's heyday: the "master" (Stefan George), the "Roman" Delius (Schuler), the "Zionist" Professor Hofmann (Wolfskehl), Hallwig (Klages), the "Sun-Youth" (Roderich Huch)–some thirty personages can be identified in the novel. The climax of Dame's adventures comes at a masquerade party at Hofmann's, where a feud arises between two factions of the self-styled "Enormous Folk," one led by the master and Hofmann and the other by Delius and Hallwig; the break is caused by the anti-Semitism of Delius and Hallwig. Dame's notebooks may have more a literary-historical than an aesthetic value. Littered with personal reminiscence and portraiture, they fall short of the singular elegance of *Von Paul zu Pedro;* but thanks in good part to the time-honored figure of the ingenuous observer, putting his amazed questions to the shrewdly cynical Dr. Sendt, Reventlow's ironic amusement at Schwabing and its extravagances is everywhere apparent. Reventlow sentimentalizes neither the recent past nor the men by whom she so willingly let herself be feted.

In the collection of stories *Das Logierhaus zur schwankenden Weltkugel und andere Novellen* (The Lodging-House at the Sign of the Wobbling Globe and Other Novellas, 1917), the new tales–

that is, those composed since the Schwabing days–are based largely upon Reventlow's travel experiences and repeatedly show an attractive woman surrounded by attentive men. Unlike the whimsical but realistic novel *Der Geldkomplex* (The Money Complex, 1916), the tales attempt to move into the realm of the supernatural or the fantastic. In these tales, as in *Von Paul zu Pedro,* Reventlow meant to profit from contemporary literary fads: Hanns Heinz Ewers and Gustav Meyrink were at the height of their popularity.

Der Geldkomplex is more idiosyncratic, an intentional and full-fledged self-dissection, once again in letters. The writer, corresponding with a friend named Maria, is in pecuniary straits and possesses the customary group of ineffectual admirers. The events of the novel, which are based on the Rechenberg-Linting episode, are less important than the manner in which Reventlow makes fun of her heroine's obsession and of the efforts of a psychiatrist to free her of it. The novel's locations are a mismanaged sanatorium, a gambling casino, and finally a nightmarish steamer–shabby settings for the high life to which Reventlow herself was so strongly drawn though she faintly despised it.

A fault of *Der Geldkomplex,* as of the short stories, lies in the urge of Reventlow–impatient about detail, and all too willing to put a charming heroine in the center of things–to encircle her alter ego with male friends who blend into one another. (Notably few subsidiary female characters appear in her work.) The same fault is apparent in *Der Selbstmordverein* (The Suicide Club), the posthumous narrative first published in her *Gesammelte Werke* (Collected Works, 1925). At the outset the novel moves away from autobiography in its depiction of the emotional despair of youth: the title refers to a suicide club among the pupils at a Munich boys' school. Nevertheless, as the male actors–young, middle-aged, and old–proliferate, the author's interest fastens more and more on Elisabeth, a frenetic girl of good family whose first love, Georg, a member of the club, has taken his own life. To replace him, Elisabeth seeks out Henning, a thirtyish and debt-ridden nobleman of exquisite manners who cannot bear the thought of regular employment. After a last fling, the two die together. Even in a book perhaps conceived as an escape from self-description, a strong (and dark) element of personal fantasy remains and flourishes.

Reventlow possesses a special voice in German letters. The claim has been made that she is a modern equivalent to Madame de Sévigné; but the opinion of an early critic, Franz Graetzer, might be more accurate–at her best, she is a gifted humorist. No one else in her time was able to smile so winningly while describing two human drives–for physical love and for money–that often degrade their victims. Neither Ibsen nor Zola, the giants of her youth, would have understood her, though de Maupassant and Kielland might have.

Letters:

Briefe der Gräfin Franziska zu Reventlow, edited by Else Reventlow (Munich: Langen, 1929);

Briefe 1890-1917, edited by Else Reventlow (Munich & Vienna: Langen-Müller, 1975).

Biographies:

Johannes Székely, *Franziska Gräfin zu Reventlow: Leben und Werk. Mit einer Bibliographie* (Bonn: Bouvier, 1979);

Helmut Fritz, *Die erotische Rebellion: Das Leben der Franziska Gräfin zu Reventlow* (Frankfurt am Main: Fischer, 1980).

References:

Hanns Arens, "Das Schwabing der Franziska von [sic] Reventlow," in his *Unsterbliches München* (Munich: Bechtle, 1968), pp. 411-416;

Mally Behler-Hagen, "Franziska Gräfin zu Reventlow," *Die schöne Literatur,* 28 (1927): 9-13;

Klaus Brockmeier, "Franziska zu Reventlow: Tagebücher 1895-1910," *Die neue Rundschau,* 83 (1972): 353-356;

Otto Flake, "Schreibende Welt," *Die neue Rundschau,* 37 (1926): 205-208;

Rudolf Frank, "Briefe der Gräfin Franziska zu Reventlow," *Die Literatur,* 31 (1928-1929): 732;

Frank, "Wahnmochings Klassiker," *Die Literatur,* 28 (1925-1926): 453-455;

Georg Fuchs, *Sturm und Drang in München* (Munich: Callwey, 1936), pp. 91-96;

Martin Green, *The von Richthofen Sisters: The Triumphant and the Tragic Modes of Love* (New York: Basic Books, 1974), pp. 92-97;

Franz Graetzer, "Die Humoristin," *Das literarische Echo,* 20 (1917-1918): 837-841;

Anselma Heine, Review of *Von Paul zu Pedro, Das literarische Echo,* 15 (1911-1912): 863;

Sophie Hoechstetter, "Ellen Olestjerne," *Das literarische Echo,* 6 (1903-1904): 1301-1303;

Josef Hofmiller, Review of *Von Paul zu Pedro, Süddeutsche Monatshefte,* 9 (1912): 489-490;

Roderich Huch, "Alfred Schuler, Ludwig Klages und Stefan George: Erinnerungen an Kreise und Krisen der Jahrhundertwende in München-Schwabing," *Castrum Peregrini,* 110 (1973): 5-49;

Huch, "Die Enormen von Schwabing: Erinnerungen aus der Zeit der Jahrhundertwende," *Atlantis,* 30 (1958): 143-150;

Ursula Kirchhoff, *Die Darstellung des Festes im Roman um 1900: Ihre thematische und funktionale Bedeutung* (Munich: Aschendorff, 1969), pp. 88-102;

Wilhelm Klüver, "Die Reventlows in der Geschichte Schleswig-Holsteins," *Nordelbingen,* 26 (1958): 210-217;

Helmut Kreuzer, *Die Bohème: Beiträge zu ihrer Beschreibung* (Stuttgart: Metzler, 1968), pp. 97-103;

Kreuzer, "Exkurs über die Bohème," in *Deutsche Literatur im 20. Jahrhundert,* edited by Otto Mann and Wolfgang Rothe, volume 1 (Bern & Munich: Francke, 1961), pp. 212-223;

Kreuzer, "Zum Begriff der Bohème," *Deutsche Vierteljahresschrift für Literaturwissenschaft,* 38B (1964): 170-207;

Fritz Martini, "Bohème," in *Reallexikon der deutschen Literaturgeschichte,* edited by Werner Kohlschmidt and Wolfgang Mohr, volume 1 (Berlin: de Gruyter, 1958), pp. 180-183;

Erich Mühsam, "Die Gräfin," in his *Unpolitische Erinnerungen* (Leipzig: Volk & Buch, 1958), pp. 189-199;

Klara Obermüller, "Das literarische München um die Jahrhundertwende," in *München um 1900,* edited by Manuel Gasser (Munich: Heyne, 1977), pp. 49-84;

Friedrich Podszus, "Nachwort," in Reventlow, *Der Geldkomplex, Herrn Dames Aufzeichnungen, Von Paul zu Pedro: Drei Romane* (Munich: Biederstein, 1958), pp. 295-304;

Margarete Privat, "Vom Werden und Wesen der Schriftstellerin Franziska zu Reventlow," *Nordelbingen,* 38 (1969): 112-113;

Ursula Püschel, "Jugendstil-Erotik: Franziska Reventlow," in her *Mit allen Sinnen: Frauen in der Literatur* (Halle & Leipzig: Mitteldeutscher Verlag, 1980), pp. 89-116;

Johann Albrecht von Rantzau, "Zur Geschichte der sexuellen Revolution: Die Gräfin Franziska zu Reventlow und die Münchener Kosmiker," *Archiv für Kulturgeschichte,* 56 (1974): 394-446;

Wolfdietrich Rasch, "Aspekte der deutschen Literatur um 1900," in his *Zur deutschen Literatur seit der Jahrhundertwende: Gesammelte Aufsätze* (Stuttgart: Metzler, 1967), pp. 1-48;

Rainer Maria Rilke, "Franziska Gräfin zu Reventlow, *Ellen Olestjerne,*" in his *Sämtliche Werke,* volume 5 (Frankfurt am Main: Insel, 1965), pp. 653-657;

Hans Eggert Schröder, *Ludwig Klages: Die Geschichte seines Lebens,* volume 1 (Bonn: Bouvier, 1966), pp. 254-323;

Irmgard Weithase, "Franziska Gräfin zu Reventlow," *Die Frau,* 38 (1930-1931): 483-489.

Albrecht Schaeffer

(6 December 1885-4 December 1950)

Ingeborg H. Solbrig
University of Iowa

BOOKS: *Amata: Wandel der Liebe* (Hannover: Ey, 1911);

Die Meerfahrt (Leipzig: Wolff, 1912);

Der Mischkrug, by Schaeffer and A. Gerlach (Hannover: Privately printed, 1912);

Heroische Fahrt (Leipzig: Insel, 1914);

Attische Dämmerung (Leipzig: Insel, 1914);

Kriegslieder (Hannover: Ey, 1914);

Die Mütter: Ein ernstes Stück (Leipzig: Insel, 1914);

Das Schicksal (Hannover: Privately printed, 1914);

Des Michael Schwertlos vaterländische Gedichte (Leipzig: Insel, 1915);

Moses Tod: Ein Mysterium (Hannover: Privately printed, 1915);

Rainer Maria Rilke (Leipzig: Insel, 1916);

Gudula oder Die Dauer des Lebens (Leipzig: Insel, 1918);

Die Opfer des Kaisers, Kremserfahrten und die Abgesänge der hallenden Korridore, by Schaeffer and Ludwig Strauß (Leipzig: Insel, 1918);

Josef Montfort (Leipzig: Insel, 1918); republished as *Das nie bewegte Herz* (Berlin: Deutsche Buchgemeinschaft, 1931);

Elli oder Sieben Treppen (Leipzig: Insel, 1919); revised as *Elli: Beschreibung eines weiblichen Lebens* (Wiesbaden: Insel, 1949);

Der Raub der Persefone: Eine attische Mythe (Leipzig: Insel, 1920);

Helianth: Bilder aus dem Leben zweier Menschen von heute aus der norddeutschen Tiefebene in neun Büchern dargestellt (3 volumes, Leipzig: Insel, 1920-1924); revised and abridged as *Helianth: Bilder aus dem Leben zweier Menschen und aus der norddeutschen Tiefebene in neun Büchern dargestellt,* 2 volumes (Leipzig: Insel, 1928);

Der göttliche Dulder (Leipzig: Insel, 1920);

Gevatter Tod: Märchenhaftes Epos in vierundzwanzig Mondphasen und einer als Zugabe (Leipzig: Insel, 1922);

Eduard Mörikes "Früh im Wagen" (Berlin: Runge, 1922);

Parzival: Ein Versroman in drei Kreisen (Leipzig: Insel, 1922);

Albrecht Schaeffer (Schiller-Nationalmuseum/Deutsches Literaturarchiv, Marbach am Nekar)

Die Saalborner Stanzen: Eine Trilogie (Leipzig: Insel, 1922);

Der Reiter mit dem Mandelbaum (Chemnitz: Gesellschaft der Bücherfreunde, 1922);

Die Wand: Dramatische Phantasmagorie in einem Aufzug (Berlin: Privately printed, 1922);

Abkunft und Ankunft (Chemnitz: Gesellschaft der Bücherfreunde zu Chemnitz, 1923);

Das Gitter: Erzählung (Stuttgart: Deutsche Verlagsanstalt, 1923);

Die Treibjagd: Novelle (Chemnitz: Gesellschaft der Bücherfreunde, 1923);

Hölderlins Heimgang oder Der goldene Wagen (Berlin: Eigenbrödler, 1923);

Das Kleinod im Lotus: Die Buddha-Legende frei nach dem Englischen "The Light of Asia; or, The Great Renunciation" by Edwin Arnold (Leipzig: Insel, 1923);
Regula Kreuzfeind: Legende (Essen: Severin, 1923);
Dichter und Dichtung: Kritische Versuche (Leipzig: Insel, 1923);
Demetrius: Ein Trauerspiel in fünf Aufzügen (Berlin: Rowohlt, 1923);
Legende vom verdoppelten Lebens-Alter (Heidelberg: Asmus, 1923);
Lene Stelling (Berlin: Privately printed, 1923);
Chrysoforus oder Die Heimkehr (Chemnitz: Privately printed, 1924);
Kritisches Pro Domo (Berlin: Stilke, 1924);
Die Marien-Lieder (Leipzig: Insel, 1924);
Die Treibjagd und zwei Legenden (Cologne: Schaffenstein, 1924);
Fidelio: Novelle (Stuttgart: Deutsche Verlagsanstalt, 1924);
Das Albrecht Schaeffer-Buch, edited by Martin Rockenbäch (Leipzig: Kuner, 1924);
Das Prisma: Erzählungen und Novellen (Leipzig: Insel, 1925);
Der Gefällige: Lustspiel in vier Akten, frei nach Diderots "Est-il bon, est-il méchant?" (Potsdam: Kiepenheuer, 1925);
Konstantin der Große: Tragödie in fünf Aufzügen (Berlin: Rowohlt, 1925);
Der verlorene Sohn: Komödie in drei Aufzügen (Leipzig: Köhler & Amelang, 1925);
Der Falke und die Wölfin: Zwei Erzählungen (Berlin: Reimer, 1925);
Die Schuldbrüder (Berlin: Deutsche Buchgemeinschaft, 1926); revised as *Die Geschichte der Brüder Chamade* (Leipzig: Insel/Berlin & Leipzig: Horen, 1928);
Der goldene Wagen: Legenden und Mythen (Leipzig: Insel, 1927);
Der Apfel vom Baum der Erkenntnis: Erzählung und Gleichnis (Heidelberg: Weitbrecht, 1927);
Mitternacht: Zwölf Novellen (Leipzig: Insel, 1928);
Das verdoppelte Lebensalter (Hamburg: Deutsche Dichter-Gedächtnis-Stiftung, 1929);
Griechische Heldensagen: Neu erzählt nach alten Quellen, 2 volumes (Leipzig: Insel, 1929-1930);
Kaiser Konstantin: Eine Zeitwende (Leipzig: Insel, 1929);
Die Sage von Odysseus: Neu erzählt nach den ursprünglichen Motiven (Leipzig: Insel, 1930);
Das Opfertier: Erzählungen (Leipzig: Insel, 1931);
Gedichte aus den Jahren 1915-1930 (Leipzig: Insel, 1931);
Nachtschatten: Vier Novellen aus kriegerischen Zeiten (Leipzig: Insel, 1932);
Der Roßkamm von Lemgo (Berlin: Deutsche Buchgesellschaft, 1933); revised as *Janna du Coeur* (Munich: Desch, 1949);
Das Haus am See: Zwei Trilogien (Hamburg: Verlag der Blätter fur der Dichtung, 1934);
Der General (Frankfurt am Main: Rütten & Loening, 1934; revised edition, Witten: Eckart, 1954);
Heimgang: Novelle (Berlin: Fischer, 1934);
Cara (Potsdam: Rütten & Loening, 1936; revised, 1948);
Aphaia: Der Weg der Götter, Völker und Zahlen (Potsdam: Rütten & Loening, 1937);
Heile, heile Segen: Sieben Geschichten für Kinder von drei bis fünf Jahren (Potsdam: Rütten & Loening, 1937);
Ruhland: Lebensbild eines Mannes (Potsdam: Rütten & Loening, 1937);
Von Räubern und Riesen: Drei Märchen für Kinder (Potsdam: Rütten & Loening, 1938);
Die Geheimnisse (Potsdam: Rütten & Loening, 1938); revised and enlarged as *Die goldene Klinke* (Olten: Vereinigung der Oltner Bücherfreunde, 1950);
Kaniswall: Novelle (Potsdam: Rütten & Loening, 1938);
Rudolf Erzerum oder Des Lebens Einfachheit (Stockholm: Neuer Verlag, 1945);
Enak oder Das Auge Gottes (Hamburg: Honeit, 1948);
Der Auswanderer: Erzählungen und Novellen (Überlingen: Wulff, 1949);
Albrecht Schaeffer: Im Schatten der Marienburg. Eine Auswahl aus seinem dichterischen Werk, edited by Walter Ehlers and Alfred Mohrhenn (Essen: West-Verlag, 1951);
Vom ursprünglichen Glauben: Gedanken eines Dichters zur modernen Theologie (Witten: Eckart, 1953);
Der grüne Mantel, edited by Ehlers (Stuttgart: Reclam, 1955);
Mythos: Abhandlungen über die kulturellen Grundlagen der Menschheit, edited by Ehlers (Heidelberg & Darmstadt: Schneider, 1958).

OTHER: Clemens Brentano, *Gedichte,* edited by Schaeffer (Leipzig: Insel, 1914);
Annette von Droste-Hülshoff, *Gedichte,* edited by Schaeffer (Leipzig: Insel, 1914);
Ernst Moritz Arndt, *Gedichte,* edited by Schaeffer (Leipzig: Insel, 1915);

Klage

O wer könnte
Einmal ruhen die Stirne,
Angeneigt an das Ewige..
Uns ist nur Erde.

Gut ist wohl
Eine Felsenwand,
Eines Baumes Gestalt —
Und am Hange das weichere Gras.
Die kühl sind alle und ruhevoll —
Wie nicht des Weibes zu glühende Brust,
Wo drinnen immer
Es Flügeln ähnlich
Von großen Höhen, von großen Tiefen rauscht.

Manuscript for a 1933 poem by Schaeffer

Friedrich Hebbel, *Gedichte,* edited by Schaeffer (Leipzig: Insel, 1917);
Oscar Wilde, *Die Ballade vom Zuchthaus zu Reading,* translated by Schaeffer (Leipzig: Insel, 1917);
Joseph von Eichendorff, *Gedichte,* edited by Schaeffer (Leipzig: Insel, 1919);
Friedrich Gottlob Klopstock, *Oden,* edited by Schaeffer (Leipzig: Insel, 1919);
Nikolaus Lenau, *Gedichte,* edited by Schaeffer (Leipzig: Insel, 1919);
August von Platen, *Gedichte,* edited by Schaeffer (Leipzig: Insel, 1920);
Leucothea: Ein Jahrbuch, edited by Schaeffer and Ludwig Strauß (Berlin: Runge, 1923);
Robert Louis Stevenson, *Quartier für die Nacht; Will von der Mühle: Zwei Erzählungen,* translated by Schaeffer (Leipzig: Insel, 1925);
Eisherz und Edeljaspis oder Die Geschichte einer glücklichen Gattenwahl: Ein Roman aus der Ming Zeit, translated by F. Kuhn, interspersed poems rewritten by Schaeffer (Leipzig: Insel, 1926);
Des Apuljus sogenannter Goldener Esel: Metamorphosen, translated by Schaeffer (Leipzig: Insel, 1926);
Homer, *Die Odyssee,* translated by Schaeffer (Berlin: Horen, 1927);
Der Hymnus auf Demeter, translated by Schaeffer (Halle: Werkstätten der Stadt Halle, 1928);
Homer, *Die Ilias,* translated by Schaeffer (Berlin: Schneider, 1929);
Roß und Reiter: Ihre Darstellung in der plastischen Kunst, edited by Schaeffer and Robert Diehl (Leipzig: Insel, 1931);
Heilige Stille: Stimmungsbilder aus der Natur, introduction by Schaeffer (Leipzig: Seemann, 1934);
Frederic Prokosch, *Die Asiaten: Roman,* translated by Schaeffer (Frankfurt am Main: Fischer, 1952).

PERIODICAL PUBLICATIONS: "Beethoven im Gespräch," *Die Hilfe,* no. 26 (29 June 1916): 425ff.;
"Gespräch aus der Zeit," *Berliner Tageblatt,* no. 152 (2 April 1920);
"Gedanke und Gestalt: Sechs Epigramme," *Insel-Almanach auf das Jahr 1926* (1926): 152-153;
"Das Haus im Feuer: Ein Gespräch," *Die Horen,* 3, no. 4 (1926/1927): 302ff.;
"Poetischer Sprachverfall," *Preußische Jahrbücher,* 208, no. 3 (1927): 312ff.;
"Die Technik der 'Darstellung' in der Erzählung: Eine Erwiderung," *Germanisch-Romanische Monatsschrift,* 15, no. 1/2 (1927): 13-18;
"Ewige Gegenwart: Ein Gespräch," *Die Horen,* 4, no. 3 (1927/1928): 200ff.;
"Kain und Abel: Epigramme und Glossen," *Das Inselschiff,* 9, no. 2 (1928): 144-147;
"1913: Beschreibung eines kritischen Jahres," *Die literarische Welt,* 5, no. 8 (22 February 1929);
"Offene oder heidnische Form," *Der Kunstwart,* 42, no. 11 (1929): 295ff.;
"Der Mensch und das Feuer," *Die psychoanalytische Bewegung,* 2, no. 3 (1930);
"Gott: Aphorismen," *Vossische Zeitung* (3 August 1930);
"Selbstdarstellung," *Die literarische Welt,* 7 (6 February 1931);
"Noch einmal: Der Feuermythos. Brief an Sigmund Freud," *Imago,* 19, no. 2 (1933): 256-259;
"Siebengang: Eine Selbstdarstellung," *Die neue Rundschau,* 45, no. 9 (1934): 313ff.;
"Die Belladonna: Gedicht," *Eckart: Monatsschrift* (September 1936);
"Der Feigenbaum: Ein Gespräch," *Eckart: Monatsschrift* (March 1937);
"Fiona oder der zerschlagene Kuß: Erzählung," *Frankfurter Zeitung,* 83, nos. 10, 12, 14, 17, 19, 21, 23, 25, 27, 30, 32, 34, 36, 38, 40 (1939);
"Der Schlüsselberg," *Frankfurter Zeitung,* 83, no. 165 (1939);
"Der letzte Wunsch," *Frankfurter Zeitung,* 83, no. 316 (1939);
"Das Versäumnis: Parabel," *die neue linie,* 10, no. 8 (April 1939);
"Verse auf den 146. Psalm," *Aufbau,* 3, no. 3 (1947);
"Die beiden Türen: Erzählung," *Neue Zürcher Zeitung,* nos. 1537 and 1553 (1947);
"Die Wahl des Todes: Erzählung," *Berliner Hefte für Kunst und Literatur,* 3, no. 3 (March 1948): 3-7;
"Die Erscheinung des Reiters," *Die Welt,* (21 August 1948);
"Der Engel: Eine Erzählung," *Zeitschrift für Freunde guter Literatur,* 2, no. 3 (March 1948): 3-7;
"Ein deutscher Verleger: Anton Kippenberg," *Staatszeitung und Herold* (New York), 22 May 1949;
"Der Pfarrer war so freundlich," *Sie: Die Berliner Wochenzeitung,* no. 30 (1949);

"Schicksal und Anteil: Erzählung," *Neue Zürcher Zeitung,* no. 1883 (1949);
"Auskunft über zwei Entdeckungen an den Formen einer Krabbe und einer Schnecke," *Merkur: Deutsche Zeitschrift für europäisches Denken,* 3, no. 3 (1949);
"Pelz: Erzählung," *National-Zeitung* (Basel), 30, nos. 239 and 527 (1949);
"Indische Legende," *Sie: Die Berliner Wochenzeitung,* no. 25 (19 June 1949): 6;
"Klage," *Das literarische Deutschland: Zeitung der Deutschen Akademie für Sprache und Dichtung,* 1 (10 December 1950): 5;
"Lazarus: Erzählung," *Die neue Rundschau,* 61, no. 2 (1950);
"Die Familie," *National-Zeitung* (Basel), 31, no. 161 (1950);
"Die Exekution: Erzählung," *Die Erzählung: Zeitschrift für Freunde guter Literatur* (Constance), 4, no. 4 (1950);
"Die Verwechslung: Erzählung," *Die neue Rundschau,* 61, no. 4 (1950);
"Neue Gedichte," *Die Erzählung: Zeitschrift für Freunde guter Literatur* (Constance), 4, no. 6 (1950);
"Der schwarze Anzug: Erzählung," *Staatszeitung und Herold* (New York), 20 August 1950;
"Unersättliches Schwert: Erzählung," *Die Welt,* 5, no. 29 (1950);
"Die Ballade von Deutschland: Geschrieben auf der Heimreise von Amerika im September 1950," *Sonntagsblatt,* no. 42 (1950);
"Der Auswanderer: Gedicht," *Merkur: Deutsche Zeitschrift für europäisches Denken,* 5, no. 12 (1951): 1147-1150.

Albrecht Schaeffer, like his older contemporaries Stefan George and Rainer Maria Rilke, attempted to restore dignity to poetry in a time of spiritual decline. His literary art was informed by the intellectual traditions of antiquity, the Middle Ages, and the romantic period. His writings were widely acclaimed because of their metrical precision, attention to form, and tremendous scope. His masterful shorter fiction includes short stories, novellas, legends, and parables.

Schaeffer was born on 6 December 1885 in Elbing, Prussia (now Elblag, Poland), to Paul Friedrich and Marie Antoinette Agnes Schäffer (all extant documents show this spelling of his parents' name). In 1890 the family moved to the northwestern German city of Hannover, where Schaeffer remained until his graduation from high school. He studied classical and modern philology at the universities of Munich, Marburg, and Berlin from 1905 to 1909. For a short time he worked as an unpaid employee for a newspaper, but could not settle down in a conventional profession. Instead, he returned to his parents' home, continued to study ancient and modern literature, and wrote poetry, epics, drama, and fiction. Later he revised and rejected many of his earlier works, most of which were composed in verse. During these years Schaeffer greatly admired the poet and aesthete Stefan George; like George and his disciples, Schaeffer rebelled against materialism and opportunism in his pursuit of a deeper understanding of life through poetry.

Schaeffer spent the year 1913 traveling to London, Paris, Vienna, and the northwestern coast of Germany. After he returned home, Stefan Zweig recommended his work to the renowned publishing house of Insel in Leipzig. In 1914 the first volumes of poetry by Schaeffer appeared under the titles *Heroische Fahrt* (Heroic Journey) and *Attische Dämmerung* (Attic Dawn). They reflect a modern sensitivity and clearly reveal his models during this early phase of his career: George, Homer, Friedrich Hölderlin, August von Platen, Hugo von Hofmannsthal, and, especially, Heinrich von Kleist.

The young Schaeffer was a typical representative of a period during which many modern literary movements emerged. It is difficult to place Schaeffer's work into a specific category at any time in his career; his writings bear the stamp of neoromanticism, impressionism, and symbolism, but they also contain echoes of naturalism, traces of surrealism and expressionism, and elements of the grotesque. Religion of a speculative, mystical Christian kind, Greece and Rome and other ancient cultures, nature, and the simple life close to the soil are themes prevalent in his works.

When World War I broke out in 1914 Schaeffer was drafted as a clerk at the bureau for disabled soldiers in Berlin; his duties enabled him to continue writing. The play *Die Mütter* (The Mothers, 1914) reflects the conventions of nineteenth-century drama. The collection of poems *Des Michael Schwertlos vaterländische Gedichte* (Michael Swordless's Patriotic Poems, 1915), which eulogizes human strength in suffering instead of glorifying war, received a favorable review by the influential critic Julius Bab in the *Berliner Tageblatt.*

In 1916, while still working at the bureau for disabled soldiers, Schaeffer met the writer, theater critic, and literary historian Ludwig Strauß, a dedicated Zionist who translated Hebrew and Yiddish literature into German. The two men became friends and collaborated on a volume of parodies of poems by George's imitators, *Die Opfer des Kaisers, Kremserfahrten und die Abgesänge der hallenden Korridore* (The Sacrifices of the Emperor, Charabanc Rides, and the Swan Songs of the Echoing Hallways, 1918). Schaeffer and Strauß also produced a yearbook, *Leucothea,* in 1923. Schaeffer was not Jewish, but he had a keen interest in the Old Testament and in Jewish thought. Strauß's influence lasted throughout Schaeffer's career.

After the war ended in 1918 Schaeffer married Irma Bekk. A year later he moved to Neubeuren, a small estate in the upper Bavarian countryside. His first three significant works of fiction appeared in 1918 and 1919: two long narratives and a similar work that has been classified both as a tale and as a novel.

Gudula oder Die Dauer des Lebens (Gudula; or, The Continuing Life, 1918) spans the time from the Napoleonic wars to the beginning of the industrial age. Gudula Trassenberg, an orphaned princess who has chosen the active life of a commoner, lives near Weimar as the wife of the sculptor Longinus Drolshagen. Longinus returns from the war severely wounded but finally recovers. In 1830 the family moves to Berlin, where Longinus and two of his sons join the revolutionary forces and die fighting on the barricades. Gudula marries an old friend of her late husband, the Scottish nobleman Sir Ronald Ramory, who is an ardent advocate of freedom and social justice. Gudula and Ronald travel to various western European countries to study political, economic, and social developments. When Ronald dies, Gudula continues their work. She meets Ferdinand Lassalle, Karl Marx, August Bebel, and Wilhelm Liebknecht, and remains a radical revolutionary until the end of her long life. This work is actually a bildungsroman with a female protagonist who realizes her aesthetic, ethical, and intellectual capabilities through meeting life's challenges.

While *Gudula oder Die Dauer des Lebens* is written in traditional language with strong neoromantic overtones, the novel *Josef Montfort* (1918) reveals the influence of Freud's psychology of the unconscious in Schaeffer's decoding of mythical motifs. (Schaeffer's privately published volume *Rainer Maria Rilke* [1916] was dedicated "to the discoverer of childhood, the extraordinary man, Sigmund Freud.") The story

Schaeffer in 1935 (Ullstein)

is narrated by Li, the Chinese servant of the young Baron Josef Montfort, a man incapable of fear. As the two men travel from one adventure to another, a mysterious double of Josef 's continually reappears; he turns out to be Josef 's twin brother Erasmus, and he finally kills Josef. The epigraph, from Baudelaire, prepares the reader for the eerie atmosphere and symbolizes Josef's personality: "The sea, your double, mirrors back your soul/Reflected in its billow's restless roll;/ Your aching heart shares its vast vacancy." In this novel Schaeffer defamiliarizes the external world; the uncanny horror becomes symbolic of a second, supernatural world that lurks in the characters' minds. The style of *Josef Montfort* became characteristic of Schaeffer; it has affinities with the styles of E. T. A. Hoffmann and Edgar Allan Poe.

Elli oder Sieben Treppen (Elli; or, Seven Stages, 1919; revised as *Elli: Beschreibung eines weiblichen Lebens* [Elli: Description of a Female Life, 1949]) is a long narrative in seven parts introduced by a verse of Hasidic wisdom. In 1925 Kurt Busse described the work as the "gradual descent of the female protagonist into chaos." In the urgent tone of Greek tragedy, Schaeffer tells the painful story of an educated woman who suffers a continuing loss of identity. Each of Elli's lovers betrays, deceives, uses, abuses, and abandons her; her kindness and devotion drag her to ruin as she falls from intellectual heights to destitution, rape, venereal disease, prostitution, and finally suicide. Shortly before her death, the word *Opfer* (sacrifice) appears on her breast. In the manner of Balzac, Schaeffer's novels share certain motifs, scenes, characters, and settings. Josef Montfort and his evil twin brother Erasmus figure in *Elli oder Sieben Treppen;* and one of Elli's lovers, the painter Bogner, is referred to in *Josef Montfort.*

Helianth: Bilder aus dem Leben zweier Menschen von heute aus der norddeutschen Tiefebene in neun Büchern dargestellt (Helianth: Episodes from the Lives of Two People of Our Time from the North German Plains Presented in Nine Books) appeared in three volumes in 1920-1924 and commanded the attention of an entire generation. For the two-volume revised and abridged edition of 1928 Schaeffer deleted the words *von heute* (of our time) from the subtitle, indicating his intention to portray timeless humanity in the novel. The work has the idealistic background of the bildungsroman, yet it is marked by a distinctly modern sensitivity. Like the protagonists of Goethe's *Wilhelm Meister* (1795, 1796, 1829), Tieck's *Franz Sternbalds Wanderungen* (1798), Novalis's *Heinrich von Ofterdingen* (1801), and Gottfried Keller's *Der grüne Heinrich* (1879, 1880), Schaeffer's hero, Georg, approaches perfection through art. In the forty-five months treated by the novel Georg sets out to find his identity and ends up as the ruler of a well-managed principality. The title evokes the Greek word *helianthos* (sunflower), as well as the Old Saxon epic *Heliand* (Savior). Schaeffer's title refers to the individual seeking God, to whom he constantly turns his soul as the sunflower turns toward the sun. In emblem books the sunflower symbolizes the good Christian who follows the sun's (Son's) course throughout his life. Historical figures such as Lassalle, Marx, Bebel, Rilke, Oskar Kokoschka, and Christian Morgenstern situate the plot in a specific historical period, but behind this world there exists another one, a timeless sphere indicated by the names of Rembrandt, Goethe, and Jean Paul.

A review by Guido Brand in *Das literarische Echo* was typical of the enthusiastic acceptance of the work when it first appeared. With regard to the reception of *Helianth,* Werner Vortriede remarked with a touch of irony in the early 1960s: "There was much beauty, excessive politeness, thoroughly relished moods, and stimulating discussions by young people who still understood how to read poetry." In 1922 Oscar Walzel pointed out many romantic elements in *Helianth,* maintaining that "Schaeffer had tried to write exactly as Jean Paul would have done if he had lived in our century." Walzel also recognized Schaeffer's many innovations, especially the treatment of perspective and the use of interior monologue, and emphasized the difference between Schaeffer's prose and that of the expressionists. In the *Germanisch-Romanische Monatsschrift* in 1926 Eduard Berend discussed *Helianth* in the context of trends in contemporary narrative technique and criticized Schaeffer for mixing narrative with dramatic techniques. Schaeffer, arguing for the autonomy of art and emphasizing that every work of literary art has its own innate "Prinzipien," its own laws of composition and narrative technique, rebuffed Berend's analysis in a 1927 issue of the same journal. Berend replied in 1928, clarifying some points Schaeffer seemed to have misunderstood, but the results of this debate were inconclusive. In his *Stilstudien* (Studies of Style, 1928) Leo Spitzer listed Schaeffer's favorite narrative devices as the interior monologue, the dream, the diary, and the epistle, and raised him to the ranks of such novelists as Dostoyevski and Joyce. But no critic emphasized adequately those features of Schaeffer's prose that can be traced to *Josef Montfort* and which remained vital to his fiction: the elements of the grotesque, fantastic, and surreal. There are passages in Schaeffer's texts that strongly remind the reader of Kafka's fictional world.

In a 1928 issue of the *Germanic Review* Otto Koischwitz pointed out Schaeffer's use in his novel of such modern forms of communication as the telegraph and the telephone and commented on the reception of the work in Europe. In Germany he noted a "community of enthusiastic admirers" of Schaeffer's literary art but also a group of critics who accused him of mixing narrative with dramatic techniques and of cheap sensationalism. In France, however, Schaeffer's work was well received. Koischwitz quoted the French critic Henri Lichtenberg, who called Schaeffer the "prince de l'imagination, créateur d'une abondance fabuleuse d'images et objets" (prince of the imagination, creator of a fabulous abun-

Portrait of Schaeffer by Herbert von Reyl-Hamisch

dance of images and objects). Koischwitz described Schaeffer's use of a technique popular among French and Scandinavian writers–the mixing of elements of naturalism and impressionism–and showed striking similarities between the narrative techniques used by Clemens Brentano in his novel *Godwi* (1801) and those used by Schaeffer in *Helianth.* In 1929 Walter Muschg dedicated his postdoctoral dissertation to a study of *Helianth,* discussing it in the context of the group of early twentieth-century writers who experimented with innovative narrative techniques and tried to develop a new theory of the novel. *Helianth* coincided with the symbolist-neoromant ic reaction against "positivistic" naturalism in France and the Scandinavian countries.

Schaeffer's observations on characteristics of poetry appeared in *Dichter und Dichtung: Kritische Versuche* (Poets and Poetry: Critical Essays, 1923). The first three chapters, including discursive reflections on Gotthold Ephraim Lessing, Eduard Mörike, and Ludwig Strauß in the context of literary theories in general, mirror the impact of the works of the art historian Wilhelm R. Worringer on Schaeffer's thought. They are followed by chapters on the ballad, sonnet, tragedy, and epic. A perceptive study of Stefan George concludes the work.

The 1920s and 1930s were Schaeffer's most productive years, during which he wrote many works in meter. Schaeffer's lyric poetry from these busy decades was collected in *Die Saalborner Stanzen: Eine Trilogie* (The Saalborn Stanzas: A Trilogy, 1922), *Die Marien-Lieder* (Songs in Praise of Mary, 1924), and *Das Haus am See: Zwei Trilogien* (The House on the Lake: Two Trilogies, 1934). The one-act drama *Die Wand: Dramatische Phantasmagorie* (The Wall: Dramatic Phantasmagory, 1922) was not intended for the stage; set in an inn near Zurich in 1797, its dramatis personae

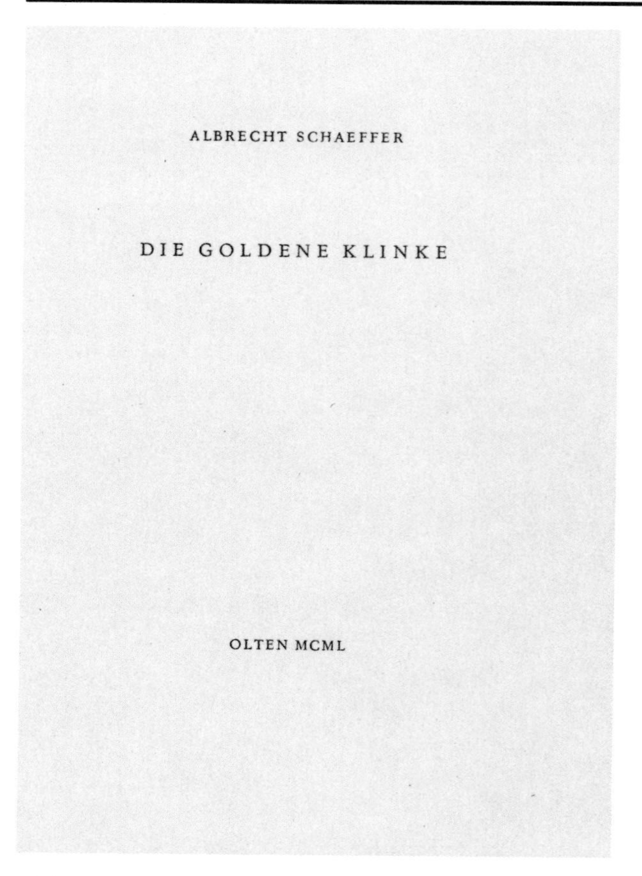

Title page of the revised and enlarged edition of Schaeffer's story collection Die Geheimnisse, *first published in 1938*

include Goethe and his friend Heinrich Meyer. *Demetrius* (1923), a tragedy in five acts, was inspired by Schiller's unfinished drama of the same title. In 1925 Schaeffer wrote *Der Gefällige* (The Congenial One), a free adaptation of Diderot's *Est-il bon, est-il méchant?;* the comedy *Der verlorene Sohn* (The Prodigal Son); and a tragedy, *Konstantin der Große,* which was praised by the critics but, like most of Schaeffer's dramas, not performed on the stage because it was inconsistent with the experimental trends of the German theater of the 1920s. The form-conscious author experimented with the genre of the epic in the neoromantic work *Gevatter Tod: Märchenhaftes Epos in vierundzwanzig Mondphasen und einer als Zugabe* (Brother Death: Fairy-Tale Epic in Twenty-Four Lunar Phases and an Additional One as a Bonus, 1922). Schaeffer's "novel in verse" *Parzival: Ein Versroman in drei Kreisen* (Parzival: A Verse Novel in Three Circles, 1922), which was enthusiastically received, may be considered a modern epic poem. The three parts are entitled "Circle of the Father," "Circle of the Son," and "Circle of the Holy Spirit." Each chapter is named for a constellation. *Parzival* opens with a quotation from the seventeenth-century mystic Angelus Silesius: "You will be transformed into what you are." The work combines the Parzival and Ulysses themes and represents, according to Rudolf Ibel, an attempt at a synthesis of "Germanic metaphysics" and "Greek love of form." Parzival meets the eternal Wandering Jew Ahasver, Saint Francis of Assisi, and the hermit and ascetic Trevrizent, all of whom become his friends; figures from Albrecht Dürer's paintings–Hieronymus, Melancholy, the Knight, Death, the Devil, and Master Erwin, the architect of cathedrals–also cross Parzival's path. At one point the hero must serve as ferryman for the dead. During his mystical journey Schaeffer's Parzival, a figure much like Rilke's figure of the poet, must transform the external world into a world of the mind. At age eighty, Parzival completes his search for the Holy Grail, which, Ibel notes, "stand in seines Wesens Mitte" (stood within his essence).

During these two decades of his greatest literary productivity Schaeffer wrote novellas, short stories, myths, legends, and children's stories; the best-known collections of his short narratives include *Hölderlins Heimgang oder Der goldene Wagen* (Hölderlin's Return; or, The Golden Chariot, 1923), *Die Treibjagd und zwei Legenden* (The Battue and Two Legends, 1924), *Der Falke und die Wölfin: Zwei Erzählungen* (The Falcon and the She-Wolf: Two Stories, 1925), *Das Prisma: Erzählungen und Novellen* (The Prism: Short Stories and Novellas, 1925), *Der goldene Wagen: Legenden und Mythen* (The Golden Chariot: Legends and Myths, 1927), *Mitternacht: Zwölf Novellen* (Midnight: Twelve Novellas, 1928), *Das Opfertier* (The Sacrificial Animal, 1931), *Nachtschatten: Vier Novellen aus kriegerischen Zeiten* (Night Shadow: Four Novellas from Times of War, 1932), and *Die Geheimnisse* (The Enigmas, 1938). Like *Helianth,* these stories are characterized by complex symbolism, the use of interior monologue and dream, elements of the fantastic and surreal, and a wealth of images. A novel, *Die Schuldbrüder* (The Brothers of Shame), was published in 1926 and revised in 1928 as *Die Geschichte der Brüder Chamade* (The Story of the Brothers Chamade).

None of Schaeffer's works has been translated into English, despite their successful sales figures and repeated printings in Germany: By 1928, 14,000 copies of *Josef Montfort,* 13,000 of *Gudula oder Die Dauer des Lebens,* and 12,000 of

Einleitung

I.

1. Zu den Eigenschaften, die wir dem Menschen auf-
bürden glauben, gehört der Drang nach Wissen oder die
Wißbegier.
2. Dem ist aber nicht so. Bei näherem Zusehen finden
wir den Drang nach Wissen räumlich wie zeitlich beschränkt, nämlich auf den europäischen Menschen
bis zurück zum Griechen des 7ten vorchristlichen Jahrhunderts und der westasiatischen Mittelmeerküste.
Die ganze übrige Welt weiß von einem solchen Wis-
sensdrang, die materielle Welt zu erkennen, ins
Innere der Natur einzudringen, Nichts.
3. Auch die hellenische Leuchte des Forschungsdrangs,
die von Thales und Anaximander bis zu Aristoteles
brannte, erlosch wieder und wurde erst im 14. Jahrhundert fern im Norden wieder entzündet in den
Geistern Galileis und Keplers, seitdem sie nicht wieder
erloschen ist.
4. Hier beobachten wir das Phänomen, daß die Forschung
ihr Auge nicht auf das Nächste, sondern auf das
Fernste, nicht nach innen, in die Materie, sondern nach
außen in den Raum richtete: erst nachdem die Gesetze
des Kosmos erkannt waren, erst als der Mensch sich
im Himmelsraum orientiert und wohnlich gemacht hatte,
wandte er sich der Nähe und dem Innenraum der
Natur und seiner eigenen Physis zu, so als ob er die
biblische Schöpfung, an die er noch immer glaubte, wieder-
[illegible]

1

First page from the manuscript for Schaeffer's introduction to Mythos, *his collection of essays on the history of civilization (Albrecht Schaeffer,* Mythos, *edited by Walter Ehlers, 1958)*

Elli were in print. Even *Parzival,* a book published in deluxe editions, sold 6,000 copies by 1939.

Whenever Schaeffer was not occupied with a major work, he tried his hand at imitative poetry and translation, especially from the ancient Greek. The translations are often quite free and romanticized. He was especially attracted to the myth of the Odyssey and used motifs from the story of Ulysses' travels in a collection of poems, *Die Meerfahrt* (The Sea Voyage, 1912). In a later collection, *Der göttliche Dulder* (The Divine Sufferer, 1920), he combined these motifs with the Parzival theme. His retelling of the myth of Persephone, *Der Raub der Persefone* (The Abduction of Persephone), appeared in 1920. Schaeffer's translation of the *Odyssey* appeared in 1927, followed two years later by his translation of the *Iliad.* Two volumes of narrative, *Griechische Heldensagen* (Greek Heroic Myths), were published in 1929 and 1930. His adaptations from English include *Das Kleinod im Lotus: Die Buddha-Legende* (The Jewel in the Lotus Blossom: The Buddha Legend, 1923), based on Edwin Arnold's epic in blank verse *The Light of Asia; or, The Great Renunciation* (1879). He also translated Oscar Wilde's *The Ballad of Reading Gaol* (1898) as *Die Ballade vom Zuchthaus zu Reading* (1917), two stories by Robert Louis Stevenson (1925), and a novel by Frederic Prokosch (1952).

Schaeffer's first marriage ended in divorce in 1929, and his son Erwin remained with his mother. In 1931 Schaeffer moved to Rimsting, Bavaria, and married a Hungarian, Olga Elisabet Heymann. In 1933 he produced the historical novel *Der Roßkamm von Lemgo* (The Horse Dealer of Lemgo).

Schaeffer's success reached its peak just before the National Socialists seized power. Although Schaeffer was not Jewish and his books were not burned, he fell victim to the many restrictions imposed by the Nazi government. Schaeffer indirectly condemned the racist doctrines of the National Socialists in *Cara,* a novel about a marriage, published in 1936. In 1937 and 1938 Schaeffer wrote *Heile, heile Segen* and *Von Räubern und Riesen,* two volumes of Märchen (fairy tales) for the three children of his second marriage. The novel *Ruhland: Lebensbild eines Mannes* (Ruhland: Episodes from the Life of a Man, 1937) depicts the fate suffered by people who live on and around Ruhland, an old Prussian estate, during and after the Napoleonic era; the main character, the nobleman Monthier, is a gentle person who inspires goodness. Thematically *Ruhland* is in line with *Gudula oder Die Dauer des Lebens.*

The setting of the philosophical novel *Aphaia: Der Weg der Götter, Völker und Zahlen* (Aphaia: The Way of the Gods, Peoples, and Numbers, 1937) is Greece during the year after Socrates' death. The sculptor Parmenides and his young apprentice Nikitas build a temple to the mysterious goddess Aphaia on the island of Aigina. Much of the text is in the form of a Socratic dialogue between Plato and Parmenides.

In 1939 the Schaeffers went into voluntary exile to the United States with their children, Dirk, Angelika, and Veit (who later called himself David), and the two children of Olga's first marriage, Klaus and Marlies. The Nazis confiscated Schaeffer's library and papers. Friends provided a house for the family in Croton-on-Hudson, New York, where Olga Schaeffer established a preschool for immigrant children from German-speaking countries; most of the children were Jewish. Schaeffer was named honorary professor of literature at Oberlin College, a position supported by the Carl Schurz Memorial Foundation and the Emergency Committee for Displaced German Scholars, but when the United States entered World War II in 1941 the position was terminated. From 1941 until the late 1940s Schaeffer lived as a free-lance writer in Croton-on-Hudson. To find a quiet environment for his work he created a study in a remodeled garage in nearby Cornwall. He frequently commuted to New York to do research at the Columbia University library and tried to improve his English by studying British and American authors. Much of his time was devoted to the revision of his own works. New stories written during these years were published in German and German-American newspapers and other periodicals.

The most significant accomplishment of Schaeffer's years in exile is the novel *Rudolf Erzerum oder Des Lebens Einfachheit* (Rudolf Erzerum; or, Life's Simplicity, 1945), published by the Neuer Verlag in Stockholm, a firm that produced many works by displaced German writers. *Rudolf Erzerum,* narrated by the protagonist and title character, is, like *Helianth,* the novel of a seeker. It is also Schaeffer's most intense presentation of the various stages of the intellectual and ethical evolution of a young man. The novel begins with Schaeffer's version of two well-known verses from Schiller's poem *Das Lied von der Glocke* (The Song of the Bell). The first word of

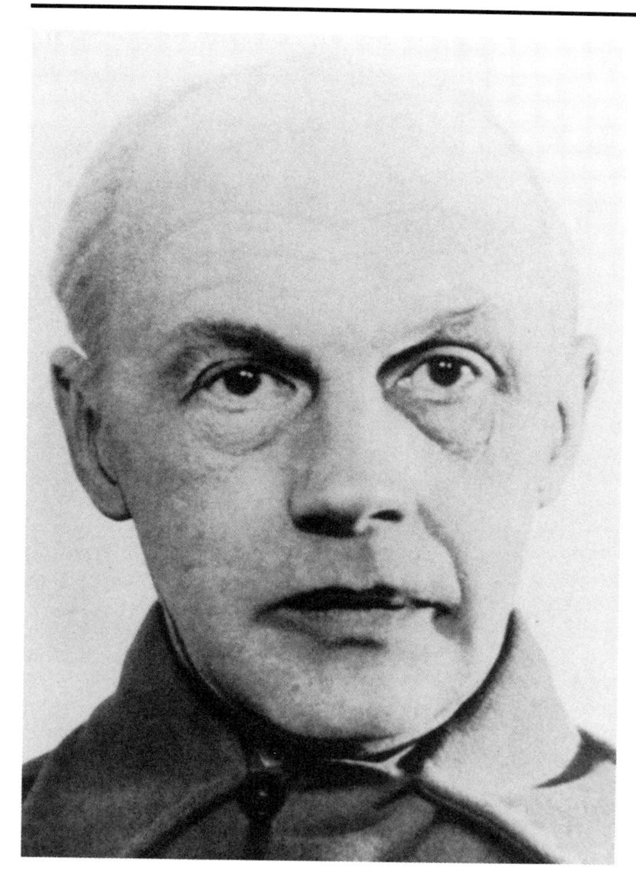

Schaeffer in later life

Schiller's verse, *Freude* (joy), has been changed to *Friede* (peace); and *Stadt* (city) becomes *Welt* (world), endowing the lines with a more universal meaning: "Friede dieser Welt bedeute,/Friede sei ihr erst' Geläute" (May peace be its first peal, peace to this world). The plot unfolds in Germany shortly after 1800, during the Napoleonic wars, but flashbacks include the United States and several European countries. This novel brings the reassuring message that there is hope for a rebirth of the human spirit after the deep, dark night of nihilism.

Janna du Coeur (1949) is a thoroughgoing revision of *Der Roßkamm von Lemgo* (The Horse Dealer of Lemgo). The revised version has as its focal point the beautiful heiress Janna du Coeur, the daughter of an English father and a German mother. The eventful life and the intellectual and ethical development of the heroine unfold in Cromwell's England and in Germany after the Thirty Years' War, a time of devastation often compared to the post-World War II period. Bertold Biermann, writing for *Die Welt* (28 September 1949), noted that the form of the work did not resemble that of the traditional novel. The novel did not find an enthusiastic audience.

In 1949 and 1950 two more volumes of Schaeffer's short fiction appeared. Some of the texts included in these collections are revisions of earlier ones. The longest narrative of the volume *Der Auswanderer* (The Emigrant, 1949) is "Joe: Porträt eines Amerikaners" (Joe: Portrait of an American), which was first published in the New York *Staatszeitung und Herold* in 1947; it is the heartwarming story of a simple but wise handyman. The volume of parables *Die goldene Klinke* (The Golden Doorknob, 1950) is a revised and enlarged version of the *Die Geheimnisse*.

During the last thirteen years of Schaeffer's life he worked on a philosophical history of civilization, "Die Schöpfungsgeschichte der Menschheit" (The History of Mankind's Creativity). About a fourth of the manuscript was published posthumously under the title *Mythos: Abhandlungen über die kulturellen Grundlagen der Menschheit* (Mythos: Treatise on the Cultural Foundations of Humanity, 1958).

Some of the dialogues from "Die Schöpfungsgeschichte der Menschheit" appear in the narrative *Enak oder Das Auge Gottes* (Enoch; or, God's Eye, 1948), which was first published in the periodical *Das Silberboot: Zeitschrift für Literatur* (1947). The story was praised for its clear style. Like several of his previous works, *Enak oder Das Auge Gottes* reveals Schaeffer's predilection for myth and his religious concerns, especially his interest in the Old Testament. The protagonist is a "reversed Job" who makes unwarranted demands; God destroys him by granting these demands.

Olga Schaeffer died in 1947, and the school she had administered for eight years had to be closed. In January 1948 Schaeffer moved to New York. Book sales were poor in Germany during the postwar years: the four occupying powers kept strict control over all cultural institutions and enterprises, especially publishing; moreover, paper was in extremely short supply. By 1950 the financial situation of the exiled author, who was living on welfare in a shabby New York boardinghouse, had grown desperate, and his friends helped to arrange his return to Germany. Schaeffer was made a member of the Mainz Akademie der Wissenschaften und Literatur (Academy of Sciences and Literature) and, on 23 November, was honored with the Literaturpreis des Landes Niedersachsen (Literature Prize of Lower Saxony). Less than two weeks later, on 4 December 1950, he died of a heart attack in Munich. His writings are considered to be of major importance for scholars interested in the literature and thought of the early twentieth century; the debates about *Helianth* are regarded as a prelude to the debates on expressionism of the late 1930s.

References:

Eduard Berend, "Die Technik der Darstellung in der Erzählung," *Germanisch-Romanische Monatsschrift,* 14 (1926): 222-233;

W. A. Berendsohn, "Schaeffers Dichtung *Der göttliche Dulder,*" *Neue Jahrbücher für Philologie und Pädagogik* (1924): 184-197;

Guido K. Brand, "Albrecht Schaeffers *Helianth* oder Vom Wege zur Vollendung," *Das literarische Echo,* 24 (1921-1922): 136-142;

Walter Breuer, "Begegnung und Selbstbegegnung in Albrecht Schaeffers *Helianth,*" Ph.D. dissertation, University of Bonn, 1961;

Kurt Busse, "Albrecht Schaeffer," *Preußische Jahrbücher,* 202 (1925): 357-370;

Max Fischer, "Erinnerung an Albrecht Schaeffer," *Das literarische Deutschland,* 7 (5 April 1951);

Ingrid Hausmann, "Die Erzählhaltung in Albrecht Schaeffers *Helianth:* Bauform, Sprachform, Symbolform," Ph.D. dissertation, University of Cologne, 1961;

Rudolf Ibel, "Albrecht Schaeffers Parzival-Epos. Ein Brief," *Der Kreis: Zeitschrift für künstlerische Kultur,* 9 (1922): 633-637;

Otto Koischwitz, "Albrecht Schaeffers *Helianth,*" *Germanic Review,* 3, no. 2 (1928): 149-167;

Ernst Kreuder, "Nachruf auf Albrecht Schaeffer," *Akademie der Wissenschaften und der Literatur* (1951): 133-142;

Rosemarie Lorenz and Werner Volke, eds., *Albrecht Schaeffer, 1885-1950: Gedächtnisausstellung zum 75. Geburtstag des Dichters* (Marbach am Neckar: Schiller-Nationalmuseum, 1961);

Peter H. Madler, "Das Bildungsgut in Albrecht Schaeffers *Helianth,*" Ph.D. dissertation, Graz University, 1956;

Alfred Mohrhenn, "Albrecht Schaeffer," *Elbinger Hefte,* 7 (1951): 57ff.;

Walter Muschg, *Der dichterische Charakter: Eine Studie über Albrecht Schaeffers "Helianth"* (Berlin: Junker & Dünnhaupt, 1929);

Karl Ludwig Schneider, "Ich blieb was ich war: Ein letztes Interview mit Albrecht Schaeffer," *Das literarische Deutschland: Zeitung der Deutschen Akademie für Sprache und Dichtung,* 1 (December 1950): 3;

Ingeborg Solbrig, "Roß, Reiter und Stern: Zu einem vergessenen Schriftsteller des Exils," in *Akten des VI. Internationalen Germanisten-Kongresses Basel 1980* (Bern: Lang, 1980), pp. 279-285;

Solbrig, "Zu Albrecht Schaeffers Kurznovelle *Die Rosse der Hedschra,*" *Germanic Notes,* 9, no. 1-2 (1978): 2-5;

Leo Spitzer, "Vergleich des Proust'schen Stils mit dem Albrecht Schaeffers," in his *Stilstudien,* volume 2 (Munich: Hueber, 1928), pp. 473ff.;

Ludwig Strauß, "Schaeffers Odyssee," *Die Horen,* 3 (1927): 464-472;

Werner Vortriede, "Albrecht Schaeffer oder die Symbole in Exil," *Neue deutsche Hefte,* 7 (1960-1961): 879-888;

Oscar Walzel, "Albrecht Schaeffer," *Germanisch-Romanische Monatsschrift,* 10 (1922): 150-162; 213-220;

Hans Wolffheim, "Sprache der Wirklichkeit: Zum Werke Albrecht Schaeffers," *Die Sammlung: Zeitschrift für Kultur und Erziehung,* 6 (1951): 181-185.

Papers:

Albrecht Schaeffer's papers are at the Deutsches Literaturarchiv, Marbach am Neckar, Federal Republic of Germany.

René Schickele

(4 August 1883-31 January 1940)

Paul Kurt Ackermann
Boston University

BOOKS: *Sommernächte: Gedichte* (Strasbourg: Beust, 1902);

Pan: Sonnenopfer der Jugend (Strasbourg: Singer, 1902);

Mon Repos (Berlin: Seemann, 1905);

Der Ritt ins Leben (Stuttgart & Berlin: Juncker, 1906);

Der Fremde (Berlin: Morgen, 1909);

Weiß und Rot: Gedichte (Berlin: Cassirer, 1910; enlarged, 1920);

Meine Freundin Lo: Geschichte aus Paris (Leipzig: Verlag der weißen Bücher, 1911);

Das Glück (Berlin: Juncker, 1913);

Schreie auf dem Boulevard (Berlin: Cassirer, 1913);

Benkal, der Frauentröster: Roman (Leipzig: Verlag der weißen Bücher, 1914);

Die Leibwache: Gedichte (Leipzig: Verlag der weißen Bücher, 1914);

Trimpopp und Manasse: Eine Erzählung (Leipzig: Verlag der weißen Bücher, 1914);

Mein Herz, mein Land: Ausgewählte Gedichte (Leipzig & Berlin: Cassirer, 1915);

Aïssé: Novelle (Leipzig: Wolff, 1915);

Hans im Schnakenloch: Schauspiel in vier Aufzügen (Leipzig & Berlin: Cassirer, 1917);

Die Genfer Reise (Berlin: Cassirer, 1919);

Der neunte November (Berlin: Reiss, 1919);

Der deutsche Träumer (Zurich: Rascher, 1919);

Am Glockenturm: Schauspiel in drei Aufzügen (Berlin: Cassirer, 1920);

Die Mädchen: Drei Erzählungen (Berlin: Cassirer, 1920);

Wir wollen nicht sterben! (Munich: Wolff, 1922);

Die neuen Kerle: Komödie in drei Aufzügen (Basel: Rhein-Verlag, 1924);

Ein Erbe am Rhein: Roman in zwei Bänden, 2 volumes (Munich: Wolff, 1925); republished as *Maria Capponi: Roman,* volume 1 of *Das Erbe am Rhein: Roman* (Munich: Wolff, 1926); translated by Hannah Waller (New York: Knopf, 1928);

Blick auf die Vogesen: Roman, volume 2 of *Das Erbe am Rhein* (Munich: Wolff, 1927); translated by Waller as *Heart of Alsace* (New York: Knopf, 1929);

Soeur Ignace: Ein elsässisches Vergißmeinnicht aus der Kongregation der Niederbronner Schwestern (Mühlhausen: Salvator-Verlag, 1928);

Symphonie für Jazz: Roman (Berlin: Fischer, 1929);

Elsässische Fioretti aus den Missionen: Lebensbild elsässischer Missionsschwestern (Colmar: Verlag Alsatia, 1930);

Der Wolf in der Hürde: Roman, volume 3 of *Das Erbe am Rhein* (Berlin: Fischer, 1931);

Die Grenze (Berlin: Rowohlt, 1932);

Himmlische Landschaft (Berlin: Fischer, 1933);

Die Witwe Bosca: Roman (Berlin: Fischer, 1933);

Liebe und Ärgernis des D. H. Lawrence (Amsterdam: de Lange, 1934);

Die Flaschenpost: Roman (Amsterdam: de Lange, 1937);

Le Retour: Souvenirs inédits (Paris: Fayard, 1938); translated by Ferdinand Hardekopf as *Die Heimkehr* (Strasbourg: Brant, 1939);

Werke in drei Bänden, edited by Hermann Kesten and Anna Schickele (Cologne & Berlin: Kiepenheuer & Witsch, 1960-1961).

OTHER: Honoré de Balzac, *Menschliche Komödie,* volume 10: *Die Lilie im Tal; Die verlassene Frau,* translated by Schickele (Leipzig: Insel, 1910);

Europäische Bibliothek, 11 volumes, edited by Schickele (Zurich: Rascher, 1918-1919);

Gustave Flaubert, *Werke,* volume 1: *Madame Bovary: Sittenbilder aus der Provinz,* translated by Schickele (Minden & Leipzig: Grethlein, 1928);

Das Vermächtnis: Deutsche Gedichte von Walther von der Vogelweide bis Nietzsche, edited by Schickele (Amsterdam: de Lange, 1938; entire edition confiscated and destroyed; republished, Freiburg: Herder, 1948).

René Schickele's literary reputation probably rests less on the success of any particular work than on his total achievement as a man of let-

René Schickele in 1929 (Ullstein)

ters. He was born in Alsace, the "heavenly landscape," as he called it, between the Black Forest and the Vosges mountains, a region that had been disputed territory and a battleground between France and Germany for many centuries. Since much of his work reflects the complicated and sometimes painful cultural and political situation of Alsace, Schickele is often thought of as an Alsatian writer. Thomas Mann, for instance, referred to Schickele's trilogy, *Das Erbe am Rhein* (The Heritage on the Rhine, 1925-1931), as the standard work of the Alsatian soul. Far from succumbing to provincialism, however, Schickele treated the plight of his country as an important international matter. "Das Elsaß ist für mich keine provinzielle Angelegenheit," he wrote, "sondern der Prüfstein für die Beziehungen zwischen Deutschland und Frankreich, die meiner Ansicht nach–besonders kulturell–das Schicksal Europas bestimmen" (Alsace is no provincial matter for me but a testing ground between Germany and France which, as I see it, will determine–particularly in cultural matters–the destiny of Europe).

He is today primarily remembered in connection with the literary journal *Die weißen Blätter*, which he edited brilliantly in Switzerland during World War I. He made it a forum for critical opinion on contemporary affairs and a leading magazine of literary expressionism; the works of many expressionists, including Kasimir Edschmid and Gottfried Benn, were published in its pages. He also published the early works of young, not yet well-known writers, among them Franz Kafka, Franz Werfel, and Walter Hasenclever. The expressionists' aesthetic and political ideas resem-

Manuscript for a poem by Schickele (Frau Anna Schickele, Badenweiler)

bled Schickele's in many ways; like them, he believed that literature and politics belong together and that writers and intellectuals should be involved in political affairs. In *Die weißen Blätter* he became a spokesman for antimilitarism, pacifism, and international reconciliation.

In style and content, some of Schickele's literary works also show the characteristics of expressionism. Two early novels, *Der Fremde* (The Stranger, 1909) and *Benkal, der Frauentröster* (Benkal, Consoler of Women, 1914) are precursors of expressionism in form and spirit. Even his last two novels, *Die Witwe Bosca* (The Widow Bosca, 1933) and *Die Flaschenpost* (The Letter in the Bottle, 1937), bear traces of that style. The manifestations of expressionism in his works are balanced, however, by mellower qualities–an aversion to extremes in style and form and a native elegance.

Today, some of his books appear dated. Fundamentally opposing styles, impressionism and expressionism, vie with one another in individual works. Two antagonistic attitudes–brilliant intellectuality and idealistic naïveté–emerge throughout and vex the reader. Nevertheless, the integrity and substance of his thought remain relevant. His best novels have a unique quality, of which Mann wrote: "Seine Bücher sind innerhalb unserer Prosa etwas absolut Ausserordentliches an Geist und Grazie, welche ihr französisches Erbteil darstellen, während eine gewisse Naturhaftigkeit, eine Verbundenheit mit Erde und Landschaft, die bis zum Panischen geht, als ihre deutsche Komponente betrachtet werden mag, die seiner Leichtigkeit Tiefe und Schwere, seiner Geistigkeit oft einen Anhauch von Dämonie verleiht" (In our prose, his books are something absolutely extraordinary in regard to spirit and gracefulness. These represent his French heritage, while a certain naturalness, a closeness to earth and landscape which approaches the realm of Pan, can be regarded as the German component. The latter imparts depth and weight to his agility and often lends a touch of the demonic to his intellectuality).

Schickele was born on 4 August 1883 in the village of Oberehnheim (French Obernai), the second son of Anton Schickele and Marie Férard, a Frenchwoman from Fontaine, Doubs. Schickele's ancestors had emigrated from Switzerland to Alsace, where they had established vineyards at Mutzig, near Strasbourg. Schickele's father had served in the French army in two wars, and his experiences had made him a pacifist. He had returned to his Mutzig vineyards convinced of the necessity of friendship between France and Germany. When Alsace became German after 1870, he entered politics. Because he was intelligent, spoke German and French, and knew local conditions and problems, he was elected Kantonskommissar; but after one term of office he had had enough of politics and returned to his grapes. He lived to be eighty. Schickele's mother was a simple, religious woman who lived a long life without ever learning German. She did not take her son's literary career seriously, and when he was elected to the Prussian Academy she thought someone had made a mistake.

Since his mother knew no German, French was spoken at home, and Schickele considered it his mother tongue. But he preferred German. "Die Sprache ist ein besonderer Saft," he wrote, "viel mehr als Blut. Ich weiß es, gerade weil das Deutsch *nicht* meine Muttersprache ist" (Language is a very particular fluid, much more so than blood. I know it especially well, because German is *not* my mother tongue). Precisely because German was the acquired language, it seemed more thrilling. When he entered the gymnasium he could hardly speak it; after a few years he could express important, personal thoughts only in German.

A bilingual poet has a serious problem, Schickele thought; only one language will serve for creative purposes. "Jeder Mensch darf auf zwei oder mehr Sprachen leben, nur nicht der Dichter. Die Sprache des Dichters vermittelt nicht Gedachtes allein, sie stellt, in einmaliger Form, einen Menschen dar, sie ist sein Bild, an die Wand einer bestimmten Sprache geworfen" (Every person may live in two or more languages, but not the poet. The language of the poet does not only convey thoughts, it represents in a unique form a human being; it is his image thrown against the screen of a particular language).

In 1901 he enrolled at the University of Strasbourg, where he met several other students who were interested in literature and who, like him, had already published an occasional poem or review. Together, they founded the magazine *Der Stürmer,* with Schickele as editor. They were hoping to promote a cultural renaissance in Alsace, but the public and the press were indifferent. By the end of 1902 the magazine's financial position had become shaky, and *Der Stürmer* ceased publication with the ninth number. An attempt to resume cultural criticism in another new periodical, *Der Merker,* failed.

Schickele spent the fall of 1903 in Paris, where he studied at the Sorbonne. At Christmas, feeling lonely, he visited an old friend, Hans Brandenburg, in Barmen and fell in love with Brandenburg's sister Anna. They were married a year later and settled in Berlin, where Schickele be-

Dust jacket for Schickele's last novel, a quixotic comedy in the form of a madman's diary

came the editor of *Das neue Magazine.* His first novel, *Der Fremde,* was published in 1909.

The main character in the book is a young Alsatian, Paul Merkel, who grows up in the confusing political situation after the Franco-Prussian War. He does not know where he belongs and feels estranged. There are traces here of Maurice Barrès's *Les Déracinés* (1897), a book Schickele had probably read. Each writer grew up in a border area and was attracted by the problem of the uprooted individual who has lost his spiritual fatherland. Both created protagonists who are artistic individuals of melancholic sensuality and who thirst for fame and love. Somewhat in the tradition of the bildungsroman, Merkel sets out on a spiritual journey as a "Pilger der Ekstase" (pilgrim of ecstasy). He is subjected to experiences which are meant to bring about his spiritual growth and to result in a deeper understanding of his own psyche. But the book suffers as a novel of education because Schickele was too young when he wrote it: the level of maturity and spiritual growth Merkel achieves is a reflection of the maturity which Schickele had himself attained. The reader is by no means convinced of the finality of Merkel's education. It is typical of Schickele's writing in this period that the novel's style is often rhapsodic; the prevailing mystical and exalted mood lies heavily on the pages.

On the whole, *Der Fremde* received favorable reviews. C. Buchholtz in *März* (December 1913) called it one of the most beautiful books of the last decade, "der Roman der elsäßischen Seele" (the novel of the Alsatian soul); he particularly praised Schickele's style. In contrast, K. H. Maurer in *Das literarische Echo* (15 March 1910) found fault with the "decadent" Paul Merkel and considered the book "unsympathisch." The novel established Schickele as a promising young writer, and his financial situation as well as his professional reputation improved notably. He had been contributing to esoteric magazines and small newspapers, but now periodicals and newspapers with national circulations began to accept everything he sent them.

In 1909 Schickele went to Paris as a correspondent for the *Straßburger neue Zeitung*. He found no incongruity in his double position as poet and journalist; to him journalism was a valid literary occupation and, even more, a way of life. His best pieces, collected in *Schreie auf dem Boulevard* (Cries on the Boulevard, 1913), include impressions of political leaders such as Jean Léon Jaurès, Aristide Briand, and Theodore Roosevelt; accounts of strikes and demonstrations; and vignettes of Parisian society. He used some of this material as background in his novel *Meine Freundin Lo* (My Girlfriend Lo, 1911).

Schickele's Paris of 1910 is gracefully recreated in this novel, which is perhaps his most popular book and was published in four editions during his lifetime. Lo is a young, attractive actress of the Théâtre Grand Guignol who is surrounded by admirers. The narrator, Henri Daul, is her lover when the story opens. Henri is an Alsatian journalist who covers political events in the French capital when he is not busy attending to Lo. His friends include Lo's former lover, the poet Variot, as well as a rising political star, Emile Cunin, who succeeds Henri in Lo's favor. Henri acquiesces in the inevitability of the loss of Lo's love. In pursuit of his journalistic endeavors, Henri takes the reader on a guided tour of Parisian nightlife, the Chamber of Deputies, Les Halles, an aviation event, and the like. The appealing characterization of an emancipated Parisian woman combined with the evocation of the Parisian ambience probably accounts for the novel's popularity. In every respect, the work is a complete change from *Der Fremde*.

In Paris Schickele also completed a volume of poetry, *Weiß und Rot* (White and Red, 1910). The work was devastatingly criticized in *Das literarische Echo* (15 June 1911) by Ernst Lissauer, who called the poetry "im allerhöchsten Masse unerfreulich, unsympathisch und unkünstlerisch" (extremely unpleasant, uncongenial, and lacking in artistry). He called Schickele "instinktlos" (lacking in intuition), "ein Dilletant," and a "Sonntagsreiter" (rank amateur). In contrast, Ernst Stadler, in the same periodical (1 June 1911), had praised the collection as "ein Buch eines im tiefsten künstlerisch empfindenden Menschen" (a book of a man with profound artistic sensibilities).

Schickele left Paris in 1911. After two years in Strasbourg as editor of the *Straßburger neue Zeitung* he moved to Fürstenberg, near Berlin, and joined the staff of the Berlin literary periodical *Die weißen Blätter,* which had recently been founded by Franz Blei and Erik Ernst Schwabach. In 1914 he published *Benkal, der Frauentröster,* a short novel consisting of twenty-eight loosely connected chapters, one of which is a play in four scenes entitled "Das tote Kind" (The Dead Child). The narrative line is somewhat difficult to follow, but the novel achieves its unity through its emotional intensity. At times it seems to be a veiled autobiography.

The events take place at an unspecified time in a country called "Mittelland" which lies between countries inhabited by the "Kremmen" on one side, and the "Langnasen" on the other. War breaks out, followed by rebellion. Eventually peace is restored. The central figure is a sculptor, Benkal, who begins as an unconventional young man and ends as an old and lonely artist. Benkal loves women, and they love him. It is woman as such who inspires his art; his passions are easily transferable: "Nichts anderes sah er, während er viele Liebschaften hatte, von denen er nur verlangte, daß sie ihn mit der Atmosphäre der Frau umgaben. Er suchte keine. Nur die Frauen waren einander so ähnlich" (He saw nothing else, while he had many love affairs of which he only demanded that they surround him with the ambience of woman. He was looking for none. But women resembled each other so much). His loves have strange names: there is Kru; Hahna, his first mistress; Gugu, his model; and Ij, the passionate great dancer who seems to him "ein weißes Tier mit einer Feuermähne. . . . Ihre graublauen Augen, in denen plötzlich rote Funken regnen konnten, hielten immer stand, ihre spitzen Brüste rührten sich nicht" (A white animal with a fiery mane. . . . Her gray-blue eyes, into which suddenly red sparks could rain, were never averted, her pointed breasts never moved). A host of women are enriched and "consoled" by Benkal and find their own authenticity in his embraces.

Benkal, der Frauentröster is a work of literary expressionism. Schickele attempts to find the most intense expressions possible to convey the book's emotional convictions. The vocabulary abounds in words typical of expressionist writers, such as "taumeln" (to reel), "schreien" (to scream), "aufgepeitscht" (whipped up), "überbieten" (to surpass), "irrsinnig" (mad). But Schickele is not consistent: pathos and irony alternate in rapid succession, and matter-of-factness alternates with grandiose epic prose.

Contemporary critics such as Kurt Pinthus in *Zeitschrift der Bücherfreunde* (January 1914) found in Schickele's style a new direction, a new narrative technique. Ernst Stadler in *Die Aktion* (1914) drew attention to Schickele's view of woman as a synthesis of *eros* and *nous*. In general, however, critical reception of *Benkal, der Frauentröster* was negative. In twenty years less than one thousand copies were sold.

Aïssé (1915), written after a trip to India, is the often told story of the eighteenth-century Circassian girl who was bought by the French envoy at Constantinople and taken to Paris, where she caused excitement in society by her beauty, natural charm, and exotic origin. Schickele uses this biography as background for a story about transmigration of souls. Aïssé is the image of the ideal beloved, a figure that haunted him all his life; even twenty years later, he mentioned her in his diaries: "Die Gestalt der Aïssé verließ mich nie. Jedesmal, wenn ich nach Beendigung einer Arbeit um mich blickte, stand sie am Weg, ein nacktes, braunes Mädchen, das mit dem Arm die Augen verbirgt" (The figure of Aïssé never left me. Every time I looked around me after finishing some work, she stood there at the roadside, a naked, brown girl who hid her face in her arm).

The collection of narratives *Die Mädchen* (The Maidens, 1920) was written in memory of an excursion to the Acropolis. Schickele was impressed by the sensuality of the caryatids of the Erechthion and by the feeling of "Sehnsucht" (yearning) they provoked in him. *Die Genfer Reise* (Journey to Geneva, 1919) is made up of essays, impressions, and lyrical descriptions, while *Wir wollen nicht sterben!* (We Don't Want to Die!, 1922) is a collection of political reflections. The books contain essays on France, Dostoyevski, and the "Good European." These pieces and his contributions to *Die weißen Blätter*, written between 1914 and 1922, are largely concerned with pacifism. For Schickele, pacifism was an attitude toward life and not a political strategy. It was synonymous with nonviolence, and it was radical. As he wrote in *Die Genfer Reise*, "Es gibt einen unverrückbaren, einen absoluten Punkt in unserem Lebensplan, wenn ich so sagen darf, die Weigerung zu töten" (There is an immovable point in the design of our life, if I may put it so, the refusal to kill). He was opposed to all forms of violence and oppression.

Yet violence and the need for power, he wrote in the play *Am Glockenturm* (At the Bell Tower, 1920), drive us all: "Die Menschen können einander nicht in Ruhe lassen. Sie verlangen in hundert Formen Gewalt übereinander" (People cannot leave each other in peace. In a hundred ways they want power over each other). In socialism he saw the political consequence and practical application of pacifism. He was convinced that the capitalist system of domestic and foreign "competitive exploitation" should be abolished. But even socialism was no guarantee of peace if it was not founded on morality. He distrusted Bolshevists because their reliance on force destroyed socialism's moral foundations.

Schickele's first literary production after the outbreak of World War I was the drama *Hans im Schnakenloch* (Hans in the Gnathole, 1917). "Ich habe den Hans lange vor dem Krieg in mir getragen" (I carried Hans within me for some time before the war), he wrote. The events of 1914 brought the problems of the play into sharp focus and heightened their relevance. As in previous works the main character, an Alsatian, suffers from the duality that life between French and German cultures has imposed upon him, and he deeply resents his predicament. The outbreak of the war brings his problems to a climax and forces decisions; his marriage is destroyed and his family is torn apart.

Schickele in 1932 (Ullstein)

Schickele intended to write a play about marriage in the psychologically and politically complex setting of Alsace. *Hans im Schnakenloch* became notorious, however, as an antiwar play. In fact, it is tendentious only in that it advocates peace, particularly between France and Germany. "Ich kann versichern, daß mir nichts ferner lag, als eine Gesinning zu proklamieren. Dazu habe ich nie die geringste Begabung gehabt" (I can assure you, that nothing lay farther from my intent, than to proclaim a political conviction. I never had the slightest talent for that), Schickele wrote in *Das literarische Echo* (1 June 1917).

French pacifists, among them Romain Rolland, were offended by the play because the French characters seemed negatively portrayed; besides, by implication, the play took a German victory for granted. Probably for this reason the German officials at first approved the play; but when the prospect of victory had dimmed in 1917, they forbade it on grounds that it undermined the fighting spirit of the troops.

In general critics reviewed the play favorably, although they were more concerned with the message they perceived in it than with its intrinsic dramatic qualities. Some wrote that Schickele had succeeded in creating a drama of the World War that had universal validity; others saw it as the drama of the "Alsatian soul." Hans Franck in *Das literarische Echo* (15 December 1916) made the point that Schickele was a "Grenzfall" (borderline case) in that he was both essayist and dramatist, journalist and poet. He saw the conflict between poet and journalist as a flaw in Schickele's artistry.

Schickele had become editor of *Die weißen Blätter* in 1915. To avoid increasingly vigilant censorship, the editorial offices were moved in 1916 to Switzerland. Schickele and his family settled in Zurich, then moved to Geneva. Because of extreme nearsightedness, he had been exempted from military service.

Under Schickele's editorship, *Die weißen Blätter* was a forum for literary criticism and contemporary, often expressionist, fiction and poetry. More than a mere literary journal, *Die weißen Blätter* advocated an antimilitarist, pacifist philosophy. Since German victory seemed almost inevitable to them in the early part of the war, the politically enlightened intellectuals associated with *Die weißen Blätter* were in favor of a postwar German diplomacy of international reconciliation and good will, and they tried to influence their readers in that direction. There was much discussion in the opinion columns of the magazine about "Imperialismus des Geistes" (imperialism of the spirit) and whether the sword is to be used in the service of the spirit or the other way around. Schickele fought in *Die weißen Blätter* against those intellectual superpatriots who saw the war as a "heroic necessity," a "gift of the heavens," and an "instrument for national purification and dedication." As the war dragged on, articles and commentaries increasingly attacked chauvinism and "Hurrah-Patriotismus." Opposition to the war became more radical and criticism of German institutions increased. Schickele's commentaries became more and more explicitly pacifistic; he now believed war to be a projection of man's internal conflicts.

Shortly after the end of World War I publication of *Die weißen Blätter* ceased. Having become a French citizen with the ceding of Alsace to France, Schickele built a house in German Badenweiler, where the mountains of the Black Forest slope down into the valley of the Rhine and where he could see the outline of the French Vosges mountains in the distance. The landscape, the people, and the recent history of Alsace provide the foundation of his trilogy *Das Erbe am Rhein*. However much the characters in the work follow their private interests, they are all touched by and often inextricably bound to the fate of their native Alsace. A record of the historical and political events in Alsace in the years following World War I makes up the rough fabric of the trilogy. Historical personages are recognizable under assumed names. The French occupation of the Ruhr and the arrest of the Alsatian autonomist leaders in 1923 are specifically described. Schickele chronicles the Alsatians' initial delight with the French and their subsequent disappointments.

The young Alsatian nobleman Claus von Breuschheim, the hero of the trilogy, is typical of his countrymen in his fierce attachment to his homeland. Despite his cosmopolitan temper and his many travels, his deepest roots remain in the soil of the Rhine valley. He represents both the Alsatian national character in all its complexities and an Alsatian ideal: a man close to his native landscape and to its human problems, a pacifist, a humanist, and a world citizen.

The first volume of the trilogy, *Maria Capponi* (1926; first published in 1925 as *Ein Erbe am Rhein;* translated in 1928 as *Maria Capponi*) tells of Claus's love for his German wife, Doris, and for his childhood friend and later mistress, the Italian Maria Capponi. He travels back and forth from the Riviera and Maria to the Rhine and Doris. His inability to choose between the southern Maria and the northern Doris reflects the Alsatian's mentality, which is said to suffer from similar difficulties of choice in regard to France and Germany. The most lyrical passages of *Maria Capponi* are not the passionate confessions of love for Maria or Doris but the evocations of the French and south German landscape. These descriptions are remarkably vivid.

In the second volume, *Blick auf die Vogesen* (View from the Vosges, 1927; translated as *Heart of Alsace,* 1929), Schickele describes the bitter awakening in Alsace after the enthusiasm of the French "liberation" in 1918 wears off: the growing mistrust, the unrest of the population that was to culminate in the aspiration for Alsatian autonomy. Claus, searching for inner peace, returns with his young son to the ancient family seat to build a new life. A conflict develops with his half-brother Ernst, a former German officer who buried his uniform after 1918 and became a French patriot. Secretly Ernst suffers from a renegade's bad conscience, and he eventually commits suicide. A penetrating analysis of a turncoat, his story touches the pathological side of the Alsatian mentality.

Set in Nice, Geneva, and Alsace, the third volume, *Der Wolf in der Hürde* (The Wolf in the Fold, 1931), concerns the spiritual destruction of the poet Aggie Ruf through her love for a ruthlessly ambitious Alsatian politician. The seduction of Aggie takes place gradually, through a loss of intellectual and spiritual innocence that transforms her from a gentle pacifist into a Marxist revolutionary. In the end she dies in an accident.

Claus, whose activities were at the center of the first two volumes, is the narrator of the third. His role in the plot is minor: he functions as Schickele's spokesman, and his philosophical pronouncements refute Aggie's ideology of violence. It is not political wisdom that Schickele's Alsatian hero has attained at the end; instead, he has discovered that happiness and his personal God are to be found in closeness to nature and to the native landscape. He says: "Was bleibt? Es bleibt, heute wie gestern, der in seiner Klarheit einmalige, stets erneuerte Mensch und die ewig schöpferische Natur–und die Zwiesprache zwischen den beiden. Manche nennen sie die Gegenwart Gottes" (What remains? What remains is the clear, unique, constantly renewed human being and eternally creative nature–and the dialogue between the two. Some call that the presence of God).

The novel *Symphonie für Jazz* (1929), written as a diversion while Schickele was working on *Der Wolf in der Hürde,* attempts to portray the moral and intellectual condition of European society after World War I. Marital problems, controversies over art and politics, social criticism, psychoanalysis, painfully contrived erotic situations, and lyric interludes are thrown together helter-skelter. The book is perhaps Schickele's least successful novel and is more outdated than any of the others because of its clichés and stereotypes.

A second collection of sketches, familiar essays, and fragments, *Die Grenze* (The Border, 1932) includes a penetrating essay on Romain Rolland, aphoristic notes, and short comments on his current reading. Some pieces are biographical, chronicling Schickele's life in Badenweiler.

In the fall of 1932 Schickele and his family moved to the south of France, living first in the Mediterranean fishing village Sanary-sur-Mer and finally in Vence, near Nice. He had observed the rise of the National Socialist party with apprehension and considered the movement a disaster. There was no political necessity for Schickele to leave Germany; as a French citizen, he had thought it prudent to stay out of German politics and had not engaged in political polemics. His exile was purely voluntary. The immediate reason to leave was his desire to spend the winter in the warmer French climate. Schickele did not sell his property in Badenweiler, but he never again saw his house or the Alsatian countryside.

The most satisfactory form for Schickele's descriptions of nature is the intimate impressionistic sketch, a number of which are collected in *Himmlische Landschaft* (Heavenly Landscape, 1933). In exquisitely lyrical prose he evokes the color and luster of flowers, the supple shapes of clouds, the capacious sweeping folds of distant mountains, and the limpidity of spring water. The countryside becomes alive. Attainment of happiness, he says, is in direct proportion to man's closeness to nature: "Um das Maß der Unschuld, der Glücksfähigkeit in sich zu ermessen, trete man vor die Landschaft" (In order to gauge the degree of your innocence, your talent for happiness, just confront the landscape). He shows in this work a high degree of craftsmanship which never allows the sumptuousness of his impressions to become mawkish. Of all his characters, Schickele said, the landscape is the most dramatic.

Schickele began work on *Die Witwe Bosca* almost immediately after settling in Sanary-sur-Mer, where most of the events of the book take place. The novel is essentially a record of spiritual and mental suffering. The widow Bosca's nineteen-year-old daughter, Sybille, is hit by a bus and crippled. At the scene of the accident she is cared for by a young man, Paul Tavin, who lives with his mother next door. The two fall in love. Paul goes to Paris, takes a mistress, then returns to Sybille. In an automobile accident she is killed, but Paul survives. A parallel plot concerns the courtship and second marriage of the widow Bosca with the notary Burguburu, who eventually strangles her but is acquitted of the crime.

Schickele contrasts two worlds: the sphere of the widow Bosca, which is dark and demonic, and the bright and happy world of the Tavins. The novel receives much of its unity from descriptions of the Provençal landscape.

Die Witwe Bosca is characteristic of Schickele's last period, showing the final development of the rich musical quality and refinement of his style. But Schickele was aware of the dangers this style represented. In his diary he wrote: "Ich darf unter keinen Umständen in der Glätte, dem Musikalischen der Sprache weitergehn. Sonst wird aus der Buhlerei mit der Sprache Unzucht. Ich bin nicht mit ihr zur Welt gekommen, habe sie mir erst als Geliebte gewählt" (I must under no circumstance heighten the smoothness, the musicality of the language. Otherwise my love affair with language becomes lechery. I was not born with it; I have chosen it as my mistress).

Schickele's avowed intention in the novel is to show the power of evil by which the devil perverts his erstwhile enemies and forces them to adopt his manner of fighting. Victims, Schickele thought, easily take on the mentality of their hangman. Although the novel is not a political allegory, Schickele's reactions to political events in Germany and to his own experiences in exile are implicitly reflected.

Sanary-sur-Mer harbored many literary refugees from Germany, including Thomas Mann, Lion Feuchtwanger, Stefan Zweig, Ludwig Marcuse, and Ernst Toller. It was a gregarious and gossipy world, centered on the cafés at the harbor side where they argued about politics and books and speculated as to when Hitler would be finished and they could go home again. Exile conferred a common bond, but the emigrants had political differences. Schickele did not like the political aggressiveness of some of the emigrants because he thought that they were adopting Hitler's methods. He objected to the "Blechmusik der journalistischen Emigration" (brassy music of the journalists among the emigrants).

The essay *Liebe und Ärgernis des D. H. Lawrence* (Love and Anger of D.H. Lawrence, 1934) had its origins in the experiences of those days. The essay was meant less as an interpretation of Lawrence than as an occasion to express thoughts that occupied Schickele at the time. For instance, Lawrence's experiences as a pacifist during World War I gave Schickele an opportunity to weave his own thoughts on war into his interpretation of Lawrence's position. He also discussed his attitude toward the Jews. The Jews, he thought, like the Greeks in Roman times, had contributed to civilization by providing a degree of restlessness and intellectual fermentation that prevented stagnation and complacency. In this context Schickele regarded Christ as the greatest "Unruhestifter" (agitator) of all times and he blamed the Christians for the so-called Jewish problem. The political weight of the essay lies in his arguments against Lawrence's belief in a "mystical authority," which, in a somewhat different sense, Schickele thought characteristic of National Socialism.

Schickele was not attuned to Lawrence's world; Lawrence's preoccupation with sex as a means of breaking through spiritual isolation was especially foreign to him. The tone of the essay—sympathetic, sophisticated, and somewhat ironic—betrays Schickele's incapacity to understand Lawrence on Lawrence's own terms.

Schickele also discusses the nature of the true artist: he is intuitive, and his experiences are original, perspicacious, and fresh. In that, says Schickele, he resembles a child. He is "a primitive" because his vision is unspoiled. Schickele's idea of the primitive includes not just a heightened sensitivity toward the wonders of the world but also visions that are distorted by demons, dreams, and signs. Such a primitive lives in the disquietude brought on by racial memories and oracles. These features mark Schickele's own work, in which remarkably lucid, lyrical descriptions alternate with obscure, distorted, violent, and bizarre images.

In the essay Schickele asserts that art and politics are entirely separate. Trusting in the persuasiveness and efficacy of the serene work of art, he absolves the poet from taking a political position: "Ein gutes Gedicht, ein schönes Stück Prosa,—müssen sie nicht in der Gewöhnlichkeit der Umgebung nach den Früchten des Paradieses duften?" (A good poem, a fine piece of prose,—do they not smell of the fruits of paradise amidst the vulgarity of our surroundings?).

The subject matter of Schickele's last novel, *Die Flaschenpost,* written in the form of a diary, is the debilitating, paralyzing loneliness of the individual who, endowed with a sensitive and highly developed conscience, stands aghast and frightened at the crossroads of civilization. It is an intensely subjective, ironic work.

Surrounded by an enchanting landscape (the locale is probably Nice-Fabron), Richard Wolke lives with his housekeeper in a villa on the Riviera. Although he lacks no material comforts, he feels insecure and needs to imagine the reassuring hand of his beautiful mother. Alfonso XIII, the former king of Spain, who moves into an adjoining house with his mistress Pipette, becomes the object of Wolke's fears that a political plot is being hatched. Soon Wolke and Pipette are in love, but later he finds out that Pipette is faithless. In the end Wolke shoots the "king," who is really only a terrorist in hiding.

In an insane asylum, Wolke burns his unpublished books and learns this truth: "Unsere Zivilisation beruht auf dem Verschweigen der Tatsache, daß die Gesunden unter dem Knüppel eines Häufleins besonders begabter Irrsinniger leben" (Our civilization is based on the concealment of the fact that the sane live under the knout of a bunch of especially talented madmen).

Die Flaschenpost is a quixotic comedy. Wolke is a charming fool, a reluctant skeptic, and an optimist who strives to escape disaster. A radical individualist, Wolke considers the state his mortal enemy. Only the individualist is truly free. Wolke's cosmological fear and anxiety are the price he must pay for his individualism. Like Paul Merkel in Schickele's first novel, *Der Fremde,* Wolke lives a precarious spiritual existence. His equilibrium is only delicately maintained.

In his only book written in French, *Le Retour* (The Return, 1938; translated into German as *Die Heimkehr,* 1939), Schickele describes the political fever that had spread at last to Alsace. The book is a collection of highly lyrical prose fragments, including short essays on communism and German-French reconciliation, and biographical pieces. His personal philosophy is always uncompromising in its demand for a free conscience: one is responsible to no one but oneself. It is remarkable that Schickele's style, which seems to have such "French" overtones when he writes in German, loses these graceful and supple qualities in French.

No longer an advocate of political engagement, Schickele came to believe that the role of the artist is to conserve art and ideals. It is not a question, he thought, of taking a political position, of choosing between democracy and totalitarianism; the problem is to heal mankind from a disease from which it will suffer under any form of government. The disease is, simply, life without God.

As the struggle between the totalitarian states and the democracies sharpened, when it seemed that this conflict could not be resolved by compromise or reconciliation, Schickele's position became unequivocal. "Die Welt teilt sich in zwei Lager, und das ist gut," he wrote to Thomas Mann in a letter dated 18 January 1940. ". . . Ich will lieber völlig unterliegen, als nur mit halbem Herzen bei einer Partei zu sein, mit geteilten

Gefühlen ihrem Sieg beizuwohnen, zur Feier eine Fahne aufzuziehn, die für mein innerstes Empfinden auf der Masthälfte stecken bliebe. Zum ersten Mal in meinem Leben bin ich Konformist und fühle mich ganz und gar auf der rechten Seite" (The world is divided into two camps, and that is good. . . . I should far rather be completely defeated than to be half-hearted in my support of my side, or to have mixed feelings about the victory or about the flag which to my innermost sentiments would always remain at half-mast. For the first time in my life I am a conformist and feel myself to be wholly on the right side).

Schickele died at Vence on 31 January 1940. He had contracted influenza, which developed into pleurisy and caused a heart complication. He was buried in the local cemetery. A memorial plaque at Badenweiler reads: "Sein Herz trug die Liebe und die Weisheit zweier Völker" (His heart bore the love and the wisdom of two peoples).

Bibliography:

Paul Kurt Ackermann, *René Schickele: A Bibliography* (Cambridge: Schoenhof 's, 1956).

References:

Friedrich Bentmann, *René Schickele: Leben und Werk in Dokumenten* (Nuremberg: Carl, 1974);

Adrian Finck, *Introduction à René Schickele* (Strasbourg: Salde, 1982);

Finck and Maryse Staiber, *Elsässer, Europäer, Pazifist: Studien zu René Schickele* (Kehl: Morstadt, 1984);

Julie Meyer, *Vom elsässischen Kunstfrühling zur utopischen Civitas Hominum* (Munich: Fink, 1981);

Joachim W. Storck, "Der späte Schickele: Ein Sonderfall der deutchen Exilliteratur," *Jahrbuch der Deutschen Schillergesellschaft,* 27 (1983): 435-461.

Papers:

René Schickele's papers are at the Schiller-Nationalmuseum, Marbach am Neckar, West Germany.

Hermann Stehr

(16 February 1864-14 September 1940)

Erich P. Hofacker, Jr.
University of Michigan

BOOKS: *Auf Leben und Tod: Zwei Erzählungen* (Berlin: Fischer, 1898);

Der Schindelmacher: Novelle (Berlin: Fischer, 1899);

Leonore Griebel: Roman (Berlin: Fischer, 1900);

Das letzte Kind (Berlin: Fischer, 1903);

Meta Konegen: Drama (Berlin: Fischer, 1904);

Der begrabene Gott: Roman (Berlin: Fischer, 1905);

Drei Nächte: Roman (Berlin: Fischer, 1909);

Geschichten aus dem Mandelhause (Berlin: Fischer, 1913); enlarged as *Das Mandelhaus: Roman* (Munich: List, 1953);

Das Abendrot: Novellen (Berlin: Fischer, 1916);

Der Heiligenhof: Roman, 2 volumes (Berlin: Fischer, 1918);

Meicke, der Teufel: Erzählung (Berlin: Hillger, 1919);

Das Lebensbuch: Gedichte aus zwei Jahrzehnten (Berlin: Fischer, 1920);

Die Krähen (Berlin: Fischer, 1921);

Das entlaufene Herz (Trier: Lintz, 1923);

Wendelin Heinelt: Ein Märchen (Trier: Lintz, 1923);

Peter Brindeisener: Roman (Trier: Lintz, 1924);

Gesammelte Werke, 9 volumes (Trier: Lintz, 1924);

Der Schatten: Novelle (Chemnitz: Gesellschaft der Bücherfreunde, 1924);

Wanderer zur Höhe: Erzählung (Vienna: Österreichischer Bundesverlag, 1925);

Der Geigenmacher: Eine Geschichte (Leipzig: Horen, 1926); American classroom edition, edited by Walter A. Reichart (New York: Oxford University Press, 1934);

Das Märchen vom deutschen Herzen: Drei Geschichten (Leipzig: List, 1926);

Gesammelte Werke, 12 volumes (Leipzig: List, 1927-1936);

Mythen und Mären (Berlin & Leipzig: Horen, 1929);

Nathanael Maechler: Roman (Berlin & Leipzig: Horen, 1929); republished in *Droben Gnade, drunten Recht,* volume 1 of *Das Geschlecht der Maechler: Roman einer deutschen Familie* (Leipzig: List, 1944);

Hermann Stehr

Über äusseres und inneres Leben (Berlin & Leipzig: Horen, 1931);

Meister Cajetan: Novelle (Leipzig: List, 1931);

An der Tür des Jenseits: Zwei Novellen (Munich: Langen-Müller, 1932);

Die Nachkommen: Roman (Leipzig: List, 1933); republished in *Droben Gnade, drunten Recht,* volume 1 of *Das Geschlecht der Maechler: Roman einer deutschen Familie* (Leipzig: List, 1944);

Gudnatz: Eine Novelle (Leipzig: Insel, 1934);

Mein Leben (Berlin: Junker & Dünnhaupt, 1934);

Der Mittelgarten: Frühe und neue Gedichte (Leipzig: List, 1936);

Das Stundenglas: Reden, Schriften, Tagebücher (Leipzig: List, 1936);

Im Zwischenreich (Breslau: Oehmigke, 1937);

Der Himmelsschlüssel: Eine Geschichte zwischen Himmel und Erde (Leipzig: List, 1939);

Von Mensch und Gott: Worte des Dichters (Leipzig: List, 1939);

Hermann Stehr und das junge Deutschland: Bekenntnis zum fünfundsiebzigsten Geburtstag des Dichters, edited by F. Hammer (Eisenach: Röth, 1939);

Damian oder Das große Schermesser, edited by Wilhelm Meridies, volume 2 of *Das Geschlecht der Maechler: Roman einer deutschen Familie* (Leipzig: List, 1944).

OTHER: *Schlesien: Ein Bildband,* introduction by Stehr (Bielefeld: Velhagen & Klasing, 1937).

Hermann Stehr was a highly regarded author during the first decades of the twentieth century. In his nine novels, thirty-one narratives, and hundreds of poems he revealed hidden aspects of human nature and proposed answers to age-old religious and philosophical questions. Some of his novels and novellas were translated into French, Norwegian, Czech, and even into Celtic and Japanese, but no English translations appeared, though an American school edition of his story *Der Geigenmacher* (The Violin Maker, 1926) did come out in 1934. Of his novel *Der begrabene Gott* (The Buried God, 1905) Hugo von Hofmannsthal said in a review: "One word I must use in describing it is grandeur. And another is reverence, and awe." Recognition also came in literary honors: Stehr received the Bauernfeld Prize in 1907, the Fastenrath Prize in 1911, and the Schiller Prize in 1913. When the Ministry of Culture established a literary academy in 1926, it invited Stehr, as one of the five greatest living German authors, to be a founding member. He won the Rathenau Prize in 1930 and the Goethe Prize in 1933. Arnold Zweig said: "He is the strongest literary force now at work in Germany." Today he has been all but forgotten, and none of his works are in print. Even in his own day they were not best-sellers: sales of his best-known novel, *Der Heiligenhof* (The Farm of the Saintly, 1918), did not reach the half-million mark. Indeed, Stehr feared that his works would be misinterpreted if they were read by the masses.

Stehr was born in 1864 to Robert and Theresia Faber Stehr in the small town of Habelschwerdt in the province of Silesia, which is today part of Poland. Since it was feared that he might not survive, he was given an emergency baptism, packed in cotton wadding, and placed by the stove. In his autobiographical sketch *Mein Leben* (My Life, 1934) Stehr observed, "It seemed as if my death and my existence were to become an undreamed dream. But there is a folk belief that those are anchored to life most firmly who were, as one might say, pushed from death into life; they must chew as bitterly on the first breath of life as on the last. This belief seems confirmed in me."

Stehr in 1929 (Ullstein)

Troubled even in childhood by the dogmas of the Catholic faith of his family, Stehr rebelled against the methods of his clerical teachers. During his training as an elementary-school teacher his rebelliousness continued to anger school authorities, and his nonattendance at church and apparent atheism resulted in the loss of his modest scholarship. Stehr's financial difficulties continued during his employment as a substitute teacher in remote Silesian mountain hamlets from 1885 to 1889. Friction between Stehr and the community was frequent. His first permanent position, where he believed his superiors hoped to "bury" him, was in the village of Pohldorf, "a rifle-shot away from endless forests." The school was situated between two villages, "deserted, as lonely as death, and under the supervision of two clerics." He developed a marked persecution complex which is reflected in his literary works of the period. In 1894, when his annual salary reached 1,000 marks, Stehr married Hedwig Nentwig. His feelings of oppression and depression were eased briefly, only to become more severe over his and his wife's recurrent illnesses and the deaths of their first three children. Since Stehr faced each conflict with the townspeople squarely, he found himself surrounded by suspicion and hatred; he was even denounced from the pulpit as a blasphemer. After each school day Stehr found it necessary to regain his composure by walking in the open air and being alone with nature. After a simple supper he would sleep a few hours before arising to study and write through the night. He wrote poetry and prose, discarding almost everything he composed. As morning approached, his mind became hyperactive. He took pills to obtain a few hours of leaden sleep before once again appearing before his 120 pupils of all grade levels. This cycle remained Stehr's routine for a decade.

All his life Stehr sought a God who would not rule the world arbitrarily. He felt so tortured that he often contemplated suicide, but literary creation brought him solace. In *Mein Leben* he relates: "The more pitilessly the blows of life beat down upon me, the more fervently did I devote myself to the visions within me. All the world's accusations, all disquietude, all my disappointments I offered for resolution to that other-worldly court presided over by poetry, the goddess whom I served. I struggled for her blessing and her sanction of a mode of existence which before my inner eye appeared possible, in my longing appeared necessary, and in my hopes seemed certain to come." Some critics consider his years in Pohldorf, externally his worst, to have been his most productive and qualitatively his best.

In 1889 and 1894 Stehr completed two novellas which were favorably received by Moritz Heimann, manuscript reader for the prominent publishing house of S. Fischer in Berlin. The stories finally appeared in 1898 in *Auf Leben und Tod* (It is a Question of Life and Death), which he called "eine psychologische Monographie" (a psychological monograph). In "Der Graveur" (The Engraver) concrete images reflect the spiritual and psychological abuse the author felt at the hands of his fellow men. When Joseph Schramm, a pious engraver, is struck a crippling blow by his drunken brother, he loses his power of speech and the ability to distinguish reality from fantasy. He cannot respond to the mockery of the townspeople because he cannot communicate with them. Hate and a desire for revenge become all-consuming. Periods of confusion alternate with lucidity, and in a moment of madness he murders an innocent man. His mind suddenly clears, the horror of his deed possesses him, and he commits suicide.

Unlike the engraver, who fell from moral and intellectual heights, Marx, the protagonist of the second story in *Auf Leben und Tod,* "Meicke, der Teufel" (Meicke, the Devil), makes only half-hearted attempts to raise himself from the depths of depravity. Wherever Marx goes, Meicke the devil-dog, an ugly, black, bristly, dirty, obtrusive beast, remains at his heels. Though Marx claims to wish to "a Ende macha mit em Elende, mit a Menschern, mit a Schnapse" (put an end to the misery, the bad company, and the liquor), his drunkenness is only replaced by licentiousness. Frau Stumpf (whose name means dull or stupid), a middle-aged widow, welcomes Marx's advances. For a time she finds happiness in his arms, but the spell is broken, and she flees his bestial gaze when she compares the pure love of her daughter Mariela, "sweet as the sunshine in May," with her own, "an endless swamp of tepid, stinking water." When Marx attempts to assault Mariela sexually, Frau Stumpf sacrifices her life to preserve her daughter's purity. Shortly thereafter, the drunken Marx kills himself. After Marx's death, Meicke is repulsed by Mariela's unblemished purity and seeks depravity elsewhere.

In 1898 Stehr completed *Leonore Griebel,* which was published in 1900. Beginning with this novel, most of Stehr's fictional works deal with marital incompatibility. (This subject may be non-autobiographical, since on his sixtieth birthday Stehr spoke of thirty years of happy marriage.) In *Leonore Griebel* Stehr expresses his belief that woman's spiritual love finds its fullest realization in her natural sensuousness: "Denn alle Geistigkeit des Weibes ist leiblich, und ihr Körper ist die restlose Fülle ihrer Seele" (For all spirituality in woman is corporeal and her body is the com-

Page from a letter by Stehr (Hermann Stehr Museum)

plete fulfillment of her soul). The biblical formulation "ohne Leib keine Liebe" (without the body there is no love) may be understood in this sense. Leonore marries before she has matured intellectually and spiritually, and without first establishing with her husband-to-be Joseph the spiritual harmony which must complement the sexual relationship. She is unable to love the child that she has conceived in less than perfect love: the barrier that separates her soul from her child's soul is the result of her distant relationship with her husband. Because the child was born only of its parents' bodies and not of a spiritual love, she kisses it with her lips but not with her soul. Lacking a spiritual bond with the child, she eventually loses interest in it.

But a longing for a deep and beautiful mystical bond of love is still alive in Leonore, and she has an affair with a traveling salesman who has been able to communicate spiritually with her and has brightened the darkness of her existence. According to the world's law, her adultery is a crime, and she is so charged by her husband. The irony is that Leonore's marriage is really no marriage at all; in order to avoid a crime against the world's law she must perpetrate a crime against her own soul. After a bitter inner struggle she renounces her extramarital relationship; her spirit slowly ebbs away until she finds release in death.

For Stehr, perfect love comes naturally from a heart which is in harmony with itself and with God. It is not a purely spiritual love, for much of its strength is derived from the physical: love that is wholly intellectual or platonic, like love that is purely sensual, is destructive and makes a permanent relationship between man and woman impossible. Perfect love combines elements of both, but in Stehr's works such a relationship proves difficult to achieve.

Gerhart Hauptmann and Stehr at Schreiberhau, circa 1928 (Dr. Benvenuto Hauptmann, Munich)

Der begrabene Gott (The Buried God), written in 1898 but not published until 1905, is Stehr's darkest work. Reflecting a personal situation which often turned his thoughts to suicide, it is so unremitting in its pessimism that contemporary reviewers maintained that they were unable to read it without periodic breaks to regain their composure. Not a trace of humor or irony relieves the sadness and suffering. Hofmannsthal wrote of the power of the novel: "It transports us to depths we have never before experienced. Here a great hand has created something out of the darkness and depths of life. Here I must say, when I read it I had a moving experience." Misunderstanding Matthew 16:24 ("If any man will come after me, let him deny himself and take up his cross and follow after me"), the devout Marie marries an embittered cripple, a cruel man who torments her with distrust and suspicion. Marie's blind faith enables her to suffer silently through an inhuman marriage. She believes that the child she is to bear will be her reward for her suffering and for having followed God's command; but when the child turns out to be ugly and deformed, "die Nacht, die sich nicht fortschaffen lässt" (the night which cannot be driven away) breaks over her. Marie revolts against God, curses her former faith, and in a fit of rage buries her picture of the Virgin Mary under the snow. She then murders her child and burns her house, saying: "Mir wern de Nacht verbrenn' of dr Erde. Darnach sein mir alle erlöst, mir und alle Menschen" (We'll burn up the night on earth. After that, we'll all be saved, we and all people). In 1900 Stehr's works gained him the recognition of the regional ministry of culture in Breslau and a transfer to a more comfortable location in Dittersbach. The bitterness, pessimism, defeat, and despair of his early works did not disappear with his transfer, but they were no longer the dominant feature of his writing.

Drei Nächte (Three Nights, 1909) is a confessional novel in which the young schoolteacher Franz Faber relates the story of his life before he gave up his position in one town and moved to another. In contrast to *Der begrabene Gott* some passages of this work are lightened by rays of hope; it is the book Stehr gave his son when he left to fight (and die) in World War I. Confession brings freedom from old psychological and spiritual bonds and permits one to turn inward to seek the dwelling place of the soul and of God. Since the soul is beyond the limits of time and place, one need not wait for the grave to find salvation.

Drei Nächte marked the end of Stehr's years of despair; his next works were stories in a generally lighter vein. Following a period of lost inspiration and restlessness occasioned by his retirement from teaching in 1911 he began work on *Der Heiligenhof*, which was published in 1918 as a two-volume, 822-page novelistic statement of his philosophic and religious views. This developmental novel chronicles the progress of Andreas Sintlinger as he turns his gaze inward and seeks the meaning of life. His pathway leads him ever deeper into the realm of the spirit until he comes to know "where the world begins." His spiritual growth is reflected in his remark that whereas he had once danced through the streets, he is now dancing within himself.

In *Der Heiligenhof* Stehr employs the "Romeo and Juliet motif" of two feuding families reconciled by the love of a son and daughter. The Brindeisener farm is in disrepair, silent, and nearly forsaken; the neighboring Sintlinger farm is alive with singing and dancing. In the contrasting fates of the two farms Stehr develops an image of the impact of love: its presence brings happiness, inner peace, and strength; its absence leads to the destruction of the family and to tragedy for its members.

Andreas Sintlinger, who has led an unruly life both before and after his marriage, is awakened to a new existence by the birth of his daughter Helene. Though blind, the child can feel what others can see. Certain that her "sight" is divine, her father grows spiritually; his daughter becomes the saint through whom he discovers the way to his true self and to God. In the different world in which he now dwells with "Heiligenlenlein" (little St. Helene) Sintlinger believes he can perceive God directly and has no need of priest or church. Nevertheless, Sintlinger is alternately ruled by faith and doubt; he sometimes sees his new world losing its harmony. Misgivings arise, and he stirs up hatred against his hostile neighbor Brindeisener, even participating in acts of cruelty and injustice.

Franz Faber, the autobiographical figure of *Drei Nächte,* visits the farm. Now a mysterious sage, prophet, rebel, visionary, or mystic–according to one's perspective–Faber communicates to Sintlinger the existence of a set of absolute laws which rule the universe, which have power even over God Himself; because of these absolutes, God cannot act arbitrarily.

In Helene's childhood Peter Brindeisener, of the neighboring farm, is her playmate; as a young man he is unruly, but the two young people are attracted to each other. On the day they declare their mutual love, Helene suddenly acquires her eyesight. Her relationship with Peter follows a normal course and includes the erotic side. Sintlinger suffers a corresponding loss of faith, becoming gloomy, distrustful, and taciturn; the bond between father and daughter dissolves as Helene turns all her attention to Peter. It gradually becomes clear that Peter is unable to become a new person; he persists in his old, undisciplined ways until Helene doubts his fidelity. The problem of the balance between spiritual and sensual love so frequently present in Stehr's works remains unresolved. Having been drawn out of the world of the soul and of God by her love for Peter, Helene is shattered by Peter's betrayal of her love and drowns herself.

At this point, Franz Faber reappears to aid Andreas Sintlinger in reaching his final goal: only when he has learned understanding, sympathy, and love for his fellow man will he be ready for life. Faber himself has attained perfect harmony with God; he is "resting in" and "living in" God. There is a wonderful calm and strength about Faber, who is described as being "like a great, kindly father of mankind." He has set out into the world to guide and serve others, expressing his discovery of his true self, his soul, and God in active love for his fellow man.

Peter Brindeisener (1924) retells the events of the previous novel from the perspective of Brindeisener, who is now a lonely, old, eccentric bookkeeper. As he grew out of his childhood he lost his divine innocence and entered the world of the senses, knowledge, and discord. His relationship with Helene was the tangible form of his longing for the divine purity of his childhood; she functioned as the light of the soul. But he fell victim to the sensual by repeated contacts with Mathinka Meixner, a farmhand employed by his father. The poison corroded his soul, and he made the error of believing that he would be permitted to continue his spiritually pure relationship with Helene despite his experience with Mathinka. In his old age Brindeisener understands that by his lineage he was predestined to follow an erroneous path, and he knows that his fate could not have been overcome except by a mystical return to the "Seelengrund" (the ground of his soul). His confession complete, Peter Brindeisener is free of his lifelong burden; he seeks absolution and reunion with Helene by drowning himself.

In "Gudnatz," a story collected in *Die Krähen* (The Crows, 1921), the protagonist is a hardened black marketeer who exploits the poor during the food shortages following World War I. Stehr says that "although the gods of morality sometimes reign even in the world of profiteers, and it has happened that the exalted God in heaven has cast his splendid aura over one of these ignoble individuals," this has not occurred in the case of Anton Gudnatz. One night Gudnatz hears, as if in a dream, the voice of a child pleading for bread. "Wie mit Fäusten gestossen" (as if struck by a fist), he springs from his bed but can find no one. The image of the starving little girl has issued from the mystical depths of his soul. Gudnatz subsequently loses his skill and self-confidence in dishonest business dealings, and his longing for his homeland grows. He embarks on a railroad journey to the region of his childhood, initially to escape prosecution and preserve his fortune; but station by

Stehr in 1933 (Ullstein)

station the train carries him away from his earthly treasures on a path to his redemption and his "eternal home." In the end Gudnatz has given away all of his money to feed hungry children.

Der Geigenmacher deals with the difficulty of artistic creation. Through training with the greatest master a violin maker learns technical perfection; unsatisfied, he leaves civilization behind and works toward true artistic perfection in the forest. Under somewhat mysterious circumstances, a girl called Schönlein (Little Beauty) appears at the violin maker's retreat. Within days a relationship of mutual love has developed between the violin maker and the girl, but his impatience for her response to his proposal of marriage causes him to intrude upon her seclusion; he encounters her naked, bathing. In amazement he cries out. His direct view of her perfect beauty before the relationship has matured results in its destruction: Schönlein leaves in haste to rejoin her mother. Inspired by recollection and intense longing, the violin maker constructs a unique instrument incorporating the essence of Schönlein, a concrete representation of the absolute. All who hear it are enchanted by "an indescribable [tonal] paradise intermingling heaven and earth." The violin maker disappears, searching the land for his lost Schönlein.

Nathanael Maechler (1929) is the initial novel of the trilogy *Das Geschlecht der Maechler* (The Maechler Family). The second volume, *Die Nachkommen* (The Posterity) followed in 1933; in 1944 these two novels were published together as *Droben Gnade, drunten Recht* (Grace on High, on Earth Justice). The final volume, *Damian,* was published posthumously in 1944. The novels are expansive developmental works which trace the Maechler family line through several generations. The first novel introduces young Nathanael Maechler as he searches for training as a journeyman tanner. As he wanders, the traditional evening prayer of the Maechler family runs through his mind, and he dwells particularly on its concluding lines, "May thou be always my Lord and I thy servant, with Grace on high and justice on earth." Overtaken by fever and delirium, he is cared for by Paula Grossmann, the daughter of a local farmer. But he rejects her love and sacrificial care and becomes involved in a purely sensual relationship which sullies his character and denies him the path to grace. In later years, despite an exemplary life of community service, his youthful misdeed spells his downfall and that of his family. Although the Catholic church grants him absolution, he can find no freedom from the bondage of fate and is unable to achieve true grace through a mystical submersion of the self in God.

The main theme of the trilogy is "Innerlichkeit" (inward focus), a condition fostering redemption and spiritual freedom. Stehr's assertion, "Die Augen sind nur ein Umweg" (Our eyesight takes us along a roundabout path), indicates his belief in the omnipresence of the divine and his conviction that the divine may be perceived only by the soul; indeed our eyes impede us in our search for God.

While Stehr allowed himself to be celebrated by the National Socialist regime as "ein Dichter der deutschen Seele" (a poet of the German soul), his circumstances in later years suggest that he may not have been aware of the true nature of Nazism: he died in 1940 in Oberschreiberhau, a small resort town in Silesia, nearly deaf and growing blind, at the age of seventy-six. Stehr did not belong to the Nazi party and refused to supply proof of his Aryan bloodlines. He was certainly not an author of the

"Blut und Boden" (blood and soil) literature desired by the Third Reich. The rural figures of such literature were positive in outlook; they were one with the land and dedicated to serving a "healthy" nation. They supported militarism, had large families, advocated German colonization of the territory to the east, and were generally of one mind concerning issues. By contrast, Stehr's works reflect the village realism of the nineteenth century: village and farm are places of struggle, and chaotic forces reveal themselves; there are scarcely any positive relationships, let alone idyllic ones. In opposition to the "Blut und Boden" image, Stehr depicts decay and degeneration, dehumanized and chaotic conditions. In all his work there is not a single character who fits the ideal of the Third Reich. It would appear that the Nazis had a poor understanding of Stehr; had they known his works, they would have condemned him as a decadent, a nihilist, or a mystic.

Letters:

Hermann Stehr und Walther Rathenau: Zwiesprache über den Zeiten, Geschichte einer Freundschaft in Briefen und Dokumenten, edited by Ursula Meridies-Stehr (Leipzig & Munich: List, 1946).

References:

Anton Aulke, "Dichtung und Weltanschauung," *Die Bücherwelt,* 24 (1927): 57-63;

Gustav Blanke, *Hermann Stehrs Menschengestaltung* (Berlin: Junker & Dünnhaupt, 1939);

Hermann Boeschenstein, "Hermann Stehr, der Erzähler-Mystiker," *Monatshefte für den deutschen Unterricht* (March 1941): 97-109;

Boeschenstein, "Sprachstilistische Merkmale Hermann Stehrs," *Germanic Review,* 9 (April 1934): 130-139;

Franz Böhm, "Hermann Stehr: Grundzüge seiner Weltanschauung," *Die Literatur,* 30 (June 1928): 507-508;

Gerhart Hauptmann, "Über ein Volksbuch," *Das literarische Echo,* no. 3 (1903): 166-169;

Moritz Heimann, "Hermann Stehr: Zu seinem 70. Geburtstag. Stehrs erstes Buch," *Die neue Rundschau,* 45 (February 1934): 191-198;

Cedric Hentschel, "Hermann Stehr," *German Life and Letters* (August 1939): 94-106;

Erich Hofacker, "Äusseres und Inneres in Stehrs Geigenmacher," *Monatshefte für den deutschen Unterricht,* 28 (March 1936): 97-105;

Hofacker, "Hermann Stehrs letztes Werk [*Der Himmelsschlüssel*], in *Hermann Stehr: Schlesier, Deutscher, Europäer,* edited by Fritz K. Richter, pp. 147-160;

Hofacker, "Die sinnlich-übersinnliche Bedeutung der Tonwelt in Hermann Stehrs Erzählungskunst," *PMLA,* 55 (June 1940): 568-578;

Hofacker, "Stifters Abdias und Stehrs Heiligenhofbauer," *Monatshefte für den deutschen Unterricht* (November 1939): 321-330;

Hugo von Hofmannsthal, Review of *Der begrabene Gott, Der Tag* (1905); republished in *Vom Geheimnis des Jenseits im Diesseits,* edited by Wilhelm Meridies (Stuttgart: Brentano, 1960), pp. 51-53;

F. W. Kaufmann, "The Style of Hermann Stehr in Its Relation to His View of Life," *Germanic Review,* 7 (October 1932): 359-366;

Hans Knudsen, "Hermann Stehr," *Zeitschrift für Deutschkunde,* no. 6 (1925): 291-299;

Stefan Lobe, "Wirkungsgeschichte Hermann Stehrs und seines Werkes," Ph.D. dissertation, University of Cologne, 1976;

Oskar Loerke, "Der Künstler und Künder Hermann Stehr," *Die neue Rundschau,* no. 2 (1934): 199-207;

Wilhelm Meridies, "Der Epiker: Hermann Stehr und sein Weltbild," *Der Kunstwart,* no. 5 (1929): 96-104;

Meridies, "Hermann Stehrs neuer Roman," review of *Nathanael Maechler, Die schöne Literatur,* 30 (July 1929): 289-294;

Meridies, ed., *Hermann Stehr: Sein Werk und seine Welt* (Habelschwert: Franke, 1924);

Meridies, *Wege zu Hermann Stehr* (Würzburg: Holzner, 1964);

Meridies, ed., *Vom Geheimnis des Jenseits im Diesseits* (Stuttgart: Brentano, 1960);

Meridies, ed., *Wangener Beiträge zur Stehrforschung* (Munich: Delp, 1971);

Erich Mühle, *Hermann Stehr: Ein deutscher Gottsucher der Gegenwart* (Stuttgart: Truckenmüller, 1937);

D. Nitschke, "Studien zum Gottsuchertum in der schlesischen Literatur der Gegenwart," Ph.D. dissertation, University of Fribourg (Switzerland), 1935;

Julius Petersen, "Wundergeige und Hochzeitsgeige," *Germanisch-Romanische Monatsschrift,* (April-June 1940): 77-86;

Robert Petsch, "Hermann Stehrs Meisterwerke, 'Der Heiligenhof' und 'Peter Brindeisener,'" *Deutsches Volkstum,* no. 1 (1925): 24-34;

Walter A. Reichart, "Hermann Stehr and His Work," *Philological Quarterly,* 10 (January 1931): 47-61;

Reichart, "Hermann Stehr: Zum 70. Geburtstag," *Monatshefte für den deutschen Unterricht* (February 1934): 33-38;

Fritz K. Richter, "Hermann Stehrs Künstlernovellen," *Journal of English and Germanic Philology,* 41 (1942): 444-450;

Richter, ed., *Hermann Stehr: Schlesier, Deutscher, Europäer* (Würzburg: Holzner-Verlag, 1964);

Rudolf Sturm, "Wirklichkeit und hohe Welt: Studien zum Werke Hermann Stehrs," Ph.D. dissertation, University of Munich, 1940;

A. E. Terry, "The Literary Significance of the Silesian Elements in the Works of Hauptmann and Stehr," Ph.D. dissertation, Stanford University, 1942;

Karl S. Weimar, "The Concept of Love in the Works of Hermann Stehr," Ph.D. dissertation, University of Pennsylvania, 1945;

Elizabeth Zorb, "Religiöse Strömungen in der schlesischen Dichtung der Gegenwart," Ph.D. dissertation, University of Freiburg, 1933.

Papers:

The Hermann Stehr Archive in Wangen, Bavaria, contains manuscripts, diaries, notebooks, and letters to and from the author.

Ludwig Thoma

(21 January 1867-26 August 1921)

Herbert Knust

University of Illinois (Urbana-Champaign)

BOOKS: *Agricola: Bauerngeschichten* (Passau: Waldbauer, 1897; enlarged edition, Munich: Piper, 1948);

Grobheiten: Simplicissimus-Gedichte, as Peter Schlemihl (Munich: Langen, 1901);

Assessor Karlchen und andere Geschichten (Munich: Langen, 1901);

Die Medaille: Komödie (Munich: Langen, 1901);

Witwen: Lustspiel (Munich: Langen, 1901);

Hochzeit: Eine Bauerngeschichte (Munich: Langen, 1902);

Die Lokalbahn: Komödie (Munich: Langen, 1902);

Die bösen Buben (Munich: Langen, 1903);

Neue Grobheiten: Simplicissimus-Gedichte, as Schlemihl (Munich: Langen, 1903);

Das große Malöhr im Juni 1903: Wahrheitsgetreu dargestellt (Munich: Langen, 1903);

Der heilige Hies: Merkwürdige Schicksale des hochwürdigen Herrn Matthias Fottner von Ainhofen, Studiosi, Soldaten und späterhin Pfarrherrn von Rappertswyl (Munich: Langen, 1904); translated by B.Q. Morgan as "Matt the Holy" in volume 19 of *The German Classics of the 19th and 20th Centuries,* edited by Kuno Francke and William Guild Howard (New York: German Publications Society, 1914), pp. 251-267;

Die Wilderer: Eine Jagdgeschichte (Munich: Langen, 1904);

Lausbubengeschichten: Aus meiner Jugendzeit (Munich: Langen, 1905);

Pistole oder Säbel? und anderes (Munich: Langen, 1905);

Peter Schlemihl: Gedichte (Munich: Langen, 1906);

Andreas Vöst: Bauernroman (Munich: Langen, 1906);

Der Schusternazi: Posse mit Gesang (Munich: Langen, 1906);

Tante Frieda: Neue Lausbubengeschichten (Munich: Langen, 1907);

Kleinstadtgeschichten (Munich: Langen, 1908);

Moritaten: Wahrheitsgetreu berichtet (Munich: Langen, 1908);

Briefwechsel eines bayerischen Landtagsabgeordneten (Munich: Langen, 1909);

Ludwig Thoma

Moral: Komödie (Munich: Langen, 1909); translated by H. Bernstein as *Morality* (New York, 1909);

Erster Klasse: Bauernschwank (Munich: Langen, 1910);

Lottchens Geburtstag: Lustspiel (Munich: Langen, 1911);

Der Wittiber: Bauernroman (Munich: Langen, 1911);

Bismarck; Kirta (Munich: Callwey, 1912);

Jozef Filsers Briefwexel (Munich: Langen, 1912);

Kirchweih: Simplicissimus-Gedichte, as Schlemihl (Munich: Langen, 1912);

Krawall: Lustige Geschichten (Berlin: Ullstein, 1912);
Magdalena: Volksstück (Munich: Langen, 1912);
Münchner Karneval: Lustige Verse (Munich: Langen, 1913);
Nachbarsleute (Munich: Langen, 1913);
Das Säuglingsheim: Burleske in einem Aufzug (Munich: Langen, 1913);
Die Sippe: Schauspiel in drei Aufzügen (Munich: Langen, 1913);
Der Postsekretär im Himmel und andere Geschichten (Berlin: Ullstein, 1914);
Der erste August; Christnacht 1914: Zwei Einakter (Munich: Langen, 1915);
Das Aquarium und anderes (Munich: Langen, 1916);
Brautschau; Dichters Ehrentag; Die kleinen Verwandten: Drei Einakter (Munich: Langen, 1916);
Der alte Feinschmecker: Ein Münchner Schwank, as Hans Georg Vogelsang (Munich: Langen, 1916);
Das Kälbchen; Der umgewendete Dichter; Onkel Peppi; Heimkehr: Novellen (Munich: Langen, 1916);
Geschichten, edited by Walter von Molo (Munich: Langen, 1917);
Heilige Nacht: Eine Weihnachtslegende (Munich: Langen, 1917);
Waldfrieden: Lustspiel in einem Aufzug (Munich: Langen, 1917);
Altaich: Eine heitere Sommergeschichte (Munich: Langen, 1918);
Gelähmte Schwingen: Lustspiel in einem Aufzug (Munich: Langen, 1918);
Erinnerungen (Munich: Langen, 1919);
Der Jagerloisl: Eine Tegernseer Geschichte (Munich: Langen, 1921);
Die Dachserin und andere Geschichten aus dem Nachlaß (Munich: Langen, 1922);
Der Ruepp: Roman (Munich: Langen, 1922);
Gesammelte Werke, 7 volumes (Munich: Langen, 1922–includes *Münchnerinnen* and *Kaspar Lorinser;* enlarged edition, 7 volumes, Munich: Langen-Müller, 1933);
Leute, die ich kannte (Munich: Langen, 1923);
Stadelheimer Tagebuch (Munich: Langen, 1923);
Gesammelte Werke, 8 volumes, edited by A. Knaus and Johann Lachner (Munich: Piper, 1956);
Gesammelte Werke, 6 volumes (Munich: Piper, 1968).

OTHER: *Der Burenkrieg,* edited by Thoma (Munich: Langen, 1900);
Bayernbuch: Hundert bayrische Autoren eines Jahrtausends, edited by Thoma and Georg Queri (Munich: Langen, 1913);
Franz von Kobell and Kaspar Stieler, *Petzmaiers Zitherspiel: Oberbayerisches,* selected by Thoma (Munich: Langen, 1916);
Ignatius Taschner, edited by Thoma and Alexander Heilmeyer (Munich: Langen, 1921).

Thoma as a law student (Ullstein)

Ludwig Thoma, satirist, political essayist, playwright, and author of first-rate stories and novels, contributed a distinctly "Old-Bavarian" note to the literary concert during Germany's Wilhelminian era. Deeply attached to the country and the plain people around the thriving Bavarian capital of Munich, he concentrated on the life of the farmers, portraying their characters, traditions, and work and, not infrequently, upholding their old ways and values against the conceits and artificialities of the increasingly bureaucratic society spawned by the industrial age. By artfully linking colorful and expressive local language to deep-rooted human problems he became one of the few writers capable of elevating dialect beyond provincial sentiment or entertaining farce to the realm of great literature.

Born in 1867 in Oberammergau, Thoma was the fifth of seven children of Max and Katharina Thoma. He spent his first six years in

Illustration by Olaf Gulbransson for Lausbubengeschichten *(1905), Thoma's best-known work*

his father's solitary forester's house in the beautiful upper Isar valley near the Tyrolian border, which he recalled often as a childhood paradise. Fairy tales of the Alpine region, hunters' stories, and actual encounters with poachers excited his lively fantasy. In the woods he met charcoal burners, lumberjacks, and raftsmen; but hunting parties also brought visitors from high society to the forestry inn, including the eccentric King Ludwig II of Bavaria. Political debates among guests, as well as illustrated periodicals, gave the boy a first inkling of the world outside, of stirring events such as the Franco-Prussian War and the founding of the German Reich by Bismarck, for whom Thoma developed a lifelong admiration. An early predilection for books, especially Wilhelm Busch's *Max und Moritz* (1865), a book of verses about boy pranksters, influenced his imagination. But Thoma recalled in his memoirs that it was most of all the security and warmth of his family as well as the peaceful landscape that shaped his early years. In 1873 the family moved to Forstenried, near Munich.

The sudden death of his father in 1874 left the family with only a small pension. Thoma's teachers at various boarding schools recognized his intelligence, but he was a difficult pupil: stubborn, lazy, yet–despite his shyness–given to jokes and pranks. He was frequently reprimanded, disciplined, even incarcerated, and could hardly await vacation time to return to his beloved mother, who in 1875 took over an inn at Lake Chiemsee.

Though Thoma was not enthusiastic about school, he devoured literature on his own. He discovered Dickens, read the German classics, liked the realists, and favored Theodor Fontane and especially the Swiss writer Gottfried Keller, whose humor and tales about country folk were to serve as a yardstick for his own literary endeavors. When he finished his trying school years, which would supply him with hilarious episodes for his best-known work, *Lausbubengeschichten* (Little Ras-

Thoma circa 1899, about the time he became editor of the satirical Munich journal Simplicissimus (Ullstein)

25. Mai 1912 Preis 50 Pf.

März

Eine Wochenschrift

Gegründet von Albert Langen

Herausgeber:

Ludwig Thoma · Hermann Hesse

Aus dem Inhalt:

Martin Andersen Nexö, August Strindberg
Hans Heinrich Ehrler, Ein Pfingstbrief an den „März"
Conrad Haußmann, M. d. R., Elsaß-Lothringen
Theodor Heuß, Das Hambacher Fest
Walter Schädelin, Das Schaf
Wilh. Hausenstein, Kunst und Religion
Dr. Alfons Goldschmidt, Strafpredigt Nr. 2

6. Jahrgang
Heft 21

März-Verlag G.m.b.H.
München

Cover for an issue of the journal Thoma founded in 1906 with Hermann Hesse, Albert Langen, and Kurt Aram

cal Stories, 1905), he intended to become, like his father, a forestry official. Yet after two semesters at the Forstakademie in Aschaffenburg he found that he was more interested in people than in forest administration. He studied law in Munich and then in Erlangen, obtaining his doctorate in 1890.

After brief periods of legal apprenticeship in Traunstein and in Munich, Thoma, shortly after his mother's death in 1894, settled as a lawyer in Dachau, near Munich. Although his eloquence served his clients well, he soon grew to dislike the legal profession. But his keen observation of people in adverse situations would amply supply him with subject matter for his writing.

It was not only his fascination with the life of the country folk but also his interest in politics that provoked Thoma to express himself in writing. With shock he had witnessed the dismissal of Bismarck by Emperor Wilhelm II, whose pursuit of national and personal greatness, observed with increasing alarm from abroad, was applauded by the German public. Thoma tended toward conservatism, and he viewed the industrial and economic expansion, accompanied by lust for power and rank, with mistrust. In Munich cafés and at beer tables he never tired of discussions on Bavarian politics, art, and culture. He also developed his skills as a story writer and journalist.

His short prose and political articles in the *Augsburger Abendzeitung* gained attention, and in December 1897 his first book, an illustrated collection of his rural stories, was published. *Agricola* was praised by critics as a naturalistic work of art, but belittled as caricature by some who recognized themselves. By the time the book appeared he had moved to Munich, where he contributed to the influential new weeklies *Die Jugend,* which grew into an important voice on modern trends in literature and the arts, and *Simplicissimus,* founded by the publisher Albert Langen, which was about to become Germany's foremost satirical journal. When Langen fled Germany in 1899 because his journal was accused of printing an "insult" to His Imperial Majesty, Thoma gave up his law practice and assumed major responsibility for *Simplicissimus,* which thrived under his editorship and was widely feared among those it attacked. The small-town conservative lawyer inclined toward comfortable smugness turned into a daring, sharp-tongued liberal critic, who, under the pseudonym Peter Schlemihl, wrote aggressive satirical verse against the complacent bourgeoisie, political oppressiveness, servility, lies, corruption, militarism, and injustice. Thoma did not spare even the emperor from his acid ridicule.

Illustration by Gulbransson for Tante Frieda, *Thoma's sequel to* Lausbubengeschichten

Thoma's volume of stories *Assessor Karlchen* (1901) contains ironical stabs at the jockeying practitioners of the law and colorful studies of the rural milieu. Having found his style and polished his skill at dialogue, Thoma tried his hand at a one-act social comedy, *Die Medaille* (The Medal, 1901), satirizing the gap between high officials speaking High German and their subordinates speaking their plain home dialect and proving themselves superior in common sense and genuine feeling at every turn. The play was Thoma's first big theatrical success. In his lengthy story *Hochzeit* (Wedding, 1902) he returned to his major theme, the everyday life of the farmers, and described the sober and practical considerations of a marriage that is to safeguard a farm's continuity from one generation to the next. Against critics who missed the element of "love," Thoma defended the farmers' values but refused to romanticize them.

Other works appeared in quick succession. A full-length comedy, *Die Lokalbahn* (The Branch Line, 1902), was enthusiastically received. His Schlemihl poems were published in three volumes, illustrated by Theodor Heine, in 1901, 1903, and 1906. He completed the masterly tale *Die Wilderer* (The Poachers, 1904). His first major

Illustration by Eduard Thöny for Thoma's comic epistolary novel Briefwechsel eines bayerischen Landtagsabgeordneten

novel, *Andreas Vöst* (1906), based on a law case, involves a clergyman who abuses his religious office for political power. The clergyman is challenged by Andreas Vöst, a masterfully characterized farmer whose frustrated struggle for justice and ultimate downfall have been compared to the fate of Michael Kohlhaas in Heinrich von Kleist's 1808 novella.

In the story *Der heilige Hies* (1904; translated as "Matt the Holy," 1914) Thoma ridicules the sanctimonious aura of an all-too-worldly priesthood. His biting public derision in *Simplicissimus* of a conference of the German Societies on Ethics brought him notoriety, a trial, and a six-week term in jail in 1906. This experience only spurred him to launch new satirical attacks. His brilliant essay against shallow rhetoric, "Die Reden Kaiser Wilhelms II" (The Speeches of Emperor Wilhelm II), was written for the journal *März,* which he founded with Langen, Hermann Hesse, and Kurt Aram in 1906. He satirized the hypocrisy of bourgeois morals and corrupt state officialdom in his comedy *Moral* (1909; translated as *Morality,* 1909).

Thoma's greatest narrative successes were *Lausbubengeschichten,* with its sequel *Tante Frieda* (Aunt Frieda, 1907), and *Briefwechsel eines bayerischen Landtagsabgeordneten* (Correspondence of a Member of the Bavarian Parliament, 1909), continued in *Jozef Filsers Briefwexel* (Jozef Filser's Correspondence, 1912). *Lausbubengeschichten* and *Tante Frieda,* written from the seemingly naive perspective of a clever schoolboy and ranked by some critics with Mark Twain's *The Adventures of Tom Sawyer* (1876) and *Adventures of Huckleberry Finn* (1884), depict roguish retaliation against the philistinism and authoritarianism of the adult world. *Briefwechsel eines bayerischen Landtagsabgeordneten* and *Jozef Filsers Briefwexel,* written in the hilarious diction and orthography of a rural representative in the Bavarian parliament, reveal the fallacies of bureaucratic processes and the preposterousness of human conduct in all areas of daily life. A dramatized farce about Filser, *Erster Klasse* (First Class, 1910), was another immediate success.

Intermittently Thoma traveled, both to escape mounting pressures in Munich and to gain wider experiences. In cosmopolitan Berlin the exotic Bavarian was lionized by high society and praised by influential critics. In Paris, through Langen, Thoma met Auguste Rodin and other members of the artistic and literary world. In Vienna he made the acquaintance of the satirist Karl Kraus and other Austrian writers. He also traveled to Italy, southern France, and northern Africa. But despite his enthusiasm for new impressions, he remained loyal to Bavaria, where he had his roots. He wore Bavarian dress, smoked a Bavarian pipe, and in 1908 built an expensive rustic house in Bavarian style near Rottach on Tegernsee. Maria Trinidad de la Rosa, a Manila-born dancer known as Marietta di Rigardo, whom he had married in 1905 after her divorce from her ailing first husband, never felt at home with his Bavarian life-style. They separated in 1910.

The crisis of his marriage and the sudden deaths of several friends and collaborators brought out Thoma's somber side. His 1911 novel *Der Wittiber* (The Widower) is a tragic tale about a widowed farmer whose affair with his maid stirs the jealousy of his self-righteous daughter and the rebelliousness of his son; the son, fearing that he will be disowned, hangs the pregnant maid in the barn. The inevitable downfall of the once-respected family, a consequence of stubbornness, bigotry, and self-interest in a closed world, reads like an archaic myth in realistic local setting. In Thoma's only tragic play, *Magdalena* (1912), a father acting within the rigid moral system of a small community kills his daughter because she has brought "shame" on family and village. It is a mature masterwork of its genre.

World War I caused a radical change in Thoma that shocked his friends and admirers. Thoma had criticized "Prussian" militarism, had caricatured the Kaiser and his officers, and had attacked feverish armament in Germany. But when the war broke out in 1914 he became patriotic, pro-Kaiser, and nationalistic; his heart was with his people, and, at forty-seven, he wanted to join the fighting farm boys. He drove to the front with gift packages and was finally accepted in the ambulance corps, serving in France and Galicia. He proudly received the Iron Cross, but in 1915 he was sent back home for reasons of health.

In his withdrawal and increasing solitude, where Heimat (homeland) seemed to become his only value, he lost touch with life and with himself; he even went so far in 1917 as to join an archconservative and anti-Semitic group, the Vaterlandspartei. But he still wrote short plays and novellas in his proven style. The theme of dying began to haunt him. He wrote a religious poem, the Christmas legend *Heilige Nacht* (Holy Night, 1917), transferring the Nativity story to a Bavarian village milieu and creating a unique lyrical gem of Bavarian dialect. In the "cheerful summer tale" *Altaich* (1918) Thoma succeeded at mild critical humor about the ambiguous blessings of tourism. An idyllic small town wants to become a health resort; its businesses utilize peculiar forms of advertising; the arrival of strangers from the city is captured in amusing portrayals of types with distinct idiosyncrasies.

After the defeat of Germany Thoma feared that the old order and way of life he valued were threatened. He was plagued by depression, self-doubt, and missed opportunities. Skeptical about the Weimar Republic, he was distrustful of leftist attempts to gain power; during his lowest political moods he anonymously attacked the republic in the reactionary local newspaper of the nearby town of Miesbach. *Simplicissimus* resumed its liberal stance of social criticism, but Thoma wrote little for it–he sensed the irritation he had caused by his shifts in philosophy. He turned to the past, completing his memoirs, *Erinnerungen,* in 1919.

In 1918 he encountered Maidi von Liebermann, whom he had first met and greatly admired in 1904 without daring to propose to her. Now he wooed her, fought for her almost desperately, hoping for a new life with her and a new creative start. But Maidi, of Jewish descent and quite different social background, sensed their incompatibility and delayed putting an end to her unhappy marriage. Thoma began to write fiction again, semiautobiographical like most of his work. *Der Jagerloisl* (1921) is a story about hunters, farmers, nature, and vacation spirit around his home area, Tegernsee. *Münchnerinnen* (Munich Women, 1922) is a novel about a dissatisfied married woman who falls in love with a student who deserts her. Set in Munich in the late nineteenth century, the novel blends colorful milieu and fine character analysis. It remained a fragment, as did *Kaspar Lorinser* (1922), which promised to become a major bildungsroman; only a few superb pages exist, however. They reflect Thoma's most mature narrative skill, which tells most where it seems most restrained. Both fragments were posthumously published in *Gesammelte Werke* (Collected Works, 1922).

His last completed novel, *Der Ruepp* (1922), is a powerful tale of the moral and social decline of a farmer (the title is his cognomen) who begins drinking and cheating only to trap himself and pull others down with him. Occasional humor in

Thoma, circa 1911, at his home near Rottach on Tegernsee

this realistic portrayal of rural life gives way to tragedy. While putting the finishing touches to this masterwork the fifty-four-year-old Thoma fell ill with stomach trouble. An operation came too late, and he died on 26 August 1921 in his home. He was buried at Rottach-Egern. In his will he had made Maidi von Liebermann his literary executor and main heir.

Early interpreters set a trend that continued for several decades: they focused on Thoma as a local phenomenon and treated his work predominantly from a biographical perspective. Thoma's many acquaintances emphasized his close ties with Bavaria and tended to see him as a popular humorist. Next to this image, supported by the broad success of his comedies, farces, *Lausbubengeschichten,* and the figure of Josef Filser, there developed a deepening perception of Thoma as a political writer, pamphleteer, and aggressive satirist creating shock effects in various quarters at different times. This perception is based primarily on his essays for the *Simplicissimus,* but also on a closer analysis of some of his stories and plays. Gradually, scholarship caught up with an achievement that had long been neglected, although Thoma himself had been quite conscious of it: the narrative art of his novels. Not only did critics recognize the universality of the human problems presented in local milieu, they also pointed to the sophistication of Thoma's deceptive simplicity of style: a blending of robust realism with sensitivity of mood, a musical and pictorial quality of language that brings his epic portrayals to life in a compelling way. Dialect is an important part of Thoma's artistic work which has made him a "classic" of modern German literature.

Letters:

Ludwig Thoma: Ausgewählte Briefe, edited by Josef Hofmiller and Michael Hochgesang (Munich: Langen, 1927);

Ludwig Thoma: Ein Leben in Briefen 1875-1921, edited by Anton Keller (Munich: Piper, 1963);

Ludwig Thoma–Ignatius Taschner: Eine bayerische Freundschaft in Briefen, edited, with notes, by Richard Lemp (Munich: Piper, 1971);

Thoma circa 1914

Lithograph of Thoma by Karl Bauer

Thoma with his Bavarian pipe

Ludwig Thoma: Vom Advokaten zum Literaten. Unbekannte Briefe, edited, with notes, by Lemp (Munich & Zürich: Piper, 1979).

Bibliography:
Richard Lemp, ed., *Ludwig Thoma zum 100. Geburtstag* (Munich: Stadtbibliothek, 1967).

Biographies:
Fritz Heinle, *Ludwig Thoma* (Reinbek: Rowohlt, 1963);
Roland Ziersch, *Ludwig Thoma* (Mühlacker: Stieglitz, 1964);
Gerd Thumser, *Ludwig Thoma und seine Welt* (Munich: Desch, 1966);
Peter Haage, *Mit Nagelstiefeln durchs Kaiserreich: Ludwig Thoma. Eine Biographie* (Munich, Gütersloh & Vienna: Bertelsmann, 1975);
Helmut Ahrens, *Ludwig Thoma: Sein Leben, sein Werk, seine Zeit* (Pfaffenhofen: Ludwig, 1983).

References:
Siegfried Beyschlag, "Ludwig Thomas Romandichtung," *Euphorion,* 47 (1953): 79-96;
Hermann Boeschenstein, "Zu Ludwig Thomas *Andreas Vöst,*" *Germanic Review,* 11 (1936): 207-213;
Friedl Brehm, *Ludwig Thoma und der Simplicissimus: Immer gegen die Machthaber* (Feldafing: Brehm, 1966);
Fritz Dehnow, *Ludwig Thoma* (Munich: Langen, 1925);
William Diamond, "Ludwig Thoma," *Monatshefte,* 21 (1929): 97-101;
Oskar Maria Graf, *An manchen Tagen: Reden, Gedanken und Zeitbetrachtungen* (Frankfurt am Main: Nest, 1961), pp. 48-75;
Edgar Hederer, *Ludwig Thoma* (Munich: Langen, 1941);
Walter L. Heilbronner, "A Reappraisal of Ludwig Thoma," *German Quarterly,* 30 (1957): 247-253;
Bernt von Heiseler, "Ludwig Thoma, der Dichter," *Die Sammlung,* 12 (1957): 25-32;

Korfitz Holm, *Ludwig Thoma und Olaf Gulbransson, wie ich sie erlebte* (Munich: Nymphenburger Verlagshaus, 1953);

Frank D. Horvay, "Ludwig Thoma's Dagger Thrusts," *American-German Review*, 29 (1962): 9-12, 40;

Calvin N. Jones, "Ludwig Thoma's *Magdalena:* A Transitional 'Volksstück,' " *Seminar*, 16 (1980): 83-95;

Richard Lemp, *Ludwig Thoma: Bilder, Dokumente, Materialien zu Leben und Werk* (Munich: Süddeutscher Verlag, 1984);

Will-Erich Peuckert, "Ludwig Thoma," *Zeitschrift für deutsche Philologie*, 71 (1951/1952): 369-373;

James P. Sandrock, *Ludwig Thoma: Aspects of His Art* (Göppingen: Kümmerle, 1975);

Bruno F. Steinbruckner, *Ludwig Thoma* (Boston: Twayne, 1978);

Donald V. White, "Ludwig Thoma as a Political Satirist," *German Life and Letters*, 13 (1959/1960): 214-219.

Papers:

Ludwig Thoma's papers are at the Stadtbibliothek Munich.

Clara Viebig

(17 July 1860-31 July 1952)

Erich P. Hofacker, Jr.
University of Michigan

Deutsche Staatsbibliothek, Berlin

BOOKS: *Kinder der Eifel: Novellen* (Berlin: Fontane, 1897);

Rheinlandstöchter: Roman (Berlin: Fontane, 1897);

Barbara Holzer: Schauspiel in 3 Akten (Berlin: Fontane, 1897);

Dilettanten des Lebens: Roman (Berlin: Fontane, 1898);

Vor Tau und Tag: Novellen (Berlin: Fontane, 1898);

Es lebe die Kunst! Roman (Berlin: Fontane, 1899); republished as *Elisabeth Reinharz, Ehe: Es lebe die Kunst!* (Berlin: Neufeld & Henius, 1928);

Pharisäer: Komödie (Berlin: Fontane, 1899);

Das Weiberdorf: Roman aus der Eifel (Berlin: Fontane, 1900);

Das tägliche Brot: Roman in zwei Bänden, 2 volumes (Berlin: Fontane, 1900); translated by Margaret L. Clarke as *Our Daily Bread* (London: Lane, 1909);

Die Rosenkranzjungfer und anderes (Berlin: Fleischel, 1901);

Die Wacht am Rhein: Roman (Berlin: Fleischel, 1902);

Vom Müller-Hannes: Eine Geschichte aus der Eifel (Berlin: Fleischel, 1903);

Wen die Götter lieben; Vor Tau und Tag: Novellen (Stuttgart: Krabbe, 1903);

Gespenster; Sie müssen ihr Glück machen: Zwei Novellen (Stuttgart: Krabbe, 1904);

Das schlafende Heer: Roman (Berlin: Fleischel, 1904); translated by Gilbert Waterhouse as *The Sleeping Army: A Story of Prussian and Pole* (London: Benn, 1929);

Simson und Delila: Novelle (Leipzig: Hesse, 1904);

Naturgewalten: Neue Geschichten aus der Eifel (Berlin: Fleischel, 1905);

Der Kampf um den Mann: Dramenzyklus (Berlin: Fleischel, 1905);

Einer Mutter Sohn: Roman (Berlin: Fleischel, 1906); translated by H. Raahauge as *The Son of His Mother* (London & New York: Lane, 1913);

Absolvo Te: Roman (Berlin: Fleischel, 1907); translated by Raahauge as *Absolution* (London: Lane, 1908);

Das Kreuz im Venn: Roman (Berlin: Fleischel, 1908);

Das letzte Glück: Schauspiel (Berlin: Fleischel, 1908);

Die vor den Toren: Roman (Berlin: Fleischel, 1910);

Die heilige Einfalt: Novellen (Berlin: Fleischel, 1910);

Drei Erzählungen: Für das deutsche Volk und seine höheren Schulen, edited by P. Beer (Berlin: Fleischel, 1910);

Ausgewählte Werke, 6 volumes (Berlin: Fleischel, 1911);

Das Eisen im Feuer: Roman (Berlin: Fleischel, 1913);
Heimat: Novellen (Berlin: Fleischel, 1914);
Eine Handvoll Erde: Roman (Berlin & Stuttgart: Deutsche Verlags-Anstalt, 1915);
Töchter der Hekuba: Ein Roman aus unserer Zeit (Berlin & Stuttgart: Deutsche Verlags-Anstalt, 1917); translated by Anna Barwell as *Daughters of Hecuba* (London: Allen & Unwin, 1922);
Roter Mohn: Erzählung (Berlin: Hillger, 1918);
Das rote Meer: Roman (Berlin & Stuttgart: Deutsche Verlags-Anstalt, 1920);
West und Ost: Novellen (Leipzig: Reclam, 1920);
Ein einfältiges Herz; Das Kind und das Venn; Ein Weihnachtsabend: Drei Erzählungen (Wiesbaden: Volksbildungsverein, 1921);
Unter dem Freiheitsbaum: Roman (Stuttgart: Deutsche Verlags-Anstalt, 1922);
Ausgewählte Werke, 8 volumes (Stuttgart: Deutsche Verlags-Anstalt, 1922);
Menschen und Straßen: Großstadtnovellen (Leipzig: Lohmann, 1923);
Der einsame Mann: Roman (Stuttgart: Deutsche Verlags-Anstalt, 1924);
Franzosenzeit: Zwei Novellen (Stuttgart: Engelhorn, 1925);
Die Passion (Stuttgart: Deutsche Verlags-Anstalt, 1926);
Die goldenen Berge: Roman (Stuttgart: Deutsche Verlags-Anstalt, 1927); translated by Graham Rawson as *The Golden Hills: A Novel of the German Vineyards* (London: Lane, 1928; New York: Vanguard, 1930);
Die Schuldige: Novelle aus der Eifel (Lahr: Schauenburg, 1927);
Die mit den tausend Kindern: Roman (Stuttgart: Deutsche Verlags-Anstalt, 1929); translated by Brian Lunn as *The Woman with a Thousand Children* (New York & London: Appleton, 1930);
Charlotte von Weiß: Der Roman einer schönen Frau (Berlin: Ullstein, 1930);
Prinzen, Prälaten und Sansculotten: Roman (Stuttgart: Deutsche Verlags-Anstalt, 1931);
Menschen unter Zwang: Roman (Stuttgart: Deutsche Verlags-Anstalt, 1932);
Insel der Hoffnung: Roman (Stuttgart: Deutsche Verlags-Anstalt, 1933);
Der Vielgeliebte und die Vielgehaßte: Roman (Stuttgart: Deutsche Verlags-Anstalt, 1935);
Berliner Novellen (Berlin: Verlag Das Neue Berlin, 1952).

OTHER: *Mütter: Acht Bilder aus dem Leben der Mutter,* introduction by Viebig (Leipzig: Seemann, 1933).

PERIODICAL PUBLICATIONS: "Wie ich Schriftstellerin wurde," *Aus dem Posener Lande,* 5 (1910): 107-112, 171-174;
"Lebens-Abriß," *Berliner Tageblatt,* 7 December 1930.

Clara Viebig, the most prominent woman writer among the German naturalists, was one of Germany's most successful authors for twenty-five years. Sixteen of her seventeen novels published through 1922 were best-sellers. Viebig's worldview and stylistic temperament were perfectly in accord with the perspective of naturalism. Literary critics considered her works to be in harmony with the spirit of the times; Hermann Bahr, a novelist as well as a prominent critic, said that Viebig was the only writer of the early twentieth century who accurately reflected the interests and concerns of the average German and that she created a "mirror of German conditions." Translations of her works into English, French, Russian, Spanish, Dutch, Finnish, and Polish spread her reputation abroad, and lecture tours took her to most European countries and to the United States. An enthusiastic American reviewer declared in the *Fatherland* (30 December 1914): "What George Eliot was to England Clara Viebig is to-day to Germany."

Viebig's parents settled in the Rhineland after coming from the eastern province of Posen (now Poznań), where her father, Ernst Viebig, had served as a high official in the Prussian administration of that former Polish territory until the revolutionary unrest of 1848. Clara Viebig was born on 17 July 1860 in Trier on the Moselle River, but the family soon moved to Düsseldorf in the Rhineland, where Viebig attended school and grew up as something of a tomboy. In her teenage years her father became seriously ill, and she was sent back to Trier to attend a boarding school operated by a family friend named Mathieu, an official of the rural court. With her good-humored "Uncle" Mathieu young Clara walked along the banks of the Moselle and received her first vivid impressions of the Eifel landscape. The region and its borderland, the Venn, consisted of an extensive heath, a high moor of volcanic earth, ancient craters, and deep, dark, often eerie crater lakes and pools. It is this land-

Drawing by Max Liebermann for the title page of Viebig's novel about sexual frustration among women in a German village

scape which Viebig's artistry so frequently portrays in all of its austere and lonely beauty.

While Uncle Mathieu made his official rounds, Viebig sat in the garden and let her imagination roam. When he returned she was eager to learn the details of the cases he had investigated. "Nicht alles taugte für Mädchenohren" (not everything was suitable for a young girl to hear), but she insisted. "Aber hat es mir geschadet? O nein! Ich bin dem Volk in seinem Denken und Empfinden nahe gekommen. Ich bin wohl erschaudert beim derben Tritt, mit dem es die Erde stampft" (But did it hurt me? O no! I came close to the people and the way they think and feel, although I was probably shocked at their coarseness and at how forcefully they expressed themselves). She found that the common people trod hard with their hobnailed boots on everything that was weak. They were sometimes insensitive and without pity, but they could also express love with a primitive energy. The people of the Eifel region followed their instincts without shame. These early discoveries were later reflected in her literary work.

Her experiences in the Eifel, Venn, and the Rhineland, and later in Posen and Berlin, aroused her sympathy for the common people. They were victims of economic hardship, but they suffered socially and intellectually as well. An objective and accurate description of their lot might bring improvement. Viebig was not inclined to introspection, and her warmheartedness toward her subjects was, paradoxically, combined with an almost cold objectivity. She portrayed the farmers and peasants of these regions just as she found them: sometimes astonishingly ignorant, but often possessing great powers of endurance that enabled them to continue the struggle for existence. Her works also showed the benefits and limitations of strict religious faith and the strength born of fidelity and love. Many letters of support came from the farmers of the Eifel, often acknowledging the accuracy of her depiction, but at times sharply critical of her portrayals of their "Dummheit, Aberglauben und Geldgier" (stupidity, superstition, and greed).

At twenty-three, after her father's death, Viebig moved with her mother to Berlin to study singing. For the next thirteen years she spent her summers with relatives in the province of Posen, an area she at first disliked because of its dissimilarity to the Rhineland. But there, too, she gradually found a personal relationship with nature and ultimately considered the region, along with the Rhineland and the Eifel, one of the three "brides" she had come to know and love.

Viebig's singing career brought her little satisfaction and insufficient income. "Following an inner compulsion," she turned to writing brief literary sketches of the landscape and people of the Rhineland. After perhaps a decade of indifferent success with these sketches, none of which has been preserved, an acquaintance gave her a copy of Emile Zola's novel *Germinal* (1885). This moving account of child labor in the coal mines triggered a sudden turn in Viebig's literary life: "Ich fieberte, ich zitterte, ich war wie niedergedonnert, ein Blitz hatte mich hell durchfahren . . . diese Gewalt der Sprache, diese Fülle der Gesichte, diese Leidenschaft der Gefühle,–so muß man schreiben, so!" (I was feverish, I trembled, it was as if I had been struck down by thunder and lightning, a transfiguring bolt passed through me . . . this power of language, this fullness of vision, these passionate emotions–one should write this way!). Viebig did not become a mere imitator of Zola but his true heir through her genuine affinity for his worldview and literary technique. In only two days of intensive work she completed a naturalistic tale about the exploitation, seduction, and lust of a peasant girl. Titled "Die Schuldige" (The Guilty One), it was at first rejected as too bold for publication, but a revised version was published along with six other novellas in her first collection, *Kinder der Eifel* (Children of the Eifel, 1897). Viebig had married Fritz Theodor Cohn, a publisher's representative, the previous year, and *Kinder der Eifel* was the first of many works by Viebig to be published by his firm.

"Die Schuldige" contains themes, concerns, and elements of style characteristic of naturalism, the late nineteenth-century literary movement that followed and countered poetic realism. Typically employing a harsh realism in which aesthetic considerations were sacrificed to the artist's attempt at a true representation of life, the naturalists often focused on the deplorable living conditions of the urban poor and the negative effects of heredity and environment; they were noted for their frank discussion of sexual questions. Naturalistic works often sought to establish causal explanations of the ills that beset mankind. To heighten realism they employed the vigorous, blunt, earthy language of the lower classes; dialect was commonly used.

Kinder der Eifel introduced the Eifel region and Trier to the literary world. Viebig's skillful blending of the character of a people with their surroundings created the regional "living landscapes" that became her literary signature. In these novellas the local dialect contrasts with the cultivated standard German of the author's commentary. Against a background of bleak and gloomy moors, Viebig allows basic human instincts free rein. "Die Schuldige" is the first of her works to display honest and open sensuality and an admission of sexual desire in women. Its motif of the deserted single mother became one of Viebig's favorites. Barbara Holzer, the hired hand, is seduced by Lorenz, the son of the farmer who employs her. Though she must accept her ultimate desertion as "ein Stück bäuerlicher Weltordnung" (a piece of the rural world order), her feeling of self-worth enables her to win a contest of wills with her socially superior partner. Before a final sexual encounter totally devoid of love, she wrings a pledge from Lorenz that he will never marry: "Liewer sehn ech dech dud vor mer, als dat ech dech ener annern laoß–hörste, Lorenz–Lorenz!" (I would rather see you lying dead before me than give you to another–do you hear me, Lorenz–Lorenz!). Barbara leaves the farm without disclosing the identity of her unborn child's father and looks forward with growing pride and joy to its birth. Later, superstitious peasants report having seen her moving like an apparition on the forested hillside before the cave where she lives with the child. The end is tragic and melodramatic: Lorenz seeks to steal the child out of fear that its discovery will doom his approaching marriage to the devout daughter of a wealthy farmer. In frenzied fear of losing all she possesses, Barbara kills Lorenz with a rusty bread knife. In the last scene she sits in her jail cell weeping; she has lost her child.

"Die Schuldige" combines the romantic forest atmosphere typical of poetic realism with the new clinical verisimilitude of naturalism. Its negative impressions regarding human nature are allowed to prevail; as in later works, the author gives no indication that an ethical or humane solution can be found.

Viebig's work during the following three years shows a marked retreat from the lively style of her original collection. *Vor Tau und Tag* (Before Dew and Day, 1898) contains several long and formally imperfect novellas in which she tries unsuccessfully to describe the complicated personalities of upper-class individuals. Her three novels of this period are conventional in style and concept and strongly autobiographical. The heroines of *Rheinlandstöchter* (Daughters of the Rhineland, 1897) and *Dilettanten des Lebens* (Amateurs at Life, 1898) are like those of other female authors of the day: they struggle to establish independent life-styles in the face of the barriers of convention. *Es lebe die Kunst!* (Long Live Art!, 1899) is somewhat better. Its heroine, Elisabeth Reinharz, is thrust into the competitive literary environment of Berlin: "Immer gepeitscht, immer gehetzt, immer gequält, unglücklich–verzweifelt–das ist die Kunst" (Always under the whip, always rushed, always tormented, unhappy–despairing–that's art). Her struggle to balance obligations to family and career seems to be a reflection of Viebig's own experiences with her young son.

With *Das Weiberdorf* (The Village of Women, 1900) Viebig was back in stride. She frankly depicts sexual starvation among women–an anticipation of Gerhart Hauptmann's *Die Insel der großen Mutter* (1925; translated as *The Island of the Great*

Drawing by H. Zille for the dust jacket of Das tägliche Brot, *Viebig's novel about the grim lives of servants in Berlin*

Mother, 1925) a quarter century later. Poor crops force the men of the community to seek work in distant steel mills. During their semiannual return home their women's pent-up sensuality is relieved, but after their departure the women's loneliness begins again. "Wie ein Rudel ausgehungerter Wölfe" (like a pack of starving wolves) the women pursue Pittchen, the only man left in the village. The women and men in *Das Weiberdorf* together seem to represent Eros. Its essence is embodied in Zeih, Pittchen's wife, whose beauty gives her power over all men. Zeih's antithesis is Bäbbi, who symbolizes the natural instinct of motherliness and who remains untouched by the pervasive sensuality; in Bäbbi, Eros is consumed and overcome. Unfortunately, the novel directs too much attention to the frustrated, sexually deprived women and neglects the positive image of the fulfilled individual. Conservative readers and critics of the time found fault with *Das Weiberdorf,* but more recent opinion views it as an effective work of social criticism and as a significant portrayal of one of the negative effects of the rapid industrialization of Germany around 1870.

Central to Viebig's worldview is a belief in the primary role of nature in human life. Animals and plants interact with their environments as elements of a totality; all are part of nature and all are interdependent. Sustained by nature and one with it, man is subject to natural forces; he is the servant of nature, not its ruler. This unity is most evident in the simple individual who is motivated by forces of hunger and love and whose life moves with the cycle of nature. Viebig wished the figures in her works to be seen and judged in their proximity to nature. All potentially share the same simplicity of life and fate; all are members of one family; and all may be conditioned by the same natural forces to think, act, and feel as a whole. Viebig employs the analogy of the river: as the river is composed of a multiplicity of drops of water which flow along together, so mankind is moved, according to natural laws, to common, unconscious expression in political and social developments. Therefore, social transformations and revolutions have the character of natural forces. The more effectively the interdependence of man and nature is conveyed by a literary work, the greater the artistic power.

Das Weiberdorf was followed by *Das tägliche Brot* (1900; translated as *Our Daily Bread,* 1909), a very different type of novel, which was hailed as a masterpiece and as the first chronicle of servants' lives in German literature. Viebig's aim in the novel is to show the joylessness of material and spiritual poverty. Set in Berlin during the final decades of the nineteenth century, *Das tägliche Brot* focuses alternately on the snobbish bourgeoisie and the narrow-minded lower-middle class, on the one hand, and their household servants, on the other. Describing the fate of rural girls who go to the city to make good only to be exploited at every turn, Viebig provides abundant examples of social distress, humiliation, setbacks, and despair. Within this framework a timeless symbolic weight is carried by Mine, the strongest female figure in any of Viebig's works. A country girl, unpretentious and strong, Mine is patient and noble like the earth in which her existence is rooted. These roots remain firm during her life in the city, and through them she can draw on the inexhaustible strength of the earth, on moral and spiritual values that enable her to overcome the misery of her externally impoverished life. She is equal to all the trials that befall her and becomes Viebig's best example of a spiritual victory over the circumstances of an urban environment.

Bertha is from Mine's hometown, but she has not put deep roots into the nourishing soil. Pretty and frivolous, full of practical wisdom gained from her midwife mother, she has come to Berlin looking for the easy life. Lacking Mine's stability and intent on quick success, Bertha fits Viebig's prescription for downfall: she becomes an Animiermädchen (B-girl) in a cheap bar and is heading for prostitution. It is evident that rural origins alone do not give strength of character: Bertha becomes one of the many proletarian figures who are dominated by the restlessness and dissatisfaction generated by the urban environment. All are rootless, and all are doomed to defeat.

Fifteen years later, Viebig published *Eine Handvoll Erde* (A Handful of Earth, 1915), a weaker sequel describing the later life of Mine, who is now married to one of the rootless proletariat. Through a benefactor Mine acquires a small plot of land outside the city. Her instinctive longing satisfied, she can once again find peace in direct contact with Mother Earth and relieve the pain and worry caused by her unstable husband.

Viebig in 1905 (Ullstein)

The historical novel *Die Wacht am Rhein* (The Watch on the Rhine, 1902) is generally considered Viebig's best work. The novel opens in 1815 with the Congress of Vienna, which aimed at territorial resettlement after the defeat of Napoleon, and closes with the establishment of the German Empire in 1871. *Die Wacht am Rhein* is set in Düsseldorf and the Rhineland during the period of Prussian political control. The friction between the Rhinelanders and the Prussians is increased because of their differing temperaments. Viebig characterizes her fellow Rhinelanders as people of optimistic and cheerful disposition who display joy in life and are disinclined to gravity. Her stereotypical Prussian is stern, a personification of the Kantian categorical imperative: he is controlled by a sense of duty and follows the dictates of a strict personal discipline. Through the reminiscences of her mother Viebig acquired a "living relationship" with the history of the period, especially the revolutionary years 1848-1849 and the age of Bismarck. *Die Wacht am Rhein* follows three generations of a family of mixed marriages, Roman Catholic Rhinelanders and Protestant

Prussians, chronicling the gradual disappearance of regional separatism and antagonisms. The Rhinelanders and the Prussians finally subordinate their separate concerns to the good of a unified Germany no longer under Prussian domination. Historical tensions and conflicts provide the driving force for the novel, molding character and establishing the framework for individuals' interdependent actions.

Military tradition, the essence of Prussia, is exemplified by Sgt. Rinke, who is rooted heart and soul in his profession and in the five elements of the military catechism: "Treue, Tapferkeit, Gehorsam, Pflichtgefühl, Ehre" (fidelity, bravery, obedience, duty, and honor). The barracks is the natural environment of the soldier, but his wife, Trina, can feel thoroughly at home only in the cheerful, comfortable bourgeois households of her native Rhineland. The husband and wife cannot overcome regional distinctions and conflicts because they are not willing to alter their basic natures. As manifested in Düsseldorf, the uprising of 1848 is not a demand for democratic freedom or an expression of socialistic ideals by a distressed third estate but an outpouring of the repugnance felt in the Rhineland for the Prussian military. As time passes, however, the two bloodlines and the opposing mentalities draw together into one spirit and one German nation. This evolution is embodied in Josefine Rinke, the daughter of Sgt. Rinke and Trina. Her progress over forty years toward a resolution of her inner conflicts is the central theme of the novel.

Das schlafende Heer (1904; translated as *The Sleeping Army,* 1929) is a companion piece to *Die Wacht am Rhein;* it, too, describes the contact of alien cultures and the struggle of a subjugated people. Prussia has gained political control over Poland, but an "army" of Poles may one day awaken to drive out the intruders. The number of Germans in Poland is small; they are primarily administrative officials, large landowners, and a few settlers from the Rhineland. The pedantic Doleschal, a former army officer and the representative of the Prussian spirit, is a counterpart to Sgt. Rinke: just as Rinke's pedantry destroyed his family life, Doleschal's punctiliousness makes his life in the community difficult. Viebig characterizes Prussian official policy as narrow-minded, intolerant, and dependent on force to achieve its goal of compelling the indigenous population to speak, think, and feel "in German" so as to destroy the Polish national consciousness. The thematic development in *Das schlafende Heer* is not as clear as in *Die Wacht am Rhein,* and Viebig had some difficulty in portraying landowners and other nonpeasant groups. Her strength lies not in the psychological differentiation of individuals but in the portrayal of the peasant masses.

To the Eifel, its landscape and its people, Viebig said she owed "das Höchste, das Schönste, das Größte" (that which was highest, most beautiful, and greatest) in her life. But nature is a hostile force to those not native to the region, who are often unable to cope with its infertile soil and harsh climate. The first and best of Viebig's so-called Landschaftsromane (landscape novels) is *Das Kreuz im Venn* (The Cross in the Venn, 1908), which describes the Venn portion of the Eifel, a high and lonely moor which extends to the Belgian border. Viebig describes this vast area: "Wie ein Meer mit Wellen und Wellchen, eine Flut, endlos, ohne Ufer, ohne Begrenzung dehnt sich das Venn, und der Wagen fährt wie ein winziger Nachen in die Unendlichkeit" (Like a sea with its waves and ripples, like a flood tide, endless, without shores, without limits does the Venn stretch out, and the [traveler's] wagon moves like a tiny boat out into the infinity). Left far behind the traveler in the invisible distance are valleys, rivers, cities, vibrant and pulsating life. In the solitude of the Venn, people become melancholy and taciturn. Heather, junipers, a few berries, scrub grass, and occasional flowers cover the earth during the short, hot summer; in the spring and fall come long rainy periods; the winter brings heavy snows and raging northwesterly winds. This inhospitable landscape takes on a life of its own; in the novel it offers almost human companionship to a lonely old man who has lost his wife and child. The native inhabitants are tough and resistant like nature itself, accustomed to the raw wind, hard work, and meager existence. Life is austere; the people are miserly, reserved, and independent; each house stands alone.

Rising above all else, like the cross on the mountaintop, religious faith dominates life, offering strength in daily life and joy on festival days. Prayer is the only weapon against sickness and death in the struggle with nature. Viebig recognizes the validity of a natural, mature, and genuine piety and accepts religious processions and pilgrimages as an expression of a childlike faith. She believes, however, that an unhealthy exaggeration in religious matters may be harmful, as is the progressive intoxication of the Echtenacher Spring-Prozession, a "pilgrimage" of 1,250 meters to a shrine, made by springing five jumps for-

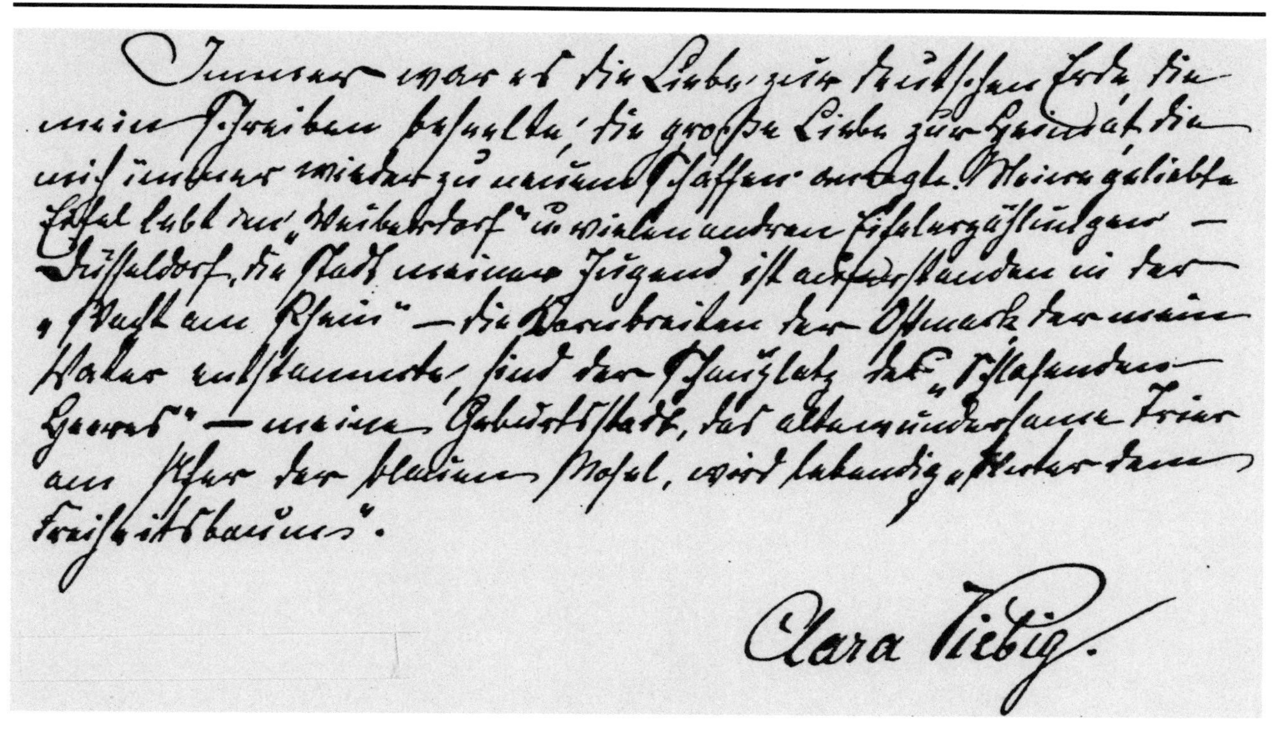

Immer war es die Liebe zur deutschen Erde die meinem Schreiben befeuerte; die grosse Liebe zur Heimat die mich immer wieder zu neuem Schaffen anregte. Meine geliebte Eifel lebt im „Weiberdorf" u. vielen andren Eifelerzählungen — Düsseldorf, die Stadt meiner Jugend ist auferstanden in der „Wacht am Rhein" — die [illegible] der Ostmark der meine Vater entstammte, sind der Schauplatz des „Schlafenden Heeres" — meine Geburtsstadt, das altehrwürdige Trier am Ufer der blauen Mosel, wird lebendig „Unter dem Freiheitsbaum".

Clara Viebig.

Page from a manuscript by Viebig (Albert Soergel and Curt Hohoff, Dichtung und Dichter der Zeit, *1963)*

ward and three back. As some 20,000 persons participate on a hot, humid Whitsunday, the combination of religious and physical excitement produces in many an intoxicating blend of spiritual and carnal sensations. To Viebig, those who spring beyond the limits of propriety demonstrate the demonic effect of religious ecstasy. Detailing the struggle for existence in the village of Eifelschmidt, the novel demonstrates that life is hard, but it is familiar and secure for those who feel the bond of nature and follow the old ways.

In the documentary novel *Die vor den Toren* (Those Outside the Gates, 1910), Viebig describes the detrimental effect of the expansion of the new capital of Berlin on the surrounding rural population, which suffers a marked deterioration of its cultural traditions and morality. The opportunistic farmers of the neighboring town of Tempelhof sell their land to speculators, then find themselves totally unsuited to life in the city: the city has taken their land, prosperity, and children and has given nothing in return. Viebig views urbanization, however, as only one stage in a cycle of migrations which eventually will bring the city dwellers to the country to strengthen their moral fiber and resiliency. Their children will one day establish themselves in farming.

Lacking naturalism's orientation toward the city and its fascination with urban misery, Viebig's fiction approaches Heimatdichtung (regional literature) in that she views life in the city as unnatural. To her the human bond with nature does not merely enhance life but is a deeply rooted and indispensable component of man's makeup. Since urban life destroys the cosmic unity of man and nature, it is an unnatural state and cannot be considered a permanent human condition.

Viebig devoted a pair of novels to World War I: *Töchter der Hekuba* (1917; translated as *Daughters of Hecuba,* 1922) concerns the period 1914-1916, and its sequel, *Das rote Meer* (The Red Sea, 1920), deals with the years 1917-1918. Both novels focus on personal concerns rather than on military and political questions. *Töchter der Hekuba,* employing Viebig's characteristic positive image of women and motherhood, rejects the naturalist's assertion of female despondency, faintheartedness, and even frivolity in times of military conflict. Distinctions of class, age, and temperament are erased as all types of women are united in a sisterhood of common cares. Women, in their courageous responses to their losses, approach the heroism of frontline soldiers. *Das rote Meer* contends that only the German leaders possessed a will to win the war. There is a feeling of brotherhood between the German and Russian

Viebig in 1925 (Ullstein)

soldiers in their common desire for peace and for more humane conditions at home.

In both novels, war is presented as an impersonal machine hostile to mankind. Viebig sounds no hurrahs, awards no medals, and shows no pride in victory. Nevertheless, her underlying patriotism is revealed when she places partial responsibility for Germany's defeat on the "Prussian spirit" of its officers, whose Standesdünkel (rigid class consciousness) has prevented the democratization of the army.

In Viebig's best novels characters function as voices of the community or the masses, of an environment or a region; the problems depicted are not those of individuals but are typical of the society or the region. Some of her less successful novels are more individualized. The deeper understanding and psychological penetration of individuals required by such works exceeded Viebig's artistic capabilities, and the portraits are often pale and unnatural. *Einer Mutter Sohn* (1906; translated as *The Son of His Mother,* 1913) deals with the struggle between environment and heredity in an adopted child; *Absolvo Te* (1907; translated as *Absolution,* 1908) and *Charlotte von Weiß* (1930) concern women who feel enslaved to their husbands and seek their freedom by poisoning their spouses; *Der einsame Mann* (The Lonely Man, 1924) describes the longing of a lonely individual for companionship and meaning in life; *Die Passion* (1926) describes the sad life of a girl who contracted venereal disease at birth.

Viebig continued her literary activity until 1935, but with diminishing skill and success. Since her husband was Jewish, her works were not published or reprinted in Nazi Germany. Her husband died in 1936; the following year she joined her son in Brazil, but homesickness brought her back to Germany in 1938. Air raids drove her from Berlin to a small town in Silesia, which she was compelled to leave in 1946 in the forced evacuation of the German population. Sick and impoverished, Viebig returned to her bomb-damaged house in Zehlendorf, on the outskirts of West Berlin. A former acquaintance of her husband's acquired power of attorney over her affairs and purchased her house for 60,000 marks; she was given the use of two rooms and a payment of 100 marks per month. He prevented her old acquaintances from visiting her, although she had always thrived on personal contacts.

On her eighty-ninth birthday Viebig received a congratulatory telegram from the East German Communist party which enumerated political goals she allegedly shared with the party, such as "the overcoming of the socioeconomic class struggle and its terrible effects." But Viebig never joined any political organization nor did she attack any political party or system in her writings. She could be considered nationalistic only in that she sought the general welfare of Germany, although not at the expense of other nations. When Viebig celebrated her ninetieth birthday in 1950, she received greetings from more than 200 well-wishers. She died on 31 July 1952 and is buried in Düsseldorf.

Modern critics are less generous than Viebig's contemporaries in assessing the literary quality of her work, and discussions of Viebig in modern literary histories are brief. Most commentators agree, however, that many of her twenty-six novels and eight volumes of novellas have lasting documentary value. Hers was an important contribution to the understanding of the German working class, both in the rural areas and in Berlin, during a period of rapid expansion and change.

References:

Victor W. Carpenter, "A Study of Clara Viebig's 'Novellen,'" Ph.D. dissertation, University of Pennsylvania, 1978;

Rudolf Danke, "Clara Viebig 90 Jahre alt," *Die neue Zeitung,* 13 July 1950, p. 7;

Hans Martin Elster, ed., *Clara Viebig* (Dresden: Lehmann & Schulze, 1920);

O. S. Fleissner, "Ist Clara Viebig konsequente Naturalistin?," *PMLA,* 46 (1931): 917-929;

Berthold Litzmann, "Clara Viebig," *Das literarische Echo,* 3 (1900-1901): 303-312;

Urzula Michalska, *Clara Viebig: Versuch einer Monographie* (Poznań: Uniwersytet im. Adama Mickiewicza W Poananiu, 1968);

Josef Poláček, "Deutsche soziale Prosa zwischen Naturalismus und Realismus: Zu Clara Viebigs Romanen *Das Weiberdorf* und *Das tägliche Brot,*" *Philologic Pragensia,* 6 (1963): 245-257;

Review of *Das tägliche Brot, Saturday Review,* 91 (11 May 1901): 610;

S. B., "Unter dem Zwang der Wahrheit: Zum Tode Clara Viebigs," *Berliner Zeitung,* 7 August 1952, p. 3;

Gottlieb Scheuffler, *Clara Viebig: Zeit und Jahrhundert* (Erfurt: Beute, 1927);

Albert Schneider, "Clara Viebig (1860-1952): Esquisse biographique et bibliographique," *Annales Universitatis Saraviensis,* 1 (1952): 392-400;

Doris Dedner Smith, "From Infanticide to Single Motherhood: the Evolution of a Literary Theme as Reflected in the Works of Clara Viebig," Ph.D. dissertation, Indiana University, 1979;

Heinrich Spiero, "Clara Viebig," *Ostdeutsche Monatshefte,* 6, no. 1 (1925-1926): 422-425;

Sascha Wingenroth, *Clara Viebig und der Frauenroman des deutschen Naturalismus* (Endingen: Wald, 1936).

Papers:

There is a collection of Clara Viebig's papers at the Staatsbibliothek Preußischer Kulturbesitz in West Berlin.

Robert Walser

(15 April 1878-25 December 1956)

George C. Avery
Swarthmore College

BOOKS: *Fritz Kochers Aufsätze* (Leipzig: Insel, 1904);

Geschwister Tanner: Roman (Berlin: Cassirer, 1907);

Der Gehülfe: Roman (Berlin: Cassirer, 1908);

Jakob von Gunten: Ein Tagebuch (Berlin: Cassirer, 1909); translated by Christopher Middleton as *Jakob von Gunten* (Austin & London: University of Texas Press, 1969);

Gedichte (Berlin: Cassirer, 1909); enlarged edition, edited by Carl Seelig (Basel: Schwabe, 1944);

Aufsätze (Leipzig: Wolff, 1913);

Geschichten (Leipzig: Wolff, 1914);

Kleine Dichtungen (Leipzig: Wolff, 1914);

Prosastücke (Zurich: Rascher, 1917);

Kleine Prosa (Bern: Francke, 1917);

Der Spaziergang (Frauenfeld: Huber, 1917); translated by Christopher Middleton as "The Walk" in *The Walk and Other Stories* (London: Calder, 1957);

Poetenleben (Frauenfeld: Huber, 1918);

Seeland (Zurich: Rascher, 1919);

Komödie (Berlin: Cassirer, 1919);

Die Rose: Skizzen (Berlin: Rowohlt, 1925);

Große kleine Welt: Eine Auswahl, edited by Seelig (Erlenbach: Rentsch, 1937);

Stille Freuden, edited by Seelig (Olten: Vereinigung Oltner Bücherfreunde, 1944);

Vom Glück des Unglücks und der Armut, edited by Seelig (Basel: Schwabe, 1944);

Dichterbildnisse (Schaffhausen: Joos & Scherrer, 1947);

Die Schlacht bei Sempach: Eine Geschichte (St. Gallen: Tschudy, 1950);

Dichtungen in Prosa, edited by Seelig, 5 volumes (volumes 1-3, Geneva & Darmstadt: Holle-Verlag, 1953-1955; volumes 4-5, Geneva & Frankfurt am Main: Kossodo, 1959-1961);

Unbekannte Gedichte, edited by Seelig (St. Gallen: Tschudy, 1958);

Das Gesamtwerk, edited by Jochen Greven, Robert Mächler, and Martin Jürgens, 12 volumes (Geneva & Hamburg: Kossodo, 1966-1975); republished with revised notes and afterwords (Frankfurt am Main: Suhrkamp, 1978);

Saite und Sehnsucht: Faksimile-Ausgabe, edited by Elio Fröhlich (Zurich: Suhrkamp, 1979);

Selected Stories, translated by J. C. Middleton and others (New York: Farrar, Straus & Giroux, 1982; Manchester: Carcanet New Press, 1982);

Romane, 2 volumes, edited by Anne Gabrisch (Berlin: Verlag Volk und Welt, 1984);

Aus dem Bleistiftgebiet: Mikrogramme aus den Jahren 1924-1925, edited by Bernhard Echte and Werner Morlang, 2 volumes (Frankfurt am Main: Suhrkamp, 1985);

Robert Walser Rediscovered: Stories, Fairy-Tales, Plays and Critical Responses, edited by Mark Harman (Dartmouth: University Press of New England, 1985).

Robert Walser, a German-Swiss prose writer and novelist, enjoyed high repute among a select group of authors and critics in Berlin early in his career, only to become nearly forgotten by the time he committed himself to the Waldau mental clinic in Bern in January 1929. Since his death in 1956, however, Walser has been recognized as German Switzerland's leading author of the first half of the twentieth century, perhaps Switzerland's single significant modernist. In his homeland he has served as an emboldening exemplar and a national classic during the unparalleled expansion of German-Swiss literature of the last two generations.

Walser's writing is characterized by its linguistic sophistication and animation. His work exhibits several sets of tensions or contrasts: between a classic modernist devotion to art and a ceaseless questioning of the moral legitimacy and practical utility of art; between a spirited exuberance in style and texture and recurrent reflective melancholy; between the disparate claims of nature and culture; and between democratic respect for divergence in individuals and elitist reaction to

Robert Walser in 1909 (by permission of Dr. E. Frölich, president of the Carl Seelig Foundation, Zurich)

the values of the mass culture and standardization of the industrial age.

Robert Otto Walser was born on 15 April 1878 in the small Swiss city of Biel, the second youngest of eight children. His father, Adolf Walser, was an easygoing, convivial man, whose forebears included clergymen, historians, and a grandfather who had left the ministry in Appenzell to write radical pamphlets in the country around Basel. Trained as a bookbinder, Adolf Walser tried to make his fortune as a merchant, but failed. Walser's mother, Elisa Marti Walser, from rural Emmenthal, was severe in temperament and died in 1894, disabled in her last years by a nervous affliction. Walser was closest to two of his siblings: his sister Lisa, who replaced their mother in running the household and later taught school, and Karl, who became a painter, set designer, and book illustrator with a successful career in Berlin. Their brother Ernst, an artistically gifted music teacher, had to be institutionalized and died at forty-three in 1916. Another brother, Hermann, became professor of geography at the University of Bern and committed suicide in 1919. None of the children had offspring.

In 1892 the resources of the family were so straitened that Walser was removed from the Progymnasium (a secondary school with a curtailed classical curriculum) and apprenticed as a clerk in a local bank. He left home in 1895 on completing the training, working first in a bank in Basel and then in Stuttgart as a clerk for two large publishers. In Stuttgart Walser pursued a career in the theater, an inclination that had surfaced in childhood, when Walser, in his own words, was "house dramatist" for the plays he and his siblings put on at home. A dramatic reading before a famous actor resulted in a judgment unequivocal enough to persuade Walser to turn to literature.

In the fall of 1896 Walser returned to Switzerland. He settled in Zurich, where he started to write while working at a variety of jobs and frequently moving from one quarter of the city to another. He broke into print in May 1898, at the age of twenty, when J. V. Widmann, Switzerland's most influential literary critic and an author in his own right, published poems by Walser in an essay in the literary section he edited for *Der Bund* in Bern. Widmann praised the poems' original language and the depth and immediacy

Walser, circa 1898, while he was living in Zurich (by permission of Dr. E. Frölich, president of the Carl Seelig Foundation, Zurich)

of sensibility in the young poet, whom he identified only as the office worker "R. W." The essay was read by the Austrian critic Franz Blei, who was then living in Zurich. At a meeting initiated by Blei, Walser showed Blei more poems, and Blei recommended that he read the German romantics to fill the gaps in his literary education.

Recognizing Walser's talent, Blei introduced him to the editors of *Die Insel,* a new, eclectic Munich literary review of high standards, with a leaning toward literary symbolism and art nouveau. Publication of Walser's early work in *Die Insel* during its short, influential history meant a running start in the young writer's career. Poems, short prose, and four short plays appeared in the magazine. The plays inspired Otto Julius Bierbaum, an *Insel* editor, to dub Walser with Victor Hugo's appellation for the young Arthur Rimbaud, "Shakespeare enfant." The poet R. A. Schröder, another *Insel* editor, perceived the uncanny power at work in the poems; Hugo von Hofmannsthal, the best-known member of the *Insel* circle, later sought out Walser for contributions to other periodicals.

The encounter with the *Insel* circle meant contact not only with sophisticated literary figures but with a social life very different from Walser's background and experience. The editorial offices of *Die Insel* were situated in the palatial Munich residence of the young author and bon vivant Alfred Walter Heymel, whose wealth underwrote the founding of the journal and who in 1899 helped start the Insel publishing house. Walser sought to adapt in two ways: probably without means of support in Munich and evidently aware of his lower social status, he suggested that Heymel employ him as manservant in his home. Contrarily, Walser for a time apparently affected fine kid gloves in imitation of the contemporary literary dandy. The experience of Munich seems without parallel in Zurich, where there is little evidence of contact with literary circles. Indeed, Walser's early years in Zurich were fired by enthusiasm for the cause of socialism.

Walser worked in Thun in the spring of 1899, in Solothurn from the fall of 1899 to the spring of 1900, and in Winterthur in the spring of 1903. He stayed with Lisa, who was teaching in the countryside near Bern; performed military service in Bern in the summer of 1903; tested the literary waters in Berlin in two brief visits; and visited Munich again in 1901. From the summer of 1903 to the end of that year he was a secretary in the home of an engineer in Wädenswil, on the Lake of Zurich.

Widmann continued support of his "discovery" by publishing in *Der Bund* all the prose pieces that were to be included in Walser's first book, *Fritz Kochers Aufsätze* (Fritz Kocher's Essays, 1904). The essays go beyond those by the fictional schoolboy Fritz Kocher and foreshadow central themes in Walser's later work. Kocher's essays, purportedly school writing assignments on topics such as friendship, courtesy, poverty, nature, and the homeland, show Walser developing a fundamental persona in his work: the precocious youth of promise but of indeterminate abilities who disarms the reader with a combination of immediacy, reflective self-awareness, the ingenue's capacity for observation, and seemingly naive commentary on the building blocks of social intercourse. Three longer, separate essays deal with the office employee, the forest, and the painter. The motives articulated in this first book foreshadow the constancy of motifs for the larger part of Walser's oeuvre, where the preco-

Walser in 1905, the year he moved to Berlin (by permission of Dr. E. Frölich, president of the Carl Seelig Foundation, Zurich)

cious youth of promise but of indeterminate abilities who disarms the reader with a combination of immediacy, reflective self-awareness, the ingenue's capacity for observation, and seemingly naive commentary on the building blocks of social intercourse. Three longer, separate essays deal with the office employee, the forest, and the painter. The themes articulated in this first book foreshadow the constancy of motifs for the larger part of Walser's oeuvre, where the precocious youth given to monologues, the inevitability of an artistic calling, the primacy of nature, and the circumscribed, unsatisfied existence of the office employee are reworked, variously combined, expanded, and refined.

Shortly after publication of *Fritz Kochers Aufsätze* Insel Verlag was sold to Anton Kippenberg, who built the firm into a publishing house of great distinction. Plans for a second book by Walser with Insel were abandoned, in part because Kippenberg did not share the enthusiasm of Heymel and others for Walser's work, in part because *Fritz Kochers Aufsätze* sold poorly and had to be remaindered. In fact, as recent scholarship has recognized, Walser had produced a work of considerable literary sophistication. In the guise of a naïf he disregarded conventional prose categories and, with the indeterminate designation "essay," was writing alternately lyrical prose, fictive letters, fantasies, sociological analyses, and unabashed finger exercises in prose.

The themes, style, and texture of *Fritz Kochers Aufsätze* are innately bold, but it is a boldness presenting itself as minimalist. Fundamental to Walser's writing is a high degree of subjectivity coexisting with a postmodernist disquiet with the idea of self. The self-presentation found through all of Walser's work is ultimately a reaction to an essential loneliness and the seeming impossibility of escape from one's environment.

In an early appreciation published in the 15 October 1911 issue of *Pan,* Max Brod tries to characterize Walser's aesthetic subtleties and artistic prowess, calling him a triple-level writer; but the broader reading public had difficulty with his writing, beginning with Kocher's essays in *Der Bund* and increasingly as Walser's prose became more demanding. The poetry so praised by editors of *Die Insel* was republished in mass-appeal newspapers to prove that "modern" poetry was deranged. Later, even Widmann rejected the "excesses" of *Jakob von Gunten* (1909; translated, 1969), a work Martin Walser ranks among the three or four masterpieces of irony in European literature.

The most noteworthy phase of Walser's career began when he joined his brother Karl in Berlin in March 1905. This was Walser's third visit to the city; returning to Switzerland in 1902 after the second visit, he had assessed the literary prospects there as so bleak that he appeared to want to abandon literature, asking Widmann to try to find him work as a copyist. In 1905 Berlin stood at the beginning of its ascendancy as Europe's most vital cultural center. Walser came into contact with this milieu only later; early in his stay he attended a school for servants, and from October to the end of 1905 he waited on nobility as "Monsieur Robert" at a castle in Upper Silesia.

Karl Walser, renowned and successful, had entrée to various sides of Berlin's cultural life: through his scenic design for Max Reinhardt, to Berlin's rich theater world; through his wall frescoes for the wealthy and powerful, to the homes of Samuel Fischer and Walter Rathenau; through his membership in the association of largely im-

Walser's brother, the artist and stage designer Karl Walser (by permission of Dr. E. Frölich, president of the Carl Seelig Foundation, Zurich)

pressionistic painters known as the Berlin Secession, to Paul Cassirer, the cousin of Robert Walser's Berlin publisher Bruno Cassirer and the philosopher Ernst Cassirer. A wealthy art dealer, Paul Cassirer stood at the hub of an important circle of creative activity in Berlin. Karl Walser's contacts ranged from established artists and editors such as Max Liebermann, Max Slevogt, Maximilian Harden, Frank Wedekind, and Hugo von Hofmannsthal, through editors and critics such as Alfred Kerr, Siegfried Jacobsohn, Efraim Frisch, and René Schickele, to younger writers such as Franz Hessel, later Robert Walser's editor at Rowohlt for the publication of *Die Rose* (1925).

In Berlin Walser's short prose began to appear in *Die Schaubühne,* a periodical covering all aspects of the theater; soon his work was being published in other well-regarded journals. Yet in the flush of achievement on completing his first novel, short prose came to seem ancillary to the production of novels. In 1906 and early 1907 he professed to Christian Morgenstern, his editor at the Cassirer firm, his commitment to the genre, regardless of its demands, stating that he would sooner join the army than earn his living writing for literary periodicals.

Walser's ambition as a novelist produced three early contributions to the expansion and refinement of German narrative forms in the twentieth century. These three novels are based on Walser's experiences: *Geschwister Tanner* (The Tanner Siblings, 1907) reworks the Zurich years; *Der Gehülfe* (The Assistant, 1908) derives from Walser's employ with the engineer-inventor in Wädenswil in 1903; and Walser's declared favorite, *Jakob von Gunten,* fictionalizes the month he spent at the school for servants in Berlin.

The novels have in common a youthful central figure in an urban or suburban setting, a figure preoccupied with the search for himself and only marginally attached to a society he observes from an indeterminate or shifting perspective. Possessing minimal plots, the novels are notable for their narrative form and for their characterizations.

Simon Tanner leaves his bank job at the beginning of *Geschwister Tanner* to protest the regimentation of the individual and the leveling of personality that are the cost for success in society. He takes occasional jobs, once as a servant in the home of a woman he has met on the street; drifts into the backwaters of the city; alternately criticizes his passivity and rails at the characterless age and at the seclusion of the rich from the poor; and maintains attachments to each of his equally self-critical siblings, to friends, and to chance acquaintances. He drifts away from Klara, the former mistress of his artist brother, whom he had loved in an idealized fashion, anticipating Rainer Maria Rilke's *Die Aufzeichnungen des Malte Laurids Brigge,* (1910; translated as *The Notebooks of Malte Laurids Brigge,* 1949). The novel ends with a provisional resolution, at best a vague sense of promise and hope. Bested in his encounter with the city, he turns away from the cult of beauty and swears loyalty to maternal earth.

The episodic composition of *Geschwister Tanner* identifies it as a novice work, but the acuity of insights in the novel and the dynamism and haunting quality of individual scenes amply compensate for the rough edges. The uneven texture of the novel reflects Simon's character: he is sometimes burdened by the certainty of personal inadequacy, at other times buoyed up by moral fervor and a yearning for "heroic" deeds. The novel is peopled with fleeting figures, individually sharp

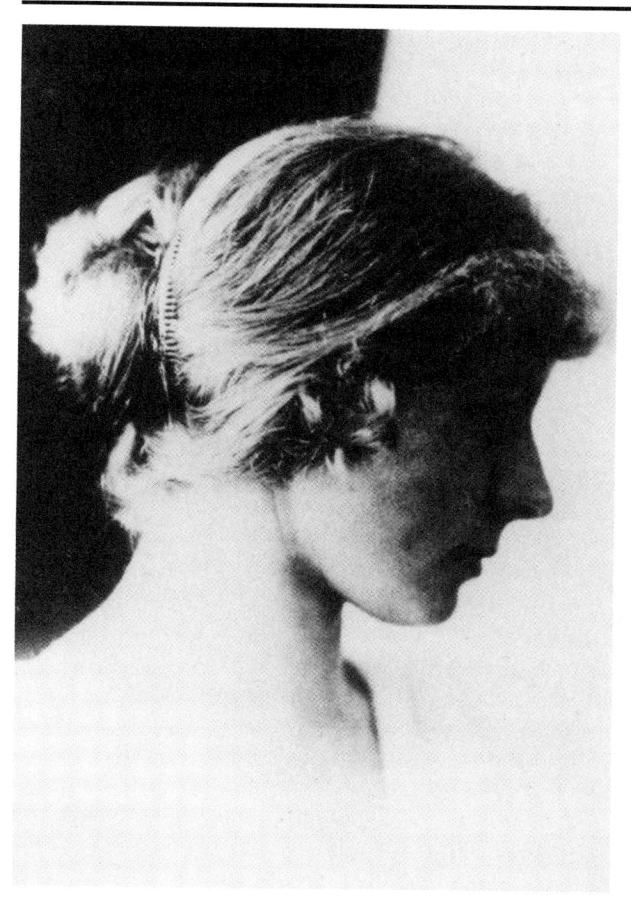

Lisa Walser, Walser's older sister, in 1901. Of all his siblings, Walser felt closest to her (by permission of Dr. E. Frölich, president of the Carl Seelig Foundation, Zurich).

and memorable, economically drawn with little concern for realistic narrative portrayal. The novel's seemingly disparate parts all contribute to the depiction of a society in flux: cities bare of refuge, families and individuals seeking new bonds to replace the inherited bonds of blood. At bottom the novel focuses on the life of the soul–its vagaries, its imagination, its inconsistencies, and its ardors.

Joseph Marti, the central figure of *Der Gehülfe* (which Walser claimed to have written in six weeks as an entry for a novel competition), is a slightly older, more temperate spiritual relative of Simon Tanner. Marti has been hired to help secure financial backing for the engineer Tobler's inventions. Having spent his legacy on an imposing villa, Tobler and his family live on a scale befitting the success to which they aspire. The inventions fail; the family deteriorates as the prospect of financial ruin becomes a reality. The proximity of commodious familial life and foundering commercial enterprise in Villa Abendstern initially tempt Marti to believe he can bridge the social distance between himself and his bourgeois employers. By the end of the novel, although he has come to love the Toblers, he recognizes his delusion and departs. Marti's interior monologues are at the center of the realistic portrayal of an age poised between the old and the new, the socioeconomic shift from seigneurial relation to an "assistant" living in one's own home to the employer-employee relation of the present.

While the form of *Geschwister Tanner* had been outwardly conventional, *Der Gehülfe* discards chapter divisions altogether. Marti and the narrator alternate in the narration and interior monologues, creating a dense narrative fabric that is intellectually stimulating and aesthetically intriguing. Franz Kafka, who, according to Brod, "loved" *Der Gehülfe,* might well have taken Walser's technique as a model for *Der Prozeß* (1925; translated as *The Trial,* 1937).

The eponymous hero of *Jakob von Gunten* is the natural descendant of Tanner and Marti. The novel is about the moral and psychological strength inhering in a lackluster existence passed in service and self-abnegation at the Institute Benjamenta, where Jakob, the last scion of an aristocratic family, has enrolled while still craving wealth, power, and high station. The masterpiece of Walser's first maturity, Jakob's journal describes the comic, sometimes grotesque events in a dreamlike school where he is clearly "overqualified," where he seeks to link–again paralleling Rilke's Malte Laurids Brigge–dignity with anonymity. His journal entries describe an intentional descent from inherited privilege to the status of ordinary person: "Ich habe den Stolz, die Ehrenarten gewechselt" (I've exchanged kinds of pride and honor). Jakob believes that the poverty and faceless anonymity the school teaches are underwritten by divine sanction.

The novel's appeal derives from the fact that Jakob's personality is instinctively at odds with precepts for the good servant. Jakob is the intellectual who praises the nonintellectual, for whom physical grace contains more knowledge than a shelfful of books, and whose new humility is a powerful stimulant for his pride. Jakob defends the mindless regimen of the school while knowing that he will always flout the rules. The novel represents a culmination of Walser's idea of service, an idea Martin Walser sees as deriving from middle-class Christian ethics, while more recent critics such as Christoph Siegrist impute a psychological context with masochistic elements.

Walser in 1949, while a patient in the mental institution at Herisau, Switzerland (by permission of Dr. E. Frölich, president of the Carl Seelig Foundation, Zurich)

Walser's discomfort with the aggressiveness of the Berlin literary scene inhibits him from unqualifiedly identifying Jakob as a writer. This reserve toward writing is found from his earliest work on: neither Tanner nor Marti is permitted more than a casual interest in writing, all impulses to the contrary notwithstanding. In an indicative passage in *Geschwister Tanner* Simon chances on the frozen corpse of the poet Sebastian, who never seemed a match for life's demands. At the end of *Jakob von Gunten* Jakob lays down his pen, even as the chronicler of the lowly in the Institute Benjamenta, assuring himself that "Gott geht mit den Gedankenlosen" (God is with the empty-headed).

Despite Walser's proud words to Morgenstern, disdaining writing for literary periodicals in favor of writing novels, his output of short prose dwarfs his production of published novels. From 1902 to 1933 Walser wrote more than 1,500 short prose works, most of which were published in periodicals ranging from exclusive literary reviews to the literary columns of newspapers.

All of Walser's books during his Berlin years were published by Bruno Cassirer. In addition to the three novels, Cassirer produced a bibliophile edition of Walser's poetry, *Gedichte* (Poems, 1909), illustrated by Karl Walser, and, a decade later, under the title *Komödie,* the four playlets originally published in *Die Insel.*

Cassirer was never especially taken with Walser's writing and declined to do a small second printing of *Jakob von Gunten,* as he had done for *Der Gehülfe.* Sometime thereafter, probably because of Walser's failure to produce a new novel, Cassirer suspended advances to Walser. The relatively steady flow of publications in periodicals that began in 1907 fell off in 1910-1911; there are no extant letters from July 1908 through October 1912, and the single bit of information from ancillary sources locates Walser in a decrepit rooming house during this period. Walser later reported to Carl Seelig that he was drinking a lot and frequenting low-class bars and amusement halls. He also spoke of constant advice he was receiving on authors he should use as models to improve his own writing: "Entweder du schreibst wie Hesse oder du bist und bleibst ein Versager" (Either you write like Hesse or you're a failure and you'll remain one) was his pointed characterization of such criticisms to Seelig. Clearly, he saw himself judged a failure at the genre in which he had chosen to prove himself.

Early in 1913 Walser returned to Switzerland. There was no longer a family home, and after sharing cramped quarters first with his sister Lisa and then with his father, Walser took a garret room in the Hotel Blaues Kreuz, a temperance hotel in his hometown, Biel. Walser lived in spare, indeed ascetic, circumstances, whether from thrift, insufficient means, or from his stated conviction that austerity was a necessary precondition for creative work. At the same time he left the proceeds from his single literary award, from the Women's League for Awards to Rhenish Poets for *Kleine Dichtungen* (Short Writings, 1914), on deposit in a German bank until inflation in the 1920s made it worthless.

Ten more volumes of Walser's work were published before he stopped writing in 1933. Except for *Komödie,* all were collections of shorter prose works. The first two volumes, *Aufsätze* (Essays, 1913) and *Geschichten* (Stories, 1914), contain material written and originally published in Berlin. Many of these pieces deal ironically with

Last photograph of Walser. He died on 25 December 1956 of a heart attack while walking in the woods surrounding the Herisau institution (by permission of Dr. E. Frölich, president of the Carl Seelig Foundation, Zurich).

the theater, Walser's unrequited love: they include fictive "mash" letters to actresses, skewed prose recountings of famous scenes from the classical repertory, arguments for and against theater, a defense of antirealistic theater, a stage phantasmagoria that equals the surrealism of later decades, a gruesome evocation of fire in a packed theater, a fairy tale performed by cats, an ovation for a novice dancer, and parodistic representations of Walser's early theatrical aspirations.

These volumes also contain pieces mirroring the vitality, rhythms, and diversions of Berlin; fairy tales or "fantasies"; and portraits of artistic personalities. The portraits, mostly of German authors of the eighteenth and nineteenth centuries but also of painters and draftsmen, include some of Walser's most memorable work. The portraits employ empathetic identification, celebration, stylistic imitation, critique, and projected self-criticism; historical details are indifferently handled. Friedrich von Schiller, Heinrich Wilhelm von Kleist, and Clemens Brentano are repeatedly subjects. An especially well-realized portrait is the 1907 piece "Kleist in Thun," a powerful depiction centering on the vain, enervating struggle to resist the compulsion to create. Walser continued to write such portraits until the end of his career; the 1929 piece "Cezannegedanken" (Thoughts on Cézanne) is a tender, comic treatment of the painter's recurrent surrender to the enticement to shape material into objects for revelatory contemplation, always at the cost of participation in "life."

The pieces in *Kleine Prosa* (Short Prose, 1917), *Prosastücke* (Prose Pieces, 1917), *Poetenleben* (Poets' Lives, 1918), and *Seeland* (Lakeland, 1919) comprise the bulk of Walser's production in Biel; the equivalent of another volume of short prose appeared in periodicals during that period but was not collected. On the whole the Biel prose lacks the boldness of conception frequently found in the Berlin prose; self-assured verve has given way to a lyrical tone between celebratory praise and gratitude. The most often cited works from the period–and the source of the lower critical estimation given the Biel work–are the descriptions of walks centered on the lakeland around Biel together with the inspiriting view of society reflected for the narrator in the nature he experiences. These descriptions are quite different from those in *Geschwister Tanner,* where nature is given a mythic dimension as the overarching parallel to human culture or the physiological ground out of which the soul arises; or from those in *Der Gehülfe,* where the beguiling beauty of nature is only an illusory refuge for Marti but, in the end, Villa Abendstern's forgiving tribunal.

Walser's classic in this subgenre is *Der Spaziergang* (translated as "The Walk," 1957), which was published separately in 1917 and revised for inclusion in *Seeland.* It is an apologia for himself as a writer sui generis and a celebration of the unprepossessing and the diurnal. Walser's objective self-assessment underlies the wit, comedy, and self-irony of this "report" on a day-long saunter through a small Swiss city. The piece has a rhythm of highs in the narrator's pleasures and imaginary speeches and lows as the night falls, the spirit wanes, and the mask is put aside. Walser's poet-artist is aware of his eccentricities and his remove from the routine of Swiss life, but *Der Spaziergang* assumes that society tolerates diversion from the norm because of its collective beneficence and its realization that it thereby warrants its humanity.

The artist portraits continue in the Biel volumes; the most notable among them are those of Friedrich Hölderlin and Charles Dickens. Walser also begins to comment on his earlier production, as in "Die Gedichte" and "Geschwister Tanner." A narrowing of focus is signaled in such titles as "Rede an einen Knopf " (Speech on a Button), "Lampe, Papier und Handschuhe" (Lamp, Paper, and Gloves), and "Tannenzweig, Taschentuch und Käppchen" (Fir Twig, Handkerchief, and Small Cap). Other pieces join comic, socially critical, and linguistically experimental elements in re-creations of obsessional patterns and parodies of bourgeois orderliness.

At the end of the Biel period Walser completed a short novel called "Tobold." The title suggests that the novel, like shorter works with the same name, reworked his experiences at the Silesian castle in 1905. The manuscript is lost, however, with no indication as to its fate or whether Walser ever submitted it for publication.

Walser moved to Bern in 1921. Looking back, he had contradictory assessments of the Biel years. In a letter to Frau Mermet, his sister Lisa's friend and Walser's most frequent correspondent in Biel and Bern, he assessed his Biel work quite positively. Later, in conversations with Carl Seelig, he called the same work too shepherd-boy-like and lacking in the esprit of urban life.

Walser was remarkably productive in Bern, with his output reaching a peak in the years 1924-1926. But only one book–*Die Rose,* published in Germany in 1925 and poorly received–appeared in the Bern years; nine other projects for books were rejected by publishers. Walser's efforts found little acceptance in his homeland; reader complaints about his pieces in the *Neue Zürcher Zeitung* and the tendency of Swiss editors to tamper with his texts led him to submit work to periodicals in Germany and in Prague.

It is clear from Walser's letters that he realized how limited the appeal of *Die Rose* would be. The book contains rarified exercises in transformations of the self, breathtaking both for their fecundity of verbal imagination and for the border area they traverse. There are also direct and allusive depictions of love, ranging from "troubadour" adoration through proud rejection to painful isolation; fictive letters; literary studies; and a notable montage piece, "Eine Ohrfeige und Sonstiges" (A Slap in the Face and So Forth).

Walser's work in Bern differs from his previous production in scope rather than in kind; earlier motifs and themes are deepened and expanded, and his union of irony and immediacy attains new heights. Movement, the structural substratum in all of Walser's work, was encompassed in his earlier writing in the ambulatory narrator as the metaphor for an infinitely variable nature. In the Bern work movement becomes a narrative grillwork of shifting reflections, recollections, empirical observations, fragmented segments of "story," and parodistic adaptations of popular literature. This narrative structuring is in the service of an unremitting portraiture of the self, a portraiture whose exposed vulnerability suggests that it is a defense against the loss of self in society. Walser's Christian-inspired awareness of tran-

Märchen.

Ich erzähle hier eine vielleicht zum Teil lächerliche Geschich-
te.
Eine Zeit lang ging's mir glänzend; ich erbte eines
Tages ein übrigens gewiß nur geringfügiges Kapital,
das mich befähigte, sorglos in den Tag hineinzuleben.
Die Tage, die vor mir lagen, glichen einer bezaubern-
schön und lockig eingerichteten Wohnung.
Welch ein poetischer Vergleich!
Ich bildete mich in voller Gemächlichkeit zu etwas wie
einem Liebhaber aus, der unter anderem in seiner
Mußezeit vergnügt dichtete. Ich wußte, ich sei irgend
etwas von Belang, oder ich bildete mir dies ebensogut
bloß ein.
Hübsche Einbildungen machen uns bekanntermaßen
fröhlich.
Nun komme ich auch sie zu sprechen, die ich liebte,
und der gegenüber ich gern mit meiner Neigung
kokettierte. Sie war gleichzeitig wenig und viel,
ich war dies ebenfalls. Bald war ich das All, bald
nur in diesem All ein Atom.
Darf ich das für Philosophie halten zu dürfen hof-
fen?
Prächtig war's für mich, wenn ich wahrnehmen konnte,

Manuscript for a poem by Walser (by permission of Dr. E. Frölich, president of the Carl Seelig Foundation, Zurich)

sience as a counter to personal ambition conflicts with his furious pursuit of recognition and acceptance as a writer.

In Bern there were new signs of Walser's preoccupation with the novel. In a then-unpublished piece written in the late 1920s, "Eine Art Erzählung" (A Kind of Tale), Walser says: "Meine Prosastücke bilden meiner Meinung nach nichts anderes als Teile einer langen, handlungslosen, realistischen Geschichte. Für mich sind die Skizzen, die ich dann und wann hervorbringe, kleinere oder umfangreichere Romankapitel. Der Roman, woran ich weiter und weiter schreibe, bleibt immer derselbe und dürfte als ein mannigfaltig zerschnittenes oder zertrenntes Ich-Buch bezeichnet werden können" (To my mind, my prose pieces constitute nothing other than parts of a long, plotless, realistic story. For me, the sketches which I produce now and again are longer or shorter chapters of a novel. The novel, on which I keep on writing, is ever the same and it might be possible to designate it a variously cut-up or divided-up Ego-book).

"Theodor," a novel written shortly after Walser moved to Bern, was the subject of protracted negotiations before it disappeared while being considered by Rowohlt in Berlin. Judging by selections that appeared in the Swiss review *Wissen und Leben* in 1923 and an evaluation by a reader of the manuscript, "Theodor" was a comic-lyrical novel with episodes in both urban and rural settings. The long fragment "Tagebuch" (Diary), written in 1926, is an indirect approach to the novel, combining critical examination of arguments for and against reportorial as opposed to imaginative fiction with a poetically oriented diary.

The most representative and most enduring narrative work from Bern is the novel *Der Räuber* (The Robber), found among the so-called microscripts–prose texts, dialogues, and verse written in a miniscule pencil script on 117 sheets of high-gloss art paper in 1924 and 1925. Seemingly illegible, the writing was at first incorrectly identified as a code. The microscripts are first drafts from which Walser made clean copies of material he submitted for publication. With the assistance of Martin Jürgens, Jochen Greven transcribed *Der Räuber* for inclusion in the collected edition of 1966-1975.

The "robber" is Walser's climactic artistic persona, an artist seeking material for a novel. The title is a play on Walser's first name and also an allusion to Karl Walser's watercolor of the adolescent Robert garbed as Karl Moor, the hero of Schiller's play *Die Räuber* (The Robbers, 1781). In the robber's exploitation of his love for Edith as material for a novel Walser varies an early motif: the diminution of reality through literature. Lack of money, lack of success, "errors" in behavior and in his writing make the robber an "outlaw" and justify his persecution–that is, pressure to marry, to conform, to belong to the community–by his fellow townspeople. At the end Edith shoots the robber while he is delivering a lecture on love from a church pulpit. The robber recovers, and there is a tentative reconciliation with Edith. The narrator's prediction that persecution of the robber will abate is questionable, given the precedence he has given his own aims. Walser's comedy trenchantly analyzes the writer's rejection by society.

Transcriptions of the microscript texts from the years 1924-1925 not transcribed by Greven and Jürgens and from which Walser had not made clean copies have been published in two volumes as *Aus dem Bleistiftgebiet* (From the Pencil Zone, 1985). Two further volumes of transcriptions, from microscripts from the years 1926-1932, are projected.

In January 1929 Walser committed himself to the cantonal mental clinic Waldau on the outskirts of Bern. In the preceding months he had been drinking heavily, had heard "voices," and had undertaken halfhearted suicide attempts. The circumstances of the committal and the summary diagnosis of schizophrenia have been questioned since pertinent documents have become available. After a few months in Waldau Walser was able to resume writing prose and verse and submitting his work to editors.

In 1933 Walser rejected an offer to live in a halfway house in the country and was forcibly removed to the cantonal institution in Herisau in eastern Switzerland. He never wrote again. He lived the life of an ambulatory patient, doing simple manual work, with liberty to undertake day trips. He appears to have received no psychiatric treatment.

In 1936 the Zurich literary critic and journalist Carl Seelig began visiting Walser in Herisau. Later, with the approval of Walser and members of his family, Seelig was named Walser's legal guardian, heir, and literary executor. In 1957 Seelig published *Wanderungen mit Robert Walser* (Hikes with Robert Walser), a valuable account of their meetings and walks together between 1936 and 1955 along with transcriptions of their conversations.

Walser seems to have wanted to leave the institution in 1938, but this intent was opposed by his family and by the directing physician. Walser died on Christmas Day 1956 of a heart attack while on a solitary walk in the hills around Herisau.

Academic interest in Walser's work began in the late 1950s and grew apace after the excellent edition of the collected works by Greven, Jürgens, and Robert Mächler began to appear in 1966. Since Suhrkamp secured publishing rights to the complete works from the original Swiss publisher, Walser has found a broad, diversified readership in German-speaking countries, and his work has been translated into many European languages.

Letters:

Briefe, edited by Jörg Schäfer, with Robert Mächler (Geneva: Kossodo, 1975).

Biographies:

Robert Mächler, *Das Leben Robert Walsers: Eine dokumentarische Biographie* (Geneva & Hamburg: Kossodo, 1966);

Elio Fröhlich and Peter Hamm, eds., *Robert Walser: Leben und Werk in Daten und Bildern* (Frankfurt am Main: Insel, 1980).

References:

George C. Avery, *Inquiry and Testament: A Study of the Novels and Short Prose of Robert Walser* (Philadelphia: University of Pennsylvania Press, 1968);

Avery, "A Writer's Cache," in *Robert Walser Rediscovered: Stories, Fairy-Tales, Plays and Critical Responses,* edited by Mark Harman (Dartmouth, Mass.: University Press of New England, 1985), pp. 179-189;

Hans Bänziger, "Die Villa Abendstern: Zu Robert Walsers Roman 'Der Gehülfe,' " in his *Schloß-Haus-Bau: Studien zu einem literarischen Motivkomplex. Von der deutschen Klassik zur Moderne* (Bern & Munich: Francke, 1983), pp. 131-145;

Walter Benjamin, "Robert Walser [1927]," in his *Gesammelte Schriften,* volume 2, edited by Rolf Tiedemann and Hermann Schweppenhäuser (Frankfurt am Main: Suhrkamp, 1977), pp. 324-334;

Peter Bichsel, "Geschwister Tanner lesen," in *Robert Walser Dossier* (Zurich: Pro Helvetia/Bern: Zytglogge, 1984), pp. 79-88;

Bernhard Böschenstein, "Theatralische Miniaturen. Zur frühen Prosa Robert Walsers," in *Probleme der Moderne: Studien zur deutschen Literatur von Nietzsche bis Brecht. Festschrift für Walter Sokel,* edited by B. Bennett, A. Kaes, and Wm. J. Lillymann (Tübingen: Niemeyer, 1983), pp. 67-81;

Guy Davenport, "A Field of Snow on a Slope of the Rosenberg," in his *DaVinci's Bicycle: Ten Stories* (Baltimore: Johns Hopkins University Press, 1979), pp. 149-185;

Werner Eggers, "Zertrenntes Ich-Buch," in *Studien zur deutschen Literatur: Festschrift für Adolf Beck zum 70. Geburtstag,* edited by U. Fülleborn and Johannes Krogoll (Heidelberg: Winter, 1979), pp. 284-297;

Hildegard Emmel, *Geschichte des deutschen Romans,* volume 2 (Bern & Munich: Francke, 1975), pp. 211-216;

Elio Fröhlich and Robert Mächler, eds., *Robert Walser zum Andenken: Aus Anlaß seines 20. Todestages am 25. Dezember 1976* (Zurich & Frankfurt am Main: Suhrkamp, 1976);

Jochen Greven, *Existenz, Welt und reines Sein im Werk Robert Walsers: Versuch zur Bestimmung von Grundstrukturen* (Cologne: Kleikamp, 1960);

Greven, "Robert Walser-Forschungen: Bericht über die Edition des Gesamtwerks und die Bearbeitung des Nachlasses, mit Hinweisen auf Walser-Studien der letzten Jahre," *Euphorion,* 64 (March 1970): 97-114;

Arnold Heinz, ed., Special Walser issue of *Text und Kritik,* 12 (1966); revised and enlarged as 12/12a (1966);

Urs Herzog, *Robert Walsers Poetik: Literatur und soziale Entfremdung* (Tübingen: Niemeyer, 1974);

Bernd Hüppauf, ed., *Provokation und Idylle: über Robert Walsers Prosa,* supplement no. 1 to *Der Deutschunterricht,* 23 (1971);

Martin Jürgens, *Robert Walser: Die Krise der Darstellbarkeit. Untersuchungen zur Prosa* (Kronberg: Scriptor, 1973);

Katharina Kerr, ed., *Über Robert Walser,* 3 volumes (Frankfurt am Main: Suhrkamp, 1978-1979);

Peter von Matt, "Die Schwäche des Vaters und das Vergnügen des Sohnes: Über die Voraussetzungen der Fröhlichkeit bei Robert Walser," *Neue Rundschau,* 90, no. 2 (1979): 197-213;

Malcolm Pender, "A Writer's Relationship to Society: Robert Walser's ' "Räuber"-Roman,' " *Modern Language Review,* 78 (1983): 103-112;

Elsbeth Pulver and Arthur Zimmermann, eds., *Robert Walser* (Zurich: Pro Helvetia/Bern: Zytglogge, 1984);

Lukas Rüsch, *Ironie und Herrschaft: Untersuchungen zum Verhältnis von Herr und Knecht in Robert Walsers Roman "Der Gehülfe"* (Königstein: Forum Academicum, 1983);

Carl Seelig, *Wanderungen mit Robert Walser* (St. Gallen: Tschudy, 1957);

Christoph Siegrist, "Robert Walser: Der Gehülfe (1907)," in *Deutsche Romane des 20. Jahrhunderts: Neue Interpretationen,* edited by Paul Michael Lützeler (Königstein: Athenäum, 1983), pp. 50-62;

Emil Stumpp, "Besuch bei Künstlern," *Sinn und Form,* 30 (1978): 239-250;

Jens Tismar, *Gestörte Idyllen: Eine Studie zur Problematik der idyllischen Wunschvorstellungen am Beispiel von Jean Paul, Adalbert Stifter, Robert Walser und Thomas Bernhard* (Munich: Hanser, 1973), pp. 71-105;

Erich Unglaub, "Robert Walser: 'Feierabend' und 'Brentano. Eine Phantasie.' Texte aus dem Umkreis der 'Insel.' Erstausgabe und Einleitung: Erich Unglaub," *Recherches Germaniques,* 10 (1980): 239-254;

Siegfried Unseld, "Robert Walser und seine Verleger," in his *Der Autor und sein Verleger: Vorlesungen in Mainz und Austin* (Frankfurt am Main, 1978), pp. 241-341;

Peter Utz, "Der Schwerkraft spotten: Spuren von Motiv und Metapher des Tanzes im Werk Robert Walsers," *Jahrbuch der deutschen Schiller-Gesellschaft,* 28 (1984): 386-403;

Karl Wagner, *Herr und Knecht: Robert Walsers Roman "Der Gehülfe"* (Vienna: Braumüller, 1980);

Martin Walser, *Selbstbewußtsein und Ironie: Frankfurter Vorlesungen* (Frankfurt am Main: Suhrkamp, 1981);

Walser, "Der Unerbittlichkeitsstil: Zum 100. Geburtstag von Robert Walser," in his *Liebeserklärungen* (Frankfurt am Main: Suhrkamp, 1983), pp. 123-154;

Hans Dieter Zimmermann, *Der babylonische Dolmetscher, Zu Franz Kafka und Robert Walser* (Frankfurt am Main: Suhrkamp, 1985).

Papers:

The Robert Walser Archive in Zurich was founded in 1973 with the support of its parent organization, the Carl Seelig Foundation. The archive is a study and research facility whose holdings comprise the whole of Walser's literary estate, including manuscripts and papers, biographical source material, and a comprehensive library of secondary literature on Walser.

Jakob Wassermann

(3 March 1873-1 January 1934)

Josef Schmidt
McGill University

Jakob Wassermann (Ullstein)

BOOKS: *Melusine: Liebesroman* (Munich: Langen, 1896);

Die Juden von Zirndorf (Munich: Langen, 1896; revised edition, Berlin: Fischer, 1906); translated anonymously as *The Jews of Zirndorf* (New York: Jewish Book Agency, 1918); translated by Cyrus Brooks as *The Jews of Zirndorf* (London: Allen, 1933); Brooks translation republished as *The Dark Pilgrimage* (New York: Liveright, 1933);

Die Schaffnerin; Die Mächtigen: Novellen (Munich: Langen, 1897);

Schläfst Du, Mutter?; Ruth: Novellen (Munich: Langen, 1897);

Lorenza Burgkmair: Karnevals-Stück (Munich: Rubinverlag, 1898);

Hockenjos oder Die Lügenkomödie (Munich: Rubinverlag, 1898);

Die Geschichte der jungen Renate Fuchs (Berlin: Fischer, 1900; revised, 1925);

Der Moloch (Berlin: Fischer, 1903; revised, 1921);

Der niegeküßte Mund; Hilperich: Zwei Novellen (Munich & Berlin: Fischer, 1903);

Die Kunst der Erzählung (Berlin: Bardt & Marquardt, 1904);

Alexander in Babylon (Berlin: Fischer, 1905); English translation (Chicago: Ziff-Davis, 1949);

Die Schwestern: Drei Novellen (Berlin: Fischer, 1906);

Caspar Hauser oder Die Trägheit des Herzens (Stuttgart: Deutsche Verlags-Anstalt, 1908); translated by Caroline Newton as *Caspar Hauser* (New York: Liveright, 1928; London: Allen, 1938);

Der Literat oder Mythos und Persönlichkeit (Leipzig: Insel, 1910);

Die Masken Erwin Reiners: Roman (Berlin: Fischer, 1910);

Faustina: Ein Gespräch über die Liebe (Berlin: Fischer, 1912);

Die ungleichen Schalen: Fünf Dramen (Berlin: Fischer, 1912);

Der goldene Spiegel: Erzählungen in einem Rahmen (Berlin: Fischer, 1912);

Der Mann von vierzig Jahren (Berlin: Fischer, 1913);

Deutsche Charaktere und Begebenheiten, 2 volumes (volume 1, Berlin: Fischer, 1915; volume 2, Vienna: Rikola, 1924);

Das Gänsemännchen (Berlin: Fischer, 1915); translated by Allen W. Porterfield and Ludwig Lewisohn as *The Goose Man* (New York: Grosset & Dunlap, 1922);

Was ist Besitz? (Vienna: Verlag Der Friede, 1919);

Die Prinzessin Girnara: Weltspiel und Legende (Vienna: Strache, 1919);

Christian Wahnschaffe, 2 volumes (Berlin: Fischer, 1919); translated by Lewisohn as *The World's*

Illusion (New York: Harcourt, Brace & Howe, 1920); original German version, revised (Berlin: Fischer, 1932);

Der Wenderkreis, 4 volumes (Berlin: Fischer, 1920-1924); volume 1 translated in part by Lewis Galantière as *World's End: Five Stories* (New York: Boni & Liveright, 1927); volume 4 translated by Harry Hansen as *Faber; or, The Lost Years* (New York: Harcourt, Brace, 1929; London: Allen, 1930);

Imaginäre Brücken: Studien und Aufsätze (Munich: Wolff, 1921);

Mein Weg als Deutscher und Jude (Berlin: Fischer, 1921); translated by S. N. Brainin as *My Life as German and Jew* (New York: Coward-McCann, 1933; London: Allen, 1934);

Der Geist des Pilgers: Drei Erzählungen (Vienna & Leipzig: Reclam, 1923);

Gestalt und Humanität: Zwei Reden (Munich: Drei Masken, 1924);

Gesammelte Werke, 11 volumes (Berlin: Fischer, 1925);

In memoriam Ferrucio Busoni (Berlin: Fischer, 1925);

Laudin und die Seinen (Berlin: Fischer, 1925); translated by Lewisohn as *Wedlock* (New York: Harcourt, Brace, 1925); translated anonymously as *The Triumph of Youth* (New York: Boni & Liveright, 1927; London: Allen, 1928);

Der Aufruhr um den Junker Ernst: Erzählung (Berlin: Fischer, 1926);

Das Amulett (Nuremberg: Schrag, 1927);

Lebensdienst: Gesammelte Studien, Erfahrungen und Reden aus drei Jahrzehnten (Leipzig: Grethlein, 1928);

Der Fall Maurizius (Berlin: Fischer, 1928); translated by Caroline Newton as *The Maurizius Case* (New York: Liveright, 1929; London: Allen, 1930);

Christoph Columbus: Der Don Quichote des Ozeans: Ein Porträt (Berlin: Fischer, 1929); translated by Eric Sutton as *Christopher Columbus: Don Quixote of the Seas* (Boston: Little, Brown, 1930; London: Secker, 1930);

Hofmannsthal, der Freund (Berlin: Fischer, 1930);

Etzel Andergast (Berlin: Fischer, 1931); translated by Brooks as *Dr. Kerkhoven* (New York: Liveright, 1932); translation republished as *Etzel Andergast* (London: Allen, 1932);

Bula Matari: Das Leben Stanleys (Berlin: Fischer, 1932); translated by Eden and Cedar Paul as *H. M. Stanley–Explorer* (London: Cassell, 1932); republished as *Bula Matari: Stanley, Conqueror of a Continent* (New York: Liveright, 1933);

Wassermann in1896, portrait by Emil Orlik (G. Grote'sche Verlagbuchhandlung, Rastatt)

Rede an die Jugend über das Leben im Geiste (Berlin: Fischer, 1932);

Selbstbetrachtungen (Berlin: Fischer, 1933);

Joseph Kerkhovens dritte Existenz (Amsterdam: Querido, 1934); translated by Eden and Cedar Paul as *Joseph Kerkhoven's Third Existence* (London: Allen & Unwin, 1934; New York: Liveright, 1934);

Tagebuch aus dem Winkel: Erzählungen und Aufsätze aus dem Nachlaß (Amsterdam: Querido, 1935);

Olivia: Ein Roman (Zurich: Verlag Neue Bücher, 1937);

Gesammelte Werke, 7 volumes (Zurich: Posen, 1944-1948);

Bekenntnisse und Begegnungen: Porträts und Skizzen zur Literatur- und Geistesgeschichte, edited by Paul Stöcklein (Bamberg: Verlag Bamberger Reiter, 1950);

Engelhart oder Die zwei Welten (Munich: Langen-Müller, 1973);

Jakob Wassermann, Deutscher und Jude: Rede und Schriften 1904-1933, edited by Dierk Rodewald (Heidelberg: Lambert Schneider, 1984).

OTHER: Hans Aufricht-Ruda, *Die Verhandlung gegen La Roncière: Roman,* foreword by Wassermann (Berlin: Fischer, 1927); translated by Bernard Miall as *The Case for the Defendant* (London: Allen & Unwin, 1929);

Joseph Conrad, *Die Schattenlinie: Eine Beichte,* translated by E. McCalman, foreword by Wassermann (Berlin & Frankfurt am Main: Suhrkamp, 1948).

During his lifetime Jakob Wassermann was much praised and much derided. His friend Thomas Mann, in one of his ironic compliments, called Wassermann a "Weltstar des Romans" (a world-best-selling novelist), while Oskar Loerke, his publisher's reader, characterized his fiction as "Edelschmarren" (gilded junk). Wassermann is today chiefly remembered as a one-book author. Whenever the short list of highbrow German detective novels is recited, it includes his *Der Fall Maurizius* (1928; translated as *The Maurizius Case,* 1929), the suspenseful story of a tragic miscarriage of justice. For many of his contemporaries, as well as for the history of German literature, however, his primary importance is based on his treatment, in much of his best and worst writing, of anti-Semitism and the Jew's quest for cultural assimilation while maintaining his Jewish identity.

The son of Adolf and Henriette Traub Wassermann, Karl Jakob Wassermann was born in Fürth on 3 March 1873. His father was a small Jewish merchant. Wassermann became secretary to a prominent literary figure, Ernst Ludwig von Wolzogen, a leading Munich writer, publisher, and satirist. Through Wolzogen he become an editor of the satirical magazine *Simplicissimus.*

In 1895 Wassermann wrote the autobiographical novel *Engelhart oder Die zwei Welten* (Engelhart; or, The Two Worlds). In this thinly disguised portrait of the artist as a young man, the depressing and tormented beginnings of the son of a small Jewish merchant in Fürth unfold with the classical themes known from many representative works of that period. Engelhart Ratgeber, the confused hero, stumbles through the botched beginnings of a bourgeois career, touching upon people and places (Vienna, Munich, Freiburg,

Dust jacket for Wassermann's 1905 historical novel

and Zurich) that were the biographical steppingstones of the author. A financially unsuccessful father and the resulting poverty for his family, a malicious stepmother taking over after the early death of a beautiful and beloved mother, a hostile German environment for an ambitious Jewish boy, the torment of enduring a hated clerical apprenticeship for a modest bourgeois career, the stupid inhumanity of military service, and clumsy attempts at establishing some kind of artistic existence are familiar motifs of autobiographical fiction of that time. He decided not to publish *Engelhart* for personal as well as artistic reasons, the latter being that the novel, with its obsessive self-centeredness, lacked cohesion. As his friend Moritz Heimann, reader at the S. Fischer Verlag, put it in a letter to him: "Die geschilderten Gestalten und Ereignisse haben keine Realität in sich, sondern immer nur dem Erzähler zuliebe" (The persons and events depicted have no real life, they are merely vehicles for the narrator). The novel was finally posthumously published in 1973.

His first published novel, *Melusine* (1896), was an account of a tangled erotic obsession he had; he later relegated it to oblivion by not including it in his collected works. His second novel, and one of his most convincing works of fiction, *Die Juden von Zirndorf* (1896; translated as *The Jews of Zirndorf,* 1918), brought him instant fame far beyond the Bavarian capital. It is a powerful description of the agony and alienation of Jewish individuals and communities in Wassermann's native region of Franconia in southern Germany. A lengthy prelude is set during the second half of the seventeenth century, when Sabbatai Zewi was proclaimed the Messiah and savior of Jews throughout Europe. The Jews of Fürth embark to meet him in Salonica; when they hear of his conversion to Islam, they settle instead in a quiet valley of the Rednitz River and found the village of Zirndorf. Wassermann, unlike other contemporary authors, avoids painting a falsely idyllic picture of the community. Statements about the intrinsic qualities of "the Jew," which abound in this novel and in Wassermann's later works, sound odd to a modern reader: "Die Juden sind ein starkes und störrisches Volk; doch sind sie nur groß, wenn ein wenig Gelingen bei ihnen wohnt, und sie sind nicht lange groß, denn sie brechen leicht in dem Erstaunen über ihre eigene Größe" (The Jews are a strong and stubborn people; but they only rise to greatness when they have acquired some modicum of success, and they do not remain great for long because, in their amazement about their own greatness, they stumble). The main plot, set in the second half of the nineteenth century, concerns young Agathon, who has to come to terms with the collective past. The plot is weak and the development of the protagonist erratic. But a host of scenes and figures come alive: Agathon's immediate family, struggling to acquire the necessities of life; Jeanette, a Jewish banker's daughter refusing to be sold into marriage; Bojesen, the sympathetic high school teacher who becomes a victim of the bigoted bourgeois institution; and a literary charlatan, Gudstikker, whose phoniness reflects much of what Wassermann came to loathe about the literary scene in Munich.

A scathing portrayal of the Munich literati can also be found in his next novel, *Die Geschichte der jungen Renate Fuchs* (The Story of Young Renate Fuchs, 1900); but by the time it was published Wassermann had moved to Vienna, where an uncle smoothed his way into society. In 1901 he married Julie Speyer, the daughter of a wealthy Viennese entrepreneur. In Vienna he enjoyed the friendship of such famous literary figures as Mann, Hugo von Hofmannsthal, and Arthur Schnitzler.

With an unerring instinct for issues smoldering under the upright facades of the Wilhelminian and Austro-Hungarian empires, he published a series of novels at a rapid pace. In *Der Moloch* (1903), which was first published in the prestigious *Neue deutsche Rundschau* in 1902, the corrupting city is the villain. In this pessimistic story Arnold Ansorge is an idealistic rural simpleton who sets out to rescue a young Jewish girl, Jutta Elasser, from a convent where proselytizers are trying to convert her. But he succumbs, instead, to the decadence of life in Vienna. Wassermann here shows increasing skill in characterization. In *Alexander in Babylon* (1905; translated, 1949) he tried his hand at re-creating history for an educated urban readership. He was to write quite a few other historical novels, always giving preference to the psychological dimension while remaining sufficiently faithful to the factual background to make the books commercially successful.

His first really mature work, *Caspar Hauser oder Die Trägheit des Herzens* (Caspar Hauser; or, The Dullness of the Heart, 1908; translated as *Caspar Hauser,* 1928), blending self-reflection with contemporary history, takes the legend of Caspar Hauser for its main plot. This story has produced many works of fiction. Hauser was found roaming the streets of Nuremberg in 1828, unable to communicate normally but obviously of some social standing; his true identity has always been shrouded in mystery, and he was suspected by some of being a cleverly manipulated charlatan. After being shuffled off to various guardians, he was finally assassinated; apparently he represented a threat to dynastic interests. In Wassermann's portrayal, the mean and pedantic last guardian, Quand, and the beastly and brutal police lieutenant, Hickel, contrast with one of the few positive characters, Clara von Kannawurf, who in vain tries to secure a safe environment for the outcast. Wassermann describes Hauser's gradual development from terrifying fear of a loathsome, harsh world to determined self-defense. Wassermann uses some theatrical effects and sensational narrative tricks, but in the main the motifs of uprootedness and lack of charity are handled with restraint and skill.

Wassermann was always plagued by self-doubt; his letters to his wife reveal the manic-

Rainer Maria Rilke (left, back row) and Wassermann (right, back row) with the publisher Samuel Fischer and his family in Rome, 1910

depressive traits of a successful author who could never free himself from his humble beginnings. His self-doubts were clearly articulated in an outburst of 21 May 1913: "And how inadequate I feel in relation to my work, how repulsive every sentence I have written seems to me, how futile every word I employ, how halting my imagination, how conflicting my emotions, how empty my pleasures! And it is just this that increases in me an inordinate desire, a fierce impulse to snatch and embrace everything; I am horribly conscious, moreover, that my strength is not equal to my desires, and that I am sacrificing my whole being to a chimera. And to make things worse there are sordid material worries, which after all *do* exist, and must be warded off and kept out of my spiritual realm like evil spirits; and then the fear that I may be proving unsatisfactory to you, that I am not giving you and the children all that is your due; here again desires come into play, cravings for luxury. . . . Self-control, faith, is of no avail. . . ."

World War I was a time of genuine agony for Wassermann, who tried to enlist as a volunteer; his wife, by then the mother of several children, thwarted all such attempts. Wassermann compensated by writing a series of novels which, although of greatly varying quality, catch the issues of fundamental social change with uncanny accuracy. What he had developed as a typical theme of modern crisis, the brittleness of marriage as an institution, in *Der Mann von vierzig Jahren* (The Forty-Year-Old Man, 1913) became an epic tale of an obsessed artist who is entangled with three different types of women in *Das Gänsemännchen* (1915; translated as *The Goose Man,* 1922). Daniel Nothafft, a self-centered composer, loses his wife Gertrud to suicide. He falls in love with her sister, Leonore, while being married to the scheming Dorothea Döderlein, but loses Leonore in spite of her love for him. In the background lurks Philipine Schimmelweis, an ugly woman whose affection turns into perverted hate and leads to the destruction of all of the composer's manuscripts and possessions. A delicate counterbalance is provided by the portrait of Nothafft's friend, the biologist Dr. Benda. Because he is a Jew, Nothafft is barred from obtain-

Fischer and Wassermann in 1926

ing a chair at a university. He rebels by going on an expedition to Africa, and his reputation becomes established in England. He then casts off his antagonistic feelings, returns to his native land, and patiently compromises in hope of a better future. This novel is one of Wassermann's most subtle and penetrating works; hardly any extravagant effects mar his treatment of anti-Semitism and the problems of modern marriage.

While *Christian Wahnschaffe* (1919; translated as *The World's Illusion,* 1920) is atypical of Wassermann's novels with regard to its international setting, it is probably the best example of his ambiguous gifts as a writer. Christian Wahnschaffe is cast against two principal heroines who dominate almost equal parts of the novel. The singer Eva Sorel rises from poverty to wealth in the artificiality of prewar Europe. She regards life as a luxurious, never-ending game of chess. In the second part of the novel the poor Jewish student Ruth Hofmann serves her fellowman with the same innate charity as St. Francis of Assisi, who is expressly mentioned as the basis for this modernization of the theme of selflessly losing oneself among the poor, the destitute, and the outcasts. Christian Wahnschaffe's conversion, brought about by the prostitute Karin, and the confession of Niels, the murderer of Ruth Hofmann, leads him to a life that is in stark contrast to the opulent world of high society from which he comes. Wassermann's depictions of high and low milieus and a multitude of noble and nefarious characters are fascinating, but his nebulous references to noble traditions of the past–besides St. Francis, the Buddha is mentioned as a church father–reveal a rather vague humanitarianism.

Like his role model Thomas Mann, Wassermann started to write essays and deliver lectures on contemporary issues, mostly of a literary sort. He stirred up heated controversy with his polemic *Mein Weg als Deutscher und Jude* (1921; translated as *My Life as German and Jew,* 1933), where he uses naive and semimystical generalizations of personal experiences to try to analyze "the Jewish character" in a hostile Gentile world. Many of his observations are compelling, but they are hardly ever followed by a clear line of reasoning. Wassermann was a popular speaker, and his many addresses show the sincerity with which he perceived his role as a seer and warning voice in the desert. But the sinister signs of his time that he caught in many gripping scenes in his novels were not matched by an equally keen eye for social analysis in his essays and speeches.

Wassermann began spending more and more time away from Vienna in Alt-Aussee, which at first was a summer retreat for his family and then became his permanent home away from his wife and children. During the early 1920s he formed a relationship with Marta Karlweis, the daughter of a popular writer and an author in her own right. They were married after Wassermann's divorce in 1926.

The dramatic changes in his private life found expression in a series of novels, of which *Laudin und die Seinen* (Laudin and His Own, 1925; translated as *Wedlock,* 1925) is typical. Laudin, a successful Viennese lawyer almost fifty years old, becomes infatuated with the shallow, scheming actress Luise Dercum. Pia, his wife of sixteen years, gradually becomes aware of the secret life of her husband. Marlene, their daughter, reacts with puzzled, distrustful consternation. The social and psychological web in which Laudin is entangled leads to his gradual disintegration. The theme of people having lived for years in conventional ways, without being conscious of themselves or their immediate environment, is

[illegible]

[illegible]

[illegible]

[illegible]

Page from a draft of the manuscript for Wassermann's short story "Adam Urbas" (Schiller-Nationalmuseum, Marbach am Neckar, by permission of Jacqueline Wassermann)

sketched in a manner reminiscent of Schnitzler. Among the weaker features of *Laudin und die Seinen* are many sensationalistic confrontation scenes.

In the collection *Lebensdienst* (My Service in Life, 1928) Wassermann provides a wide variety of impressions, opinions, polemics, and literary reflections that reveal the oscillating character of his artistic temper, which consisted of flashes of brilliance and a rich variety of emotions. Quick-witted, impressionistic retorts are more common than penetrating analyses, and Wassermann's ponderous tone is more pompous than profound.

The novel *Der Fall Maurizius* deservedly won high acclaim from the beginning. The plot is loosely based on the case of Carl Hau, who, though innocent, was sentenced to life imprisonment. Wassermann's victim, Leonhart Maurizius, is condemned because of his self-imposed silence: he is protecting the real murderess, Anna Jahn, who has done away with her sister, Elli Hensolt, Maurizius's insanely jealous wife. After a long prison term–Wassermann is said to have taken Dostoyevski's *The House of the Dead* (1861-1862) as a model in portraying the bleak and despairing atmosphere of confinement–Maurizius is pardoned only to find that Anna has become a stale and stultified member of the bourgeoisie. But this story is secondary to the main narrative, the classical expressionist motif of a son's hatred for his father. Etzel Andergast, a teenager, finds out that eighteen years previously his father, the public prosecutor, had failed to ascertain the facts in Maurizius's case. The father refuses to reopen the case but grants Maurizius a pardon. The father had divorced his wife over a comparatively minor misdeed, and the son had became estranged from her; at the end, Etzel is reunited with his mother, and his father becomes insane because of his obsession with the "unresolved" court case. In his search for the truth Etzel encounters a sordid world of blackmail, infatuation, cynicism, and inhumane institutions. A powerful villain, Warschauer-Waremme, on whose perjury the conviction rested, narrates a moving story of how his Jewishness made him an outcast and criminal; his description of time he spent in the United States, particularly in Chicago, reflects Wassermann's impressions during a lecture tour of America in 1927. Wassermann saw the novel as an epic trial of his society's lack of understanding of true justice; but the outstanding feature of the tale is the author's ability to view a multitude of characters and events through diverse perspectives. The cumulative effect of seeing the same events unfold through the eyes of the narrator, the searching mind of a teenager, and the encrusted formalism of a legal professional is still haunting.

The commercial success of *Der Fall Maurizius* led Wassermann to extend the story of Etzel Andergast into a trilogy of novels. In *Etzel Andergast* (1931; translated as *Dr. Kerkhoven,* 1932) the drifter Etzel comes under the spell of Dr. Kerkhoven, who had been an ordinary general practitioner until he met Major Irlen, an African veteran whom he tried to cure of sleeping sickness. From Irlen Kerkhoven has gained extrasensory powers that endow him with unusual insight into the human psyche. His patient Andergast, however, betrays his confidence and becomes the lover of Kerkhoven's wife, Marie. Thrown out by Kerkhoven, Etzel ends up in the solitude of a "magic mountain" atmosphere in the Upper Engadine in Switzerland, where he undergoes a spiritual healing process. He also finds solace in the company of his mother, and the novel ends on an optimistic note. Familiar motifs of earlier stories, including marital struggle and anti-Semitism, resurface in the novel, which also reveals a return of Wassermann's old foibles: a penchant for melodrama, overbearing emotionalism, and simplification.

The last novel in the trilogy, *Joseph Kerkhovens dritte Existenz* (1934; translated as *Joseph Kerkhoven's Third Existence,* 1934), published after Wassermann's death in Alt-Aussee in 1934, is a broad canvas where characters and themes often get lost in an impenetrable maze of events. Etzel has married Marie; Dr. Kerkhoven is drawn into the life story of his patient Alexander Herzog; faced with his own terminal illness, Kerkhoven embarks on a spiritual journey for the last year and a half of his life. The dominant theme, however, is the persecution of Jews: Chaim Herzog is beaten by his classmates; Karl Imst and Jeanne Mallery are destroyed by their unjust imprisonment. The novel reflects Wassermann's growing fear of political developments in Germany; he wanted his audience to see where hatred, intolerance, and fanaticism could lead. But not even he could foresee the colossal social destruction that was in the making.

Wassermann became a favorite target for the National Socialists as a perverse and deviant author typical of his race. After World War II Wassermann did not join the ranks of "rediscovered" novelists of the past, such as Stefan Zweig and Jo-

Hermann Hesse, Thomas Mann, and Wassermann on holiday at Lenzerheide in 1933 (Marta Feuchtwanger, Pacific Palisades, California)

seph Roth. While some of his novels were republished, it was during this time that his status as a one-book author *(Der Fall Maurizius)* was established.

In 1973, on the 100th anniversary of his birth, his native city of Fürth published a solid monograph with an exhaustive bibliography. The Langen firm–now Langen-Müller–that had published his first works made an attempt at reissuing his more famous novels. But only in the 1980s did the critic Peter de Mendelssohn start a systematic reprinting project of Wassermann's major works; his premature death has made the undertaking an uncertain one. Dierk Rodewald's 1984 edition of some of Wassermann's essays reveals that Wassermann's reflections obfuscate rather than help to clarify the issues that eventually led to the mass murder of Jews.

The audience for whom Wassermann wrote his novels recognized him as a representative voice of their society. His career spanned more than three and a half decades of continuous prominence and acclaim. But no matter how successful and influential Wassermann was as a novelist and critic during his lifetime, most of his work seems today to belong to an irretrievable past.

Letters:

The Letters of Jakob Wassermann to Frau Julie Wassermann, edited by V. Grubwieser, with biographical notes by Frau Julie Wassermann, translated by Phyllis and Trevor Blewitt (London: Allen & Unwin, 1935); enlarged German edition published as *Briefe an seine Braut und Gattin Julie, 1900-1929* (Basel: Bücherfreunde, 1940);

Geliebtes Herz: Briefe, edited by A. Beranek (Vienna: Zwei Berge-Verlag, 1948).

Biographies:

Julie Wassermann-Speyer, *Jakob Wassermann und sein Werk* (Vienna & Leipzig: Deutsch-Österreichischer Verlag, 1923);

Siegmund Bing, *Jakob Wassermann, Weg und Werk des Dichters* (Nuremberg: Fromann, 1929);

Marta Karlweis-Wassermann, *Jakob Wassermann: Bild, Kampf und Werk. Mit einem Geleitwort von Thomas Mann* (Amsterdam: Querido, 1935).

References:

John C. Blankenagel, *The Writings of Jakob Wassermann* (Boston: Christopher Publishing House, 1942);

Eleanor Frankle, "Dostoievsky et Wassermann," *Revue de Litterature Comparee,* 19 (1939): 43-64;

Walter Goldstein, *Der Mann von sechzig Jahren* (Berlin: Künstlerdank, 1933);

Jakob Wassermann: Ein Beitrag der Stadt Fürth zu seinem 100. Geburtstag am 10. März 1973 (Fürth, 1973);

Franz Koch, "Wassermanns Weg als Deutscher und Jude," *Forschungen zur Judenfrage 1* (Hamburg: Hanseatische Verlagsanstalt, 1937);

Fritz Martini, "Nachwort," in Jakob Wassermann, *Der Fall Maurizius* (Vienna & Munich: Langen-Müller, 1971);

Peter de Mendelssohn, "Nachwort," in Wassermann, *Joseph Kerkhovens dritte Existenz* (Munich: Langen-Müller, 1982);

Charles Wassermann, "Nachwort," in Wassermann, *Schläfst Du, Mutter? Meistererzählungen* (Munich: Langen-Müller, 1984);

Holger Zahnow, " 'Der Fall Maurizius,' Jakob Wassermanns analytische Erzählkunst," *Archiv für das Studium der neueren Sprachen und Literaturen,* 221 (1984): 241-265;

Stefan Zweig, "Jakob Wassermann," *Die Neue Rundschau,* 23 (1912): 1131-1145.

Papers:

Most of Jakob Wassermann's papers are at the Deutsches Literaturarchiv of the Schiller-Nationalmuseum in Marbach am Neckar, Federal Republic of Germany.

Arnold Zweig

(10 November 1887-26 November 1968)

Liliane Weissberg
Johns Hopkins University

Arnold Zweig (Arnold Zweig Archiv, Deutsche Akademie der Künste, Berlin)

BOOKS: *Der englische Garten: Sonette* (Munich: Hyperion, 1910);

Aufzeichnungen über eine Familie Klopfer; Das Kind: Zwei Erzählungen (Munich: Langen, 1911);

Die Novellen um Claudia (Leipzig: Wolff, 1912); translated by Eric Sutton as *Claudia* (New York: Viking, 1930; London: Secker, 1930);

Abigail und Nabal: Tragödie in drei Akten (Leipzig: Rowohlt, 1913; revised edition, Munich: Wolff, 1920);

Ritualmord in Ungarn: Jüdische Tragödie in fünf Aufzügen (Berlin: Hyperion, 1914); revised as *Die Sendung Semaels: Jüdische Tragödie in fünf Aufzügen* (Leipzig: Wolff, 1918);

Die Bestie: Erzählungen (Munich: Langen, 1914);

Geschichtenbuch (Munich: Langen, 1916);

Bennarône: Eine Geschichte (Munich: Roland, 1918);

Entrückung und Aufruhr, poems by Zweig and lithographs by Magnus Zeller (Frankfurt am Main & Berlin: Tiedemann, 1920);

Das ostjüdische Antlitz, text by Zweig and lithographs by Hermann Struck (Berlin: Welt-Verlag, 1920);

Drei Erzählungen (Berlin: Welt-Verlag, 1920);

Söhne: Das zweite Geschichtenbuch (Munich: Langen, 1923);

Gerufene Schatten (Berlin: Tillgner, 1923);

Das neue Kanaan: Eine Untersuchung über Land und Geist, text by Zweig and lithographs by Struck (Berlin: Horodisch & Marx, 1925);

Lessing; Kleist; Büchner: Drei Versuche (Berlin: Spaeth, 1925);

Frühe Fährten (Berlin: Spaeth, 1925);

Regenbogen: Erzählungen (Berlin: Spaeth, 1925);

Die Umkehr des Abtrünnigen: Schauspiel (Berlin: Soncino-Gesellschaft, 1925); revised as *Die Umkehr* (Potsdam & Berlin: Kiepenheuer, 1927);

Der Spiegel des großen Kaisers: Novelle (Potsdam & Berlin: Kiepenheuer, 1926; revised edition, Leipzig: Reclam, 1949);

Caliban oder Politik und Leidenschaft: Versuch über die menschlichen Gruppenleidenschaften, dargetan am Antisemitismus (Potsdam & Berlin: Kiepenheuer, 1927);

Juden auf der deutschen Bühne (Berlin: Heine-Bund, 1927);

Der Streit um den Sergeanten Grischa: Roman (Potsdam & Berlin: Kiepenheuer, 1927); translated by Sutton as *The Case of Sergeant Grischa* (New York: Viking, 1928; London: Secker, 1928);

Pont und Anna (Potsdam: Kiepenheuer, 1928);

Herkunft und Zukunft: Zwei Essays zum Schicksal eines Volkes (Vienna: Phaidon, 1928);

Die Aufrichtung der Menorah: Entwurf einer Pantomime (Berlin: Soncino-Gesellschaft, 1930);

Laubheu und keine Bleibe: Schicksalskomödie (Berlin: Kiepenheuer, 1930);

Adolf Zweig (third from left), Zweig's father, in front of his saddler's shop in Kattowitz

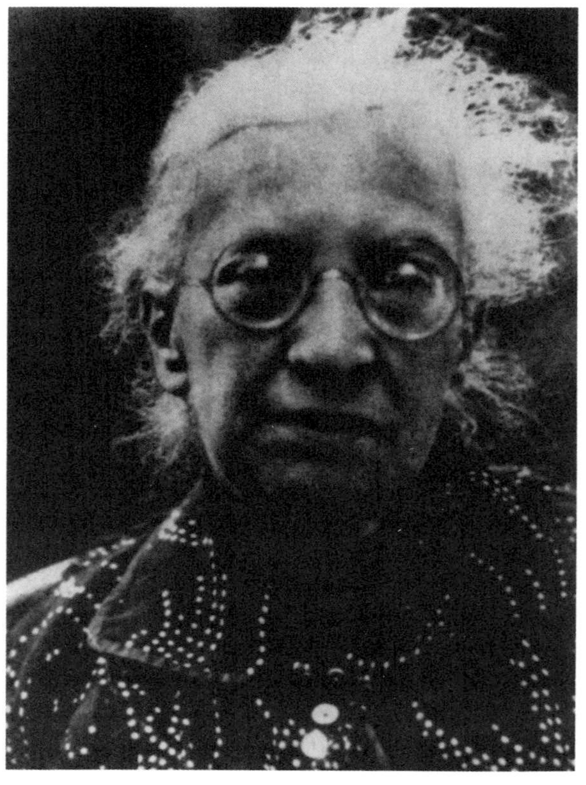

Zweig's mother, Bianca van Spandow Zweig

Junge Frau von 1914: Roman (Berlin: Kiepenheuer, 1931); translated by Sutton as *Young Woman of 1914* (New York: Viking, 1932; London: Secker, 1932);

Knaben und Männer: Achtzehn Erzählungen (Berlin: Kiepenheuer, 1931);

Mädchen und Frauen: Vierzehn Erzählungen (Berlin: Kiepenheuer, 1931);

Goethe in neuer Dichtung, by Zweig, Albrecht Schaeffer, and Wolfgang Goetz (Berlin-Charlottenburg: Wegweiser-Verlag, 1932);

De Vriendt kehrt heim: Roman (Berlin: Kiepenheuer, 1932); translated by Sutton as *De Vriendt Goes Home* (New York: Viking, 1933; London: Heinemann, 1934);

Spielzeug der Zeit: Erzählungen (Amsterdam: Querido, 1933); translated by Emma D. Ashton as *Playthings of Time* (New York: Viking, 1935; London: Secker, 1935);

Die Aufgabe des Judentums, by Zweig and Lion Feuchtwanger (Paris: Europäischer Merkur, 1933);

Bilanz der deutschen Judenheit 1933: Ein Versuch (Amsterdam: Querido, 1934); translated by Eden and Cedar Paul as *Insulted and Exiled: The Truth about German Jews* (London: Miles, 1937);

Erziehung vor Verdun: Roman (Amsterdam: Querido, 1935); translated by Sutton as *Education before Verdun* (New York: Viking, 1936);

Einsetzung eines Königs: Roman (Amsterdam: Querido, 1937); translated by Sutton as *The Crowning of a King* (New York: Viking, 1938; London: Secker, 1938);

Versunkene Tage: Roman aus dem Jahre 1908 (Amsterdam: Querido, 1938); republished as *Verklungene Tage* (Munich: Desch, 1950);

Ha-Kardon shel Wandsbek, Hebrew translation by Awigdor Hameiri (Haifa: "Sifriat Poalim" Workers' Book Guild, 1943); revised German version published as *Das Beil von Wandsbek: Roman, 1938-1943* (Stockholm: Neuer Verlag, 1947); translated by Sutton as *The Axe of Wandsbek* (New York: Viking, 1947; London: Hutchinson, 1948);

Ein starker Esser (Vienna: Verkauf, 1947);

Allerleirauh: Geschichten aus dem gestrigen Zeitalter (Berlin: Aufbau, 1949);

Die Kulturschaffenden und der Kampf um den Frieden (Berlin: Kulturbund zur demokratischen Erneuerung Deutschlands, 1949);

Stufen: Fünf Erzählungen aus der Übergangswelt (Berlin: Kantorowicz, 1949);

Bonaparte in Jaffa: Historisches Schauspiel (Berlin: Aufbau-Bühnenvertrieb, 1949);

Über den Nebeln: Eine Tatra-Novelle (Halle: Mitteldeutscher Verlag, 1950);

Der Elfenbeinfächer, volume 1 of *Ausgewählte Novellen* (Berlin: Aufbau, 1952);

Westlandsaga: Erzählung (Berlin: Rütten & Loening, 1952);

Rede zur Eröffnung der deutschen Bauakademie (Berlin: Deutschen Bauakademie, 1952);

Gruß an Christian Morgenstern (Leipzig: Insel, 1953);

Die Feuerpause: Roman (Berlin: Aufbau, 1954);

Der Regenbogen, volume 2 of *Ausgewählte Novellen* (Berlin: Aufbau, 1955);

Soldatenspiele: Drei dramatische Historien (Berlin: Aufbau, 1956);

Früchtekorb; Jüngste Ernte: Aufsätze (Rudolstadt: Greifenverlag, 1956);

Die Zeit ist reif: Roman (Berlin: Aufbau, 1957); translated by Kenneth Banerji and Michael Wharton as *The Time Is Ripe* (London: Gibbs & Phillips, 1962);

Fünf Romanzen (Berlin: Aufbau, 1958);

Literatur und Theater, volume 1 of *Essays* (Berlin: Aufbau, 1959);

A Bit of Blood and Other Stories (Berlin: Seven Seas, 1959);

Novellen (Berlin: Aufbau, 1961);

Zwölf Novellen (Leipzig: Reclam, 1962);

Traum ist teuer: Roman (Berlin: Aufbau, 1962);

Symphonie Fantastique: Zwei Novellen (Leipzig: Insel, 1963);

Dramen (Berlin: Aufbau, 1963);

Jahresringe: Gedichte und Spiele (Berlin: Aufbau, 1964);

Was der Mensch braucht: Erzählungen (Leipzig: Reclam, 1967);

Aufsätze zu Krieg und Frieden, volume 2 of *Essays* (Berlin: Aufbau, 1967);

Über Schriftsteller, edited by Heinz Kamnitzer (Berlin & Weimar: Aufbau, 1967);

Furchen der Zeit: Ausgewählte Geschichten (Frankfurt am Main: Fischer, 1973).

OTHER: Georg Büchner, *Sämtliche poetische Werke, nebst einer Auswahl seiner Briefe,* edited by Zweig (Munich: Paetel, 1918);

Heinrich von Kleists sämtliche Werke, 4 volumes, edited by Zweig (Munich & Berlin: Paetel, 1923);

Gotthold Ephraim Lessings gesammelte Werke, 3 volumes, introduction by Zweig (Berlin: Voegels, 1923);

Zweig with his sister Ruth and brother Hans, circa 1892

From left: Adolf, Bianca, Ruth, Hans, and Arnold Zweig, circa 1905

Zweig in 1905

Oscar Wilde, *Werke,* 2 volumes, edited by Zweig (Berlin: Knaur, 1930);

The Living Thoughts of Spinoza, Presented by Arnold Zweig, introduction by Zweig, translated by Eric Katz and Barrows Mussey (New York & Toronto: Longmans, Green, 1939; London: Cassells, 1939); original German version of Zweig's introduction published as *Baruch Spinoza: Porträt eines freien Geistes* (Leipzig: Insel, 1961);

Hilde Huppert, *Fahrt zum Acheron,* edited by Zweig (Berlin: VVN, 1951).

No better example may be found for the different emphases of literary history in the German Democratic Republic and in the Federal Republic of Germany than the case of Arnold Zweig. Zweig was the most celebrated living author in the German Democratic Republic, where he lived from 1948 until his death in 1968. Many of his novels have been published in large editions there. Festschriften appeared on his birthdays, and in 1962 Johanna Rudolph edited a book, *Arnold Zweig,* to serve as a guide for school festivities honoring the author and his work. In 1958 the Aufbau-Verlag in Berlin began to publish Zweig's collected works. Not all the works that were published in the German Democratic Republic are still in print, but Zweig remains a well-known writer and the subject of much scholarly work.

In the Federal Republic, on the other hand, Arnold Zweig has been the "other Zweig"–in reference to the Austrian author Stefan Zweig–and nearly forgotten. There, he still seems to be known mainly as the author of a single book, *Der Streit um den Sergeanten Grischa* (1927; translated as *The Case of Sergeant Grischa,* 1928). While Zweig was celebrated in the East during the 1950s and 1960s, most of his books were not available in West German bookstores, and only in very recent years have a few of his novels appeared in a paperback series.

Zweig was born on 10 November 1887 in Glogau, Silesia (now Glogów, Poland), the oldest of three children. Zweig's father, Adolf, had been a saddler; after his marriage to Bianca van Spandow he entered the thriving business of his parents-in-law, grocers whose trade was primarily with the military personnel stationed in Glogau. The economic situation of the Zweig family worsened drastically when the Prussian ministry of war prohibited Jews from supplying the army with agricultural goods. In 1896 the family moved to Kattowitz (now Katowice, Poland) where Adolf Zweig resumed his old profession as a saddler.

In the same year, Arnold Zweig entered the Oberrealschule in Kattowitz, interrupting his studies for a year to work in a bookstore. At school he formed lasting friendships with the future painter Ludwig Meidner, the future poet Arnold

Zweig (seated, second from left) in the graduating class of the Kattowitz Oberrealschule (nonclassical secondary school), 1907

Ulitz, and the future philologist Rudolf Clemens. He played the violin at musical gatherings and developed an interest in music that he would later ascribe to many of his fictional characters and that would also influence his conception of literature itself. Zweig graduated in 1907 and began to study German literature, English, French, philosophy, psychology, and art history at the university in nearby Breslau. He studied in Munich in 1908-1909, in Berlin from 1909 to 1911, in Göttingen in 1911-1912, in Rostock in 1912-1913, and in Munich again in 1913-1914. During these years of wandering Zweig became fascinated by the writings of Friedrich Nietzsche. He attended lectures by Edmund Husserl and Georg Simmel, and these philosophers became lasting influences on him. He also read the works of the utopian socialist Gustav Landauer, the socialist Zionist Franz Oppenheimer, and the Jewish philosopher Martin Buber. Zweig's interest in the fate of the Jewish people guided much of his early writing. During his last years of study at the universities of Rostock and Munich, Zweig began research for a dissertation on Paul Jakob Rudnick, a student of the Enlightenment poet Johann Wilhelm Ludwig Gleim; the thesis was never completed.

Zweig's first intention had been to become a teacher of modern languages, but he had already begun to write fiction during his university years. While Zweig's earliest literary attempts date from his last year in high school, his first serious literary work was written during his early years in Munich. The manuscript for a fragmentary novel about a musician, "Die Stationen des Johannes Grimm oder die Vergitterten" (The Stages of Johannes Grimm; or, Behind Bars), has been lost. In 1908 Zweig published some of his poems in an almanac edited by a Munich student organization, and he began work on a novel that would not appear until thirty years later, when it was published as *Versunkene Tage* (Days Faded Away, 1938). Like its author, the main character of this novel is a devoted reader of Nietzsche.

In the summer of 1909 Zweig returned to Kattowitz and founded, together with some former schoolmates, a bimonthly literary magazine, *Die Gäste* (The Guests). In the six issues that appeared Zweig published poems, essays, a first ver-

First page from the manuscript for the novel fragment "Die Stationen des Johannes Grimm oder die Vergitterten," written during Zweig's early years in Munich (Arnold Zweig 1887-1968: Werk und Leben in Dokumenten und Bildern, *edited by Georg Wenzel, 1978)*

Zweig in 1911

Zweig in 1912. He began studying the violin while a student in Kattowitz.

Zweig's cousins, Beatrice and Miriam Zweig, circa 1913

sion of his drama *Abigail und Nabal* (Abigail and Nabal, 1913), and narratives.

In 1911 Zweig published his first book of fiction, *Aufzeichnungen über eine Familie Klopfer* (Notes about a Family Named Klopfer, 1911), which includes two novellas. The title story, the history of a Jewish family narrated by one of its last members, was influenced by Thomas Mann's *Buddenbrooks* (1901; translated, 1924). A year later *Die Novellen um Claudia* (translated as *Claudia*, 1930) was published; its introductory chapter had already appeared in *Die Gäste* as a separate narrative. The book was Zweig's first major success.

Die Novellen um Claudia consists of seven novellas that follow the courtship, marriage, and married life of the rich and beautiful Claudia Eggerling and the gifted scholar Walter Rohme. The novellas are narrated from the perspectives of Claudia, Rohme, and a third-person narrator; the fourth novella, in which Claudia's mother looks through old photographs on the day of her daughter's wedding, serves as the centerpiece. In each of the novellas events are filtered through the sensibility of its protagonist, but the presentation of private emotions combines with reflections on what art should be, on the moral integrity of the artist, and on the role of the receptive audience.

In 1912 Zweig completed *Ritualmord in Ungarn* (Ritual Murder in Hungary), a tragedy that was published in 1914 but banned by war censorship; Zweig received the Kleist Prize for it in 1915. A collection of Zweig's short fiction, *Die Bestie* (The Beast), also appeared in 1914. The volume contains six stories and three sketches derived from war incidents that Zweig had read about in the newspapers. The stories testify to Zweig's naive belief in the truth of the propaganda published by the press early in the war. The title story reflects upon the deaths of German soldiers on a Belgian farm. In the mid 1940s Zweig planned to integrate this tale into a novel, "Gesang aus dem Abgrund" (Song From the Abyss), but he never completed the project; in 1952 he included a revision of "Die Bestie" as the first story in his volume *Westlandsaga*. Published with an explanatory note, this version emerges as a much more complex tale that describes the lives and social backgrounds of a group of German soldiers who have murdered one another, and whose deaths caused the execution of an innocent Belgian farmer.

Zweig was drafted into the army in April 1915 and spent the following years as a common soldier near Lille, in the south of Hungary and Serbia, and at the western front at Verdun. On 5 July 1916, while on leave, he married his cousin Beatrice ("Dita") Zweig, a painter. After thirteen months at Verdun Zweig became a member of the press division of the Ober-Ost section in Lithuania and Russia. The war ended in November 1918, and Zweig returned to Berlin.

During his youth Zweig had contracted tuberculosis of the eyes, and in 1916 his eyes had started to bleed. In the years that followed, this malady, despite constant treatment, at times rendered him virtually blind.

In 1919 he spent a term at the university of Tübingen, studying literature and sociology, but soon abandoned his studies. He and his wife moved to Starnberg near Munich in October 1919; their first son, Michael ("Michi"), was born there a year later.

Since 1918 he had been a contributor to Siegfried Jacobsohn's *Weltbühne*, and he also wrote for other journals. At this time Zweig regarded himself as a socialist and a Zionist, and he received threats on his life after the Hitler putsch in 1923. In 1924 Zweig and his family moved to Berlin, where he became an editor of the *Jüdische Rundschau*. His second son, Adam, was born in the same year. His essays on Gotthold Ephraim Lessing, Ewald von Kleist, and Georg Büchner appeared as a book in 1925.

In his essayistic work of the 1920s Zweig reveals his idealistic Zionism and his involvement in the fight for better social conditions for the Jewish immigrants to Germany from Poland, Russia, and other eastern states. *Das ostjüdische Antlitz* (The Face of the Eastern Jew, 1920), an essay with lithographs by Zweig's friend Hermann Struck, testifies to the exotic "otherness" the Eastern Jews represented for Zweig. The achievements of German Jews are described in *Juden auf der deutschen Bühne* (Jews on the German Stage, 1927). His reading of Sigmund Freud's work led to his *Caliban oder Politik und Leidenschaft* (Caliban; or, Politics of Emotion, 1927), an analysis of anti-Semitism as a Gruppenleidenschaft (emotion of the group).

Zweig sent a copy of *Caliban* to Freud, initiating a friendship that would last until Freud's death in 1939. He met Freud only a few times, but their correspondence is marked by an affection that turns Zweig into "Meister [Master] Arnold" and Freud into "Vater [Father] Freud." Zweig had learned about himself through

Zweig in 1914, the year his short-story collection Die Bestie *was published*

Zweig with Beatrice and Miriam in 1914

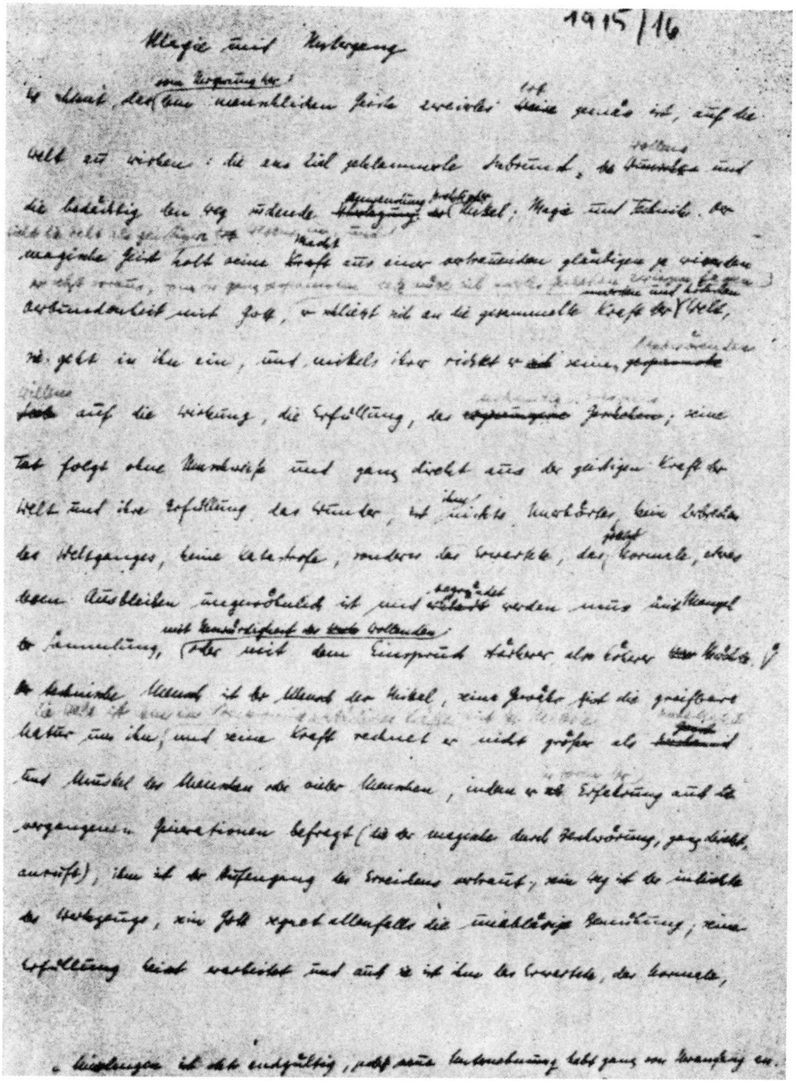

*First page from the manuscript for Zweig's essay "Magie und Untergang," written circa 1915-1916 but not published until 1978 (*Arnold Zweig 1887-1968: Werk und Leben in Dokumenten und Bildern, *edited by Georg Wenzel, 1978)*

Freud's writings and through psychoanalytic treatment, and wanted to bring the insights of psychoanalysis to his literary work. Zweig's understanding of psychoanalysis, however, was often met by reservations on Freud's part.

Zweig's novella *Pont und Anna,* begun in 1925 but not published until 1928, poignantly illustrates Zweig's interpretation of Freud's theory of the effect of shock upon memory. Laurenz Pont, a Baumeister (builder: an old-fashioned term for architect), is in love with the dancer Anna, who tires of his admiration for her. While in Italy hoping to overcome his love for the girl, Pont receives a telegram that informs him of Anna's murder. The news of her death triggers recollections of events in his youth that had been long forgotten, providing him insights into his own nature. In its discussion of art and the artist, as well as in its description of Italy, *Pont und Anna* bears similarities to Mann's *Der Tod in Venedig* (1912; translated as *Death in Venice,* 1925), but peculiar to Zweig is the ease with which Pont can combine the love for his wife and small child with that for the much younger Anna. This concept of the "neue Moral" (new morality) is a recurrent theme in much of Zweig's later fiction.

In 1927 Zweig published his first and best-known novel, *Der Streit um den Sergeanten Grischa* (translated as *The Case of Sergeant Grischa,* 1928). Because of his poor eyesight, in composing this

Arnold and Beatrice Zweig in their wedding picture. They were married on 5 July 1916 while Zweig was on leave from the western front during World War I.

work Zweig adopted the method of dictating a draft to a secretary, having it read back to him, and then dictating the next draft. The novel was completed during a two-month period in 1927 and first published in serial form in the *Frankfurter Zeitung* under the title *Alle gegen Einen* (All against One). It was an immediate popular and critical success.

Zweig had first shaped the material as a drama, *Das Spiel vom Sergeanten Grischa* (The Play about Sergeant Grischa), which was written in 1921. Both works are based on an anecdote Zweig had heard while serving on the eastern front: a Russian prisoner escaped from a German prison camp, was recaptured by the Germans, produced a false name, and was accused of being a Bolshevik spy. Although his identity was cleared up, he was sentenced to death as an example. The play was not produced until 1930, when Zweig reworked it for a production of the Berlin Theater am Nollendorfplatz, where it was staged by the Russian director Alexander Granowsky and drew attention because of the novel's reputation.

The soldier Grischa Paprotkin, alias Bjuschew, is an innocent victim; the order to execute him is given by General Schieffenzahn, who sets wartime rules above all human concerns and who is involved in a power struggle with General Lychow, the area commander. General Lychow, his staff officer Paul Winfried, the press secretary and writer Werner Bertin, the nurses Bärbel Osann and Sophie von Gorse, and the common soldiers who know Grischa try to help him and, in their failure to do so, become victims of the war themselves. This failure provides all of these characters with a lesson about power structures and the logic of the war. Zweig would proceed to recount the consequences of this lesson–and lessons like it–in his later novels.

The general humanistic concerns of *Der Streit um den Sergeanten Grischa* made it attractive to a large audience that was able to agree on condemning the war even if it was unwilling to subscribe to the author's socialist politics. It is not a single war that is at the center of Zweig's novel, but all war. The novel calls for this universal interpretation from its very beginning. The introduc-

Card sent by Zweig to his sister Ruth from Montmedy, near Verdun, March 1917

Zweig in June 1919, about the time he was a student at Tübingen

Zweig in 1920 (Arnold Zweig Archiv, Deutsche Akademie der Künste, Berlin)

tion of the first character–"Es steht ein Mann im dicken Schnee, unten am Fuß eines schwarz angekohlten Baumes, der spitzwinklig in gute Höhe ragt mitten im verbrannten Walde, schwarz auf vielfach zertretener Weiße" (A man stands in the deep snow, at the foot of a tree turned into black coal that is pointing up in a sharp angle in the midst of a burnt wood, black on a trampled down white)–is preceded by a paragraph indicating both a cosmic scope and the narrator's distanced position: "Die Erde, Tellus, ein kleiner Planet, strudelt emsig durch den kohlschwarzen, atemlos eisigen Raum, der durchspült wird von Hunderten von Wellen, Schwingungen, Bewegungen eines Unbekannten, des Äthers, und die, wenn sie Festes treffen und Widerstand sie aufflammen läßt, Licht werden, Elektrizität, ungeahnte Einflüsse, verderbliche oder segnende Wirkungen" (The earth, Tellus, a small planet, whirls busily through the coal-black, breathless icy space that is drained by hundreds of waves, vibrations, movements of the unknown, of the ether, which, if they strike something solid and flare up, become light, electricity, unsuspected influences, destructive or beneficent effects).

Soon after the publication of this book, Zweig began outlining what he first conceived as the "Trilogie des Übergangs" (Trilogy of Transition). *Der Streit um den Sergeanten Grischa* was to be the center of this trilogy, with *Erziehung vor Verdun* (1935; translated as *Education before Verdun,* 1936) covering preceding events and *Einsetzung eines Königs* (1937; translated as *The Crowning of a King,* 1938) covering later events. Each novel was to focus on a different character, such as Grischa or Paul Winfried. Zweig intended to let the increasingly critical minds of his characters provide commentary on the events depicted.

Despite these plans, Zweig first continued his "Grischa cycle" with *Junge Frau von 1914* (1931; translated as *Young Woman of 1914,* 1932), a prologue to *Erziehung vor Verdun. Junge Frau von 1914* concentrates on the early years of the war, ending with Werner Bertin's marriage to Lenore Wahl, the daughter of a wealthy German-Jewish banker. Lenore's parents have opposed the marriage, but the "social need" to have a family member in the army finally leads to their agreement and a wedding during Bertin's leave. On one of her visits to Bertin Lenore becomes pregnant. Zweig's account of her changing attitude to Bertin, and of her feelings before and after she has an abortion, provides a parallel to Bertin's war experiences.

Zweig interrupted work on his World War I cycle after the publication of this novel. In February 1932 he traveled for the first time to Palestine, where friends such as Struck had already settled. Zweig's trip combined visits to his friends with an exploration of the possibility of moving to Palestine himself. He was impressed by many of the achievements of the Jewish immigrants, but his experiences of the country under English rule, the tensions and even warfare between its Jewish and Arab inhabitants, apparently disillusioned him. After his return to Berlin in April 1932, Zweig wrote *De Vriendt kehrt heim* (1932; translated as *De Vriendt Goes Home,* 1933), the first of his novels set in Palestine.

De Vriendt kehrt heim is based on the case of Jacob Israel de Haan, an orthodox Dutch Jew who had immigrated to Palestine. A teacher at the government law school, de Haan was a member of the anti-Zionist, religious Agudat-Israel movement who worked against the establishment

Beatrice (left) and Arnold Zweig with Miriam Zweig, 1920

Zweig with his first son, Michael, in Starnberg, summer 1921

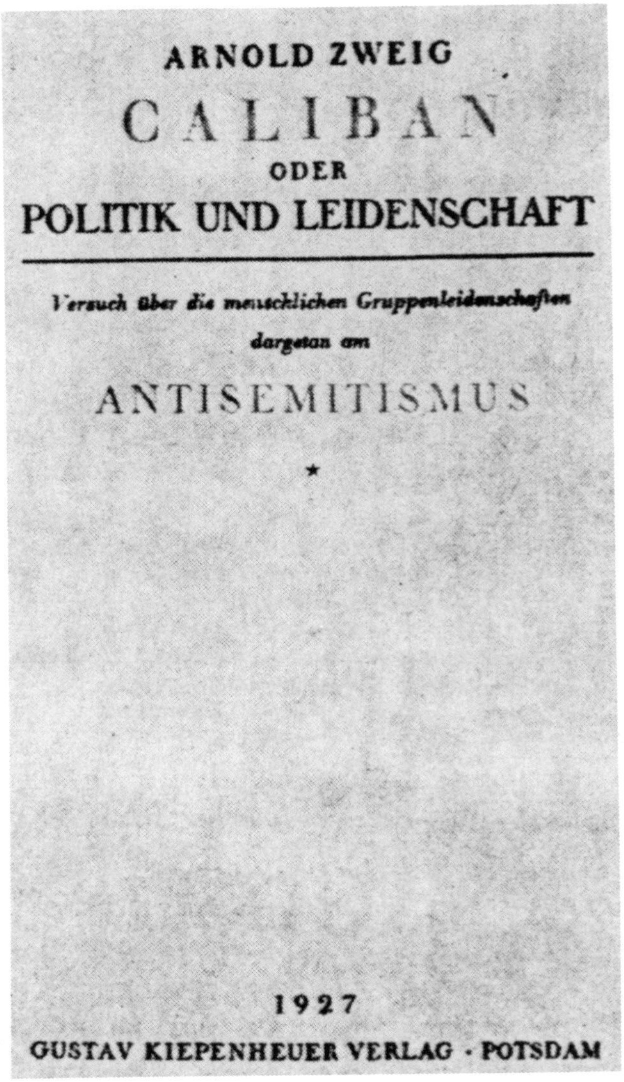

ARNOLD ZWEIG

CALIBAN

ODER

POLITIK UND LEIDENSCHAFT

Versuch über die menschlichen Gruppenleidenschaften dargetan am

ANTISEMITISMUS

★

1927

GUSTAV KIEPENHEUER VERLAG · POTSDAM

Title page for Zweig's study of anti-Semitism, based upon his reading of Sigmund Freud's work

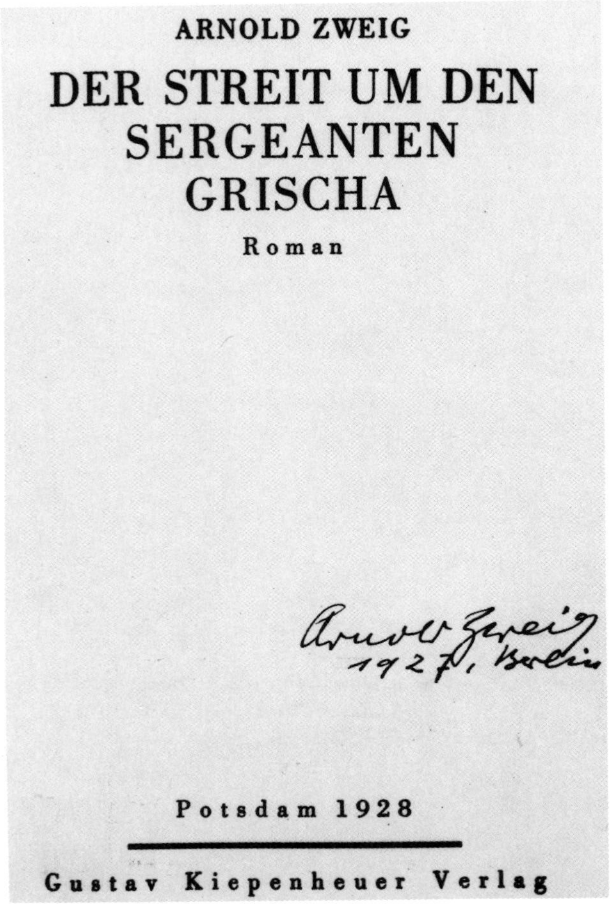

ARNOLD ZWEIG

DER STREIT UM DEN SERGEANTEN GRISCHA

Roman

Arnold Zweig
1927, Berlin

Potsdam 1928

Gustav Kiepenheuer Verlag

Autographed title page for Zweig's first novel, his most successful work

of a Jewish state and was the object of many attacks by the Zionists, who saw him as a traitor to the Jewish cause. The news that de Haan was having an affair with a young Arab boy caused a scandal and led to a student boycott. In 1924 de Haan was murdered; the crime remained unsolved, though there was some suspicion that he was killed by the Arab boy's relatives to avenge the family's honor.

Zweig structures his novel as a detective story in which he explores the psychology of the victim and his murderers. By placing the murder of de Vriendt in 1929, five years after the actual event, Zweig is able to combine the description of this case with that of the later unrest in Palestine. De Vriendt's murderers are not the relatives of the Arab boy but a pair of young Jewish immigrants. The novel's focus is on the politics of Zionism: have Jews come to Palestine to play the oppressor as a new Herrenrasse (master race)? One of the characters in the book, the engineer Eli Saamen, gives a problematic answer: "In Europa kämpfen wir gegen die Unterdrückung als Staatsbürger, hier aber um unser Prestige als Semiten" (In Europe, we are fighting against the oppression as citizens, here for our prestige as Semites).

When Zweig returned to Berlin he found that the political situation there had worsened. On 10 May 1932 the journalist Carl von Ossietzky was sentenced to an eighteen-month jail term for "treason." In protest Zweig, Lion Feuchtwanger, Ernst Toller, Leonhard Frank, and many others accompanied Ossietzky to the jail in Tegel where he was to serve his sentence. The National Socialists were rapidly gaining power, and Zweig decided to return to Palestine with his family, leaving Germany on 14 March 1933, shortly after Hitler's formation of a new government. *De Vriendt kehrt heim* was Zweig's last novel published in Germany before his emigration. The manuscripts he left behind in Berlin were seized by the Gestapo.

Zweig spent a few months in Sanary-sur-Mer in the south of France, which also provided refuge for Heinrich and Thomas Mann, Bertolt Brecht, Franz Werfel, and Feuchtwanger. Zweig and Feuchtwanger had met in Munich in 1922 and later had become close friends in Berlin, where both were engaged in reinterpreting the concept of the historic novel. Feuchtwanger remained in France until 1940 and then moved to the United States. An extensive correspondence kept their friendship alive.

In December 1933 Zweig moved to Haifa, Palestine, following his wife and children, who had traveled there a few months earlier. Haifa became their home for the next fourteen years. His sister Ruth lived with them for a short period, but later decided to immigrate to Argentina with their brother Hans. Beatrice's sister Miriam lived nearby. Zweig's German citizenship was revoked in 1935, but the next year he received a Palestinian passport and was able to travel again. He went to Vienna in 1936 to consult an eye specialist and to New York in 1939 to participate in the P.E.N. congress. He became a member of the Ausschuß zur Vorbereitung einer deutschen Volksfront (Committee for the Preparation of a German Popular Front), which was constituted in Paris in June 1936 under Heinrich Mann's chairmanship. Throughout this period he continued to work on his World War I novels. *Erziehung vor Verdun,* published in Amsterdam in 1935, and *Einsetzung eines Königs,* which appeared two years later, completed the cycle as Zweig had planned it in the late 1920s.

The events of *Erziehung vor Verdun* follow those of *Junge Frau von 1914*. Christian Kroysing, a young soldier, discovers mismanagement of the food supply in his division at the western front. The officers who manage the supplies to their own advantage send Kroysing into battle, where he is killed. Werner Bertin relates this story of "murder" to Christian's brother Eberhard, an officer, who then wages a private war against Christian's former superior Niggl and other members of his division. In the end, Niggl is rewarded with a medal, and Eberhard dies in a hospital during an air raid. Kroysing's case, however, as well as the experiences and the political engagement of his working-class comrades Lebehde and Pahl, teach Bertin much about the interests which benefit from war.

Einsetzung eines Königs takes place in the last years of the war. The officer Paul Winfried, from *Der Streit um den Sergeanten Grischa,* who is stationed at the eastern front, witnesses the intrigues of the German officers and politicians who are trying to install either a Saxon or a Swabian king in Lithuania–in total disregard of the wishes of the occupied people and with much naiveté concerning the future of the German domination over these lands. On a visit to his future parents-in-law in Swabia Winfried transmits a message to the Swabian Duke of Trek. The consequence is a "lesson" arranged by his superior, the Prussian officer Clauß, who sends Winfried to a

Alle gegen Grischa / Roman 1.
von Arnold Zweig

1. Buch: Die Flucht

1. Kapitel: "Die Zange."

Die Erde, ein kleiner Planet, sprudelt emsig durch den kohlschwarzen, atemlos eisigen Raum, der durchströmt wird durch Hunderten von Wellen, Schwingungen, Bewegungen eines Unbekannten, des Aethers, und die, wenn sie auf Widerstand ihnen Leben gibt, Licht werden, Elektrizität, unbekannte Einflüsse, verderbliche oder segnende Wirkungen. Sie hat, umgeben von ihrer schweren, wolligen Lufthülle, auf ihrer elliptischen Bahn die fernste Kurve hinter sich, die sie am weitesten von ihrem Lebensquell, der Sonne, abhält; unaufhaltsam kreisend arbeitet sie sich dem Muttersterne wieder zu. Da prallen die Strahlen der Sonne erregender in ihren Bereich; die Atmosphäre gerät in Gärungen, rasende Winde stürzen von den kalten Polen überall zu den schon wärmeren Landgebildenen, in denen es sich, gelockt von der Magie des wieder näheren Lichtes, zu regen beginnt, zu keimen. Die Welle des Lebens auf der Erde beginnt langsam anzusteigen; in den Menschen vollziehen sich, wie Jahr für Jahr, befremdende Wirkungen.

Es steht ein Mann unten am Fusse eines hohen dunkelgrünen Baumes, spitzwinklig in die Höhe gewachsen und umgeben von einer Schar gleicher Gesellen. Der Mensch, gekleidet in viele Hüllen, versenkt die Hände in die Taschen der einen, blickt vor sich hin und denkt. „Butter", denkt er, „anderthalb Pfund, und zweieinhalb Pfund Mehl von den Bauern, und ein gespartes Brot. Ja, das wird's tun. Damit kann sie wieder eine Weile aushalten. Ich geb's Fritzke mit, der morgen auf Urlaub fährt. Vielleicht tausch ich meinen Tabak gegen eine Büchse Schmalzersatz ein; wenn ich von der Löhnung eine Mark drauflege, rückt der Küchenbulle damit raus. Butter," denkt er, „anderthalb Pfund," und so beginnt er, den Inhalt des Paketes, das er an seine Frau zu schicken beabsichtigt, wieder in

First page from the manuscript for Der Streit um den Sergeanten Grischa *(1927) (Arnold Zweig Archiv, Deutsche Akademie der Künste, Berlin)*

Zweig at his home in Berlin, September 1929

Zweig with Lily Offenstadt at a ski resort in the Tatry mountains in Czechoslovakia in the winter of 1932-1933

Beatrice and Arnold Zweig in Haifa, Palestine, where they lived from 1933 to 1948 (Marta Feuchtwanger, Pacific Palisades, California)

work camp as a spy. After Winfried's true identity is revealed, he dissociates himself from his former idol and identifies with the oppressed.

Zweig introduces minor characters from earlier novels in the cycle, providing a sense of continuity and recognition for the reader. He also quotes historical figures, such as Rosa Luxemburg. Members of the party in power are given fictional names, though it is possible to connect some of them with historical personages. General Albert Schieffenzahn, for example, seems to have been modeled on Erich Ludendorff, and Albin Schilles resembles the industrialist Hugo Stinnes.

The political message of *Einsetzung eines Königs* is sharper than that of the earlier volumes of the cycle, and it enjoyed less popular success than its companion volumes. All of these novels are didactic in a broad sense and describe the political education of the characters. This education, often produced by single events, levels the differences between characters such as the poor Jewish writer Werner Bertin and the semiaristocratic Winfried, favored nephew of General Lychow and a believer in the old Prussian ideals. Zweig's main characters are often artists, intellectuals, or reflective bourgeois who progress from their vaguely humanist convictions to a socialist interpretation of events. Ultimately Werner Bertin is the true protagonist of the cycle, not only because Bertin's "education" seems to parallel Zweig's own experiences and development but also because he has to translate his experiences into aesthetic form. When he enters, Bertin has already written a novel called *Liebe auf dem letzten Blick* (Love at Last Sight); he emerges from the war as a writer with strong social engagement, a student of Georg Büchner as well as a chronicler of actual events. Zweig's novels demonstrate the influence of the Russian nineteenth-century novelists and Theodor Fontane; his style has moved from the early *Novellen um Claudia* toward a more realistic treatment of events. *Einsetzung eines Königs* already bears, moreover, the traces of the essayistic excursions into the realm of historic facts that are characteristic of Zweig's later style. Since the novels in this cycle were written out of chronological sequence and with long interruptions, it is not surprising that there are discrepancies among them. Some events are described or interpreted in different ways in different novels, providing evidence of Zweig's growing political engagement.

Das Beil von Wandsbek (translated as *The Axe of Wandsbek,* 1947) is Zweig's only novel set in Germany during the Hitler regime. After reading about the suicide of a Hamburg executioner in the Prague *Deutsche Volkszeitung* in 1937, Zweig wrote the novel to probe the reasons that might have led to the act. Albert Teetjen, a butcher, accepts the job of executing four communist prisoners to earn the money to save his business. He becomes both a murderer and a victim. After the deed becomes known his store is boycotted, but what seems to be a moral issue becomes ambiguous. He is blamed and blackmailed for not splitting his "fee" with other members of his SS troop, and he is also presented as the victim of an economic system that makes it impossible for a small, independent businessman to survive. Although Teetjen seems to become critical of the early National Socialist promises to provide help for the petty bourgeoisie, he is also unwilling to become part of the working class. Zweig later insisted that Stine, Teetjen's once religious wife, is the main character of the novel. At first unaware of her husband's deed, she is the first to choose suicide because of their situation; Teetjen soon follows. The shipowner Footh, who arranged Teetjen's job, thrives under the new regime. Heinrich Koldeway, the director of the prison and a student of Nietzsche, and Käte Neumeier, a doctor whom he later marries and a liberal turned party member, both discover Freud and define Hitler as a psychopath. The danger of the political disengagement of intellectuals in the pre-Hitler years is ironically presented in a vignette that describes the visit of Claudia and Walter Rohme, the main characters of *Novellen um Claudia,* to Hamburg.

Zweig described the work as an "Anti-Nazi novel" to distinguish it from his antiwar novels. It was first published in a Hebrew translation of an early draft in 1943. The next year Zweig sent a carbon copy of his manuscript to Feuchtwanger in California. Feuchtwanger edited it heavily and sent it to his Swedish publisher, who brought out the revised German version in 1947.

Zweig's years in Haifa were difficult. Poverty and lack of recognition were difficult to bear. There was hostility toward him as a German writer and no demand for his work; Zweig was never able to write in Hebrew. In 1938 he sustained a concussion in a car accident and was unable to work for months.

In Palestine Zweig became disenchanted with a Zionism that wanted to deprive him of his language and that gave him no chance to publish his work. Before 1933 he had dreamed of a Juda-

Zweig visiting Marta and Lion Feuchtwanger at the Villa Valmer, their home at Sanary-sur-Mer, France, in 1936 (photograph by Stefan Lorant, courtesy of Archiv Marta Feuchtwanger)

ism that would stand for a Stammeseinheit (unified nation) supporting German-Jewish culture. Now he not only saw himself deprived of his language but observed Jews cheating newly arrived Jewish immigrants. Palestine was not the country Zweig had dreamed of, and he increasingly doubted that it could ever become that country. There was also an uncanny likeness between the behavior of Jews toward Arabs and the imperialism of German capitalists that he had described in his novels about World War I. In April 1942 he and Wolfgang Yourgrau founded the journal *Orient*. In *Orient* Zweig supported socialist politics in Palestine and insisted on the importance of German Jews using their own language. Zweig and his paper were frequently attacked, and the journal ceased publication after a year.

In 1942 Zweig became a cofounder of the Liga Victory, an organization that tried to procure supplies for the Soviet army. Zweig had become a member of the Gesellschaft der Freunde des neuen Rußland (Society of Friends of the New Russia) in 1926, but the war years drew him closer to the country that was, he thought, offering to help create a new Germany.

Zweig remained in Palestine after the end of World War II but left shortly before the founding of Israel in May 1948. He flew first to Prague and then to Berlin. The emerging German Democratic Republic needed a writer of Zweig's stature and was willing to provide him with attractive working conditions. Zweig was happy to become a German author again, able not only to find a readership but also to help create a state that would have learned the lessons of peace that he had offered in his books. After a few months' stay at what remained of the Hotel Adlon, Zweig moved to a villa in Niederschönhausen. His wife suffered a nervous breakdown upon their return to Germany and was under medical care for the next two years.

The former Zionist became a German state

author. Shortly after his arrival in Berlin, Zweig became a leading member of the Kulturbund zur demokratischen Erneuerung Deutschlands (Cultural Committee for the Democratic Renewal of Germany). During the following year he participated in the World Peace Congress in Paris and became a member of the parliament of the German Democratic Republic. Heinrich Mann had been elected the first president of the Deutsche Akademie der Künste (German Academy of Arts) of the German Democratic Republic, but he died in California in 1950 before his intended return to Berlin. Zweig was named his successor and moved into the president's villa. In 1953 he became honorary president, and Johannes Becher, who was seen as a more vigorous supporter of the new party program, became president. In 1952 Zweig had made his first trip to the Soviet Union to attend the celebration for the centenary of Nicolai Gogol's death in Moscow. He also traveled to Vienna and to Italy, both for official purposes and for medical reasons.

Zweig's public offices, especially in the early years of his return, did not leave him much time for writing. For his German audience his fame largely rested on *Der Streit um den Sergeanten Grischa* and *Erziehung vor Verdun,* and they expected lectures, speeches, addresses, and prefaces evaluating literary works. *Der Streit um den Sergeanten Grischa* had attained symbolic qualities that also became attached to Zweig: he was the German who returned from exile. He was also remembered as the friend of Hanns Eissler, Johannes Becher, and Bertolt Brecht, and as the person to whom Kurt Tucholsky wrote his last letter before his suicide in 1935.

Zweig had started work on a memoir of his relationship with Freud, "Freundschaft mit Freud" (Friendship with Freud), in 1944, but although he continued to work on this book it was never completed. A few excerpts from the manuscript were included in Georg Wenzel's *Arnold Zweig 1887-1968* in 1978. Zweig also began to revise his previously published fiction and considered film versions of his work.

Zweig had decided to expand his cycle of World War I novels to include at least seven books, to be called collectively "Der große Krieg der weißen Männer" (The Great War of the White Man). The novels he published over the following years are mostly reworkings of older material. *Die Feuerpause* (Ceasefire, 1954) recounts the events in *Erziehung vor Verdun* as narrated by Werner Bertin himself. In a 1951 letter to

Postcard from Zweig, in Haifa, to Lion Feuchtwanger, 1938 (Marta Feuchtwanger, Pacific Palisades, California)

Feuchtwanger, Zweig stressed the didactic intentions of his project: "Zur Schulung der jungen Schriftsteller, um den Unterschied zwischen subjektiver und objektiver Epik an ein und demselben Material nachzuweisen, kann es kaum eine bessere Gelegenheit geben" (There cannot exist a better opportunity to teach young writers the differences between subjective and objective narrative on the same material). Laurenz Pont, the architect from *Pont und Anna,* also reappears in *Die Feuerpause.*

Zweig planned to complete his cycle with two volumes dealing with the prewar period and the early war years–"Aufmarsch der Jugend" (The Youth Marches Up) and "Wahrheit und Lüge" (Truth and Lie)–and a third volume, "In eine bessere Zeit" (Toward a Better Time), that would sketch the events between 1919 and 1945; this volume remained unwritten. "Aufmarsch der

Zweig and Sigmund Freud, with whom Zweig corresponded from 1927 until Freud's death in 1939

Zweig's car after the 1938 accident in Haifa in which he suffered a concussion

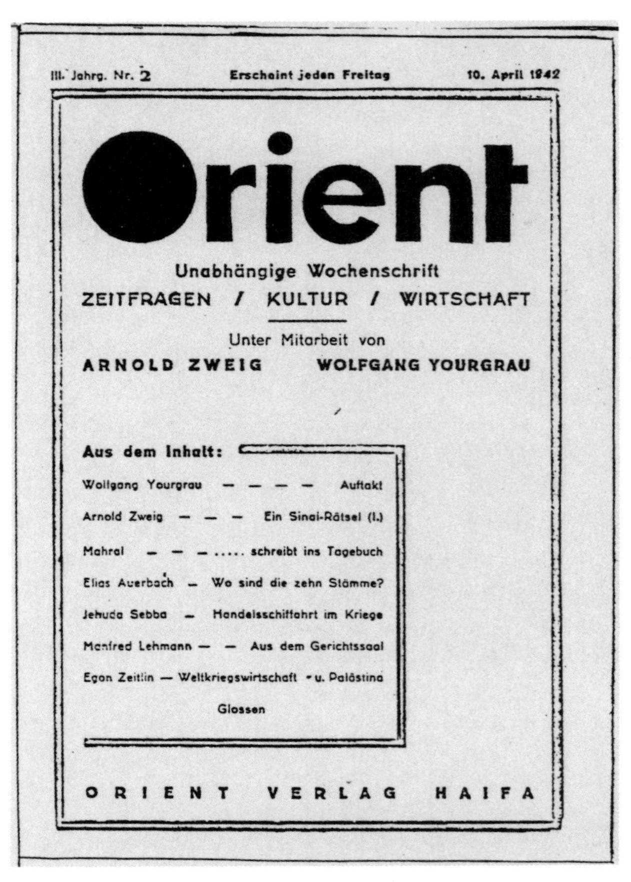
III. Jahrg. Nr. 2 Erscheint jeden Freitag 10. April 1942

Orient

Unabhängige Wochenschrift
ZEITFRAGEN / KULTUR / WIRTSCHAFT

Unter Mitarbeit von
ARNOLD ZWEIG WOLFGANG YOURGRAU

Aus dem Inhalt:

ORIENT VERLAG HAIFA

Cover of the journal Zweig coedited with Wolfgang Yourgrau in Haifa

Zweig circa 1943

Zweig on the day after his sixtieth birthday

Zweig delivering an address at the Paris World Peace Congress, 1949

Zweig with the Marxist composer Hanns Eisler and Eisler's wife Louise, summer 1951

Zweig with figurines from his ivory collection, 1957

Zweig receiving the Lenin Peace Prize in Moscow in 1958

Jugend" and "Wahrheit und Lüge" became one book, *Die Zeit ist reif* (1957; translated as *The Time Is Ripe,* 1962), set during the years before World War I. The novel's omniscient narrator describes the relationship of Lenore Wahl and Werner Bertin, intellectuals who have not reached the political awareness that would lead them to react against the system. Lenore's grandfather, who looked favorably upon Bertin as an admired writer in *Junge Frau von 1914,* now appears as a person conscious of the peasant roots of his family and sympathetic with the cause of the Russian people. Bertin's discussions with workers demonstrate that he still has much to learn, but also that he is on the way to an understanding of social and political forces. As in the other novels of the cycle, Zweig draws upon his own experiences, and Bertin's early literary achievements seem to refer to Zweig's own works. Thus, Zweig self-critically depicts his former self as an example of a bourgeois writer who lived for the arts and undefined humanistic ideals while remaining blind to political realities.

In *Die Feuerpause,* Zweig was unable to turn a narrative experiment into a successful novel; *Die Zeit ist reif* is likewise a failure. Workers often speak with unconvincing foresight and sophistication in long commentaries on political events that reflect on causes and consequences. The style of some passages–for example, the description of Bertin and Lenore's trip to Italy–is reminiscent of Zweig's earliest work. At times the book reads like a travel guide to a world of sun and youth.

An outline exists for "Das Eis bricht" (The Ice Breaks), but the novel remained incomplete; one chapter was published as *Ein starker Esser* (A Heavy Eater, 1947). *Ein starker Esser* narrates the occurrences of the year 1918, from the peace treaty of Brest Litovsk in March, to the November revolution in Russia, to the constitution of the Weimar Republic.

In all of his novels Zweig introduces narrators who can comment from a distance and refer to past and future events, including those unknown to the protagonists. At the center of each novel is a "case" that brings together public and private concerns, legal and moral issues.

Zweig's protagonists are middle-class intellectuals; he never wrote what one might call a proletarian novel. Georg Lukács, in his discussion of Zweig's four earliest war novels, compared Zweig's use of workers as characters to Büchner's use of the mob in the drama *Dantons Tod* (Danton's Death, 1835): as a mere backdrop to the action. In Zweig's later novels, this "background" has become more prominent without being completely integrated into the novel, and his characters have lost some of their complexity. Eberhard Hilscher has attributed the lively style of Zweig's novels to the fact that they were dictated, and therefore reflect everyday style. In his later novels, however, the disadvantages of this method are more apparent; the style seems to change abruptly from formal to casual, and many passages seem closer to essays than to dialogue.

For the subject of his last completed novel, *Traum ist teuer* (The Price of Dreaming, 1962), Zweig turned again to Palestine. The novel is a final statement of the extent to which Zweig subscribed to psychoanalysis. His narrator/protagonist Richard Karthaus is a psychiatrist who temporarily leaves his wife, Helen, and his children to immigrate to Palestine, where he joins his secretary and lover, Jeanne. Jeanne seems to be inspired by Zweig's former secretary, Lily Offenstadt, who had immigrated to Haifa with her husband and who had saved a few of Zweig's early manuscripts. In Palestine, Karthaus joins the English army and is involved in an adventurous plot revolving around one of his patients, a Greek soldier named Kephalides. The moral of this novel is summed up by Karthaus: "Ich habe es von A bis Z mit durchlebt, es hat auch mich an den Rand des Verzweifelns und wieder zurück gerissen, mich belehrt. Traum könne sehr teuer kommen–der politische einer mittleren Linie wie der private eines Ausgleichs, Ehegefühls zwischen Frau und Freundin" (I have lived through all of this from A to Z, it has brought me toward the verge of despair and back, and has taught me about the price of dreaming–of that of the political dream of a middle way, as well as of that of a private one of a balance, a feeling of being married to wife and lover). But Zweig fails in his attempt to subsume Karthaus's personal wishes in a political statement.

Zweig received the National Prize first class in 1950, an honorary doctorate from the University of Leipzig in 1952, the International Lenin Peace Medal in 1958, and the National Medal of Merit in gold in 1962. He was president of the East German P.E.N. Center from 1957 to 1968. In the German Democratic Republic he was an official writer who served as a didactic exemplum.

While Zweig supported East German and Soviet politics in essays and official statements, his lifelong interest in Freud was looked at askance by party liners. East German critic Eberhard Hilscher describes Zweig's belief in psychoanalysis rather patronizingly, as if it were a harmless whimsy. Although Zweig was celebrated in East Germany, *Das Beil von Wandsbek* was not widely distributed, and a film version of the book was withdrawn after completion in 1951 because, according to Zweig, the author showed too much sympathy with his hero. Zweig had problems staging his plays, and although he accepted the excuse that there were no appropriate actors, he was also concerned that a Festschrift such as the 1952 issue of *Sinn und Form* would become a "Pflästerchen . . . um eine Wunde zu verkleben" (patch . . . to cover a wound). Zweig once called himself an "Überrest" (leftover) from a previous generation. *Die Zeit ist reif* is the only one of his later novels to receive critical acclaim in East Germany, and even it was regarded as flawed. East German publications of his fiction, as well as the sixteen-volume edition of his works published by the East Berlin Aufbau-Verlag in the late 1950s and early 1960s, were intended for the general reader rather than for the scholar. Not all of his books were included in this edition, and some of his manuscripts remain unpublished.

While Zweig could count on an audience and support in the East, the West has viewed him with indifference. For many years after the war West German publishers seemed hesitant to distribute the works of an author published in the East, and only quite recently has there been a stronger interest in Zweig. While his work has received much critical attention in the German Democratic Republic, in West Germany he has remained a subject for foreign scholars. For example, two dissertations on Zweig's work that were published in West Germany in 1977 and 1980 were by English scholars, Geoffrey V. Davis and David R. Midgley.

Zweig's importance in West Germany in the 1960s can perhaps best be seen in the "Springer affair." Early in September 1967, shortly after the Arab-Israeli war, newspapers owned by the

Beatrice and Arnold Zweig at Bad Liebenstein, September 1962

Zweig dictating to his secretary, Ilse Lange, in 1967

Zweig in 1967 (Ullstein)

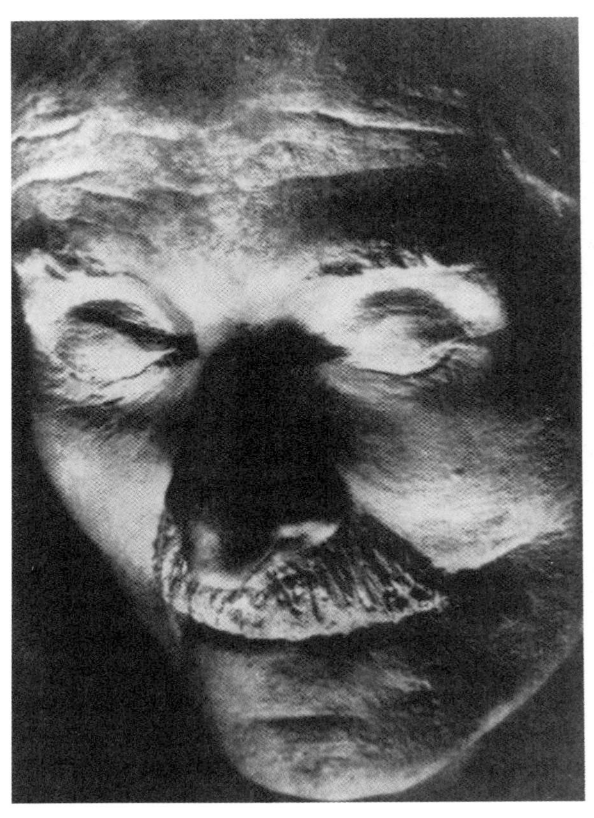

Zweig's death mask, by Gerhard Thieme

Arnold and Beatrice Zweig's grave at the Dorotheenstadt Cemetery, East Berlin

Springer concern printed a story they had received from the West Berlin news agency Tarantel Press. According to the story, Zweig had informed friends in Israel that he was dissatisfied with living in East Germany and regretted having left Haifa. Zweig responded sharply in a letter published on 10 September in the official East German newspaper *Neues Deutschland*: "Noch niemals, selbst nicht im braunen Reich des Herrn Goebbels, sind derartig faustdicke Lügen über mich verbreitet worden. . . . Seit Jahren habe ich erklärt, da ich mich nirgendwo so heimisch fühle wie in unserer Deutschen Demokratischen Republik. Die Schwindler bestätigen mir wieder einmal die Richtigkeit meiner Entscheidung" (Never, not even in the brown Reich of Mr. Goebbels, have such tremendous lies been spread about me. . . . For years I have declared that nowhere else do I feel so much at home as in our German Democratic Republic. These swindlers have once again confirmed me in the soundness of my decision). Günter Grass criticized the Springer press on a West German television news show and was threatened with a libel suit. In the same year Grass published an account of the case as a West German scandal.

Zweig wrote to Feuchtwanger in 1958: "In den zehn Jahren, welche ich bisher in der DDR verbrachte, habe ich durchaus gelernt, mich den Realitäten nicht zu widersetzen, aber auch nicht nachzugeben, dort wo ich recht zu haben glaube wie etwa im Falle Freud. Man kann nicht zaubern und bekommt ein Staatswesen nicht geschenkt, in welchem die politischen Grundtatsachen besser als je in Deutschland gestaltet werden. Muß ich dafür in Kauf nehmen, was ich in Palästina niemals getan hätte, so weiß ich, daß ich in Palästina ohne die Hilfe von Freunden ziemlich kläglich eingegangen wäre" (In the ten years that I have spent in the GDR up to now, I have learned well not to resist given facts, but also not to give in when I believe that I am right, as in the case of Freud. One cannot do miracles, and one does not receive a republic as a gift, in which the fundamental political facts are created better than ever in Germany. If I have to experience things that I would never have accepted in Palestine, I also know, that I would have perished there quite miserably without the help from friends). Nine years later the West German press forced Zweig to one of his last, and certainly most vehement, declarations of support for the German Democratic Republic. He was, with pride, a writer of this new republic. Zweig died in Berlin on 26 November 1968.

Letters:

Sigmund Freud–Arnold Zweig: Briefwechsel, edited by Ernst L. Freud (Frankfurt am Main: Fischer, 1968); translated by Elaine and William Robson-Scott as *The Letters of Sigmund Freud and Arnold Zweig* (New York: Harcourt Brace Jovanovich, 1970);

Der Briefwechsel zwischen Louis Fürnberg und Arnold Zweig: Dokumente einer Freundschaft, edited by Gerhard Wolf and Rosemarie Poschmann (Berlin: Aufbau, 1978);

"Alfred Döblin–Arnold Zweig: Briefwechsel," *Neue deutsche Literatur,* 26, no. 7 (1978): 134-143;

Lion Feuchtwanger–Arnold Zweig: Briefwechsel 1933-1958, 2 volumes, edited by Harold von Hofe (Berlin: Aufbau, 1984).

Bibliographies:

Zinaida V. Zitomirskaja, *Arnold Zweig* (Moscow: National Book Bureau, 1961);

Ilse Lange, ed., *Findbuch des literarischen Nachlasses von Arnold Zweig (1887-1968)* (Berlin: Akademie der Künste der DDR, 1983).

Biographies:

Eberhard Hilscher, *Arnold Zweig: Brückenbauer vom Gestern ins Morgen* (Halle & Saale: Sprache und Literatur, 1962); revised as *Arnold Zweig: Leben und Werk* (Berlin: Volk und Wissen, 1967; revised again, 1978);

George Wenzel, ed., *Arnold Zweig 1887-1968: Werk und Leben in Dokumenten und Bildern: Mit unveröffentlichten Manuskripten und Briefen aus dem Nachlaß* (Berlin: Aufbau, 1978);

Manuel Wiznitzer, *Arnold Zweig: Das Leben eines deutsch-jüdischen Schriftstellers* (Frankfurt am Main: Athenäum, 1983).

References:

Arnold Zweig: Ein Almanach. Zum 75. Geburtstag (Berlin: Aufbau, 1962);

Arnold Zweig zum siebzigsten Geburtstag: Eine Festschrift (Berlin: Aufbau, 1957);

Geoffrey V. Davis, *Arnold Zweig in der DDR: Entstehung und Bearbeitung der Romane "Die Feuerpause," "Das Eis bricht" und "Traum ist teuer"* (Bonn: Bouvier-Herbert Grundmann, 1977);

Günter Grass, *Der Fall Axel C. Springer am Beispiel*

Arnold Zweig: Eine Rede, ihr Anlaß und die Folgen (Berlin: Voltaire, 1967);

Jürgen Happ, *Arnold Zweig, "Der Streit um den Sergeanten Grischa": Probleme des Aufbaus mit besonderer Berücksichtigung der Entwicklung der Grischagestalt* (Stockholm: Almquist & Wiksell, 1974);

Heinz Kamnitzer, *Erkenntnis und Bekenntnis: Arnold Zweig 70 Jahre* (Berlin: Aufbau, 1958);

Eva Kaufmann, *Arnold Zweigs Weg zum Roman: Vorgeschichte und Analyse des Grischaromans* (Berlin: Rütten & Loening, 1967);

Georg Lukács, "Arnold Zweigs Romanzyklus über den imperialistischen Krieg 1914 bis 1918," in his *Schicksalswende: Beiträge zu einer neuen deutschen Ideologie* (Berlin: Aufbau, 1948), pp. 273-313;

David R. Midgley, *Arnold Zweig: Zu Werk und Wandlung 1927-1948* (Frankfurt am Main: Athenäum, 1980);

Fritz J. Raddatz, "Zwischen Freud und Marx: Arnold Zweig," in his *Traditionen und Tendenzen: Materialien zur Literatur der DDR* (Frankfurt am Main: Suhrkamp, 1972), pp. 279-300;

Marcel Reich-Ranicki, "Der preußische Jude Arnold Zweig," in his *Deutsche Literatur in West und Ost: Prosa seit 1945* (München: Piper, 1963), pp. 305-342;

Johanna Rudolph (Marianne Gundermann), *Der Humanist Arnold Zweig* (Berlin: Henschelverlag, 1955);

Rudolph, ed., *Arnold Zweig* (Berlin: Deutscher Kulturbund, 1962);

George Salamon, *Arnold Zweig* (Boston: Twayne, 1975);

Sinn und Form, special Zweig issue (1952);

Annie Voigtländer, *Welt und Wirkung eines Romans: Zu Arnold Zweigs "Streit um den Sergeanten Grischa"* (Berlin: Aufbau, 1967).

Papers:

Arnold Zweig's papers are in the Arnold Zweig Archiv at the Akademie der Künste of the German Democratic Republic, East Berlin.

Appendix
Historical and Cultural Premises of German Fiction

Introduction

Modern German literature poses special problems for the American reader. There is the obvious barrier of language: while many of the most significant works of the period have been translated into English, even the most accomplished translations cannot do justice to the nuances of the original works; and most of the secondary literature is inaccessible to those who cannot read German. But quite aside from the linguistic hurdles that stand between the original and the reader, there are great cultural and historical barriers to understanding. It is, for example, impossible to understand the writings of Thomas Mann without some comprehension of the works of Friedrich Nietzsche, of Richard Wagner's opera and operatic theory, of Arthur Schopenhauer's philosophy, and of German political and social history of the nineteenth and twentieth centuries–just to mention the most obvious influences. And the case of Thomas Mann is not atypical. An understanding of Nietzsche is likewise useful when one takes up the novels of Hermann Hesse, but more than a casual acquaintance with Oriental religions will also be necessary for the reader who wishes to plumb the depths of such works as *Siddhartha, Der Steppenwolf,* or *Narziß und Goldmund.* The world of German fiction is for the most part a somewhat forbidding one, for it has been a tradition in German letters, since at least the time of the publication of the baroque novels of Christian Weise and Daniel Caspar von Lohenstein in the seventeenth century, that literature of the first rank (*Dichtung*) must edify and educate. German literature is didactic, engaged, and philosophical to a degree unknown in the Anglo-Saxon literary tradition. These features will be especially noticed not just in the writings of Mann and Hesse, but also in those of Heinrich Mann, Hermann Stehr, Kurt Eisner, Jakob Wassermann, Albrecht Schaeffer, Robert Walser, and even Lou Andreas-Salomé.

For these reasons publisher and editor felt it necessary to provide several supplemental texts that illuminate historical and cultural premises of central European literature. The essays included here serve either to introduce the reader to significant extraliterary influences, such as the music of Wagner and the "philosophy" of Nietzsche, or to provide a broader framework for an understanding of the entries on individual writers. Additionally, it was the editor's goal to include essays that interpret key works from more than one standpoint, and to choose–where possible–excerpts or articles such as Michael Hamburger's "Premisses" that have themselves become classics of a kind.

–James Hardin

Writers and Politics: 1871-1918

Ronald Gray

In 1871, four years before the births of Thomas Mann and Rilke, three years before that of Hofmannsthal and three years after that of Stefan George, the political unity of the German people was achieved; after twenty years of manœuvring the King of Prussia was crowned by Bismarck Emperor of Germany. This was the culmination of a movement that had begun at least a century before, and which fulfilled even older aspirations. For six hundred years the area in which German was the chief language had consisted of independent states, more than four hundred at times, owing at most a nominal allegiance to Holy Roman Emperors who did not always rule over even their personal domains. Before that, it had never been more than part of a larger whole whose very structure weakened its coherence. Yet it had always been ruled by kings of German origin, and the memory of it as a great German political power was still alive. Bismarck's manœuvres, cutting out the non-German elements which Austria-Hungary might have brought in, now gave hopes of realizing a unity not Holy or Roman, but an Empire. As if in confirmation of the new strength accruing from the achievement, the economy developed by leaps and bounds. The industrial revolution, long under way in Britain, had hung fire in Germany until this moment: now, with the railway net already complete, the new factories and mines enjoyed unparalleled facilities. The population grew from 41 millions in 1871 to 65 millions in 1913, industry and foreign trade boomed, for almost the first time German colonies were established abroad, while at home the first "welfare state" provided workers' insurance, subsidies for opera and drama, compulsory further education. Such rapid and widespread developments, affecting every class, had not been experienced in the whole course of German history.

The success was not only in the political and economic sphere but also in that of the arts. It is true that for some twenty years no new names of international reputation appeared. In opera, however, there was one great work to crown almost immediately the political victory. The production at Bayreuth in 1876 of Wagner's tetralogy *Der Ring des Nibelungen* has properly been called the first national achievement of the united German nation; Bayreuth showed signs of becoming the shrine of German culture, a place of pilgrimage symbolizing the great rebirth. "Im Vertrauen auf den deutschen Geist entworfen" were the first words in Wagner's dedication of *The Ring* to Ludwig II of Bavaria: "Composed out of confidence in the German Spirit." Yet it is also significant that the concluding music of *Götterdämmerung*, the end of the tetralogy, was intended to express a mood of deliverance from all rebirth. The gods perish, Brünnhilde rides exultantly into the flames of Siegfried's funeral pyre, to enter the "wunsch- and wahnlos / Heiligstes Wahlland."[1] She is "redeemed from rebirth,"[2] her desires and illusions forsaken, and yet she is now in a "realm of choice": it is she who will choose her destiny henceforward, in harmony with the pure gold of the ring which has now returned to its true home in the depths of the Rhine. Whereas the gold had been formerly used in the selfish interests of both Wotan and Alberich, it gleams now in an eternal present, perfect in its sheer existence, subject to no man's claims on it. In this symbolism there is a good deal to be learned about the spirit of the new Germany. How far it was consciously understood nobody can say. Certainly the ideal of identification with an undivided, unappropriated Being in a synthesis beyond all individuation, was to be prominent in German literature as well as in politics from this time on, as was also the belief in total annihilation as a path to this end. Wagner's work had a prophetic quality.

The new literature, however, distinct in mood, presuppositions and preoccupations from that of the mid-century, did not emerge until the generation which had grown up within the Wilhelmine Empire reached maturity. When it came, in the 1890's, it bore witness to the perplexity in which the younger men now found themselves. From now onwards, for the next fifty years and more, German literature was to be concerned above all with the overcoming of the blackest pessimism. The Naturalist authors,

Hauptmann, Sudermann, Arno Holz and Johannes Schlaf, portrayed the misery of life in the industrial regions and cities now developing; the neo-Romantics, Rilke, George, and Hofmannsthal, turning their backs on this,[3] looked for the spiritual comforts of total isolation. In the 1900's the forebodings of catastrophe, heralded by the armaments race and the crises of Algeciras and Agadir, are reflected more and more: they can be felt in Rilke's poem "Spätherbst in Venedig," in George's cycle of prophetic poems *Der Stern des Bundes,* as also in Mann's *Der Tod in Venedig,* where the passages dealing with the outbreak of cholera often read like an account of an even greater evil. Indeed, when the war came, it was greeted by all three of these writers as an end to the pretense of civilization with which they had been living for the past thirty or forty years.

There had been a certain falsity, a certain self-conscious and self-doubting assertiveness, about the Wilhelmine Empire from its beginning, to judge by the novels of its severe though still tolerant critic, Theodor Fontane. One thinks of the husband of Effi Briest, in the novel of that name, who insists on the rigid observance of a duel to the death in defence of his wife's honour, but who in his heart no longer believes in the traditional code, so that his adherence to it is both coolly formal and ruthlessly exacting; or one thinks of the comical family pride of the industrialist in *Frau Jenny Treibel:* "Wir sind die Treibels: Blutlaugensalz und Eisenvitriol!" But the most stringent criticisms were those of Nietzsche, whose first *Unzeitgemäße Betrachtungen* appeared in 1873. Nietzsche castigated the illusion that by means of the recent victory over France there had come about a victory for German culture. It was rather, he affirmed, a victory for military discipline, courage, leadership, and obedience, qualities valuable in themselves which had, however, merely established the "culture-philistine," a smug product of pedantic schoolmastering who was completely without true German-ness and creative power.

There was also opposition from a different quarter. For while the parliamentary voting system heavily favoured the propertied classes, and while the Reichstag itself was constitutionally powerless to overthrow any government, the Social Democrat (Marxist) vote increased in forty years from 124,000 to over 4,000,000 in 1912, and the Catholic "Zentrum," conservative in tendency but jealous of its confessional interests, polled in the same year nearly 2,000,000 out of 12,000,000 votes cast. The potential opposition was thus, by that time, about half of the active vote. The literary record leaves little trace of this, for with very few exceptions men of letters paid no regard to the political and religious doctrines which, given the opportunity, could have radically changed German society. The study of the literature and philosophy in these years thus gives a one-sided emphasis to neutrality or acceptance. All the same, the results are revealing, if only of the fundamental beliefs shared by those in power and some at least of their most influential critics. Doctrines apart, no literature was ever more concerned with national, political and religious themes than this one, not even the literature of the ancient Hebrews.

At first sight, there appears to be little in common between those who opposed the new Empire. Nietzsche had no interest in the schemes for social welfare introduced by Bismarck, and would have attacked the portrayal of industrial life given by Naturalist authors as an intolerable yielding to the sense of pity. His ideal of Germanness, the criterion by which he found the new culture wanting, was aristocratic and pagan, anti-democratic and anti-Christian; its contrasts were not "good" and "evil" but "noble" and "mean." He had no criticism to offer of the way in which Bismarck had brought the Empire into being or of the way in which it was maintained; he was not concerned with the "Kulturkampf" between Catholics and Government, or with the colonial question. As his ideas developed after *Unzeitgemäße Betrachtungen* they dealt rather with the individual, and with society only in so far as it restricted or promoted the individual's growth towards the supreme form, the Superman. For Nietzsche, traditional morality was merely the means by which the weak and powerless sought to hamper the natural energy of the strong, it was the expression of a slave-mentality. His mood was optimistic, "saying yea" to all manifestations of life, whether cruel or kindly, savage or civilized; it was pessimistic, in so far as it perceived the present "all-too-human" nature of mankind; ultimately it was beyond either pessimism or optimism, seeking to transcend humanity in living a life of sheer instantaneous, unreflective action.

At the heart of Nietzsche's thought is a desire to live what would otherwise have been called, in Christian terms, the life of the lilies of the field, although he would have added to this the life of the beasts of the jungle. The fascination of his work lies in the flashes of insight it provides into the possibilities of such existence. In fact it sometimes appears that his real intention is to transform human nature once and for all by an almost Christlike insistence both on its hypocritical evil and on a generous toleration, in attendance on the promptings of the spirit. In this connection, one may quote the passage in which he speaks of wars as a curative means ("eine Brutalitäts-Cur") for decadent nations only, whereas more healthy nations have no need of them.[4] Here his meaning might seem to be that war, like the unjust anger of one's neighbour, is an evil to be understood and endured, if not actually forgiven, as an essential as well as an inevitable consequence of men being what they are. On the other hand, another passage from the same work gives an entirely different colour to the thought. Here Nietzsche declares that such a highly civilized and therefore decadent humanity as that of contemporary Europe needs not only wars, but the greatest and most terrible wars, if it is to restore itself to eminence and health; it needs "that deep impersonal hatred, that cold-blooded murderousness coupled with a good conscience, that communal, organizing zest in the destruction of the enemy,"[5] without which it must cease to exist. From sayings like these it becomes clear that whatever Nietzsche's ultimate aim may have been–and he does speak of it elsewhere, however ambiguously, as the innocence of a child–so far as the immediate practical task was concerned, he incited to war. Germany, in his eyes, was decadent: the way to health led through a deliberate cultivation of cold-blooded murderousness. By some process of homeopathy, perhaps, the decadence would be overcome.

Nietzsche's criticism of the Empire thus became an attack on hypocritical attachment to outdated, Christian standards, which were for him the very source of hypocrisy. At the same time, his conception of health was so much a matter of accepting human nature in its totality that his main object became self-awareness–or, more accurately, self-oblivion after self-awareness had been achieved. Thus his observations on human nature, penetrating as they often are, are made in order to affirm that nature in the long run, indeed to accept it with joyful abandonment, to achieve a kind of synthesis of affirmation and negation. His doctrine of the Eternal Recurrence, in which he offered a kind of test whereby the quality of affirmation might be judged, reveals this paradox. It asks the question whether, confronted with the prospect of living the same life over again an infinite number of times to all eternity, men would be ready to do so not resignedly, in the consciousness of the inadequacies it contained, but with delight in every moment of it. The genuinely affirmative answer is given only by the Superman, and what distinguishes him from the Christian or Jewish saint who might also answer affirmatively is that for the saint there must always remain some duality; the saint will delight in the work of a loving and good Creator, and thus not escape grief at the world's defection, whereas for the Superman God is dead, and there remains only the dynamic creativity of living beings. Or, to put the point in another way, it may seem to the saint as much as to the Superman that God does not exist–the Psalms are full of laments which almost amount to such a realization–but while the one continues to praise the divine love and justice, the other concludes that they are never to be thought of again.

To give a proper account of Nietzsche's thought, which is thus constantly running so close to Judaeo-Christian ideas as to require the most scrupulous distinctions, is impossible within a few pages. He was, as he felt, driven to his conclusions not by any mere Machiavellianism, not by arguments of expediency, but by the deepest of religious concerns, and by the desire to have life more abundantly. He demanded courage, endurance, self-sacrifice, as well as barbarism, cruelty and parasitic self-preservation, and the core of his teaching is really as ineffable as the force that moves lions and butterflies, if there is one. However, certain conclusions can fairly be drawn even without full definition. In the light of the doctrine of the Eternal Recurrence, the criticisms of Bismarck's Reich, made in Nietzsche's earlier days, would have to end in an affirmation of the very conditions he had criticized. It would always remain, it is true, an affirmation tempered with knowledge, a "knowing" optimism rather than the blind and smug one he had attacked. But his aim was an unhypocritical assertion of the life of the pirate and the *condottiere,* by those who had it in them to live such a life, and an unenvying submission to such men on the part of those unwilling to use their Will to Power. That this aim was qualified at times by other considerations is largely irrelevant to the practical effects his teaching was bound to have. Certainly, there is nothing in his teaching which seriously detracts from such an aim. And thus, for the majority of his sympathetic readers, rightly or wrongly, the conclusion most readily to be drawn was one which would promote the militarism and expansionism of the German state as it already existed. It was merely necessary to clear the mind of cant, the kind of cant which Wilhelm II displayed when he imagined himself at the time of the Chinese campaigns as a Crusader against Asiatic paganism. For the Emperor to have attacked China in the full knowledge of his Will to Power would, in Nietzschean terms, have been no sin.

It is a strange paradox that Nietzsche's doctrines, so interpreted (and I am concerned here solely with their propensity for practical interpretation), look like a rationale for the actual conduct of the state in which he lived, the conduct of Bismarck rather than of Wilhelm II. Bismarck was highly aware, more so than any other statesman of his time, of the complexities of human nature; he had a more clear-sighted view both of his own purposes and of the situations by which they might be fulfilled. While his whole aim was to promote the strength of Prussia, he had no illusions about the qualities of the Prussians, so that his unsentimental patriotism seems at times wholly pointless. For liberals and socialists he had a shrewd contempt, together with a surprising ability to detect serviceable qualities in an adversary. His attitude towards the Polish insurrections in 1861 seems to have all that Nietzsche could have required in the way of awareness and ruthlessness. "Strike the Poles," he wrote in a private letter, "in such a way that they will despair of their lives; I have every sympathy with their situation, but if we want to exist we cannot do anything else but *exterminate* them. The wolf, too, is not responsible for being what God has made it, but we kill it nevertheless, if we can."[6] It is difficult to see on what grounds Nietzsche might have faulted such frankness. The situation is clearly seen, the rights of the enemy acknowledged; there is no spurious appeal to justice, and the religious reference has just the same implications as Nietzsche's atheism had: the claims of self-assertion are overriding. Since it was on the basis of such an attitude that the Empire had been founded, Nietzsche's objections must often imply that Germany's real weakness was the lack of more Bismarcks. Nietzsche was ambiguous, it is true, and could speak of the Superman at times as of some ideal far beyond the reach of contemporary humanity; in so far as this was, on the other hand, an ideal to be inculcated in the present, it could only promote the Bismarckian spirit.

Moreover, Nietzsche's writings came to be widely known–from the 1890's onwards–at a time when historians and politicians were beginning to become more and more strongly aware of Germany's dynamic power and of her claim to a place among the Great Powers. Men of great influence held the view that world history, by virtue of some trend immanent in it, was lifting Germany to dominance as though on the topmost shoot of a newly flourishing tree.[7] Nietzsche's "Will to Power" could be readily interpreted as yet another aspect of this immanent driving force, and his teaching on the subject was easily understood (or misunderstood?–one can never be quite sure) to mean that frank acceptance rather than hypocritical virtue was the one thing needful.

Nietzsche's influence was dominant on almost all the major writers of the ensuing decades, up to and beyond the 1930's, although it naturally altered in emphasis with each individual. Closest to him in spirit was Stefan George, whose poetry, beginning with evocations of pagan splendour, ended in 1926 with prophecies of a new Empire led by a core of dedicated Supermen. In the period before 1914 George was above all concerned, in his poetry, to combine the Dionysian qualities of the German with the Apolline calm and clarity of the Roman and Italian, a fusion which is deeply indebted to Nietzsche's thought. What he at length achieved, despite the great poetic sensitivity of many of his lyrics, was an obtrusive formalism together with an ecstatic call to battle which could easily be taken as an incitement to war on behalf of Wilhelm II's Empire.[8] Equally close to Nietzsche was the Swiss Carl Spitteler, whose lengthy epic poem *Olympischer Frühling*, refurbishing the Greek myths with Nietzschean meaning, appeared between 1900 and 1910. (Although Switzerland was politically independent, German-speaking Swiss were already beginning to feel the tug of their racial affinity with a nation whose recent achievements were so impressive.) Others more or less in the same tradition were Thomas Mann, Rilke and Hofmannsthal, of whom there will be more to say later.

Even the Naturalist authors were not so far removed from this kind of thought as might be imagined, for while European Naturalism was generally positivistic, the German form had features linking it rather with the main currents of mysticism or quasi-mysticism in the nineteenth century. Thus, while the theoretical ideal of the movement was a photographic realism, this had certain connotations not found elsewhere. Arno

Holz, the leading theoretician, attempted the most complete reproduction of Nature in the so-called "Sekundenstil," whereby actions were described as they happened, second by second, and even the most insignificant events such as the tapping of a tree-branch against a window, or the shrivelling of a fly in the wax surrounding a candle-wick, were given as much prominence as events essential to the narrative. The relevance of such incidents was immaterial: they happened at the same time, and were therefore included. In addition, all Naturalist authors reproduced exactly local dialects and tricks of speech; they gave precise instructions for the furnishings of indoor scenes in stage plays, and tended to write plots which had no clear beginning or end, but "ran off into the sand" with the inconsequentiality and lack of pattern of life itself as they saw it. The theory–so far as that goes, for it was not rigidly observed by all authors–was summed up by Holz in a phrase which has had some currency, despite its apparent absurdity. "Art," he wrote, "has a tendency to become Nature again. It does so in proportion to the means at its disposal, and the way they are used."[9] The point to be observed here is not the broad generalization, which cannot apply to such forms of art as music, architecture, or ceramics, and only in a limited sense to painting or literature, but rather the notion that Art tends to become Nature *again.* There is no doubt that Holz thought of the best art as actually being Nature, much as Schiller thought that the best artists "were" Nature, while inferior art was for him restricted by its media, and by the lack of skill of the artist, from achieving such an identification. The ideal was thus not so much a reproduction of Nature as the creation of a work so identical with Nature (whatever that might be) that it stood as a natural object in its own right. In addition, however–if we take Holz literally–this was evidently in some way a return to Nature: at some time, presumably, Art and Nature had been one, and the present tendency of Art was to revert to this unity. It is plain enough, from the assumptions it makes, that this way of thinking has the same kind of pattern as that of the general tradition already outlined. An initial unity is broken up by some process of individuation, there is an ensuing period of dividedness, and an ultimate return to the first state. Holz's theory, for all its pretensions to scientific exactness, owes its form to what we may call, in the widest sense, a neo-Platonist tradition. It implies, as much as ever Mann or Rilke's work did, an acceptance of the given situation, and differs from them only in its freedom from speculation or doubt.

Indeed, while Naturalists in other countries were often reformists imbued with a deep sense of the need to put right injustices–Zola's defence of Dreyfus is a case in point–there is no such sense in the German school. It is true that M. G. Conrad demanded, in his manifesto published in *Die Gesellschaft,* that writers should seek out and expose the ills of society with ruthless frankness. Yet Conrad's novels, imitative of Zola's, have the reputation now of being written very much in the spirit of the contemporary "Prachtkerl." On the other hand, there was an appeal to Bismarck for a state subsidy to writers which seems scarcely compatible with freedom to criticize, and a suggestion that Naturalist authors should not concern themselves with the sick and decadent, but with the promotion of the simple virtues of the average citizen.[10] Even Gerhart Hauptmann, the leading dramatist of the movement, might be thought to have sympathized with this attitude, at least in his earliest play. Whether *Vor Sonnenaufgang* is a *pièce à thèse* may be open to doubt. It is difficult to interpret as a tragedy since the hero is endowed with such high-minded callousness as to destroy all sympathy for him. Certainly, a young man who abandons a woman with whom he is deeply in love on the eugenic grounds that, were she to bear children, they might inherit the dipsomania of her relatives, and who leaves her so abruptly as to cause her to take her life, shows too little human feeling to be accounted a tragic protagonist. And if the play is not taken as tragedy, it must appear rather as advocating the course taken by the hero, unpalatable though it is, in the interests of that healthier society which usually seems to be his real concern: the circumstances of the play do then take place, as the title puts it, "before the dawn," the dawn of a disinfected world in which loving will present no problems. It is easier to believe that this was Hauptmann's intention–that he shared the hero's eugenic principles and therefore regarded his decision as a "tragic" necessity–than that he thought it possible to make a mean-spirited action into the crux of his play. The contemporary emphasis on "health," to the disregard of all forms of "sickness," lends weight to the former interpretation.

A much more mature work of Hauptmann's, though written only a few years later, is his play *Die Weber.* There is no possibility of interpreting this as a *pièce à thèse;* rather, the play impresses by the generosity displayed towards all the characters, industrialists and workers alike, and the sense it conveys of a relentless fate overcoming all efforts at amelioration of the weavers' poverty. Neither the employer nor the weavers themselves are responsible: he is hamstrung by foreign competition, they revolt because their conditions of work are beyond endurance; and yet the suppression of the revolt by the militia at the end of the play seems to be equally a part of the workings of Fate. *Die Weber* is, for all its vivid characterization, its powerful tempo, and its skilful presentation of a mass-movement, a quietistic work, helplessly recording a disaster from which no political escape is envisaged. In this perhaps it reflects its author's other preoccupations, for Hauptmann was already writing at this time in a symbolical vein and on supernatural themes. Within thirty years, Naturalism itself having remained powerful for a decade and a half, Hauptmann had shed most of his concern with social issues and had turned to the sexual mysticism of his short story, *Der Ketzer von Soana,* in which a priest abandons his Christian religion for a Dionysian vitalism.

Hauptmann in his youth had least in common, of all the major writers of his time, with Nietzschean doctrine; far less than the poet Richard Dehmel, whose welcome to "our human beast-divineness"[11] plainly echoes Nietzsche's ambiguities. In his trend towards eroticism, however, Hauptmann was moving with the times which were shortly to see the frenzies of Expressionist drama, and were already in the first decade of the twentieth century witnessing the naked portrayal of sexual appetites in the plays of Frank Wedekind.

The bridge between Naturalism and Expressionism is made in Reinhold Sorge's play *Der Bettler,* written in 1911. In this the acts alternate between Ibsenesque realism and stylized scenes in which spotlights stab fiercely on a darkened stage at choruses of airmen and prostitutes, chanting in staccato rhythms. Sorge's hero, an "autobiographical" one, feels intensely the desire to work for humanity at large, and thus far shares the social concern of the Naturalists, but envisages his ideal in terms of an inexpressible revelation which he is called on to announce, and so comes closer to the Expressionist school. The play is also the culmination of Sorge's efforts to come to terms with Nietzschean thought, bringing momentarily into blurred identity the two streams which had been in progress since the early 1890's.[12] From now on, it is more difficult than hitherto to make any clear distinctions of category. The more rationalistic spirit of Naturalism, scientific in its pretensions, gives way to dynamic ecstatic philosophies of intoxication; the "Heldenlosigkeit" of the Naturalist plays gives way to the presentation of orgiastic masses in which the individual disappears from view.

However, despite the increasing emphasis on zestful living and Dionysian self-identification, many writers of the Wilhelmine Empire felt a sense of shame in their profession. A flood of "Künstlerromane" was published around the turn of the century, novels in which the "artist," whether painter, musician, or poet, is presented as effete, sexually impotent, crippled with doubts of his own capacities, unproductive in contrast with a robust society that has no place for him. Although the roots of this genre go back at least as far as Goethe's *Torquato Tasso,* it has never formed so large a part of German literature as it did between 1890 and 1920. Thomas Mann's Tonio Kröger was not alone in thinking that no banker, or any other respectable member of society, could properly demean himself by indulging in creative literature. The inferiority of the artist to the man of action is one of the major themes of these years. It is the theme of Arno Holz's and Johannes Schlaf's sardonic picture, in *Papa Hamlet,* of a down-at-heels, out-of-work actor, written in a spirit of smug Philistinism, as it is also of the more generous though sentimental novel, *Das Gänsemännchen,* by Jakob Wassermann. Heinrich Mann's story *Pippo Spano* treats of the same subject, which recurs in scores of others, including the early works of Hermann Hesse, *Peter Camenzind* (1904), *Gertrud* (1910), and *Roßhalde* (1914). The artists in these works are relatively helpless, able only to accept with an ironical reserve, to withdraw into self-centred isolation, or to succumb to a crushing defeat at the hands of "Life." Thoroughgoing protest or confident satire does not exist except in such works as the witty, prolix tragedy of the Austrian Karl Kraus (written between 1915 and 1917), *Die letzten Tage der Menschheit,* the comedies of Carl Sternheim, and the novel by Heinrich Mann (Thomas Mann's brother), *Der Untertan,* censured on the outbreak of war for its attack both on the person of the Emperor and the society he led.

With the widespread sense of inferiority goes also a sense that the artist is a pretender to feelings he does not truly have, or an actor playing a part required of him by society rather than a man speaking in his own person. The most conscious manifestation of this sense is Thomas Mann's novel *Felix Krull,* begun in 1911, the autobiography of a character (an artist only in Mann's very broad usage) who adapts himself with astonishing ease to every situation, and who displays, with rare exceptions, just those feelings which people most expect of him. It appears also in painting, especially in the portrait by Lovis Corinth of himself as a Bacchanalian, a work painted in 1905 which is of some significance for the times. The heavily jowled face, crowned with ivy, seems about to express triumphant laughter, but the wide-open mouth is awry, the eyes have a pained look, and the whole expression is equally close to hysterical tears: the masquerade is frankly portrayed as a desperate pretence. In a not dissimilar way, the rather earlier paintings by the Swiss Arnold Böcklin, mostly taking myth or heroic legend for their subject-matter, are rendered with a derisive mockery. One thinks of his "Venus Anadyomene" in which a pallid society lady, undressed rather than naked, rises from the sea on the back of a squid-like monster with goggling headlamp eyes; or of his "Ruggiero liberating Angelica," where a black-mustachioed hero in armour puts a protecting arm round a flabby heroine clutching her fingers between her teeth, while the severed head of a dragon leers up at her as though ironically commiserating with her at her new peril. Böcklin seems as aware as Corinth of the impulse to make the grand gesture, and yet is unable to do so, in his artistic integrity, without at the same time deriding his own highly finished achievement. Like many of the men of letters, both these artists felt the need of some dynamic to replace the dreariness of mechanical routine in a newly industrialized society, and yet remained conscious of the spurious quality of self-conscious striving after such a goal. It is just such a consciousness as Felix Krull has in mind when he explicitly asks the reader to accept the operetta-hero he himself represents, and to forget the ageing actor behind the cosmetic mask. There are also, however, stories in which degradation is more nakedly and viciously portrayed. Gustav von Aschenbach's cosmetic rejuvenation in *Der Tod in Venedig,* his pretence at youthful vigour, is degrading; we are not explicitly asked to forget the mask in his case. Heinrich Mann's story, *Professor Unrat,* treats the theme of a respectable citizen's fall from grace in decidedly unambiguous fashion. Here the parallel to Aschenbach is a worthy elderly schoolmaster who becomes infatuated not with a beautiful boy but a cabaret artist ("die *Künstlerin* Rosa Fröhlich" as she is always called); his equivalent of Aschenbach's journey to Venice is the attempt to live in her sphere of Bohemian generosity and easy-going unconventionality; his degradation is the moment when, having debauched the whole town in which he lives, he is arrested for theft and deluged with filthy water. Where Thomas Mann is, however, always aware of a dual possibility, of condemnation and approval running hand in hand, Heinrich portrays his hero with a pitiless fury whose only purpose seems to be to wreak vengeance on some image of authority. *Professor Unrat* loses interest as a novel, not because it pretends black is white, but rather because it presents a world so completely black that none of its features can be distinguished.

By 1914 the dilemma of men of letters had become apparent. There was, on the one hand, the feeling of inadequacy expressed in Hofmannsthal's famous "Chandos" letter (entitled "Ein Brief "), in which he confessed his inability to use any of the traditional concepts of religion and metaphysics or to come to any settled conclusion about any topic whatsoever: a kind of paralysis or "ligature," to use the jargon of the eighteenth-century quietists, in which awareness of the ineffable made all attempt at expression seem indecent. Related to this was the dilemma of Aschenbach and Tonio Kröger, both of whom saw in the phrase "tout comprendre, c'est tout pardonner" an inducement to unbearable laxity, an antinomianism which they both desired and abhorred. The same difficulty confronts Arthur Schnitzler in his stories and plays, particularly in *Professor Bernhardi,* in which an attempt at decisive moral protest peters out in a series of justifications of all the parties involved. Frequently, as here and in Hauptmann's *Die Weber,* the indecisiveness is due to a scrupulous care in avoiding prejudiced condemnation. There is also, however, as in Thomas Mann, a tendency to conclude that since nothing is justified everything is justified, or, as in Nietzsche, that the concepts of good and evil are nullified and need to be replaced by new values of daring assertiveness. This too brings its dilemmas, for Rilke the dilemma of confronting death as a part of life, for Mann that of mocking his own creations. The attempt is therefore made to merge the contraries in one, to welcome contradictions as inherent in all intenser forms of living and thus to escape their inhibiting influence. Stefan George, living among a group of poets whose stress lay all on irrationalism, "Rausch," intoxication, opposed them with the demand for clarity, formal excellence, "Helle": his poetry was to be the fusion of both, and the boy-god Maximin whom he discovered and revered was said to display the living embodiment of these contraries. Rilke sought, in the "Dinggedichte," to combine a subjective perception with complete objectivity; he sought contact with others through a love which should also be intransitive, to live and write a replete isolation which should also, paradoxically, be all-embracing. Thomas Mann oscillates between Schopenhauer's denial and Nietzsche's affirmation of the Will, and yet stands outside both. Yet the dilemmas are not felt to be solved, nor is there, among the writers in the Nietzschean tradition, any intention of solving them: it is rather a matter of accepting the dilemma as an integral part of existence.

Occasionally, it is true, some reference is made to the traditional Christian standards, which despite the general decline in religious belief had by no means lost their grip on the population at large. Thomas Mann frequently ended his novels with some form of quasi-Christian statement; several of Rilke's poems, and a few of George's, at least treat of Christ, as does the novel by Gerhart Hauptmann, *Emanuel Quint*. On the whole, however, it was to some form of Buddhistic belief that writers felt an affinity. Schopenhauer had ended the main exposition of his philosophy with an explicit comparison with the Buddhists' Nirvana; Nietzsche had seen in Buddhism at least a more acceptable religion than Christianity. Rilke, while he wrote a poem in denigration of Christ, wrote another in praise of the Buddha; Hermann Hesse's post-war novel *Siddhartha* was an interpretation of Buddhist teaching, and Franz Werfel's dramatic trilogy *Spiegelmensch* had as its theme the Buddhist conception of selfhood. In the years before 1914 no writer or poet of note within the German Empire held any Christian convictions or was sympathetically inclined to any, and even in "Catholic Austria," where Kralik's "Society of the Grail" (Gralbund) represented a movement unknown in Germany, the only outstanding poet of Christian persuasion was the Protestant poet Georg Trakl. In Trakl's poetry the forebodings of war are expressed with sombre intensity. There is no ambiguity about his work, nor any form of irony; the dark landscapes of his poems, like his moods, are unassuaged by any philosophical reflections. His constructions are for the most part a seemingly fortuitous assemblage of unconnected passages, and when a peaceful mood emerges from them, as it does surprisingly often, it is the result of a particular mood which may be broken again as a new poem begins to form. Trakl is distinguished by his complete lack of any systematic "Weltanschauung," and was thus less well equipped, in one sense, to meet the horror of the war when it came. The spectacle of slaughter on the Eastern Front, which he was one of the few pre-war writers to witness in person, was overwhelming; his inability to give any help, as a member of an ill-equipped medical detachment, to the wounded men he had expected to tend, drove him within a short while to take his own life. His defencelessness against experience, the frankness with which he sets down his lyrical moods, his simplicity and directness and the almost inarticulate grief in many of his poems make him a kind of Woyzeck in the society of his own day. By comparison, and despite Trakl's ultimate despair, the turning towards Christian belief in Hofmannsthal's version of the morality-play *Everyman* looks facile.

The outbreak of war in August 1914 was greeted in Germany as in England with tumultuous enthusiasm, much of it naïvely patriotic or chauvinistic.[13] The Social Democrat party alone was divided, its Marxist wing under Karl Liebknecht opposing the vote for war-expenditure; but of 110 members of the party in the Reichstag, only fourteen were thus opposed, and none opposed the majority in the House itself. German workers went to war to meet the threat of Russian autocracy, as their English counterparts did to defeat German imperialism. The middle-class man was likely to see in the foreign opposition to Germany's belated rise to power a hypocritical refusal to allow what other nations had already achieved through war. There was also the unashamedly militarist view that Germany was entitled to assert herself as a world-power; what the Netherlands and Sweden had temporarily achieved by force of arms in the seventeenth century, and what England and France enjoyed at this day, was not to be denied to the most populous nation in Central Europe. The new Empire was now to win its spurs as others had done. The long process since the Reformation, which had had such startlingly rapid results for the Dutch and the Swedes, was now felt to be reaching its culmination. As the great sociologist Max Weber wrote in a letter of April 1915, "we have proved that we are a people of great culture (großes Kulturvolk): human beings who live amidst a refined culture, yet who can even stand up to the horrors of war (which is no achievement for a Senegalese!) and then, in spite of it, return basically decent like the majority of our soldiers–this is genuinely humane. . . ."[14] The war, seen in such a spirit, was a sign of Germany's awakening from decadence; the insistent self-consciousness of the awakening hid the doubtfulness which it might have revealed.

For Rilke, a citizen of the Austro-Hungarian Empire by birth, although German by inclination, the war was a revelation. In a way quite untypical of his normal mood, he proclaimed that at last, out of the lifeless sham of the preceding years, a god had arisen, men were truly in the grip of emotion, no longer mild and reasonable but giving vent to the terrible impulses within them. A few days later the reports of bloodshed and destruction, together with his own gentle nature, made him pause in doubt whether this could truly be the fearful god himself: there appeared to be no awareness in him, but only savage destructiveness:

Ist er ein Wissender? *Kann*
er ein Wissender sein, dieser reißende Gott?[15]

(Is he one of those who know? *Can*
He be such a one, this tempestuous god?)

This fury seemed purely barbaric, not that deliberate murderousness in the knowledge of the necessity for barbarism, which Nietzsche would have welcomed. It was a manifestation of the Will in its primal integrity, not in its conscious self-affirmation. Rilke turned therefore to the task of bringing about this self-knowledge. The war must be lamented, in order that it might be more duly praised. His own hesitation must be swallowed up ultimately in abandonment to the driving impulse of the times:

Sei euch die Klage nicht schmählich. Wahr erst
wird das unkenntliche, das
keinem begreifliche Schicksal,
wenn ihr es maßlos beklagt und
dennoch das maßlos,
dieses beklagteste, seht: wie ersehntes begeht.

(Let not lament seem disgraceful. This faceless, incomprehensible destiny cannot come true till you have lamented it measurelessly, and yet, lo, have engaged on this measureless, most lamentable thing as though it were dearly desired.)

Rilke's desire is not that the war should end or the destruction cease. It is rather that the war should "become true," that it should arouse both the fullest acceptance and the fullest rejection. The lament should be entered upon as though what was lamented were at the same time what was most desired. Without this, the existential experience of war would not attain complete truth, for war needed this dual response in order to come into its fullest range of being. In this way Rilke came to make his own affirmation of existence, fully in the Nietzschean sense. Yet his desire for truth of experience was curiously diminished by his deliberate welcome to illusion. The culture he defended still did not exist, but it must be asserted as though it did exist and as though it had cosmic significance; the beliefs he held were not authoritative and yet must be held to be so:

Nun seid ihr aufs Eigne wieder beschränkt.
Doch größerist es geworden. Wenns auch
nicht Welt ist, bei weitem,–nehmt es wie
Welt!

(Now you are restricted again to what's yours. But it has grown larger. Even though it is not a whole world, by far, take it as a whole world.)

Rilke's achievement as a poet is a matter to which more thought will be devoted later. His political views, with their paradoxicalness, have a peculiar significance in the present context. This determination to affirm what was recognized as inadequate has an unexpected echo in the words of the forerunner of National Socialism, Moeller van den Bruck, when he declared that Germany was "strong as a state, and consequently strong in military matters, in everything that had to do with defence, but extremely weak in possessing anything to defend."[16] The deliberate cultivation of what Rilke called a sham is one of the strangest aspects of German thought in these years.

Thomas Mann's attitude to the war–his achievement as a novelist is of course another matter–did not differ essentially from Rilke's, and was expressed first in his essay *Friedrich und die große Koalition,* dated December 1914 and published in 1915 together with his letter to a Swedish newspaper in defence of German policy. In effect, it is at once a criticism and a justification of Frederick the Great's Prussia and of the Wilhelmine Empire. Mann does not give the sentimental picture of "der olle Fritz," the good-hearted old pirate, that many of his readers might have liked. He emphasizes the king's brutal cynicism towards his subjects, his flouting of common decencies, the savagery of his instructions to his troops. He suggests that Frederick was probably the father of bastards as well as a homosexual, and makes no pretence that he had any moral justification for the invasion of Silesia and the partition of Poland. But at the same time he portrays the almost incredibly tenacious will-power in Frederick, the faith in his own ability to encounter the greatest odds, his immense industriousness, his social reforms and financial successes. "Germany today," he concluded, "*is* Frederick the Great. It is his struggle that we have now to carry through to the end, that we must fight again."[17] Mann felt for Frederick an admiration which his frankness did not diminish. Indeed such frankness was in itself a justification. The Germans, he asserted, were more deepsighted than other nations, and more manly in their endurance of what they were able to see: they knew the evil in themselves and despised civilization because it hid that evil under hypocritical pretences, preventing its true expression. For them war meant an end to the corrupting ease of peaceful times, and thus their conduct had a moral justification lacking in the conduct of other nations; it was a deliberate expression of the totality of human nature: "this is a matter of brutality for intellectual reasons (eine Brutalität aus Gedanklichkeit), an intellectually based will to become worthy of the world, to qualify in the world."[18] "Germany's whole virtue and beauty . . . is unfolded only in war." "The German soul is too deep for civilization to be for her a high value, let alone the highest value."

All this sounds reminiscent of Nietzsche's "Brutalitäts-Cur," and there are times at which, in this essay, Mann seems to see the brutality he now advocates as a step towards a "Third Reich" in which the liberal ideals of 1848 will be realized in a fusion of might and right.[19] This notion of war as a cure for decadence, rather than as a healthy activity in itself, plays a part in the collection of occasional pieces written by Mann in the next few years and published under the title *Betrachtungen eines Unpolitischen*. Indeed, Mann does not seem to have been over-proud of what had been, perhaps, an ill-considered outburst, or at least of some of the more fanatical passages it contained. In the *Betrachtungen* he lays frequent emphasis on the civilized qualities he had recently disdained. "Good breeding," he wrote, "is the sphere in which I live and breathe; I love, indeed at bottom I respect only what is kindly–crudity offends me, personal hatred I fear, and suffer from that which I deal out as much as from that which I bear, although I know very well that in order to live out humanity to the full one must experience hatred both actively and passively."[20] There are many passages to a similar effect–to much the same effect, indeed, as Hans Castorp's dream of the "Grail" in *Der Zauberberg*, insisting on courtesy, reverence and love as essential human qualities. But, again as in the dream, there is also a recognition of the cruelty inherent in human nature and in life itself, finding expression here in racial hatred, jingoism, wild and dark accusations against the enemy coupled with a persistent affirmation of the homeland's moral right to be brutal and a denial that it could possibly be so. Mann's attitude is ultimately detached and quietistic: "The horrors of war may set your hair on end–well, my hair stood on end at a birth which lasted thirty-six hours. That was not human, it was *hellish,* and so long as that continues to exist, war can continue to exist, for all I care."[21] Birth, like war and death, was part of life; far from attempting to assuage the pangs of either, Mann preferred to accept both, seeing in each a "mystical element" common to all fundamental feeling, whether of religion or of love. Or rather, Mann seems to have had such a preference, for in the preface later added to the rest he both associates and dissociates himself from the views he had expressed, claiming that they were no more than a daily record of his varying opinions. The contradictions they contain are thus paradoxically regarded both as worthy and as unworthy of attention. But this is characteristic also of Mann's fictional work at least up to this date: it has the same ambiguous affirmations and denials. And as in Nietzsche, the practical results are notable for the support they give to society as it exists at the moment.

During the war-years, those who had been most influenced by Nietzsche published almost nothing of a literary kind. Rilke and Mann restricted themselves (as far as publication is concerned) to the political utterances just described, George was silent, Hofmannsthal was principally occupied with the definition of a Christian, conservative tendency in Austrian history from which he hoped for some unification of the rapidly disintegrating, multi-national Empire of Franz Josef.[22] Hermann Hesse published only the tales of *Knulp* (1915), a figure in the Romantic tradition of Eichendorff's *Taugenichts* who provided an escape from the present reality rather than a confrontation with it. Sorge, whose play *Der Bettler* had been followed almost at once by his conversion to Catholicism, wrote only two more plays, both of them now almost forgotten, before his death at the front in 1916. The Expressionists, all of them young men, and often serving soldiers, published poems of agonized horror whose impact was not fully felt until after 1918. The one writer of international reputation who continued both to write and publish throughout the war was a man remarkably different from most of his predecessors, Franz Kafka.

Kafka did not become widely known until the late 1920's, after the posthumous publication by his friend Max Brod of his three unfinished novels, and suffered an almost complete eclipse in Germany from 1933 till 1945. The greater part of the works he himself was prepared to publish did appear, however, between 1912 and 1919. They are distinguished from most of the works so far discussed in that they have no explicit political concern whatsoever. Apart from Zionism, Kafka had no political interests, and in so far as he was concerned with society, it was the bureaucracy of the Austro-Hungarian Empire, of which he himself was an official, which claimed his attention and formed the subject-matter of his two major works, *Der Prozeß* and *Das Schloß*. In each of these novels the central character is confronted with a mysterious organization which both makes the most exacting demands on him and preserves to the end an inscrutable superiority; K. and Josef K. alike are left exhausted by their efforts at penetrating the mystery. On this account, Kafka's detractors have been prone to see in his work a lack-lustre acquiescence in the society of his day.[23] To hold this view, however, is to see in the two K.'s a kind of Tonio Kröger, whereas in fact neither of them makes any such acknowledgment of the "Bürger's" superiority as he does. Where Tonio concludes with the expression of "Bürgerliebe" and with contempt for the greatest works of art and philosophy, Kafka's heroes continue throughout to assert their inability to solve their riddles. They are frustrated men, sometimes desperately anxious to be accepted by society, sometimes wishing to stand completely apart, but constantly persuaded of the impossibility of either. That they are also neurotically prone to see this as their own guilt rather than that of society is a mark of Kafka's own situation, not of any desire for easy accommodation. There is never–this is a further mark of distinction–any philosophy of synthesis informing Kafka's work. Nor does he in his short stories set out to illustrate the workings of a system of beliefs, already held, but, as a rule, to explore the situation of his characters in an ignorance as complete as the reader's of what the outcome will be.[24] His usual method relies too much on the inspiration of the moment to allow of any such appearance of form as Mann's work has. By the same token, although Kafka's fictional *alter ego* desperately seeks some sense of community, he is never willing to accept such a sense at the cost of his conscience.

This scrupulousness of Kafka's makes generalized interpretation misleading: his stories and novels do not bear out one common solution of a problem, but have a wide variety of moods, each regulated by the particular context. (It is absolutely clear, for example, that *Das Schloß* was never meant to end like *Der Prozeß*.[25]) The task of interpretation is even further complicated by the suggestion that Kafka's work is of allegorical and religious significance. For Kafka himself was certainly occupied for most of his life with Jewish and Christian theology, particularly that of Kierkegaard, and this is reflected even in his purely literary writing. In much the same way as K. and Josef K. struggle against a mysterious authority, Kafka struggled with his convictions, both that there must be a point of view from which it was possible to see the world as good, and that to express such a view in human language was an intolerable act of *hubris*. He could not escape from this dilemma through self-affirmation, or through such affirmations of meaninglessness as his recent admirers have made.[26] To him the Absurd remained absurd, never to become acceptable and never to be accounted for in philosophical terms. So far as complete ignorance of God's existence was concerned, he was in the Nietzschean situation, but not of it, and would never make that change of front which sought to make an intolerable world tolerable or even welcome. Dreams of punishment, meaninglessness, the Absurd, dread, retain their full import to the bitter end, not paradoxically turning into praiseworthy values or "gratuitous" facts of existence.

Despite his unorthodoxy as a Jew, Kafka has seemed to some writers[27] to typify the faith of

Judaism, at least in the respect that no amount of awareness of God's absence and of present misery weakens his belief in God's faithfulness. Kafka wrote as he did in the conviction that the worst could be said and experienced by men without stain to the divine perfection. (What orthodox Jew today, in the light of the concentration camps, to say nothing of Jewish history since the Dispersion, could believe otherwise?) His religious aphorisms, never published although apparently prepared for publication, are full of this conviction, and if his stories do not reveal it, that is probably because he saw his task primarily as that of a modern novelist, recording experience rather than conquering it, remaining open to every facet of his own moods. In this, he is a man of his times: Tolstoy, Dostoevsky, Dante, the English Metaphysicals did not feel the need to exclude their religious beliefs from their artistic work. The same determination to remain firm by the inspiration of the moment, with all its quietistic implications, must account for that tendency of Kafka's to lengthy developments of minutiae, which interrupts the fascination his grim narratives often exert. Yet in his insistence on living out his tragic life as a writer to the full, without recourse to irony and without laying claim to a belief he could not wholeheartedly affirm, Kafka stands opposed to every German writer of his time, with the sole exception of Georg Trakl.

K. never reaches the Castle; Josef K. never learns the nature of the guilt with which the Court charges him. The one is executed by officials of the Court, the other, we are told by Max Brod, was to have received permission to stay in the village, outside the Castle's walls, only on his deathbed. It may seem from this as though the alternative to the tradition of acceptance and affirmation were despair to the point of annihilation, and it is true that there are stories of Kafka's which suggest such terms of choice. The man fantastically transformed into an insect in *Die Verwandlung* is swept away with the rubbish after his death, leaving his unreflective family to enjoy a happier existence. The "Hunger-artist," in the story of that name, is a man of the past whose hungering, apparently symbolical of the hunger after righteousness, is no longer appreciated by the world at large: he too is swept away with the refuse, to be replaced by a wild beast who takes the public's fancy rather better. It is as though Kafka were allegorizing here with some prescience the tendency of his times, in which such a preference was already showing itself. The gruesome story *In der Strafkolonie* might be interpreted in a similar way. The machine of torture described here, by means of which men formerly gained enlightenment, evidently stands for the traditional conception of redemption through conviction of guilt. The explorer who flees from the scene after the machine has broken in pieces could well be taken to represent that contemporary attitude which shuns all suffering as an obscenity. Yet to make such interpretations into a message from the author, as though he himself sought to shun suffering and to inculcate such an attitude in his readers, is to make Kafka less of an artist than he is. He makes these endings to his stories in his awareness of his own times: "hungering" and the endurance of torment are outmoded, and the public would rather live in ignorance of them. However–"You can shut your eyes to the suffering of the world," he wrote in his notebook, "that is the one suffering you might be able to avoid." In each of these stories there is at least a moment, fleetingly glimpsed, when the sufferer shows signs of a purity of spirit which passes unnoticed by the world around him. These are very faint gleams, barely recognizable and perhaps not even consciously felt by Kafka to exist. In times of extreme self-consciousness, however, when messages were being proclaimed by writers on every side, such tentativeness and such unwillingness to make any parade of insights were one way in which a writer of scrupulous integrity could continue to write without a completely overwhelming sense of shame. They were perhaps not the only way; Kafka's neurotic imbalance partly accounts for them. But they were at least not corrupted by willing self-contradiction. They had no political implications: the drift towards the concentration camps could not have been halted by such a mode of writing, even had it become widely known before the Nazis seized power. But at least those for whom release from the camps was as unforeseeable as was Kafka's release from his own, mental torment could have faced their extermination with a similar composure–as some did.

---

1. "Desireless, illusionless, most sacred realm of choice" (R. Wagner, *Gesammelte Dichtungen*, ed. Julius Kapp, Leipzig, n.d., II, 286). Wagner deleted these words from the final version of the libretto of *Götterdämmerung*, saying that the music expressed the ideas contained in them with far greater precision.

2. *Loc. cit.*

3. Rilke, however, treated of the new cities in his early works, the *Book of Hours*, and in *Malte Laurids Brigge*, though not in the spirit of the Naturalists.

4. Nietzsche, *Menschliches, Allzumenschliches*, vol. II, para. 187.

5. *Op. cit.* vol. I, para. 477.

6. Quoted in Erich Eyck, *Bismarck and the German Empire*, 2nd edn. (London, 1958), p. 68.

7. For instances, see Ludwig Dehio, "Ranke and German Imperialism," in *Germany and World Politics in the Twentieth Century* (London, 1959; German edn., 1955).

8. E.g. the last poem of *Der Stern des Bundes.*

9. *Deutsche Literatur in Entwicklungsreihen*, "Vom Naturalismus zur neuen Volksdichtung," vol. I (*Naturalismus*), ed. W. Linden (Leipzig, 1936), p. 83.

10. *Op. cit.* p. 66.

11. "unsere menschliche Tier-göttlichkeit." R. Dehmel, *Aber die Liebe* (Fischer, Berlin, n.d.), p. 180.

12. One of Sorge's unpublished plays, for a sight of which I am indebted to Mr. R. Hinton Thomas, reveals something of the uncertainty in which Nietzsche left young men at this time. A group is seen discussing Nietzsche's views in the reading-room of a public library, and particularly the question whether Nietzsche intended to preach the killing of the infirm. One of the group leaves, and returns to announce that he has just killed a cripple. Thereupon Nietzsche or his spirit enters the room and turns off the light, declaring that those who really understand him can read him in the dark.

13. Cf. the early chapters in Ernst Toller, *Eine Jugend in Deutschland.*

14. Quoted in J. P. Mayer, *Max Weber and German Politics* (London, 1944), p. 57.

15. Quotations from Rilke's *Fünf Gesänge* are from his *Ausgewählte Werke* (Insel, 1948), vol. I, pp. 335-341.

16. A. Moeller van den Bruck, *Das dritte Reich*, 3rd edn. (Hamburg, 1931), p. 303.

17. Thomas Mann, *Friedrich und die große Koalition* (Berlin, 1915), p. 15.

18. *Op. cit.* p. 123.

19. The "Third Reich" had not at this stage its later implications. Mann may have had in mind its use by Ibsen in *Emperor and Galilean*, where it means a kind of Kingdom of Heaven on earth, a synthesis of body and spirit.

20. Thomas Mann, *Betrachtungen eines Unpolitischen* (Berlin, 1922), p. 458.

21. *Op. cit.* p. 477.

22. See Hofmannsthal's legend-creating essays on national heroes: Prince Eugène, Grillparzer, and Maria Theresa; also the study of these in *Hofmannsthal's Festival Dramas*, by Brian Coghlan (Cambridge, 1964).

23. E.g. Günther Anders, *Kafka pro und contra*, and E. Burgum in *The Kafka Problem*, ed. A. Flores.

24. This would appear to be untrue of *The Trial* and of *America*, of which the final chapters exist, though the chapters immediately preceding them do not.

25. See further my "The Structure of Kafka's Works: A reply to Professor Uyttersprot" in *German Life and Letters* (October, 1959). My own attempt at such a unitive interpretation in the appendix to *Kafka's Castle* (Cambridge, 1956), I now think, was mistaken, although I would not say the same of the argument in the main body of the book.

26. E.g. Maurice Blanchot and Samuel Beckett. Cp. Maja Goth, *Franz Kafka et les lettres françaises, 1928-1955* (Paris, 1956).

27. E.g. Martin Buber, *Two Types of Faith* (London, 1951), also in *The Twentieth Century Views Kafka*, ed. Ronald Gray (Englewood Cliffs, N.J., 1962).

Reprinted from The German Tradition in Literature 1871-1945 *(Cambridge: University Press, 1965), pp. 19-45.*

Premisses

Michael Hamburger

1

"Research indicates that the commonest or most commonly-voiced English objection to German literature has it that this literature is wordy, philosophical, humourless, highly abstract, and crammed with details. In brief, heavy-handed." This is the weightiest of the eight reasons for what he calls "non-liking towards German literature" discussed by Mr. D. H. Enright in a recent article, *Aimez-vous Goethe?*[1] Though he writes as a non-specialist Mr. Enright regards the objection as largely invalid, and his other essays on German writers confirm that he does not share the prejudices which he analyses with insight and wit; but in an earlier essay, included in his book *The Apothecary's Shop,* he finds Rainer Maria Rilke guilty of "highbrow baby talk" in the *Duineser Elegien,* a judgement worthy of Mr. Kingsley Amis and other contemporary English writers who approach all foreign literature with suspicion and disdain–if they approach it at all. Mr. Enright has expressly dissociated himself from this new parochialism, yet that casual remark sticks in the mind, if only because one can imagine how deeply shocking it would be to the great majority of German critics who have written books or essays on Rilke.

The remark brings one up against one of the fundamental differences between the premisses of most of the more serious modern German writers–or most of the modern German writers who are taken more seriously–and the premisses of their nearest English counterparts. German and English attitudes to these writers tend to reveal the same fundamental difference. Very briefly it amounts to this: more often than not these German writers assumed prophetic or priest-like functions which very few English writers have assumed in modern times. (D. H. Lawrence is an exception.) In an age of cultural pluralism, they claimed or assumed that their work was of exemplary importance as a source of spiritual or moral leadership. The claim or the assumption goes back to a time when secular literature and philosophy took over functions which had formerly been the prerogative of the clergy–to the eighteenth-century Enlightenment and Weimar classicism. Yet, for reasons which will be examined here, late nineteenth- and early twentieth-century German writers were singularly ill-equipped to exercise such functions in a socially effective way. Rilke's "highbrow baby talk" was accepted as high metaphysical doctrine by one of many minority groups; but its effectiveness was cancelled out by the appeal of other lone prophets to other minority groups. Hugo von Hofmannsthal summed up the dilemma when he remarked: "It is hard to fight against a dominant society, but harder still to be forced to postulate a society that does not exist."[2] Even this awareness of the dilemma is far from being characteristic of the German writers after Nietzsche; Hofmannsthal was an Austrian. The dilemma may become a little more palpable after a cursory glance at two books that deal not with literature but with social history and the history of political ideas.

2

In his lecture *The Tradition of Authority, Democracy and Social Structure in Germany,*[3] Professor Ralf Dahrendorf shows how the German hankering after absolute authority was inseparable not only from a fear of social tension and diversity but an incapacity to cope with them. The German literary cult of "inwardness" and of social utopias must be seen in this light. About utopianism Professor Dahrendorf writes: "In reality Utopia, that is, a society without conflict, always turns out to be dangerously close to the totalitarianism of a suppression of all opposition." As for the "inwardness" which Mr. Enright certainly had in mind when he spoke of Rilke's "highbrow baby talk," again Professor Dahrendorf relates it to attitudes characteristic of the whole nation: "I think it can be shown that in Germany private virtues are characteristically highly valued by society, whereas in the Anglo-Saxon countries the public virtues dominate." Mr. Enright's criterion of maturity, by which Rilke is found wanting, rests on this Anglo-Saxon preference for public virtues. Professor Dahrendorf goes on to observe how the German preference for private virtues was built into the educational system:

> Throughout their school life, children spend but a few hours of the day, generally in the mornings, at school; the rest of the time "belongs to the family." Under these conditions, a type of school is almost inevitably created in which the public virtues of getting on with others and living together are repressed by the private virtues of learning and individual assiduity. Thus, the individual is introduced to society by being held at a distance from it. Until recently, one of the basic assumptions of German educational thinking was that the school is supposed to build up a "spiritual world" in the child besides and even against the "real world. . . . The "unpolitical German" is a result of the rank and order of family and school in German society.

The representative or exemplary status assumed by and sometimes granted to modern German writers may seem to contradict what has been implied about their tendency towards a cult of inwardness; but where the cult of inwardness is general to the point of being built into the educational system, the contradiction is less acute than it seems. The German preference for private virtues did not lead to individualism in the British sense of the word, for British individualism is both measured and manifested against a social or public setting, whereas the "spiritual world" to which Professor Dahrendorf refers was regarded as separate from and superior to the domain of public virtues. That each writer should also have set up his spiritual world as an example to others, points back to the dilemma which I have touched upon, to the nonexistent society of which Hofmannsthal complained, and the need to posit one. Utopianism–and this could include some of the more extreme forms of German nationalism in the past–is the desperate resort of an inwardness that longs to impose itself as a social norm, not only to posit a society in its own image, but to create one. British writers on the whole have been able to take the existence of society for granted. But for its awareness of an existing society, and its cautious and moderate tone, Mr. Eliot's *The Idea of a Christian Society* is one instance of a utopianism that might be comparable to the utopianism of German writers, and the anarcho-syndicalist tracts of Sir Herbert Read also show that social utopias are by no means incompatible with Anglo-Saxon attitudes. The decisive difference is that the British establishment is both capacious and adaptable enough to digest such utopias and their progenitors, while the complexity of British tradition guarantees that no minority creed can be as potentially disruptive as the lone prophecies or utopias of the German writers.

Conformism and a "non-political" passivity are the reverse side of German "inwardness," just as fanatical nationalism is the reverse side of the isolation that was bound to result from the exclusive cultivation of private spiritual worlds. "Many people everywhere and at all times," Professor Hans Kohn wrote in *The Mind of Germany*,[4] "have succumbed to the demonic temptation of power, but German intellectuals sanctified this acceptance with the halo of a philosophy which they extolled for its deep or realistic understanding of the alleged forces of history." In Professor Kohn's survey of the peculiar collaboration and interplay between ideas and politics from the early Romantic period to the two world wars, one is struck once again by the importance accorded to philosophers and imaginative artists. By no means all of these lent their support to nationalism. From Goethe and Hölderlin to Heine, Nietzsche, Hermann Hesse and Thomas Mann it was the German intellectuals, too, who offered the most radical and penetrating criticisms of German megalomania, very often because their quarrel with Germany was a quarrel with themselves. As Professor Kohn demonstrates, historicism or fatalism was one distinguishing feature of extreme nationalism in Germany–though a fatalism which deliberately or unconsciously confused the will to power with historical necessity. The appeal of such a creed, conveniently translated into the language of religion and metaphysics by a long succession of influential writers and teachers, was too strong for all but a few independent minds. "After 1866," Professor Kohn finds, "Germany knew neither a true conservatism nor a true liberalism."

Yet in 1919 Hermann Hesse could warn the Germans: "With the help of your Emperor and of Richard Wagner you have made of the 'German virtues' an operatic display which no one in the world took seriously but yourselves. And behind this pretty humbug of operatic splendour you allowed your dark instincts, your servility and your swagger, to proliferate." Three years later the Lutheran theologian Ernst Troeltsch said in a lecture that the nationalist aimed at nothing less than "a total and fundamental dissolution of the idea of a universal natural law," and pointed to the "curious dualism" of Germany that tended to "brutalize romance and romanticize cynicism."

Professor Kohn sees modern German history as a struggle between "western" and "eastern" casts of mind. Here "western" stands for reason and enlightenment, "eastern" for the irrationalism and anti-rationalism of the Germanophiles (his name for the extreme nationalists, probably by analogy with the Russian Slavophiles, though Heine's word for them, Teutomaniacs, is far more apt). But to adopt these geographical terms is to run the risk of fostering another political myth; and in fact Professor Kohn shows a marked bias towards south-west Germany as against Prussia. In his account of the "western" opposition to the Teutomaniacs he includes the Austrian Hofmannsthal, but does not so much as mention the Prussian novelist Theodor Fontane, a writer much less ambiguously on the side of sweetness and light than Nietzsche, Stefan George, Rilke, Thomas Mann or even Goethe, all of whom he cites in his account of the ineffectual resistance to Teutomania.

Granted that philosophical and literary ideas permeated German policies and institutions to an extent that has no parallel in Britain–who would think of including Blake or Keats in a study of British political thought?–no history of ideas alone can possibly get to the heart of a phenomenon that consists in the denial of reason. Such a phenomenon calls for a combination of social, psychological and semantic analysis which Professor Kohn does not attempt. Many of his quotations can make no sense at all to an English reader unfamiliar with the emotive overtones of German words like *Schicksal* (fate), *Geist* or–during the Second World War–of Professor Martin Heidegger's combination of these words with his own numinous terminology. It is also true that a single case like that of Heinrich von Kleist, who moved from the extreme "western" to the extreme "eastern" position in the course of a few years, contributes more to one's understanding of the psychological and social roots of Teutomania than a whole compendium of miscellaneous opinions and events. As it is, Professor Kohn's interpretation sheds little light on the "servility and swagger," the "brutal romanticism" and "romantic cynicism" on which Troeltsch and Hesse remarked. Nor does he illumine the crucial paradox that it is the lack not only of independence of mind, but of public virtues, which creates the vacuum so often filled by fanatical corporative creeds.

His conclusion that West Germany has now returned to the "western" fold, because the centre has shifted from Prussia to the Rhineland, and that all the circumstances forbid a revival of aggressive nationalism, would be more convincing if it were supported by evidence of a parallel change in the social and psychological conditions, such as Professor Dahrendorf provides in the lecture quoted and in his article "The New Germany."[5] Teutomania, by its very nature, shows a suicidal disregard for circumstances. As for the "eastern" and "western" trends or the clash or ideologies as such. Again it is Professor uous generality. Professor Kohn's book has the sub-title "The Education of a Nation," but he does not tell us whether West German education has broken the tyranny of autocratic parents and teachers, themselves at once servile and overbearing, whose brutalizing effect on German life was much more immediate than any conflict between "eastern" and "western" trends or the clash or ideologies as such. Again it is Professor Dahrendorf's analysis that helps to fill the gap. If contemporary German literature is another reliable guide–and one cannot be sure just how far it is–the pattern of conformity and revolt, rather than community and independence, is less conspicuous than before, though still apparent. Professor Kohn contrasts the present dearth of "greater writers or musicians" with the "rich but confused cultural and artistic flowering on the one hand and a wave of violence on the other" after 1918, but he overlooks that the flowering sprang from roots established before 1914, and seems unaware of the distinction of much contemporary writing in Germany. More of that later. Professor Kohn and Professor Dahrendorf agree that the social and political structure of Germany has undergone a drastic change. "National-Socialism," Professor Dahrendorf concludes, "was the German revolution; after 1945 there was no way back to the society I have described."

3

Until recently, German literary criticism, too,

tended to treat writers as though they were pure repositories of "spiritual worlds" and exemplary values, untainted by worldly involvements. Much of this criticism, therefore, seemed to exist in a social and political vacuum, except where it served didactic ends, harnessing imaginative writers of the past to ideologies which they might or might not have approved when alive. It is a British scholar, Professor W. H. Bruford, who has provided a sociological study of the little principality for ever associated with the brief "classical" period of German literature. As he reminds us in his book, *Culture and Society in Classical Weimar, 1775-1806*,[6] as long ago as 1803 Mme de Staël was struck by the indifference of Wieland, Goethe and Schiller to European politics; and these representatives of Weimar classicism were more directly involved in society than most of their Romantic successors. Goethe, after all, was a statesman and administrator, Schiller an historian, Wieland an educationalist and writer of political novels. Yet, to a degree almost incomprehensible to non-Germans, culture and society tended to be regarded as separate, if not as mutually hostile, domains. Culture, more often than not, was identified with *Bildung*, with an individual's cultivation of his inner life, while society was left to take care of itself.

More than any other comparable work, Professor Bruford's helps to explain this state of affairs during the period covered by his study. He does so by relating the literary works of Wieland, Herder, Goethe, Schiller, and Fichte to their non-literary activities at Weimar, and by investigating the social structure of the Dukedom itself–down to statistics of salaries and industries, such as they were. In this way he has not only filled the vacuum for students and readers, but made it far easier to see how the vacuum came about in the first place. Goethe's diverse interests and activities are presented against the background of other Weimar figures, from the Duke and Dowager Duchess to their ministers, functionaries and other subjects, not excluding Jungfer Wenzel who acted as messenger and carrier at the time of Goethe's correspondence with Schiller. There are detailed accounts of all the plays, operas and other entertainments put on at Weimar in those years, the commercial enterprises of F. J. Bertuch, the various periodicals of those years, and their circulation. Though Professor Bruford concentrates on a single period and a single locality–and there is something almost fortuitous about the literary prominence of this tiny Thuringian state–he has added a chapter on later developments in Germany and the growing schism between culture and society. The concept of culture itself, and its history, are examined in an appendix. Professor Bruford acknowledges the precedent of Mr. Raymond Williams's approach to English literature of the same period, but he has the merit of having broken down a much more formidable barrier; and in his earlier book on *Theatre, Drama and Audience in Goethe's Germany*, published in 1950, he had adopted a similar all-round approach.

Social and political interests are no less apparent in the works of other British writers on German literature, such as Professor Barker Fairley, Professor Roy Pascal and Professor R. Hinton Thomas, than they are in the brilliant studies of the French critic Professor Robert Minder. That characteristically German genre, the *Bildungsroman*, is a case in point. As Professor Pascal has shown,[7] the peculiarity of the *Bildungsroman* is that its young hero is an outsider who gradually makes his peace with society. The reasons for this peculiarity have already been touched upon: German individualism tends to take the form of "inwardness," rather than outward independence and non-conformism, and German society has tended towards a rigid conformism of outward behaviour that refuses to accommodate the exceptional or merely vital individual, who is driven back into the isolation of his embattled "spiritual world." It follows that the individual's integration into society–which used to be taken for granted by the major English, French and Russian novelists–becomes a theme of special importance and urgency. Since this integration is very apt to fail, another characteristically German variety of the novel–of which Goethe's *Werther* is the prototype–revolves around the dilemma of isolated and thwarted inwardness. Professor Pascal, who has a marked preference for the realists, scarcely deals with this latter variety; but his strictures on novels of the other kind, including even such masterpieces as Goethe's *Wilhelm Meisters Lehrjahre* and Keller's *Der grüne Heinrich*, always point to the basic dilemma. He observes that the *Bildungsroman* rarely takes us beyond the point of reconciliation, so that the reader is left with the fear that the hero's subsequent life–the maturity so precious to the author–will be one of barren and boring conformism, free from conflict only because it is a capitulation. This helps to explain why so many of Professor Pascal's subjects–the nineteenth-century novelists Gottfried Keller,

Adalbert Stifter, Jeremias Gotthelf, Wilhelm Raabe and Theodor Fontane–have not won the international public they would seem to deserve. Not even the two Swiss novelists or the Austrian could do full justice to the social institutions of their time without a certain loss of vision, passion or intensity. Professor Pascal goes so far as to write of the Germans in general that "they have been happiest in the symbolic world of music, and Wagner, rather than any novelist, represents their highest achievement in epic form." For that very reason, the symbolic almost mystical realism of Stifter, or the didactic realism of Gotthelf–who became a novelist despite himself, in the process of composing moral tracts for the Swiss peasantry–may be more interesting to non-German readers than the *études de mœurs* of Raabe or Fontane, writers far less parochial in outlook and far closer to the mainstream of European fiction in their time. Yet it is difficult to understand the neglect of Theodor Fontane's studies in Prussian society, with their fine balance between love and scorn of the Junker class. If these novels fall short of the highest achievements of realistic fiction outside Germany, it is Dr. J. P. Stern who tells us why in a distinguished book, *Re-interpretations.*[8]

4

Its publication has scarcely been noticed in this country. With the exception of three or four writers, German literature remains a special case–or the province of specialists. If a book on German literature is to reach anything that could be described as a general public, its thesis too must be general, and the more sweeping its diagnosis of the special case, the better the prospects of receiving general attention. Yet criticism proper is apt to be defeated not only by this need, but by the perpetual need to "introduce" individual German writers as though they had just landed from Mars, to summarize the plots of all the works discussed and to translate any passage quoted or analysed. No wonder, therefore, that such books as Dr. Stern's are rare, and that some of the most excellent writers on German literature in this country–Professor Eudo C. Mason for instance–have chosen to publish their most important books in Germany. It is reasonable enough that strictly scholarly research should be made available where the demand for it is greatest; but critical works are another matter, and the state of affairs I have outlined is serious enough, especially since it is beginning to extend to French studies also. There is all the more cause, in any case, to welcome the few writers and publishers who defy it.

Nor does publication abroad necessarily solve the problem. The best English criticism of German literature, including both Dr. Stern's and Professor Mason's, tends to be written from a standpoint and in a manner peculiarly English, and both the standpoint and the manner may not be easily acceptable in Germany, as in the case of E. M. Butler's *The Tyranny of Greece over Germany,* which many German readers found positively offensive. Clearly, it is as difficult for German readers not to resent the assumption that their literature is a special case as for honest English critics to avoid it. Tact, tolerance and humility are called for on both sides. On the German side, for instance, it is necessary to understand that British critics have been struck by the strangeness of German literature ever since Carlyle, who did more than anyone to make it respected here in the first place, and that recent history alone does not account for the proliferation of works that stress and explain this strangeness. On the British side, and this is where Dr. Stern's book is quite uncommonly helpful, what is needed is a greater readiness to understand the very different premisses of the German imaginative writers; above all the primacy so often accorded to the inner life of individuals rather than to social life, social tensions and social morality. If German literary criticism too often strikes English readers as a contribution to metaphysics or to hagiography, English literary criticism must too often strike German readers as a contribution to sociology or behaviourist psychology; and much the same is true of many poems, plays and novels–the subjects of that criticism–but of novels especially.

German prose in the nineteenth century, from Goethe to Fontane, is the subject of Dr. Stern's book. His main studies are devoted to Grillparzer, Büchner, Schopenhauer, Heine, Stifter and Fontane, but there are illuminating and relevant passages on many of their contemporaries. These writers, and the whole period, are even less familiar to most English readers than those that immediately preceded and followed them; but Dr. Stern rightly sees them as pointing forward to specifically modern developments not only in German literature but in all Western literature. "The conclusion to which the most characteristic works of nineteenth-century German prose have led me," he writes in the Preface,

> is that they are distinguished above all by their special combination of the prophetic and the archaic, of the existential and the parochial, of the elements of worldly innocence and reflective profundity. They are almost always behind their times, and often peculiarly relevant to ours.

Dr. Stern, then, has a thesis to develop, and the special case of German literature is never far from his concerns. What is admirable about this book, however, is that he does not drive the thesis through the criticism, but has enough confidence in the rightness of the thesis and the intelligence of his readers to provide patient and penetrating expositions of literary or philosophical works in their own right. At the same time the criticism proper is always supported by observations on society, politics and cultural background, so that he succeeds in conveying a singularly rich and many-sided impression of the whole period, and indeed of peculiarly German features ever since the Middle Ages (as in his comparison between the *Chanson de Roland* and the German *Rolandslied*). The chapter on Grillparzer includes a wry, sympathetic but devastating analysis of Austrian literary culture, with special emphasis on Vienna, and up to modern times. Here Dr. Stern's own early un-English background has proved a distinct advantage; but his terms of reference elsewhere are quite decidedly English, and he rarely misses an opportunity to draw pertinent comparisons with English writers. Though French and Russian prose writers are also frequently cited, Dr. Stern's central argument about the nature of realism–an outstanding instance is the discussion of *Madame Bovary, Anna Karenina* and Fontane's *Effi Briest*–is firmly rooted in ethical and social preoccupation that will be immediately understood in this country, as they would not be in Russia, France or Germany. . . .

Since it is attained in quite a number of twentieth-century works of literature, Dr. Stern may have been wise to confine himself to the period of "poetic realism," though he indicates Thomas Mann's debt to Theodor Fontane and quotes Rilke's lines about later generations who "are not very reliably at home in the interpreted world." His criterion could very well be applied to other twentieth-century writers, as he points out in a brief Epilogue; but these "more radically alienated" writers would have brought him up against a situation no longer characteristically, or exclusively, German. The inclusion of lyrical poetry, as he is well aware, would also have strained his thesis and demanded further concessions to Schopenhauer's aesthetics. (Heine is treated primarily as a prose writer, and that seems unobjectionable–not only in the context of Dr. Stern's book.) Significantly, even Flaubert's realism is shown to be of a kind not unrelated to the "reinterpretations" of Dr. Stern's German subjects, because Flaubert's aestheticism and pessimism alienated him from social sympathies, however minutely accurate his social observation. It is Tolstoy who is celebrated as the true and exemplary realist.

Yet it must be stressed again that Dr. Stern's main argument does not prevent him from entering deeply and unreservedly into the works of the German writers with whom he is principally concerned. The brilliance, profundity and originality of Georg Büchner, for instance, are not only acknowledged once more, but re-enacted and re-defined; and though Büchner's disillusionment with revolutionary politics led to an obsession with solitude, futility and incommunicability that anticipates the extreme alienation of twentieth-century writers, Dr. Stern also does justice to the stark humanism of Büchner's vision and recognizes his importance as a forerunner of Brecht's "epic theatre." In the same way, the unique beauty–as well as the unique tedium–of Adalbert Stifter's prose is brought out, and it is to be hoped that both Stifter and Fontane will become a little better known in this country when Dr. Stern's studies have been assimilated. The inept and ill-informed criticism so frequently meted out to modern German authors by general reviewers in England is partly due to obstinate prejudice, but such knowledge of the antecedents as Dr. Stern provides would at least elicit second thoughts about the cruder generalizations.

In the post-war period many of the younger German authors have shown a social consciousness that compares very favourably with that of their contemporaries anywhere else in the world. Heinrich Böll, for example, is a novelist to whom social reality is quite literary sacred, out of a religious commitment that accords very well with Dr. Stern's conception of realism. The ambivalence that bedevilled Thomas Mann's attitudes to society and politics, so that he was precariously balanced between a "non-political" aestheticism and a conscientious devotion to "progress"–frequently toppling over into one or the other absurd extreme–has been left behind. The post-war writers, even including the poets, are pretty clearly divided between realism on the one hand–in Dr. Stern's sense of the word–and various forms of abstraction or concretion on the other. If very few expectations can now be carried from the social world into the work of art, that is hardly surprising after what happened to the social world in the past three decades. (Many of the writers in question, whether realist or otherwise, have accepted their part of the responsibility for what happened to the social world.) Most important of all, perhaps, none of these writers could possibly be charged with parochialism. A poet like Hans Magnus Enzensberger–who, incidentally, chooses to live in Scandinavia rather than in West Germany–has a range of reference that marks him as a citizen of the world; of the new world, that is, with its terrifying trend towards uniformity.

The danger of parochialism is more acute in this country, and not least in its literature, both imaginative and critical. If German literature has erred in the direction of "inwardness," and it certainly did so in the period covered by Dr. Stern, for reasons which he has gone far towards explaining, the social preoccupations of British writers and critics are in danger of becoming not only parochial but barren. Imagination, for one thing, is being cramped by a literalness quite different from Dr. Stern's notion of realism. Even poetry, too often, only accomplishes on a mercifully small scale what those almost nightly television plays accomplish at unbearable length: to reproduce our drab realities with a drab efficiency, without transforming anything, without enriching or refining our experience. One cries out for a little more inwardness, for social irresponsibility, if need be, for imagination at all costs. The endless reiteration of social trivia has become our form of parochialism. The tedium of Stifter's minute descriptions is more than bearable in comparison, because his descriptions are animated by a loving concern with things which, like Rilke's, not merely reproduces, but transforms them. It would be a pity indeed if Dr. Stern's main argument were to be used only as another stick with which to beat German literature as a whole, when his book would serve as an aid to our understanding of its oddities and a valuable incentive to the study of specific works.

5

Many non-specialist readers and critics are prepared to accept a large measure of social alienation in twentieth-century writers. What they find much more difficult to accept is the degree to which this alienation was anticipated by German writers of the late eighteenth and early nineteenth centuries. Miss Kathleen Nott's review of the collected stories of Heinrich von Kleist is one example of the misunderstandings that can arise from sheer ignorance of elementary facts and premisses. This highly intelligent critic dismissed Kleist as follows:

> Mr. Greenberg quotes Georg Lukács on the despairing isolation of Kleist's characters; and from Thomas Mann we are given the notion that Kleist might have picked up his solipsism from Kant. (I find it staggering that Kant could upset *any* writer with warmth of imagination.) Anyway, I am sure that there is something in all this, but not much: and I fear that we may now be in for a spate of thesis-hunting about Kleist. Mann informs us that the stories fill us "with anxiety and terror . . . all our affects are confounded." Our *senses* possibly: Personally I find them frenzied, as if far too many characters were all shouting their heads off at once. . . .

It is conceivable that Miss Nott would have disliked Kleist's stories even if she had been familiar with the background and in a position to dispense with the Preface and Introduction to the *Collected Stories*. Yet in that case she would have known that the source of the notion she dismisses is not Thomas Mann at all but Kleist himself in his letters, and that his so called "Kant crisis" has been a commonplace of literary history for well over a hundred years; also, that what makes the crises interesting is the very perversity of Kleist's misreading of Kant. Nor could she have added that "Kleist uses this deafening frenzy as a device to make your flesh creep"–when his desperate sincerity is attested by all the documents–or that "the 'Horror' is all very Gothick."

The misunderstanding has implications more disturbing than Miss Nott's dislike. Although Carlyle wrote about him in 1827, Heinrich von Kleist's stories were presented to American and English readers as a new discovery due to the admiration of Kafka and Thomas Mann for a writer who died in 1811. In a preface written for the American edition Thomas Mann congratulated the publishers on their courage in making Kleist's stories available; that must have been some time before 1955, the year of Thomas Mann's death. The American edition appeared in 1960, and nearly three more years had to pass before this courage was matched by a British publisher. Better late than never, is the obvious response; but one can't help smiling a little at the excitement with which the translator, Mr. Martin Greenberg, records his discovery of Kleist–by way of Kafka's diaries! When will the Germans get around to discovering that extraordinary new writer Sir Walter Scott? Didn't James Joyce mention him somewhere? Neither Thomas Mann nor Mr. Greenberg thought of mentioning that Kleist has been a German classic for at least a century. Hence Miss Nott's quite unjustified fear that we may now be in for a spate of thesis-hunting about Kleist. The theses were written long ago.

Casual reference might also have been made to one or the other of such facts as that Kleist has been translated and written about in this country for a good many years; that some of his plays have been performed in England, even on television; that two of them are available in a paperback volume in *The Classical Theater* series (Anchor Books)–hardly a recondite publication, one would have thought–and a different translation of one of these in another paperback book (Library of the Liberal Arts, New York); that essays on Kleist appeared in *The Times Literary Supplement* in 1953 and 1954, in *Partisan Review* in 1955, and in my critical book *Reason and Energy* (1957); that the paperback collection *Great German Short Stories* included a story by Kleist as recently as 1960; or that recent books in English on Kleist include Richard March's short study in the Bowes and Bowes series, a new edition of Professor E. L. Stahl's *The Dramas of Heinrich von Kleist*, and *Heinrich von Kleist: Studies in his Works and Literary Character* by Professor Walter Silz. Since Mr. Greenberg mentions none of these facts, Miss Nott may be less to blame for failing to notice that Kleist was not discovered yesterday, or that neither Thomas Mann's preface nor Mr. Greenberg's introduction adds anything substantial even to the English literature on Kleist.

At least one of Thomas Mann's remarks, in fact, points to his astonishing limitations as a literary critic, "The only genre hardly cultivated by Kleist is the lyric," Mann wrote, "and we may well ask why he chose to bypass it, why this extraordinary master of poetic rhetoric, whose plays abound in magnificent flights of poetry, could never get himself to speak directly and freely *in propria persona*." Lyrical poetry is simply identified with personal confession, as though the poet's "I"–when he chooses to introduce it–were not as much a fiction as any narrative "he" or "she"; and Kleist's strictly dramatic verse is treated as though it were comparable to the passages of lyrical poetry that can be extracted from plays by less thoroughly dramatic writers.

Nor was there any good reason why Kleist should "get himself" to produce anything so inconsistent with his peculiar genius for the rendering of character in the grip of events. Kleist, as he once admitted, wrote only because he could not help it–that is one reason why his plays and stories are unlike any other written in his time, "Gothick" or otherwise. As usual, Thomas Mann the critic was too patently using another man's work as a pretext for talking about himself; and what he really tells us is why he, Mann, a much more deliberate and self-conscious writer than Kleist, had to wrap up *his* self-confessions in would-be critical essays.

These observations are not meant to reflect on Miss Nott or on the publishers and translator of Kleist's collected stories, nor even on Thomas Mann's contribution to the volume, but on the perpetual need to begin from scratch in "introducing" the best German writers to an English-speaking public, and to the curious misunderstandings to which such belated "discoveries" can give rise. The need to enlist the support of Thomas Mann for a project so urgent in itself, and so long overdue, is another symptom of the same state of affairs.

Miss Nott's dislike or–"non-liking"–of Kleist is a different matter. Kleist's stories are not "wordy, philosophical, highly abstract" or "crammed with details"–to quote Mr. Enright's common objection–but they are "humourless" if we take humour to rest on common sense, detachment and equanimity. Among all the extant documents about Kleist's extraordinary life, there is only one striking account of his laughter; according to his friend Zschokke, it took hold of Kleist when he was trying to give a reading of his tragedy *Die Familie Schroffenstein* to a circle of friends. This suggests a very remarkable affinity with Kafka, whom Max Brod reports as being overcome by the same kind of sinister hilarity while reading his work aloud. If the "black humour" of Kafka or Mr. Samuel Beckett is admissible, Kleist was not even humourless–quite apart from the broader, more Shakespearean or Hogarthian humour of his comedy *Der zerbrochene Krug*. Miss Nott's non-liking must be due to Kleist's "frenzy," his addiction to the absurd–his experience of "the strange institution that is his world," as he called it, prompted him to place all his characters in situations of extreme perplexity or stress–and his distrust of reason. More than anything else it is the irrationalism of so much German literature since the Romantics that makes it distasteful to British readers.

6

"Poetry is something more than good sense," S. T. Coleridge once remarked, "but it must be good sense at all events; just as a palace is more than a house, but it must be a house, at least." Coleridge was not talking about Kleist or Kleist's contemporaries, the German Romantics, but he could well have been; his remark explains why the German Romantics are hardly known or read in this country, though their influence on the French Symbolists was decisive and pervasive. German Romanticism, of course, has very little to do with what is meant by the Romantic Movement in England. In his book *German Romantic Literature*[9] Professor Ralph Tymms found it necessary to devote a whole introductory chapter to "Romanticism as a word and concept in German literature." Not surprisingly, for a long time English critics were in the habit of treating Goethe and Schiller–the pillars of German classicism–as Romantics; for Wordsworth, Coleridge, Shelley and Keats would have not qualified as Romantics in Germany.

With few exceptions, the German Romantics were fantastic to a degree quite incompatible with the practice of major English writers; fantastic is the word, for they differed from their Classical predecessors in cultivating free fantasy. Because it was deliberately cultivated, this free fantasy was often an incongruous mixture of imagination and fancy, in Coleridge's sense of the words; if it had been wholly one or the other, the author of *Kubla Khan* could not be cited against the movement in general. Pure imagination is subjective, but its appeal is unlimited. Imagination becomes eccentric only where it is impure. It is the admixture of fancy and reflection that created the phenomenon known as "romantic irony."

The eccentricity of German Romanticism has clearly troubled its British historian. Professor Tymms is prepared to go a long way with the German Romantics, as one can see from the scope and thoroughness of his study, but he refuses to follow them into palaces that will not serve as houses. If anything, his good sense is a little too adamant; he is a reliable guide, but one feels that his initial enthusiasm for the subject has not withstood the long labour of exploration. Perhaps the subject itself was too large. Certainly Professor Tymms took on a strenuous task when he decided to deal with the philosophical, political and aesthetic aspects of a movement that included writers so diverse as Friedrich and Wilhelm Schlegel, Tieck, Novalis, Brentano, Eichendorff, Hoffmann and Heine.

What makes the German Romantics most interesting to modern readers is their investigation–sometimes deliberate, sometimes involuntary–into the subconscious mind. This is the trend that led not only to modern depth psychology, the most anti-Romantic of all the sciences, but also to Symbolism, Expressionism and Surrealism. Novalis and E. T. A. Hoffmann had the strongest influence on their French successors. Professor Tymms is less in sympathy with the political trends of the movement which–with few exceptions–were either reactionary or apocalyptic; reactionary, because the Romantics were in reaction against eighteenth-century rationalism and materialism, to the point of preferring an idealized vision of the Middle Ages; apocalyptic, in so far as they projected this vision into the future. Novalis's essay on *Christendom or Europe* is the outstanding example of this dual tendency. Aesthetically, the German Romantics were divided between the cult of popular art forms–the fairy tale in prose, the *Volkslied* in verse–and the awareness of their own sophistication. Philosophically, most of them were drawn to the extremes of subjective idealism, if not to solipsism, and Novalis's famous critique of Goethe's *Wilhelm Meisters Lehrjahre* is typical in its objection to Goethe's excessive concern with social values and public virtues! Nothing could be further from Professor Pascal's misgivings about the *Bildungsroman* or Dr. Stern's requirement of realism.

Yet just as Kleist's glorification or the puppet's freedom from cramping self-consciousness anticipates many later forms of anti-intellectual vitalism, so the more daring theories and fantasies of the German Romantics anticipated many twentieth-century developments both in and outside Germany. Here again non-social or anti-social inwardness combined "the prophetic and the archaic, the existential and the parochial" to a degree unmatched in any other literature of that period. However reasonable and well-founded our non-liking, reason itself demands some attempt to understand that astonishing combination.

So far I have dealt with British approaches to German literature. (French, Italian and Swiss approaches are rarely as explicitly censorious, though Professor Robert Minder, for instance, is as acutely aware as any British critic of German anomalies, and insists on judging German literature against the background of theological and philosophical traditions, of social institutions and of the class structure. The same is true of Professor Walter Muschg, the Swiss critic, whose passionate commitment distinguishes him from the partisans of "autonomous" scholarship and the analysts of "autonomous" art.) It remains to look briefly at German critical approaches and to ask how far recent critical literature shows the kind of changed perspective that one would expect from the conclusions of Professors Dahrendorf and Kohn.

Until quite recently at any rate, the German word *Literaturkritik* had little of the dignity or authority of the English term. To most Germans it suggested the newspaper *feuilleton* or, at best, the book review section of the more serious periodicals. What the highly respected and far more serious professors of literature professed was not literary criticism, but *Literaturwissenschaft* or *Literaturgeschichte,* products of the scientific positivism and historicism of the nineteenth century. Neither discipline was necessarily associated with critical acumen or with literary grace, let alone with the polemical sharpness and passion of mere literary journalists. By the middle of the nineteenth century the function of the great literary critics proper–men like Lessing, Herder, Schiller and the Schlegels–had been divided between academic specialists on the one hand, professional journalists on the other. Independent critics who belonged to neither class rarely exerted an influence comparable to that of English critics from Matthew Arnold to T. S. Eliot. In several cases–Rudolf Borchardt and Walter Benjamin are examples in this century–their position was precarious, if not positively desperate, and their fame largely posthumous. Germans still find it difficult to understand the literary-cummoral authority of a critic like Dr. Leavis–an authority that has so little to do with academic status or with scholarship in the German sense. It need hardly be pointed out that it was the "purity" and "autonomy" of *Wissenschaft* that made it so easy for German academics to continue their work under National-Socialism; certain adjustments were required, of course, but *Wissenschaft,* basically, was politically and morally uncommitted.

To a much more considerable extent than in this country, too, it was from philosophy and science that literary scholars derived their aesthetic criteria, their methods of research and their strictly "objective" presentation of the results. (The academic thesis is an international survival still imposed on students for reasons which few teachers could now defend.) German literary scholarship, therefore, could develop its formidable pseudo-scientific apparatus and procedures in a sphere as remote from the social and moral concerns of English critics as from controversial issues of any but a strictly factual or methodological kind. True, it was a scholar (if not a philosopher) who did his best to demolish this autonomous, and thus only too amenable, machine; but long after Nietzsche's blasting of both historicism and positivism–fact for fact's sake, method for method's sake, knowledge without end, amen–the irreparably damaged machine could still be used against him. Nietzsche in turn became the subject or object of the very scholarly procedures which he had thoroughly invalidated. Much in the same way, even now the influence of Professor Martin Heidegger's thought and terminology is apparent in a great many works of academic criticism, not only of those poets–Hölderlin, Rilke and Trakl–who have served him as philosophical springboards. Even Heidegger, it seems, is grist to the academic mill; and Professor Marianne Thalmann, in her stimulating study *Romantik und Manierismus,*[10] can quote a sentence from Heidegger's *Holzwege* whose implication for scholars is more deadly than anything in Nietzsche: "Thinking begins only at the point where we have discovered that thinking has no more stubborn adversary than reason, that reason which has been glorified for centuries." Heidegger's own approach to literary works may be in line with this dictum; works of scholarship, including even those as free from pedantry as Professor Thalmann's, are not and cannot be.

Martin Heidegger, of course, was committed enough, even in 1933, when he addressed his students as follows:

> Out of the resolve of German students to hold their ground towards German destiny

> in its extreme trial, there comes a will to the nature (*Wesen*) of the university. This will is a true will inasmuch as the German students, by virtue of the new university statutes, are voluntarily placing themselves under the law of its nature (*Wesen*) and so defining that nature (*Wesen*) for the very first time. To give oneself laws is the supreme freedom. The much-lauded "academic freedom" will be expelled from the German university; for this freedom was false, because only negative. . . . The concept of freedom of the German student will now be brought back to its truth. From it in future will grow the commitment and service of the German students.
>
> The *first* commitment is that to the unity of our people. . . .[11]

And so forth, on to the "honour and destiny of the nation," the "intellectual [*geistige*] mission of the German people," and the three kinds of service corresponding to the three commitments; "labour service, military service and knowledge service (!) [*Wissensdienst*]."

The whole passage, fortunately, defies translation into English. The tense used is that of military orders–a feature of Heidegger's style brilliantly parodied by Günter Grass in his novel *Hundejahre.* The word which I have rendered as "students" is *Studentenschaft*–"studentry," as it were–and its function is to telescope a great number of individuals into a corporative abstraction. Elsewhere these individuals become "*the* German student" and all the German universities become "*the* German university." Heidegger's vocabulary alone accomplishes a *Gleichschaltung* which excludes the very possibility that any one student might have a will of his own. In the passages not translated here, he adds his own existential halo (or miasma) to such established phantom-words as *Geist, Schicksal* and *Wesen;* and the whole performance serves to convince the young scholars of Germany that their freedom consists in conformity, their will in obeying the new laws. The whole performance, too, would be incomprehensible but for the peculiar function of German intellectuals ever since Hegel and Fichte. What Heidegger was providing here is not philosophy, as we understand it, but secularized theology; and the religion it expounds is the religion of nationalism.

This particular commitment is a thing of the past; but the implications both of Nietzsche's anti-positivism and Heidegger's hatred of reason may have contributed to the much greater readiness of German critics, both academic and non-academic, to accept the modernist revolution in literature as a *fait accompli.* Professor Thalmann's study of the early German Romantics is not alone in reminding us that in German literature the roots of modernism can be traced back without difficulty to the eighteenth century and beyond it. At present, therefore, even critics with a mainly historical orientation find it much easier to come to terms with the aesthetic and ontological premisses of modern writers, such as James Joyce or Samuel Beckett, whom many English academic critics still tend to treat as outsiders or freaks. (D. H. Lawrence, so dear to a whole school of English critics, is rarely mentioned in similar contexts, perhaps because his preoccupations were the moral and social ones which remain more characteristic of English than of German criticism.)

Nietzsche also predicted that aesthetic values would come into their own after the breakdown of metaphysical and ethical systems. Recent German criticism has excelled in the stylistic and structural analysis of single works and in the historical study of genres, themes, symbols and forms. The still very marked insistence on the exact classification of genres, especially the shorter forms of prose fiction, may strike some English readers as another misapplication of the methods of natural science to the study of literature: and Professor Benno von Wiese, in his survey of the German *Novelle,* admits that it has become harder to classify recent works. Herr Günter Grass's *Katz und Maus,* he points out, lacks all the characteristics of the *novella,* as which it is described.

Another striking post-war development is the narrowing of the gap between academic scholarship and literary criticism on the one hand, criticism generally and imaginative writing on the other. This is partly due to the prominence of professors who are also writers, such as Professor Walter Jens, who is a classical scholar, literary critic and novelist, or Professor Walter Höllerer, active not only as a lecturer in German, but as a poet, editor, and theorist of new literary movements. Höllerer's critical study *Zwischen Klassik und Moderne* examined the transitional post-Romantic period and showed how many of its writers anticipated the problems, if not the solutions, of later generations. The series of critical books, *Literatur als Kunst,* now edited by Professor Höllerer, includes a study of Clemens Brentano by the poet Hans Magnus Enzensberger–originally written as an academic thesis–and a personal tribute to Kafka by Herr Martin Walser, the novelist and playwright. The effect of such cross-fertilizations can be seen in the readiness of other academic critics to deal with contemporary writing.

A later collection of essays by Herr Enzensberger is a remarkable instance of that passionate commitment of the whole man which is still rarely to be found in German criticism. Enzensberger's *Einzelheiten*[12] suggests analogies not only with German polemical writings by Karl Kraus, Kurt Tucholsky and Theodor Haccker, but with English critics like George Orwell or Professor Raymond Williams. Enzensberger analyses such phenomena as the language of the periodical *Der Spiegel,* the new paperback industry and its sociological implications, modern tourism, and the reactionary tendencies concealed behind the current West German cult of all things *avant-garde.* On all these subjects he is well-informed, eloquent, witty and refreshingly radical. Only the concluding essays–almost a manifesto–on poetry and politics suggests that he has not yet resolved all the complexities of his themes. Here he finds it difficult to face the fact that many of the writers he admires were far from sharing his generous humanism, and that innovation in the arts is by no means inconsistent with beliefs and attitudes of which he cannot approve.

Another non-academic critic must be mentioned at this point, if only because his point of view is as far removed as possible from Herr Enzensberger's. Herr Albrecht Fabri is a purist who believes that no non-aesthetic consideration is relevant to the appreciation of literature. Quite as trenchant as Herr Enzensberger, and an impeccable stylist, he presents his critical insights as briefly as possible, often in the form of aphorisms or dialogues. His aim is to achieve in criticism something of the concentration and elegance of the works to which it is devoted; and his book *Variationen*[13] does give the same kind of pleasure as a well-made imaginative work. His belief in the autonomy of art does not prevent him from showing uncommon psychological acumen, as when he connects the word *Kunst* with the adjective *kühn* (bold) or asserts that "phrase-making is a sort of avarice." Paradoxically, therefore, he becomes a moralist by virtue of his aestheticism; and the boldness and spareness of his own manner succeed better than any argument in convincing us that he is right about art.

Prolixity remains the besetting sin of much academic criticism in Germany. In Herr Manfred Gsteiger's Preface to his collection of essays, *Literatur des Übergangs*[14]–the title points to a preoccupation with flux and change not confined to this critic–we read that one of the essays, on Stefan George's translations from Baudelaire, was originally planned as a full-scale study but has been "reduced to its substance" here. Herr Gsteiger is a learned, but non-academic, critic with extraordinarily wide interests. His subjects here range from mediaeval literature to the style of Calvin and the poetry of M. René Char. Like other prominent contemporary critics, such as Herr Max Rychner and Professors Spoerri, Staiger and Muschg, he writes from the peculiar perspective of Switzerland, to whose literature he devotes a stimulating essay; and one distinction of all these Swiss critics, academic and otherwise, is that they do reduce their critical writing "to its substance."

Professor Emil Staiger's recent book, *Stilwandel*[15] differs from most of his best-known studies in not being confined to the analysis of single works. Yet this seeming concession to the historical approach is deceptive. Like so much German criticism at present, his book traces the evolution of certain literary genres and style, but the emphasis, as ever, falls on the analysis of specific works, many of them works which have received little critical attention. As ever, too, even his remarks on familiar works, like Goethe's *Götz* and ballads, are revelations, not reiterations of stale facts. He deals with the interpretation and application of Aristotle's principle of *mimesis* from Gottsched to the *Sturm und Drang,* with the development of the German ballad from Gleim to Goethe and Claudius; with Herder's merits and shortcomings as a critic, and with Tieck as an originator of German Romanticism. The last section confirms and complements Professor Thalmann's reappraisal of this unequal, exasperating, but nevertheless important writer, whose very vacuity made him a unique receptacle of the *Zeitgeist.*

The philosophical definition of tragedy is the subject of a short but pithy treatise by Dr. Peter Szondi.[16] In the first part he quotes and comments on the theories of twelve philosophers and writers, from Schelling and Hölderlin to Nietzsche and Hebbel. In the second part he analyses plays by Sophocles, Calderon, Shakespeare, Gryphius, Racine, Schiller, Kleist and Büchner with reference to these theories and his own conclusion that tragedy is "a specific form of the dialectic."

The evolution and genealogy of modernism are the principal subjects of several distinguished works. Professor Edgar Lohner's *Passion und*

Intellekt[17] is primarily a study of Gottfried Benn's poetry, but includes an historical introduction extending from the German Romantics–once again–through the French Symbolists to such twentieth-century poets as Jimenez, Signor Ungaretti and Wallace Stevens; and throughout the text there are frequent comparisons with other modern poets, French, Italian, English and American. Some of the same ground is covered by Dr. Kurt Leonhard in *Moderne Lyrik,*[18] though there is more stress on modern German poetry other and later than Gottfried Benn's. The book, intended mainly as a guide for students, includes a little anthology of poetical manifestos, beginning–yet again–with an early Romantic, Novalis, leaping on to Nietzsche and ending with some of the younger living poets. This is preceded by a kind of glossary of current critical terms which incorporates a good deal of hard thinking and sound judgement, as does the main body of the text; and another appendix provides biographical and bibliographical information about a large number of twentieth-century German poets.

Two other outstanding collections of critical essays deal mainly, though not exclusively, with twentieth-century literature. Professor Wilhelm Emrich, best known for his work on Kafka, sees the development of modern art as the inevitable consequence of social and existential factors, especially of the alienation induced by modern industrial environments. Even writers who resist modernism as such, he argues, show the effect of this alienation; and the belief in "absolute" or autonomous art is a necessary response to the meaninglessness of "so-called reality" in the industrial age. This is one of several recurrent and unifying themes in his collection *Protest und Verheissung,*[19] though he too begins with the Romantics and deals with Goethe and Schiller, as well as twentieth-century writers from Hauptmann and Wedekind to Hofmannsthal and Kafka. His rehabilitation of Arno Holz, a name omitted from Dr. Leonhard's list of prominent twentieth-century poets, is consistent with his main argument in the important essays *Literaturrevolution 1910-1925* and *Die Literaturrevolution und die moderne Gesellschaft.*

The title of Dr. Reinhold Grimm's book *Strukturen*[20] points to his dominant interest. In the opening essay he investigates two types of dramatic structure, the pyramid and the roundabout, and shows how the latter pattern tends to take over not only in Brecht's epic theatre, but, long before Brecht, in several plays by Gerhart Hauptmann. On certain matters he arrives at the same conclusion as Dr. Peter Szondi from a starting-point quite different from Dr. Szondi's philosophical premisses. What Professor Emrich has done for Arno Holz, Dr. Grimm does for the translator Karl Klammer (more widely known by his pseudonym K. L. Ammer in connexion with Brecht's notorious plagiarisms), proving that Klammer's translations from Villon, Maeterlinck and Rimbaud influenced not only Brecht, but Trakl and Benn–the last a survey of Benn criticism in Germany and elsewhere.

For all their diversity, such post-war publications permit the conclusion that the gulf between literary scholarship and criticism proper has been very considerably narrowed, if not wholly bridged, partly because the "scientific" and historical approach to literature has lost much of its justification and prestige, and is now regarded as one of many possible approaches at the most. Professor Staiger is a scholar and an academic, but he writes with the sensibility, precision and lucidity of the best prose stylists; and even where his theme is historical, what he writes is literary criticism. Many of the other works touched upon here break through the frontiers of academic disciplines to a new awareness of the indivisibility not only of literature, but of culture. As Dr. Grimm remarks, even "national literatures" are a creation of the nineteenth century; and so, one may add, is the exclusive study of those national literatures. Professor Emrich, in his way, is as passionately concerned with the social, cultural and ontological implications of literature as Herr Enzensberger, the free-lance critic, poet and satirist, is in his.

It may well be that students are not only overwhelmed by the sheer quantity of critical books now available, and stunned by the sheer bulk of those of them which have not been "reduced to their substance," but also baffled by the diversity of current approaches and the frequent overlapping of subjects. Yet certain common preoccupations, like the reawakened interest in the early Romantics, the study of "structures," rather than historical periods, and the wish to understand the evolution of contemporary themes and styles, are conspicuous in works that have little else in common. Several critics who derive from Marxism–the philosopher Professor Ernst Bloch, Professor T. W. Adorno and Professor Hans Mayer, to mention the most distinguished–have made substantial contributions to the West German discussion of such topics both in and outside the universities. An *embarras de choix* is one of the hazards of a pluralistic culture; and it is the acknowledgement of this pluralism–so much in contrast with Professor Heidegger's appeal to the corporative "will" of the students in 1933–which bears out Professor Dahrendorf 's claim that, for West Germany at least, there is no way back to an order based on terrible simplifications.

---

1. In *Encounter,* Vol. XXII, No. 4, April 1964.
2. Hugo von Hofmannsthal: *Aufzeichnungen* (Frankfurt 1959), p. 59.
3. Delivered at the German Institute, London, on 7 March 1964.
4. London 1961.
5. *Encounter,* Vol. XXII, No. 4, April 1964.
6. Cambridge 1962.
7. In *The German Novel,* Manchester 1956.
8. London 1964.
9. London 1955.
10. Stuttgart 1963.
11. Reprinted in *Nation in Widerspruch,* Hamburg 1963.
12. Frankfurt 1962.
13. Wiesbaden 1959.
14. Berne 1963.
15. Zurich 1963.
16. Frankfurt 1961.
17. Neuwied and Berlin 1961.
18. Bremen 1963.
19. Frankfurt and Bonn 1960.
20. Göttingen 1963.

Reprinted from From Prophecy to Exorcism: The Premisses of Modern German Literature *(London: Longmans, Green, 1965), pp. 1-28.*

Germanophilism

Hans Kohn

The Nature of the State

In his *Reflections of a Nonpolitical Man,* Thomas Mann, stressing the similarities between Russia and Germany, asked, "Don't we also have our Slavophiles and our Westernizers (*zapadniki*)?" He alluded to the fact that during the nineteenth century two trends of thought vied in influencing Russia's development. One trend wished to integrate Russia as closely as possible with the West and make it part and parcel of the European development. The other trend insisted, for the sake of Russia and of world civilization, if not of world salvation, on the need of preserving Russia's distinctiveness from Europe, her original Slav character and traditions which were regarded as superior to those of the West. These Slavophiles felt that capitalism and rationalism doomed the West and they opposed to the rotting West the alleged social justice and love of peace characteristic of Russia. The West was torn by party conflict and social struggle whereas Russia formed a true community. The Slavophiles were convinced that the approaching struggle between Russia and the West would, for reasons of her moral and social superiority, end with Russia's victory. Though this Slavophile thought was strongly influenced by German Romanticism, the Slavophiles regarded Germany as forming part of the hostile and doomed West.

A similar struggle between Germanophiles and westernizers went on in late nineteenth century Germany and was intensified after 1914. As in Russia, the dividing line between the two camps was not clearly drawn. Many westernizers harbored Germanophile sentiments, many Germanophiles adopted and helped to develop western techniques. There were, of course, fundamental differences between Russia and Germany, based upon their different stage of technological and economic development and upon their different spiritual traditions. Russian Slavophilism was on the whole deeply Christian, identifying Russia and her mission with the national Russian Orthodox Church. No such identification was possible in Germany. Even Lutheranism was not specifically German though of German origin: for instance in Scandinavia, Lutheranism had developed differently from the German model. Some Germanophiles–before 1933 only a tiny minority–dreamt of a specific form of Christianity or turned to the pre-Christian German gods. Many Germanophiles were found in the Protestant camp. They all shared with the Slavophiles the conviction of their moral and social superiority over the West, of which they knew very little. Their one-sided perspective made them overestimate Germany's strength and treat the West with contempt.

Like Slavophilism in Russia, Germanophilism expressed itself in the emphasis on a state concept different from the western one and on its superior value. Ernst Troeltsch and others have pointed out how German political and social thought after 1806 developed in a direction opposite to that of the general trend of western thought which until then had been shared by Germany. In the eighteenth century politics was considered the art of assuring a good life for man, of creating the conditions which would enable men to live, as they should live, a worthy human life. The doctrine of man's individual rights, including the right of the pursuit of happiness, was a logical outcome of this concept of politics. This concept has continued as the dominant one in the political thought of the English-speaking countries.

German political thought after 1806 came under the one-sided influence of Machiavelli's realism and of the *raison d'état, die Idee der Staatsräson,* a concept for which, characteristically, there is no English equivalent. Politics now became a technique of acquiring, preserving, and expanding power. The state was no longer a society established by men for securing as far as possible the good life for its members and of reconciling conflicts of group interests. Instead it was regarded as an instrument of power which had no higher purpose than itself, a system of domination of men over men based upon force; that was the characteristic definition given by a leading German social scientist, Max Weber (*ein auf Gewaltsamkeit gestütztes Herrschaftsverhältnis von Menschen über Menschen*). At the same time the state as embodiment of the nation or the folk was raised to the highest dignity. The human individual, basic to the western state concept, was replaced by the higher organic individuality of the state or nation.

One of the early expressions of this Germanophile view of the state was presented by Ranke in his *Dialogue on Politics*. He opposed the western liberal view that power was merely an instrument to further the general welfare. The state for him was not a member of an international community, not a "subdivision of something more general, but a living thing, an individual, a unique self. . . . The position of the state in the world depends on the degree of independence it has attained. It is obliged therefore to organize all its internal resources for the purpose of self-preservation. This is the supreme law of the state." Such a theory, as Ranke himself acknowledged, "relegates politics to the field of power and of foreign affairs where it belongs." Each state has the tendency to grow incessantly according to its own unique and specific nature.

In commenting on Ranke's view, Professor Theodore H. von Laue pointed out its momentous consequences for German political thinking. Ranke's view implied a break with western developments; it expressed Prussia's refusal to follow the more pacifist western evaluation of international relations. Ranke's philosophy "was one of the landmarks in the revolt against the West, upholding against the advocates of western liberalism a new Prussophilism which in time grew into a Germanophilism. . . . His theory . . . was carried forward . . . in a destructive but inevitable chain reaction into Slavophilism, Sinophilism, Indophilism, etc. Wherever the standards of the most advanced western nations clashed with local traditions, a similar ideological revolt was the logical consequence of local nationalism. The Prussian and German revolt was the first one. It supplied the essential guides of thought for all subsequent ones. And up to the present it is the most odious rebellion only because it occurred so near the heart of Western Europe, in a situation in which the competition between western universal liberalism and local nationalism was very close."

Germanophilism insisted, to a degree unknown to Christian Slavophilism, on the power character of state and politics and on the precedence of foreign over domestic policy. It shared with Slavophilism the conviction of its country's unique spiritual character, of its moral superiority over the West, and of the legitimacy of its claim to leadership. Adolph Lasson, who was born the year after Hegel's death and died the year before the First World War ended, was a Hegelian who taught philosophy at Berlin University. The *Kantstudien* in 1918 called Lasson "the torch bearer of universal idealism." This strange universal idealist wrote in 1871, in his *Principles and Future of International Law:* "The more powerful state is the better state, its people are the better people, its culture is a superior culture. Whoever suffers defeat must acknowledge that he deserved it. The victor can be sure not that he is good but that he is the better one of the two." Strangely enough, this philosophy of 1871 was not accepted by the Germans in 1918. But in 1882 Lasson was so convinced of the strength of Germany that his *System of the Philosophy of Law* asserted that "the decision of war is just. The victorious people will become the leading, the model people."

In a similar spirit Otto von Gierke, the greatest exponent of the Germanic point of view in the interpretation of legal history, wrote in his *The German Folk Spirit in the War* (1915): "If we achieve our war aims the triumph of our arms will bring about the triumph of the truth. For in world history success utters the decisive word. Even those formerly incapable of being taught this, will now realize that success in war is not an accident, but rather the outcome of eternal laws, in which God's rule reveals itself." Gierke upheld this point two years later in "Our Peace Aims" in which he not only demanded wide annexations but also proclaimed the victor's right to determine the existence of the defeated. At the same time the historian Erich Brandenburg contrasted in "Wilson and World History" (*Tägliche Rundschau,* January 31, 1917), Anglo-American and German concepts of state. To the Germans the state "does not exist to protect the interests of its citizens, it is rather the power organization of a people and has primarily the task of securing the latter's independence, individuality and rank in the world. . . . Consequently the relationship between the state and the individual is here entirely different from what it is on the other side of the Ocean." Nations as conceived by Wilson–or, as Brandenburg forgot to add, by Kant–could organize themselves into a league of nations. That was not the case with states as understood by most modern Germans. The nature of such states lies in their growth as power organizations in sharp competition with other states.

Many people everywhere and at all times have succumbed to the demonic temptations of power, but German intellectuals sanctified this acceptance with the halo of a philosophy which they extolled for its deep or realistic understanding of the alleged forces of history. Modern German thought turned away from rational natural law and the universal ideas of the eighteenth century and conceived universal history as the progressive differentiation of nations according to each one's peculiar character. German historians, while increasing the perfection of their methods, became more and more provincial in their horizons. They knew little of foreign countries and conditions. This was not due to the fact that they did not travel.[1] Goethe and Kant traveled less, and yet while living in small provincial towns their horizons were world-wide, and they were sympathetically concerned with events and movements everywhere. They never regarded Germany's situation as peculiar or unique. The leading German scholars at the turn of the century made little effort to understand western thought. They knew that the West emphasized individual liberty and that it regarded war as a misfortune. They saw therein proof of the superficial optimism and humanitarian sentimentalism of the West. In their enthusiastic affirmation of the German state the German historians educated their people to accept wars as a contest of moral energies. They saw their nineteenth century history, from Goethe to their own age, not as a decline, not as a loss of value-substance, but as a steep ascent to a higher and more permanent reality. This feeling was expressed by Friedrich Meinecke in his first major work, *Cosmopolitanism and the Nation-State* (1907), which he dedicated, in recollection of the "great times" through which they had lived together, to his nationalistic fellow-historian, Erich Marcks, Bismarck's biographer.

This power-proud smugness was as superficial and optimistic as were the most shallow expressions of western liberalism but it contained less consideration for humanity and carried more dangerous implications. In 1870, Rudolf Haym, professor of the history of literature at the University of Halle and biographer of Herder, wrote in the preface to his *Die Romantische Schule* of the "confident and joyous work of progress on the foundations, won as by a miracle, of power-proud national independence." Thirty years later when the last New Year's Eve of the nineteenth century was celebrated in the home of the famous liberal theologian Adolf von Harnack, a neighbor, Max Delbrück, brother of the historian Hans Delbrück, in a spirit of buoyant confidence proposed the toast to "the greater Germany, the greater navy" of the new century.

This spirit of power-proud self-confidence spread from the universities to the secondary and elementary schools, where it became oversimplified. At that time German schools devoted much time to a recent history and its glorious fulfillment. William II, opening a conference of Prussian school principals in December, 1890 called upon teachers to bring up nationalistic young Germans, and not young Greeks or Romans. "More than ever, the instruction in history must provide an understanding of the present, and especially an understanding of our country's position in the present. For this purpose, German history, particularly that of modern and contemporary times, must be stressed." As the result of a study of textbooks of that time, Walter Consuelo Langsam found that "the material presented in books and in the school rooms appeared to have been much more militaristic in spirit than either the government regulations or the courses of study seemed to demand."

This nation-centered self-glorification made the period around the turn of the century a time in which people lived with a feeling of unshakable security and great expectations. This smugness was felt throughout the western world in general; it was nowhere more pronounced than in Germany. The people, from the Emperor to the farm hand, from the university professor to the village schoolmaster, were convinced that history demanded them to enter *Weltpolitik* and that they were the *Weltvolk* of the immediate future. In the preface to the third printing of *Cosmopolitanism and the Nation-State* Meinecke regarded the war of 1914 as "the event which will definitely raise us to the rank of the leading world nation" (*der uns endgültig zum Weltvolke erheben soll*). Yet neither German leaders nor intellectuals were able to think in a world-political framework. The Germans entered the war of

1914 unprepared for the trial of strength which they were to face. They had no understanding of the real and moral forces of the outside world. They overestimated the advantages of sheer military preparedness and of organizational discipline. In all decisions military and technical points of view took precedence over political and moral ones. Under those conditions the defeat in the war came as an unexpected shock. It ran counter, the Germans were deeply convinced, to the laws of history and of divine justice.

Of the innumerable expressions of this Germanophilism, it will suffice to quote one chosen on account of the importance and influence of the correspondents involved: the letter which Houston Stewart Chamberlain, whose book was then the leading best seller,[2] as twenty years later Spengler's was to be, wrote to William II on November 15, 1901. Chamberlain, who was born an Englishman, a well-read and well-traveled author of serious books on Kant, Goethe, and Wagner, thanked God that he had become a German. "It is my deep conviction, which I have gained as a result of my long years of study, of those solemn hours when the soul wrestles with the divine for understanding as Jacob wrestled with the Angel, that the moral and spiritual salvation of mankind depends upon what we call the German (*das Deutsche*). In that moral world order of which Your Majesty has sometimes spoken, the German element now forms the pivot. The language itself irrefutably proves it, for scholarship, philosophy and religion cannot advance one step today, except in German. . . . Because the German soul is indissolubly tied up with the German language, the higher development of mankind is tied up with a powerful Germany, a Germany which is spread far over the earth and everywhere maintains, and imposes upon others, the sacred heritage of its language. The *Realpolitik* of the German Reich which cannot be sufficiently sober and matter-of-fact, nevertheless signifies, at least in my eyes, something different from the policy of other nations. . . . Only a planned organization embracing the minutest detail, not the free civilization of emancipated individuals as it exists with the English speaking peoples, can assure German victory. Political liberty for the masses is an obsolete idea (*hat abgewirtschaftet*); but through organization Germany can achieve everything, everything! In that respect no one can equal her."

As a man of non-German origin Chamberlain was perhaps more enthusiastic about Germany than most Germans. But the sentiments he expressed were typical. He did not understand that Germanophilism could not provide the foundation of a sober and matter-of-fact *Realpolitik*. Intoxicated by the knowledge that the German was different from, and better than, other nations, the Germans discarded Bismarck's sober foreign policy. Adalbert Wahl, professor of history at the University of Tübingen, saw the task of the state in its will to make the unique and specific character of its own people triumph in all political and cultural fields, a philosophy which Bismarck would neither have approved nor understood. Such a philosophy ran counter to the conduct of a realistic foreign policy in Bismarck's style as well as to the building of a peaceful international society as envisaged by Gladstone or Woodrow Wilson.

Conservative Germanophilism

German political development suffered from the absence of conservatives and of liberals in the western sense of the word. Germany had neither a Disraeli nor a Gladstone, neither a Theodore Roosevelt nor a Woodrow Wilson. Its liberals–to name only two of the most famous, Max Weber and Friedrich Naumann–were not primarily concerned with individual rights but with national power. They opposed autocracy and aristocracy not for the sake of liberty but on account of their insufficiency when it came to safeguarding and enhancing Germany's position as a world power. To that end they wished to modernize, and to a degree westernize, Germany's political and social structure.

Before 1918 the liberals had no practical influence. This was equally true of the leading representatives of conservative thought. Whereas the liberals based their program on power politics the conservatives took their stand on cultural and ethical grounds. But they were so reactionary in their political and economic outlook that they lost themselves in romantic dreams far removed from the reality of the modern age. Their influence did not even reach the conservative parties, which in smugness and philistinism outdid the less conservative parties and had become merely the champions of economic interests and social privileges.

One of the remarkable representatives of conservative thought under Bismarck was Paul de Lagarde, professor of oriental languages at the University of Göttingen. In his *Deutsche*

Schriften he proposed the return to true Germanism–which meant the end of interdependence with other civilizations. The adoption of Roman law, the influence of the Enlightenment, modern urbanization and parliamentarism, all of these threatened the very foundations of Germany. Lagarde opposed Bismarck and the new Germany on two grounds: they conformed too closely to the modern pattern and they spurned ethical principles. According to Lagarde the development of personality was a German principle. But Bismarckian Germany was too centralized and bureaucratic, tending to suppress individuality. Only a self-sufficient Germany, whose own individuality, eternal and divine, was developing according to its own laws, could develop German personalities.

In Lagarde's eyes the Bismarckian Reich lacked ethos; it adored success and power. This was not surprising because it had been established by irresponsible followers of Machiavelli. "It will be difficult," he wrote, "to find anything bleaker (*trostlos*) than the fatherland's history between 1871 and 1890." Where were the ideas which could guide national life? Glorification of the state was not one of them, Lagarde insisted, nor was the accumulation of wealth. Rather, both tended to corrupt the true life of the nation, which as a divine creation embodied a high moral principle. What the Germans needed was not so much external as inner unity. To that end Lagarde wished to replace Protestantism and Catholicism, which divided Germany, with a German national church. Such a church would be able to arouse the German sense of nationality, "the invisible force which lives in everything that grows and thrives in Germany, and to bring out in every single German that divine image which is in him from birth." Thus Lagarde's national church would transform the whole nation into a religious body outside of which there would be no salvation for the members of the nation.

Sceptical of the whole Christian tradition, Lagarde clung to the true teachings of Christ without being able to define them. Like many others, Lagarde made a sharp distinction between Jesus on the one hand and Paul and Augustine on the other, regarding the latter two as destroyers of the true Christian spirit. Lagarde never went so far as to wish to revive the old German gods, though he stressed the value of old Germanic traditions. He never took part in the Wotan-cult, which had then become acceptable to a few writers, thanks partly to Wagner's resurrection of the Germanic myths. Among others, the novelist Felix Dahn and the playwright Ernst von Wildenbuch made use of the new cult. In a poem "Allvaters Anrufung" (1884) the latter called upon Wotan to stand always and everywhere on Germany's side and to give her strength in her struggles. "We, of thy blood, God of the Germans, approach Thee; we, lost among alien folk, call upon Thee, Father of All!"

Wir, von deinem Blut geboren,
Gott der Deutschen, nahen dir,
Wir, in fremdem Volk verloren,
Dich, Allvater, rufen wir!

The conclusions which Lagarde drew from his idealistic ethics ran counter to the whole modern development. For that reason Thomas Mann approved of Lagarde in his *Reflections of a Nonpolitical Man.* "One must clearly understand," Lagarde wrote, "that voters constitute a people as little as a canvas and color molecules constitute a painting by Raphael. . . . Individuals as such, that means as egoisms, are in opposition to the people. The people's voice is not heard at all when single individuals speak, of whom the people consist. The people speaks only when the soul of the people (*Volkheit*) speaks through the individuals, that is to say when the consciousness of the fundamentally common roots, common to all individuals, is awakened and finds a common response of the great events of history" (e.g. great wars). . . . "As regards individual laws, the people really has nothing to say, even if everyone votes. Where universal suffrage is regarded as a blessing one does not weigh the votes, one counts them. My students should recognize that this immoral method of arriving at a political decision is immoral."

Needless to say Lagarde was not an admirer of democracy. "The principles of 1789 can find even less application in Germany than in France. They originated out of pure theory, not out of any real necessity or truth. Under Louis Philippe the French lost the merciless honesty of their fathers, who at least had strong convictions and were ready to murder and die for them. Thus these principles have no claims to being universal principles. The specific Celtic taste which they imported from Paris made them for Germans neither more palatable nor more justifiable. Celtic egalitarianism could make Germany, which is by nature aristocratic, only more un-German and thereby unhappy." Lagarde was convinced that in his time liberty and self-government were impossible in Germany. Before Germany could become ripe for self-government a small elite would have to be created through an entirely new system of education. This elite would be selected not by birth but by ethical and intellectual endowment, and working on behalf and for the people, it would be able at some future time to realize self-government for Germany. But of course, Germany could never be governed by the people themselves.

It is important to note that Lagarde's ethical idealism was confined to the Germans. In international relations he indulged in an aggressive imperialism going far beyond anything known in the age of bourgeois imperialism. He was an opponent not only of the domestic spirit of Bismarck's Prussian German Empire, but also of its moderate foreign policy. He demanded the creation of a greater Germany which would include the lands and peoples of the Habsburg monarchy and expand beyond into southern and southeastern Europe. He disagreed with Bismarck's pro-Russian policy. He saw in Russia a force in which all that he disliked, "Catholicism, Judaism and North America," were symbolically represented. He was convinced of the inevitability of a Russo-German war. Such a war would open the possibility of the settlement of German farmers throughout eastern Europe. "By pushing the Muscovites back we could find room next door to us for those Germans who are now lost to us by emigrating to America, and at the same time we could create conditions for an independent, non-Russian development of the southern Slavs which would thereby no longer be dangerous to us. . . . May Russia be kind enough to move voluntarily some five hundred miles into Asia where there is room enough. May she give us sufficient access to the Black Sea so that we can settle our beggars and peasants in Asia Minor. If Russia does not accede to our wishes, she will force us to exercise the right of eminent domain, and that means war. . . . This policy is somewhat Assyrian, but there is no other alternative for us."

Lagarde's fundamentally unpolitical ideas about Germany were shared by the author of a book which appeared anonymously in 1890. Entitled *Rembrandt As Educator. By a German,* it aroused immediate and widespread attention. In the year of its publication it went through thirteen printings. The following year the thirty-seventh much enlarged and revised edition was published. Though the book was widely discussed in the 1890's and enthusiastically supported by Rudolf Eucken, a popular professor of philosophy at the University of Jena, it really came into its own only after 1918, a decade after the death of its author, Julius Langbehn. What made him popular after 1918 and prevented his full success in the 1890's was his insistence upon race as a decisive factor in human life. Langbehn rejected the division of nations according to political frontiers, history or language. "Blood is mightier than political nationality and mightier even than language; blood affinity inescapably produces spiritual affinity." Langbehn concluded from his assumption that blood determined men and that inborn qualities were more important than acquired ones. Upon this hereditary element rested, according to him, the natural superiority of aristocracy as a social-political system over democracy.

In his emphasis on race Langbehn went far beyond Lagarde. He also had no part in Lagarde's Greater Germany program with its eastward expansion. Langbehn was a Low German, born in the then Danish Schleswig-Holstein. The Low Germans were for him the true born aristocrats. His racialism was distinctly Low German, not German, and the Low German race included the Dutch and a large part of the English, and even New Englanders. "Bismarck, Cromwell, William of Orange, Shakespeare, Rembrandt, Beethoven–two Germans, two Dutchmen, two Englishmen–these are the most beautiful flowers and leaves in this [Low German] wreath . . . and this glorious wreath circles the North Sea, the Low German Sea."[3] He contrasted the Low German spirit with that of Berlin-Borussia which, through Bismarck, had triumphed in Germany. In Prussia, Slavic, French, and Jewish influences corrupted the Low German character. Prussian discipline was good but it had brought with it arrogance, brutality, a lack of moral seriousness and the irresponsibility of the rulers. Langbehn regarded William II as a man who dissipated the inheritance of his ancestors. "Do you know of a German intellectual," Langbehn asked, in November, 1900, "who strongly and seriously opposes this personality which now radically dominates Germany? I do not know of one. And can you understand the consequences of this? I can. The people is becoming demoralized and brutalized if they are not so already." Langbehn found the atmosphere in Bismarckian Germany soul-destroying. "Present day Germany succumbs more and more to an increasing moral rottenness. I feel neither the inclination nor the calling to counteract this. Certain historical processes cannot be arrested. May the well-deserved curse be fulfilled."

Langbehn put his hope in the German youth. "At the time of the old *Burschenschaft*, German youth rose for the ideal interests of the fatherland," he wrote. "It fought hostile forces in Germany's inner life and thereby prepared a later national resurgence. Today the situation in Germany is such that a similar impulse is required; some signs even point to this possibility." Langbehn appealed to the German youth–and to that end helped disseminate Lagarde's writings–to form a new nobility, an elite of social aristocrats who would put upon their banner two words: German honor. German honor meant above all a struggle against materialism, against the capitalistic mentality, against the mechanization of intellectual life, and against the typically German educated barbarian. Art seemed to Langbehn superior to scholarship, which was mechanical, abstract and international. "Everything now depends," wrote Langbehn, "on the preservation of the continuity of folk life. It is a principal task of our day to dig ancient folk rights out of the soil, and one of the most important fundamental rights of the German folk is its right to a thoroughly native art, a thoroughly native intellectual life. Therein the German heart must be the determining factor." But Langbehn insisted also on measure and moderation as a criterion of all true art and opposed romantic ecstasy. For that reason he dismissed Wagner. "Wagner wishes to dominate and he dominates, but for how long? . . . Wagner does not offer simplicity and quiet greatness and yet these are the core of all true art and of all folkdom. That stunning and intoxicating element which is so characteristic of Wagnerian art is entirely un-German. He out-Meyerbeers Meyerbeer."

In the later editions Langbehn altered two of his original positions. On the one hand he denounced Jewish influence more strongly; on the other hand his attitude toward Christianity became more positive. Born of a Protestant family–his mother was a pastor's daughter–Langbehn left the church at the age of twenty-four and turned against Christianity. After the publication of his book he came under the influence of his fellow Holsteinian Momme Nissen, who in 1900 became a convert to Catholicism. Living as a hermit and shunning all political activity, Langbehn abandoned his emphasis on race before his death in 1907. Yet his book had a greater influence on German youth after 1918 than Lagarde. Before Nissen–Langbehn's literary executor–died, in 1943, the book had reached its ninetieth large printing.

A third conservative thinker was Konstantin Frantz, the son of a Protestant pastor. For many years in Prussian governmental service, he left the service and Berlin in 1873 and withdrew to Saxony where he died in 1891. Frantz became Germany's foremost advocate of federalism and thus gained in influence after 1945. Though he was a declared enemy of Bismarck's Reich, he was neither a democrat nor even a friend of a moderate constitutional monarchy. Bismarck's Germany was not a true Reich, he complained, but imitated France's political and social immorality, becoming an eastern replica of France, *ein östliches Frankreich*. In a mad power-drive Bismarck's empire had abandoned German morality and the German principle of federation. Yet a true federation of all central European peoples, not their annexation by Prussia, was demanded by the world situation.

Frantz regarded the United States and Russia as the two real great powers of the future; he felt that only a federated central Europe under German leadership could check their imperialism. He wished to recreate the German Confederation which would include Germany and the Habsburg lands as the nucleus of a wider central European federation. There were undoubtedly sound elements in Frantz's political vision. He believed in the federal principle on all levels of political life. He demanded a friendly relationship between the Germans and the western and southern Slavs, especially the Poles, and respect for every nationality. He wished to found politics on a moral basis which in his case was not purely Germanic as it was with Lagarde, but Christian and universal. "Where will it lead us if we replace the Gospel by a so-called *Realpolitik* which divests itself in principle of all ideal demands and strives only for national power and greatness and wishes to confine our mind within the narrow sphere of alleged national interest? It will certainly not lead us to a system of peace. . . . Good God, what is not being done in the name of progress, even if it leads to catastrophe! But what are your Germanias, your Borussias, your Berolinas, and similar images which you call up before the eyes of the nation, so that it will pay homage to it? What else but the most tasteless inventions of artificial refurbished paganism. And the sacrifices which these new idols will demand will be human sacrifices!"

Frantz not only rejected modern nationalism; he also rejected democratic constitutionalism and demanded the return to a true or premodern national economy based upon transformed medieval institutions. The Prussian state, even before Bismarck, appeared to him, as it did to many German liberals, to be an embodiment of modern principles in economy and administration. Whereas the liberals praised Prussia for it, Frantz blamed Prussia for undermining "the Christian-Germanic principles." In his pamphlet "National Liberalism and Jewish Domination" (*Der National-liberalismus und die Judenherrschaft*, 1874), he saw Berlin as the center from which the Jews and the stock exchange dominated Germany. The year 1866 meant in his eyes the final triumph of the pro-capitalist, pro-Jewish policy. "This most desirable situation for the Children of Israel we owe to Herr von Bismarck who has done more for them than has ever been done before." Frantz maintained that by descent and tradition a Jew always remained a Jew and that the Jewish religion was inseparably tied up with Jewish nationality. Therefore he saw only one solution, to exclude the Jews, who were by nature aliens, from German life and to have them lead their own segregated life. The violent anti-Semitism of Frantz was not religiously or racially motivated: it had its roots in his rejection of modern ideas of liberalism and emancipation. In the same way his concept of Europe was not that of Nietzsche or of the good Europeans: it was antiwestern and excluded not only Russia, but also France and above all England. It was a Germano-centered Europeanism based upon antiliberal foundations, a romantic longing for a renewal of the medieval nonnationlist Holy Roman Empire, pacifist and Christian. In his utopian way Frantz longed for the rebirth in Germany of a deep and authentic Christianity, freed from divisive church ties, a Christianity based at the same time on exact science. Through federation and true religion Germany would point the way for mankind. Frantz concluded his *Federalism as Guiding Principle for the Social, Political and International Organization* (1879) by quoting Friedrich Gentz: "Europe which fell through Germany's fault, shall rise up again through Germany."

Though some of the ideas of the Germanophile conservatives bear a resemblance to some National Socialist ideas–and how could it be otherwise?–it would be a profound mistake to see in these romantics forerunners of National Socialism. Their ethos and their concern with cultural and spiritual values were entirely alien to National Socialism. The conservatives were profoundly opposed to the vulgar adoration of the masses, of technology and organization which characterized the National Socialists, in spite of their authoritarianism, as it characterizes Communism. But by their hostility to western liberalism, by their disregard of the fundamental importance of the modern rights of man, these conservatives contributed to that mental and moral confusion, out of which later, when war and chaos had brutalized the masses, a mass movement could grown from which they would have shrunk in horror.

Yet even without the National Socialist last act of the tragedy Germanophilism had a dangerous implication. It emphasized, as Slavophilism did, uniqueness (though not always on racial grounds) and separate destiny. Germany had the task of regenerating Europe, so Frantz believed. George's disciple Friedrich Gundolf, himself a scholar of high rank, spoke for many highly cultured and prominent Germans at the turn of the century when he wrote, comparing Germany with the West: "Only Germany is not yet 'completed'–how often did this incompletion torment and intimidate us, when we faced the form, the sureness, the perfection of the Latins and the Celts! Around all German figures there seemed to hover a chaos of yet indeterminate forces. But our people, the only people in possession of a wealth that is still intact and formless and, at the same time, of a creative force to mould that wealth, the only people, in short, which is still young, is thereby entitled and in duty bound to regenerate Europe." A Russian Slavophile could have written in the same terms about Russia.

Liberals and the Power State

More disturbing than the failure of the conservatives to understand western thought, was the similar failure on the part of the German liberals. The depth of the misunderstanding is indicated by the fact that even in the German Federal Republic of the 1950's Ernst Moritz Arndt is apparently regarded as a liberal. It was Arndt who wrote in his *Germany and Europe* that "Germany needs a military tyrant who is capable of exterminating whole nations."

When we think of influential and representative liberals at the beginning of the twentieth century, the names of Friedrich Naumann and Max Weber come to mind first. Both were men of high personal integrity, both, with a perspicacity rare among the members of their class, were interested in social reforms which they regarded, however, as a means to strengthen the power-state. There was no philistine smugness in their views. They were critical of the government and the people and fully understood the need for modernizing Germany's political and social structure. But the idea of the German power-state was central to all their thought. They explained the emphasis upon the need of growing national power–realistically, not ethically–by pointing to Germany's uniqueness. They believed that Germany, as a stepchild of history, had come very late into her own and that as a stepchild of geography she found herself in a most vulnerable location.

Of the two men Weber was the younger and more influential. The son of a National Liberal member of the Reichstag, Weber studied jurisprudence and became one of Germany's leading scholars in the social sciences. He never questioned, as Frantz did, the German power-state as constituted by Bismarck. Throughout his life he differed from Bismarck by being, like Lagarde and Frantz, anti-Russian. From 1892 on he was critical of the Kaiser and also became critical of Bismarck's legacy, not because he saw any flaw in its fundamental conception but because he became convinced that Germany as constituted in the 1890's was not strong enough to succeed in carrying out her mission as a great power.

As a student in Berlin Weber listened to Treitschke. In 1887, in a letter to his uncle Hermann Baumgarten, who was highly critical of Treitschke's influence upon the students, Weber defended Treitschke by putting part of the blame upon his fellow students. His characterization of the young generation in the late Bismarck period agreed with Nietzsche's and Lagarde's strictures: "If among my contemporaries there did not exist the adoration of militaristic and other ruthlessness, the cult of so-called realism and philistine contempt for all those aspirations which hope to reach their goal without appealing to the worst side of men's character,–then the innumerable and often harsh cases of one-sidedness, the passionate struggle against other opinions, and the predilection, under the powerful influence of success, for what one calls today *Realpolitik*, would not be the only impression which the students take away with them from Treitschke's lectures. Under these conditions, however, Treitschke succeeds in degrading serious and conscientious work, which is interested in truth alone. He calls forth a boorish self-conceit (*flegelhafte suffisance*), which becomes insupportable here even in conversation, and an unusual coarseness (*ungemeine Roheit*) in judging everything which is not purely opportunistic."

In the atmosphere of uncritical adoration of the German regime which prevailed in academic circles, Weber was one of the very few to foresee the catastrophe to which the Kaiser's regime was leading Germany. On December 14, 1906, he warned Naumann against supporting the Emperor. "The degree of contempt with which we are met as a nation abroad (in Italy, the United States–everywhere), and justified contempt–that is decisive–because we tolerate *this* regime of *this* man, has become a factor of greatest importance in world politics. We are becoming isolated, because this man rules us in this way, and *because we tolerate and excuse it.*" Weber knew where the responsibility lay: not only with the Kaiser "who was dealing with politics from the point of view of a young lieutenant," but with the whole system of sham-constitutionalism and with the Conservative Party, which prevented its change. "The dynasty of the Hohenzollern," he wrote again to Naumann on November 18, 1908, "knows only the corporal's form of power: to command, to obey, to stand to attention, to boast." But the fault was not the Kaiser's alone. "Don't overestimate the quality of the person; it is the institutions and your lack of temperament, which are responsible. Both are the result of Bismarckism and the political immaturity which it promoted. . . . Bismarck's terrible annihilation of all independent convictions among us, is the reason, or one of the main reasons, of all the defects of our situation. But do we not bear at least the same responsibility for it as Bismarck does?"

Yet Weber never doubted the principles on which Bismarck and the Hohenzollern had established the Reich of 1871. The *Machtstaat* idea was, as J. P. Mayer, the great student of Toqueville, writes, the *Leitmotif* of Weber's thought, it never changed throughout his life and it survived the downfall of the Hohenzollern monarchy. "Bismarck's example made Weber understand the lesson of Machiavelli's *Principe*." In reality, Weber, like most German scholars, never understood the implications and limitations of

Machiavellianism. He was "unable to see the moral element inherent in any political power."

As a young man Weber joined the Pan-German League and the Association for Social Policy (*Verein für Sozialpolitik*). The latter was founded by the "socialists of the cathedra," professors who advocated an active interest in the betterment of the workers. These men regarded the struggle against English and French economic and political liberalism as the mission of Germany, whose ethically superior national social community confronted the individualistic or atomistic democracy of the West. The Association sought, as its program stated, the union of state, people, and economy for the advancement of national greatness. One of its moving spirits was Adolph Wagner, whose nationalism, according to Professor Evalyn A. Clark fused irrational romanticism, ruthless *Realpolitik,* Pan-Germanism, and racialism. He taught economics in the 1860's at the University of Dorpat (today Tartu in Estonia) then a town in Russia's Baltic provinces inhabited mostly by Germans. From his association with the aggressive nationalism of the borderland, Wagner took over its insistence on the supreme importance of maintaining and spreading one's own national language and destroying that of the enemy nation by means of schools and economic pressure. From Treitschke and the whole climate of opinion of *Machtpolitik* and social Darwinism, Wagner appropriated the belief in the forcible assertion of national superiority. "The nation must assert its right over all individuals within it and prove its right to existence among other nations by a war of all against all in which only the stronger survive."

In 1870, when Wagner was called from Dorpat to the University of Berlin, he published *Alsace-Lorraine and Its Recovery for Germany,* a pamphlet whose point of view was too extremist even for Treitschke. It claimed Germany's right to bring all people of Germanic descent–the Dutch, the Flemish, the Swiss, and others–home into the new German Reich. The same spirit of Pan-Germanism animated Wagner's *Vom Territorialstaat zur Weltmacht* ("From Territorial State to World Power," 1900) and *Gegen England* ("Against England," 1912). But his outlook was broader than that of most Pan-Germans. He was sincerely interested in improving the lot of workers and peasants: the workers to wean them away from Marxism to patriotism, and the peasants because he saw in them "the fountain of youth of our military power."

In 1878 he helped Pastor Adolph Stöcker, court chaplain in Berlin, found the Christian Social Workers Party. Stöcker combined a thoroughly conservative point of view with modern mass agitation methods. He wished to prevent the Marxist social revolution by sound social reforms, based on a Christian foundation. He saw, as did Frantz, Marxism, liberalism, capitalism, and the Jews as the enemy, finding a common root in all four of them. He became, as Professor Koppel S. Pinson called him, "The most volatile, stormy, and controversial political agitator and demagogue of the Second Reich. In this agitation anti-Semitism was his most formidable weapon." Stöcker was largely responsible for the Conservative Party adopting anti-Semitism as part of its platform. "Previously anti-Semitism had been represented," a German writer quoted by Pinson remarked, "only in various small splinter parties; now it became the legitimate property of one of the biggest parties, of the party nearest to the throne and holding the most important positions in the state. Anti-Semitism had become close to being accepted at the highest level of social respectability." The alliance between the Conservatives and Stöcker did not last. In 1887 a political party basing its program entirely on anti-Semitism competed for the first time in the Reichstag elections.

In 1881 Friedrich Naumann, a Lutheran pastor's son who himself became a pastor, helped Stöcker to found the nationalist and anti-Semitic German Student Association. Later on Naumann abandoned Stöcker's ostensibly Christian outlook. Under Max Weber's influence, he no longer regarded politics as applied ethics, but as a method to assure Germany's power position. He developed into "a nationalist, whose lifetime of public service sought its object in strengthening the German nation." One of the ways to strengthen it was to win the adherence of the workers, whose importance in modern industrial society he fully understood, to a sense of civic responsibility and awareness of the importance of the power-state.

Weber's inaugural lecture at the University of Freiburg (1895) changed Naumann's outlook. In this lecture the brilliant young economist discussed the relationship between the nation-state and political economy. Characteristically he started from the nationality conflicts in Prussia's eastern provinces, the economic and social struggle between the Germans and the Poles. He proclaimed Germany's right to strengthen and broaden the German character of the Polish provinces. The economic and social policy of the nation-state must be governed by national egotism, the famous *sacro egoismo,* as the Italian nationalists called it. "It is not our task to pass on to our descendants peace and human happiness," Weber said, "but the eternal struggle for the maintenance and enhancement of our national way .... The power and interests of the nation ... are the last and decisive interests which economic policy has to serve.... The national state is for us the secular power organization of the nation and in this national state the *raison d'état* is for us the ultimate yardstick for economic considerations." Therefore the economic policy of the German state and the value standards of the German economic theorists could only be German, making international economic co-operation and scholarship impossible and undesirable.

In her biography of Weber, his widow wrote that he demanded "from economy, technology and governmental machinery first of all, that they be the proper pillars for Germany's great-power-position.... His passion for the national power state sprang clearly from an innate instinct which no reasoning could call in question. The powerful nation is the expanded body of a powerfully endowed man; its affirmation is his self-affirmation." Germany was Weber's ultimate norm. Economic and political leaders were only justified in Weber's eyes if they recalled this fundamental truth to the people. Germany's domestic situation caused Weber to be deeply concerned about the future. The Junker class, which had done so much to raise Germany's power, was decaying and the bourgeoisie and the workers were in Weber's opinion, politically too immature to assume the responsibility for Germany's power-position. "An immense task of political education lies before us," he told his fellow scholars, "and there is no more serious duty for each one of us than to collaborate in the political education of our nation which must remain our ultimate aim." Unfortunately the German scholars were hardly qualified for this task, and Weber's infatuation with the power-state did not make them better qualified.

Looking back upon the road traveled by Germany between 1871 and 1895, Weber in his inaugural address asserted that the unification of Germany was meaningless if it meant the end and not the beginning of German world-power-politics (*wenn sie der Abschluss und nicht der Ausgangspunkt einer deutschen Weltmachtpolitik sein sollte*). At that time Weber was still a member of the Pan-German League. He left it soon afterwards, not because he disagreed with its imperialism but because he objected to its rigid antilabor policy. Twenty years later, during the First World War, Weber fully adhered to his position of 1895. "If we did not wish to risk this war, we might just as well have dispensed with the creation of the German Reich." Like so many others, he saw–and not without justification–that the spirit in which the Bismarckian state was founded conditioned its future dynamic drive for greater power and expansion, an urge for constant growth without concrete, limited political or economic aims. This sheer power drive belonged to the realm of metapolitics, which raised it above the level of reasonable discussion. Naumann well expressed it when he wrote, "You must have the will to conquer something, anything in the world, to be something."

Weber's inaugural address made Naumann change from his emphasis on a Christianity winning and helping the proletariat, to a social policy supporting imperialist expansion. In his weekly *Die Hilfe* (The Help), with its significant sub-title "God's Help, Self-Help, Brotherly Help," he asked in July, 1895: "Is not Weber right? Of what use is the best social policy if the Cossacks are coming? Whoever wishes to concern himself with domestic policy must first secure the people, fatherland and frontiers. We must consolidate national power." To Naumann, socialism made sense only when it was linked with German nationalism. It must recognize the precedence of foreign policy.

In 1896 Naumann founded the National Social Party. In discussing its program Weber protested against the humanitarian and Christian elements which then still existed in Naumann's draft. "We must face without illusion the one fundamental fact," Weber insisted, "the inevitable eternal struggle of men against men on this earth." Social Darwinism, then fashionable throughout the western world, made a deep impression on Naumann and Weber. They did not apply it so much to economic life as to international power-politics. When Hellmuth von Gerlach attacked Prussia's policy against her Poles, which reduced the Poles to second class citizens, Weber countered that the opposite was true: "We alone made out of the Poles human beings" (*Wir haben die Polen erst zu Menschen gemacht*). Such views expressed by leading German liberals who today are regarded as representative of German liberalism help one to understand the German catastrophe.

The membership of the Pan-German League did not consist, as is often assumed, mainly of Prussian Junkers, but of the academic intelligentsia and the upper middle class. Naumann himself, though he had nothing in common with the Pan-Germans' reactionary antilabor views, agreed largely with their foreign policy. His sincere domestic liberalism supported an illiberal imperialism. "Before 1914," Professor William O. Shanahan writes, "no one propagated the German liberal view more effectively than Friedrich Naumann. To this task he applied his warm and sympathetic personality backed by the resources of his quick intelligence. He charmed his generation with a wit and style previously unknown in German politics or political journalism. To eloquence he added the magic of a lucid prose. His pen could ease Germanic sentences of their pedantic burdens. He could simplify erudition and he could dignify the commonplace. His literary gifts compensated for lack of originality to give his political writing a luster which reflected the hopes and aspirations, as well as the doubts and fears of Wilhelmian liberalism."

Naumann's and Weber's chauvinism was enhanced by their knowledge of Germany's political immaturity. They felt that no real national unity existed in Germany and that no common ideals, no agreed-upon social compact bound the various warring classes, parties, and religions together. They doubted the continuity and vitality of the Reich. They dreaded its enemies without and its inept leadership within. They forgot that their own imperialism created and united their enemies and that despite their grumbling, their half-hearted toleration gave Wilhelm II a free hand as a later generation was to give to Hitler. This longing for true national unity became intensified in the Weimar Republic with its sharper conflict of classes and *Weltanschauungen* and formed the most important single idealistic appeal of National Socialism. It was the weakness of Weber's and Naumann's nationalism–as it was later that of National Socialism–that it had no human or universal ideas to offer to inspire the Germans, but only a *sacro egoismo* and a cult of power for its own sake, adorned by some vague metaphysical ideas about German destiny.

Weber's attitude in the First World War and in 1918 bore out his Pan-Germanism. "It is open to doubt," J. P. Mayer writes, "whether Weber's war aims were *de facto* much different as compared with the war aims of the *Alldeutsche* (Pan-Germans). More subtle they certainly were. Weber still firmly believed in the conception of the State as power-State, a conviction to which he adhered to his death. Germany, the German people was *his* supreme law." When Weber addressed a Munich meeting called by the Progressive Liberals in October, 1916–his first public address in nineteen years–he explained the historical meaning of the war. He saw its cause in Germany's development as a great power which the Germans had to go through, not out of vanity but out of their responsibility before history. Otherwise, Weber feared, the world would have been divided between–and its civilization determined by–the regulations of Russian officials on the one hand and the conventions of Anglo-Saxon society on the other, perhaps with an infusion of Latin *raison.* Against this dreadful prospect the small Germanic peoples, the Scandinavians, the Dutch, and the Swiss, could do nothing, but Germany could and therefore had to fight "because we can throw our weight on the scales of history, therefore we have the duty before history, before posterity to throw ourselves against those two powers which threaten to engulf the whole world. Our national *honor* ordered us to do it . . . and this war concerns *honor*, and not territorial changes or economic gain."

As the war revealed more and more the weakness of the Reich's social and political structure, Weber ascribed the responsibility for the poor quality of Germany's leadership no longer to the Kaiser, but to Bismarck. "Bismarck left behind as a political heritage a nation without any political education, far below the level which, in this respect, it had reached twenty years earlier. Above all he left behind a nation without any political will, accustomed to allow the great statesman at its head to look after its policy for it. Moreover, as a consequence of his misuse of the monarchy as a cover for his own interests in the struggle of political parties, he left a nation accustomed to submit, under the label of constitutional monarchy, to anything which was decided for it, without criticizing the political qualifications of those who now occupied Bismarck's empty place and who with incredible ingeniousness took the reins of power into their own hands." Bismarck's legacy survived the catastrophe of 1918 and so led to that of 1933.

A man of Weber's views could hardly be helpful when the time came to establish democracy and to adapt the new Germany to peaceful coexistence of nations. Weber, who even after the armistice continued to admire Ludendorff, went to see him shortly before the armistice in an effort to persuade him to surrender as a true heroic soldier to the enemy. The hearts of the two men, Weber's widow wrote, "were beating with the same feeling of heroic patriotism" (*schlugen gleich in heldischem Patriotismus*). In his conversation with the General, Weber explained his concept of democracy: "In democracy the people elect their leader, in whom they have confidence. Then the chosen leader says: Now shut up and obey! People and parties are no longer allowed to interfere with him." Ludendorff of course replied that Weber's democracy might be acceptable to him. Weber went on: "Afterwards the people can judge–if the leader made mistakes, let them hang him!" On the strength of this interpretation of democracy Weber insisted on Article 41 of the Weimar constitution, which stipulated the election by the people of the Reichspresident. Article 48 of the constitution gave the president extraordinary powers in times of emergency and these powers became in the hands of Hindenburg the main constitutional instrument for ending the constitution. Yet Weber was regarded by many as the hope of liberalism for the Weimar Republic.

Weber had as little understanding of an international order based on peace as he had of domestic democracy. After the acceptance of the Versailles treaty, he declared that he would from then on concentrate on the one problem: how to get once more a great General Staff for Germany. Before and after the armistice, he repeatedly demanded that should Polish troops invade Danzig or Thorn (Toruń), a German irredenta must be bred (*gezüchtet*) and a nationalist revolutionary terrorism must be set in motion. In talking with students he insisted that the first Polish official who dared set foot in Danzig must be shot. In his eyes it was inevitable (*unvermeidlich*) to follow such a method. Weber's incitement to terrorism (which as the events after 1945 proved was in no way inevitable) was followed, and naturally broadened beyond the limits which Weber might have set.

In a letter to Friedrich Crusius, professor of classical philology at Munich, Weber wrote on November 24, 1918, that Germany had to start anew as she did after 1806, but this time with greater speed and energy. He expressed this with strong Germanophile overtones. "We have shown to the world, 110 years ago, that we–and *we alone*–were able to be one of the great cultural peoples under foreign domination. *This* we shall demonstrate again! Then history, which has already given us–and *us alone*–a second youth–will give us also a third one. I have no doubt about it . . . ." Weber took his reference to a second youth from Treitschke. His insistence that the Germans *alone* were able to be one of the great cultural peoples under foreign domination was mistaken: he could have easily remembered, for instance, that the Italians of the Renaissance were a very great cultural people under foreign domination. In fact, Italians and Germans have never regained as an independent nation the level of cultural creativity obtained under foreign domination. This is of course no plea for foreign domination but a warning against the belief that national independence is necessarily favorable to culture.

The essence of Weber's political thought and the unfortunate influence of his "liberalism" on Germany can best be summed up in the words of a recent American interpreter of Weber and Spengler, Professor H. Stuart Hughes: "In a less extreme and apocalyptic form Weber's vision of the future has disconcerting resemblances to Spengler's." Both were Germanophiles in their attitude toward democracy and the West. "Weber's hankering after personal leadership–along with his ineradicable nationalism–is enough to make us question the whole basis of his political thinking."

Naumann's political thought was far less scholarly but due to his religious roots, more complex than Weber's. "I am a Christian, a Darwinist and an Imperialist," he gladly proclaimed. But of this trinity, Christianity was the weakest member. It abdicated before the supposed necessities of history. Illustrative of his attitude was Naumann's reaction to the famous speech with which Wilhelm II in the summer of 1900 sent German troops off to China to crush the Boxer uprising. He admonished them to take no prisoners and to spare no lives. The soldiers were to leave a record in history similar to that of Attila's Huns, "so that the name German will be confirmed by you in China for one thousand years in such a way that at no time again will a Chinese dare to look askance at a German." These words which were characteristic of many of Wilhelm's utterances, aroused sharp criticism in some German liberal and socialist papers. Naumann, against the protest of Friedrich Paulsen and others, defended the Kaiser. A nation which wished to rise in the world would have to be hard. Politics, he wrote, had nothing to do with applied ethics but were only a technique to use in the power struggle. There was only one part of the Emperor's speech to which Naumann objected. Wilhelm called the war against China a vehicle for the propagation of Christianity, an interpretation of religion by a Christian monarch which Attila certainly missed. The Emperor wished to fuse inhuman power politics with the Gospel. Naumann went to the other extreme. He recognized no connection between ethics and politics. "We fight," he wrote, "because we are a nation, not because we believe in the Gospel. For the sake of the Gospel we send missionaries, for the sake of politics we send naval captains. Crusades are undertaken for the sake of the Holy Cross; our soldiers go to Peking for the sake of our power." That both attitudes, that of the Emperor and that of the liberal spokesman, would degrade Christianity as well as European power politics in the eyes of the Chinese, and ultimately work against both, was beyond the understanding of the two men.

Naumann took a similar position on colonial questions. Public opinion in Germany, as in other European countries at the time, was deeply divided on some of the horrors connected with colonial expansion in Africa. But perhaps it was only in Germany that a leading liberal came forward in defense of heinous inhumanity in backward areas. Against the prevailing liberal opinion in Germany, Naumann joined the Pan-Germans in defending Karl Peters, who, after being an instructor in philosophy at Berlin University, opened up and governed East Africa for Germany. In 1896 a murder charge forced his dismissal. In Naumann's eyes Peters' inhumanity was more than outweighed by his service to German expansion. Naumann regarded Peters as a symbol of Germany's world-power aspirations, which should not be tarnished by public criticism based on moral grounds. The arguments which he advanced–the precedence of respect for the realities of national existence over moral law–were fundamentally the same as those advanced about the same time by the French anti-Dreyfusards. But the anti-Dreyfusards were not regarded as liberals and did not regard themselves as such. Naumann of course had moral justification for his attitude; he proudly contrasted German candor about colonial brutality with British liberal hypocrisy in condemning colonialism while continuing to practice it. That the British liberals from Gladstone on tried to humanize colonialism escaped Naumann's attention.

Needless to say, Naumann supported to the hilt German naval armaments with their accompanying risk of war with Britain. Nietzsche's admonition to "live dangerously" fascinated Naumann and many of his contemporaries. "Expansion means great danger," Naumann wrote. "But without such risks there is generally no political greatness. Without daring no individual and no people has ever become strong." Naumann was convinced that world civilization depended upon Germany's growing strength; no sentimental considerations could be allowed to interfere with it.

The heady wine of imperialism even went to the head of the contributors to Germany's leading liberal intellectual monthly *Neue Rundschau.* It published in 1907 an article which demanded German expansion into the Barbaric lands east of the Vistula. Germany's enlightened national interest required, the Russians were told in a periodical deservedly famous for its intellectual and aesthetic standards, the dissolution of the Russian empire and the subordination of eastern and southeastern Europe to German administration and settlement. It was not the German government nor the Prussian army which harbored such plans; they were discussed openly by German intellectuals. That they frightened Russia–as Germany was frightened not by any concrete plans of the Russian government but by the vague aspirations of Pan-Slav intellectuals–is understandable. They helped to bring about the unexpected Anglo-Russian Entente of 1907 as they had engineered, at least unwittingly, the equally surprising Anglo-French Entente Cordiale of 1904. Professor Sell rightly insists that when after 1918 liberal apologists for Germany claimed that only a small reactionary Pan-German minority before the war had advocated expansionism, the facts were otherwise.

Theodor Heuss warned in his biography of Friedrich Naumann (1937) that one ought to beware of the misunderstanding that democracy was for Naumann a kind of ethical demand (*eine Art von sittlicher Forderung*). Democracy was to him a means of strengthening the nation. Only a democratic Germany, in Naumann's sense of the word, would in the age of industrialism which Naumann fullheartedly accepted, find enough healthy soldiers and skilled workmen to realize Germany's historical task. Only a democratic state would be able to channel the great potential strength latent in the people for the good of the nation. To that end the workers must receive full political rights and their well-being must be assured. These rights, however, could not be based upon the natural rights of man. Naumann despised such theories which he regarded as obsolete (*ein überwundener Standpunkt*). For him rights could only be based on power. A nation struggling for more power could not indulge in the sentimentality of natural law. "In our political activity we do not wish to imagine that we shall thereby enhance the happiness of individuals, . . . our concern is not happiness but the duty we have to fulfill towards the nation in which we were born." Naumann was convinced that he was thinking historically, and that historical thought in the realm of politics was infinitely superior to ethical thought. He never asked himself whether his interpretation of history, which was supported by most German historians of his day, corresponded to the real forces moving the world in modern times.

Under these circumstances it is not surprising that Naumann was among the most determined opponents of the ratification of the Treaty of Versailles. After the ratification he became an advocate of a purified Pan-Germanism. The Germans outside the frontiers of the Reich had to be included into the German nation. The folkish German faith–"*der volksdeutsche Glaube,*" as Theodor Heuss calls it–became Naumann's guiding principle: "The spirit which now unites all Germans from Riga to Strasbourg, from [northern] Schleswig to Bozen [in south Tyrol], is rising up now more mightily than ever before (*der steht jetzt erst recht auf*)!" Thus, a few days before his death, Naumann set the tone for the nationalism of the Weimar Republic.

The German Reich, defeated after an unprecedented effort, was to rise again mightier than ever before. The previously scorned principle of national self-determination, of the natural rights of men and peoples, was to become the instrument of Germany's revenge. Most liberals and socialists in the Weimar Republic refused to accept the eastern borders of the new Germany and the principle of self-determination for the Poles. (The Germans were, however, not the only people to interpret self-determination one-sidedly in their own favor and to deny it to their neighbors.) All of the liberals and socialists demanded the expansion of the Reich to include Austria and thus to enlarge Germany after defeat by much more land and population than she had lost in her Polish, French, and Danish borderlands. None asked themselves whether France, her territory devastated and her population dwindling, could agree to face after her hard-won victory a Germany superior in population and potential power to the one which had been so formidable in 1914. In 1919 German liberal thought was as German-centered as it had been before 1914. The experience of the First World War taught the German liberals nothing. Though in the event of Germany's victory they would have demanded vast territorial gains and huge indemnities, they regarded with sincere horror the loss to Germany of her non-German borderlands, which Germany had acquired by the partitions of Poland and her annexations of 1864 and 1871.

The Drift to War

The war of 1914 and the events of 1917 marked the great divide in modern history. The Second World War only brought into relief what had happened in the previous war, which marked the end of the four-century-old phase of European world leadership. During that period this leadership asserted itself all over the globe and thereby prepared an unprecedented intercourse and interdependence among all continents and civilizations. The Germans and the other great European powers, however, regarded the First World War as another struggle for hegemony in Europe; none realized its true implications. This incomprehension of the character of the war made its resumption twenty years later possible and perhaps inevitable. All the participants in the first war, with the exception of Leninist Russia, continued their pre-First World War policies fundamentally unchanged after 1918.

Before 1914 the democratic forces in Germany were growing in numbers but not in influence. They were the opposition, but the opposition in Bismarckian Germany played a different role from that in western countries. The opposition was not an alternative government but was regarded by the government as a force hostile to the State, even if it represented a majority of the voters. In the last prewar Reichstag elections of 1912 the Social Democrats emerged as the strongest single party. More than 85% of the electorate went to the polls, and of them more than one-third voted for the Social Democrats, who received more than 4,200,000 votes and had 110 representatives in the Reichstag. The second strongest party in votes and deputies was the Catholic Center Party. In 1912 the Progressive Liberals, a democratic group to the left of the National Liberals, received more votes than in any previous Reichstag election. In addition four smaller parties in the Reichstag were in opposition to the Bismarckian Reich–the Poles, with eighteen deputies; the Alsatians, who in the course of more than forty years had not become reconciled to their separation from the French fatherland, with nine; the Guelphs who continued to protest the annexation of Hanover by Prussia in 1866, with five; and the Danes of northern Schleswig with one. Together the opposition parties counted 276 out of a total of 397 deputies.

Twice in 1913 the Reichstag voted a motion of nonconfidence in the Government, in January because of the expropriation of Polish-owned estates for the purpose of settling German colonizers and in December because of the famous Saverne affair. In that little Alsatian town the long smoldering tension between Alsatians and Germans came to a head as the result of the high-handed and illegal behavior of German officers. The military and civilian authorities backed and rewarded the officers, against the protests not only of the Alsatians but of many Germans. The Chancellor who defended the government point of view was Theobald von Bethmann Hollweg, a man of generally moderate and civilian views. Thus once more, to quote Professor Pinson, the camouflage character of German parliamentary institutions became manifest, and the source of real power was still there where Bismarck had placed it, in the Emperor and the high command. Throne and Altar as the seat of all power in the period of Metternich had been replaced by Throne and Army. It was hardly an improvement. "In Prussia," wrote Wickham Steed in *The Times* (London) of January 12, 1914, "the army is supreme, and through Prussia, the army rules Germany. This is the first lesson of the [Saverne affair] for those who lightly imagine the German Empire to be even as other states."

The Saverne affair demonstrated to Europe the military character of the German government and the semicolonial attitude which it assumed toward its Polish, Alsatian, and Danish citizens. Even a conservative professor like Hans Delbrück protested, out of deep concern for Germany's future, against this attitude. He was Treitschke's successor as professor of history at Berlin and as editor of the *Preussische Jahrbücher.* "If there really existed a way to transform the two and a half million Poles into Germans," Delbrück wrote in 1894, "one could then seriously discuss the government's policy. But . . . too many of our German politicians are like this: If only the word national is mentioned, they begin to roll their eyes, pound on the desk, and breathing hard they shout 'energy'! One would think that we are on the verge of declaring war on Russia, of conquering Holland, and of being obliged to transport all our Poles and also our Jews and Social Democrats to Africa." But instead, only some small scale measures were being taken. "In reality we would like to exterminate all the Poles, but actually we limit ourselves to expropriating several hundred Polish estates and paying the highest compensation; we annoy them with some language regulations, we do not appoint Poles to the better civil service posts, and we teach Polish children the German language in an unintelligent rather than an intelligent way. Away with such a policy of pinpricks, which is as unworthy of a great nation as it is useless."

To Delbrück it was inconceivable that less than half a century later the Germans would carry through some of the radical policies which were implied in the big words used at the turn of the century. But he realized that these extreme statements, through they were followed by no real action, did irreparable moral harm to Germany. They proved, as a young German historian Annelise Thimme remarks in her brilliant biography of Delbrück, the existence of a spirit which if unloosed one day would have devastating consequences. The Prussian government, Delbrück wrote, received its proper coloring from the bureaucracy "which always saw only the immediate object, the authority which has to assert itself, the adversary who has to be crushed, but disregards the moral and other consequences which are out of its immediate province (*Ressort*)."

Delbrück was one of the most likeable among the German historians. Like practically all of them he started as an archconservative. As editor of the *Preussische Jahrbücher* he defined its position in 1884: "For the Emperor, against the Pope, against federalism, against parliamentarism and against capitalism."[4] In this programmatic declaration Delbrück did not even mention the socialists. Opposition to them was at that time tacitly understood. Like some other German historians, Delbrück slowly developed toward a more liberal conception, though his heart remained even in the 1920's faithful to the *ancien régime.* But more than other German historians he was sensitive to ethical questions. He condemned the persecution of minority groups not only because of the repercussions such a policy was bound to have on Germany's relationship with her neighbors but because of the deterioration of the German national character which he saw as a consequence of such a policy. "I regard the effect," he wrote in 1907, "of our policy against the minorities on the German national character as equally important and equally calamitous. We are facing the task of developing among us a more refined respect for law and a higher regard for the individual, in which respect we are manifestly lagging behind the English-speaking nations. But the acceptance of the principles which we employ in our policy against the minorities, even if one should regard them as politically necessary, blunt the respect for law among our officials, and in view of the fact that public opinion did not only not oppose but even approved our policy, this border war against the minorities depresses our whole ethical-political life and thus revenges itself upon us." Delbrück took a similar stand against the persecution of the Danish minority. He protested the expulsion of some Danes from northern Schleswig. "Even worse than the brutality which arouses the horror of the civilized world," he wrote in 1898, "is the delusion that we can achieve by such means lasting successes in the struggle among nationalities." Turning against his fellow historian Erich Marcks, who supported extreme measures against the Danes, Delbrück sadly remarked in 1911: "This has been the essence of religious or political fanaticism: that it silences criticism and that it blurs, even on the part of men who are otherwise intelligent and reasonable, the insight into the simplest and most manifest facts."

But Delbrück never doubted that the Prussian German state was the best of its time. Like the other German historians he pressed forward for a German *Weltpolitik.* The continental hegemony achieved by Bismarck was no longer enough. In the interest of mankind, of civilization, of the freedom of the small nations Germany had to break British hegemony on the seas. Delbrück's demand for the construction of a powerful German navy took precedence over concerns for domestic policy and liberty. Later on he was not as incautious as many of his colleagues or Naumann were. Writing in the *Preussische Jahrbücher,* in 1905, he understood very well that it was the building of the German navy and not economic competition which provoked British fears. A defeat in a naval war with Germany would mean for Britain, Delbrück recognized, the end of her great power position. But he was determined that Germany should take a leading role in the future "War of the English Succession," which Max Lenz predicted at the time of the Boer War. Delbrück was convinced that out of England's defeat a new world balance of power would emerge in which Germany would be recognized as an equal by Britain on the seas.

Ludwig Dehio in his *Germany and World Politics in the Twentieth Century,* the most original reinterpretation of the international situation at the beginning of the century, has shown the influence on German *Weltpolitik* exercised by Ranke's theory of continental power-politics. It made the German historians, and through them public opinion, underestimate the strategic and moral role of maritime power. Therefore they could seriously believe that Germany in her war against England would find allies among all the smaller nations. "We hope," one of them wrote, "that sooner or later, other nations who are oppressed by the yoke of English supremacy at sea will also pluck up courage and decide to shake off their yoke. It is our aim to complement the balance of power on land with the balance of power at sea .... The effects of German naval armament are clearly making themselves felt in the peripheral territories of the Pacific. Japan is developing into a position of power, and we may soon hear the cry, Asia for the Asians. The rise of Islam points in the same direction. The dream of a world governed by the white race is beginning to dissolve."[5] It was Germany's duty to help create this future by fighting England and her obsolete hegemony.

No one put it more strongly than Friedrich Meinecke who in republishing Ranke's "The Great Powers" interpreted the First World War as a German struggle against universal monarchy which he accused the British of wishing to establish. "Universal maritime supremacy is only another form of universal monarchy, which cannot be tolerated and must, sooner or later, fail. England is fighting against the spirit of modern development. . . . Her significance as a world nation and a world civilization, which we recognize, will not suffer if the balance of power, which she has tried in the past to restrict artificially within the limits of Europe, is extended to include the oceans and the world beyond. Only then will every nation have the free breathing space it requires."

German public opinion before 1914 was systematically prepared by historians and publicists for the War of the English Succession, for the moral need of a new division of the world, in which Germany had to play the leading role.[6] For her historical mission, and not for the defence of her commerce, Germany needed naval equality with the British. "Although foreign observers often overestimated the power of the Pan-German League in specific cases," Professor Dehio writes, "their suspicions later proved to have been, on the whole, too modest. Though they may have exaggerated the influence of the Pan-Germans in the Foreign Ministry, this influence was indisputably at work in the Admiralty, whose chief, and not Imperial Chancellor, was the man of destiny in the years before the war." The common desire of those Germans who thought about foreign policy–obviously a minority, though their ideas trickled down to the masses through popular journalism–was to eliminate English maritime supremacy.

Germany's hopes of mobilizing the lesser powers in a war against Britain was in vain. Napoleon had harbored similar hopes. He was convinced of the mastery of the world if he could conquer Britain. In this struggle he claimed to represent the interests of mankind and to defend the liberties of all peoples against British universal monarchy. These peoples however did not agree: they feared Napoleon and the French more than the English. The English employed the advantages of commerce and inspired jealousy; Napoleon used the means of war and imposed tyranny. In the chapter "*Du caractère des nations modernes relativement à la guerre*" of his *De l'esprit de conquête et de l'usurpation dans leurs rapports avec la civilisation européene* (1813), Benjamin Constant saw in war the instrument of the past, in commerce that of enlightened civilization: "War and commerce are only two different means of arriving at the same goal–the possession of what one desires. Commerce is an attempt to receive by agreement what one no longer hopes to conquer by force. A man who would always be the strongest, would never think of commerce. It is experience which, in demonstrating to him that war–this is to say, the employment of his force against that of another–is exposed to various resistances and checks, leads him to have recourse to commerce–that is to say, to a more pleasant and certain way of compelling the interests of others to consent to what accommodates his own interest. . . . Carthage, fighting with Rome in ancient times, had to succumb; it had the force of circumstances against it. But if the fight between Rome and Carthage were taking place today, Carthage would have the universe on its side (*Elle aurait pour alliés les moeurs actuelles et le génie du monde*)." Constant warned the French, unfortunately with as little effect as a similar warning to the Germans would have had later, against the spirit of military glory, an ancient and hallowed spirit but one opposed to modern civilization which was animated by the commercial instinct prevailing over "the narrow and hostile emotion which people masked with the name of patriotism." Constant called war a savage and passionate impulse, commerce on the other hand, a civilized and rational calculation. He called upon the French to draw closer to England, "that noble country, the generous asylum of free thought, the illustrious refuge for the dignity of the human race." Though Constant was not a man of lofty character he had a clearer insight into the forces of modern times and the aspirations of civilized people than most German historians who personally were men of much greater integrity.

The German philosopher Max Scheler added a pseudo-Marxian interpretation to the anti-English agitation which later became fashionable. Germany's struggle against Britain, transferred to the international stage, represented the rise of the proletariat whose revolutionary ethos was expelling the bourgeois *beati possidentes* from their paradise. In such a struggle Germany was to be supported, in their supposed self-interest, by all other have-not nations. But this was not to be. The German attitude before 1914 forced Britain into agreements with France and Russia. Before 1914, as before 1939, Britain made repeated efforts to arrive at an understanding with Germany. At both times she was rebuked. When she finally declared war on Germany, the majority of mankind was on her side. Germany's faith that the wind of history was swelling her sails as she set forth against England proved to be a miscalculation.

The War

During the war Germany shifted her main targets. At the beginning there was an upsurge of anti-British feeling. The Germans had expected, and because of their feeling of superiority accepted, war against Russia and France. Twenty-five years later the same attitude prevailed with regard to Poland. However, Britain's declarations of war both in 1914 and in 1939 came as a surprise and–in spite of all the anti-British agitation in Germany which preceded the conflict–were regarded as treachery motivated by envy. "*Gott strafe England* (God punish England)" was the most popular German slogan in 1914. When victory against Britain was slow in coming and when the mighty German fleet proved of no avail and turned out to be a poor investment, the Germans shifted their arguments about their mission and purpose in the war. In his *Der Genius des Krieges* Max Scheler proclaimed that it was Germany's task to unite the whole continent against Russia. The other European nations would certainly realize that only a mighty Germany stretching from the Baltic to the Mediterranean could defend them against Russia's towering threat. In their claim that they were leading and protecting the West against the threat from the East, Napoleon's France and the Germany of Wilhelm and Hitler acted, to quote Professor Dehio, "like the man who sets a house on fire and then invites the other occupants to help him put it out." After 1918 Germany regarded France as her main enemy and German historians like Erich Marcks and Erich Brandenburg hoped to find in Britain an ally against France, while other Germans preached cooperation with Russia against the West.

At the beginning of the war Werner Sombart, one of the leading economists of his generation–once a Marxian socialist–gave classical expression to anti-British feeling. In his *Händler und Helden* he contrasted the nation of shopkeepers with the nation of heroes. The term itself was not of German invention. In his novel *The Young Duke* (1831) Disraeli had referred to the English as "indeed a nation of shopkeepers." As early as the eighteenth century a British economist Josiah Tucker in his *Four Tracts on Political and Commercial Subjects* (1766) wrote: "A shopkeeper will never get the more custom by beating his customers, and what is true of a shopkeeper is true of a shopkeeping nation." Heroes, of course, had interests and habits different from those of shopkeepers. Sombart stressed the ancient and dominant German tradition of love for war, condemned Kant's pacifist writings as senile, and regarded Nietzsche as "merely the last singer and seer who descending from heaven announced to us the tidings that from us would be born the son of God whom he called superman."

Sombart was wrong about Kant and Nietzsche; in his case an economist spurred on by war became himself a kind of dithyrambic singer and seer. "German thought and German feeling," he proclaimed in 1915 in a typically Germanophilic fashion, "express themselves in the unanimous rejection of everything that even distantly approximates English or western European thought and feeling. With deepest disgust, with exasperation and resentment the German spirit has risen against the ideas of the eighteenth century which were of English origin. Every German thinker, even every German who thought in a German way, has always resolutely rejected all utilitarianism and eudaemonism. . . . We must recognize everything which resembles western European ideas or which is even distantly related to commercialism as something much inferior to us."

Sombart dedicated his book to the young heroes fighting the enemy and reminded them that the struggle must go on even after they returned from the battlefield. "I pray that the ideas contained in this book," Sombart wrote at the end of his dedication, "might become the seed which falls on fertile soil and will bear fruit a thousandfold times." Sombart's wish was fulfilled. He praised war as the greatest ethical force and Treitschke as the man who had best described its moralizing influence. "Militarism is a supreme manifestation of the heroic spirit. It is the highest form of union of Potsdam and Weimar. It is Faust and Zarathustra and the Beethoven scores in the trenches. . . . Above all, militarism means the primacy of military interests in national life. Everything that refers to military matters takes precedence with us. We are a nation of warriors. The highest honors in the state are paid to the warriors. . . . All other branches of the life of the people, especially the economic one, serve military interests."[7]

Sombart welcomed the war as Germany's great opportunity to heal the wounds western civilization had inflicted on her before 1914. Before the happy event of the outbreak of the war Sombart confessed that, like so many others, he had been deeply pessimistic about the future of culture. Now everything was changed. Great times were here. "The miracle happened, the war came. A new spirit surged forth out of a thousand sources." It was the old German heroic spirit that had smoldered under the ashes. "We Germans [are culturally independent]. No people on earth can give us anything that we really need, in the field of scholarship, technology, art, or literature. From no people on earth can we learn anything about domestic policy, the constitution or administration. Let us think of the inexhaustible wealth of Germanism which includes every real value that human culture can produce." Sombart had no use for the idea of the good European. He did not wish the Germans to develop into Europeans, but into ever better Germans. "How," he asked, "could a European emerge from a mixture of a heroic German and a calculating Englishman? If a European would emerge who would think half as a shopkeeper and half as a hero, that would mean the elevation of the Englishman but the degradation of the German." That, of course, would not be desirable.

Sombart found it natural for England with her imperialist greed to expand. Germany, he asserted, had no similar desire. She was not driven by greed. "If it is necessary that we expand so that our growing people have space to develop, then we shall take as much land as we regard as necessary. We shall also put our foot where we think it essential for strategic reasons to maintain our unassailable strength. Therefore, if it is useful for our power position on earth, we shall establish naval bases in perhaps Dover, Malta, and Suez. Nothing more. We do not wish to expand at all. For we have more important things to do, we have to develop our own spirit, we have to keep the German soul pure, we have to take precautions against the enemy, the commercial spirit, invading our mentality. This task is tremendous and full of responsibility. For we know what is at stake: Germany is the last dike against the muddy flood of commercialism which threatens to cover all other people because none of them is armed against this threat by the heroic spirit *(Weltanschauung)* which alone provides protection and salvation."

A Slavophile like Dostoevsky might have written in much the same style, only he would have appealed to the truly religious and not to the heroic spirit. Again like the Slavophiles, Sombart proclaimed his people the chosen people of modern times. He showed a certain modesty by declaring that the Germans were "the chosen people of this century." He saw the Germans surrounded by hatred and incomprehension because they were the chosen people. "Now we understand," Sombart wrote, "why other people hate us. They do not understand us but they fear our tremendous spiritual superiority." Like the Slavophiles, Sombart was convinced that foreigners could not understand Germany. But he made exceptions for a very few prominent personalities,–perhaps he thought of Houston Stewart Chamberlain–"whom a kind fate has lifted up to the towering heights of the German spirit" *(die ein gütiges Schicksal in die Flughöhe des deutschen Geistes emporgetragen hat).*

A similar Germanophilism inspired many other German scholarly writings of the period. Max Scheler proved that the openly acknowledged war ethic of the Germans was superior to the cunning business ethic of the English. For spiritual, not for political, reasons Scheler praised the war against England. The war, he wrote, arouses the Christian ideal of love much more than peace does, which is only a nonwar of people who exchange goods and rely on the principle, Do nothing to me and I shall do nothing to you.[8] Scheler was even ready to accept England as a partner in a coalition led by Germany against Russia and the rest of the world–as soon as England was cured of her English malady, a malady which Scheler defined as an overevaluation of commerce and money making, of favoring the natural sciences above the humanities, of misunderstanding civil liberty.

It was quite clear that the views of Sombart and other leading German intellectuals did not make it easy for Germany to win moral support during the war. When Matthias Erzberger, a member of the Center Party, undertook such a task early in the war, he ran into almost unsurmountable difficulties. One of them, as Klaus Epstein, Erzberger's biographer, writes, was "the utter indifference shown to what influential people in the neutral countries thought about Germany. To serve as propagandist for a nationalist, militarist, and semiautocratic country, whose war effort was challenging the liberties and equilibrium of Europe, was to assume a task where great successes could not be expected."[9]

On July 8, 1916, 1,314 intellectuals, among them 352 university professors, submitted a memorandum supporting the most extreme Pan-German war aims. The initiator of the petition was Reinhold Seeberg, professor of theology at Berlin University. Many thousands more sent in their signatures later. A memorandum drafted by Delbrück and opposing extreme annexationism received no more than 141 signatures. Only after the failure of unrestricted submarine warfare in July, 1917, could Erzberger have a very vague peace resolution adopted by the Reichstag and to this Ludendorff was bitterly opposed. But even the moderates who desired a negotiated peace hoped that it would open the door for further advances once Germany had recovered and, above all, disintegrate the western coalition. The struggle of the more moderate elements in the Reichstag to assert themselves did not help; it increased the "hopeless confusion that prevented Germany from developing any coherent foreign or domestic policy." The real power in Germany, though without any constitutional authority, remained in the hands of Ludendorff.

This whole spectacle increased the distrust of German war aims abroad. Returning from a trip into neutral countries, Delbrück recognized that "the fear of German despotism . . . was one of the most effective facts and strongest factors in favor of the enemy," which Germany had to take into account. He asked publicly whether the peace resolution of the Reichstag was ever meant sincerely. Two months before the German collapse Delbrück in vain implored the German government to repudiate the Pan-German demands. Even outside the Pan-German camp, German public opinion insisted at a time when defeat clearly loomed on the horizon upon Germany emerging from the war in so strong a position that no one and no coalition would ever again dare to attack her. Delbrück was one of the very few who dared to point out that a power which was so strong as to be superior to any coalition would represent a permanent and unacceptable threat to the outside world. "The world demands, and has a right to demand," he wrote, "that the German people give it a guarantee, that the Pan-German spirit, the spirit of arrogance, of the cult of power, of paganism is no longer the German spirit." In quoting this passage Dr. Thimme added: "Today we shall hardly be able to say that this was an exaggeration. Rather, Delbrück underestimated the general acceptance of Pan-German thought." The events after 1918 proved how strong a hold Pan-Germanism and Germanophilism retained on the German mind.

Their disastrous effects were deepened by the acceptance of war as the supreme test of human worth and by the praise bestowed upon this attitude as a typically Prussian or German virtue. The defenders of this attitude acted from high idealistic motives. Characteristic in this respect was Walter Flex, a young officer who fell in battle at the age of thirty. Flex, who was born in Eisenach, a city in the Grand Duchy of Saxony-Weimar, embraced the ideals of Prussianism with great moral earnestness. Before the war he was tutor to Bismarck's grandchildren and played an active part in the German youth movement. Among his war poems, the "Oath to the Prussian Flag" achieved the greatest popularity. It idealizes the man who overcomes all love of self and every trace of self-will and devotes his whole life and soul to Prussia. The two lines

> *Wer auf die preussische Fahne schwört,*
> *Hat nichts mehr, was ihm selber gehört.*

(A man who swears an oath on the Prussian flag no longer has anything that belongs to him) were an inspiration to many young Germans before and after 1918.

Flex became even more popular through his war novel *The Wanderer Between Two Worlds* (1916).[10] It is the story of his friend Ernst Wurche, who was killed in battle and to whose memory Flex dedicated the book. When Flex visited the mother of his dead friend, she asked him softly after a long silence: "Did Ernst participate in an attack *(Sturmangriff)* before his death? I nodded yes, 'That was his great wish,' she said slowly, as if she rejoiced, despite her suffering, that something about which she had been long anxious had been fulfilled. A mother certainly must know what the deepest wish of her child is. And that must have been a deep wish, about whose fulfillment she had been anxious even after his death. Oh you mothers, you German mothers!"

From the novel, which became a favored book with the youth of Germany, two sentences were widely quoted: "To serve as a lieutenant means living as a model for one's men; to show them how to die is of course only a part of this model life. Many men are capable of showing others how to die–but it will always be a much finer achievement to show them how to live. It is also more difficult. . . . How to remain pure and yet to grow to maturity–that is the finest and most difficult thing in the art of living." Wurche always carried in his knapsack a small volume of Goethe's poems, Nietzsche's *Zarathustra,* and the New Testament, all of them well-thumbed. He had intended to become a Protestant pastor and had just begun his theological studies when war broke out. His case, Professor S. D. Stirk points out, proves the close connection of the best kind of Prussianism with a definite and confident Protestant piety. Professor Pinson has shown the influence of pietism on the rise of German nationalism. There was in German Protestant nationalism a deeply ingrained religious enthusiasm and earnestness.

The elevation of nationalism to an almost

The elevation of nationalism to an almost religious personal pathos has rarely been so clearly experienced as by some idealistic German youth in 1914. Flex himself has referred to the religious character of his national devotion in a letter: "I am today as willing to volunteer for the war as on the day it broke out. I am willing not, as many think, out of national but out of ethical fanaticism. What I wrote of the eternity of the German people and of the world-saving mission of Germanism *(der welterlösenden Sendung des Deutschtums)* had nothing to do with national egoism but is an ethical faith which can realize itself in the defeat or as Wurche would have said, in the death in battle of a people. . . . I have always maintained that human development reaches its most perfect form for the individual and his inner development in his love for his nation. I believe that the German spirit reached in August, 1914 a height no other people had previously seen. Happy the man who stood on this peak and does not need to descend again. This is my faith, my pride, and my happiness, which lifts me above all personal worries."

As religion has done in the past, nationalism too can misuse and pervert some of man's noble sentiments. A cosmopolitan tolerance alone can prevent these misuses and perversions. But Germans were little inclined to such a tolerance, for which pragmatic people–or shopkeepers as Sombart called them–are perhaps better predisposed. Defeat in the First World War did not disillusion the Germans in their ideals. On the contrary, it confirmed them in their belief in their distinctness and in the moral superiority over their victors. Again this one-sided perspective led them to overestimate their strength and to despise and challenge the West.

---

1. When, in 1904, Friedrich Paulsen, professor of philosophy and education at Berlin University, traveled in England, a country to which he had always felt drawn in so many ways, the reactions of this truly liberal scholar were typically German. "In Germany, far into the middle classes, people have the idea that the policeman's business is to order them about; in England, everyone regards him as a man who is there for everyone's safety and protection. In England, everybody is a citizen, in Germany, everybody is a subject. At least another century will have to go by before we can attain this self-assured attitude toward the State. Perhaps we shall never attain it. The relation of a German to the State is based principally on the place he holds in the army, whereas that of an Englishman is based on the part assigned to him in the political and judiciary organization of the State. So long as that holds good in Germany–and I do not see how it could be altered, our external political situation being what it is–the great majority of Germans will continue to identify the State with the person of the supreme war lord on the one hand and with that of the noncommissioned officer on the other. And after all it cannot be denied that our military discipline has its good side, too; it has been remarkably successful in instilling into our population a taste for good deportment, orderliness, and cleanliness. In England I have heard my wife exclaim more than once: 'One would have to go a long way in Germany to see such slovenliness among both sexes of the lower classes!' "

2. Even the English translation, *Foundations of the Nineteenth Century,* went through five large printings between November, 1910 and June, 1914.

3. Langbehn loved Venice and found there a people akin to the Low Germans. "It is a truly aristocratic city. If Rembrandt had not been a Dutchman he would have deserved to have been a Venetian. That is equally true of his person as of his art. At the mouths of the Po and of the Rhine the inhabitants combine the strong sense for home which is characteristic of inhabitants of marshlands with the wide horizons which characterize seafaring people. . . . Venice the single aristocratic city of former days, faces North America, a whole democratic continent of today. Yet it should not be difficult for the present Germans to choose between these two models. Venetianization is superior to Americanization."

4. *"Für die kaiserliche Partei, gegen den Papst, gegen den Partikularismus, gegen den Parlamentarismus und gegen den Kapitalismus."*

5. In this passage, written in 1916, Otto Hintze meant by the white race primarily the English. Other German historians, like Erich Marcks, tried to frighten the British with the claim that the United States was more dangerous to England's future than was Germany. Marcks thought that the First World War might be followed by a struggle between the two Anglo-Saxon empires for Canada and Australia.

6. The desire to replace England went back to the middle of the nineteenth century, though it was then expressed, not by scholars and certainly not by responsible politicians, but by men of letters. A prominent Viennese literary critic, Ferdinand Kürnberger, published in 1855 a novel *Der Amerikamüde,* in which he portrayed a German immigrant disenchanted with America. Kürnberger himself was never in the United States. His portrayal of the country, so different from

that of Goethe, was influenced by the unhappy German poet Nikolaus Lenau, who had gone as a pioneer to the wilderness on the banks of the Missouri river and became understandably disillusioned. America seemed to him a vast continent where men and culture were doomed to decay. He anticipated Spengler's judgment when he characterized American life and institutions as typical examples of *Bodenlosigkeit,* lack of rootedness in the soil or nomadism.

Kürnberger's hero shared Lenau's disgust with the United States. Living a quarter of a century later and having shared in the nationalist exuberance of 1848, he was also an enthusiast for Germany's unity and power. Envisioning the future of America and his share in it, he wrote: "What the German farmers in Pennsylvania were able to do unconsciously, to preserve German life through a whole century so strongly that even today whole communities of theirs do not understand one English word, should I be less able to do, with my enthusiastic consciousness of German kind and culture? I am not afraid of it. No, I shall last, a German in Yankeedom, and the fall which I foresee for this racial mixture can worry me . . . little." What seemed a writer's phantasy around the middle of the nineteenth century, Germany's rise in place of England, became at the end of the century the concern and desire of influential German public opinion. *Der Amerikamüde* is interesting today in the light of developments just prior to and following the First World War.

7. *"Militarismus ist der zum kriegerischen Geist hinaufgesteigerte heldische Geist. Er ist Potsdam und Weimar in höchster Vereinigung. Er ist Faust und Zarathustra und Beethoven-Partitur in den Schützengräben. Vor allem wird man unter Militarismus verstehen müssen das, was man den Primat der militärischen Interessen im Lande nennen kann. Alles, was sich auf militärische Dinge bezieht, hat bei uns den Vorrang. Wir sind ein Volk von Kriegern. Den Kriegern gebühren die höchsten Ehren im Staate. . . . Alle anderen Zweige des Volkslebens dienen dem Militärinteresse, insbesondere auch ist das Wirtschaftsleben ihm untergeordnet."*

8. *"In diesem grossen Erlebnis aber liegt eine metaphysische Erkenntnisbedeutung des Krieges, . . . Auf höchster Stufe geht uns in jener Gottinnigkeit heiliger Liebe, in der wir uns schon als Menschen, ja darüber hinaus als Inbegriff aller persönlichen Geister, alle als Brüder und als Kinder eines göttlichen Vaters fühlen und sehen, die ganze Ausdehnung des geistigen Reiches auf."*

9. Even Erzberger started in 1914 with an extremist program which demanded the annexation of all of Belgium and the French channel coast; the acquisition of the iron ore of Briey-Longwy; the separation of Poland, the Baltic provinces and the Ukraine from Russia and their constitution as satellites of Germany and Austria; the creation of a German African empire, including the Belgian and French Congo; and finally huge reparations of at least 10 billion marks and the payment of Germany's entire national debt, in addition to establishing funds to provide for German veterans and for their housing needs. Only gradually did Erzberger abandon these war goals. He remained a nationalist though with greater moderation until 1917. He had the wisdom, Professor Epstein writes, "unlike most of his annexationist colleagues, to abandon such foolish aims in the further course of the war."

10. The copy available to me shows that over 480,000 copies were sold. His collection of "poems and thoughts from the battlefield" called *Vom grossen Abendmahl* reached, in the edition available to me, a printing of 120,000 copies.

Reprinted from The Mind of Germany: The Education of a Nation *(New York: Scribners, 1960), pp. 262-305.*

The Novel of Impressionism

Jethro Bithell

There is no clear cut between the naturalistic novel and the impressionistic novel. The transition is gradual; with some writers there is no complete break, and with others what really happens is that they continue the poetic realism of the prenaturalistic period, though with a more literal conception of reality. Taking the later phase of novels *en masse,* what remains in them of the naturalistic program is that the *milieu* may still be presented in detail; this, however, is no longer wearisome. The *Milieuroman* merges into the *Charakterroman,* the difference being that while in the former the *milieu* swamps the characters in the latter the *milieu,* though still emphasized, serves as a background against which the characters stand out in vivid relief, and that these characters, instead of being the chemical product of the *milieu,* dominate it.

Typical of the change-over is the work of Emil Strauss (1866-1956). A Swabian from Pforzheim, he gravitated to Berlin, and there moved in Gerhart Hauptmann's and Dehmel's circles; that is, in close touch with naturalism. Then he migrated to Brazil, but returned to Germany, and turned farmer in the Schwarzwald near Freiburg. He thus acquired a fund of experience which the doctrinaire naturalists–encysted in theories–cannot lay claim to. And experience shapes his heroes as it shaped him; they plunge into life, go wrong, make good, and so can face up to whatever fate may bring. This heroic conception of life is the direct opposite of the surrender to fate or rather to environment and mental state of the naturalists. Moreover, this development of character is altruistic: *"Du kannst die Welt nur vollenden,"* Strauss says, *"indem du dich vollendest."* In addition Strauss as a Swabian brings to his fiction Swabian *Gemüt* and a certain leisureliness of narration. He repeatedly gives impressions of Brazil (in his drama *Don Pedro* as in the short stories of *Menschenwege* and *Hans und Grete,* and elsewhere), but quite simply–what exotic impressionism is can be seen at a glance by comparing his Brazilian pictures with Dauthendey's descriptions of Mexico. His novel *Der Engelwirt* (1901) is made up of old-fashioned irony: a Swabian landlord has no boy by his wife, and tries for one with the servant, Agathe; but she presents him with a daughter! He emigrates with Agathe and the girl to Brazil, where Agathe dies, and where he is cheated of all he has. A sadder and a wiser man, he returns to home and wife; and the point of the story is that this good woman, whose character is finely drawn, welcomes him. The next novel, *Freund Hein* (1902), created a sensation; not, however, because it was a literary masterpiece (it is far from that), but because it was an attack on the examinational tyranny of German secondary schools. As *Anklageliteratur* it should be naturalistic; but Strauss just tells the story, and lets the accusation emerge from the facts. There is rather impressionistic than naturalistic consistency in the psychogrammatic notation of a boy's mental torture. The hero is Heinrich Lindner; in local pronunciation he is Heinerich, Heiner for short; but "Freund Hein" is a euphemism for Death. He is the grandson of a virtuoso on the violin, and the son of a lawyer who, in his own green youth, had been addicted to music, but had forced himself to relinquish this passion because it interfered with his legal studies. He expects his son, who has this hereditary gift for music, to practise the same self-control; but in Heiner the gift amounts to genius. He is already a composer, and do what he will he cannot tear himself away from the passion of his soul. He is physically incapable of reaching the required standard in mathematics, and is refused promotion to the 6th form. Desperately he shuts himself up, and grinds away at this detestable study–in vain; and when in the following year he is again refused promotion to the higher class he shoots himself. The discussion is twofold: the school motto, *non scholae sed vitae discimus,* is shown to be arrant humbug: the pupil is relentlessly sacrificed to the school, while individual bent and capacity are ignored. Actually Heiner is already a first-class musician, and the leaving certificate is not essential to him. The second theme is the tyranny of father over son; and this particular father, though he is as good as gold, is hopelessly incapable of seeing that his belief in the character-forming virtues of school discipline is sheer idiocy. Life, not school, forms character, is the moral of Strauss's work generally. As a contrast to Heiner–the German dreamer in the cruel grip of life–there is the figure of an active rebel, a boy poet who has read Darwin; he has been expelled from one school, and scamps the dull routine of the second simply because it is too slow and pedantic for his quick and practical mind. This boy will surmount his fate. In *Kreuzungen* (1904) the way to a true life is opened out; the hero throws up his post to live, without marrying her, with a girl who is pregnant by him. But passion fades; and when the girl realizes that merely a sense of duty is chaining the man to her she makes way, with cool determination, for another woman. Love is a hard test of character; what matters is not the wrong sort of experience, but the will to get over it. *Der nackte Mann* (1912) is a historical novel of Strauss's native town of Pforzheim; the theme is the struggle, at the beginning of the seventeenth century, between Calvinists and Lutherans. *Das Riesenspielzeug* (1935), with its anti-Socialist and anti-Marxist virus, belongs to Nazi *Blut- und Bodenliteratur*. The "giant toy" is a farm in the Black Forest, and the hero turns from the culture of the schools to the nation-serving life of farm and field. Strauss's Novellen have readability (*Menschenwege,* 1898; *Hans und Grete,* 1910; *Der Schleier*–by common consent a masterpiece–1931).

It is customary to pair Emil Strauss with Hermann Hesse (1877-). Both are Swabians–Hesse from Calw in Württemberg; and both are vagabonds in sunny climes–Hesse is almost as Italianate as Paul Heyse or Isolde Kurz. He also to begin with shows the impress of pre-naturalistic models (e.g. of Gottfried Keller in the irony of *Peter Camenzind* and the first two collections of Novellen); here, however, the radical difference between Strauss and Hesse emerges–whereas Strauss hammers his characters out of hard dramatic experience Hesse, who has the morbidity of the true neo-romantics, dreams his characters into soft lyric moods and leads them gently through pain and pleasure to the peace of death. Moreover, Hesse develops–his later novels are finely philosophical and psycho-analytical; while Strauss remains the preacher of salvation by hard knocks. Strauss ends as a purveyor of Nazi doctrine; Hesse in later years was treated, somewhat gently, as a diseased and spineless Nordic who uses that Jewish infamy of psycho-analysis to undermine the sanity of his race.

Hermann Hesse began with an ironical analysis of the artistic temperament: *Hinterlassene Schriften und Gedichte Hermann Lauschers* (1901), and followed this up with a kind of inverted *Künstlerroman: Peter Camenzind* (1904); the artist divests himself of his artistry and levels himself to the humdrum existence of the ordinary mortal; here we have, not (as with Thomas Mann) the contrast with the tortured mentality of the artist of the happy normal being, but a sheer decadent surrender of personality. At least on the face of it: an ironical treatment of the glorification of the artist (*Künstlerverhimmelung*) may be the undertone; or, more likely, persiflage of the author's self. Hesse was the son of a missionary, and he was sent to the Protestant Theological College at Maulbronn[1] to be fitted for the same calling. Actually he earned his living for a time as a bookseller. Like Peter Camenzind he was a scholarship boy who failed in his calling and found himself again by lake and mountain as a child of nature. Peter Camenzind returns to his native Swiss village of Nimikon; Hesse too elected to live in Switzerland, though not till 1912; previously he had lived at Gaienhofen on the Lake of Constance. In *Unterm Rad* (1905) the autobiographical element is glaring: the hero goes from Calw to the Seminary at Maulbronn, breaks down under the strain of study, is sent home ill, and drowns himself. As in Strauss's *Freund Hein*–which may have influenced Hesse–the school system is blamed for the lad's martyrdom; in both novels there is a ring of reality in the gentle unfolding of the process of mental exhaustion. In the following novels the psychology deepens gradually. *Gertrud* (1910) has a musician for hero, and tells a tale of marital failure and of fading skill. *Rosshalde* (1914) is finely psycho-analytical. Veraguth, a famous painter, lives at Rosshalde, his country estate, but in an *atelier* in the grounds, while his estranged wife lives in the mansion. Man and wife meet for meals only. There are two sons: one, at the university, takes the mother's side (*Sohn-Vater-Kampf*); the other, Pierre, is a child. Veraguth would separate from his wife if she would let him have Pierre, all that remains to him in life except his work; but this she will not agree to. This state of affairs is revealed to an old friend, a rubber planter in the Far East, who spends a holiday at Rosshalde; he by cautious questioning probes the painter's state of mind, and shows him where healing might lie–in separation, even at the price of relinquishing Pierre. The boy dies of meningitis, and the painter is free to go to the blazing tropics (where there are lovely native women to paint–and love . . .) with his sunburnt and happy friend. The problem–whether love for a child should chain a man to a hard wife–is the same as that of Ricarda Huch's *Vita Somnium Breve,* but there is more verisimilitude in Hesse's picture of the suffering husband, who, immured in loneliness, lives doggedly on in the hypnosis of resignation, an illusory contact with a wife who has never had any feeling for his needs. Domiciled now in Switzerland, a hotbed of psycho-analysis, Hesse was himself treated by a pupil of Jung, when he fell ill as a result of mental stress during the War; he then wrote a series of typically psycho-analytical novels. *Knulp* (1915), the story of a vagabond lover, ranks with its description of *Wanderqual* as closely related to the substance of the great novels and reflects what may be interpreted as Hesse's own abandonment of the masculine principle of *bürgerlich* for the feminine principle of the nomadic life and Bohemian freedom (see also his poem *Auf der Reise*). In *Klein und Wagner* (1919) the schoolmaster Wagner murders his wife and children and Klein is conscious that in his heart of hearts he approves the deed; Klingsor in *Klingsors letzter Sommer* (1920) is similarly convinced, as he goes his way *zu den Müttern,* that all feelings, even cruelty, are good because they are stirrings that lead to a reversal of personality and a renewal of self. In *Demian* (1919)–as in Friedrich Huch's *Mao* (1907)–there is a minute delineation of states of adolescence as determined by the uprooting which school life means and by the chemical changes in the body before and after the shock of puberty; the psycho-analytic probing through a blanket of occultism reveals the two worlds of a boy's mind, the world of parents, home, and duty, and the luring forbidden world of mystery which begins with the servants in the kitchen and stretches out to drink and girls and bold ideas that frighten at the first impact and then grow familiar as friends; they who domineer in this other world are those with the mark of Cain–this, as it turns out, is merely the sign of superiority in strong faces which the inferior Abels fear. The (Byronic) fascination of Cain is in the face of Demian (? = demon), the school friend of the hero Sinclair[2]; rumour has it that Demian and his mother live as lovers. The kernel of the book is the conception of the mother: of her a boy has two images, one physical, the other ideal; in this novel the ideal image is transferred to Demian's mother, to "Frau Eva," i.e. any mother, the mother of all; and the story ends with a promise that she will come to Sinclair when wanted–incest in symbol, since Sinclair and Demian are respectively the timid or angelic and the aggressive or demonic aspects of one character. The conception is a daring and delicate symbolization of the all-folding, cradling function of motherhood and motherliness: that creeping to breasts is one instinct in childhood and maturity, and in a woman's embrace man is always a child; any child's mother is his wife to be; any man's wife is his mother and ideal, whose brooding face has called him from the deeps to her bosom; "mother" is alpha and omega, the far fountain spring and the vast safe harbour of love. The new morality in a world now breaking in pain through the shell must (as music does already) harmonize the two worlds, sundered at present by convention: love + sex, mother + vampire, man + beast, God + devil. *Siddhartha* (1922) is permeated with the Indian quietism with which Hesse had made himself familiar when, in 1911, he had fled from "*die Verrohung unserer Kultur*" to India. The novel is an attempt to weave what is on the face of it Indian philosophy, but is in the heart of it a considered Bolshevization of morality, stage by stage, into the story of a boy's relations to his father and the world. *Siddharta* is the completion of *Demian*: as in *Demian* one personality is split into halves (angel and demon), so it is in the later novel into the ever-seeking Siddharta and his friend Govinda, who is obedient to doctrine (heterodox and orthodox). In *Demian* boy moves ever nearer to mother as the centre of emotion; in *Siddharta* boy moves ever farther away from father, for a boy's experience of life is newer and therefore more true than the faded experience of a father; in mother boy surrenders self, for love absorbs all to create anew; he finds himself away from father (the son-father motive of expressionism explained by psycho-analysis). The hero of Hesse's novel *Der Steppenwolf* (1927), Harry Haller, an artist, calls himself "the wolf of the steppes": the steppes are the wastes of existence in which the artistic temperament is shut out from the peace and comfort normal beings enjoy (the smell of furniture polish which he sniffs as he passes the first-floor flat on his way to his lonely attic rooms reminds him of the lost world, the world of mahogany, early rising, duty, mother). There can be no harmony when one is two, wolf and man, with the wolf snarling at the man. The man loves Mozart, poetry, ideals, peace; the wolf has wild urges, but in the higgledy-piggledy of society the wolf is penned with the sheep (the genius lives in contiguity with an alien crowd, and must adapt himself–or be slaughtered). Really one is more than two: personality is divided into chess-pieces: the individual has a multiple personality, he is wolf, tiger, monkey, bird of Paradise, and these are suppressed by wolf as wolf is suppressed by *Bürger*. Hermann, the friend of Haller's youth, is Hermine, who casts over him the spell of the hermaphrodite; she (he) is also the fresh and uncrumpled Pierrot with whom he dances. The mystic union of joy is the merging of personality in the mass: a fox-trot mingles us in a mass and makes us one. Haller is shown a mirror in which he sees himself as Haller and wolf of the steppes, each trying to devour the other: he is told that in order to extinguish the reflection he has only to laugh at it (humour begins when we learn not to take ourselves seriously). The novel ends in a medley of interfused symbolic craziness, like a film in which one picture is shot through another. There is a Magic Theatre, admission to which is by a trifling suicide; the doors of the closed boxes bear the legend: *"Alle Mädchen sind dein: Einwurf eine Mark"* (= all the girls I love are mine, for spirit pierces spirit). Mozart (a genius who–pigtail and girlish grace and Rococo–had harmonized the artist's and middle-class life) turns somersaults and plays trills with his heels; Haller pulls Mozart's pigtail, it lengthens, and carries Haller into icy space. Mozart appears again in evening dress, tinkers up a wireless set, and remarks that radio, though it projects music where it does not belong, does not destroy it: as radio cheapens the sublime, so does life in this Magic Theatre (*"nur für Verrükte"*) of the world; the lesson is to laugh at it, not destroy it. With this consoling thought–"the gallows humour of life"–suicide is not necessary. Hesse's next novel, *Narziss und Goldmund* (1930) is perhaps his masterpiece; it is at all events fascinating with its soft rhythm and its patient unravelling of psychic complications. Here again we have the old German progress from *tump* to *wîs*; the result is the proof, not that cloistered purity is the divine ideal, but that the life of the senses as much as the ascetic's flight from reality is service to the divine purpose–all ways lead to God. The dualism of existence is interpreted as a conflict of the paternal and maternal principles: paternal is the urge to abstract thought and the contemplative life; maternal is the tyranny of the senses. But only the maternal principle is creative; the paternal and therefore hard and masculine principle interprets–and should guide–its weak and pathetic contrary, the thinker "obsessed with fine distinctions." Thus Narziss is guide and mentor, and unselfish lover, of Goldmund, nature's darling, the doomed voluptuary and poet-dreamer; we first find them together as novices in a medieval monastery, and even then Narziss by patient questioning reveals to Goldmund his own inner nature. Narziss rises to be Abbot of the monastery; Goldmund, sent out to collect herbs on the moors, is initiated by a nut-brown gipsy; he disrobes her, and discovers beauty. Thereafter his life is that of the wandering scholar; woman after woman gives herself to him (*"die Weiber sind so gierig"*); characteristically the only one who turns contemptuously aside from his bloom and beauty is a Jewish girl whom he finds strewing her raven hair with the ashes of her father, whom the Nordic Christians of Germany have burnt by the waysided; he knows she will be seized and violated, for she too is a lone wanderer, but he takes leave of her "as if she were a queen." She teaches him that there is the will to die (*Sterbenwollen*) as well as the necessity of dying (*Sterbenmüssen*); and later he knows that life is ripe when the will to die is reached. This stage the belovèd vagabond attains when at long last women look at him as one spent and unseductive. The only thing worth living for, he had told Narziss, is copulation; and yet he has lived for more than woman. "Your eyes are never merry," says a girl who loves him, "they seem to say that all this only lasts a minute." He comes to realize that only creative art can save beauty and feeling for yet a little while from the Dance of Death; and he attaches himself to a great carver of wood, and creates as his first masterpiece the image of Narziss as the Apostle John–his expression of the worship of his contrary. He dreams of recapturing a fleeting mystery–the look in a woman's eyes in the spasm of copulation; and this distortion and contraction, this leap of fire and the fading of it, he has seen too in the eyes of a peasant woman over whom he held a candle when she was giving birth to a child; for rapture and pain, he realizes, are the same. His final masterpiece, he dreams, is to be his dead mother's face, which appears to him in dreams; but as age withers him it is no longer a personal face but that of all the women he has loved, the face of Eve, of the *Urmutter,* which lures to rapture, to birth, and, as the last grasp of her love, to death. But ere he has time to shape the mystery of her face she folds her hands round his heart and shapes him–to the will to death, to the fading of the fire she wakes. And before he dies Narziss, the lonely scholar with the fine face shaped by thinking, has bent over him and kissed him with the only kiss that life grants him. In *Der Kurgast* (1925) and *Die Nürnberger Reise* (1927) there is again the problem of nature's urges and the controlling function of the mind, and in the latter we read that nature is, as flowers are, lovely but fast fading, while reason, though it wearies, is durable as gold. *Morgenlandfahrt* (1923), with its secret league of sterling characters, comes still nearer to the synthesis of these opposites which is symbolically achieved in *Das Glasperlenspiel* (1943). This story of the bead-game, in the province of Kastalien round about the year 2400, shows mathematics and art in unison contriving control of the functions of existence. These bead-players live like monks, sundered from "the forbidden and inferior world," devoting themselves to the works of the spirit, as happened in Goethe's *pädagogische Provinz* in the *Wanderjahre.* In days following the havoc of a great war, which has brought degradation to mankind, the bead-players in the peace of their Alpine valley practise this game of glass pearls which, "*der Inbegriff des Geistigen und Musischen,*" synthetizes intellectual disciplines and in which all dissonance becomes unison. The purpose of their order is to rescue the world from that degradation of mind which had come from the "warlike age," "*das feuilletonistische Zeitalter,*" and to safeguard order, norm, reason, law, and measure. The protagonist is Josef Knecht, whose life is chronicled from his early orphan days till he rises to be Magister Ludi, the High Priest of this gameful religion. But he is initiated into historical studies by Pater Jacobus (what is quoted points to Jakob Burckhardt as model), and he learns that all historical phases are transitory. He realizes, too, that the bead-players preserve cultural values, but do not create them, and he observes that everything tends to change to its contrary. Thus he himself, Knecht by name, is Master of the Order. He discovers that he is not merely a Castalian, but a human being as well, and that as such his concern is with the world as a whole and not with a fraction of it. And so he sets out to find his earthly transformation, breaks way into the common life, and is drowned in a mountain lake.

Of Hermann Hesse's critical and essayistic work *Blick ins Chaos* (1920) has three essays on Dostoieffsky, whose influence on his fiction is clear, while *Dank an Goethe* (1946) details his debt to the sage of Weimar. The essays of *Krieg und Frieden* (1949), in particular *Der Europäer* and *Zarathustras Wiederkehr,* reflect Hesse's reactions to the World War II. His *Briefe* (1951), with date from 1927 to 1951, are addressed to correspondents who have sought his advice and to his contemporaries (Thomas Mann, Oskar Loerke, André Gide, C. G. Jung, Theodor Heuss, etc.) and are in essence self-interpretation.

As a lyric poet Hesse is traditional in form: *Gedichte* (1902), *Unterwegs* (1911), *Musik des Einsamen* (1915), *Trost der Nacht* (1928), *Stunden im Garten* (1936; an epic idyll), *Orgelspiel* (1940), and the complete edition *Die Gedichte* (1942 and 1947). His early verse draws from the common fund of romantic themes, moods, and imagery; for his mature poetry the key is the *Zweisinnigkeit* of his great novels, the saga of man passing "*im Zickzack zwischen Trieb und Geist durchs Leben*"–"*Bald Mönch, bald Wüstling, Denker bald, bald Tier.*" Often sensuous, vividly limned and coloured, but rarely subtle, they lack the compelling spontaneity of a poet proper; the verse is indeed *en marge* of the novels, in which, however, the ideological clash is consistently presented and defined, whereas in the poems it is scattered and fragmentary. They are pondered in patience, not poured forth in passion; that is, they are not *Rauschkunst*; and, moreover, there is a restricted range of theme and *ewige Wiederkehr* both in Nietzsche's sense and in the sense of iteration. One is tempted to say that, though in the novel Goldmund is clearly Hesse, the poems are thought out and morally contrived by Narziss, although of course this might mean that in them there is the synthesis the novels seek.

Gottfried Keller's ironic manner and Swiss sagacity come natural to Jakob Schaffner (1875-1944), who, born in Basel, began as a shoemaker's apprentice, and made use of his journeyman's experiences in his first novel, *Die Irrfahrten des Jonathan Bregger* (1905). Schaffner's ideal hero is a good European without religion except that of the solidarity of nations on the path of human brotherhood and progress. His ironic handling of customs and character sunders him from the *Heimatkünstler,* but in his descriptions of Swiss life, as in his village tale *Die Erlhöferin* (1908), he is vivid and close to reality. His great effort is *Konrad Pilater* (vol. I, 1910, vol. II, 1922), an autobiographical novel on the scale and pattern of Keller's *Der grüne Heinrich.* In *Der Bote Gottes* (1911) he goes back to the Thirty Years War. *Der Dechant von Gottesbüren* (1917) reflects his reactions to the First Great War. Religious problems provide the woof and weft of the trilogy *Johannes* (1922), *Die Jünglingszeit des Johannes Schattenbold* (1930), *Eine deutsche Wanderschaft* (1933). The great city is the background of *Der Mensch Krone* (1928). By the prominence he gives in his novels to the clash of Catholicism and Protestantism in Switzerland Schaffner ranges himself alongside Enrica von Handel-Mazzetti. He has attempted popular history in his *Geschichte der schweizerischen Eidgenossenschaften* (1915).

Ironic handling of life is the salient element in the novels of the two cousins, Friedrich Huch and Rudolf Huch; but since the literary clan of the Huchs–Ricarda Huch is Rudolf 's sister–have their home center at Brunswick it is natural that in their case the influence of Wilhelm Raabe should supplement that of Gottfried Keller. There is an implied didacticism in the novels of Friedrich Huch (1873-1913), but it is not conveyed with the breezy directness of Emil Strauss, it shines forth rather from a subtle quizzical treatment of human frailty and futility and would be scurrilous if it were not so sly. Born in Brunswick he studied philology, and was a tutor in various families. His first novel, *Peter Michel* (1901), has affinities with Hermann Hesse's *Peter Camenzind*: in both a dreamer of the feminine type–Peter Michel is obviously once again "der deutsche Michel"–is disillusioned by life, and is shown in the closing pages as a smug, contented Philistine. In Hesse's novel, it is true, the hero is exceptional, a died-out artist, while Peter Michel is any German, or indeed any normal being anywhere who sees the dreams of his youth fade into the light of common day. That this common man we all know is represented in the novel by a teacher is part of the satire; and since Friedrich Huch was himself a teacher by trade he should know the depths of dullness of this profession; to a teacher reading the sad story the consolation must be that there *is* the spice of poetry in Peter–before he is ruined by routine and environment. Peter Michel is the usual scholarship boy who rises to be a secondary teacher; incidentally the description of school life is more life-like than in the other novels which show up the Philistinism of academic existence–the teachers are humdrum enough, but the headmaster here, though wrapped in routine and cramped by cant, displays tact in the exercise of his authority. Famous is the chapter in which one of the masters is accused by another of jeopardizing the morals of his boys by having a mistress: the headmaster is aware of the facts, but saves the school an excellent teacher by assuming that the delinquent (more or less) intends to regularize the situation by marrying the lady (he does not, but keeps his post). The novel stands out by its presentation of the son-mother motif: Peter is forced into opposition to his mother, particularly when she tries to keep him moral by getting him married. Marriage, the novel demonstrates, is the stamp of respectability, but it may brand deep. All the poetry of the tale (and there is a deeply probing psychology in the weft of it) is in the suppressed sexual emotion of Peter before his marriage, and that dulling of this vibrant emotion into the animal paternal functions which is the normal result of marriage. As a grammar school student Peter dreams himself into a sensitive love of Liesel, the daughter of the *Kantor* with whom he lodges; at the university, amid the bestial orgies of German student life (unsparingly pictured), his dreams of her keep him clean; however, as the course of events shows, what he loves is not Liesel but his dream-picture of her: when he sees his headmaster's wife he has an optical illusion that *she* is Liesel, and loves her even when it is clear that she is not; for *she* is now his dream-picture or his ideal woman. The situation is tensely dramatic, particularly in Chapter VII, which is masterly in every detail: the headmaster, sure of his wife, leaves her with Peter in a room where the red lamp-shade symbolizes what might be demonic danger–if the characters were not in the grip of respectability. The headmaster's wife talks it over with him, and sends him back to Liesel; but she–the only Bohemian in the book–refuses to marry into the teaching profession, though she does very energetically take him into the forest and seduces him (the only lapse of his exemplary career); finally she marries a Graf, and is a shining light of society–which is also life as it is. And thus we know that all a teacher (particularly) has to hope for is to grow mouldy, and to put up with his wife and children–and colleagues; and to talk grandiloquently of the contentment of home and duty. Marriage keeps Jean Paul's *Schulmeisterlein* in the clouds; Peter Michel it brings down to pipe and slippers and sloppy sentiment. In his next three tales Friedrich Huch specializes in the somewhat painfully detailed transcription, deduced by adult divination, of processes in the minds of children and growing youth, and of the relations of parents to these processes. If his children have attraction, it is that of constructed models. In *Geschwister* (1903) two girls represent the dualism–familiar in medieval literature as *Weltflucht* and *Weltfreude*–of the brooding religious bent and the need of pleasure and company, with Hagen, the tutor of the girls' brother, as the man between the two. In *Wandlungen* (1905), the sequel to *Geschwister,* the boy of the previous tale and his relations to his father (*Sohn-Vater-Kampf*) move into the center of interest, with the father's second wife (the woman with a past) estranging the two by her shallow character. In *Mao* (1907) the *Kinderpsychologie* is still more searching. A family who were poor but are now rich live in an old patrician house. The only son, Thomas, goes to the elementary school, and brings home the smell of the class, which is painful to him. He is exquisitely sensitive, and for that reason is bound to be tortured in the rough-and-tumble of school life. The book thus falls into line with the studies of school life in Emil Strauss's *Freund Hein* and Hesse's *Unterm Rad.* As a satirist of Philistinism Friedrich Huch pairs with Carl Sternheim; he has less glitter, but more depth. And he is more depressing; for while Sternheim makes the respectability look like a huge joke Friedrich Huch, quietly but pitilessly, pictures it as a sea of idiocy in which we are all submerged. A few dreamers, dangerously gifted, struggle to rise out of it; but either, like Peter Michel, they are sucked back or, like Pitt, the hero of *Pitt und Fox* (1908), they are isolated at the rim of decency. The title of the story was no doubt suggested by a remark of Goethe that he could not help picturing Pitt as a pug-nosed broomstick and Fox as a fat pig. The names stick from boyhood to two brothers who are elaborately contrasted, more or less as Wolfram von Eschenbach contrasts Parzival, as a dreamer swayed by moods, problematic and baffled, with Gawân, the shallow and insinuating masterful man who takes the women the other might have had if he had not been decent. For Pitt, who studies philosophy, the problem life presents is the conflict of will, feeling, and action; and, as the novel shows, the conflict is due to distance from "primitivity," in which willing, feeling, and acting synchronize. Other problems of the day fill out the action: the son-father conflict, the right of the unmarried mother to refuse to marry her seducer. The most striking thing in the book is the delicate way in which the physical feelings of Elfriede–who falls in love with Pitt–and the restraint imposed upon the two by good breeding are indicated: her longing for embraces is foiled by Pitt's gentlemanly aloofness, and the point made is that the female undergoes a sexual awakening in contact with a male whose attitude is one of intellectual interest and sympathy: for Pitt, Elfriede is a lady, not sex. Pitt is sexually awakened by a simple girl–the daughter of Fox's landlady–of whom by the accepted code of student (that is, Philistine) morality he has a right of possession: he is too decent to exercise this right and it is taken by his brother. The novel ranks as a penetrating study of sexual phases; the Dickensian element–an almost affectionate delineation of whimsicalities–fails by comparison with the English model. Friedrich Huch's last novel, *Enzio* (1910), is yet another in the long list of *Künstlerromane*: the hero has music and a sensuous response to beauty in his blood–his father is a conductor; and his musical career is ruined because he cannot control his sex impulses. He has a student's affair with a simple and very charming girl of the people; Enzio is condemned, not for this experience–to Friedrich Huch natural and beautiful–but for his disreputable drifting to worthless creatures. Admirable is the contrast of this restless genius with a cultured girl whose name, Irene, symbolizes her nature; when she hears the tale of his loose living she breaks off her engagement to him, and he skates down the river till the ice breaks and rids the world of one who has been spoilt, not shaped, by what should be the best life can offer. The lesson of the book is that life and work are parallels: Enzio loves music as he loves his women, but in both spheres he is tossed about on the waves of impulse; work and love should be *terra firma* for artist and lover to build his sanctuary on.

In the novels of Rudolf Huch (1862-1943) the fling-back to pre-naturalistic models is declared and decided. He fluttered the dove-cotes by his two pamphlets launched against naturalism, the over-estimation of Gerhart Hauptmann, Maeterlinck, Helene Böhlau, and against other crazes of a degenerate day (*Mehr Goethe,* 1899; *Eine Krisis,* 1904), and shaped his style on that of Goethe and Wilhelm Raabe. He satirizes the life of small towns in *Aus dem Tagebuche eines Höhlenmolches* (1895), *Der Frauen wunderlich Wesen*

(1903), *Komödianten des Lebens* (1906), and *Die Rübenstedter* (1910). His best novels are *Die beiden Ritterhelm* (1907), *Familie Hellmann* (1908), and *Talion* (1913); and in these there is something of the morbidity of subject he had scorched in his pamphlets. There is delightful humor in *Wilhelm Brinkmeyers Abenteuer* (1911), *Altmännersommer* (1925), and *Humoristische Erzählungen* (1936). Generally speaking Rudolf Huch's aim was to educate the *Bürger* to a realization of the vacuity of his existence; he is in this respect the most academically minded of a group to which belong Friedrich Huch, Heinrich Mann, Carl Sternheim, and Leonhard Frank.

Eduard von Keyserling (1855-1918) is an impressionist in the true sense of the word: there is in all his work a nervous refinement of style, and the goal of his characters is not a moral mastery of life but sensuous enjoyment of it. For him, when love ends, life is over. His affinity is with that master of sensitive Danish prose, Hermann Bang,[3] whose works, with their subtle delineation of culture-worn aristocrats, had a great vogue in impressionist Germany; but it is inevitable that he should be compared with Friedrich Spielhagen, for both depict the junkers of north-east Germany. The region of Spielhagen's predilection is Pomerania, that of Keyserling is his native Courland, but the junker type is in the characterization of both essentially similar. There is, however, a difference which moves them worlds apart–while Spielhagen describes these landed gentry as an outsider of radical and even revolutionary views (though with a suppressed admiration for a socially superior class) Keyserling takes it for granted that their qualities are the prerogatives of their class. And these qualities–the most questionable to us are the right to adultery and the manorial right (exercised by all males of the family) to any girl on the estate–to Graf von Keyserling represent vitality ("*Lebenskraft*"), adventure, "the pleasurable sensation of the beast of prey" ("*angenehmes Raubtiergefühl*"). These junkers have no morality, but they have *Herrenmoral.* However–and this is the note of his work–the characters he chooses to depict are not the bold bad Baltic barons who live a full life, but the exceptional, thwarted dreamers of the stock, those whom their finer feelings force to stand by in the gnawing bitterness or helpless sadness of resignation, while their inferior but robust brethren seize life where it offers. "*Wir, an denen das Leben vorübergeht,*" might be the motto of his works; and what happens in tale after tale is no happening at all, but just the melancholy inspection of what might have happened–"*Ereignis in der Ereignislosigkeit.*" In his novel *Dumala* (1907) the pastor of a parish is in love with the wife of the lame lord of the manor, but he knows she has a lover, and comes near to murdering him; all that he has of life is to gaze at a lighted window on which his lady's shadow is cast. In *Seine Lebenserfahrung,* one of the stories of *Bunte Herzen* (1908), a man who knows he is preferred puts off his courage to sin till the woman goes off for sheer boredom with an insignificant rival. In actual life Eduard von Keyserling was anything but a bold bad baron. The third son of the lord of the manor at Paddern in Courland (then in Russia), he was educated at Dorpat University; and, apart from a period when he managed the ancestral estate for his brother, he was exiled from the life which he sees in a mystic beauty of landscape through the haze of a dream. When, after the conclusion of his studies, he resided in Vienna, he appears to have been attracted to Socialism, and to have been disillusioned by contact with the movement; his experiences at this time are assumed to form the basis of his novel *Die dritte Stiege.* In Vienna began the disease which was to lay him low; from 1897 onwards he suffered (like Heine) from a spinal disease due to syphilis, and became blind in 1907. Of decisive importance was a stay in Italy: here–an almost traditional experience of German writers[4]–his mind opened out to the magic of his northern homeland; and, like him, his dreams came home–if only, as in *Schwüle Tage,* to die. In 1899 he settled in Munich. After 1914 he wrote no more.

Keyserling's naturalistic novels *Rosa Herz* (1883) and *Die dritte Stiege* (1890) have as little importance as his dramas (*Din Frühlingsopfer,* 1899; *Der dumme Hans,* 1901; *Peter Hawel,* 1903); the dramatic sketch *Benignens Erlebnis* (1905) has the vain snatching at life and happiness of the Novellen. As a delineator of North German aristocracy Keyserling is often ranged with Fontane; but the comparison is illusory–Fontane, with the sympathetic understanding of an outsider, gives his characters just as they are, as quite ordinary gentlemen, with their class prejudices and snobbishness, their tricks of conversation: in Keyserling's aristocrats there is decay–not so much the moral decay which Spielhagen sees, but the decay of blood quickened by experience (actual or in dream) of alien ways, of the mellow culture of the West or the hot passion of the South. Thus in *Schwüle Tage* (1906) Ellita, prisoned in her impoverished manor, excites her school-boy cousin, whose own blood is restlessly stirring in dream, by dancing the bolero under the forest trees. She has given a last spell of happiness to the lad's Casanova-like father, who has come home, stricken with disease, to die–but not before he has healed their secret sinning by arranging Ellita's marriage with an officer: she–"*eine Blüte der adligen Kultur*"–must sacrifice life to be true to her class; and the boy dreamer, by accident, sees her (a *Herrenweib*), in her last rendezvous with his father before her marriage, threaten the worn-out old rake with her riding-whip. Admirable in this masterly Novelle is the fitting of human moods to the tense atmosphere: plain and forest swelter in the late summer heat, and with the breaking of the gathered storm comes the catastrophe of marriage to Ellita, death by morphia to the exhausted lover, and disillusionment to the sensitive boy. The striking feature here as elsewhere is the delicacy of the characterization: we see vividly the suffering lines on the old rake's face, the physical exasperation of Ellita, the languid pose of an invalid and faded lady of her mother, the baffled wonderment and impatience of the boy, and the idiot-like receptivity of the barefoot girl who relieves the pressure of the boy's blood. Not less masterly is the contrast of the two types of women in *Beate und Mareile* (1903). "Die weisse Beate" is once again the "blossom of culture," ruling her manorial hall in a kind of silvery radiance; *Schlossherrin* rather than wife, not sensual because by the exigency of rank she may not be ("*Verlieben*," she says, "*fand ich lächerlich; Verlieben gehörte zur Kammerjungfer*"). Mareile is the daughter of the Inspector on the estate, earth-born and the full-blown flower not of culture but of passion; and when the gush of passion has spent itself and the manorial reveller returns to the cold decency of home he knows that henceforth for him life is to watch life go by: chastity is an essential of *tenue*, but stagnant. In this identification of vitality and sex Keyserling–he is utterly erotic–is of course not true to the junker type, in whom notoriously martial qualities come first; but the obsession is veiled by his association of it with the landscape, visionary in his notation–sweeping plains, brooding forests, park and pond by the manorial home, and with the extremes of the climate folding the mood of the moment. In sheer impressionism of landscape-coloring Keyserling is unsurpassed; for instance: "*Still und sandig lag das Land da, Überall gelber Sand; Wiesen, Felder und Gärten lagen darauf, wie eine verblasste Stickerei auf einem blind gewordenen Goldgrund.*"

Hermann Stehr (1864-1940), a Silesian and a saddler's son who began life as a village schoolmaster, is above all a visionary, a mystic seeking religious certainty. In youth he had his own mental crisis: brought up as a Catholic he studied Darwin and began to doubt; for his change of faith he was persecuted by his official superiors, and found relief from his suffering in writing stories. His Darwinian positivism gave way to a Maeterlinckian fatalism which, he says, is rooted in the Silesian character: "*Wir Menschen halten doch immer nur die Fäden in den Händen, das Schicksal aber webt, was es will. . . .*" Reason is, therefore, of no account in the government of life: the beginning of faith must be in a "*grundentstiegene Unsicherheit.*" Not reason decides the course of a man's life; and free will is like a doctor trying to cure a grievously sick man: man's fate is in his blood. Stehr, therefore, sets himself the task of piercing into those undiscovered regions of the soul where fate grows; that is, to plunge deep into subconsciousness and the urge of the senses; until he reaches his final conviction that "*das Denken ohne Bewusstsein erlebt die Bewegung des Weltalls, und das Gefühl, das sich nicht kennt, die Empfindungen Gottes.*" Stehr's own mental conflict is reflected in his first work, the short stories of *Auf Leben und Tod* (1898) and the novel *Der begrabene Gott* (1905). His conquest of mystic faith is symbolized in *Drei Nächte* (1909), in which Faber appears, a dismissed elementary teacher, the mouthpiece of Stehr himself. Faber reappears in *Der Heiligenhof* (1918), the scene of which is not, as is customary with Stehr, in his native Silesia but in Westphalia (as is also the case in the short story *Meister Cajetan,* 1931). *Der Heiligenhof* is one of the most alluring–though perhaps the most illogical–of those novels which have *Wandlung* for their theme. Here conversion is equivalent to a turning inward of thought in the person of the hero, a Berserker type of farmer, as the effect of his conviction that his blind daughter is holy, and that her holiness proves the spirituality behind reality of life. Now his reformed character earns for his farm the name which is the title of the book. The mystical idea is that which Gerhart Hauptmann weaves into *Und Pippa tanzt*: only the blind see; or, in other words the outer reality seen by the eyes of the body is corruption, while the inner reality visible to the soul is imperishable beauty. In the life behind life, and there alone, is the peace that passeth understanding, and clarification is a processs that must come out of one's own deeps ("*Selbstheiligung*")–the idea of salvation by another was invented by priests, but the muddiest pool grows clear of itself when peace comes to it within itself. The girl's sight is restored, however, by the miracle of her love for Peter Brindeisener, the son of her father's inveterate enemy (the Romeo and Juliet motif in a rural setting once more), and the religious faith of the Heiligenbauer almost founders when this daughter, because marriage with her boy is impossible, drowns herself in a pond. He recovers his faith only in the conviction that what had come to him by the accident of the girl's blindness must be regained by his own soul stirred to its deeps and consciously piercing to the light of divine truth. *Der Heiligenhof* is in some sort a companion volume to Hauptmann's *Emanuel Quint*–both novels continue the seventeenth-century mysticism of Jakob Böhme, and in both hallucinations and fixed ideas constitute religion. Stehr, with his type of the new *Seelenmensch,* is already the *Gottsucher* of the expressionists; but in *Der Heiligenhof* the *Wandlung* of which the expressionists are so fond occurs with the impossible suddenness of the conversion in Masefield's *Everlasting Mercy.* At bottom Stehr's mysticism is not so much Silesian as Maeterlinckian: it is not the New Jerusalem beyond the horizon, but a mirage.

Stehr's next novel, *Peter Brindeisener* (1924), is a sequel to *Der Heiligenhof.* Peter Brindeisener, for the love of whom the blind girl had gone to her death, relates his own experiences in the form of a confession. The chief interest is in the exposition of Stehr's somewhat bloodless attitude to sex. In other novels of Stehr social problems are handled. *Leonore Griebel* (1900) has a *femme incomprise* for heroine; the pathological problem of a finely strung woman's decay by the side of a hopelessly prosaic husband and her indifference even to the child she bears him (she regards it as his and as another shackle of dull domesticity) is patiently interpreted. Stehr's one drama, *Meta Konegen* (1905), is related in theme: the heroine is neglected by her husband, who is engrossed by his struggle to free schools from clerical interference. The two late novels *Nathaniel Maechler* (1929) and *Die Nachkommen* (1933) deal in chronological sequence with the evolution of political ideas. Nathaniel Maechler is a tanner's apprentice who is infected with the ideas of the 1848 revolution; gradually he learns to subordinate himself to the welfare of the community–which safeguards the family. His descendants, however, in the illusive outer splendour and inner poverty of imperialist Germany, are criticized for their selfish defection from this totalitarian self-effacement. Stehr's Novellen fail because of their lack either of concentration or clearness. His first collection, *Auf Leben und Tod* (1898), is drab naturalism. *Der Schindelmacher* (1899) is, for Stehr, violent and even melodramatic: the hero transfers his farm to his niece, who humiliates him to the dust; the ghost of his dead wife appears, and goads him to vengeance. He rages like King Lear, smashes the furniture, mows the corn, and hangs himself in the corner where his wife died. As a Silesian Stehr should have that knowledge of the gnomes of the mountains which goes to the making of so many *Märchen.* But a *Märchen* which a child cannot understand is, as a *Märchen,* damned; and *Wendelin Heinelt* (1909), Stehr's most famous *Märchen,* is merely a cryptic elaboration of the theme that happiness is not the golden gift of the sprites of the underworld. The short story *Der Geigenmacher* (1926) is the fanciful symbolic *Märchen* of a maker of violins who loves and by his passion loses a maid, Schönlein, and then in the passion of his grief carves a magic violin, as though out of his own heart, rounds and smooths it to the shape of Schönlein's body, and from its chords conjures forth the music of Heaven. He had made perfect violins before he found Schönlein; but their music was not divine. Only suffering and privation ripen a master's magic gift.

Any valuation of Stehr today can only be provisional. German critics maintain that only a German can appreciate him; apparently a downweighted brain is needed, and a patience unconscious of length of time. To read *Der Heiligenhof* is a heroic task. Stehr has the plodding mind of an elementary teacher; he grinds on and on to the end. His style, laden as it is with laborious thinking, has a level and heavy rhythm; nor has it the flashes of flame of the mystics proper–the ultimate effect is that of an imposing mass of solidly constructed truth, not that of revelation fired with the sublime ecstasy of faith. The mysticism is that of a schoolmaster whose class has expanded to a nation; and probably only the German nation could be fascinated by novels so religiously formative.

Some at least of the tales of Jakob Wassermann (1873-1934) may be ranked as *Heimatkunst*: born at Fürth, where he began life as a clerk, he describes Franconia, and with great intimacy Nuremberg: in *Die Juden von Zirndorf* and other tales he is the accredited interpreter of the spiritual and physical environment of the Franconian Jews. But, since Wassermann is a Jew, his native province is not so much Franconia as a world of ideas, unctuously Oriental to a great extent in substance and presentment, although, in his autobiographical sketch *Mein Weg als Deutscher und Jude* (1921), he has energetically asserted his claim to all the German heritage of soul and language. The declared aim of his laboured writing is to bring about the birth through tribulation of spirit of "the new man," simple, humble, and good, who calls himself brother to the outcast, and will kneel (in *Christian Wahnschaffe*) even to a criminal who has raped and murdered a little girl. (A murderer is innocent, runs the argument in Stehr's *Der Heiligenhof,* in the depths of his soul, just as on the ocean bed there is peace while tempests rend its surface; we shall see that the expressionists proper will show that not the murderer but the murdered is guilty.) Wassermann's didactic tendency clearly runs parallel with that of Hermann Stehr, but there is a wide disparity in their technique: Stehr leads up to his *Seelenmensch* by inner experiences which illumine and purify the soul they awaken; Wassermann's characters are transformed in a welter of crass sensationalism which has elements of Eugène Sue or of the *Police Gazette.* If only by reason of this lurid excitement and concentration on physically criminal types one is forced to question the permanent value of Wassermann's writings. Of interest there is no lack; the obvious reason for his comparative failure is that the cerebrally evolved characters act, not dynamically, but to illustrate the theory (proclaimed in *Christian Wahnschaffe*) that to reveal humanity the novelist must "sink himself into sick souls," and unveil what is secret and hidden by "inquisition" into the causes of moral disease. Wassermann's creed as a novelist is set down in the treatise *Die Kunst der Erzählung* (1904). "*Ich will nicht die Verknüpfung äusserer Erlebnisse geben,*" he says, "*sondern die Wirrnis der inneren; ich setze keinen Ehrgeiz darin, Fäden zu knüpfen und zu lösen.*" He means that he would not prune and shape his matter to a logical cohesion, but light up the inextricable confusion of human happenings by allusive symbol and give them the significance of a myth. Dream and myth are poetry; the psychologist's interpretation is a naturalistic negation of poetry; it is a shameless exposure, not an imaged illumination. The psychologist of present-day literature, Wassermann says in another treatise, *Der Literat als Psycholog* (1910), is the very contrary of poet, he is "*der Literat,*" "*der vom Mythos losgelöste Mensch, der auch von der Gesellschaft losgelöste Mensch.*" The technician, probably, is not tied to his technique, or falls below it; but there is considerable originality in his method, though the influence of other writers is patent: e.g. of E. T. A. Hoffmann and Jean Paul in certain of his Novellen (*Der niegeküsste Mund,* 1903), of Balzac in his linking of novel to novel by the migration of characters, and of Dostoieffsky in his exhaustive illumination of the soul of outcasts.

Wassermann made his reputation with *Die Juden von Zirndorf* (1897), in substance a withering exposure of Jew mentality. In the prologue the Jews in Fürth and Nuremberg, who live in a close racial community, hear that at Smyrna a Messiah has arisen; and they would go out to him with caravans, but news comes that he has gone over to Islam. They found a village, Zionsdorf, which the Christians corrupt to Zirndorf. There remains the problem whether the Messiah was really a renegade and a cheat, or a typical Jew who goes where profit is. In the second part a new Saviour arises, Agathon Geyer, in Zirndorf itself; but he saves himself only by overcoming the narrow spirit of the law. *Die Geschichte der jungen Renate Fuchs* (1900) is built up on one of those typical theses of Wassermann which to sober sense must seem absurd. In this novel a character who is obviously a copy of Peter Altenberg utters the portentous aphorism: ther is an indestructible asbestos soul, and every girl has it, even if she falls. Renate Fuchs is a Munich lady engaged to a duke; she leaves him to run away with a student. She wades through all the filth of the world–she falls to a demonic creature who is recognized as a study of Wedekind–before she is reborn as that which her name signifies, and as the new woman who has a night of love with Agathon Geyer, the Saviour of the previous novel, ere he dies, and she bears him the first child of a new era: Beatus. In *Der Moloch* (1902) Wassermann first handles the obsession which recurs in *Der Fall Maurizius: summum jus, summa injuria.* Arnold Ansorge, an innocent country youth, is horrified by a legal crime committed against a Jew, goes to Vienna (*der Moloch = die Grosstadt*) to seek a righting of the wrong (the influence of Kleist's *Michael Kohlhaas* manifests itself here as also in *Casper Hauser* and *Der Fall Maurizius*), but is himself contaminated by the miasmic life of the city, and in hopeless self-contempt shoots himself. *Alexander in Babylon* (1905) has something of the exotic splendour and the rich Oriental coloring and sensationalism of Flaubert's *Salammbô,* but the theme is essentially that of the medieval epic of *Alexander:* even the mightiest conqueror must depart from his conquests, and have his mouth stopped with dust. What is the use of life, the sulphur-faced young king asks, if I cannot keep it? Of all Wasserman's novels *Casper Hause oder die Trägheit des Herzens* (1908) is that into which he has put most clearly the perhaps naïve religious teaching which was so dear to his heart. The events narrated are historical; and, though Wassermann has interpreted them with obstinate wilfulness and obsessional bitterness, he has changed them but little in details. In the summer of 1828 a boy appeared in the streets of Nuremberg who could neither walk nor speak. His story, Wassermann says, has all the elements of an ancient myth: he is like an inhabitant of another planet straying into this world as if by miracle. A contemporary jurist wrote a treatise, *An Example of a Crime against a Human Being,* to prove that Caspar was a legitimate prince of the house of Baden. The key to the mystery, as provided by the novel, would be that the morganatic wife of the Grand Duke of Baden had done away with her husband's son by his consort, a stepdaughter of Napoleon; whether with her knowledge or not, the boy had been kept immured in a dark tower and suddenly released by his jailer; and as soon as opportunity offered the reigning dynasty caused him to be assassinated. This prince imprisoned from birth in a dark tower and thrust out into the light of day at maturity is a theme familiar in German literature from the translations of Calderon's *La vida es sueño*; it was to be used again by Hofmannsthal in *Der Turm.* Wassermann uses the story as a ready-made exemplification of his faith in pure humanity: Arnold Ansorge in *Der Moloch* had been such an innocent depraved by contact with wickedness, but he had had some conception of human depravity, whereas Caspar Hauser has the utter innocence of a new-born babe. The problem then is: is it possible for a grown-up person to be as morally white as the driven snow? The answer is in the affirmative; for Caspar Hauser is an angel, and would remain an angel if the world would let him. But his keepers torment him, and force him to lie. And inevitably–for he has a face of girlish gentleness, brown curls glossed like those of animals that live in the dark, the light brown eyes of a frightened fawn, flesh that smells like honey–the wife of his keeper attempts what Potiphar's wife attempted. What is wrong with the world is that we have got *Trägheit des Herzens,* sluggish hearts or hearts that won't wake up and glow in the worship of innocence and justice. This famous phrase was to be blazoned like a diamond in the forefront of their programme by the expressionists. But by Wassermann's showing no expressionist fervour would save humanity so long as there are dynasties of princes: their juridical system is an abomination, and innocence is a myth . . . In *Caspar Hauser* Wassermann tracks evidence with the relentless inquisitiveness of a criminologist and pronounces upon it with the apodictic certainty of a judge. In the novels which follow he plunges ever deeper into the investigation of strange crimes, and tends to interpret them as the effect of primitive urges, or, another adept in the occultism of the period, he hints at psychic transferences. In the short stories of *Die Schwestern* (1906) he presents a trio of women who are sisters in the morbidity and suffering of their souls: Joan of Castile, the mother of the Emperor Charles V, who takes about with her the painted corpse of her husband Philip the Fair, in which a watch takes the place of a heart; a washerwoman hanged for murder in Fleet Street in 1732; the daughter of the President of the French Republic in 1830 who opens her veins in a cell. *Das Gänsemännchen* (1915) is one of the most notorious handlings of a man's cohabitation with two wives. Wassermann's story is probably modelled literally on the life-story of the poet Bürger, who cohabitated with his wife's sister as well as his wife. The hero of Wassermann's novel is a musician in Nuremberg, and the symbolic title is taken from the figure of a man with a goose under each arm on a fountain of one of the city market-places. The brunt of thé story is the tragedy of the artist, the myth of the eternal enmity between the creative man-mind and the earthly woman-mind: "*Das Ewig-Weibliche zieht uns hinab.*" The main feature of *Christian Wahnschaffe* (1919) is that a rich man's son does what Buddha did: he turns his back on wealth and rank, and lives with outcasts. In the four volumes of the cycle *Der Wendekreis* (the first novel, 1920, has this title; then follow *Oberlins drei Stufen,*1922; *Ulrike Woytich,*1923; and *Faber oder die verlorenen Jahre,* 1924) the idea of psychic discontinuity comes into play–an individual is made up of various *I's* which come to the surface under the pressure of events; and this idea continues in *Laudin und die Seinen* (1925). Then in a trilogy of novels Wassermann probes his way to what he conceives as a new cerebralogically attested system of ethics and religion. *Der Fall Maurizius* (1928) is the most ambitious detective novel in German literature, but *qua* detective novel it is incredibly naïve and boring. Very irritating is Wassermann's technique, here relentlessly applied, of *Entschleierung*–striptеasing should be the translation of the word: there is a mystery which is revealed shred by shred. Etzel Andergast, a boy of sixteen, sets out to unravel a murder mystery. His father, an attorney general, had procured the verdict; and he too, after Maurizius, the man condemned for the murder, has been doing penal servitude for eighteen years, renews the investigation by sitting with the prisoner day by day in his cell (!), listening to his interminable self-dissection. Etzel runs away to Berlin, where he ingratiates himself with the man who had been the chief witness at the trial, a homosexual Jew scholar, Waremme, who is clearly modeled on du Maurier's Svengali. Maurizius, married to Elli, had passionately loved Anna, Elli's sister, a strange creature compact of positive and negative qualities (with her "*ichlose Selbstischheit*" she is "*narzisshaft,*" "*Frau Holle im Schnee,*" "*eine seelenlose Lemure,*" "*eine Leiche, die man galvanisieren muss*"). Anna has been violated by Waremme, and she is hypnotically controlled by him as Trilby is by Svengali; and, though she fired the revolver and killed her sister, Waremme's diabolical will directed her aim. The real purpose of the novel, apart from the inquisition into problematical mental states, is the bitter Communistic accusation of German justice and of justice generally, continued from *Der Moloch* and *Caspar Hauser. Etzel Andergast* (1931) is the sequel to *Der Fall Maurizius*: the titular hero is now the pupil of a medical specialist, Joseph Kerkhoven, who pierces into the innermost mind of the crowd of characters. *Joseph Kerkhovens dritte Existenz* (1934) takes up the threads again. *Bula Matari* (1932) and *Christoph Columbus* (1929) mark the culmination of Wassermann's morbid skill in the delineation of strange characters. It has been said that the heroes of his tales were fantastically baroque, as unreal as (say) Lohenstein's Arminus: here he dissects historical characters, and lays bare what he considers to be their secret soul–together with its disease. In *Bula Matari* he illuminates the inner psychology of Stanley. To him Stanley is a type of *conquistador*–a *conquistador* not merely of vast new spaces of earth but of his own mysterious urges, and of "the quagmire of life." What makes the book alluring is the obvious influence of another adept in strange mentalities, Joseph Conrad: the whole book is indeed planned more or less as an interpretation of Conrad's *Heart of Darkness* by the light of Stanley's psychological experiences; perhaps, indeed, as an interpretation of the mysterious psychology of Conrad's tragic hero generally. Whether this interpretation is not too naïvely Freudian may be questioned: at all events Wassermann cannot understand Stanley's ostensibly clean sheet of erotic experience unless there is an assumption of paederasty; the explorer's bewilderment at the collapse of the subordinates he had left in charge of the rearguard in the Emin Pasha Relief Expedition is questioned as either naïveté or puritanical pretence, since it must be clear that these normal British men had succumbed to the erotic allurement of the African jungle. Only religious heroism of character (Livingstone, Stanley) can lead out of this poisonous inertia of the jungle, or symbolically the quagmire of life in general (*Trägheit des Herzens*), while those who have not this heroic strength of will (Emin Pasha, Stanley's subordinates) seek deeper and deeper into it. Wassermann's Columbus is a drastic case of *Entheroisierung:* he is a creature of impulse rather than discoverer, sailing the seas blindly, and "buried in his own dark self, a joyless exile." Wassermann is mainly concerned in denouncing the destruction by dynastic and religious greed of a symbiotic community.

Stehr's obstinate seeking for a new religion and Wassermann's programmatic Buddhism are symptomatic of the change that takes place in the novel after 1900 in the choice of hero: the great personality (Nietzsche's *Adelsmensch*), who has replaced the decadent *Nervenmensch,* tends to be a *Gottsucher,* or at all events he seeks some new moral way of escaping from the quagmire of life;the progression to the humanistic or communistic hero of the expressionists is typified by the sequence of Wassermann's social rebels. Many of these novels of the new century are, since they describe the development of the hero from youth through maturity through weal and woe, *Bildungsromane* or *Entwicklungsromane* more or less in the old sense; but the best of them are so intensely personal that they have been classified as *Bekenntnis- und Bildungsromane:* in their pages the author reveals himself.

The work of the two brothers Heinrich and Thomas Mann has from first to last this blending of confession and mental evolution, and at the same time criticism of society, gently ironic in the work of Thomas, corrosive in that of Heinrich, who has been called the German Juvenal. The two brothers are scions of an old patrician family of Lübeck. Their grandmother was a Brazilian creole, a skilled musician; she is the "southern" mother, passionate and artistic, who in Thomas Mann's novels stands in stark contrast with the solid and practical German temperament of the men of the old stock. In Thomas the German temperament prevails and controls his slow, carefully considered and polished style with its sad rhythms; in Heinrich the romance blood is credited with the hectic rush of the sentences, with his gorgeous coloring, and with his Italianate rut of passion.

Heinrich Mann (1871-1950) reveals his own personality, particularly in his Novellen, by those of his characters who are artists and poets. Mario Mavolto in *Pippo Spano* (one of the short tales of *Flöten und Dolche,* 1904-5) is self-portraiture; he is a poet who, forced to observe life, remains outside it; this disgust with art is again expressed in *Die Göttinnen* by the painter to whom it would be happiness if he could contemplate beauty without having to paint it. Art is revealed as "a perverse debauch" that enervates its victim to such an extent that he is incapable of real feeling. Heinrich Mann's novels may be divided into two classes; the first class, the scenes of which are mostly in Germany, are caricature of the grotesque genre, in intent social criticism and culminating in a kind of political propaganda; the second class are as a rule localized in Italy, and though they may be classed as *Bekenntnisromane,* since they reveal the author's orgiastic mind, are riotous paeans of life lived at fever heat in a world where common sense and goodness and pity do not count. *Im Schlaraffenland* (1901) caricatures and excoriates the stock-jobbers and literary hacks of Berlin; it is a picture of Sodom in which all the sinners are not worth a decent man's kick. The hero, obviously modeled on Maupassant's Bel Ami, is a *littérateur* who lives by love. *Die Jagd nach Liebe* (1904) transfers these literary orgies to Munich; its most lurid scene is when an actress who is to play Monna Vanna disrobes herself and finds the man before her dead. *Professor Unrat* (1905), well known as the film *The Blue Angel,* has for hero a grotesque schoolmaster who, tracking his pupils to a tavern where they wait on a light o' love, is himself drawn into her coils, marries her, loses his post, and avenges himself on his fellow-citizens, his former pupils, by luring them through his wife to debauch. The picture is repulsive; but Heinrich Mann is applying the method of Balzac: by exaggeration he aims at showing the terrific power of instincts and of passions latent in any respectable individual; a Philistine, or an immaculate Methodist is a potential monster of vice, for, since virtue is vice reversed, intensity may be equal in a different direction, just as rising (according the observer's standpoint) is falling upwards. In *Zwischen den Rassen* (1907) Heinrich Mann fights out over the conflict in his own blood between north and south, spirituality and sensuality: the heroine, like the author, is half South American. The Romance lovers pounce on their women, while the Germanic hero timidly waits. *Die kleine Stadt* (1909) begins as an idyll in a little Italian town where the clerical party try to prevent an itinerant troupe of actors from producing their shows. But the action quickens to the passionate love-story of the young tenor and a beautiful girl he sees behind the door of the convent. In *Die Göttinnen oder die drei Romane der Herzogin von Assy* (1902-3), Heinrich Mann's most ambitious work, all this southern fever seethes into delirium. To blame his creole blood for the ravishing rut of it all is hardly scientific; much of it is due to his residence in Italy and still more to his cult of d'Annunzio, who, moreover, appears, thinly disguised, as one of the characters. "I have discovered a new genre," one of the characters proclaims, "the hysterical Renaissance!" This term hits the nail on the head: the characters (*unbedenkliche Abenteurer, stolz und düster nach Grösse, blutbefleckt frei und unverwundbar*) are weaklings to whom their perversities are heroic strength; the keynote of the trilogy is the discord between desire and capacity. As in a German novel written a century before, J. J. W. Heinse's *Ardinghello,* the wickedness is a phantasmagoria, not a ruthless unfolding of strength as in the authentic history of the *cinquecento.* Conrad Ferdinand Meyer, himself a weakling worshipping the strong, had delineated Renaissance voluptuaries with the credibility of an historian; Heinrich Mann sees only one side of their mentality: worship of beauty unhampered by the moral law, and therefore lust, not love. The scene is set on a vast scale–the Duchess rules by right of beauty from Dalmatia to Venice, Rome, Naples–but the inner meaning shrinks: she is in the first novel Diana achieving freedom, in the second Minerva ruling the realm of ideal beauty in art, in the third Venus seizing joy (*Frieheitssucht, Kunstfieber, Liebeswut*)–but in reality as the novel shapes we see her, in the first two novels empty and aching, and in the third Venus vulgivaga and nothing more. Nietzsche's doctrine of Dionysian joy is here like a cup drained to the dregs: a boy is loved to death at Capri; there are violations and sadism; there is a bout of lesbian love by experts staged and watched like a boxing-match; a robust English dame, Lady Olympia, moves through the tale, coming from the ends of the earth and emerging at parties to whisper, with a velvet voice, to some stranger or other: "*Heute nacht sind Sie mein Geliebter– . . . Meine Gondel wartet.*" But the trilogy stands out in the history of literature both by reason of its extreme tendency and of its style. It stands on the threshold of expressionism, first because it is the *ne plus ultra* of Nietzschean *Schrecklichkeit,* and therefore nearest to the inevitable reaction from ideals of picturesque depravity dear to impressionism; and, secondly, because the style, so feverish that it rushes along in a succession of pictures, has passed beyond the coldly gemmed and chiselled style of impressionism, and is already *Rauschkunst,* the ecstatic style which presents life (*das rasende Leben*) in cinematographic flashes. It is strange to find so antireligious a writer as Heinrich Mann among the *Gottsucher,* and no doubt *Mutter Marie* (1927) is rather a dispassionate study of religious conversion than a confession of personal belief in the efficacy of faith. Baroness Marie Hartmann recognizes in the heir of a general the son whom, twenty-five years before, when she was a servant girl, she had abandoned on the rim of a street fountain. And–horror of horrors! (but somewhat in the nature of the Ninon de l'Enclos motif)–she finds that her love for the boy is that of a woman for the male as well as that of a mother. She seeks a refuge in religion, and makes a hectic confession in the Hedwigskirche in Berlin. *Eugénie oder die Bügerzeit* (1928), with its description of life in Lübeck in Geibel's days, is a side-piece to Thomas Mann's *Buddenbrooks*–but at a great remove. The historical novels *Die Jugend des Königs Henri Quatre* (1938) and *Die Vollendung des Königs Henri Quatre* (1938) represent a declension from the heights of literature to the level of Feuchtwanger and *hoc genus omne.* The first novel relates the king's career to his victory at Arques in 1589. There is a vivid picture of the Queen Mother, Catherine dei Medici, whose sinister cunning is contrasted with the frank joyousness of the young king. Coligny too stands out, and the massacre of St. Bartholomew as the climax is descriptively fine. The construction is episodic, and the skein of the story is tangled. *Der Atem* (1949) is a hectic attempt to write in the ultra-expressionist style of the day.

The psychological and personal trend of Heinrich Mann's work develops, like that of his brother, in the direction of the regeneration of society by democracy; he ended as a declared friend of the Soviet Union. His political and social satire culminates in the trilogy *Das Kaiserreich* (*Der Untertan,* 1914–the officials; *Die Armen,* 1917–the proletariat; *Der Kopf,* 1925–state policy), a scathing denunciation of the Wilhelminian state which is all the more daring as the first novel of the series was in course of publication when the War broke out. There was a question of prosecution for *lése-majesté,* and presumably only the absorbing excitement of the War prevented it; the obvious portraiture of notabilities alive or dead may have been too illusive to ensure a conviction, but the mockery of the All-Highest was in plain terms. In *Der Untertan* the career is set forth of Diederich Hessling, the son of a factory-owner; he shows sadistic tendencies at school, is hardened by his experiences as a corps student, and has the usual affairs with women. He develops a fanatical admiration of the Hohenzollerns, and for that reason loathes the Socialists. In *Die Armen* Diederich is now Generaldirektor Geheimer Kommerzienrat Hessling. As a political move he introduces profit-sharing, a system under which the workers are worse off than they were before. The troubles and struggles of the proletariat are depressing reading, and are not helped by the melodramatic intrigue: Balrich, a young worker, has a trump card in his hand, for he can prove financial villainy in his employer's family; he learns Latin and Greek, and turns agitator. The struggles against capitalists helped by dynasty and State prove hopeless; Balrich gives up his books and returns to the life of a suppressed worker; and the novel ends with the picture of him and his fellow-workers marching away to the War along beflagged streets. In *Der Kopf* public life is described by one character as a private affair–the personal struggle of Wilhelm II with Social Democracy. As a *roman à clefs* the novel has historical interest. Secretary of State Lannas is understood to represent Bülow. There is no need to give the key to Knack, the iron and steel magnate, with his daughter Bellona. Tolleben is stated in the novel to be "like Bismarck." The agitation of the industrialists, supported by Admiral von Fischer, to make the fleet strong enough to annihilate the British fleet is a vital element of the intrigue: England and France are under the thumb of the Jews, and hence are the deadly foes of Germany. Round these pillars of the State flit and flash two glittering scamps, Terra and Mangold. Mangold marries Bellona, becomes secretary to Graf Lannas, and rises to be Chancellor. Terra personally advises the Kaiser to abolish the death penalty: then it will not be possible to charge him with lusting for mass murder by means of war. The Kaiser is at first impressed, but then replies in very vulgar German. When the War is lost Terra and Mangold, in 1918, die a picturesque death: linking arms, they shoot each other and fall in the shape of a cross, to the music of a military band playing outside. In spite of the political filth the novel would be comparatively clean if it were not for the women–of the key characters as stated. The verdict must be that as a crossword puzzle the cycle is exhausting, while as fiction it is too dirty even for real life. In his preface to *Die grosse Sache* (1931), which continues the political and social novels, Heinrich Mann expatiates on his conception of the *Bekenntnisroman:* a novel, he says, should always be a sort of confession made by the author to himself but also to his contemporaries. The action is compressed into a period of three days.

Nothing could be more different from the whipped haste and the darting radiance of Heinrich Mann's style than the quiet flow and the guarded flame of Thomas Mann's (1875-1955) writings. The ever-recurring theme in his tales (short and long) is the glaring contrast between the normal man (*der Bürger*), who is fit to live (*lebenstüchtig*), and the artist or poet (*der Künstler*), who is not fit to live (*lebensuntüchtig, "unheilbar unbürgerlich"*). Thomas Mann's artist is another version of Schnitzler's over-ripe decadent; but whereas Schnitzler's creature dies under kisses as under a gradual anaesthetic, Thomas Mann's artist is tortured by the inescapable contemplation of his normal fellow-men with blue eyes and the rosy glow of health and no self-consciousness. The "citizen" is cased in his insensitive skin as in thick armor; he lives a charmed life, while the artist, to whom beauty is full of arrows, is assailed and driven despairing into the lonely corners of self-contempt. The artist is shut out inexorably from life; he is an outcast, a cripple, often an attitudinizing fraud. Something of this strange conception of the artist may be due to the vogue about 1900 of Lombroso's *Man of Genius;* but it is also by way of reaction from the old romantic *Verhimmelung* of the poet as one born in a golden clime, dowered with heaven knows what, ambrosial-locked, adulated, in short Tennyson or Paul Heyse or Wedekind's *Kammersänger,* or Hofmannsthal's *Tizian.* There is only one previous author with whose interpretation of the tragedy of the artist Mann's can be compared. But in Gottfried Keller's *Der grüne Heinrich* the lesson that life lies away from dream and mental effort is rather to be gathered by the wise than thrust to the front of all eyes; Keller's significance here is rather in the example of his own life–he, a great and sensitive artist, turned his back on art and letters and did his tedious duty for years as *Staatsschreiber* of the canton of Zurich. To go farther back, Goethe was lost for years in the common round of duties useful to his fellow-men: was he then a traitor to his genius or, for a period, sane?

Thomas Mann wrote *Buddenbrooks* (1901) when he was twenty-five; it made him a reputation which he progressively consolidated. It is a story of the parallel decay in the fortunes of a merchant's family in Lübeck and in the capacity for life of the members of it as succeeding generations take on more and more of the polish of culture. Through all Thomas Mann's work winds the grey thread of this idea that degeneration is the fruit of culture, that with culture goes physical decay. One ghastly detail recurs with unpleasant frequency: the carious teeth of the cultured; the last of the Buddenbrook dynasty suffers agonies and in the end dies from the diseased teeth. Two of Mann's characters (the author Spinell in the short story *Tristan* and the fat, degenerate husband in *Luischen*) are beardless in manhood (like Conrad Ferdinand Meyer before his Indian summer). It is in this conception of catastrophe springing, not from the classic conception of "tragic guilt" or the romantic conception of uncontrollable passion, but from a natural and inevitable process like that of seeding after flowering, that Thomas Mann is an innovator; to have proved with a slow, painstaking logic supported by all the evidence of science that culture is death (and with this idea he interweaves the still more tragic conception that love is death) is to have earned a secure seat with the immortals who have struck out into new paths in literature. The lesson is, in *Buddenbrooks* as in the following stories, enforced by an intricate use of symbol; e.g. though the Buddenbrooks die guiltless and in utter decency the last head of the firm, the immaculate senator Thomas, falls into a puddle in the streets and is brought home stained and bleeding to die; or, in plain terms, physical decay brings back the flower of gentility to the gutter. The technique of the novel is on the whole masterly, with its slow contrasts of character and its minute rendering of the *milieu* of an ancient Hanseatic city; faulty, perhaps, is the Dickens-like caricature of the eccentrics and villains; and very dubious is the use of leit-motifs, i.e. the wearisome repetition of facial and personal peculiarities and tricks of diction and gesture. This not only tends to bore if not to irritate the reader, it limits the characters; that is, at a certain moment they *must* say a certain thing or make a certain gesture–they are bound up in the piffling trammels of their personal habits instead of having unrestricted freedom of movement and self-revelation. To this practice, however, Thomas Mann keeps; thus in *Königliche Hoheit* Imma always speaks "with pouted lips," and the Grand Duke always sucks his upper lip.

The most poignant expression of the artist's tragedy, perhaps, is in *Tonio Kröger* (1903), the story of the Lübeck boy with a correct father and an exotic, passionate mother; he strays into art and longs to get back to decency, and is not surprised that when he returns as a famous author to his native city he is nearly arrested under suspicion of being a criminal. The three collections of short stories *Der kleine Herr Friedemann* (1898), *Tristan* (1903) and *Das Wunderkind* (1914) contain more than one acknowledged masterpiece. Asceticism and joy in life, or in other words dualism, are the theme of the short tale *Gladius Dei* and of the literary drama *Fiorenza* (1905). In *Gladius Dei* a religious fanatic declaims against the flaunting indecencies and the display of physical beauty in Munich, the typical art-city of our days; in *Fiorenza* Savonarola faces and defies Lorenzo dei Medici, while Florence, symbolized as the courtesan Fiore, has to choose between the two, between ascetic spirituality (*Geist*) and art that snares the senses. In *Königliche Hoheit* (1909) the individualism of the impressionists turns to the altruism which the expressionists were soon to proclaim: a prince (with a withered hand–bold symbolism before 1914!) stands for the artist or unusual character; he achieves salvation by sacrificing himself for the good of the community. The problem of the extraordinary personality here finds its solution, which is (in Mann's own words) that turning of the mind to democracy, common service, companionship, love, which had been proclaimed in the previous year in Heinrich Mann's novel *Die kleine Stadt*.

The problem of the artist is handled with painful incisiveness in *Der Tod in Venedig* (1913): a German author, ripe in years, with his work already in the schoolbooks, goes for a holiday to Venice; here, to his own horror, he falls in love with a beautiful boy, cannot tear himself away, dies. The negative solution is positive in scope: the romantic adulation of beauty is shameless ("*liederlich*"); the hero, if he had not been a romantic artist, might have controlled himself, might have left Venice and returned to duty.[5] The septentrional artist is softened and corrupted by the balmy south; but there is peril, too, in the indolent and consciousless east: the boy is a Pole, and smitten already with an incurable disease. The meaning of *Der Tod in Venedig* is clear enough in the hero's communings with himself: beauty, virtue, wisdom are, as Plato taught, divine; but of these only beauty is at once divine and visible to the senses; and since the artist works by the apperception of the senses, beauty is the artist's way to the spiritual. But how can he whose way to the spiritual goes through the senses attain wisdom and dignity? Is not this a devious way of sin that is bound to lead astray? The poet cannot take the way to beauty but Eros joins him as guide. . . . Poets are like women, passion is their exaltation, and their yearning must be for love. Mann's grim picture of the doomed artist is relieved by his interpretation of Schiller's character in the short tale *Schwere Stunde* (in *Das Wunderkind*): it is the physical incapacity caused by the overweight of mind that isolates the artist; the true artist, however, conscious of his frailty but also of the nobility of his task, develops the "heroism of weakness" (*Heroismus der Schwäche*): Schiller, too, is doomed by disease, and realizes how terrible his fate is when he compares himself with Goethe; but he finds consolation in the thought that it is harder to be a hero than to be a god. Here, too, there is an acknowledgment by Mann that the artist may be god-like and raised above criticism: Goethe, "*der Göttlich-Unbewusste*," creating by inspiration and not by knowledge, is worlds away from the man of letters to whom creation is a craft learned by rote and practised in tortured isolation.

This preoccupation with the problems of degeneration and disease culminates with Thomas Mann in his vast symbolic interpretation of life: *Der Zauberberg* (1924), perhaps the most deeply planned novel since *Wilhelm Meister*. Hans Castorp, the last scion of a patrician family in Hamburg, comes on a visit to his cousin, who is a patient at a sanatorium for consumptives at

Davos; he comes for three weeks, he remains seven years, and leaves the place to fall in the Great War–rescued by a great cataclysm, returned from dream to duty. The Magic Mountain is a symbol of Europe before the First Great War; it is a questioning of all culture. The Magic Mountain is the world of the dead: the doctor in charge is Rhadamanthus, all reckoning of time is lost, the inmates eat greedily (it is a life from copious meal to meal), and fall in love, the diseased with the diseased. Hans Castorp is in love with a Russian lady (Madame Chauchat): that is, the cultured love beauty–but beauty is only the phosphorescence of a dead body. This, again, is the old medieval view of life which we call dualism. Life itself, Hans Castorp discovers, is the equivalent of death: for life is a process of decomposition just as takes place in the body after death; the only difference is that in life there is chemical renewal.[6] Disease quickens the greed for food and love: so does culture. Hans is X-rayed: he sees his skeleton. But he keeps consciousness of the world of duty; there is a contrast between the bright daylight of the world of duty without and the soft moonlight in which he lingers hallucinated; afar is manly dignity, on the Magic Mountain there is Claudia Chauchat (like *Vrou Werlt* of medieval days) *"schlaff, wurmstichig und kirgiesenäugig."*

In *The Magic Mountain* all the resources of modern psychology, science, and criticism are massed and irresistibly brought into action in support of the thesis. There is an almost impossible delicacy in the use of psycho-analysis: e.g. sexual processes are suggested by the moving up and down of a pencil in a case unconsciously haunting the memory of a schoolboy, and there is some play, very effective in the diseased effulgence of *The Magic Mountain,* with the word *Liebe* as suggestive of two soft yielding lips with a fierce vowel like a red tongue shooting between them. Mann's most penetrating use of psychoanalysis is perhaps in the short tale *Unordnung und frühes Leid* (1926), in which a baby of a girl falls sick with erotic feelings for an adult: Prince Charming in a fairy-tale up to date. The self-irony of a criminal in *Bekenntnisse des Hochstaplers Felix Krull* (1938) serves as a variant of Mann's usual contrast of normality with artist morbidity, and expands the thesis hinted at in *Tonio Kröger* that there are affinities between artistry and criminality. A fragment of the Krull tale had been published in 1922; it was added to in the edition of 1954 (*Der Memoiren erster Teil*). As we have it now it is a picaresque novel in the sense of the English eighteenth century. Another story long known to exist was made available in 1931, but in French only, as *Sang réservé.* It is a translation, published in Paris, of *Wälsungenblut,* of which there had been a privately printed edition (1922) for the author's friends. This more or less suppressed tale served the Nazis as a stick to beat the author with: two Jews, they point out, twin brother and sister, commit incest on a bear-skin in the brother's bedroom after attending a performance of Wagner's *Walküre.*

In Hermann Hesse's *Narziss und Goldmund* the dualism of flesh and spirit is presented as two separate halves which are nevertheless one: for even abstract ideas, as Goldmund with his concrete vision points out, are sensuous images; the mind cannot reason save by sense; the immaterial is only an image of the material. In Thomas Mann's great series of four novels *Joseph und seine Brüder* (*Die Geschichten Jaakobs,* 1933; *Der junge Joseph,* 1934; *Joseph in Ægypten,* 1936; *Joseph der Ernährer,* 1942) Joseph is flesh and spirit in one; in him the flesh is sanctified by the divine law, but the spirit is in control of the flesh, and this by the consciousness of consecration to the higher life. Thomas Mann's purpose in this immense work is, therefore, as moral and "cultural" (to use a Nazi word) as possible; and there is Nazi doctrine in the detailed account of the Nordic wandering of first culture, including the solar myth, from Atlantis. What is not Nazi doctrine is the demonstration that higher culture–the consciousness of mind (*Geist*)–is historically Jewish, and that culture really is the sublimation of the sense of duty as obedience to those instincts of refinement which sunder man from brute. Thomas Mann in these volumes interprets history–and therefore life–as an eternal recurrence (*ewige Wiederkehr,* p. 102) of myth, which is in origin a symbolization of nature processes; and culture, he shows, is the effort of man to extricate his mind from the swathing folds of these myths by piercing to the sense of the symbol. Knowledge unifies the myriad myths of history and religions as the multiple but identical imaginative shaping, ever repeated though varied, of processes mysterious and miraculous to the primitive mind, particularly the sexual act (= burial in the pit), birth (= resurrection from the pit), and death (= birth; for all that is buried–as: seed in slime–is reborn). The divine is split into male and female; but these are one, because they are one principle. The animal gods of Egypt are easily intelligible as deifications of the animal functions of man: the "*baumelnde Hoden*" of the god-bulls, the phallic spears of temples reared at the sun, and so much besides that Thomas Mann with gentle irony illuminates. The most daring interpretation is that of the Resurrection of Christ as *ewige Wiederkehr* and as a birth-myth: "*Bôr*" means so much–hole, prison, pit, underworld; and in Mann's story a stone is rolled away from the pit into which Joseph has been cast by his brethren. But though the elucidation of procreation myths is the crimson thread that binds the succession of tales, there is interwoven too in moving fashion a picture of the gradual creation of the idea of God by Abraham, Isaac, and Jacob: God as He evolves for them is that which consecrates to higher duties (that is, to humanity and culture); and if Jewish religion, created as it is by the spirit, still retains in veiled form the sexual symbols by which primitive man imaged his gods Joseph (and by implication Christ, as Joseph returning) marks the ultimate spiritualization of life. If there were only this far-cast net of thought in the work, it would be philosophy rather than literature; but to the general reader the lure of the tales will be in the superb characterization, particularly of Jaakob, a monumental and tragic figure; and in the vivid poetic realism of certain episodes–the birth of Reuben, Jaakob's marriage-night with Rachel and the nine times repeated frenzied union. Most curiously elaborated is the temptation of Joseph by Potiphar's wife; and if Philipp von Zesen in his seventeenth-century novel of *Assenat und Joseph* (1670)–a related experiment in the cramming of encyclopedic knowledge into a tale showing the present in the past–makes this lady psychologically possible, Thomas Mann gives inevitability to her stung passion–not only is her "husband" a eunuch priest, not only is she obsessed by the phallic ritual of Egyptian deities, but the poignancy of the situation is accentuated because Potiphar (a super-refined sybarite and gourmand) has been and is a second father to Joseph: as Joseph resists the woman he sees before him not only the face of his own father but that of his second father as well; it is indeed a composite face, with sterner features–those of God. Parental and divine inhibition therefore give the spirit strength to resist the flesh. And yet there is no defence of asceticism or even of chastity in the story: the chastity of priests and vestals is ruthlessly laid bare in all its futility; but Joseph is reserved–that is, sexual functions are for a purpose foreordained by God. The meaning of Mann's Joseph thus is that he simplifies the chaotic and fleshly symbols of the divine to what he himself is–spirit purified (more literally, superior and more cultured intellect). To spirit (*Geist*) the eternal peril is the flesh, the undying sphinx which, crouching, hides its sex, but which, male or female, is all sex and cruel clutching claws.

The action of *Lotte in Weimar* (1939) returns ostensibly to modernity–the date is 1816–, but the foundation matter is still myth, the myth or legend of *The Sorrows of Werther*. The main theme, however, is that of the loss of a writer's productivity as the pitiless years take their toll. Lotte visits Goethe in Weimar and finds him, not so much aged as lost to life, as life is in female fancy. Goethe as we see him, stiffened and sterile, in *Lotte in Weimar,* exemplifies one of the main tenets stated in Mann's next novel, *Doktor Faustus* (1947): "Choose good, you vegetate; choose evil, you attain knowledge and you create." The narrator is Serenus Zeitblom, Ph.D., a grammar school teacher. In the two years from 1943 to 1945 he writes down the story of an old schoolfellow and lifelong friend, Adrian Leverkühn, who had died in 1940. They had studied together at Halle; Zeitblom philology, Leverkühn theology. Very clear in the story is the contrast of *Bürger*–Zeitblom, and *Künstler*–Leverkühn. Or, otherwise contrasted, they typify *Moralismus–Ästhetentum.* Leverkühn's study of theology at Halle is the first approach to the atmosphere of the Faust legend; however, he changes over to music. Zeitblom writes during the course of World War II; he is an anti-Nazi, but finds it prudent to keep quiet. The main idea of the book is that Dr. Faustus is Germany, the collapse of which is symbolized in the last musical works of Leverkühn, *Apocalipsis cum figuris* and *Wehklag Dr. Fausti. Die vertauschten Köpfe* (1940) is an Indian legend ironically treated: an Indian woman attempts to produce a perfect husband by conjuring her friend's head on to her husband's body, and vice versa, only to find that the new heads adapt themselves to the bodies on which they are transposed. *Das Gesetz* (1944) continues in brief form the Joseph novels: it is the story of Moses and his passing of the Red Sea. In *Doktor Faustus* Mann had outlined the plot of a musical composition by Leverkühn: *The Birth of Pope Gregory;* this points forward to his next novel in chronological order, *Der Erwählte* (1951), the story of yet another nominal sinner. The source is the epic *Gregorius* by the Middle High German poet Hartmann von Aue, a medieval counterpart of the Greek legend of Oedipus; that is to say, it is a handling of the involuntary incest theme. The legend is ironically treated; indeed there are parodistic elements. *Die Betrogene* (1953) is a short novel–ironical once again: a widow of fifty falls in love with a young American whom she has engaged to teach English to her son; the explanation is that, after reaching the climacteric, she has a return of menstruation; this she identifies with a *Seelenfrühling,* a *Neuerblühen* (one is reminded of Goethe's *wiederholte Pubertät*). She has a renewed sensitiveness to scents; while out walking she gets a whiff of musk, follows it up, to find that it is the effluvium of a heap of rotting vegetable matter with excrements–the womb of nature. Therefore: *Moderduft und Liebeslust.* The explanation turns out to be that she is suffering from cancer of the womb.

One of the illuminative essays of *Leiden und Grösse der Meister* (1935) deals with Wagner; the others interpret Goethe, Platen, Storm, and Cervantes. Time itself has played ironically with this ironist; always (as a born patrician) a conservative–in spite of his advanced thinking–he defended Germany during the First War (*Gedanken im Kriege,* September 1914) as the embodiment of "*Kultur*" against the mere "*Zivilization*" of the allies; and in a further 1914 essay, *Friedrich der Grosse und die grosse Koalition* (published 1915), he found "the urge of destiny, the spirit of history" in Frederick's defiance of Europe. Other collections of essays and speeches are *Betrachtungen eines Unpolitischen* (1918); *Rede und Antwort* (1922); *Bemühungen* (1925); *Die Forderungen des Tages* (1930); *Goethe und Tolstoi* (1923); *Freud und die Zukunft* (1936); *Achtung, Europa!* (1938).

Georg Hermann (1871-1943) was ranged among the disciples of Thomas Mann when, in 1906, his novel *Jettchen Gebert* won him lasting fame. The outline of the story does indeed suggest *Buddenbrooks:* the Geberts are Berlin patricians and merchants, and there is something of an implication that culture brings incapacity for business in the person of Uncle Jason, who has a distant resemblance to Christian Buddenbrook, not however as the fool of the family but as one by the bent of his character forced apart from his family, an *enfant terrible,* a man about town and a wit, a collector of rare books as well as of costly porcelain; he speaks himself (in distinctly Mannsian terms) of his "*seelische Empfindung des Ausgeschlossenseins von der Familie, dem Bürgertum, dem Staat.*" The spirit of the story is, however, different from that of *Buddenbrooks;* and where in details of technique, such as the ticketing of individual characters by recurrent phrases and long passages in which season and weather move in lyric unison with the story, both authors, no doubt, are directly imitating Dickens. Decay by culture is certainly not the theme: the revered ancestor, the Court Jeweller of his day, had culture (of the Voltairean sort) to his finger-tips, and he combined a robust capacity for life with fine feelings (*Lebensstärke und Sinnenfeinheit*), while his brother, Uncle Eli (the patriarch among the Geberts, a blunt old fellow whose culture runs to carriages and horses) and two of his children, Salomon and Ferdinand, have less fineness of nerves but undiminished capacity for business. The decay is in the reverse direction to that of *Buddenbrooks,* except, of course, in the case of Uncle Jason. The main reason for Uncle Salomon's and Uncle Ferdinand's lack of intellectual interest is family environment: they have both married Jacobys, Polish Jewesses from the Posen district, squat little women with "eyes like two black currants in a fat bun." And here we have the obvious theme of the story: the stark contrast and the unending conflict between two types of Jew represented by the Geberts and the Jacobys–and the Berlin patricians, being honest and restrained, must be outmaneuvered by the unscrupulous, bumptious immigrants from the dirty East. The Berlin Jews have the indifference to ritual of men of the world; the Posen Jews put all their narrow pride of race into the observance of every racial rite. The pride of race of the Berlin Jews springs from quite a different source–they consort with Christians, but they are true to their tribe because of age-old memories of unjust persecution. And when the heroine of the tale, Jettchen Gebert, falls passionately in love with a handsome young Christian, Dr. Kössling, an author at the beginning of whatever career the future may have in store for him but therefore to sound business men for the present a social outcast, the family with a good conscience are adamant. Uncle Eli and Uncle Jason would indeed not withhold consent, but as members of the family they must uphold its tribal authority. And so by cruel moral pressure Jettchen is forced into marriage with a loathsome cousin, Julius Jacoby, just arrived with all his green pushfulness from Posen. His two aunts arrange the affair. The reader, well informed of Jettchen's strong will and intellectual leanings and her physical revulsion (her fine nerves shiver at his approach as if her two hands touched a toad in the dark) would expect her to elope rather than yield; but–and it comes as a dramatic surprise–she *cannot* resist, because she is a good Jewess as well as a passionate lover: she is an orphan–her father had been killed fighting for Prussia against Napoleon, a volunteer with Jason, who came off with a lame leg; and she has been brought up, with all a father's care and affection, for twenty years by Uncle Salomon, who now is entitled to present the bill which Jettchen must pay. Like one hypnotized she goes through all the agony of the marriage festival, but at its close steals out into the starry night. The sequel, *Henriette Jakoby* (1908), falls below the level of *Jettchen Gebert*: there is too little in the way of action and the painting of moods is too extensive. The marriage, of course, is a failure from the first, and Henriette takes refuge with Uncle Jason. Gradually the truth dawns on her that Uncle Jason loves her. The relations with Kössling are renewed, and in a weak moment she gives herself to him. Then she realizes that Uncle Jason's love is more to her, and she commits suicide. Jettchen is one of the most charming ladies in recent German literature. We see her, a perfect little housewife, preparing the immense family banquets; and we admire her with Dr. Kössling's eyes when in the first chapter we find her going to market (like a dainty Doulton lady) in her silver grey taffeta gown, coal-scuttle bonnet tied by pink buds, lavender gloves and long-fringed Cashmere shawl and velvet bodice. The presentation of the *Biedermeierzeit,* the period of 1840 with its crinolines and daintily figured stuffs, its stately *intérieurs* with massive furniture and costly porcelain, is generally praised as scholarly, accurate, and for all its gentle irony appreciative. How delightful it is to go with Jettchen and her aunt for a summer holiday in sylvan Charlottenburg, and to hear why Uncle Ferdinand's family prefer the more open solitudes of Schöneberg! Altogether *Jettchen Gebert* must be given high rank as more or less (in spite of an occasional false note due to Dickens worship, to which German novelists are prone[7]) a Jewish classic, and certainly the one Berliner Roman of the period which is likely to live. The Berlin novels of the naturalists failed because, as *Milieuromane,* they subordinated character to *milieu*; *Jettchen Gebert* succeeds because, over and above its masterly and detailed presentation of the *milieu* of a given period, it creates vividly individualized characters and handles racial and social problems with inner knowledge and keen insight. Georg Hermann's other works show him still a master of irony, but he does not again find a theme of so simple an appeal as *Jettchen Gebert.* In *Heinrich Schön junior* (1915) he again shows his knowledge of art matters; the theme–that of Don Carlos–is a young man's love for his stepmother in the Potsdam of 1844. *Kubinke* (1911) is yet another Berlin novel, but of our own days: Emil Kubinke is a barber's assistant who, meshed in the toils of three calculating females, hangs himself to avoid marriage with his *fiancée* while faced with two affiliation orders.

Animal symbolism as an interpretation of human character by implied comparison reaches its high-water mark in Kipling's *Jungle Book.* In German literature there is nothing nearly so good. Bölsche's *Das Liebesleben in der Natur* is, as a start, too scientific for pure literature, while Hermann Löns's *Mümmelmann* and Waldemar Bonsels' *Die Biene Maja und ihre Abenteuer* (1912), *Himmelsvolk* (1915), and *Mario und die Tiere* (1927) play about the surface. Waldemar Bonsels (1881-1952) is a Holstein man and has that love of sea-faring and far lands that Holstein men often have. His *Indienfahrt* (1916) is too peacefully dream-like for exotic thrills, the radiant vagabond of his numerous stories is never more than a hero for happy people, and the theosophical doctrine he propounds has no tangibility.

---

1. Where Hölderlin studied before proceeding to the higher Seminary at Tübingen.

2. Hesse signed this novel with the name of Emil Sinclair. Sinclair is the name of Hölderlin's friend.

3. Born in 1858, Hermann Bang lived in Berlin. His first novel–*Hoffnungslose Geschlechter* in German–has for hero the last decadent scion of a noble race. In his later works he has Maeterlinck's conception of fate as a secret force which breathes around us. With the short stories of *Leben und Tod* his attitude to life moves to a naïve hedonism: we can defy fate, and snatch what fleeting joys we can: "*es gibt nichts als den Trieb; der allein ist Herr und Meister*"; "*Blut ist Blut; das will sieden, bis es matt ist oder kalt ist.*" Keyserling's *Herrenmenschen* have the frightful sensation of loneliness of Bang's characters, due to the tragic intensity of their feeling that there is nothing in life but this snatching at pleasure which *must* be shot with pain because it passes, and because in the face of fate, which ironically permits it, it is so mean.

4. Typical is Heinrich Mann's confession: "*Ich ging,*

sobald ich konnte, heim nach Italen. Ja, eine Zeitlang glaubte ich zu hause zu sein. Aber ich war es auch dort nicht; und seit ich dies deutlich spürte, begann ich etwas zu können."

5. Dr. D. M. Hall, in her dissertation *The Venice Legend in German Literature since 1880,* has made it seem likely that one of the sources of the book was the unabridged edition of Platen's diary (ed. Laubmann und von Scheffler, 1896-1900). In a speech on Platen (in *Leiden und Grösse der Meister*) Thomas Mann takes the poet's homosexuality for granted. Another possible source is *Ein Vermächtnis* (1911), the diary of the painter Anselm Feuerbach.

6. *Der Trieb unserer Elemente geht auf Desoxydation. Das Leben ist erzwungene Oxydation.* Novalis.

7. The influence is most marked in the novels of Wilhelm Raabe (1831-1910) and Max Kretzer. Stefan Zweig deals with Dickens in *Drei Meister.*

Reprinted from Modern German Literature 1880-1950, *third edition (London: Methuen, 1959), pp. 279-320.*

The 'Twenties and Berlin

Alex Natan

To write about the 'twenties in Berlin serves as a reminder that Berlin was then not only the capital of Germány but also the center of Germany's cultural life. First nights in theatres and cinemas, outstanding art exhibitions, daring opera premières and concerts with ultra-modern programmes, architectural experiments, were initiated in Berlin, and were later repeated, modified, or transformed in the provinces. This fact is of crucial importance to an understanding of Berlin in the 'twenties and an appreciation of the parochial character of the cultural life in the Federal Republic deprived of the focal point that once was Berlin.

The 'twenties in Berlin did not start on the first day of the decade nor did they end with its last day. They blossomed for a far shorter period, perhaps from the autumn of 1923 onwards, when inflation reached its end, to a hot summer night in August 1928. These few years, now so sentimentally steeped in a rosy afterglow, were rightly described as "the time between two twilights," between the collapse of Imperial Germany and the suicide of the Weimar Republic. But why try to resuscitate what by rights ought to be dead but still lives on as the "Golden 'twenties?"

When, in Spring 1968, at the end of the impressive production of Seneca's *Oedipus* in London's National Theatre a tremendous phallus was carried on to the stage and the Bacchantes began their dance in honor of the God of Thebes who had cleansed their town from archetypal sin, the music accompanied this ritual with a popular hit-song of the 'twenties: "Yes, We Have No Bananas." At this moment a friend of mine whispered to me: "Isn't it breath-taking? To you it must be like an emotive revival of Berlin in the 'twenties. . . ."

Most of the documentary evidence about the 'twenties in Berlin are records written by those who had then lived in the metropolis and had been personally involved in its important events. It is therefore necessary to understand that these diaries and notes are identical with a personal recollection or confession. However, one should be on one's guard when discussing the literary and artistic aspects of this period with young people today who seem to be dazzled by their image of what Berlin once represented. To a rather vociferous section of the contemporary intellectual world Berlin seems to have been turned into a myth, to have emerged as a fabulous city of sheer make-believe anticipating a permissive society to a degree which even London has failed to achieve.

In probing deeper into this myth of a city which hardly any of its present admirers had actually known forty or fifty years ago, one often finds that admiration stems from Christopher Isherwood's brilliant novels of Berlin. *Mr. Norris changes trains* (1935) and *Goodbye to Berlin* (1939) display a most engaging but hardly impartial or analytical panorama of the alleged corruption of Berlin and of the insecure moral position of the bourgeois intellectuals. I am the last to deny that both novels offer a suggestive and often compassionate guide to the more lurid aspects of metropolitan nightlife and its dubious denizens. However, one should not overlook the fact that Isherwood actually arrived in Berlin in 1932, when the 'twenties were over and Hitler's lust for power already cast deep shadows over things to come. Isherwood only knew Berlin at the height of the political and economic crisis. What he reports about the 'twenties stems from hearsay.

I have already touched upon the misleading fact that the "Golden 'twenties" hardly filled the decade but can easily be encompassed between the end of the inflation in the autumn of 1923 and the climactic last day of August 1928, when Bert Brecht's *Dreigroschenoper* with music by Kurt Weill was staged for the first time. I attended this premiere, which became one of the most meaningful experiences of my life. In the theatre Berlin's sophisticated bourgeoisie, pampered and complacent during those five "fat" years following the revolution that never took place applauded not only a biting satire of its own brittle existence but also–if unwittingly–the menacing approach of a political extremism which was to turn its superficial security into perilous quicksand. Shortly after the Brecht first night came the bank crashes, economic depression, ever-increasing unemployment, and ultimately the short-lived triumph of those reactionary forces which had retained their influence from that decisive milestone in November 1918 when the German Social Democrats committed the act of historical treason by strangulating the incipient social revolt through their pact with those powers which had only the day before been the stalwart pillar of throne and altar.

Fifty years of counter-revolution have passed. A real revolution never took place in Germany. Only the army and the navy went on strike. No great landowner was dispossessed, no factory was ever nationalized and in no industrial enterprise were the workers allowed a right of co-management. And which revolution would have ever been so magnanimous as the November revolution in Germany which granted full freedom of the press to its arch-enemies? Only very few revolutionary minds, dreaming of an age for a new man, the coming of which had been proclaimed by the Expressionists, intended a genuine reconstruction of the social fabric. They could not tolerate the thought that nothing would be altered and everything revert to the shallowest materialism after a war which had destroyed the happiness of millions of people. The kings had indeed departed but the generals remained. They were taken on the pay-roll of the Social-Democrats. Their "Freicorps" drenched Germany in blood and trampled the "Neue Zeit" of which the young generation sang into the mud and mire with their jackboots. All this happened primarily in Berlin. It is all too easy to forget that Berlin's 'twenties began with disappointed hopes, with blood and tears, with political and social disenchantment. The dreams of a new and possibly egalitarian society and the faith in a new man had been nipped in the bud violently and decisively. Yet the glamorous attraction of Berlin in the 'twenties still continues to fascinate a generation born after the Second World War. We who were then young and very much alive can only shrug our shoulders and quote François Villon: "Où sont les neiges d'antan?"

One of the fundamental misconceptions of the Berlin myth is that this short period had indeed given birth to all those movements in the arts and sciences which are all too readily associated with Berlin in the 'twenties. Talking to young people of today one is taken aback to hear them telescoping Expressionism in literature and painting, the science of psychoanalysis, the science of the psychology of the subconscious, the adventures in architecture, music and the applied arts, the provocative trends in philosophy and sociology, as if all had occurred almost simultaneously in Berlin.

In fact, a glittering kaleidoscope of talents and creative forces was concentrated in and around Berlin and provided the source for the legend of the 'twenties. Four years of the carnage of war had severely inhibited these talents. When the war ended, the flood-gates opened and the creative forces gushed forth, uninhibited everywhere, not only in Berlin, not only in imitative Germany, but all over Europe. They exercised a tremendous impact on the cultural revolution of the Western world. For man neither remained the measure of all things nor the centre of the world. The epoch of the Renaissance was finally over. The 'twenties signified, however, the end and a new beginning of what Robert Musil described as "the disintegration of anthropocentric behavior." Berlin offered a particularly good vantage point for observing this transformation.

For this cultural revolution was to be witnessed everywhere: in the Cubist paintings of Picasso, Braque and Gris, in the abstract compositions of Archipenko and Kandinsky, in the Futurist theories of Marinetti, in the Surrealism of Aragon, Breton and Elouard. Dadaism was born and propagated in the Cabaret Voltaire in Zürich. Stravinsky and Schönberg had already shocked the concert-going public before the war. Most of the poets and writers who came into their own during the 'twenties had already made their mark before the outbreak of the war. All these trends could be observed in Paris as well as in New York, even in staid London and in frivolous Vienna, simply because all these new ideas and new impulses no longer remained the privilege of a small minority but became the property of a changing society, of what the German sociologist Max Weber called "Massendemokratie."

Berlin stood at the receiving end of this cultural turbulence but it was not its creative birthplace. Admittedly Berlin's theater and cinema productions had achieved a remarkably high standard. But a closer scrutiny will readily reveal that Berlin's famous first nights belonged to the period before rather than after 1923. It is too easily forgotten, for instance, that the explosion of Expressionist drama had already spent its main force when the 'twenties dawned. Wedekind had died in 1918 and the plays of his last years had proved second-rate. Sternheim, the caustic satirist, wrote his cycle of mordant comedies against middle-class morality all before 1914. From this time dated also the anti-war poems of Werfel, Stadler and Heym. The significant reviews and periodicals of Expressionism, such as *Die Aktion, Der Sturm* and *Die weißen Blätter* all flourished in the pre-war years. The younger generation of Expressionists, such as Barlach, Kornfeld, Hasenclever, Bronnen, Unruh, Goering and Sorge had also written their dramatic manifestos before and during the war. Even Toller's famous *Die Wandlung* was finished in 1917. What all Expressionist writers had in common was a determination to kindle a new outlook on life in the midst of a solid world of bourgeois prejudice. Hence the Imperial censorship was determined not to give them a public hearing. But a way was discovered to circumvent the censor. Matinées to which only club members were admitted were formed and already produced daring novelties during the war. When the censor disappeared in 1918 a flood of new plays and new productions could be seen all over the country, foremost in Berlin. It was the time when inventive producers like Jessner, Fehling, K. H. Martin and Piscator dominated the Berlin stage and made it a focus of new experiments in style and interpretation. It was equally significant that the great magician Max Reinhardt chose just this moment to exchange the turbulent waters of Berlin for the sager pastures of Vienna because the foundations of the German bourgeoisie seemed to be dangerously underminded, at least for the time being. In short, what was exciting in the Berlin theatre took place mainly between 1918 and 1920. When conservative forces were back in the saddle, Jessner, the director of the State Theatre, was criticized and censured in the Prussian parliament, and Schnitzler's charming dialogue *Der Reigen* prosecuted because it allegedly undermined morale and public order. The great experimental phase of Berlin's stage petered out with the end of inflation when the forces of yesterday relentlessly returned to power.

The same phenomenon can be observed in the development of Expressionist art. The "Blaue Reiter" group lasted for only three years (1911-14). Afterwards Klee returned to his native Switzerland. So did Kirchner. Macke and Marc were killed during the war and the sculptor Lehmbruck died soon after in 1919. Since the arts had ceased to be the privilege of those who used to be their patrons their works could now be exhibited to a greater public.

And yet Berlin possessed some justification to be proud of its position as a leading avant-gardist center between 1923 and 1928. It was then that a new style was developed which became significant for the whole period and which really put its stamp on the Berlin of the 'twenties. This was "Neue Sachlichkeit," an attitude of mind which recognized the supremacy of material facts and worshipped materialism as an ideology. It produced the "Zeitstück," a kind of dramatic documentation which regained popularity in the German drama of recent years (viz. Dorst's *Toller*). These plays dealt with contemporary issues, seen in retrospect and reflecting very sharply the social and spiritual currents and problems of recent and present German history. One remembers those "Zeitstücke" which came to grips with the moral and spiritual difficulties of German adolescence, such as Klaus Mann's *Anja und Esther,* Peter Martin Lampel's *Revolte im Erziehungshaus,* Christa Winsloe's *Mädchen in Uniform* and Ferdinand Bruckner's great success *Krankheit der Jugend.* Theodor Plivier and Friedrich Wolff dramatised contemporary political events and presented them in Berlin, thus provoking much discussion and partisanship. But what used to set Berlin on fire is now completely forgotten because all these dramatic efforts were time-bound and did not possess what the Germans so admire, namely, "Ewigkeitswert." And then Bert Brecht, who made Germany's outstanding contribution to the post-war European theatre, appeared. Although a native of the Bavarian provinces he spent his formative years in the capital. It is hardly an exaggeration to say that Berlin made Brecht. The proposition has been advanced that the five "fat" years of Berlin culminated with the first night of Brecht's *Dreigroschenoper,* whose philosophy is expressed by Brecht's famous dictum: "The world is poor; man is evil," a telling obituary of the 'twenties. Brecht reversed the basic creed of Expressionism that "man is good." In him social cynicism identifies itself with a revolutionary challenge, directed at the "rich" and demanding social upheaval: "Erst kommt das Fressen, dann kommt die Moral." First the poor, too, must be allowed to cut themselves their share from the large loaf. During that August evening in 1928 the bourgeois audience relished the antics of Macheath and his gang of cut-throats. Brecht intended them "to represent bourgeois types, and their exploits to reflect bourgeois morality" (H. F. Garten). The poet wrote: "The robber Macheath must be represented by the actor as a bourgeois character. The partiality of the bourgeoisie for robbers can be explained from the fallacy that a robber is not a bourgeois. This fallacy derives from another fallacy: a bourgeois is not a robber." Berlin had not long to wait to discover the correctness of Brecht's forecast: there was no difference between bourgeois and robber, for both became ardent Nazis.

This vogue of "Neue Sachlichkeit" manifested itself also in the visual arts. Georg Grosz, stimulated by the Dadaist technique of photomontage, became the outstanding representative of the trend to express a grim realism in his paintings by choosing the terrible and repulsive side of war as the main theme of his work. He became the center of a significant controversy when a reactionary judge sent him to prison for having depicted Christ on the cross with a gas-mask in his famous "Ecce Homo." Those in power allowed those out of power a certain amount of leeway in Berlin. However, as soon as a member of the cultural minority dared to criticize the hollow mentality of the ruling class it clamped down on him ruthlessly. And indeed, Georg Grosz, tried mercilessly to caricature and thus to dissect the real "Gesicht der herrschenden Klasse" ("face of the ruling class"). In vain–he realised the truth behind the deceptive veneer of the Weimar Republic and left for the United States before the 'twenties were ended.

It has been said that Berlin was less a center of productive and creative forces than a successful catalyst for the dissemination of new values, new ideas, new forms and shapes in the usual arts, music and so on, and there was evidence enough for such a belief. Berlin could boast three opera houses and an annual concert programme which was certainly the envy of other European capitals. At the beginning of the 'twenties the repertoire of the opera houses was still traditional: Richard Wagner, Richard Strauss, plenty of "verismo," interspersed with the minor figures of German romanticism. Like lightning Igor Stravinsky's *Soldier's tale,* produced for the first time at the end of the war in Lausanne, heralded a new era which reached its climax with Arnold Schönberg and his dodecatonal system. Schönberg's experiments encouraged Alban Berg to compose his Büchner opera *Wozzeck* whose production under Erich Kleiber on 14 December 1925 proved probably the highlight of the feverish musical life of Berlin which also welcomed annually conductors like Bruno Walter, Toscanini, Stokowski, R. Strauss, Furtwängler, Fritz Busch, Klemperer, Mengelberg and many others.

Berlin was also the centre of Germany's budding film industry. Siegfried Krakauer in his fascinating book *From Caligari to Hitler* has drawn attention to a sinister pattern which he finds in all German films of importance. As a reflection of the miscarried attempt of a revolution such films as *Dr. Caligari, Der müde Tod,* or *Dr. Mabuse* portrayed the individual soul faced with the unavoidable alternative of tyranny and chaos. *Die Nibelungen,* shot in 1922, already stressed the inexorability of fate and destiny, patterns which were resumed in the film pageantry of the Nazis. The great days of the German experimental film, usually shot in the suburb of Babelsberg, were significantly over, when the five "fat" years set in and produced films which were primarily aimed at the entertainment of the bourgeoisie.

All these new trends, of which only very few actually originated in Berlin itself, polarized, nevertheless, in the capital of the Weimar Republic. The town acquired the reputation of a focal spectrum which knew how to attract the most divergent forces and, in return, granted them unlimited scope to play out their dynamism. Yet there were millions of people who still went regularly to church, who read Agnes Günther or Vicki Baum, if not Stefan George and the new heralds of the post-war youth movements. Many, many people longed for the "Golden Age" of Wilhelminian vainglory or helped to get the new craze for sport started. They all remained totally immune to the glittering panorama Berlin's West End had to offer or were determined to bring it to an abrupt and even bloody end. Yet the question remains why the artistic and intellectual life represented such an exciting force for such a short time and that so many forces blazed the path into this new and uncharted world of "Neue Sachlichkeit." While Paris remained hide-bound to tradition and hampered by much plush and self-adulation Berlin enjoyed the advantage of not possessing any past. The town was singularly devoid of buildings of architectural interest, partly because Berlin became very late a capital, partly because the Hohenzollerns preferred Potsdam as their near-by residence.

Lacking tradition, which London, Rome or Vienna possessed Berlin found it easier to become the centre of forces which were hardly rooted on the banks of the Spree. Berlin was an ideal point of departure for the experiments of an avant-garde. They have now assumed the proportions of a nostalgic age for people who did not experience them. One should never forget that a social revolution did not take place in 1918. After some months of unrest the policeman was back in his place and guarded the bourgeois's peace, security and order. As long as these guardians of the state remained undisturbed the writer and the artist could spread their wings unclipped, certainly more undisturbed in Berlin than in the provinces. All that really happened in the 'twenties was that "the more realistic saxophone replaced the coachman's romantic bugle." Anyone who wishes to understand the brittleness and the hectic mostly self-deceptive fever of Berlin's 'twenties should read once more any of four books which all appeared significantly at the end of this period. Their authors had all welcomed the Expressionist dawn of an epoch which promised a new age of green pastures for a free man. They all had lost every ounce of their illusions by 1930. These are the books: Alfred Döblin's *Berlin Alexanderplatz,* Robert Musil's *The Man without Qualities,* Ortega y Gasset's *The Revolt of the Masses,* and Karl Jasper's *The Spiritual Situation of our Times.* All four books express the deep resignation of their writers. Hitler was already knocking at the gates!

Who thinks today of Berlin only as an exciting and sparkling dream, as a perpetual "happening" of mental and physical high-powered "trips" misses the under-current of the revolution that never was. Anyone who was born in Berlin and sang in 1918 "Mit uns zieht die neue Zeit" perceived the pulse-beat of the disillusions and frustrations of the restored "good old days" underneath the glittering, alluring but so deceptive facade in the 'twenties. Nobody can deny that life then in Berlin was exciting and a breathtaking merry-go-round. But all who knew the ironical attitude of the Berliner towards the events of life, witnessed the interment of the man who once saw a vision of a new age which was now shattered by the harsh reality of the old establishment. Georg Kaiser's most telling drama is probably *From Morn to Midnight.* It is the story of a bank clerk who embezzles a large sum of money and strives, within the compass of a single day, to make up for a lifetime of frustration. Finally he is thoroughly disillusioned and shoots himself. Georg Kaiser's last stage direction which, to me, is synonymous with the real significance of Berlin in the 'twenties runs like this: "His groaning rattles like an Ecce . . . his breathing hums like Homo."

To have spent one's formative years in the Berlin of the 'twenties was certainly an education in itself which supplied unlimited stimulation for the rest of one's life. Until Hitler, the history of Berlin was the history of Germany; afterwards it became, for a time, the history of the world. It has always been the most un-German of Germany's cities, otherwise President Kennedy could never have said, "I am a Berliner." Imagine saying this of Bielefeld or Weilheim! The Berliner would be the first to draw a sharp dividing-line. For he, as a big-city character, is tough and cynical, and has always been somewhat unpopular with his own countryman. The satire and irony have set him aside from the rest of the Germans. How he copes with life and thus also digested the manifold attractions of the 'twenties is better told through a little anecdote. In 1848 a street urchin stops whistling as Field Marshal Wrangel approaches. "Because of my uniform?" asks the flattered Wrangel. "No," shouts back the irreverent boy, "when I see you I want to laugh, and when I laugh I can't whistle!"

Reprinted from Affinities: Essays in German and English Literature, *edited by R. W. Last (London: Wolff, 1971), pp. 280-289.*

The Conversion of an Unpolitical Man

W. H. Bruford

It is a fortunate accident for the understanding of German thought about the relationship between culture and politics, as it developed under the pressure of events between the later years of the Wilhelmine Reich and the foundation of the Federal Republic, that Thomas Mann, a supremely articulate, conscientious and intelligent witness of these events, felt himself impelled to speak his mind about them, not only symbolically in his novels and stories, but directly in essays and speeches on current affairs. Studying these writings, particularly the *Betrachtungen eines Unpolitischen* and the two volumes of *Reden und Aufsätze* (1965), one is led to the conclusion that Thomas Mann has few if any rivals as the representative of the best German thought and feeling, the enduring German conscience, in the most disturbed and tragic half-century of German history.

It is well known that Mann's political views underwent what looks like a complete reversal, though he often disputed this interpretation, seeing his whole life's effort as directed towards a fuller humane life for all. His example may at least show how it was possible for a patriotic German conservative to grow into a supporter of the Weimar Republic, an impassioned opponent of Hitler and, in his last years, a convinced democrat who, as an American citizen, deliberately lived in Switzerland and declared himself to belong to no party but that of "humanity."

At the beginning of the First World War Thomas Mann was thirty-nine years old and was quickly rejected for military service, but in the general unrest and suspense he found himself unable to continue the creative writing he had planned and begun before the war–the *Zauberberg* was the chief item–until he had cleared up his ideas about the rights and wrongs of the war and particularly about the question singled out by Allied propaganda, the attitude on both sides to freedom and democracy. After writing in the first year of the war his historical sketch *Friedrich und die große Koalition* and two patriotic articles, he spent more than two years on a series of essays on the war-aims question which he published in 1918 as a book of over 600 pages, *Betrachtungen eines Unpolitischen.* It is a tedious, rambling book which shows little of the psychological penetration, witty irony and shapeliness of his novels and stories, but one can well believe that some inner compulsion made him go on and on, endlessly rehandling the same basic themes: the contrast between the literary artist and the man of letters, between German "Kultur" and Western civilization, between middle-class stability in a hierarchic society and modern notions about progress and democracy. His intentions, as he remembered them a generation later, are put succinctly in a letter to Hermann Hesse (8 February 1947): "The pacifism of the political journalists, Expressionists, Activists of that time got on my nerves as much as the self-satisfied moralism of Allied propaganda, half Jacobin, half Puritan, and I defended in reply to it an unpolitical and anti-political Germanity, Protestant and Romantic in essense, which I felt to be the basis of my existence."

These abstractions however do not explain the bitter personal tone of the book, which is due to differences, only partly political, between Thomas Mann and his elder brother Heinrich. Both had been bent on writing from an early age, Thomas no doubt at first in imitation of his four years older brother and following the same models, but determined in his dour way to do better and before long succeeding. They spent most of 1896-8 happily together in Italy, supported from home, but the novels they both began then, *Buddenbrooks* and *Im Schlaraffenland,* had already shown their different preoccupations, and the differences had grown greater with time. Heinrich was always too slapdash and crude for Thomas's taste, and Thomas too little concerned with social and political problems for Heinrich's. There were differences in their friends and way of life too, especially after Thomas had married (in 1905) into a wealthy and cultivated Jewish family. His respectability and artistic asceticism were as distasteful no doubt to Heinrich as much about Heinrich was to him, his bohemianism, his theatrical friends and mistresses, and his provocative studies of bourgeois life like *Professor Unrat,* the novel of the film *The Blue Angel,* one of Marlene Dietrich's early triumphs. In the first year of the war Heinrich was annoyed by his brother's patriotic article "Gedanken im Kriege" and responded by veiled criticism of him in his essay "Zola" late in 1915 in *Die weißen Blätter,* where he masks himself as Zola and paints a lurid picture of Germany under Wilhelm II, calling it France under Louis Bonaparte. Thomas, as his note-books show, rejected his brother's activism, his idea that literary men and politicians should combine against reaction.[1] The man of intellect, according to Thomas, would only make a fool of himself by attempting direct action. He should be content to influence thought. He particularly resented what he took to be barbed references to his own writing, in which he was accused of toadying to the establishment and of misplaced ambition. For six years the brothers would have nothing to do with each other, and they were not fully reconciled for some years after 1922, when Thomas toned down and abbreviated the *Betrachtungen* in a new edition.

The opponent whom Thomas Mann criticizes throughout the *Betrachtungen* under the name of "der Zivilisationsliterat" is therefore in the main his brother. A letter to Ernst Bertram (25 November 1916) speaks explicitly of the need he has long felt of symbolizing and personifying the differences of outlook, which are the curse of Germany, in his brother and himself. "There is no German solidarity and final unity," so that Germany is not really a nation. His own natural stance was unpolitical, an attitude of intellectual freedom, but as he said later, he was "a man of balance" and instinctively leaned to the left if the boat heeled over to the right, so he sounds perhaps more chauvinistic than he really was.[2] Anyhow, he quite deliberately expresses his full approval of the system of government of pre-war Germany, for instance in this passage at the end of the introduction:

> I proclaim my deep conviction that the German people will never take to political democracy, for the simple reason that it cannot take to politics at all; and I feel that the much abused "authoritarian state" is the form of government suited to it, best for it and at bottom what it desires.[3]

The typical middle-class German like himself is indifferent to politics, Mann says, because he is so much more interested in the things of the mind, and this devotion to culture is good because it tends to make him humane.[4] There are other ways of explaining the German indifference to politics, as we shall see in discussing Troeltsch, and the cultivated are by no means always humane–Vercors was to illustrate this point unforgettably in *Le silence de lamer.* But the history of "Bildung" makes the assumption a natural one for a German, as earlier chapters have shown. Mann's "teachers" Schopenhauer, Nietzsche and Wagner are all brought in to prove that "the political element is missing in the German idea of 'Bildung.' "[5] Mann quotes Nietzsche's third *Unzeitgemäße Betrachtung:* "All states are badly organized where anyone but members of the government needs to be bothered with politics, and they deserve to come to a bad end through these shoals of politicians." When Mann speaks of the middle-class man, the "Bürger," he is thinking, he tells us, of those who had come through the age of Goethe, which had "atomized the Bürger into a human being," as Turgeniev puts it, that is, made him into a "Romantic individualist," a person in his own right, not just one of his prince's subjects among many, a "philistine." Things have changed in the Bismarck era, he has to admit, and some would say that the typical "Bürger" has become a capitalistic-imperialistic "Bourgeois" (he is thinking of Sombart's *Der Bourgeois*), a mineowner perhaps, ready to sacrifice thousands of lives for his own enrichment.[6] Mann's only reply to this fatal objection to his thesis is to say that he himself is not such a Bourgeois, but the product, like Hans Castorp, of a north-west German city democracy, patriarchal and conservative, never much concerned, he admits, about social and political questions but devoted, with the sense of duty and diligence of a good "Bürger"–like his Tonio Kröger or Gustav Aschenbach–to his art. His present home is in Munich, which has some claim to be a city of the arts, though it certainly has its coarser elements too. But Mann has a good word for the modern business man in other cities too, regarding him as a "Leistungsethiker," a firm believer in the traditional middle-class gospel of work–we saw the type in Hans Castorp's home town in the Protestant north–and associating him with his hero Nietzsche, "the most thoroughgoing and fanatical ascetic among thinkers."[7] It was this same spirit of "Durchhalten," of choosing the hard way and holding on to the end, that he had found in Germany in 1914 and celebrated in his book on Frederick the Great.

It had long been predictable that Heinrich

would not share the brother's patriotic enthusiasm. In the letter of 17 February 1904 in which Thomas tells him about meeting Katja Pringsheim, his future wife, he already speaks about Heinrich's move towards "Liberalism" and doubts whether he himself will ever follow. "To begin with, I understand little about 'freedom.' For me it is a purely moral and spiritual concept, the equivalent of 'honesty.' (Some critics call it 'coldheartedness' in me.) But political freedom does not interest me at all." He can only understand Russian literature which, he agrees, is tremendous, as having resulted from enormous pressure. "What *does* 'freedom' mean? The very fact that so much blood has been shed for the idea makes it for me something strangely *un*free, something quite medieval. . . . But I suppose I don't know anything about these things."[8] Thirty years later, during the campaign against Hitler, it might have embarrassed Mann to be reminded of this passage, but as it stands it is quite understandable in a man of culture and an artist who had come to maturity in the "Nineties." At the end of 1913, enquiring about Heinrich's progress with *Der Untertan,* his best social-critical novel (published 1918), Thomas, very depressed at the time through family worries and overwork, speaks of his "incapacity to find his bearings intellectually and politically" as his brother has contrived to do.[9] He speaks too of "a growing sympathy with death, which is part of my make up: it was the problem of decadence which always absorbed me, and that is probably what prevents me from being interested in progress." *Buddenbrooks* of course, though it was the story of several generations of a German merchant family in the nineteenth century, had hardly mentioned the social consequences of the Industrial Revolution, the growth of a working class, the problems of its life and the beginnings of socialism. The changing manners of successive generations had been brilliantly suggested, but the theme had been an idea from Schopenhauer, their weakening hold on life as they became gradually more sensitive to ideas and art and music. As Mann says in his "Lebensabriss" (1930), to explain how he shared, at the outbreak of the 1914 war, the "solemn feeling of German intellectuals that they were in the hands of fate, a belief that contained so much that was true and false, right and wrong," he was "disposed by native endowment and education rather towards the moral and metaphysical than towards the political and social."[10]

This marked intellectualism, combined with what must have seemed even to him later a strange blindness to social and political realities, lies behind Mann's often repeated praise of German devotion to "Bildung" in the *Betrachtungen,* and his equally warm approval of his country's capacity for obedience.[11] What seems important to the German people, he writes, is "Bildung" and the morality which stems from it. "Playing politics makes people coarse, vulgar and stupid. Envy, insolence and rapacity are the lessons it teaches. Only the cultivation of the mind makes men free. Institutions matter little, convictions are all-important. Become better yourself! and everything will be better." Freedom of the mind will only survive as long as order is maintained by some powerful central authority, preferably a strong monarchy which leaves religion, art and scholarship free. "I want objectivity, order and decency. If that is philistine, a philistine I will be."[12] Sayings like these could be paralleled, as we have seen, in Goethe and Wilhelm von Humboldt, whose conception of culture was also aristocratic, based on a status society of graded ranks. But Thomas Mann finds support for his views also in more dubious quarters. He would like to see his country adopting the organic political philosophy of the Romantic Adam Müller, whom he cannot praise too highly, but he sees a further movement towards the radical-democratic as inevitable.[13] That is why he is "unpolitical." "From the very fact that mind, philosophy, superior thought have obviously no further part to play in politics, it follows that intellectual life must be kept separate from that of politics, leaving this to pursue its own fated course while itself rising above any such fatality to serene independence."

Another laudable capacity which Mann finds particularly well developed in the Germans, alongside that for "Bildung," is that for self-subordination without loss of dignity. "Pride, honour and delight in obedience seems to-day to be a German idiosyncrasy and a source of intellectual bafflement."[14] He thinks of a cadet saluting an officer hardly older than himself, with delighted alacrity and a sort of humour, as if it were all a romantic game. "Only someone who is nothing at all has an interest in emphasizing human equality." This is a very flattering way of describing a German characteristic which seems to have been almost proverbial for centuries. The eminent jurist Friedrich Karl von Moser wrote in 1758: "Every nation has its own principal motive. In Germany, it is obedience, in England, freedom, in Holland, trade, in France, the honour of the King."[15] Herder in *Humanitätsbriefe* spoke of the Pope who already referred to Germany as "terra obedientiae," and Goethe, to Eckermann in 1828, contrasted the effect which "the blessing of personal freedom, the consciousness of the English name" had, even on children, with the habitual attitude of apprehension which he saw when he looked through his window at German children playing in the snow. Mann's praise of cheerful obedience sounds like an over-explanation when one remembers Bergson's comment on the attitude towards authority in the early "closed communities" in which he thinks man may first have acquired the social instincts which became the basis of moral obligation, an attitude of unquestioning obedience from habit. "Une subordination habituelle," he says, "finit par sembler naturelle, et elle se cherche à elle-même une explication."[16]

In putting forward these views, Thomas Mann frequently appeals for support to the great tradition of German humanism coming down from Goethe and his contemporaries, and continued in Schopenhauer and Nietzsche, by each in his own, at first sight perhaps rather surprising way. "Bildung," he writes, "is a specifically German idea; it comes from Goethe, it got from him the connection with the plastic arts, the sense of freedom, civilized outlook and worship of life in which Turgeniev used the word, and through Goethe this idea was elevated into an educational principle as in no other nation."[17] It makes people impatient with idle talk, for instance about politics, and it must be admitted "that 'quiet' culture, which Goethe contrasts with the French way, that is, with politics, encourages a quietistic attitude and that the profoundly unpolitical, anti-radical and anti-revolutionary nature of the Germans hangs together with the primacy which they have given to the idea of 'Bildung.' " It has also been said however, for example by Gustav Freytag, and Thomas Mann agrees with him, that Germany's cultivation of scholarship, literature and art first for a long time purely for their own sake, contributed towards the growth of political nationalism, because "their pure flame tempered the gentle disposition of the Germans with its glow, and steeled it gradually for a great political struggle."[18] Thomas Mann uses this as an argument for holding that his brother's activistic democracy is unnecessary and quotes Goethe's words to Luden in 1813, to the effect that though he had been able to forget the "political wretchedness" of Germany through art and scholarship, the comfort they gave was a poor substitute for the consciousness of belonging to "a great, strong, respected and formidable (yes, he used the brutal word 'formidable') people." Does it not look, Mann adds, as if Goethe had regarded Germany's great period of culture as one of preparation, and that he was consciously working for the future "day of glory" when Germany would be unified and would rule?[19] So although every German intellectual feels a very strong temptation to revert to the old condition of non-participation in politics, of watching with an ironical smile from the side-lines, he doubts if any will fail to respect and defend Germany's great struggle for power and influence, even though it may be admitted that Bismarck, "the man of power," was in many ways, when one thinks of the old Germany, a disaster. Anyhow, he finds it quite natural that the "world power of the mind" ("Weltvolk des Geistes"), grown to mighty physical strength, had taken a deep draught at the spring of ambition. It aspired to become a world power, and if God so willed, *the* world power of reality, if necessary (and clearly it would be necessary) by means of a violent breakthrough. Had not Spain, France, England all had their hour of world power and glory? When the war broke out, Germany fervently believed that her hour had struck, the hour of trial and of greatness.

In spite of his admiration for Adam Müller's "organic" political theory and in spite of his full acceptance of German war aims, as he saw them, and of such acts of war as the invasion of Belgium, the sinking of the "Lusitania" and unrestricted submarine warfare, Thomas Mann has strong reserves about the powers that should be exercised by the state. He does not like too much organization and resists any "enslavement of the individual by the state," though the "ethical socialism, generally called State Socialism" is acceptable, as opposed to "Marxist socialism with its rights of man." He is with Lagarde (*Deutsche Schriften,* 1878) against Hegel with his state-idolatry.[20] He quotes with approval Lagarde's statement that the state should stand in the same relation to the nation as the "Hausfrau" does to the master of the house, when she relieves him of all externals so that he can get on with "the really essential things"–a nice illustration of the paternalism which is so deep-seated in the German social tradition! What Lagarde wanted was rule by technical experts, including men who had learnt the business of administration in local government, but excluding professional parliamentarians, so that there should be no opportunity for "everyone to join in journalistic chatter about everything." It is not surprising that his views were to be frequently brought up later by apologists for totalitarian rule, with its total rejection of "talking shops."

Thomas Mann's views during the First World War about the basic political assumptions of his countrymen are not entirely representative because they are those of a professional writer, always very much concerned about the interests of his profession in particular, as is clear for instance immediately after his discussion of Lagarde's ideas, when he makes a special plea for consideration for the "aristocratic and individual," the "uniquely gifted mind," i.e., for literature and art, in the years of economic strain which he foresees as inevitable after the war.[21] It is interesting therefore to compare Mann's reply to Western propaganda with that made about the same time by an equally distinguished German intellectual with an entirely different background, the theologian, historian and sociologist Ernst Troeltsch, in a lecture given in Vienna in October 1915 and printed in the *Neue Rundschau* of January 1916.

In this lecture Troeltsch acknowledged that the ideal of political freedom had originated in the West and that when, in the eighteenth century, it spread to Germany, it exercised a considerable influence there, though it was quickly adapted to German institutions and traditions. He admitted certain real differences in outlook between Germany and the West, some of them not entirely to Germany's credit. Germany was in truth less advanced than the West, for instance, in that certain medieval forms of society (he was thinking of the semi-feudal Prussian Junker) had lingered on there too long in the modern industrial world. The differences were partly due to the necessity of restricting the application of Western ideas of freedom in a continental state in an exposed position, because of its need of a strong central authority. (Bismarck made the same point forcefully when, in his Reichstag speech defending the army estimates on 6 February 1888, he said that Germany, being exposed to attack on at least three flanks, felt herself compelled to remain united and strong: "The pike in the European carp-pond prevent us from becoming carp. ") But the chief cause of the differences between Germany and the West was that she had developed a different idea of freedom in general, and therefore different forms of political freedom from those prevailing in the West.

The British notion of freedom, Troeltsch explained, had resulted from the merging of feudal traditions with the stubborn individualism of the Puritans and Dissenters in the age of the English Revolution of 1688. The country gentry, in alliance with the merchant class, developed the sense of independence and personal initiative as the main features of British freedom, and provided it with a parliamentary basis. Further contributions came from the experience of a nation of pioneers in their colonial enterprises, from the free expansion of British commerce in the early capitalistic age, from memories of many past achievements and from the secure international position won by this "Herrenvolk" and ascribed by it to just the qualities mentioned. The monarchy, the high aristocracy and the established church were regarded as national institutions, not as hindrances to freedom. They had largely adapted themselves to the nation's needs and exercised a useful social function. Only in the nineteenth century had French democratic ideas broken into this system and attained some influence.

This analysis is apposite to our study of the German unpolitical man because it reminds us of the many features in our national history to which there was in 1914 no parallel in German experience, so that as the sociologist Troeltsch saw the questions in dispute in war propaganda, it was quite unreasonable to look for the Englishman's idea of political and personal freedom among his own countrymen, when their institutions and the history behind them were so different. Troeltsch went on to describe in some detail British, French and American ideas of personal and political freedom as products of history, before defending the German idea of freedom on historical and philosophical grounds. The German idea had been influenced on the theoretical side by Locke and Rousseau, he thought, and on the practical side by the British constitution and the events of the French Revolution. But fundamental modifications of these borrowed ideas had been effected in German institutions by Stein, Scharnhorst and Boyen, and in German political theory by Kant, Fichte, Hegel and others.

"Freedom," Troeltsch writes,

> in the sense of sharing in the determination of state policy, is not for us the cre-

> ation of the will of the government by counting heads, nor the control exercised over an agent by his client, but free, conscious, dutiful devotion to the whole entity constituted by the state, the nation and their history. As the expression and essence of the whole community, this totality must be freely willed and continually recreated in its own activity. Thus princes and officials regard themselves as the first servants of the state and the citizen feels himself to be a member of the state organism. All are organs of one sovereign whole, and in dutiful devotion unceasingly create it. This freedom consists of duties rather than rights, or at least of rights which are at the same time duties. The individuals do not compose the whole, but they identify themselves with it. Freedom is not equality, but the service of the individual in his due place and function. In this lies the dignity and the active influence of the individual, but also the cause of his being restrained and confined to a particular function. In this lies the dignity and the active influence of the individual, but also the cause of his being restrained and confined to a particular function. All the political gains resulting from national unification–equality before the law, parliamentary assemblies, universal military service, are adapted to express this spirit. It is the "mysticism of the state" which in our great thinkers and historians has felt itself to have affinities with Plato . . . and which finds expression in varying degrees in all the great German creations of the century.

Troeltsch's interpretation of the German conception of freedom and attitude to the state is clearly a much subtler and more elaborate explanation of the relationship of the individual to authority which Thomas Mann calls "obedience," and it has the same counterpart in Troeltsch as in Thomas Mann, the idea of "Bildung." In the same lecture in Vienna, Troeltsch pointed to the close analogy between the idea of the state as a super-individual entity, and that of the church, as community and as institution. Free surrender of oneself as a matter of duty and conscience to the state resembled the self-surrender of the faithful to the church, and had in fact developed out of it. In the same way the inward-looking habit of mind, the stress on personal religion, had been secularized, he said, into the pursuit of personal culture, the "self-perfectionism," to translate the expressive Russian term, of Goethe and his age. "Bildung" was the necessary complement to the German attitude to the state, just as personal religion had been to self-subordination to the church. Conditions in the little despotic states of the old Germany had turned men in upon themselves, causing them to seek in what Schiller calls "Das Ideal," the realm of ideas and imagination, a compensation for the shortcomings of "Das Leben," the ugly realities around them. This was the kind of personal independence still most highly valued by the best Germans, Troeltsch claimed, the attitude to life of the Greek philosophers and poets, as the Germans of Wincklemann's age had come to see them. Troeltsch did not therefore believe that in prewar Germany Potsdam had displaced Weimar, to speak in the familiar symbols. They were both, he believed, active forces still, and must remain so, if the German attitude to the state was not to become rigid and lifeless, or personal culture sentimental, over-intellectual and politically indifferent, "unpolitical."

After Germany's defeat Troeltsch, like Thomas Mann, revised some of the views he had put forward early in the war. The result is to be seen in a lecture packed with thought, *Naturrecht and Humanität in der Weltpolitik,* given in Berlin in 1922 and published in the following year, just after the author's death. Thomas Mann's review of it will be mentioned later, but as a parallel to his development, some leading ideas from the lecture about the differences between the German system of ideas in politics, history and ethics and that of western Europe and America, as Troeltsch saw them in 1922, may best be discussed at this point. The second lecture is devoted to a fuller exposition of the modifications of the received European tradition in political theory brought about by the German writers and thinkers of what Troeltsch calls the Romantic Counter-revolution, beginning with Herder and culminating in Hegel, and much concerned with what we now call Historicism, and with "organic" notions about a group-mind. The new ideal was "half aesthetic and half religious, but instinct throughout with a spirit of antibourgeois idealism," which rejected the natural-law theory of society and the idea of the natural rights of man, the theory which culminated, according to Ernest Barker, in the American Declaration of Independence in 1776 and the French Revolution of 1789.[22] The German Romantic theory emphasizes not "social atoms on a footing of equality with one another" and "universal laws of nature," but personalities and their unique realization of the capacities of Mind (Geist). Not only single individuals but groups and nations are thought of as unique personalities, "all struggling together and all developing thereby their highest spiritual powers." Instead of the old idea of Progress, on the basis of reason, well-being, liberty and purposive organization, directed towards the unity of mankind, the theory puts forward that of Development. Development takes place in a world in which different and complementary cultures contend with each other in a sort of race, in which first one people and then another by great effort goes into the lead, enjoys hegemony for a time and then hands on the torch to the next. The general resemblance between this conception and Thomas Mann's ideas in the *Betrachtungen* is clear. After the war Troeltsch advocated a return in many respects from this "heroic" theory of history, familiar to us from Carlyle's *Heroes and Hero Worship,* to something nearer to the common European tradition, which had in fact been elaborated most fully by German professors in the seventeenth and eighteenth centuries, down to Kant. He wanted the specialists to show more "active vigour and practical sense" and to think more about cooperation than rivalry with other nations, in order to shape a better future. They must pay special attention, he thought, to the Rights of Man, and to the working out of an ordered system of relations between states. These were liberal ideas, but in home affairs Troeltsch was not yet prepared to accept German Socialism, any more than Thomas Mann at this time. He also emphatically rejected the fashionable cynicism of Spengler's *Untergang des Abendlands.*

Since the Second World War, one of the most interesting attempts to explain the very slow progress of liberal ways of thinking in Germany before her defeat in 1945, and the apparently successful beginnings of democracy in the Bundesrepublik, has been made by Ralf Dahrendorf, drawing on his experience not only in Germany, but in England and the United States. Dahrendorf has repeatedly put forward the view that what may be called the feudalism, in the widest sense, of eighteenth-century Germany did not disappear while the new industrialism of the following century was transforming the country. It survived in the unshakably paternalistic and authoritarian habits of thought and feeling predominant among the Protestant civil servants of all grades, the soldiers, diplomats and landed aristocracy who remained devoted to the old Prussian tradition of the state, and it spread to captains of industry. The Weimar Republic had very little success with its half-hearted attempts to dislodge this "establishment," and it was only the fanatical determination of the National Socialists, in their pursuit of totalitarianism, to destroy the power of the aristocracy, the higher bureaucracy and rival older élites of every kind which, paradoxically, cleared the ground for a modern democracy in the end. Even the men of the resistance of 1944 would have wanted to restore the old authoritarianism, Dahrendorf says, and Peter Hoffmann, perhaps the best historian of the movement, agrees that they were "revisionists." Instead of pairing "Bildung" with this spirit of obedience, as Thomas Mann does, Dahrendorf speaks of "nonparticipation," the cultivation of the private rather than the public virtues, as the dominant attitude in German society, praised in literature and practised in politics, and he finds the same kind of submissive attitude to authority in the family, in education, in the Church, in industrial relations and in the law. There is always the feeling that some father figure may be relied upon to produce the best possible solution of any conflict of opinion or interests, whereas in countries which really believe in solving problems by rational discussion, such differences are accepted as inevitable, bound to crop up again when circumstances change, and therefore best regulated by tentative measures, subject to later revision. We have had ample evidence in our texts of authoritarianism and the cultivation of the private virtues, and Dahrendorf's sociological ideas are a valuable supplement to Troeltsch on the German conception of freedom and Thomas Mann on "culture" and "obedience."[23]

The first public sign of a marked change in Thomas Mann's political opinions came on 15 October 1922, nearly four years after the end of the war, when he made a long speech in Berlin at a big meeting arranged to celebrate the sixtieth birthday of Gerhard Hauptmann, who had already come to be regarded as the Goethe of the new Weimar Republic and played up nobly. The speech was printed, under the title "Von deutscher Republik," in the November *Neue Rundschau,* a Hauptmann number.[24] As Mann expected, this pronouncement came as a surprise even to many good friends, most of whom thought of him after the *Betrachtungen,* as did the general public, as an unrepentant conservative. He took care to try the speech out before an invited group, which included Heinrich, on 6 October, and he had already written to some friends about it, to Arthur Schnitzler, for instance, a month before this. Even in December he was still writing, for example to Ida Boy-Edd, to explain his motives for the step. From the selection of his letters published by Erika Mann (Volume I, covering 1889 to 1936, appeared in 1962), it seems that while maintaining all along his belief in the value of German culture, in particular of Weimar humanism, for a tragically divided world–the message of the "Schnee" chapter in *Der Zauberberg*–he had long been undecided about his narrower political allegiance after the German revolution, the imposed peace and the setting up, after long discussions in the Constituent Assembly, of the Weimar Republic. While correcting the proofs of the *Betrachtungen* he expressed his fears, in a letter to Philip Witkop of 23 May 1918, some four months before the end of the war, that "the whole of Europe might have to go through the Bolshevik phase" and yet, he added, "the belief in 'freedom' is also impossible for mankind today. What belief is left?" Here of course he ascribes his own views to the whole of mankind. On 2 April 1934, a year after leaving Germany, he was to write to René Schickele, discussing the feeling in the country in early Nazi days, that things were bad and there was much dissatisfaction, "but the German people is good at putting up with things, and as it has no liking for freedom, but feels itself neglected under it, it will seem to itself in better shape under the harsh discipline of the new constitution, and still be 'happier' than under the Republic." His own conversion to "freedom," i.e., a belief in democratic government, had by then long been complete, but it had taken him over a decade completely to overcome his deep distaste for politics.

In the last year of the war he was still, as we saw, outspokenly unpolitical and anti-democratic. On 19 June 1918 for instance he wrote to Fritz Endres: "The conversion of the German people to politics! Yes, yes. If only it would not result in democracy, in democracy as a 'constitution' in every sense, political and spiritual, in the stooping of Germany to democracy, and among other things, to its bowing the knee to that wretched *Real-Politik* which Wilson has summed up in the phrase: 'Opinion of the world is the mistress of the world.' " This was written when the Treaty of Brest-Litovsk had already shown what kind of a peace the High Command would impose on the West if victorious. We have no comment by Thomas Mann on this, on the hurried concessions to parliamentary democracy when Prince Max of Baden was made Chancellor on 3 October 1918, or on the proclamation of a republic, first in Bavaria, where Mann lived (7 November) and then in Prussia (9 November) and the Kaiser's flight to Holland. The Manns lived through the anxious days of Kurt Eisner's idealistic but incompetent government, followed after his assassination (21 February 1919) by six weeks of chaos and then by a short-lived Soviet republic. Eisner had been a "literat," a journalist and writer, and the Soviet government included amongst its leaders the Expressionist poet Ernst Toller. It was suppressed after three weeks by the roving Free Corps of ex-soldiers, and in the middle of this period, on 21 April 1919, the Manns' youngest son Michael was born at their house in Munich, to the sound of heavy gun fire and after an anxious wait for the doctor, held up by the closing of a bridge. All the families around were plundered and harassed by the "Reds," but the Manns escaped, owing to Toller.

In his *Doktor Faustus,* Thomas Mann makes Serenus Zeitblom, the narrator of the story, responsible for the following impression of a political meeting in Munich at the time of the Soviet republic in the spring of 1919. It has every appearance of being a bit of autobiography:

> The word "painful" is not too strong if I try to characterize the impression made on me, as a purely passive observer, by the meetings in Munich hotel rooms of certain "Councils of Intellectual Works" etc. which came into existence at that time. If I were a novelist, I could perhaps describe a meeting of this kind, a meeting at which some man of letters, a dimple-cheeked sybarite not without charm, might give the address on the subject of "Revolution and the love of man" and start a free, diffuse and confused discussion, kept going by the most unlikely types, such as only came to light for a moment on such occasions, clowns, maniacs, ghosts, trouble-makers and esoteric philosophers–I could give a vivid description, I say, of such a helpless and futile council-meeting from my agonizing memories. There would be speeches for and against the love of man, for and against the officers, for and against the people. A little girl would recite a poem; a soldier in field-grey might be prevented with difficulty from going on reading from a manuscript that began by addressing the

> audience as "Dear citizens and citizens' wives!" and would no doubt have taken up the whole night; an evil specimen criticized all previous speakers mercilessly, without honouring the meeting with any positive opinions of his own–and so forth. The behaviour of the audience, which delighted in rude interjections, was turbulent, childish and coarse, the chairmanship incompetent, the atmosphere terrible and the result less than nil.[25]

At about the same time in 1919, if we may believe *Mein Kampf,* Hitler, as "education officer" of a Munich regiment, attended a meeting of the "Deutsche Arbeiterpartei" at which Gottfried Feder spoke–"These associations sprang up everywhere, only to disappear ingloriously after a short time," he says–and having taken part in the discussion, Hitler was invited to the next committee meeting, in "Das alte Rosenbad," a low-class inn:

> I went through the dimly lit main dining-room, which was empty, found the door to a side-room and had the "session" before my eyes. In the half-light of a broken gas-lamp four young fellows were sitting at a table, among them the author of the little pamphlet, who immediately greeted me cordially and welcomed me as a new member of the "German Workers' Party" . . . The minutes of the last meeting were read and passed. Then it was the turn of the Treasurer–the association had in its possession in all seven marks and fifty pfennigs–this report too was accepted and minuted.

Then the correspondence, half a dozen letters, was read and there was a long discussion about the answers to some of the letters. "Terrible, terrible. It was a pettifogging society of the worst description. So this was the club they wanted me to join?" However, he did, and it became the National Socialist Party.[26]

At the end of March Mann wrote to Ponten that there was much that seemed to him humane and good in communism. It aimed at abolishing the state and ridding the world of the poison of politics, a goal which no one could object to, though proletarian culture was something to be avoided at all costs. When Kurt Martens asked him that summer for a word of comfort and advice for the people, to be published in his *Münchener Neueste Nachrichten,* Mann had to refuse, as he felt this was not the time and he had nothing helpful yet to say. But to Gustave Blume a week later (5 July 1919), in a long letter in reply to evidently friendly comments from a stranger on the *Betrachtungen,* he says that now that the great German tradition from Luther to Nietzsche and Bismarck, which he had been defending in his book, is regarded by many even in Germany as dead and dishonoured, the only thing to do is to try to adopt a contemplative, fatalistic attitude, read Spengler and look upon their defeat as the inevitable final stage of an ageing civilization. Life may be quite tolerable under Anglo-Saxon dominance and the old Germany will be remembered, even if only with Romantic nostalgia. Six months later Mann gives strong approval to Count Keyserling's plan for a School of Wisdom at Darmstadt, saying in a letter of 18 January 1920 that nothing is more important than to provide German conservatism with solid intellectual foundations. He even writes an open letter to the Count which ends with a vision of a future Germany devoted to culture, like German music transformed into reality, a model for the nations.[27] The little volume of two idylls, *Herr und Hund* and *Gesang vom Kindchen,* which came out printed on war-time paper in the summer of 1919, conveys the spirit of those years in Mann's life when he was living quietly in Munich as a good family man, coping as well as he could with the dangers and problems of the day and gradually finding his way back to creative writing. There are bitter lines in the last canto of the *Gesang,* about the "questionable victory" and the still more questionable peace which was coming, and Mann is far from rising to the level of his obvious model, *Hermann and Dorothea,* in reformulating the great commonplaces, but the baptism scene does bring us near to the man and the writer in those unhappy days when "die sorgende Wirtin" can only provide for her guests at the baptismal supper as well "Wie die Blokade es zuließ der kalt gebietenden Angeln."* It is the baptism of the youngest daughter, Elisabeth, on 23 October 1918, which is described. In Mann's letter to Bertram (2 February 1922), the letter in which he tells one of the godfathers at the baptism ceremony about his reconciliation with Heinrich, and his approaching Goethe-week lecture in Frankfurt-am-Main, he says that he has had no

*"As the blockade of the Angles allowed, in their cold regulations."

time to be sentimental in the years since the war, when he has had to fight for existence while physically under-nourished himself. The thought which entirely absorbs him at the moment, he says, is that of a new, personal fulfilment of the ideal of "Humanität," of Weimar humanism, as opposed to abstract Rousseauistic humanitarianism–the sort castigated in the *Betrachtungen.* This is what he is going to talk about at Frankfurt, in the presence of President Ebert, before the performance of *The Magic Flute.* Hauptmann is to speak before *Egmont.* It was part of his essay on "Goethe and Tolstoi" that he read on 1 March 1922.

In "Von deutscher Republik" and more forcibly in the preface to the text published in the *Neue Rundschau,* Mann repudiates the suggestion that what he is saying is incompatible with the message of the *Betrachtungen.* "This message of encouragement for the Republic exactly continues the line of thought of the *Betrachtungen* and applies it to present conditions, and the conviction behind it is as before, without restriction, the same belief in the humane German tradition." Like E. M. Forster, Mann does not really call for more than "Two Cheers for Democracy." He hopes that this demonstration of support by a notorious "Bürger" will do the Republic some good, but he is careful to "define it first," as he said in the letter to Ida Boy-Edd later, "and how! Almost as the opposite of what to-day exists! But just for that reason: the attempt to breathe something like an idea, a soul, a spirit into this miserable state without citizens, seemed to me not a bad thing to do."[28] What he has in mind is the kind of reformed state which he thinks the young Germans of 1914 had set out to fight for. He obviously wishes to persuade people to give up thinking, as almost all Germans naturally did, that this form of government is simply the result of military defeat, and to win over its chief opponents, the young and the middle-class, for what is generally called democracy, though he prefers to call it "Humanität," to persuade them to transfer their patriotism to this Germany, in spite of its new name. At the same time he dissociates himself from the militant young conservatives of the "Frei-korps," with what he calls their "sentimental obscurantism, which organizes terror and brings disgrace on their country through hideous and insane murders," and he pays a warm tribute to their latest victim, Walther Rathenau, the late Foreign Minister. One of his chief motives for coming forward in this courageous and public-spirited way seems to have been his disgust at the behaviour of the Free Corps, who formed, of course, the nucleus of the National Socialist movement. *His* conservatism must be humane and cultivated, in the tradition of Goethe and Nietzsche, as he understands him. There is surely room for something more truly German than the "imperial gala opera" provided for them by "that talent" (the Kaiser). "That was amusing, but it was an embarrassment." They had hoped their neighbours in Europe did not hold *them* responsible–though they did–and had turned back to culture. But now there is at last the possibility of a unified culture, of a political form which really expresses the whole national life. In any case, as he had already reminded them, this was no time for dreams of a restored monarchy. "The Republic is a fate, and one towards which 'amor fati' is the only proper attitude. That is not too solemn a word for the matter, for the fate in question is no trifle. So-called freedom is no joke or relaxation. . . . Its other name is responsibility, a word which reminds us that freedom is a heavy burden–especially for the brains of the country." Mann went on to remind his audience of what a Russian writer had recently told them about the social responsibility which had long rested on the shoulders of writers in Russia, tacitly admitting that German literature had been too little concerned about social questions. The rest of this over-long address, which Mann himself later, in 'Kultur und Sozialismus' (1928)[29] was to contrast unfavourably with the *Betrachtungen* as a piece of writing, is mostly taken up with long quotations from Novalis, brought in, as it were, to make his case respectable, by showing that already in Romantic times Novalis had seen the necessity of combining novelty with conservatism in national affairs. He had proposed bringing in the church, as in the Middle Ages, to reconcile and guide the divided laity, and Mann finds a modern substitute for the church in humanism, "Humanität," which he has learnt through Walt Whitman, recently translated by Hans Reisiger, to equate with democracy. A comparison of these two writers, the original germ of this lecture, leads Mann to the theme, familiar from the *Zauberberg* and earlier works, of the "sympathy with death," or the past, which developes into a strengthened resolve to serve life.

The much shorter speech "Geist and Wesen der deutschen Republik," which Mann was invited by a group of republican students in Munich to give at a meeting held in memory of

Walther Rathenau in June 1923, is clearer and more eloquent than "Von deutscher Republik." It is not the main speech of the meeting, the tribute to Rathenau, but a very appropriate introduction, in which Mann tries dispassionately to explain what, as it seems to him, the new form of government means, or can be made to mean, for his country. Given goodwill, he is convinced that it can serve the most desirable national purposes, his ideal being the fulfilment of German "Menschlichkeit," the good life as their best traditions conceive it, which will only come through "the unity of state and culture"–the phrase familiar from the earlier speech. Mann starts from the German idea of "Bildung". . . . It is of course the German middle class that he has chiefly in mind, as he speaks to these students, and what he rightly stresses is something which he has only recently become aware of himself, namely that this in many ways so admirable ideal of personal culture is incomplete while it continues to neglect the political dimension. The failure hitherto of the educated German to take an active interest in the political element in social life, that, he sees now, is the root cause of middle-class opposition to the idea of a republic, that is, of self-government. "When we are asked to pass from inwardness to objective reality, to politics, to what the nations of Europe call 'freedom,' it seems to us a warping of our nature, indeed the destruction of our nationhood."[30] Admitting that that is their natural reaction as Germans, Mann continues, "is it German to maintain that our national character cannot and should not be improved?" For him the answer is no, and what is particularly needed to complete the German make-up is a sense for the objective, for politics and "freedom." Isn't this perhaps what Hölderlin may have meant when in *Hyperion* he calls his countrymen lacking in harmonious development, "not whole men, but fragments and patchwork?" Does he not mean that true humanity includes inner and outer, the personal and the objective, conscience and action, and that the Germans, as "Bürger" and men, broke off the process of development prematurely, before it included a political sense?

Appealing, as usual, to the authority of the German classics, Mann interprets Goethe's *Wilhelm Meister, the* "Bildungsroman," as a poetic prevision of Germany's progress, in due time, from inwardness to concern for objective goals, the political sphere, republicanism, and not just as a monument of personal culture and pietistic autobiography. From being occupied at first exclusively with his own development, Wilhelm comes to be interested, in the *Wanderjahre,* in education generally, for his son's sake, and finally in the sphere of social relations and the role of the state, "undoubtedly the highest stage of the human." Give the present-day German time enough, and he will go through the same stages and come to see that all-round culture, to be complete, must include a sense of political responsibility. The conditions of life resulting from the war and the peace are far from being favourable to this advance at present. People abroad can have no conception of the humiliating hardships the great majority have to endure at this time (the height of the inflation), "they do not know that German mothers must wrap their babies in newspapers for lack of linen"–commandeered by the French. For all this the new regime receives the blame. External political pressure (the occupation of the Ruhr) encourages political pessimism, the philosophy of brutality (of the Free Corps). An ominous paragraph follows about alarming movements of ideas in the post-war world outside, which puts concisely the message Hans Castorp hears from Naphta. A widespread feeling of depression like the mood that followed the Napoleonic wars has given rise to inhumane action–Bolshevism in Russia, Fascism in Italy, Horthy's regency in Hungary and certain shady movements in France are instanced. (Mann does not mention of course that Hitler had led a demonstration in Munich in January. The putsch led by Ludendorff and him was to come to November.) Democracy, individualism, liberalism, personal freedom are already meaningless and obsolete ideas to many in these movements, and are being replaced by their opposites, individualism by group loyalty, freedom by iron discipline and terror. They all crave for the absolute, and obscurantism is the inevitable result. But he does not believe that in the country of Goethe, Hölderlin and Nietzsche, who were not liberals indeed, but good humanists, the exploitation of anti-liberal ideas can succeed. "The republican youth of Germany," he concludes, "understands that 'Humanität' is the idea of the future, the idea to which Europe will struggle through, with which it will inspire itself and for which it must live–if it does not wish to die."

With these two pronouncements Thomas Mann had defined the political attitude which he was to maintain for the rest of his life. His reference to obscurantism was the first of the long series of outspoken attacks which he was to make on National Socialism, and it came as we have seen in the very year of the attempted "putsch" by Ludendorff and Hitler in Munich, some ten years before Hitler came to power (in January 1933) and Mann's exile began. Now that the editors of successive collected editions have brought together as many as possible of Mann's occasional speeches and essays, one is amazed at the quality and quantity of the great novelist's output of writing about current affairs, produced when he was at the height of his creative powers and probably always gave his best hours to his art. The author of *Buddenbrooks* and *Der Zauberberg* was on any showing one of the leading European novelists of his day and he had already more than once been considered for the Nobel prize for literature before it was awarded to him in 1929. It was inevitable that he should frequently be asked for his opinion on current questions, and he was conscientious about his representative duties as a leader in art and thought. Conscience as well as regard for his own good name compelled him to write about the dangers he saw coming and occasionally to reply to one of the innumerable attacks that were levelled at him after 1922, not only by the gutter press, and increasingly as the National Socialist movement grew. In what follows, only a few of Mann's essays and speeches can be briefly discussed, always with the aim of following the development of his thought about the need for a new attitude to politics on the part of the educated German.

Mann did not speak about politics at any length in the 1920s after the two pieces discussed, but one or two reviews and short articles, as well as the debates in *Der Zauberberg* and remarks in letters, show that he remained consistently liberal, if not yet quite ready for socialism. A review published on Christmas Day, 1923, of the lecture on *Naturrecht und Humanität in der Weltpolitik* by Ernst Troeltsch discussed above, says that Troeltsch was not content simply to analyse the differences he saw between German "political-historical-moral" thought and that of the West and America, bringing out the contrast between the ideas of the German-Romantic counter-revolution and the older Western political philosophy based on natural law. Troeltsch also warmly advocated Germany's return to the main line of development, proving that he too had changed his ideas since the end of the war, and in the same direction as Thomas Mann. Many Germans, the reviewers says, even some "who had long dwelt in the Magic mountain of Romantic aestheticism and studied it deeply," had lately been thinking, though less precisely, along similar lines, and certain confessions (his own, of course) had been badly received and treated as the talk of a base renegade. Although he understood this backward-looking conservatism, he was determined not to be diverted from his friendly attitude to the demands of life, and pointed to the example of Switzerland, and German parts of Austria, where there had been no such divergence of political thought. He hinted that Germany should not close its mind to the idea of the League of Nations, which was in the same natural-law tradition.[31] Stresemann was to take Germany in of course in 1926.

In 1924, asked for a comment on the fifth anniversary of the proclamation of the Weimar Constitution, Mann says that it is of course not perfect, but it is a manifestation of a will and capacity to live which are admirable and astonishing, when one remembers the circumstances in which it was created. He speaks of the German people's unparalleled resilience, not only in recent history. Though it always resists the idea of change, it acts as if it accepted the motto chosen for it by its greatest poet: "Stirb and Werde." He follows this up by quoting very appositely a page from the drama *Empedokles* by Hölderlin, whose post-war vogue was at its height, interpreting it as a vision of a truly democratic society.[32] There are several references even in the selection of letters edited by Erika Mann to the reception of Thomas Mann's apparent swing towards liberalism by German opinion as reflected in the press. They were mainly hostile and frequently inaccurate, but he seldom had time or any wish to reply. One witty and spirited retort however, published in *Die literarische Welt,* is reprinted in *Reden und Aufsätze*[33] and the response to this in other periodicals is discussed in a letter to its editor on 2 March 1928.[34] The offending article had been a quite inaccurate and apparently almost libellous comment in the *Berliner Nachtausgabe* on a conversation between Mann and a young Frenchman in Munich, printed in a Paris newspaper. Mann had been working for years for a good understanding between France and Germany, he had had a splendid reception in Paris in 1926 (fully described in his *Pariser Rechenschaft*)[35] and several leading French writers had visited Berlin. The nationalist press in Germany had reacted in what seemed to Mann its usual stupid way. "Nationalism," Mann had explained to his French interlocutor, "is with us inevitably and disastrously stricken with lack of talent, it does not count intellectually, it cannot write or exercise any fascination in a higher sense, it is pure barbarism. A curse, a metaphysical interdict hangs over it, it is the unforgivable sin against the Holy Ghost, and a writer who succumbs to it degenerates without hope of recovery." France, on the other hand, had really distinguished nationalist writers like Barrès.

Although Mann claimed, as we have seen, that the ideas expressed in "Von deutscher Republik" were not inconsistent with those of the "Unpolitical Man," he repeatedly repudiated the views of the German nationalists after the war, as we see for instance from his letter to Arthur Hübscher of 27 June 1928, after Hübscher had criticized his emendations of the *Betrachtungen* in the second edition. He insists in this letter that he has no liking for politics and belongs to no party. He only wants to defend what is reasonable and humane, and therefore in his sense "German." "There are some kinds of narrow-mindedness and malice which my intelligence and character cannot stand. I openly admit that I want to have nothing to do with people (like some Munich professors!) who after the murder of Rathenau said: 'Bravo, that's one out of the way!,' and that I find the Munich middle-class press dreadful." He has no golden message for the young and has never tried to be a leader. "All that men like me could hope to do would be to set an example to confused young people–and that only through modesty, caution and good will."[36]

In "Kultur und Sozialismus" Thomas Mann brings up to date the reflections on the ideas behind German politics which he had begun in the *Betrachtungen*. The essay was published in *Preussische Jahrbücher* in April 1928. He still claims to be consistent with his former self, but he admits now that he had left out of consideration in his book the fighting war in all its sordid reality, with all the material side of its origins, conduct and aims. It was possible for the war of ideas to obscure the ugly realities for him because of his unpolitical idealism as a middle-class German with an insufficiently examined conception of culture. At the end of the war, he believes, it was harder for the Germans to bear the shock of the collapse of their system of ideas, their "Kultur," than the facts of military defeat and political collapse. Those who held on to their traditional idea of culture could not help looking upon the democratic republic as something foreign to their country's real nature. The Germans have difficulties in adapting themselves to their new form of government because all the psychological preconditions are lacking. The great Germans recognized abroad, Luther, Goethe, Schopenhauer, Nietzsche, George, were not democrats, and it was they who created the German idea of "Kultur," with the capital "K" which aroused so much feeling abroad in the war. "Kultur" is etymologically the same word as "Kultus" with its religious connotation (cf. "Kultusminister") and Germans have long felt a quasi-religious, almost mystical respect for culture (he is evidently thinking of both self-development–"Bildung"–and of objective culture, the arts and sciences–"Kultur"). The German attitude towards the serious theatre, so different from that of the West, is a striking example. Ideally the theatre has come to be a sort of temple in Germany, to which you go for the good of your soul, as to a good concert or art-collection, whereas in the West the aim of amusement predominates, perhaps arising to social satire. Mann thinks only of the dramatists who have gradually evoked this response, and one misses some consideration of the social and even political background, the patronage of petty princes and later of towns, and behind that the division of the old Germany into a multitude of small states with few temptations towards power politics, and prestige reasons for favouring the arts. Instead we have some vague and unconvincing sociological theory about the "Gemeinschaften" or communities making up a "Volk" supporting a "Kultur," and on the other hand the "Gesellschaft" or society in a "Nation" with a mere "Zivilisation." "The concept of the nation is historically bound up with democracy, whereas the word 'Volk' corresponds to the really German, that is culturally-conservative, unpolitical way of thinking, opposed to any atomic form of society."

"German socialism," Mann continues, "the invention of a Jewish social theorist educated in Western Europe, has always been felt by devotees of German culture to be a foreign element, at variance with our folk tradition, and simply anathema for them: justifiably, insofar as it leads to the undermining of the cultural idea of folk and community by that of the social class. This disintegration has in fact already proceeded so far that to talk about folk and community to-day seems pure romanticism."[37] In spite of being based on the study of economic facts and not on idealistic metaphysics, socialism has a stronger appeal for intelligent people at present than conservatism with all its romantic aura, being so much better attuned to the requirements of everyday life. The social-democratic policy about legislation, the rationalization of government and administration, and the international organization of Europe is much more sensible than that of its opponents. To illustrate the barrenness of conservatism, Mann points to Stefan George's complete lack of interest in social themes and problems, maintaining as he does Nietzsche's similarly patrician attitude, and he ends with an appeal to the educated middle class to support not of course communism, with its fanatical idea of a proletarian dictatorship, but moderate German socialism.

Mann repeated some of these views about socialism in his "Deutsche Ansprache–Ein Appell an die Vernunft," a speech made on 17 October 1930 in the Beethovensaal in Berlin, apparently on his own initiative, so that he has to apologize at the beginning for seeming to assume the role of a second Fichte, and addressing the German nation. He had come to Berlin to give a reading from his works on the following day, but in view of the result of the general election a month earlier, in which the National Socialists had gained 18% of the votes, after a year or two of economic depression and a succession of political crises, he felt it would be fiddling while Rome burned if he did not, as a public figure, make some effort to warn the country about the seriousness of the situation and to "appeal to reason" even at the eleventh hour. The election of 14 September has shown, he says, that the country is being carried away by the shrill catchwords of fanaticism. He briefly reviews events since the war, condemning the Versailles Treaty as intended to hold the Germans permanently down, but resulting in the present chaos. The Weimar Constitution has defects, but no one has concrete proposals for overcoming them. The phenomenal success of National Socialism is due to public discontent with the political and economic situation, combined with the widespread feeling that an epoch is ending, the era dating from the French Revolution with its liberal principles based on the power of reason–freedom, justice, education, progress. There are many signs now of a revolt against reason, of a tendency to invoke instead the dynamism of passion, of ecstasy, the dark unconscious powers of the mind. The half-educated have a barbarous craze for words like "rassisch, völkisch, bündisch, heldisch" and the dangerous political romanticism they express. The old decencies are "bourgeois," dictatorship by force prevails in Finland, Russia, Italy, and in Germany fanaticism is preached as a gospel of salvation. The leaders in this movement pretend to the outside world to have renounced force in the settlement of foreign disputes, and their frenzied patriotism is vented in hatred of their political opponents and the pursuit of a totalitarian state. Only the Catholics have an ideology that is secure against them. The bogy of communism gives them their hold over the middle class, but he insists that social democracy is something quite different, repeats the phrases used about it in "Kultur und Sozialismus" and ends with warm praise for Stresemann's achievement of a peaceful revision of Versailles. It was a brave effort, made in spite of noisy interruptions and disorder in the hall caused by National Socialists and Conservative extremists, but things had gone too far to be much affected by Thomas Mann's thinking aloud before an audience of intellectuals. The lecture did not of course pass unnoticed by the nationalist popular press, and it was greeted with howls of derision and abuse. Thomas Mann wrote a long article early in 1931, "Die Wiedergeburt der Anständigkeit," suggested by a revival he had just seen of Ibsen's *Pillars of Society*, in which he contrasts the idealism of Ibsen's day with the temper of his own time. He discusses in particular the effect of the fashionable preoccupation with the irrational when its slogans filter down to the half-educated, and he attacks with bitter irony the "childish conceit" of a Hamburg reviewer of the "Deutsche Ansprache."

Thomas Mann had maintained in 1923, in "Geist and Wesen der deutschen Republik," that to be truly humane, Germans needed to develop the political interests and capacities which they had hitherto neglected, in their exclusive pursuit of Kultur. He often comes back to this idea as his central new insight, that the political is not opposed to humane culture, but a part of it. In "Kultur und Sozialismus" (1928), as we saw, he went on from a detached liberalism to a moderate socialism, repelled as he was after the war by the backward-looking and narrowly nationalistic parties of the right, with their fringe of irresponsible and violent young, whose excesses were soon matched and outdone by the new party of National Socialists with their fanatical racism, and the terror-tactics they developed, ostensibly to protect the country from Communism. Thomas Mann's "Rede vor Arbeitern in Wien" of 22 October 1932 marked for him the beginning of a new epoch in his life and thought, he declared in his opening words, being his first speech as a middle-class writer to an audience of working-men and socialists. What he said was very much the same as he had written in "Kultur und Sozialismus" four years earlier, but we find here for the first time an unambiguous plea for compassionate socialism and the express repudiation of the normal indifference of the educated in Germany to social questions, as something beneath their consideration. The second half of the speech repeats the substance of his attack in "Deutsche Ansprache" on the National Socialists and their "philosophy."

An address which was to have been read for Mann at a meeting of a Socialist society in Berlin (the "Sozialistischer Kulturbund") on 19 February 1933 is "Bekenntnis zum Sozialismus," an open declaration of his belief in socialism. The meeting never took place, because Hitler became Chancellor on 30 January, but the text of the proposed address was published in the society's periodical. It is a renewed and more explicit expression of support of the Republic, arising out of his conviction that thinking people of middle-class origin should side now with the workers and Social Democracy. His main argument is contained in the following paragraph:

> As a man of this kind I feel deeply how dishonest and life-repressing it is to look down scornfully on the political and social sphere and to consider it of secondary importance compared with the world of the inward, metaphysics, religion and so forth. This way of comparing the respective values of the inward, personal world and the life of society, contrasting metaphysics and socialism, for instance, and representing the latter as lacking in piety and sanctity, as a merely materialistic desire for happiness in a termite society, is not admissible today. It is not admissible, in a world as anti-divine and bereft of reason as ours, to represent man's metaphysical, inward and religious activities as inherently superior to his will to improve the world. The political and social is one aspect of the humane. The interest and passion for humanity, self-dedication to the problem of man, sympathy with his lot, this interest and this passion are concerned with both aspects, that of the personal and inward and also that of the external arrangement of human life in society.[38]

Mann appeals this time to Nietzsche as his authority from the great German past, quoting from *Also sprach Zarathustra* (Die Reden Zarathustras, Von der schenkenden Tugend, 2) the passage about remaining faithful to the earth, and bringing fugitive virtue back to the earth, to give it a meaning, a human meaning. "That is the materialism of the spirit, a religious man turning towards the earth," Mann adds, and socialism is just this refusal to bury one's head in the sand, and the resolve to tackle the problems of collective life, to humanize it. It is in this sense that Mann is a socialist. He is a democrat because of the fundamentally humane ideas, like that of freedom, on which democracy is based. It is natural that some of the young should have reacted against these abstract ideas in favour of the native traditions of their own "Volk," but their romantic notions are being manipulated by the Right for its own ends. The heroic age of nationalism was the nineteenth century, when it was still in Germany a revolutionary idea for which men went to prison, but now it belongs to the past. "Every man of feeling and understanding and every respectable politician knows that the peoples of Europe can no longer live and prosper in isolation, but that they all depend on each other and form a community destined to march together, a community which should be recognised and made into a reality." The European idea, it will be seen, was something quite familiar to Thomas Mann long before the Second World War, and in the middle of the war, in one of the fifty-five wireless talks he addressed to Germany through the BBC, the one for August, 1941, he assured his listeners that the world would need Germany, and Germany would need the world, when the war was over. "Germany will never have been happier–and it knows this at heart even now–than as a member of a world at peace and unified in freedom, and depoliticized through the curbing of national autocracy. Germany is just made for such a world, for if ever 'Machtpolitik' was a curse and distorting unnatural pose for a people, it was that for the fundamentally unpolitical Germans."[39]

It was Hitler's rise to power which finally brought about in Thomas Mann what he called "Die Politisierung des Geistes," the final conversion of the Unpolitical Man. Looking back at the end of the war he wrote to Hermann Hesse on 8 April 1945:

> We have all, under severe pressure, experienced a kind of simplification of our ideas. We have seen evil in all its horror, and in doing so–it is a shame-faced confession–we have discovered our love of the good. If *Geist* [spirit, mind] is the principle, the power that wills the good, the anxious attentiveness to changes in the image of truth, "divine care" in a word, which strives for an approach to what is right, enjoined, behoving, here below, then it is political, whether it likes that title or not. Nothing living, I think, can get round the political today. A refusal is also a political decision, one in favour of the wrong cause.

Heinrich Mann had been deprived of his German citizenship before his brother and had led the "Popular Front" of émigrés in Paris, but from 1936 Thomas Mann became the intellectual leader of the German intellectuals in exile. He wrote in 1937 the preface to the first number of *Maße und Wert,* their periodical published in Stockholm, and to the first numbers of the following two volumes. All were manifestos, and they had been preceded by his solemn warning against the dangers in store from Hitlerism for Europe in "Achtung, Europa!" in 1935. From 1938 till the end of the war he lived in America and made a number of political speeches there, as well as writing the radio addresses already mentioned. At the same time he was finishing the long *Joseph* novel and writing *Doktor Faustus,* in which Serenus Zeitblom, the narrator, describes incidentally the conditions of life and the atmosphere around him as he writes. From chapter XXXIII on it is a picture of Germany since 1918 that is presented to us in this way, at first from Mann's own memories and after 1933 from the reports of others. Serenus is obviously the mouthpiece of Thomas Mann, and he undergoes the same development in his political views as we have followed in his creator.

"Achtung, Europa!" is the text of a message from Thomas Mann which was read in French at the meeting at Nice in April 1935 of the "Comité de la Coopération Intellectuelle." National Socialism is not mentioned by name, because it was not until the following year that Thomas Mann lost his German citizenship, following his open letter of 3 February 1936 to Eduard Korrodi in the *Neue Zürcher Zeitung,* in which he expressed his conviction that nothing good could result from the present German regime, for Germany or the world. The address is an indictment of those responsible for the moral and intellectual debasement of "the masses" which is in progress in many countries. "The decisive point is that they (the new young) know nothing about 'Bildung' in its higher and deeper sense, about self-improvement, individual responsibility and exertion, and make things easy for themselves instead in the collective."[40] They like marching and singing songs which are a mixture of debased folksongs and leading articles. "These young people enjoy for its own sake the feeling of abandoning care and seriousness and losing themselves in a mass movement, with hardly a thought for where they are going." Their leaders do not try to raise the masses by education, but only to rule them by working on their instincts, by propaganda. The cultivated nations look on bewildered, but Mann warns them that their tolerance in present circumstances may lead to war and the end of civilization.

Mann's immediate personal reaction to the news from Germany after he had left it on a lecture tour to Holland, Belgium and France in February 1933 is fully documented in the printed pages from his diary of 1933 and 1934, "Leiden an Deutschland."[41] Anger and scorn inspire comments and descriptions full of bitter satire when the Führer speaks to the nation, for instance, on "Kultur," but there are also pages of reflections on the nature and history of politics, where the germs of later speeches and articles are to be found. In a couple of pages written apparently late in 1934, for instance, we find Mann acknowledging more clearly than before how much Germany has to learn from other countries in the by no means despicable art of politics:

> Politics as the "art of the possible" is indeed a sphere resembling that of art in that, like art, it mediates creatively between mind and life, idea and reality, the desirable and the necessary, conscience and action, freedom and necessity, morality and power. It includes harsh, necessary, amoral elements . . . and one remembers in this connection the statesman who, at the height of his successes, when he had succeeded in uniting his country and making of it a great power, declared that he did not know whether he could still count himself among the decent people.[42]

If it completely forgets its ideal side and reduces itself to brute force and deception, it easily degenerates into a devilish and criminal activity, incapable, for all its terror and destruction, of lasting effects.

Nations which have politics in their blood have an instinctive capacity for reconciling, at least as they see things, their political actions with their conscience. They will the means, but never quite lose sight of human decency and morality as ends. Germany on the other hand shows its political incapacity by its clumsy misunderstanding of these niceties. "Though by no means evil by nature, but gifted in the direction of the spiritual and ideal, it considers politics to be entirely a matter of murder, lies, deception and violence, something completely and one-sidedly filthy, and as soon as it thinks the moment has come for it to give itself over to politics, it practises the art according to a corresponding philosophy. The French say: 'If a German wants to be ingratiating, he jumps out of the window.' That is also what happens when he wants to play politics. He thinks he must behave in such a way to frighten people out of their senses . . . The variety of things that 'raison d'état' has to cover and explain, for a German turned 'political,' goes beyond saying." But in reality, "politics is a function of human society, the totality of the human mind includes an interest in it, and just as man does not belong exclusively to the realm of nature, so politics is not wholly concerned with evil. But the German thinks that it is, and it is therefore no wonder that politics distorts, poisons and ruins him." The danger to the world that results from the existence at the heart of Europe of a power with such a beast-of-prey philosophy of politics is obvious. In his declaration in the *Betrachtungen* that politics is a dirty business, Thomas Mann had had domestic politics mainly in view, and here the whole emphasis is on foreign affairs, international politics, but there is evidence all the same that his point of view has changed from that of the typical German, as he described it now after the rise of the Nazis, to the more enlightened conception ascribed here to nations with a native flair for politics.[43]

This idea of the uncultivated one-sidedness of the unpolitical German is strongly stressed in Mann's editorial introduction to his new periodical *Maß und Wert* in 1937, where the diary entry we have quoted is repeated almost word for word. After discussing the current misconception of politics in Germany, he says again:

> Totality–there is only one, humane totality, the totality of the humane, of which the social and political is a segment and component part. The German "Bürger" did not know that. He thought he could, for the sake of his inwardness and culture, negate politics, "steal away from under it," as Richard Wagner said, and many of Germany's calamities have resulted from his mistaken notion that it was possible to be an unpolitical cultivated man.[44]

What is happening now is that the German has gone from one extreme to the other and has "totalized politics, the state," which is far worse, for to force the whole of life into a political strait-jacket is a crime, with criminal consequences. The new periodical is dedicated to the service of freedom and "Humanität" but not of "Humanität" just in the classical sense, which neglects one aspect of the humane, but of a new, perfected conception of humanism still in the making.

After 1938, when Thomas Mann settled in the United States, similar ideas about the relationship between culture and politics are still the burden of his principal speeches, often made to Americans of German origin. In his "Rede auf dem deutschen Tag in New York" in 1938, for example, he repeats that it is a mistake to think of culture and politics as necessarily opposed to each other, and to look down on the one from the heights of the other. He sums up his message in the sentence: "It was a mistaken belief of the German 'Bürger' that it was possible to be an unpolitical man of cultivation." The results of that error are now plain to all, Germany's lack of political instincts, the over-compensating worship of the state and of power, and the inhumanity which results from this.[45] In "Das Problem der Freiheit" he comes back next year to the question of the tensions between democracy, based on the idea of freedom, and socialism, based on that of equality. He recalls Goethe's and Heine's attitude to the problem and declares again that a purely individualistic and intellectual "Humanität" constitutes a danger for "Kultur" which, properly understood, means the totality of the humane, including the social elements. To make politics absolute, on the other hand, as dictatorships and Bolshevism do, means the end of freedom, which depends on the maintenance of a just and reasonable, a "humane" balance between the claims of the individual and the social.

Even so private an occasion as the dinner in honour of Heinrich Mann on his seventieth birthday–he had only recently escaped to America from occupied France–evoked a speech from his brother which revolved round the now familiar antithesis of culture and politics. It is one of a whole series of speeches which these literary brothers addressed to each other on birthdays. As Hermann Kesten wrote about this occasion:

> When we celebrated Heinrich Mann's seventieth birthday it was just like old times: Thomas Mann pulled out a manuscript and congratulated from it. Then his brother pulled out his bit of paper and expressed his thanks, also from the typed page, while we sat at dessert, a score of men and women, and listened to German literature in its home circle. Feuchtwanger, Werfel, Mehring, the Reinhardts and some film people were amongst those present.[46]

In his speech Thomas Mann succeeds in giving a new turn to the now familiar thought about political institutions forming an essential part of a civilization, and about the fatal flaw in the habitual way of thinking of the cultivated classes in Germany, that it was too little concerned with the practical problems of social and political life. He quotes with strong approval some sentences from an unnamed English critic who, while deeply admiring German culture, is always depressed to find German poets and philosophers being led by their thought in the end "to the edge of an abyss–an abyss from which they could not withdraw, but must fall into headlong,–an abyss of intellect no longer controlled by any awareness of the sensuous realities of life." Nietzsche seems to Mann a tragic example, and he contrasts his "intoxicating doctrine of the anti-humane" with occasional letters, like the one about the disastrously early death of the Emperior Frederick III, Queen Victoria's son-in-law, "the last hope for German freedom," letters which reveal, he thinks, the real man behind "the romantic poem that was his work." The "realities of life" are inescapable to-day, and he is convinced that an epoch is beginning when the arts will simply have to distinguish again, on religious and moral grounds, between good and evil. Heinrich, he says, had been one of the first moral critics of his age, in books like his *Untertan, Professor Unrat* and *Die kleine Stadt.* He praises too his untiring campaign against Hitlerism, and at the darkest moment in the war, expresses his own confidence that as a victory for Hitler would result in a world completely given over to evil, a negation of all humane aspirations, there will come a revolt against this nihilism as of the elements themselves, and "iron facts" will crumble away before decent human feeling. He repeated this eloquent passage in that month's broadcast to Germany.

At the end of the German war Thomas Mann gave a lecture in English on "Germany and the Germans" in the Library of Congress (29 May 1945), in which he attempted finally a brief sketch of the German national character on a historical basis.[47] There is no question here of attacking the "bad" Germany in the name of the "good." He insists that there is only one Germany, and that what he says is the result of his own experience as a German, a piece of self-criticism. Germans are much given to self-criticism, he says, being highly introspective by nature, and it is this inward-looking habit of thought, the source of the German passion for "Bildung" and also of German ineptness in practical politics, which is again his real subject. He neither excuses nor accuses, but tries to understand, as a citizen of provincial Lübeck who has become a cosmopolitan American. Lübeck, he recalls, had something quite medieval about it, not only in its appearance but in the suggestion of irrational depths he found in its spiritual atmosphere. It is the author of *Doktor Faustus* who is speaking, putting into plain English some of the ideas he was to convey symbolically in his coming novel, in which a modern Faustus, modelled on Nietzsche, in part suffers the lot of Germany herself. He wants to convey in his lecture, he says, that the German mind has made a secret compact with this demonic.

How had this come about? Partly, he suggests, through the Reformation. Martin Luther (the counterpart of Faust in the popular imagination) was superlatively German, Mann thinks, in his introspectiveness combined with a mystical musicality, for example. He does not like him, for his anti-Europeanism, and for the combination he finds in him of choleric robustness and coarseness, lyrical tenderness and crass superstition, but he acknowledges his greatness and his enormous influence on German history. "He was a freedom-hero–but in the German style, for he understood nothing about freedom," about political freedom, that is, siding as he did with the princes in the Peasants'. Revolt, unlike Tilman Riemenschneider, one of Mann's heroes. "Luther's anti-political devotion to the rulers, the product of German-musical inwardness and unworldliness, has not only stamped itself in the course of the centuries on the subservient attitude of the Germans to their princes and all official authority. It has not only created, or at least favoured, the German dualism of boldest speculation and political immaturity. It is also representative in a monumental and defiant way of the typically German falling-apart of the desire for nationhood and the ideal of political freedom. For the Reformation, like the rising against Napoleon later, was a nationalistic freedom movement."[48] The passage which follows these words was broadcast by Mann to Germany as part of his address on 2 April 1945. It is to this effect that political freedom in Germany has always meant freedom from foreign domination, the freedom to be German and nothing else, nothing more, whereas in democratic countries it means the freedom of the individual, a moral freedom. German freedom had really meant militant slavishness, and the Nazis had hoped to extend it to the whole world.

The trouble is that the Germans have never had a real revolution like the French, whose idea of a nation was born in their revolution and includes the ideals of civic freedom and European unity. It was greeted as a liberalizing idea, even abroad, whereas German patriotism, even in the days of Jahn and Maßmann during the "Wars of Liberation," had a crude and boorish way with it which antagonized Goethe, for example, as the very antithesis for the super-national culture which was his ideal. The failure of the Germans to achieve civic freedom in any of their attempts at revolution, in 1848 or 1918 for example, had given them a strange idea of politics. The passage already quoted from the preface to *Maß und Wert* (p. 258) is repeated here, about the Germans going berserk when they take to politics, instead of practising it as the art of the possible, with due regard for moral values.

Why is it, Mann asks himself, that in German history evil so often results from good? There is surely something demonic about it. Take the capacity for "Innerlichkeit" which has so long been a German characteristic, the delicacy and depth of feeling, the unworldly absent-mindedness which went along with love of nature and a deep seriousness of thought and conscience in so many Germans and lies behind the achievements in metaphysics, in music and in the inimitable German "Lied." This quality inspired the Reformation, a mighty emancipation, yet how much evil followed after, the division of Europe, the Thirty Years' War and all the devastation and suffering it brought about! The great Romantic movement was another expression of "Innerlichkeit," and its positive achievements are undeniable, in literature and literary theory, in folk-lore, linguistics and history, and in many other fields. Enthusiasm and vitality marked all its efforts, the wish to pierce beyond useful knowledge to the irrational sources of life. It was music revolting against literature, mysticism against clarity, a willingness to face the dark sides of experience and history, putting power higher than intellectualism and rejecting all rhetorical attempts to whitewash reality. "Here is the link between Romanticism and that realism and machiavellism which achieved in Bismarck, the only political genius Germany has produced, its victories over Europe." His German unification was not at all democratic, his Reich was a pure power state aiming at European hegemony, a dangerous mixture of vigorous efficiency and dreams of past greatness, Romanticism endowed with every technical skill. "Nothing great in literature and art came out of Germany now, that had once been the teacher of the world. It was only strong. But in this strength and beneath all the organized efficiency the Romantic germ of sickness and death was still at work. It was nourished by historical misfortune, the sufferings and humiliations of a lost war. And German Romanticism, descended to a pitiful mass level, the level of a Hitler, erupted into hysterical barbarism, into a drunken fit and convulsion of conceit and crime, which is now reaching its dreadful end in national catastrophe, a physical and psychical collapse without parallel."[49]

The melancholy story of German "Innerlichkeit" shows, Mann concludes, that there are not two Germanies, a bad and a good, but only one, whose best gifts turned through some devil's art to evil. The bad Germany is the good one gone wrong, the good one in misfortune, in guilt and collapse. It is not for him to throw stones, for he too is a German. Can we dare to hope that after this catastrophe some better form will be found for Germany than a national state, that the first tentative steps will be taken towards a world in which the national individualism of the nineteenth century will be softened and perhaps finally disappear, giving the mass of the good in Germany more favourable conditions to grow in?

---

1. Thomas Mann-Heinrich Mann, *Briefwechsel 1900-49*, ed. H. Wysling, S. Fischer-Verlag, 1968, intro. p. 1.

2. Thomas Mann, *Briefe,* I, 1889-1936, ed. Erika Mann. S. Fischer-Verlag, 1962, p. 354 (To Karl Kerenyi, 20 November 1934).

3. Thomas Mann, *Betrachtungen eines Unpolitischen,* Berlin, 1920, p. xxxii.

4. *Ibid.* p. 74.

5. *Ibid.* p. 79.

6. *Ibid.* p. 108.

7. *Ibid.* p. 118.

8. Thomas Mann-Heinrich Mann, *Briefwechsel,* pp. 25f.

9. *Ibid.* p. 104.

10. Thomas Mann, *Reden und Aufsätze* I, Stockholm, 1965, pp. 548f.

11. *Betrachtungen,* p. 244.

12. *Ibid.* p. 246.

13. *Ibid.* p. 254f.

14. *Ibid.* p. 490.

15. *Reliquien,* quoted by F. Meinecke, *Weltbürgertum und Nationalstaat,* München and Berlin, 1922, p. 27n.

16. *Les deux sources de la morale et de la religion,* Paris, 1932, p. 33.

17. *Betrachtungen,* p. 517.

18. *Ibid.* p. 273.

19. *Ibid.* pp. 273ff.

20. *Ibid.* p. 267.

21. *Ibid.* p. 270.

22. See *Natural Law and the Theory of Society,* 1500-1800, by Otto Gierke, translated with an introduction by Ernest Barker, Cambridge, 1934. The 1922 lecture by Troeltsch is printed in translation at the end of vol. I and discussed in the introduction.

23. Ralf Dahrendorf, *Gesellschaft und Demokratie in Deutschland,* München, 1965, p. 442. See also "Conflict and Liberty," *Brit. Journal of Sociology,* vol. XIV.

24. Now in *Reden und Aufsätze,* II, pp. 11-52.

25. *Dr Faustus,* Stockholm, 1948, pp. 522f.

26. *Mein Kampf,* München, 1933, I, p. 240.

27. *Reden und Aufsätze,* II, pp. 341-51.

28. *Briefe,* I, p. 202.

29. Published April 1928 in *Preussiche Jahrbücher.* Reprinted in *Reden und Aufsätze,* vol. II, pp. 387-97, Stockholm, 1965.

30. *Reden und Aufsätze,* II, p. 55.

31. *Reden und Aufsätze,* I, pp. 375ff.

32. *Ibid.* pp. 378ff.

33. *Reden und Aufsätze,* II, pp. 776ff.

34. *Briefe,* I, p. 278.

35. *Reden und Aufsätze,* I, pp. 431-519.

36. *Briefe,* I, p. 281.

37. *Reden und Aufsätze,* II, p. 394.

38. *Ibid.* pp. 426-32.

39. *Ibid.* p. 198.

40. *Ibid.* p. 516.

41. *Ibid.* pp. 432-514.

42. *Ibid.* p. 507.

43. *Ibid.* pp. 507ff.

44. *Ibid.* p. 534.

45. *Ibid.* p. 138.

46. Thomas Mann-Heinrich Mann, *Briefwechsel,* p. 339.

47. *Reden und Aufsätze,* II, pp. 313-15.

48. *Ibid.* p. 323.

49. *Ibid.* p. 333.

Reprinted from The German Tradition of Self-Cultivation: "Bildung" from Humboldt to Thomas Mann *(Cambridge: Cambridge University Press, 1975), pp. 226-263.*

The Making of a People

J. M. Ritchie

Anti-Semitism was not an ever present element in the works of the forerunners of National Socialism, for there were also other "inferior" races, as was often demonstrated by authors from the periphery of the German-speaking world. One such was more concerned about the Slavs than the Jews: Erwin Guido Kolbenheyer survived the collapse of the Nationalist Socialist regime.[1] To the end he never saw any necessity to revise his opinions or to doubt in any way the intellectual path which had led him to accept Adolf Hitler and "the movement" as the solution to Germany's problems. Clearly he was a writer rather than a politician and he can perhaps be excused for failing to see the implications of the nationalist line he personally followed and also advocated in his novels, dramas, poetry and pamphlets. Born in Bohemia, he saw at an early age the disintegration of the Austro-Hungarian Empire and the rise of the militant Slav. The German language, the one single factor which seemed to hold the whole rambling Empire together, was forced to give way to Czech as the language of administration. For him this seemed to mark the beginning of the end of the Sudeten Germans. In fact the dissolution of the Austro-Hungarian Empire was to take another fifty years, but nevertheless his basic attitudes were formed at an early age–the desire to preserve the German language and resentment against the Slavs, combined with longing for a greater German fatherland. Little wonder that the *Anschluss* with Austria, which Hitler brought about, was welcomed by such people. When Kolbenheyer started his career as an author he was the typical apolitical German intellectual; however, he was born into an age in which the world of aesthetics was being radically politicized and he gradually moved further and further to the right, in what was to become a characteristic manner for the time. The frontiersman became more German than the Germans. Living in Germany after the war he found the republic less than satisfying and was soon denouncing the shortcomings of the parliamentary system. His position has been described as close to that of Thomas Mann's *Reflections of an Unpolitical Man.* They shared the same rejection of democracy, ostentatious conservatism, belief in a German mission for Europe, dependence on Nietzsche as a model of the precarious and paradoxical radical conservative, approval of the war mania of July 1914 in Germany, insistence on a powerful Germany as a precondition for European peace, a metaphysical conception of the *Volk,* a tendency to equate Goethe with Bismarck, a view of the leader as exponent of the people, and an admiration of the German performance in war. Yet although Kolbenheyer and Mann both started off expressing beliefs of this kind, Thomas Mann was to develop into a strong defender of the republic and an enemy of National Socialism, while Kolbenheyer was to come more and more to denounce the one and acclaim the other. Probably the difference between them lay in the very fact that Kolbenheyer was a border German. As Kolbenheyer the Sudeten German saw the Slavs as the enemy, this made him only too ready to accept nationalistic concepts. But Kolbenheyer was a true intellectual who had studied philosophy, psychology and natural sciences. He was no crude racist: instead he attempted to apply *biological* concepts to problems of social and cultural history and as a result developed a vast historical panorama, in the manner of the time, which he called the *Bauhütte–Elements of a Metaphysic of the Present* (1925). At the core of this philosophy Kolbenheyer sees something he calls Plasma, the fundamental stuff of life; from this, through the plant, animal and human world, he builds up a universal picture embracing races and people, but also families and individuals. The heart of the matter, however, is the "white race" and the need for the young and healthy (Germanic) race to take over the leadership from the old and exhausted (Romance-Mediterranean) race: what he demonstrates in mystical pseudo-scientific terms is *Volkwerdung,* the ineluctable progress of a race like the Aryans to leadership and maturity. Mysticism, soul, heart, life he conceives of as characteristic elements of the German race; civilization, the profit-motive, quantification and logic he rejects as un-German, and his projection of such qualities on to an external enemy (be it Jewish, Mediterranean or Slav) was to prove only too "convergent" with the NS ideology. Indeed it has been pointed out that what Kolbenheyer claimed as the first true and correct view of history was an almost direct forerunner of Rosenberg's *Myth of the Twentieth-Century*.[2] Kolbenheyer's political activity was mainly in the twenties and thirties when in many essays and pamphlets he propagated the national revolution, but his major essays, *The Biological Foundations of the Liberation Movement in the People* (1933) and *The National Revolution and the Revival of the German Spirit* (1933) give some indication by their titles alone of the thrust of his biological view.[3] By 1932 he had joined the NSDAP, because it meant for him liberation from the claims of Versailles and also the possibility of a greater Germany. Germans inside Germany itself were in his view much less aware of the biological imbalance than were the Germans outside. Hitler's political actions did justice to what for Kolbenheyer were the natural facts. Hitler came from the Austrian border, and so he could see things from the outside. His whole life was devoted to Germany as a whole. It has been argued that the difference between Hitler and all other nationalist extremists lies in the importance he placed on the German/Austrian Slav frontier and the conclusions he drew from his awareness of it. This was certainly what appealed to Kolbenheyer. It did not make him an out-and-out supporter of the regime–he was too much of an individualist for that, yet he was prepared to go a long way in his polemics against the opposition, attacking Romain Rolland, defending the burning of books, and repeating his conviction that German nationalism was only the preliminary stage on the way towards the ideal of a Europe united under German leadership. In time Kolbenheyer became "the figurehead of Nazi cultural support for the Sudeten Germans" by accepting the presidency of the Sudeten German Cultural Society. This meant that to some extent he was in a position to help some literary colleagues who fell foul of the regime. So, for example, in 1933 he was able to effect the release from Dachau of Karl Bröger, the worker-poet whose poems about the camaraderie of the First World War the Nazis exploited. But there can be no suggestion that he in any way acted against the regime or engaged in any kind of resistance. In effect he supported the Hitler regime right up to 1945, though he claimed afterwards to have been totally unaware of the horrendous crimes committed in the name of National Socialism. He himself was never anti-Semitic and said he knew nothing of the policy directed at the extermination of the Jews. Without doubt it was Kolbenheyer's Sudetenland background combined with his "biologically" based ultranationalist beliefs which led him into the National Socialist camp. At the same time he was sensitive, as were so many of the nationalist writers, about what he felt was the lack of recognition afforded his works (despite all the prizes) and was prepared to engage in practically any ideological contortion in order to prove that the National Socialist ideology accorded with his own, if this meant he could gain the recognition he felt he rightly deserved. His Bauhütte philosophy had not brought enough recognition, nor had his novels and plays, though much admired, brought him the wider recognition he sought. So perhaps, when he felt his creative powers decline, he moved more into the directly political sphere. It cannot be said to have been to his ultimate advantage. Certainly his reputation as a writer now remains severely tarnished and few will be prepared today to give serious consideration to the once much-acclaimed Paracelsus trilogy which projected its hero as a genius and artist, whose life and work, culminating in "Third Reich of Paracelsus," sums up the "German" values of depth and feeling, religiosity and strength.

Another writer equally rooted in the cultural traditions of the Austro-Hungarian Empire, and one destined to become just as much of a pan-German nationalist as Kolbenheyer, was Joseph Weinheber. At first sight this prophet of pure form and poetry seems the last person one would expect to find among the uniformed ranks of the brown-shirted barbarians; yet he claimed to have been converted to National Socialism at an early stage and he certainly remained one of its most prominent figureheads on the cultural stage right to the very end. Like many of his generation he went through a Nietzschean phase with "pride in loneliness, delight in perverse evil and affirmation of life," yet the working-class young man trying to make his way in the world of letters never really had the strength, confidence or social poise to put these ideals into practice. What he clearly wanted more than anything else was acceptance, recognition and fame. As an Austrian he shared some of Hitler's cultural background and certainly developed one feature associated with Hitler's Austria, namely anti-Semitism. Like many he also felt excluded by the "other" literature: indeed it was only with the national revival in 1933 that his eventual breakthrough came. By that time Weinheber had connections with the Austrian NSDAP, though as a party it was still illegal, because it threatened the stability of the Austrian republic.[4] His collection of poems *Nobility and Decline* betrays no direct references to events of the time, and yet the divisions of the collection were remarkably consonant with Nazi tastes, especially the grandiose classicism of his verses on classical models, his variations on the Nazi favourite Hölderlin, his attempts at the "pure poem," and his "Hymn to the German Language."[5] Weinheber specialized in denunciations of the decadence of the age, from which the poet withdraws into isolation or against which he reacts with existential heroism. In effect Weinheber shared the reactionary distaste for democracy, disliked the republic, developed an extremely nationalistic view of German culture, and was anti-Socialist and ambitious. Will Vesper took up his work, and by March 1935 Weinheber was being invited to give broadcasts on the German radio. His longing for recognition in Germany and not merely in Austria was about to be more than satisfied. He received an honorary doctorate, he was awarded the title of professor by the Austrian government, he was awarded the Mozart Prize and he visited Germany where he met Kolbenheyer, with whom he had much in common. Not surprisingly the butcher's son from the city bought a house in the country and attempted to show by his poetry that he too was rooted in the soil. Yet it was not for this kind of poetry that he became widely known or famous, but rather for *Wien wörtlich,* a cycle of poems about the ancient city of Vienna. Weinheber set his sights very high. Repudiating competitors like Rilke, George, Hofmannsthal and Werfel, he strove to raise himself to the level of the great masters of the past by taking as literary models the Greek, Latin and Italian verses of Sappho, Alcaeus, Homer, Horace, Dante and Michelangelo, and the works of German authors who had preceded him–Hölderlin, Mörike, Droste-Hülshoff and Goethe. Weinheber had in other words a fixed idea of what constituted *real* poetry, and aspired to reach it by imitation. In such an age, however, it was impossible to withdraw into the timeless sphere of pure poetry and so he also wrote a hymn in praise of the *Anschluss,* various poems to the Führer, and a "Hymn to the Munitions Worker."[6] His Nietzschean love of what was great and his amoral love of grandeur for its own sake led the "pure" poet to commit himself totally to National Socialism, despite or perhaps even because of the ruthlessness and brutality of it. Here at last was the oneness of the *Volk* he looked for, uniting German and Austrian. History was being made and he was part of it. Politics meant something other than party political manoeuvring. The *Volk* had spoken as one. His "Hymn to the Home-coming" was written for the celebrations for Hitler's birthday, held in the Burgtheater in Vienna on 20 April 1938; it consists largely of a comparison between Hitler's return to Austria and Odysseus' return to his beloved Ithaca after long years of wandering. It concludes:

> This in the name of the people!
> This in the name of the blood!
> This in the name of suffering:
> Germany, eternal and great,
> Germany, we greet you!
> Führer, sacred and strong,
> Führer, we greet you!
> Homeland, happy and free.
> Homeland, we greet you!

The *Volk,* the blood, the Führer, Germany, the homeland–this is Nazi language unadorned. With poems like this and his "Austria 1934" he "prostituted his honour in the cause of political murderers and blackmailers."[7] He was not an unworldly idealist who could be exploited by the Nazis for propaganda purposes: he was a realist determined to demonstrate his political reliability to the new masters. Needless to say he was not completely blind, yet such criticism of the movement as he expressed from time to time tended to be after the manner of the believer rather than the doubter, admitting that foreigners were perhaps right to describe the National Socialists as barbarians, but claiming that this was because they could be aware only of the external trappings of the national upsurge, not of its essence and true nature. Similarly, the Austrian in him felt some resentment from time to time at German interference in Austrian matters, but this did not stop him from penning a panegyric when the insignia of the Empire, the supreme symbols of Austria's cultural heritage, were removed from Vienna by the new German masters and taken to Nuremberg. The declaration of war indissolubly linked Austria's fate with that of Germany, and Weinheber's literary destiny even more with victory for the regime. The war for him was not about mere conquest, but about the survival of the white race, the triumph of the German cultural mission. Throughout the course of the war, nevertheless, Weinheber avoided all jingoistic poetry and instead devoted himself to what seemed on the surface much loftier ideals. In the same way as he had previously appeared as the poet of pure form, so now he strove to cultivate the word in its purest form. The lofty, almost biblical ring of the title, *Here is the Word,* gives some idea of his intentions. In this he is in line with a powerful German tradition from the turn of the century on, marking a reaction against the abuse of language in the age of mass communications (not least in the journalistic language of newspapers) and the distortion of language by mass political parties. But Weinheber, who felt he had a special relationship with Goebbels, was clearly not one to see direct applications of his critique of language to an expose of the propagandistic distortions of National Socialism: his linguistic theories are more in line with those of a Jünger. In the volume *Leaves and Stones* (1934) Jünger's essay "In Praise of Vowels" appeared. This was an exercise which had been attempted elsewhere (notably by Rimbaud), but in this case the outcome was rather different. Rainer Stollman uses this example as the climax and culmination to his book on "the aestheticisation of politics."[8] Weinheber's exercises in the inner form of the word, or the symbolic significance of particular letters of the alphabet, are somewhat similar, and by no means stop him from finding reasons for extreme nationalism. As Ridley points out, in an earlier collection like *Nobility and Decline* it was but a small step from the "Ode to the Letter of the Alphabet" to the "Hymn to the German Language" and later, in the lectures on language which he gave to students at the University of Vienna, he still found reasons for the defense of Blood and Soil writing. Significantly, language was for Weinheber not a means of communication, but a mystical entity expressive of an immutable racial essence: and this mystical essence was essential for the war effort, for ultimately in "loyalty to the German language lay the only true hope of victory."[9] By the end Weinheber found himself more directly involved with the struggle for German victory than he had expected would be necessary for a German poet. By 1944 the war was going so badly that all belletristic publications were banned and his *Here is the Word* could not be printed. Air raids destroyed the stocks of his other works, while he himself daily expected to be called to military or munitions service. By the end of 1944 the man who in the First World War had somehow escaped military training or service at the front was in the *Volkssturm,* and when the Russian tanks reached his village the following year he took an overdose of morphia and died: it is not clear whether this was by mistake because he was an addict, whether in terror at the thought of falling into Russian hands, or in despair at the collapse of the regime, to which he had become too closely attached. A remarkable number of people are still sufficiently impressed by Weinheber's formal talents to think of him as a real poet.

A writer from an entirely different part of the German-speaking world, but one nevertheless whose extreme patriotism and love of the German soil led him into close contact with National Socialism, was Hans Grimm.[10] This author's real life took him outside Germany to the colonies and yet his literary life was to become intimately bound up with Germany itself, with the nationalist movement, with Blood and Soil and with National Socialism. After leaving Germany Hans Grimm lived for years in South Africa as trader, farmer, reporter and writer. He also lived later in German South West Africa. On his return to Germany he bought the Lippoldsberg Cloister House and made it into a national literary and cultural centre. Grimm was a prolific writer and the complete edition of his works contains dramas, stories and novels as well as collection of essays. Of particular interest is his African narrative *The Judge in the Karu* (1926), not only for its style and African background, but also for the author's fairly explicit statement of his belief in the superiority of the white race over the black. However, his most successful book was his massive novel of 1,300 pages called *People Without Living Space* (1926). The title was immediately taken up and exploited as a political slogan by the National Socialists, although Adolf Hitler was more interested in *Lebensraum* in the East and had no desire at that time to become involved with England, the world power, over colonial demands. Nevertheless the whole concept appealed to the ultra-nationalist factions in Germany. As F. L. Carsten has put it:

> Of all the political slogans current in Germany in the 1920s and 1930s, none exer-

> cised a stronger influence on the youth of the country in school and university than that which proclaimed that Germany needed more space, that the nation–to be able to live–required more *Raum*. Deprived of its colonial empire by the Treaty of Versailles without any justification–thus the young were taught in the German schools–the Germans had become a *Volk ohne Raum*, a nation without living space.[11]

This message is explicitly proclaimed by the author in the very first chapter of the book, entitled "Homeland and Constriction." In his own rather pretentious and inflated style the author appeals to all German men and women, boys and girls of all classes and walks of life to raise their arms to God, so that together in their millions He may be made aware of the horrific nature of the German fate. This will be revealed through the story of one simple German whose fate will be representative for that of His people. To answer any superior doubter who might claim that the German people will always live, he then examines more closely what is meant by living. The sick man lives, the thief lives, the whore lives and worm eats worm–"but the German needs living space around him and sun above him and freedom inside him, in order to become good and fine. Is he to have waited centuries in vain for it?"

The hero of *Volk ohne Raum,* Cornelius Friebott, is a Low German, born (as Lulu von Strauss und Torney was to put it) in the most German part of the country and by the most German river, the Upper Weser. He shares the typical fate of the landworker of the end of the nineteenth century through being forced to tear up his roots in the soil and move into the big city. Where this leads is shown by the fact that he is no longer involved in healthy work, but instead is subject to the machine. He declines into a worker, a member of the proletariat, and even goes so far as to desert his peasant background completely and become involved with the Socialists! As a result of activities on behalf of the Social Democrats he is dismissed and sentenced to imprisonment. At this point he leaves this Germany of class warfare and emigrates to South Africa, which proves to be a land of opportunity for a German like himself who is prepared to work hard. He joins the Boer Army to fight against the British, is wounded, captured and imprisoned. This whole section of the book, needless to say, not only provides plenty of adventure and excitement, but also permits the author to express his resentment against the colonial, imperialist British, who treat Germans as second-class citizens. Further excitement comes when the hero moves to the new German colony, fights the Hottentots, prospers on a farm and makes money in the diamond rush. This whole wonderful world collapses on the outbreak of the World War, when he is again exposed to rough treatment at the hands of British authorities. Indeed he is even sentenced to death merely for killing an African in self-defence; but he escapes from British territory to Portuguese Angola, is rearrested and finally shipped back to Germany. By this time the war is over and he finds his homeland is in a depressed, defeated state and makes it his duty to tour Germany, conveying to his countrymen the message of *Lebensraum.* During one of his speeches calling upon Germany to awaken he is killed by a stone thrown by a worker in the crowd. His message is taken up, however, by the author Hans Grimm, who from the very first page figures prominently in the novel; the book is written to carry on the torch from the point where Cornelius Friebott was violently forced to put it down.

There is no doubt whatsoever that this blockbuster of a book is a "good read." For one thing it is almost deliberately not modern or difficult in its style, for another Grimm has a great deal of natural, narrative drive, and he tells a good, adventurous yarn, setting it against an exotic background. It is true that there are many digressions and the author tends to preach at his readers; but there is also no doubt that it was as much the message as the story that made the book sell in hundreds of thousands of copies. According to Carsten it had reached the half million mark before 1938, and even after the Second World War it was still selling well, though sales have now declined and the whole ethos of the book has dated. Grimm, the outspoken exponent of colonial imperialism, was quite clear in his own mind about the superiority of the Nordic *Herrenvolk* over other inferior races, and it was this racism which was quickly identified and praised by Nazi critics in the 1930s.

> Hans Grimm shows the particular difficulties which ensue for the worthy Germans as against other colonial peoples, quite simply from the superiority of the race . . . *Volk ohne Raum* belongs among those works in our literature which will last and in which most distant generations will

> experience the true nature of the people, the eternal power of its being and the voice of its blood, shuddering before the weight and magnitude of its Fate.[12]

An early doctoral dissertation which examined Grimm as one who "prepared the way for the Nordic view" came to the conclusion that the political ideas of Adolf Hitler and Hans Grimm converged at four main points: in the general question of race, in the particular question of the place of the Jews, in the stress given to the significance of the Aryan as Nordic man, and finally in the question of the German stance *vis-à-vis* England.[13] Apart from the basic idea of *Lebensraum,* the novel's militant nationalism also appealed to NS ideologues. Grimm released emotions and struck chords which could not fail to have their effect on a receptive public. But it must also be remembered that though he consciously acted as a propagator of the Nordic world view, he was more of an old-fashioned, crabbed national conservative than an out-and-out Nazi. Indeed he never joined the party and always avoided the formula *Heil Hitler.* While it is true he allowed himself to be elected Senator of the Literary Academy and accepted a high position in the Reichsschrifttumskammer he never made any secret of his doubts about Hitler and about Goebbels' literary policies. In the period between 1933 and 1945 he published only two speeches and he never received any of the many cultural prizes of the Third Reich. His relationship with Goebbels was a tense one, because the Doctor found it impossible to make Grimm toe the party line. Grimm remained the individualist who approved in general of what was happening, but disapproved of any restriction on his personal freedom. Of course, as the "poet of the national epic," enjoying a special relationship with Goebbels, his position was a unique one, and he could get away with more than many of his less prominent colleagues. Nevertheless, his life under National Socialism was strange. Like many, he dried up as far as creative writing was concerned, but his great wealth enabled him to develop widespread activities, most notable of which were the Lippoldsberg Literary Gatherings, to which he invited leading German national-conservatives like Edwin Erich Dwinger, Moritz Jahn, Rudolph Alexander Schröder and Paul Alverdes.[14] Even after 1945 meetings still took place there at which Kolbenheyer, Schumann and Pleyer engaged in discussions about Germany's place in the new Europe. Grimm himself remained completely unchanged and true to himself. Like a Christian defending the early church and primitive Christianity Grimm continued to defend "original" National Socialism. It was his opinion that there was nothing wrong with the movement, indeed it had attempted a great deal that was right for Germany and for Europe. It was only through Hitler's paranoia that it had gone wrong and crimes and excesses had crept in. Grimm remained one of the incurables. Attempts to rediscover him and find new readers for his works failed. As for the old readers, they had been ready to die for their belief in *Lebensraum* and when the war came they did so:

> Their graves are to be found from the Arctic Circle to the Caucasus, but Hans Grimm lived to deny vociferously any responsibility for the events of the Third Reich. It is true that he was not a National Socialist and differed from them in certain matters. Rather he was an extreme Nationalist. In Germany nationalism of a violent and antiwestern type has a much stronger tradition than national-socialism; this kind of fervent nationalism is much more likely to stage a come-back than Hitler's brand of German fascism.[15]

Another author, of an entirely different type, but nevertheless one who, like Grimm, could claim that he was never a National Socialist, one who, like Grimm, preached a nationalism of an extremely violent, anti-democratic kind; and one who, like Grimm, gave thousands of young Germans ideals to live and die for, was Ernst Jünger, who is still writing to this day. Countless studies have been devoted to Ernst Jünger, not least in an attempt to discover the extent to which he was or was not associated with National Socialism, but no satisfactory conclusion has yet been arrived at.[16] Admirers and defenders of this brilliant stylist, philosopher, botanist, aesthete and adventurer are almost as numerous as those who describe him as "one of the most dangerous of all fascist thinkers." Ernst Jünger is constantly changing, modifying and manipulating his writings and so any quotation from his work can be countered by its opposite. Yet despite the contradictory nature of his place in the conservative revolution, and of his personal and ideological relationship with National Socialism in general and with Hitler and Goebbels in particular, there is no doubting the role of war in his writings. This was for him, as indeed for all his generation, the fundamental experience, the primal vision, and to it he constantly returns. Born in Heidelberg into a solid middle-class home, his youth seems to have been characterised by the same paralysing boredom and longing for release that was to find literary expression in a play like Wedekind's *Spring Awakening,* in novels like Musil's *Törless* and Hesse's *Under the Wheel,* or in the poets of the immediate pre-war expressionistic generation. In 1910 Georg Heym wrote in his diary: "It is always the same, so boring, boring, boring. Nothing happens, nothing, nothing, nothing. If only something would happen, which wouldn't leave this stale taste of everyday things." German middle-class youths of this generation seemed to have been filled with disgust at the deadly poison of ennui, with hatred of the money-grubbing business mentality, and with contempt for the merchant's longing for safety and security. They were brim-full not with the spirit of adventure, but with the longing for an explosion, for some liberating action of any kind. Jünger shared these feelings and it was not surprising that in 1913 he ran away from home to join the Foreign Legion and only returned on the promise of a chance to join an expedition to Africa to climb Kilimanjaro. When the war came he delayed only long enough to take the emergency School Leaving Certificate before joining up. By the end of 1915 he had reached the rank of lieutenant and had become a shock-troop leader. He survived the war but not without wounds. In the final chapter ("My Last Storm") of *Storm of Steel* (1920) he amuses himself in hospital counting the number of times he has been hit:

> I found that I had been hit in all fourteen times; six times by rifle-bullets, once by a shrapnel bullet, once by a shell splinter, three times by bomb splinters, and twice by splinters of rifle bullets. Counting the ins and outs, this made precisely twenty punctures, so that I might confidently with that Roman centurion, Holkschen Reiter, take my place in every warlike circle.

Before the end of hostilities he was made a Knight of the Order "Pour le mérite," the highest possible decoration in the German armed forces. He was a national hero. Jünger remained in the army after the war, and it was during this time in the twenties that he started to write. All his titles reveal war as the central experience: *Storm of Steel* (1920); *Struggle as Inner Experience* (1922); *Storm* (1923); *Copse 125. A Chronicle of the Trench Fighting* (1915); *Fire and Blood. One Small Segment from a Major Battle* (1925); *The Adventurous Heart* (1929); *Total Mobilisation* (1931). The last title, based on one of Jünger's own concepts, is yet another example of a literary-intellectual idea which was taken over and turned into reality by the National Socialists.

Jünger's first and perhaps most influential work, *Storm of Steel,* reveals his literary starting-point. As the subtitle indicates, it was written as "The Diary of a Storm-Trooper-Leader." It was first published at the author's own expense, and indeed at first sight it does look like the amateurish effort of a typical regimental officer. Jünger signs himself a volunteer (that is not conscript), then lieutenant and company commander, he names his regiment (of which he is inordinately proud) and gives full military details of regimental casualties. The aim of the book is to be *sachlich* (objective), a term taken up later as the style of the post-war generation; yet despite such claims Jünger is far from being an exponent of the New Objectivity, and in many ways is closer to Expressionism, a movement of which he was certainly aware. His style is in fact not so much objective as visionary and apocalyptic, without the more glaring stylistic excesses of the Expressionists. What started off as a fairly technical military account, of direct interest only to a limited number of specialists, came in time to be read as one of the key books of the period. But it was not until the wave of war books started in 1928 that this came about. Then Mittler the publisher, who had re-issued *Storm of Steel* in 1922, brought out a third edition of 10,000 as a counter to the pacifism and anti-militarism of Remarque's *All Quiet on the Western Front.* It was only then that a book which had been read almost exclusively in army and Stahlhelm circles began to be read by a far wider public and that Jünger began to be characterised in the reviews as a propagator of militarism, and as a central figure in the process of mental rearmament. In this the author's self-dramatisation and the "legend" that surrounded him, together with his personal charisma, did a great deal to further his new literary and intellectual career and he began to emerge as a German author to place alongside Lawrence and Malraux.

> Gide praised *Storm and Steel* as the finest piece of writing to come out of the war. Certainly it is quite unlike anything of its time–

> none of the pastoral musings of Siegfried Sassoon or Edmund Blunden, no whiffs of cowardice as in Hemingway, none of the masochism of T. E. Lawrence, or the compassion of Remarque. Instead Jünger parades his belief in Man's "elementary" instinct to kill other men–a game which, if played correctly, must conform to a chivalric set of rules.[17]

After the war Jünger withdrew from the army into the study of botany, entomology and marine biology. Here again he appears at first sight to be following the typical nationalist path towards that crude form of Darwinism the National Socialists were able to adopt because semi-scientific slogans like the "Stuggle for Existence" or the "Survival of the Fittest" permitted them to rationalize the elimination of the gypsies and the extermination of the Jews as inferior races. But Jünger was far too much of a real scientist to be taken in by such pseudo-science and besides he leaned towards the kind of biology concerned with Linnaean classification rather than eugenics. Jünger became that contradiction in terms, the conservative intellectual, the man-of-action turned scientist, the aesthete and bibliophile. In effect the super-cool Prussian had all the hallmarks of the *dandy*, namely contempt for the masses, contempt for political parties, radical individualism and indifference to the banality of commonplace matters. Patriot and nationalist he certainly was, but with his contempt for the realities and compromises of the political game he tended to move more and more into the realms of pure theory. And yet he could not stay away from politics–he had to feel that he was playing an important part. By 1925 he was writing political articles and by 1927 he was back in Berlin mixing with Kubin, Brecht, Dr. Goebbels and Toller. Jünger's political opinions were as mixed as the company he kept: in fact he moved from the Stahlhelm variety of nationalism through the youth movement to Niekisch's National Bolshevism, that "Prussian Communism which hated capitalism, hated the bourgeois West and hoped to graft the methods of Bolshevism onto the chivalric ideals of the Junkers."[18] Jünger was as friendly with Niekisch as he was with anyone, and helped his wife and child when he was arrested by the Gestapo in 1937. Jünger probably did earnestly desire the alliance of workers and soldier-aristocrats who would abolish the middle classes. He probably did, more than anything else, hope to win over the workers to the national cause, but this did not make him totally committed to National Bolshevism–he just was not capable of total commitment. He was not a political careerist, he was more like one of the irresponsible littérateurs he himself despised. He attacked Socialism, democracy, pacifism, but most of all he attacked the middle classes and the Weimar Republic, calling instead for an authoritarian state under the guidance of a great national leader, if necessary a dictator. In effect there was little difference between his political attitudes and those of the National Socialists. The main difference was that Jünger was a true conservative revolutionary. He really wanted revolution. What he admired therefore was the *early* NSDAP, before it adopted the legality policy, before it became a mass party prepared to make accommodations with the hated middle classes and the almost equally despised capitalistic and commercial centers of power. He admired Hitler and heard him demonstrate his demagogic magic. Yet although he dedicated his book *Fire and Blood* "to the national Führer," he probably felt he could never accept Hitler, with his obsession about the Jews, any more than he could Ludendorff with his obsession about Freemasons. Jünger seems to have been closer to the original Goebbels wing of the party, because it corresponded more to his own ideal of dynamic revolutionary *élan*. And yet, despite his distant admiration for Hitler and his personal closeness to Goebbels, he never joined the party, though most of his nationalistic collaborators on *Arminius* (for example Blunck, Johst, Stoffregen, Jungnickel, Müller-Partenkirchen, Steguweit, Beumelburg, Fechter, Schauwecker, W. Weiss) did accept the NSDAP as the proper organ of the new nationalism. Apart from his dislike of *all* party political organizations and his predilection for the purity of theory, he disagreed with the NSDAP on various matters. He thought the party was wrong about the *Landvolkbewegung*, that revolution of the peasants which the NSDAP condemned, and he rejected the racial policies of the NSDAP (though for his own special reasons). But all this seemed like hairsplitting to contemporaries for whom Jünger appeared to be as close to National Socialism as it was possible to be. Differences between them disappeared in the light of the far greater number of correspondences and at the time liberal and left-wing critics quite rightly recognized in Jünger a gifted National Socialist and regarded him as one of the intellectual leaders of their party. Most readers and admirers of Jünger landed up in the party, for in it they found the realization of all he had argued most effectively for. All the not inconsiderable energy he generated, the continual reminders of the war just past and the possibility of the ones to come, the impossibility of accepting the republic, the longings for authoritarian military-style Germany, all this worked to the benefit of the mass movement. His *Total Mobilisation* (1931) showed how his goals would be achieved, namely through the collapse of the liberal system, the necessary loss of individual freedom, the transition to totalitarian structures, whose prime goal would be the military mobilization of all collective efforts "right down to the very seamstress at her sewing machine." In this same passage he also developed what was to become the policy of *Gleichschaltung* put into practice by the NSDAP when it came to power:

> To develop powers of such dimensions, it is no longer sufficient to arm the sword-arm–what is essential is arming to the very marrow, arming right down to life's finest nerve-ends. To realise this is the task of total mobilization, by which all the energy-capacity of the modern world which is so widespread and so complex can by one single movement at the control panel be fed into the great grid of military power.[19]

This vision of the Nationalist Socialist state seemed to many observers, including some in the party hierarchy itself, to be already foreshadowed in Jünger's abstract work *The Worker,* which extended the total state of war to the whole of society and made the individual into someone without rights and privileges, a mere functional cog in a completely planned society. Here again all the National Socialists had to do when they came to power was to turn the blueprint into reality:

> *The Worker* is a vaguely formulated machine-age utopia whose citizens are required to commit themselves to a "total mobilization" . . . in the undefined interests of the State. The Worker, as Jünger understands him, is a technocrat. His business, ultimately, is war. His freedom–or rather his sense of inner freedom–is supposed to correspond to the scale of his productivity. The aim is world government by force.[20]

Jünger, however, merely wrote the words and conjured up the visions: he played no part in turning them into the horrific reality of the Third Reich. Instead he withdrew once again from politics, declined consideration for the Academy, rejected the possibility of a seat in the Reichstag representing the NSDAP, and asked the *Völkischer Beobachter* not to publish him without permission. Yet undoubtedly he did great service to the party by his war books, for throughout the course of the Nazi regime they poured from the presses in carefully prepared editions. All the reality of the original reports and diary entries had now been refined into glorious visions of fateful events, presenting the younger generations with models for heroic behaviour and inviting them to follow the examples of the earlier generation of front-line fighters who had paved the way for the national awakening resulting in the Third Reich. Many accepted this invitation, joined the armed forces and died.

Joseph Goebbels is thought of now as a man of the spoken word, while his name is almost synonymous with the use of propaganda in the political sphere: yet his career started off in a much more conventionally literary fashion. As a university student he seems to have been unusually restless, changing universities many times, though he was far from well-off–indeed he relied heavily on a scholarship from the Catholic Albertus Magnus Society. In 1920, however, he eventually settled in Heidelberg, where in November of the following year he submitted a dissertation on "Wilhelm von Schütz: a Contribution to the History of Drama in the Romantic School," and gained the title of "Doctor." For the rest of his life he proudly insisted on being addressed as Dr. Goebbels. In his early years he wrote extensively and it is only because of copyright and legal problems that his literary writings remain unpublished to this day. The Goebbels archive contains many notebooks with unpublished verses, poems, prose passages and essays. There is one drama with the title *Heinrich Kampfert* and manuscripts with "Romantic" titles like "Those Who Love the Sun," or "A Roaming Scholar am I." Many of the early poems have titles equally redolent of romantic kitsch, and there are also parts of a religious drama called *Judas Iscariot.*[21]

In his early years Goebbels made many attempts to break into writing and publishing (for example, into the circle round Gundolf)–but without success. Fortunately, however, one of his literary works is available for study, namely his novel *Michael: a German Fate through the Pages of a Diary.* In *European Witness,* published after the war in 1946, Stephen Spender drew attention to this novel, not because it was a forgotten masterpiece, but because a novel written by a common murderer would excite considerable interest, and here was a book written by one of the greatest murderers of all history. Published in 1929, four years before the Nazis came to power, it was never discussed outside Germany and hardly at all inside Germany. And yet, as Spender rightly saw, it contains in literary guise "all the Nazi and Fascist symptoms."[22] This is what makes it still compulsive reading to this day. Goebbels, the master orator, could exercise some of the same magnetic power over his reader. What Goebbels offers first of all is comradeship–the camaraderie of the front-line fighter–for his book is dedicated to his friend Richard Flisges, who had died six years earlier. In 1918 his friend had come back from the war "wounded arm still in sling, grey helmet on head and chest covered with medals." With this friend he lives through the trials of the difficult post-war period and replies to its problems with cries of "Revolution! Defiance! Resurrection!" The book is to be a sign of the times, a symbol for the future, showing in exemplary manner a type of German youth characterized by will, faith, work, passion and sacrifice–for the fatherland! The language of this short novel is exclamatory and ecstatic after the fashion of Nietzsche's *Thus Spake Zarathustra*; and indeed Nietzsche's name is often invoked (needless to say in a manner and context of which he would not have approved). There are also many literary references, not least to Goethe, but these are merely the external trappings of culture. The essence of the book's message is its anti-intellectualism: its appeal to the blood rather than to the brain. The German youth of the time, in its Faustian creative drive, is described as waiting in its millions for a new dawn, a new way of life which will come like a storm to sweep away the old and bring in the new. And youth is always right, not old age and maturity! So the protagonist returns from the battlefield (which Goebbels himself, because of his physical condition, never saw), and as the representative German "rises like a phoenix from the ashes" to confront the peace in his beloved homeland Germany. The heroic life of the front-line soldier now lies behind him, the less exciting life of the university student lies ahead. But even here the New Man (according to the developing Nazi doctrine as adumbrated for the hero) is described not only as the soldier, which he has been, but also as the peasant rooted in the soil, which he always will be: "I stand with both feet on the hard soil of the homeland. Around me is the smell of the soil. Peasant blood mounts up slow and healthy within me." That is what makes it possible for him to live life to the full, unlike the city-dweller or intellectual. As for the universities, they are full of pale faces and bespectacled highbrows and are certainly not where "the future leaders of the nation" are to be found. Science and study are denounced as the death of common sense, and intellect as a hindrance to the formation of real character.

When Michael, the hero of the novel, meets a girl called Hertha at the university, the discussion between them is about the combination of poet and politician in one and the same person. The credo expressed is clear: the statesman is also an artist of a kind. The *Volk* is for him what the stone is for the sculptor.The relationship between a Führer and the masses is the same as that between painter and paints. Politics is the creative art of the state, just as painting is the creative art of the painter. "To turn the masses into a Volk and to form the Volk into a state, that has always been the fundamental essence of all true politics." From this, it is an easy step to war. War is the simplest form of life affirmation:

> Struggle the moment man sets foot on this earth. Struggle till the moment of leaving it, and in between stretches never-ending war for a place at the feeding-trough. One only has real regard for what has to be conquered or defended.

Peace has to be fought for, not with the palm frond, but with the sword; there is no such thing as equality; the natural world is anti-democratic–these are the arguments put forward, and as the debate continues Michael develops his ideas on *Volkstum*, Socialism and capitalism to the point where Hertha points out that even when talking about politics he thinks like an artist, and notes that this is a dangerous combination. But this does not stem the flow of the poet-politician. Again he develops proto-fascist ideas, this time about the role of women in society. The woman's duty is to be lovely and bring children into the world. When she accuses him of being "reactionary," he takes up the challenge by attacking fashionable, liberal ideas of what this means: "If modern means unnatural, utter collapse, putrefaction and deliberate corrosion of all mortality, then I am being reactionary." The language used in this attack on modernity is particularly significant, especially in the use of the term *Zersetzung* (corrosion) which was to become one of the key concepts for National Socialist attacks on all modern literature.

Many critics then and now have doubted whether there ever was such a thing as a National Socialist *Weltanschauung*. Michael has no doubts that his primitive, crude life doctrine is indeed a *Weltanschauung*, "not one worked out and arrived at by the power of reason and logic, but one which has grown organically and is therefore capable of resisting all attacks." His *Weltanschauung* has nothing to do with culture: it relies on belief, including the belief that Another and Greater is on the way, "who will one day arise among us and preach faith in the life of the Fatherland." Significantly, too, Michael is convinced that this coming genius will consume him, indeed consume a whole generation of youth, called upon to make the supreme sacrifice for the great cause. The demand for total sacrifice was to become one of the most attractive of all the appeals of National Socialism to the hearts and minds of the young.

Michael the poet continues his struggles with himself and with Christ, though it is clear that he has moved a long way beyond orthodox Christianity. His Christ is a hard unrelenting one who declares war on money and uses a whip to drive Jewish money-changers out of the temple. The fierce tirade against the Jews is in what was soon to become the accepted style in National Socialist Germany. Jews make Michael physically ill; Jews have despoiled his people, soiled his and the Germans' ideals, lamed the force of the nation, contaminated its customs and ruined its morals; with the Jew it is them-or-us! This whole vicious catalogue of the supposed features of the Jew culminates in the statement: "Christ cannot have been a Jew. I do not have to prove this scientifically, it is so!"

After this it is not surprising that Michael proceeds to compound his own peculiar brew of anti-Semitism and anti-Marxism. Christ was the first great opponent of the Jews and this is why they killed him, because he frustrated their aim to conquer the world. The Jew is the lie personified, while in Christ the Jew nailed truth to the cross. Christ first gave form to the concept of sacrifice; this was corrupted by the Jews into getting others to make sacrifices for them. The true sacrifice is Christian Socialism, Jewish sacrifice is Marxism. From specious arguments Michael arrives at the strange but peculiarly fascist conclusion that the real struggle is that between Christ and Marx, Christ representing the principle of love, and Marx the (Jewish) principle of hate. All this, strangely enough, is argued out within the context of a discussion of Expressionism and Modern Art:

> Our decade is absolutely expressionistic in its inner structure. This has nothing to do with how fashionable the word is. We people today are all Expressionists. People who want to form the world from inside out. The Expressionist builds himself a new world within himself. His secret and his power is passion. His mental world usually breaks against reality.
> The soul of the Impressionist is the microscopic picture of the macrocosm.
> The soul of the Expressionist is the new macrocosm.
> A world in itself.
> Expressionistic sensation is explosive.
> It is an autocratic feeling of being oneself.

Goebbels is said to have had a weakness for Expressionist art and at an early stage in the party's development it seemed possible that Expressionism would be adopted as the artistic mode of the party. The matter was in doubt for some time. In the novel, however, there are no such doubts and this section finishes with the ominous declaration: "this whole foreign rabble will have to be removed!"

While in the first part of the novel Michael has engaged partly in exclamatory monologues and partly in discussions with Hertha, in the second part, after they separate (she being perhaps still too bourgeois to follow the young poet-revolutionary on his fateful path), he meets up with a Russian student with whom he also engages in significant and wide-ranging talks. At first he is attracted by Ivan's revolutionary fervor and love of Russia, but soon he is just as repelled as he was initially attracted. It has been suggested that this encounter between Ivan and Michael in fact represents a more fundamental confrontation, namely between the Russian and the German, and also indicates Goebbels' own National Bolshevism. In the end Michael, like Goebbels and National Socialism, decides that Ivan is the enemy who must be destroyed. Michael stops being a student. "Soldiers, students and workers will build the new Reich. I was a soldier, I am a student, a worker I will be." With his hatred of the cowardly bourgeois this is the course for him, especially for one who wants to make history. He leaves the university and works in a mine. In his simple worker's room he has the Bible and *Faust*. The end of the novel is sudden and unexpected. He hears that Ivan has been the victim of a political assassination and he himself is killed in an accident soon afterwards. A letter from a miner to Hertha Holk tells her that Michael died with a smile and that in his copy of Nietzsche's *Zarathustra* he had marked the passage: "Many die too late and some die too early. Strangely still sounds the lesson! Die at the right time."

Michael is not much of a novel. It is told in the form of diary entries and consequently has little or no plot and little or no shape or form. The style is exclamatory as it follows the exaltations and depressions of the student hero, who does little but talk. However, Michael does have faith in his own personal "demon," he does have crude political beliefs which he expresses in "poetic" language, ideas which in normal circumstances would be dismissed as primitive rubbish, were it not for the fact that they were also the common currency of a nationalistic wave which was to assume total power over a whole nation. And it must be admitted that the novel and its ideas must have had the power to attract those it aimed at, namely the disgruntled youth of a defeated people. Stephen Spender is correct in observing that *Michael* is genuine in so far as it captures the sense of defeat, of reaction against post-war decadence and of national humiliation. He is right too to look beyond this and sense in *Michael* an ennui with the modern world, which deliberately seeks release through conflict and chaos. Above all he sees in *Michael* the attraction of evil. The hero who has announced the coming of the Great One goes by chance to a political meeting and immediately falls under the spell of an unnamed speaker of sinister power. Like one who has slumbered and had strange dreams and visions, he is suddenly awakened, as Germany too awakens to the call from the Leader:

> That evening I sit in a big hall with a thousand others and see him again, hear him who awakened me.
> Now he stands in the midst of a loyal congregation.
> He seems to have grown in stature.
> There is so much strength in him, and a sea of light gleams from those big blue eyes.
> I sit among all those others, and it seems as if he is speaking to me quite personally.
> About the blessing of work! Whatever I only ever felt or guessed at, he puts into words. My confessions and my faith: here they gain shape.
> I feel his strength feeling my soul.
> Here is young Germany, and those who work in the blacksmith's shop of the new Reich. Anvil till now, but hammer before long.
> Here is my place.
> Around me are people I never saw and I feel like a child as tears well up in my eyes.

Goebbels was to become the master myth-maker, creating heroes out of such unlikely figures as Schlageter and Horst Wessel. It is more than likely that here too he was creating a myth, round the moment of his own spiritual awakening to the light of National Socialism. He probably did not hear Hitler speak in 1922, as the novel claims. In fact he was working in a bank and on the Stock Exchange, calling the prices. It was not until 1925 that he actually did meet Hitler. Once he did, however, he never looked back and his career took off like a meteor. Nevertheless it is equally true, as Stephen Spender claims, that *Michael* is the key to his later success:

> One has to go back to Goebbels' first work, a novel called *Michael*, published in 1929, to discover that the real Goebbels is essentially the Nazi Goebbels, from the days when he was a rebellious student at Heidelberg to his dramatic death in the Reichschancellory in 1945.[23]

In the novel the poet hero struggles more or less successfully to write a vast religious drama on the theme of Christ and (as has been noted) parts of just such a Christ drama with the title *Judas Iscariot* are to be found among his unpublished works. Goebbels fancied himself as a dramatist and used to entertain his guests with readings from another drama called *The Wanderer*.[24] This play, though it remained unpublished, did reach the public stage. *The Wanderer* is a play with a prologue, eight scenes and an epilogue that follows the "stations of the cross" form familiar from the Expressionist theatre. Equally expressionistic is the elimination of individual psychology and the reduction of the dramatis personae to representative figures: the prologue is taken up by a confrontation between poet and wanderer, the first scene (Poverty) has Man and Woman, the second (Church) has Deacon and Chaplain, the third (Industry) Director General and Captain of Industry, the fourth (Stock Exchange) Stock-Market

Baron and Private Secretary, the fifth (Sex) Gent and Prostitute, the sixth (Party) Politician and Worker, the seventh (Government) Minister and Counsellor, the eighth (Death) only Death. The epilogue completes the circular form by coming back to the poet and wanderer of the prologue. In this play Goebbels once again returns to his own position *vis-à-vis* Hitler. In the same way as the poet here becomes the mouthpiece of the wanderer, who is the harbinger of a new faith and a new will to take a stand against the sufferings of Germany, so too Goebbels, the Gauleiter of the Berlin NSDAP, becomes the most fervent of his master's voices. The most striking feature about the play is that all eight scenes represent a negative catalogue of the German misery, without the presence anywhere of the slightest ideology. What he does is merely to reject all democratic and Socialist endeavors and, by defamation of them, strengthen the irrational wish for an authoritarian Germany under the guidance of a strong leader. So the Germany of the time is denounced as decadent, and the poet despairs because he believes that everything noble, great and beautiful is doomed to decline. In the chaos, corruption and immorality of the modern world, he meets the wanderer, who is the proclaimer of the Truth and exponent of an unshakable faith in a new life. He gives the poet insight into the life of the time, a life filled with suffering in a society driven by lust for money. The problems of a sterile, dogmatic Christianity are contrasted with a religion of action. The real "God" of the age is shown to be Mammon, while Death stands grinning over the chaos. The individual scenes are linked by a voice from the darkness, which comments on what the poet has seen, giving guidance where necessary, till in the epilogue the exhausted poet is uplifted by the wanderer, who imparts to him a faith in morality and bravery with which to return to the people. His mission will be to awaken the people to this message: "Be strong and believe!" This is the call which it is hoped the play will convey to all who are capable of hearing, moving hearts and opening eyes to the certainty of a new Germany of honour, purity and political and moral greatness.

Various attempts were made by the NSDAP to set up theatre groups which would travel the country bringing this kind of message to the people and it was in the context of one such group that Goebbels' play was performed.[25] It must be said that such Nazi theatre groups were far from successful, but by 1932 when *The Wanderer* was performed in Chemnitz the situation had changed drastically, as a report from the *Chemnitzer Tageblatt* makes clear. By this time Goebbels was known as the famous Berlin Gauleiter, agitator in the grand manner, propagandist and organizer. He was also known as a dazzling journalist from his articles in the *Angriff,* and in his book, *Struggle for Berlin,* which had just appeared. The *Tageblatt* reporter reminds his readers that Goebbels had been in Chemnitz only a short time before, addressing a mass gathering of 12,000 who hung on his lips as they sat surrounded by 1,000 Storm Troopers. How different from the time six years before, when he spoke in the Marble Palace before a much smaller crowd and with only a few dozen SA men as stewards! Then his audience had been made up mainly of Communists and the evening had ended with the bloodiest political meeting Chemnitz had ever experienced with not a pane of glass, not a chair, lamp or beer glass remaining intact. It was against a background of such conflicting memories as these conjured up in the local press that Goebbels' play *The Wanderer* was now performed. Of course, there is not a mention in the play of National Socialism, of Hitler or of the SA directly; nevertheless the message still came across loud and clear. The need of the hour, it emerged, was not simply a new faith, but a *fanatical* faith. Marxism, parliamentarianism, liberalism, all such democratic solutions have failed, and only the great leader can guide Germany out of the dark night. According to the newspaper report Goebbels' play succeeded in putting this simple message across and the Chemnitz theatre enjoyed a wonderful evening, yet despite its programmatic nature Goebbels' play did not succeed in finding a more permanent place in the theatre repertoire. Chemnitz was not Berlin and the Gauleiter's play never did reach any of the major theatres. Clearly it shows the same faults as the author's *Michael.* The language is exclamatory and ecstatic, and altogether the play, like Goebbels' novel, betrays far too much of its expressionistic origins. Besides, despite its essentially abstract nature, the play did deal with subjects which held all sorts of special dangers in Nazi Germany. Had poverty disappeared with the end of the Weimar Republic? Had the Christian Church disappeared in an essentially heathen state? Were there no more money-greedy capitalists or stock-market speculators? Was sex a completely taboo subject? Had the party solved the problem of its relationship with the workers? Worst of all, what was one to think of the figure of Death looming over the land? Altogether it is not surprising that Goebbels' expressionistic play disappeared almost as quickly as it appeared.

---

1. A. D. White, "The Development of the Thought of Erwin Guido Kolbenheyer," unpublished D. Phil. thesis, University of Oxford, 1967.

2. Willy A. Hanimann, *Studien zum historischen Roman 1930-1945* (Frankfurt a.M., 1981). For a general approach see G. P. Hutchinson, "The Nazi Ideology of Alfred Rosenberg: a Study of his Thought, 1917-1946," unpublished D. Phil. thesis, University of Oxford, 1977.

3. See Daniel Gasman, *The Scientific Origins of National Socialism* (New York, 1971), for a discussion of Social Darwinism. For biology applied to literature, see Dr. Ludwig Büttner, *Gedanken zu einer biologischen Literaturbetrachtung* (Munich 1939). For music Donald W. Ellis, "The Propaganda Ministry and Centralised Regulation of Music in the Third Reich: the Biological Aesthetic as Policy," *Journal of European Studies*, no. 5 (1975), pp. 223-38.

4. Klaus Amann, "Die Literaturpolitischen Voraussetzungen und Hintergründe für den 'Anschluss' der österreichischen Literatur im Jahr 1938," *Deutsche Philologie*, vol. 101, no. 2 (1982), pp. 216-44.

5. The first section is "classical" ("antike Strophen"), there are variations on Hölderlin, followed by a heroic trilogy, and a long section on the pure poem.

6. There is a Weinheber poem to the Führer in Loewy, *Literatur unterm Hakenkreuz*, 3rd edn (1977), p. 284.

7. With regard to Weinheber I follow the line taken by H. M. Ridley, "National Socialism and Literature," unpublished PhD. thesis, University of Cambridge, 1966.

8. Rainer Stollmann, *Ästhetisierung der Politik. Literaturstudien zum subjektiven Faschismus* (Stuttgart, 1978), p. 175.

9. Ridley, "National Socialism and Literature," pp. 262-3.

10. Hans Sarkowicz, "Zwischen Sympathie und Apologie: Der Schriftsteller Hans Grimm und sein Verhältnis zum Nationalsozialismus," in Karl Corino (ed.), *Intellektuelle im Bann des Nationalsozialismus* (Hamburg, 1980), pp. 120-35.

11. F. L. Carsten, "Volk ohne Raum. A Note on Hans Grimm," *Journal of Contemporary History*, vol. 2 (1967), pp. 221-27.

12. Hellmut H. Langenbucher, *Volkhafte Dichtung der Zeit*, 3rd edn (Berlin, 1937), p. 344.

13. J. Wulf (ed.), *Literatur und Dichtung im Dritten Reich* (Gütersloh, 1963), p. 295.

14. Paul Alverdes was the editor of the journal *Das Innere Reich* published in Germany during the Third Reich. It tried to reach a "better" public but was *never* in opposition.

15. Carsten, "Volk ohne Raum," p. 227.

16. Roger Woods, "Ernst Jünger and the Nature of Political Commitment," unpublished D. Phil. thesis, University of Oxford, 1981, to appear in 1982, published by Akademischer Verlag, Stuttgart. Still an excellent introduction is J. P. Stern, *Ernst Jünger. A Writer of our Time* (Cambridge, 1953). For the most recent survey, see W. Kaempfer, *Ernst Jünger* (Sammlung Metzler 201, Stuttgart, 1981).

17. Bruce Chatwin, "An Aesthete at War," *New York Review of Books*, 5 Mar. 1971, p. 49.

18. Ibid.

19. E. Jünger, *Die totale Mobilmachung* (Berlin, 1931), ch. 3.

20. Chatwin, "An Aesthete at War," p. 49.

21. Roger Manvell and Heinrich Fraenkel, *Doctor Goebbels. His Life and Death* (London, 1960), pp. 19-33; Helmut Heiber, *Goebbels* (London 1972), pp. 7-30.

22. Stephen Spender, *European Witness* (London and New York, 1946). See also Marianne Bonwit, "Michael, ein Roman von Joseph Goebbels im Licht der deutschen literarischen Tradition" in Hans Mayer (ed.), *Deutsche Literaturkritik der Gegenwart* (Stuttgart, 1971), vol. 4, pp. 490-501.

23. Spender, *European Witness*, p. 180.

24. Bruno Fischli, *Die Deutschen-Dämmerung. Zur Genealogie des völkischfaschistischen Dramas und Theaters* (Bonn, 1976), pp. 231-6, pp. 352-3.

25. See George L. Mosse in Reinhold Grimm and Jost Hermand (eds.), *Geschichte im Gegenwartsdrama* (Stuttgart, 1976), pp. 24-38.

Glossary of German Terms and Abbreviations

Anschluss: The Union of Austria with Germany in March 1938

Ausbürgerung: Depriving exiles of citizenship and nationality

Blut und Boden: Blood and Soil, the slogan of Nazi agrarian Romanticism

Bund Proletarisch-Revolutionärer Schriftsteller (BPRS): League of Proletarian-Revolutionary Writers

Bundesrepublik Deutschland (FRG): Federal Republic of Germany

Deutsche Arbeiterpartei (DAP): German Workers' Party founded in 1919 by Anton Drexler. The forerunner of the NSDAP

Deutsche Demokratische Republik (GDR): German Democratic Republic

Endlösung: The Final Solution. After other "solutions" including exile, this meant the plan to exterminate all the Jews in areas under German control

Entartung: Departure from the racial purity, degeneration

Freikorps: Free Corps. Right-wing paramilitary units which came into existence in different parts of Germany after 1918

Führer: The Leader (Adolf Hitler)

Gauleiter: The Gau (an old Germanic word) was a region. The Gauleiter was a District Leader of the Nazi Party

Gestapo (Geheime Staatspolizei): Secret State Police, later incorporated into the main security office of the Reich and headed by Heinrich Müller

Gleichschaltung: Literally switching on to the same current. In effect this meant coordination and subordination of all aspects of life to Nazi Party doctrine

Heimatkunst: Homeland art and literature

Hitlerjugend (HJ): Hitler Youth

Kampfbund für deutsche Kultur: League of Struggle for German Culture founded in 1929 by Alfred Rosenberg

Konzentrationslager (KZ): Concentration camp

KPD *(Kommunistische Partei Deutschlands):* German Communist Party

Lebensborn: Spring of Life. Part of the program for breeding pure Aryans in an SS stud farm

Lebensraum: Living Space. Although taken over from Grimm's African novel this came to be applied to expansion into central and eastern Europe

Nationalsozialistische Deutsche Arbeiterpartei (NSDAP): Nazi for short. The National Socialist Workers Party developed out of the earlier DAP–see above

Parteiamtliche Prüfungskommission (PPK): The Nazi Party Supervisory Commission to check Nazi party publications

Rassenschande: Defilement of racial purity by marriage or sexual intercourse with a member of an "inferior" race

Reichskanzler: Reich Chancellor, i.e. Adolf Hitler

Reichskristallnacht: The night of 9 November 1938, the great pogrom against the Jews in Germany. The crystal refers to the smashing of glass

Reichskulturkammer (RKK): Reich Chamber of Culture

Reichsschrifttumskammer (RSK): Reich Chamber of Literature

Reichstag: Parliament. The Reichstag Fire of 27 February 1933, burning down the Parliament buildings, marked the start of the Nazi reign of terror eliminating all opposition

Rotfrontkämpferbund: The Red Front Fighters' Association was the Communist equivalent of similar right-wing bodies

Schutzstaffel (SS): Literally Protection Squads. These black-shirted groups, formed in 1925, were Hitler's personal bodyguard. They grew from this to become the most powerful body in National Socialist Germany under Heinrich Himmler

Schutzverband Deutscher Schriftsteller (SDS): German Writers Defence Association

Schwarze Korps, Das: The Black Corps. This was the official weekly paper of the SS

Sicherheitsdienst (SD): The security service of the SS was founded in 1932 and directed by Reinhard Heydrich

Sozialdemokratische Partei Deutschlands (SPD): The Social Democratic Party, outlawed in 1933

Sozialistische Einheitspartei Deutschlands (SED): The Socialist Unity Party of the German Democratic Republic

Stahlhelm: Steel Helmet. National ex-serviceman's organization founded in 1918 by Franz Seldte

Sturmabteilung (SA): These Storm Troopers or Brownshirts were founded in 1921 and came under the control of Ernst Röhm. He and his followers were eliminated in the infamous massacre of June 1934, the Night of the Long Knives

Völkisch: From *Volk,* hence national, racially pure, ethnic

Völkische Beobachter, Der: The Racial Observer. The official newspaper of the Nazi Party

Volksgemeinschaft: Community of the People. This indicated the classless form of national solidarity to which the regime aspired

Volksgenosse: Genosse means "comrade." The Nazis moved the concept away from class to race. Hence the term means racial comrade, a member of the German race

Fuller information in Robert S. Wistrich, *Who's Who in Nazi Germany* (London, 1982)

Reprinted from German Literature under National Socialism *(London & Canberra: Croom Helm/ Totowa, N. J.: Barnes & Noble, 1983).*

Checklist of Further Readings

Baumgart, Reinhard. *Aussichten des Romans oder hat Literatur Zukunft? Frankfurter Vorlesungen.* Munich: Deutscher Taschenbuch Verlag, 1970.

Bennett, Edwin K. *A History of the German Novelle,* second edition, edited by H. M. Waidson. Cambridge: Cambridge University Press, 1961.

Berman, Russell A. *The Rise of the Modern German Novel: Crisis and Charisma.* Cambridge & London: Harvard University Press, 1986.

Bithell, Jethro. *Modern German Literature 1880-1950,* third edition. London: Methuen, 1959.

Boa, Elizabeth and J. H. Reid. *Critical Strategies: German Fiction in the Twentieth Century.* Montreal: McGill-Queen's University Press, 1972.

Borcherdt, H. H. *Geschichte des Romans und der Novelle in Deutschland.* Leipzig: Weber, 1926.

Bosmajian, Hamida. *Metaphors of Evil: Contemporary German Literature and the Shadow of Nazism.* Iowa City: University of Iowa Press, 1979.

Bracher, Karl Dietrich. *The German Dictatorship: The Origins, Structure, and Effects of National Socialism,* translated by Jean Steinberg. New York: Praeger, 1970.

Chick, Edson. *Dances of Death: Wedekind, Brecht, Dürrenmatt and the Satiric Tradition.* Columbia, S.C.: Camden House, 1984.

Childs, David. *Germany since 1918.* New York: Harper & Row, 1971.

Closs, August, ed. *Introductions to German Literature,* 4 volumes. London: Cresset Press, 1967-1970.

Craig, Gordon A. *Germany 1866-1945.* New York: Oxford University Press, 1978.

Demetz, Peter. *Postwar German Literature.* New York: Pegasus, 1970.

Duwe, Wilhelm. *Ausdrucksformen deutscher Dichtung vom Naturalismus bis zur Gegenwart: Eine Stilgeschichte der Moderne.* Berlin: Schmidt, 1965.

Eisner, Lotte. *The Haunted Screen,* translated by Roger Greaves. Berkeley: University of California Press, 1969.

Emmel, Hildegard. *Geschichte des deutschen Romans,* 3 volumes. Bern: Francke, 1972, 1975, 1978. Translated by Ellen Summerfield as *History of the German Novel,* 1 volume. Detroit: Wayne State University Press, 1984.

Emmel. "Roman," in *Reallexikon der deutschen Literaturgeschichte,* second edition, volume 3. Berlin & New York: De Gruyter, 1977, pp. 490-519.

Garland, H. B. *A Concise Survey of German Literature,* second edition. London: Macmillan, 1976.

Garland, Henry B. and Mary Garland. *The Oxford Companion to German Literature.* Oxford: Clarendon Press, 1976.

Gray, Ronald. *The German Tradition in Literature, 1871-1945.* Cambridge: Cambridge University Press, 1965.

Hamburger, Michael. *From Prophecy to Exorcism: The Premisses of Modern German Literature.* London: Longmans, 1965.

Hamburger. *Reason and Energy: Studies in German Literature,* revised edition. London: Weidenfeld & Nicolson, 1970.

Hatfield, Henry. *Modern German Literature: The Major Figures in Context.* Bloomington: Indiana University Press, 1968.

Heller, Erich. *The Disinherited Mind: Essays in Modern German Literature and Thought.* Cambridge: Bowes & Bowes, 1952.

Jones, M. S. *Der Sturm: A Focus of Expressionism.* Columbia, S.C.: Camden House, 1984.

Kracauer, Siegfried. *From Caligari to Hitler: A Psychological History of the German Film.* Princeton: Princeton University Press, 1947.

Kunisch, Hermann. *Die deutsche Gegenwartsdichtung.* Munich: Nymphenburger Verlag, 1968.

Kunisch, ed. *Handbuch der deutschen Gegenwartsliteratur,* second edition, 3 volumes. Munich: Nymphenburger Verlag, 1969-1970.

Langer, Lawrence. *The Holocaust and the Literary Imagination.* New Haven: Yale University Press, 1975.

Lukács, Georg. *Die Zerstörung der Vernunft.* Berlin: Aufbau, 1954.

Mann, Klaus. *The Turning Point: Thirty-Five Years in This Century.* New York: Fischer, 1942.

Martini, Fritz. *Deutsche Literaturgeschichte von den Anfängen bis zur Gegenwart,* sixteenth edition. Stuttgart: Kröner Verlag, 1972.

Mosse, George L. *The Culture of Western Europe: The Nineteenth and Twentieth Centuries, an Introduction.* Chicago: Rand McNally, 1961.

Mosse. *Nazi Culture: Intellectual, Cultural and Social Life in the Third Reich,* translated by Salvator Attanasio and others. New York: Grosset & Dunlap, 1966.

Natan, A., ed. *Swiss Men of Letters: Twelve Literary Essays.* London: Wolff, 1970.

Osterle, Heinz D. "The Other Germany: Resistance to the Third Reich in German Literature," *German Quarterly,* 41 (January 1968): 1-22.

Pascal, Roy. *The German Novel: Studies.* Manchester: Manchester University Press, 1956.

Reed, Donna K. *The Novel and the Nazi Past.* New York & Bern: Lang, 1985.

Ringer, Fritz K. *The Decline of the German Mandarins: The German Academic Community, 1890-1933.* Cambridge: Harvard University Press, 1969.

Robertson, J. G. *A History of German Literature,* sixth edition, edited by Dorothy Reich and others. Edinburgh & London: Blackwood, 1970.

Soergel, Albert and Curt Hohoff. *Dichtung und Dichter der Zeit,* 2 volumes. Düsseldorf: Bagel, 1961-1963.

Sokel, W. H. *The Writer in Extremis: Expressionism in Twentieth-Century German Literature.* Stanford: Stanford University Press, 1959.

Steiner, George. *Language and Silence.* New York: Athenaum, 1967.

Viereck, Peter. *Metapolitics: From the Romantics to Hitler.* New York: Knopf, 1941. Revised and enlarged as *Metapolitics: The Roots of the Nazi Mind.* New York: Capricorn, 1961; second edition, 1965.

Waidson, H. M. *The Modern German Novel: A Mid-Twentieth Century* Survey. London & New York: Oxford University Press, 1960.

Welzig, Werner. *Der deutsche Roman im 20. Jahrhundert.* Stuttgart: Kröner, 1967.

Ziolkowski, Theodore. *Dimensions of the Modern Novel: German Texts and European Contexts.* Princeton: Princeton University Press, 1969.

Contributors

Paul Kurt Ackermann .... *Boston University*
Dieter W. Adolphs .... *Michigan Technological University*
George C. Avery.. *Swarthmore College*
Katherine R. Goodman .... *Brown University*
Erich P. Hofacker, Jr... *University of Michigan*
Herbert Knust .... *University of Illinois (Urbana-Champaign)*
Michael M. Metzger .... *State University of New York at Buffalo*
Josef Schmidt .... *McGill University*
George C. Schoolfield .... *Yale University*
Egon Schwarz.. *Washington University*
Ingeborg H. Solbrig.. *University of Iowa*
H. M. Waidson .... *Swansea, U.K.*
Liliane Weissberg.. *Johns Hopkins University*
Hanna A. Zolman .... *Los Angeles, California*

Cumulative Index

Dictionary of Literary Biography, Volumes 1-66
Dictionary of Literary Biography Yearbook, 1980-1986
Dictionary of Literary Biography Documentary Series, Volumes 1-5

Cumulative Index

DLB before number: *Dictionary of Literary Biography,* Volumes 1-66
Y before number: *Dictionary of Literary Biography Yearbook,* 1980-1986
DS before number: *Dictionary of Literary Biography Documentary Series,* Volumes 1-5

A

B

C

D

E

F

G

H

I

J

K

L

M

N

O

P

Q

R

S

T

U

V

W

Y

Z